"After the start of planning education at Liverpool University (1907), the planning teaching exploded in post-war societies and recently in the awaking of new economies in the south. This first international handbook offers a unique insight in the common grounds, enabling a cross-fertilization of experiences over the world."

Willem Salet, University of Amsterdam

"This insightful book is timely at the start of modern urban planning's second century. I predict that reviewers of the 50-year anniversary edition, writing in 2070, will find that planning education is even more highly valued by society and that the emerging normative themes reviewed in the current edition dominate the curriculum."

Chris Webster, Dean of the Faculty of Architecture, The University of Hong Kong

"I appreciate the authors for this wonderful and unique compilation on pedagogy of planning education and highly recommend it to educators as this book bridges the gap between various schools of planning from different parts of the world. This book paves the way for a global discussion on this very important subject concerning planning education. Hopefully, additional pedagogical approaches will be added to this book over a period of time."

Utpal Sharma, Director, Institute of Architecture & Planning, Nirma University, Ahmedabad

"Bringing together informative chapters on the essence of planning and its pedagogy, on core components, specialization subjects and emerging topics in planning education, and on approaches to professional competency assessment, *The Routledge Handbook of International Planning Education* is a must-read for those who teach planning and research in planning. I found it an enjoyable and informative read, as well as a valuable sourcebook on how planning education is evolving and being delivered in different international contexts."

Prof.Dr. Ela Babalık, METU, Ankara

"*The Routledge Handbook of International Planning Education* promises to be the most influential and widely used guide to the how, what, and why of planning education. The perspectives and advice tendered by this distinguished and diverse assemblage of planning educators will ensure that all of us do what we do more effectively. It has no equal."

Christopher Silver, PhD, FAICP, Department of Urban and Regional Planning, University of Florida

"The ongoing conversation on how planning training travels across international borders is more relevant than ever. This volume provides a conceptually astute and carefully curated range of papers that considers the geographic and sectoral dimensions of this. It is a rich resource for planning educators as well as those in related disciplines."

Nancy Odendaal, University of Cape Town, Chair of the Association of African Planning Schools

"This handbook is a great compendium of theories and practices that celebrate planning education. At the same time, it catapults planning as a dynamic contemporary disciplinary field taught in universities. A must-read reference for planning educators throughout the world."

Juan Ángel Demerutis Arenas, Professor/researcher at the University of Guadalajara and President of the Association of Latin American Schools of Planning and Urbanism (ALEUP-Asociación Latinoamericana de Escuelas de Urbanismo y Planificación)

"Providing broad and diverse contributions to planning education coming from English-language scholarship, from methodologies to emerging and traditional areas of analyses and practice, this handbook provides a powerful opportunity to share common knowledges, creative experiences, and practices related to planning in different contexts, emphasizing solidarity and empowerment of social groups over competition."

Heloisa Costa, Federal University of Minas Gerais and ANPUR

THE ROUTLEDGE HANDBOOK OF INTERNATIONAL PLANNING EDUCATION

The Routledge Handbook of International Planning Education is the first comprehensive handbook with a unique focus on planning education. Comparing approaches to the delivery of planning education by three major planning education accreditation bodies in the United States, Australia, and the United Kingdom, and reflecting concerns from other national planning systems, this handbook will help to meet the strong interest and need for understanding how planning education is developed and delivered in different international contexts.

The handbook is divided into five major sections, including coverage of general planning knowledge, planning skills, traditional and emerging planning specializations, and pedagogy. An international cohort of contributors covers each subject's role in educating planners, its theory and methods, key literature contributions, and course design.

Higher education's response to globalization has included growth in planning educational exchanges across international boundaries; *The Routledge Handbook of International Planning Education* is an essential resource for planners and planning educators, informing the dialogue on the mobility of planners educated under different national schema.

Nancey Green Leigh is Associate Dean for Research in the College of Design and Professor of the School of City and Regional Planning at the Georgia Institute of Technology. She is the author of more than 50 articles and three books, including *Planning Local Economic Development* (with E. J. Blakely), now in its sixth edition, *Economic Revitalization: Cases and Strategies for City and Suburb* (with J. Fitzgerald), and *Stemming Middle Class Decline: The Challenge to Economic Development Planning*. She previously served as Vice President of the Association of Collegiate Schools of Planning, President of the Faculty Women's Interest Group, and was co-editor of the *Journal of Planning Education and Research* from 2012 to 2016. She was elected a Fellow of the American Institute of Certified Planners in 2008. Her current research, funded by the U.S. National Science Foundation, focuses on the impacts of robotics and automation diffusion on industry and employment in urban and regional economies.

Steven P. French is Dean of the College of Design and Professor of City and Regional Planning at Georgia Institute of Technology. He previously served as Director of the City Planning program, Director of the Center for Geographic Information Systems at Georgia Tech, and Associate Dean of Research. French's teaching and research activities focus on sustainable urban development, land use planning, GIS applications, and natural hazard risk assessment. He is the author or co-author of more than 25 refereed journal articles and four books, and has served on the editorial boards of the *Journal of the American Planning Association*, *Journal of Planning Education and Research*, *Journal of the Urban and Regional Information Systems Association*, and *Earthquake Spectra*.

Subhrajit Guhathakurta is Professor and Chair in the School of City and Regional Planning as well as Director of the Center for Spatial Planning Analytics and Visualization (CSPAV) at the Georgia Institute of Technology. He was previously Associate Director of the School of Geographical Sciences and Urban Planning at Arizona State University (ASU) and among the founding faculty members of ASU's School of Sustainability. He is the immediate past co-editor of the *Journal of Planning Education and Research* and is on the editorial board of the *Journal of the American Planning Association* and several other urban planning journals. He is a member of technical advisory boards of the Association of Bay Area Governments and the Atlanta Regional Commission.

Bruce Stiftel is Professor Emeritus at the School of City and Regional Planning at the Georgia Institute of Technology. His most recent books are *Adaptive Governance and Water Conflict* (co-edited with John T. Scholz) and *Dialogues in Urban and Regional Planning*, Volume 2 (co-edited with Vanessa Watson and Henri Ascelrad), and he served as consultant to UN-Habitat in production of the *World Cities Report 2016*. He previously served as President of the Association of Collegiate Schools of Planning, co-editor of the *Journal of Planning Education and Research*, founding chairperson of the Global Planning Education Association Network, and member of the Planning Accreditation Board. He is a member of the editorial boards of *Planning Theory*, *International Planning Studies*, *Journal of the American Planning Association*, *Journal of Comparative Urban Law and Policy*, and *Town Planning Review*, and represents the Global Planning Education Association Network to UN-Habitat's University Network Initiative.

Jessica L. H. Doyle received her doctorate from the School of City and Regional Planning at the Georgia Institute of Technology. Her research focuses on metropolitan-level differences in rates of Latino entrepreneurship. She has previously published in *Planning Forum, Carolina Planning Journal, plaNext,* and *Megaregions: Planning for Global Competitiveness* (Island Press, 2009).

THE ROUTLEDGE HANDBOOK OF INTERNATIONAL PLANNING EDUCATION

*Edited by Nancey Green Leigh, Steven P. French,
Subhrajit Guhathakurta, and Bruce Stiftel*

JESSICA DOYLE, ASSISTANT EDITOR

Routledge
Taylor & Francis Group
NEW YORK AND LONDON

First published 2020
by Routledge
605 Third Avenue, New York, NY 10017

and by Routledge
2 Park Square, Milton Park, Abingdon, Oxon, OX14 4RN

First issued in paperback 2022

Routledge is an imprint of the Taylor & Francis Group, an informa business

© 2020 Taylor & Francis

The right of Nancey Green Leigh, Steven P. French, Subhrajit Guhathakurta, and Bruce Stiftel to be identified as the authors of the editorial material, and of the authors for their individual chapters, has been asserted in accordance with sections 77 and 78 of the Copyright, Designs and Patents Act 1988.

All rights reserved. No part of this book may be reprinted or reproduced or utilised in any form or by any electronic, mechanical, or other means, now known or hereafter invented, including photocopying and recording, or in any information storage or retrieval system, without permission in writing from the publishers.

Trademark notice: Product or corporate names may be trademarks or registered trademarks, and are used only for identification and explanation without intent to infringe.

Publisher's Note
The publisher has gone to great lengths to ensure the quality of this reprint but points out that some imperfections in the original copies may be apparent.

Library of Congress Cataloging-in-Publication Data
Names: Leigh, Nancey Green, editor. | French, Steven P., editor. | Guhathakurta, Subhrajit, editor. | Stiftel, Bruce, editor.
Title: The Routledge handbook of international planning education / edited by Nancey Green Leigh, Steven P. French, Subhrajit Guhathakurta, and Bruce S. Stiftel.
Description: New York : Routledge, 2019. | Includes bibliographical references and index.
Identifiers: LCCN 2019013680| ISBN 9781138958777 (hardback : alk. paper) | ISBN 9781315661063 (e-book)
Subjects: LCSH: City planning—Study and teaching (Higher) | Regional planning—Study and teaching (Higher)
Classification: LCC HT165.5 .I58 2019 | DDC 307.1/2160711—dc23
LC record available at https://lccn.loc.gov/2019013680

ISBN: 978–1–03–240132–4 (pbk)
ISBN: 978–1–138–95877–7 (hbk)
ISBN: 978–1–315–66106–3 (ebk)

DOI: 10.4324/9781315661063

Typeset in Bembo
by Swales & Willis Ltd, Exeter, Devon, UK

CONTENTS

List of Contributors x

PART 1
Introduction 1

1 Introduction 3
   Nancey Green Leigh and Bruce Stiftel

2 Education and Demonstration of Professional Competence 12
   Andrea I. Frank

PART 2
Pillars of Planning Education 29

3 Planning History 31
   Robert Freestone

4 Teaching Planning Theory in China 44
   Kang Cao, Qinshi Li, Xiaolan Li, and Li Zheng

5 Planning Law 55
   Richard K. Norton

PART 3
Pedagogy 67

6 Designing Core Curricula 69
   Jessica L. H. Doyle and Bruce Stiftel

7	Planning Technology *Jennifer Minner, Jennifer Evans-Cowley, and Nader Afzalan*	78
8	Role of Studios and Workshops *Judith Grant Long*	90
9	Gender *Dory Reeves*	100

PART 4
Planning Skills   115

10	Written, Oral, and Graphic Communication *Hemalata C. Dandekar*	117
11	Research Design and Practice *David Hsu*	127
12	Quantitative Methods *William J. Drummond*	134
13	Qualitative Methods *Sai Balakrishnan and Ann Forsyth*	145
14	Spatial Analysis *Subhrajit Guhathakurta*	162
15	Leadership *Michael Neuman*	174

PART 5A
Traditional Subjects of Specialization   185

16	Local Economic Development Planning *Nancey Green Leigh and Lynn M. Patterson*	187
17	Regional Economic Development Planning *Edward M. Bergman and Edward Feser*	196
18	Planning at the National Level *Daniel Galland and Frank Othengrafen*	206

19	International Comparative Planning *Frank Othengrafen and Daniel Galland*	217
20	Land Use Planning *Nicole Gurran*	227
21	Environmental Planning *Christian Zuidema and Gert de Roo*	238
22	Transportation Planning *Andrea Broaddus and Robert Cervero*	253
23	Housing and Real Estate Planning *Katrin B. Anacker*	265
24	Urban Design *Barbara Faga*	275

PART 5B
Essential Subjects of Planning Sustainable Places — 293

25	Climate Change *Ward Lyles and Mark Stevens*	295
26	Water Resources Planning *Caitlin Dyckman*	305
27	Planning the Just City *Rachel Garshick Kleit and Rebecca F. Kemper*	323
28	Food Systems *Alfonso Morales and Rosalind Greenstein*	332

Index — *342*

CONTRIBUTORS

Nader Afzalan is Visiting Assistant Professor at the University of Redlands, the chair of the American Planning Association (APA)'s Technology Division, and the co-chair of the APA's Smart Cities and Sustainability Taskforce. Prior to earning his Ph.D. from the University of Colorado, he spent seven years working as a project director, urban planner, and designer on projects focused on socio-economic revitalization of downtown areas, redevelopment of historical towns, and ecological planning. His collaborative approaches to land use and environmental planning, civic technologies, and smart cities have been presented and published in the U.S. and internationally in the Middle East and Europe.

Katrin B. Anacker is Associate Professor at the Schar School of Policy and Government at George Mason University. She received her Ph.D. from The Ohio State University, where she was a Fulbright Fellow, and previously taught at Virginia Tech's Metropolitan Institute. A former co-editor of *Housing Policy Debate*, she now serves as the editor for *Housing and Society* and the review editor of the *Journal of Planning Education and Research*. Dr. Anacker is the editor of *The New American Suburb: Poverty, Race and the Economic Crisis* (Routledge, 2015), co-editor of *Introduction to Housing* (University of Georgia Press, 2018), and co-editor of *The Routledge Handbook of Housing Policy and Planning* (2020).

Sai Balakrishnan is Assistant Professor of Urban Planning at Harvard University's Graduate School of Design. Prior to that, she was an Assistant Professor in International Development at the Edward J. Bloustein School of Planning and Public Policy at Rutgers University; she has also worked as an urban planner in the United States, India, and the United Arab Emirates, and as a consultant to the UN-Habitat in Nairobi, Kenya. Through her research and teaching interests, Balakrishnan focuses on institutions for managing rapid urbanization, comparative land use planning, and property rights. She is currently developing a book manuscript on the rapid urbanization and land conflicts along highways in India.

Edward M. Bergman is Professor Emeritus at the University of North Carolina (1972–1995) and Vienna University of Economics and Business (1995–2009), where he taught regional planning and science and conducted research in the United States and the European Union. His recent research has focused on economic integration, technological diffusion, academic mobility, commercialization of university research, industrial clusters, regional innovation systems, and infrastructure.

Andrea Broaddus has worked in the field of transportation planning since 1997 and is now a Lecturer in City and Regional Planning at the University of California, Berkeley. She holds a Ph.D. from the Department of City and Regional Planning at the University of California, Berkeley, and has seven years of experience teaching graduate and undergraduate courses in transportation planning. Her research focuses on travel demand management.

Kang Cao is Associate Professor at the Institute of Urban Planning and Design at Zhejiang University in Hangzhou, China. She received her doctor of science degree in human geography from Nanjing University and from 2005 to 2007 taught in the School of Geography at Beijing Normal University. Her research mainly concerns planning theory study, especially philosophical tradition and evolvement mechanism of planning theory. She is the author of *A Brief History of Modern Urban Planning in the Western World* (Southeast University Press, 2010).

Robert Cervero is Professor Emeritus and former chair of the Department of City and Regional Planning at the University of California, Berkeley, and Director of the University of California Transportation Center. His research focuses on the intersection of urban transportation and land use systems.

Hemalata C. Dandekar is a licensed architect in the state of California and a former Head and Professor of City and Regional Planning in the College of Architecture and Environmental Design at California State University, San Luis Obispo. She is also a member of the board of directors for the San Luis Obispo County Housing Trust Fund. A former Director of the School of Planning and Landscape Architecture at Arizona State University (ASU), Dr. Dandekar is the editor of *The Planner's Use of Information* (Planners Press, 2003).

Gert de Roo is Professor of Spatial Planning and head of the Department of Spatial Planning and Environment at the Faculty of Spatial Sciences at the University of Groningen. From 2011 to 2015 he served as President of the Association of European Schools of Planning (AESOP). He is also the editor of AESOP's InPlanning Digital Platform, and since 2010 has edited the Ashgate Publishing Series on Planning Theory. Most of his research and publications focus on decentralization processes, in particular those concerning physical and environmental planning, and he has participated in numerous environmental planning initiatives in the Netherlands.

Jessica L. H. Doyle received her doctorate from the School of City and Regional Planning at the Georgia Institute of Technology. Her research focuses on metropolitan-level differences in rates of Latino entrepreneurship. She has previously published in *Planning Forum*, *Carolina Planning Journal*, and *plaNext*, and co-authored, with Catherine L. Ross, a chapter in *Megaregions: Planning for Global Competitiveness* (Island Press, 2009). She is also a mother of two.

William J. Drummond is Associate Professor of City and Regional Planning at the Georgia Institute of Technology and Director of the Master of Science in Geographic Information Science and Technology (MS-GIST) program. With Arthur C. Nelson, he is the co-author of *Handbook for Economic Development Geographic Information Systems* (US Economic Development Administration, 1998).

Contributors

Caitlin Dyckman is Associate Professor in the Department of City Planning and Real Estate Development St Clemson University. She earned a Ph.D. from the University of California, Berkeley, and a J.D. from the University of California, Davis. With both a legal and a planning background, her research focuses on national and international management issues where land (and its uses) meets water. Her work has concerned state water planning and interstate allocation dispute resolution; water rights restructuring in response to climate change and changing demand sectors; coastal and shoreline management innovations; integration of municipal and household-level water conservation opportunities into urban planning; and planners' roles in federally funded watershed-based planning.

Jennifer Evans-Cowley is Provost and Vice President for Academic Affairs at the University of North Texas, having previously served as Vice Provost for Capital Planning and Regional campuses at The Ohio State University and Associate Dean for Academic Affairs and Administration for Ohio State's College of Engineering. She is the editor of *Essential Readings in Urban Planning* (Planetizen Press, second edition 2014) and author of the *Report on the Nature of Online Dialogue in the Planning Academy* for the Association of Collegiate Schools of Planning (ACSP)'s Task Force on Professional Dialogue in 2016.

Barbara Faga is Professor of Professional Practice in Urban Design at the Edward J. Bloustein School of Planning and Public Policy of Rutgers University, following a 30-year career as an author, professor, and professional urban planner. While at EDAW (now AECOM) she served as chair of the board of directors from 1996 to 2005. She is the author of *Designing Public Consensus: the Civic Theater of Community Participation for Architects, Planners, and Urban Designers* (Wiley, 2006) and the co-editor, with Harley J. Etienne, of *Planning Atlanta* (Planners Press, 2014).

Edward Feser is Provost and Executive Vice President at Oregon State University, having previously served as Internim Vice Chancellor and Provost at the University of Illinois at Urbana-Champaign. His expertise is in regional economic development, innovation and technology policy, public policy and management, strategic planning, and regional economic modeling. Since 2010, Dr. Feser has served as a senior research fellow with the Center for Regional Economic Competitiveness in Arlington, Virginia.

Ann Forsyth is Professor of Urban Planning at the Harvard School of Design, where she directs the Master's in Urban Planning program and is also Co-Director of the Healthy Places Design Lab. She has also previously taught at Cornell University, the University of Minnesota, and the University of Massachusetts. She is the author or co-author of five books and over 180 refereed and magazine articles, chapters, monographs, edited collections, and book reviews; in addition, she has written dozens of professional reports, reprints, and works in other media. Dr. Forsyth has won over 60 awards, citations, named lectureships, and fellowships for individual and collaborative professional and research work.

Andrea I. Frank is Senior Lecturer in Planning and Urban Design at the University of Cardiff. She is also a Fellow of the Higher Education Academy, a member of the Spatial Planning and City Environments (SPACE) research group, and an affiliate researcher of the Sustainable Places Research Institute. Her areas of expertise include land use and spatial planning, sustainability and environmental issues, public participation, GIS, policy exercise/gaming and scenario planning, creativity techniques, and urban design. With Christopher

Silver, she is the co-editor of *Urban Planning Education: Beginnings, Global Movement and Future Prospects* (Springer, 2018).

Robert Freestone is Professor of Planning in the Faculty of Built Environment at the University of New South Wales. His research interests lie in the development of modern planning theory and practice in Australia, heritage conservation, metropolitan restructuring, and planning education. He has won several state and national awards for excellence in planning scholarship from the Planning Institute of Australia since 1995, including the 2011 national award for research and scholarship for his book *Urban Nation: Australia's Planning Heritage*. He was president of the International Planning History Society (2003–2006) and a board member of the Society for American City and Regional Planning History (2015–2019).

Steven P. French is Dean of the College of Design and Professor of City and Regional Planning at Georgia Institute of Technology. He previously served as Director of the City Planning program, Director of the Center for Geographic Information Systems at Georgia Tech, and Associate Dean of research. French's teaching and research activities focus on sustainable urban development, land use planning, GIS applications, and natural hazard risk assessment. He is the author or co-author of more than 25 refereed journal articles and four books, and has served on the editorial boards of the *Journal of the American Planning Association*, *Journal of Planning Education and Research*, *Journal of the Urban and Regional Information Systems Association*, and *Earthquake Spectra*.

Daniel Galland is Associate Professor of Urban and Regional Planning at the Norwegian University of Life Sciences (NMBU) and chair of the Excellence in Education Board of the Association of European Schools of Planning (2017–2020). He is also part-time Associate Professor at Aalborg University in Denmark and has been Visiting Scholar in the School of Urban Planning at McGill University (2013) and the Institute of Urban and Territorial Studies at the Catholic University of Chile (2012). His research and teaching experience are in planning theory, metropolitan planning and international comparative planning.

Rosalind Greenstein is Lecturer in Urban Environmental Policy and Planning at Tufts University. She has previously taught urban planning and policy at the University of North Carolina, Chapel Hill, the University of Wisconsin-Madison, Clark University, and Jackson State University. She was the founding chair of the Department of Economic and Community Development at the Lincoln Institute of Land Policy, where her department addressed the distribution of the costs and benefits of development. She is the co-editor (with Yesim Sungu-Eryilmaz) of *Recycling the City: The Use and Reuse of Urban Land* (Lincoln Institute of Land Policy, 2004).

Subhrajit Guhathakurta is Professor and chair in the School of City and Regional Planning as well as Director of the Center for Spatial Planning Analytics and Visualization (CSPAV) at the Georgia Institute of Technology. He was previously Associate Director of the School of Geographical Sciences and Urban Planning at Arizona State University (ASU) and among the founding faculty members of ASU's School of Sustainability. He is the immediate past co-editor of the *Journal of Planning Education and Research* and is on the editorial board of the *Journal of American Planning Association* and several other urban planning journals. He is a member of technical advisory boards of the Association of Bay Area Governments and the Atlanta Regional Commission.

Contributors

Nicole Gurran is Professor in the Sydney School of Architecture, Design and Planning at the University of Sydney. She has led and collaborated on a series of research projects on aspects of urban policy, housing, sustainability, and planning, funded by the Australian Research Council (ARC), the Australian Urban and Housing Research Institute (AHURI), as well as state and local government. Her numerous publications include *Urban Planning and the Housing Market: International Perspectives for Policy and Practice* with Glen Bramley (Palgrave Macmillan, 2017), *Politics, Planning and Housing Supply in Australia, England and Hong Kong*, with Nick Gallent and Rebecca Chiu (Routledge, July 2016), and *Australian Urban Land Use Planning: Principles, Policy, and Practice* (Sydney University Press 2011, 2007).

David Hsu is Associate Professor in the Department of Urban Studies and Planning at the Massachusetts Institute of Technology. His research focuses on the design, planning, governance, and operation of energy and water networks; energy access and adoption of new technologies; and new technologies and strategies to control distributed energy sources, electric vehicles, and stationary storage. Current projects include studies of policies and tools for planning green infrastructure, funded by the US Environmental Protection Agency, and deployment of experimental microgrids in rural India, funded by the Tata Center for Technology and Design at MIT.

Rebecca F. Kemper is a Ph.D. candidate in City and Regional Planning at Ohio State under the guidance of Dr. Bernadette Hanlon. Rebecca is interested in modeling urban social dynamics through complexity science. She has been an invited guest instructor at the University of Seoul, South Korea, Kent State University, and the University of Cincinnati. She also served as a research assistant for the Weinland Park neighborhood HUD Community Challenge Grant and works with Ohio State's Food Innovation Center.

Rachel Garshick Kleit is Associate Dean for Faculty Affairs in the College of Engineering and Professor of City and Regional Planning, both at the Ohio State University. Dr. Kleit has written on the social network impacts of housing programs that mix incomes, the HOPE VI program, housing self-sufficiency programs, housing choice processes for low-income people, and on the role of the public housing authorities in the future of affordable housing. Additionally, she has been working on a stream of research addressing poverty more broadly, including the equity impact of economic development policies and the dynamics of fringe banking.

Nancey Green Leigh is Associate Dean for Research of the College of Design and Professor of the School of City and Regional Planning at the Georgia Institute of Technology. She is the author of more than 50 articles and three books, including *Planning Local Economic Development* (with E. J. Blakely), now in its sixth edition, *Economic Revitalization: Cases and Strategies for City and Suburb* (with J. Fitzgerald), and *Stemming Middle Class Decline: The Challenge to Economic Development Planning*. She previously served as Vice President of the Association of Collegiate Schools of Planning, President of the Faculty Women's Interest Group, and was co-editor of the *Journal of Planning Education and Research* from 2012 to 2016. She was elected a Fellow of the American Institute of Certified Planners in 2008. Her current research, funded by the U.S. National Science Foundation, focuses on the impacts of robotics and automation diffusion on industry and employment in urban and regional economies.

Qinshi Li works at the Hangzhou City Planning and Design Academy, having received her master's degree of engineering from Zhejiang University in 2018. Her research interests include the diffusion of zoning concept in China, on which she has published papers and made a presentation at the ICCCASU conference in 2017. In addition, she worked as a teaching assistant of the Planning History class in 2017 and has also published papers on process teaching.

Xiaolan Li is a graduate student in the Department of Regional and Urban Planning at Zhejiang University, China. He received his bachelor degree from Zhejiang University. His research mainly concerns planning theory study, especially the issue of the dissemination of planning ideas. He also studies new ways of planning education.

Judith Grant Long is Associate Professor of Sport Management and Urban Planning at the University of Michigan. Dr. Long is an internationally recognized expert on the planning and finance of sport and tourism districts. Her first book, *Public-Private Partnerships for Major League Sports Facilities* will soon be offered in a second edition. Long has recently completed a two-volume series entitled *Olympic Infrastructures*, which provides graphic inventories of the construction of venues, villages, and ancillary venues for the summer and winter Olympics. Her current book project, *Olympic Urbanism: Rome to Rio*, analyzes the promises and legacies of building for the Olympic Games. Long has also written several articles addressing sport and tourism issues, including the economic impacts of the Tour de France, and the fates of former major league stadiums and arenas built in the 1960s and 1970s. A certified city planner, Long also sits on the board of the Sports Innovation Lab, the Coliseum conference, and is an academic advisor to the National Executive Forum on Public-Private Partnerships in Canada.

Ward Lyles is Assistant Professor in the Urban Planning Program at the University of Kansas. His research and teaching interests center on the intersection of people, the built environment, and the natural environment. He has published articles in the *Journal of Environmental Planning and Management*, *Cityscape*, the *Journal of Planning Literature*, and *Natural Hazards Review*, and is the co-founder of Madison Magnet, a social-capital-oriented non-profit organization based in Madison, Wisconsin.

Jennifer Minner is Associate Professor in City and Regional Planning at Cornell University. She is focused on methods of care, conservation, and sustainable adaptation of the built environment. Additionally, her research emphasizes analytical and participatory mapping; equity, reinvestment dynamics, and public space; and creative and critical approaches to technology. A former chair of the Olympia Heritage Commission and past president of the MidTexMod (central Texas) chapter of Docomomo US, she has published in *Urban Studies*, *Economic Development Quarterly*, *APT Bulletin: The Journal of Preservation Technology*, and the *Journal of the American Planning Association*, among others.

Alfonso Morales is Professor and also Vilas Trust Awardee in Urban and Regional Planning at the University of Wisconsin-Madison. In 2014 he initiated the Kaufman Lab for the Study and Design of Food Systems and Marketplaces; he is also the principal investigator, founder, and program director of MIFI Markets, a program that uses data-collection strategies to help farmers' markets. He is the co-editor, with Julie Dawson, of *Cities of Farmers: Problems, Possibilities and Processes of Producing Food in Cities* (University of Iowa Press, 2017) and, with John S. Butler and David Torres, of *An American Story: Mexican-American Entrepreneurship and Wealth Creation* (Purdue University Press, 2009).

Michael Neuman is Professor of Sustainable Urbanism at the University of Westminster. His prior appointment was Professor of Sustainable Urbanism in the Faculty of the Built

Environment at the University of New South Wales in Sydney, Australia, where he served as Director of the Infrastructure Research Cluster, chair of the Built Environment Node of the Australian Climate Change Adaption Research Network for Settlements and Infrastructure, and Associate Director of the City Futures Research Centre. His books include *Engendering Cities, The Futures of the City Region, The Imaginative Institution, Building California's Future*, and *Coordinating Growth and Environmental Management Through Consensus Building*. Since 1995 he has been principal of the Michael Neuman Consultancy.

Richard K. Norton holds a joint appointment as Professor in the Urban and Regional Planning Program and Professor in the Program in the Environment at the University of Michigan. He serves on the planning law committee of the Michigan Association of Planning (MAP) and has written friend-of-the-court appellate briefs to the Michigan Court of Appeals and the Michigan Supreme Court on behalf of the American Planning Association and MAP regarding planning and zoning disputes in the state. His most recent research has focused on the challenges of managing shorelands along the Laurentian Great Lakes.

Frank Othengrafen is Professor of Urban and Regional Planning at the Faculty for Spatial Planning at TU Dortmund. Before his appointment at TU Dortmund he was Associate Professor for Regional Planning and Governance at Leibniz Universität Hannover (2013–2019) and Visiting Professor for Regional Planning and Development at HafenCity Universität Hamburg (2010–2012). He has research and teaching experience in the fields of urban and regional planning and governance, planning theory, international comparative planning, and planning culture.

Lynn M. Patterson is the principal planner for B+C Studio, a landscape architecture, design, and planning firm based in Atlanta, where she specializes in economic development. She has provided site selection services for Fortune 100 and 500 companies and helped to negotiate state and local incentives She holds a Ph.D. in planning from Georgia Tech and has taught at Georgia Tech and Kennesaw State University; she is also a co-founder of Mango Tree Foundation, Inc., a non-profit organization that seeks to assist women globally to pursue sustainable business opportunities.

Dory Reeves is Principal, Reeves and Associates; chartered fellow of the Royal Town Planning Insitute, and associate of the New Zealand Planning Institute. Her professional practice experience, teaching, and research involve equality and diversity, management skills for effective practitioners, and academic literacy. She co-led the national project Te Whaihanga, a multi-partner project under the auspices of Ako Aotearoa (the National Centre for Tertiary Teaching Experience), to better prepare built environment professionals to work with Māori. Her most recent book is *Management Skills for Effective Planners* (Palgrave Macmillan, 2016).

Mark Stevens is Associate Professor in the School of Community and Regional Planning at the University of British Columbia. He is also Chair of the school's Masters of Community and Regional Planning program. His current research interests are in meta-research and municipal land use planning.

Bruce Stiftel is Professor Emeritus at the School of City and Regional Planning at the Georgia Institute of Technology. His most recent books are *Adaptive Governance and Water Conflict* (co-edited with John T. Scholz), and *Dialogues in Urban and Regional Planning,*

Volume 2 (co-edited with Vanessa Watson and Henri Ascelrad), and he served as consultant to UN-Habitat in production of the *World Cities Report 2016*. He previously served as President of the Association of Collegiate Schools of Planning, co-editor of the *Journal of Planning Education and Research*, founding chairperson of the Global Planning Education Association Network, and member of the Planning Accreditation Board. He is a member of the editorial boards of *Planning Theory*, *International Planning Studies*, *Journal of the American Planning Association*, *Journal of Comparative Urban Law and Policy*, and *Town Planning Review*, and represents the Global Planning Education Association Network to UN-Habitat's University Network Initiative.

Li Zheng is a plan and program manager at Liangjiang Development & Investment Group Co Ltd. in Chongqing, China. She received European Union Erasmus Mundus full scholarship in 2013 and got her master's degree of science in both Radboud University Nijmegen and Cardiff University. She participated in a China-German joint research in the Academy of Spatial Research and Planning (Akademie für Raumforschung und Landesplanung, ARL) on Germany's spatial planning system in 2015. Her research mainly concerns spatial planning, especially the evaluation of spatial plan implementation. She also focuses on public service delivery and regional development policy studies.

Christian Zuidema is Assistant Professor of Spatial Planning at the University of Groningen. In 2013 he was named the university's Lecturer of the Year. He has published in *Landscape Research*, the *Journal of Cleaner Production*, *Energy Policy*, and *Urban Design and Planning*, among others. He is the author of *Decentralization in Environmental Governance: A Post-Contingency Approach* (Routledge, 2016) and the co-author, with Gert de Roo and Jelger Visser, of *Smart Methods for Environmental Externalities: Urban Planning, Environmental Health and Hygiene in the Netherlands* (Routledge, 2016).

PART 1

Introduction

1
INTRODUCTION

Nancey Green Leigh and Bruce Stiftel

Higher education's response to globalization has included growth in planning educational exchanges across international boundaries. This handbook addresses the interest and need for understanding how planning education is developed and delivered in different international contexts. It also informs dialogue on the mobility of planners educated under different national schema.

Contributors to the handbook write about general planning knowledge, planning skills, traditional and emerging planning specializations, and pedagogy. They cover the role of their topics in educating planners, the theory and methods of their subject, key literature contributions, and course design.

This handbook comes at a time when there are growing concerns about retrenchment of the globalization that has characterized the world economy and international society since the end of World War II. This "deglobalization" has the potential to undo and destabilize much of the progress and international cooperation that has improved the lives of so many throughout the world. The corollary is the rise in nationalism whereby, as Duara (2018) observes, "the relationship between national political movements and economic development has taken a more sinister turn, exposing the tension between *self* and *other* that lies at the heart of all forms of nationalism."

Globalization's impacts, of course, have never all been positive. While a marked increase in trade and communications in the post-WWII era made nations more interdependent and wealthier, there has also been rising social and economic inequality that has contributed to the rise of nationalism. The associated protectionist tendencies, which have intensified recently, are weakening global supply chains that will lower economic growth, limit migration, and increase human suffering. These protectionist tendencies also erode the cooperation and interdependence among nations that is widely acknowledged to be necessary for solving critical global problems such as climate change.

One could argue that a handbook focused on international planning education has diminished relevance in an era of deglobalization. However, we would argue that it is more than relevant: it is greatly needed. Thirty years ago, from his study of planning schools, Niebanck (1988) found "planning as the principal means by which the human community can confidently sustain itself on this planet." We can see his statement as a heady self-validation, as well as a heavy challenge.

The enterprise we call planning education bears many of the traits of any teaching program—classes meet, homework is prepared, exams are taken—but, it is also unique in breadth of aspirations, spirit of collaboration, and experimental approach. If planners are to usefully address the challenges of rapid urbanization, economic development, disaster preparedness, climate change, social justice, and resource sustainability, they must develop capacities for prediction, analysis, and intervention that defy textbook prescriptions, and most of all, they must be prepared for lifelong learning and renewal. With this, the first *Handbook of International Planning Education*, the editors and authors have sought to capture the essence of that unique education in ways that can richly inform curricular and pedagogic choices by city and regional planning faculties across the globe.

Today's planning schools are as diverse as the institutional and cultural communities they serve. Design is the predominant theme in Latin-American, Mediterranean, and East Asian schools; policy the focus in Anglo-American and North European schools. Western country planning favors bottom-up, inclusive planning processes; in the East, top-down, centralized planning is more common. Land use and urban design represent the bulk of city planning in many countries; integrated planning involving infrastructure, housing, jobs, and sanitation is seen as essential in others (Sanyal, 2005; UN-Habitat, 2009, 2016).

The pedagogy flowing from these substantive differences is also diverse. Perhaps the more expected differences distinguish lecture hall from studio, theory debates from methods practice, but cultural norms affect pedagogy as well. Teachers are sometimes seen as authorities who cannot be challenged; at other times the give and take of a mutual learning community is expected. While planning education is often delivered at small scales, resource limitations can dictate mass education formats (Frank & Silver, 2018).

Planning academic staff can be equally diverse. In many institutions, a doctoral degree is the expected entry credential; in others, professional post-graduate degrees predominate; or the teaching staff may have only a first degree. Normal assignments may encompass teaching and research, full-time teaching may be expected, or the institution may fund only a part-time salary, with staff expected to maintain professional practices (UN-Habitat, 2009).

What is increasingly obvious to many observers is that despite this diversity, or perhaps because of it, learning across national boundaries is necessary. It was not long ago that international cross-fertilization among planning schools was severely limited, with North to South transfers dominating, often as alumni of European and North American schools moved into teaching positions in the Global South (Stiftel & Mukhopadhyay, 2007; Stiftel, Watson, & Acselrad, 2007). That unidirectional flow is increasingly omnidirectional and, today, there is growing recognition that many of the best planning ideas originate in countries that did not use to be idea exporters. There is also growing diversity in the international flow of planning students and faculty. In recognition of this fact, this handbook, while largely drawing from English-language scholarship, features authors from multiple countries and features research and case studies from around the world.

Describing a global process for movement of planning ideas across national groupings and networks leading to *contingent universals*, Healey (2010) observed: "... none of this stitching together of disparate networks and structuring dynamics reduces the diverse particularities of the individual contexts in which planning work is done." Roy (2011) calls for a critical transnationalism forging transnational solidarities, embedded in yet transcending national systems of governance. She references widely-known exemplars of innovative planning practice, such as the Singapore Model of unprecedented economic growth maintained by a well-ordered city. These exemplars from abroad enable what she calls a "crucible of informed debate" among stakeholders in a place. Sanyal (2010) asks us to remember culture has always been open to influence from abroad and today's planning cultures have characteristics that resulted from external influence:

"What is necessary is that we address the challenges of globally-linked problems by identifying the common ground—a global social commons—which would emphasize commonality over differences, and valorize linkages and 'contamination' over purity of cultures."

The Planning Schools Movement that began with formation of the (US) Association of Collegiate Schools of Planning in 1959, and spread to planning school associations in every major world region, has been key to facilitating cross-fertilization among planning educators (Stiftel, 2009; Stiftel & Watson, 2005). Today, while language and national boundaries are still powerful, planning educators read many of the same journals and attend many of the same conferences, at least much more than they used to.

Structure of the Book

To lay out key issues and practices of planning as taught in tertiary education institutions around the world, we commissioned 28 chapters by 42 authors based in ten countries. These chapters are organized into five sections, described below. After beginning with consideration of the accreditation and quality assurance in planning schools, chapters review pedagogy in common core subjects. We then turn to elective subjects and conclude with the role of studios and workshops.

The authors use their experience and research to identify issues and suggest approaches, but readers must localize each subject. National planning systems have to be taken into account. Higher education practices in specific countries have to be reflected. The context of the program in its university and the skills and ideas of the faculty have to be considered.

1. Introduction

Andrea Frank anchors the discussion with a review of the connections between planning education and organized professional planning practice in Chapter 2. She illustrates accreditation systems in place in France, Germany, Poland, the United Kingdom, the United States, and elsewhere, as well as changing approaches to competency assessment. Although there are differences among quality assurance systems administered by government or by professional bodies, these systems tend to work effectively when there is an organized planning profession that speaks with a clear voice.

2. Pillars of Planning Education

The third, fourth, and fifth chapters examine common core subjects. In Chapter 3, "Planning History," Robert Freestone insists that the past should be part of every planning education, but too often, it is not. Few planning programs have a historian on staff and available literature underserves much of the world. Still, well-articulated, successful models are presented for standalone planning history courses as well as modules focused on urbanism, joint development of history and theory, thematic history and city history.

China is a relative newcomer to planning theory, discussed by Kang Cao, Qinshi Li, Xiaolan Li, and Li Zheng in Chapter 4. Procedural planning theory is widely taught in graduate programs in China, but the approaches are highly diverse and both theories and examples are predominantly taken from abroad. The authors advocate for development of a more nationalized literature and pedagogy, but predict these will be a long time in coming.

In Chapter 5, "Planning Law," Richard Norton stresses that planners need enough knowledge of law to avoid errors in their practice. His review of planning law pedagogy suggests that the subject is best taught as a broad, interdisciplinary, highly-integrated cross-section of traditional and circumscribed academic and professional legal doctrines and practices. This involves foundational knowledge, technical skills, and application.

3. Pedagogy

The next chapters specifically address issues in the delivery of planning teaching. In Chapter 6, "Designing Core Curricula," Bruce Stiftel and Jessica Doyle suggest that the US-originated model of planning as rational, comprehensive decision making framed required core courses in planning in many countries for many years. The *generalist with a specialty* concept led to core curricula framing general knowledge, planning skills, and values. That model has evolved and core curricula now more widely reflect national planning systems, with debates about content common in schools and reflective of the background of academic staff and the employer/professional contexts in which schools operate.

Jennifer Minner, Jennifer Evans-Cowley, and Nader Afzalan provide a review of the fast changing and wide-ranging use of technology in planning education in Chapter 7. They reflect on five areas of innovation: expansion of means of delivery, new organization of university-based learning, uses of planning support systems in the classroom, growing diversity of data sources for planning, and proliferation of new technological tools in planning practice. After analyzing these innovations, they suggest collaboration with practice is vital to technological currency, and that technology should be the basis to foster creativity and critical thinking on the part of planning students.

Judith Grant Long examines the role of studios and workshops in Chapter 8. Studios and workshops are defining components of many planning programs, often relied upon to give tangible reality to book-based introductions from other courses. Studios have challenges, not the least of which is pressure for efficiency in higher education, but they remain highly valued and almost universally used. New instructional technologies have expanded the possibilities in studios, including multi-institutional partnerships.

Gender and its position in planning education is the focus of Chapter 9 by Dory Reeves. While there is substantial recognition of the importance of gender in how cities are experienced and in how planning is practiced, consideration of gender in the planning classroom has been quite limited until recently. Reeves reviews treatment of gender in planning classrooms in four Anglophone countries, persuasively showing the power of gender analysis, and suggests links between planning education and the United Nations' Sustainable Development Goal 5: Gender Equality and Empowerment of Women.

4. Planning Skills

The next six chapters are concerned with planning research skills common across nearly all planning education, regardless of location or specialization. For example, with rapid change in communication technologies and increased globalization of local economies, communication skills are even more vital than they used to be for effective planning practice. In Chapter 10, "Written, Oral, and Graphic Communication," Hemalata Dandekar discusses current practice and emphasizes that despite the rapidly changing landscape, the fundamentals of good communication remain in place, with preparation and organization as important as ever.

In Chapter 11, "Research Design and Practice," David Hsu examines the teaching of research design in planning schools from the perspective of cultural understanding and investigator trust. He begins with the understanding that these "soft" skills are not usually part of the formal curriculum, and lays out strategies for promoting trust in research participants and clients in order to raise the impact of planning research.

"Quantitative Methods," Chapter 12, is a nearly universal course in planning curricula. Author William Drummond provides an overview of teaching methods for understanding how cities grow and decline, forecasting the future, and tracking progress in goal achievement. He considers the impact of new learning philosophies and technologies, as well as choice of software in the context of foundational tools, database methods, statistical methods, and analytic methods.

Sai Balakrishnan and Ann Forsyth examine qualitative methods in Chapter 13, focused on core subjects. They recognize that qualitative methods are useful both as formal research tools and as less formal, more practical day-to-day activities in planning practice. Beginning with justifications for qualitative methods in research as complementary to quantitative methods, they illustrate some of the many contexts in which practicing planners use qualitative tools to identify and systematize planning information and they compare strategies for supporting validity and reliability in qualitative research. They also consider the potential for generalizability from qualitative studies and key ethical questions.

In Chapter 14, Subhrajit Guhathakurta reviews spatial analysis, tools for understanding urban form, and accessibility. Within a framework of understanding heterogeneity in urban land uses, equity, and exposure vulnerability, he discusses spatial clustering, network analysis, and site suitability analysis.

To be effective, planners must understand leadership. In Chapter 15, Michael Neuman asks how leadership can enhance planning practice. Recognizing that leadership is conditioned by culture, Neuman considers future orientation, situational awareness, cultural awareness, communication, and concern for the greater good as aspects of leadership that planners find useful.

5a. Traditional Subjects of Specialization

Chapters 16 through 28 present elective subjects of planning curricula, but these have been split into two categories. The first set of chapters cover specializations that have longer histories of being taught in planning schools, while the final chapters cover emerging specializations of particular interest as planning incorporates issues having to do with the "triple bottom line" of economic, social, and environmental sustainability.

Local economic development planning is distinguished from its regional counterpart by spatial focus and emphasis on the local economy within larger contexts, observe Nancey Green Leigh and Lynn Patterson in Chapter 16. It can also be distinguished within the larger economic development field by the unique role of planners. Informed by broader planning values, local economic development planners distinguish growth from development, and seek solutions that reduce inequality and increase sustainability while promoting resilient economies. From this perspective, the authors review tools to strengthen market-based development, including economic profiling, industry analysis, workforce analysis, brownfield redevelopment, microenterprises, and tourism.

In Chapter 17, Edward Bergman and Edward Feser review pedagogy for regional economic development planning. Between the two extremes of fully top-down, state-led planning and unmoored market-led development lies the recognition that trade often occurs between regions, and that economic activity has specific, and spatially measurable, spillover effects; therefore, regardless of the organization of the local and national economy in which they live and work, all planners need to think about economic development regionally. Bergman and Feser outline the key topics—employment clusters, anchor components, industrial recruitment, and workforce training—and suggest effective approaches to instruction of both theory and method.

In Chapter 18, Daniel Galland and Frank Othengrafen examine national planning. They show how national planning is linked to political ideology and how the field has adapted to global changes from the 1980s, including responses to neoliberalism and the movement toward strategic spatial planning. They illustrate with examples from Denmark and Germany, showing how the teaching of national planning has reacted to broader shifts in planning thought from rationalism to communication.

Othengrafen and Galland address international comparative planning in Chapter 19. While "international" appears in many course titles, courses with substantial comparative or multinational content are relatively few in number. Where they exist, they can be powerful complements to courses that focus on planning in one country, building repertoires of lessons and reflections, and encouraging adoption of techniques new to the home context. This chapter suggests how to use such courses to best effect and gives valuable illustrations.

Land use planning is the focus of Chapter 20 by Nicole Gurran. Understanding the processes and operational techniques of land use planning is critical for implementing strategic spatial policy across all scales of urban governance and geography. Therefore this chapter provides an overview of land use planning, including a discussion of most common theories and methods, a summary of key arguments and rationales for justifying public intervention in the urban development process through land use regulation, and an articulation of normative principles to guide planners' use of such interventions. After outlining justifications for land planning in economic theory, Gurran suggests key components to sustainability in land use, and illustrates successful programs. She ends with suggestions of key literature.

Christian Zuidema and Gert de Roo discuss environmental planning in Chapter 21. They begin by distinguishing major approaches to the field, both land use oriented and more general, resource-focused and concerned with pollution control. While environmental concerns have long been part of planning practice and teaching, there is no particular "canon" for environmental planning, which is by its nature interdisciplinary. They outline key areas of planning approaches to environmental questions, including ecology, ethics, standards, and regulation, and discuss the differences between reactive and proactive approaches to environmental policy integration. They conclude with a discussion of how interacting levels of governance influence environmental policy-making, with an emphasis on the role of central governmental planning.

Andrea Broaddus and Robert Cervero discuss transportation planning in Chapter 22. With twin foci of roads and transit, this specialty typically aims at addressing accessibility and mobility of people and movement of freight. Forecasting and modeling methods, once quite standard, are undergoing considerable renewal in the age of big data. The authors recognize considerable variation in course content and approach, including differing degrees of interdisciplinarity.

Chapter 23 by Katrin Anacker examines housing policy and housing markets with particular attention to planning for housing affordable to low-income households. Housing is a normal curricular component in the US, Canada, Australia, the Netherlands, France, New Zealand, and some Eastern European countries; it is typically not found in planning schools in England, Germany, and some other European countries. Curricular components address both supply and demand, with finance key to both. Programs seeking to expand home ownership and to curb homelessness are included.

The overview of traditional specializations closes with Barbara Faga's discussion of urban design. Once ubiquitous, urban design instruction is now highly variable across regions and specific schools, sometimes leading to strident debate. Urban design instruction is often heavily studio-oriented, frequently with the involvement of architects.

Introduction

5b. Essential Subjects of Planning Sustainable Places

Ward Lyles and Mark Stevens survey climate change pedagogy in Chapter 25. A relative newcomer to planning curricula, climate change mitigation and adaptation is taught with wide variation across schools. Stevens and Lyles lay out key decisions necessary to formulate the approach in a given school and review other organizational and pedagogical choices. These choices parallel the varying ways in which climate action is structured in planning practice.

Caitlin Dyckman's discussion of water resource management is presented in Chapter 26. Water supply is often taken for granted by city dwellers, but globally potable water is out of reach for hundreds of millions, and increasingly, water supplies are inadequate to demand. As a result, practice is in rapid flux with new technologies of increasing importance and conservation strategies in wide use. Dyckman reviews these issues as well as pricing, demand forecasting, flooding, and stormwater management.

Chapter 27 by Rachel Garshick Kleit and Rebecca F. Kemper considers planning the just city from a perspective anchored in the American Institute of Certified Planners' code of ethics. While the planning profession has enshrined social justice in its codes of professional conduct, and many of its agreed-upon ethical standards would, if followed precisely, contribute to the making of just cities, the idea of the "just city" is not universally present in planning teaching. The authors describe a pedagogy of dialogue to help students advance equity planning, engagement, and diversity in their practices. The chapter is designed to serve as a template for a seminar that leads students through a semester-long thought process, to help them consider the role of social structure in replicating societal inequity.

Finally, food systems planning is the focus of Chapter 28, by Alfonso Morales and Rosalind Greenstein. This relatively recent addition to planning curricula seeks to improve nutrition, health, employment, and land use through advances in agriculture, processing, distribution, and sales. Morales and Greenstein review syllabi from a broad sample of countries, comparing course structures, foci, and pedagogic approaches. Sometimes surprising linkages across many planning specializations are revealed.

Conclusion

This first *Handbook of International Planning Education* is limited to approaches to planning education that meet the criteria of the three English-language national planning education accreditation bodies: American, British, and Australian. We note these are distinct from English-language national planning *professional* accreditation or certification bodies. We acknowledge there are important non-English-language national planning education accreditation organizations, but translating and incorporating their approaches to planning education was beyond the scope of efforts to produce this handbook.

A few words about the differences in planning nomenclature found in different global regions are in order. What are called courses in Europe are called degree programs in the USA. And what are called courses in the USA are subjects or modules in Europe. Usage in other countries typically follows one of these two systems. Academic staff are called faculty members or just faculty in some countries. In other countries, the term faculty may refer to an entire team of academic staff members organized by disciplinary groupings, or what might be called a school or a college elsewhere. We have not standardized usage of these terms; instead, each chapter's author(s) makes the choice of terms to use.

In many respects the planning education begun at the University of Liverpool in 1907, Lvov Technical University in 1913, University of Karlsruhe in 1915, and the University of Illinois in

1917 shares ambitions and content with planning schools today (UN-Habitat, 2009). There is still the commitment to improve the experience of city dwellers. There is still the intent to draw science into planning decisions. There is still a broad, interdisciplinary orientation.

In other respects, planning education would be almost unrecognizable to students from the early twentieth century. While our early predecessors saw planning as essentially a large-scale version of architecture, today's planning educators see planning as the integration of a wide range of urban and regional policy areas, including community and economic development, housing, transportation, water, sanitation, parks, health and human services, and more. While early planning education was geared to staff top-down national planning projects and elite blue-ribbon planning commissions, today's planning educators are insistent on inclusivity in participation, transparency, and distributed control. While early planning schools taught modeling with wood, today's schools insist on proficiency in data analysis and modeling. The evolution of planning education has been a long arc of change bending toward social scientific legitimacy, policy integration, inclusiveness, social justice, and digital proficiency. Policy and design fashion has influenced planning education, sometimes introducing lasting extensions such as environmental protection, economic development, and resilience.

The global differences across planning education remain profound: design versus policy; land use versus comprehensive; nationally driven versus locally based. Planning educators must localize their teaching to reflect political systems, legal and cultural contexts, and often, resource availability. No solution, however well tested or thought through, travels perfectly into a different context; we anticipate, and hope to learn from, seeing the suggestions in this book modified and added to as its readers apply their local knowledge and understandings.

The goal of the editors of this first *Handbook of International Planning Education* was to make a significant contribution to a global conversation about planning pedagogy that would continue in subsequent editions, bringing new voices into the conversation. This handbook is a testament to both the course of the long arc toward inclusive, integrated, scientifically-sound planning, and the lasting nature of the differences across planning schools. What is clear today is that planning educators have much to learn from each other. Relaxing assumptions that seem inviolable in our own contexts leads to innovation and ultimately to the *contingent universals* that support a *global social commons*, advance planning practice, and improve communities and quality of life.

References

Duara, P. (2018). Development and the crisis of global nationalism. Retrieved from www.brookings.edu/blog/future-development/2018/10/04/development-and-the-crisis-of-global-nationalism/

Frank, A. I., & Silver, C. (2018). *Urban Planning Education: Beginnings, Global Movement and Future Prospects*. Heidelberg: Springer.

Healey, P. (2010). The transnational flow of knowledge and expertise in the planning field. In P. Healey & R. Upton (Eds.), *Crossing Borders: International Exchange and Planning Practices* (pp. 1–26). London: Routledge.

Niebanck, P. L. (1988). Planning education: Unleashing the future. *Journal of the American Planning Association*, 54(4), 432–442. doi:10.1080/01944368808976670

Roy, A. (2011). Commentary: Placing planning in the world—Transnationalism as practice and critique. *Journal of Planning Education and Research*, 31(4), 406–415. doi:10.1177/0739456x11405060

Sanyal, B. (2005). Hybrid planning cultures: the search for the global cultural commons. In B. Sanyal (Ed.), *Comparative Planning Cultures* (pp. 3–28). New York: Routledge.

Sanyal, B. (2010). Similarity or differences? what to emphasize now for effective planning practice. In P. Healey & R. Upton (Eds.), *Crossing Borders: International Exchange and Planning Practices* (pp. 329–350). London: Routledge.

Stiftel, B. (2009). Planning the paths of planning schools. *Australian Planner*, 46(1), 38–47. doi:10.1080/07293682.2009.9995289

Stiftel, B., & Mukhopadhyay, C. (2007). Thoughts on Anglo-American hegemony in planning scholarship: Do we read each other's work? *Town Planning Review*, 78(5), 545–572. doi:10.3828/tpr.78.5.2

Stiftel, B., & Watson, V. (2005). Global integration in planning scholarship. In B. Stiftel & V. Watson (Eds.), *Dialogues in Urban and Regional Planning* (Vol. 1, pp. 1–14). London: Routledge.

Stiftel, B., Watson, V., & Acselrad, H. (2007). Global commonality and regional specificity. In B. Stiftel, V. Watson, & H. Acselrad (Eds.), *Dialogues in Urban and Regional Planning* (Vol. 2, pp. 1–24). London: Routledge.

UN-Habitat. (2009). *Planning Sustainable Cities: Global Report on Human Settlements 2009*. Nairobi: United Nations, Human Settlements Programme.

UN-Habitat. (2016). *Urbanization and Development: Emerging Futures: World Cities Report 2016*. Nairobi: United Nations, Human Settlements Programme.

2
EDUCATION AND DEMONSTRATION OF PROFESSIONAL COMPETENCE

Andrea I. Frank

Introduction

Urban, city, regional, or spatial planning is practiced in many countries around the globe. Planners work in government departments, city councils, regional development agencies, private sector consultancies as well as in not-for-profit companies. Overall, planners engage with both design-focused tasks, including physical land use planning, and policy-oriented tasks, such as economic development, environmental protection, historic conservation and community planning (e.g., Rodwin and Sanyal, 2000; Dalton, 2001; Stiftel, et al. 2009; Hoch, 2012).

In the classification of occupations from the International Labour Organization (2012), planners are categorized as engineering professionals together with architects, surveyors and designers[1] (as opposed to craftspeople or members of a trade). Professions, according to Kerr et al. (1977) exhibit comparatively high levels of:

1) Expertise (derived from prolonged education and training in a body of knowledge);
2) Autonomy (derived from the freedom to choose the means to examine and solve problems);
3) Commitment (derived from personal interest in the pursuit of one's chosen specialty);
4) Identification (derived from the identification with fellow professionals through formal association structures and external reference);
5) Ethics (derived from agreed codes of conducts, ensuring impartial service and ethical behavior);
6) Standards (derived from commitments to continued professional development and policing the conduct of fellow professionals).

These characteristics are reflected emphatically in membership criteria and standards specified by professional bodies for planners. They also align with ILO's (2012) classification of planning as an occupation at *skill level 4* meaning that planners need to be able to perform complex problem-solving and decision-making tasks that demand creativity and draw on an extensive body of knowledge in a specialized field. Planners require excellent literacy and numeracy as well as communication skills in order to understand complex written material and communicate complex ideas via different media, e.g., Caves and Wagner (2018).

Professional competence or expertise in planning, which is formally defined as subject-specific (theoretical) knowledge and the skills to apply this knowledge in context, enables an individual to conduct work in a proficient manner. Knowledge and skills for planning are usually obtained through 3–6 years of postsecondary education. Admission into the profession may require additional periods of supervised on-the-job training, and/or an examination. This chapter first reviews the status of the profession and regulatory requirements associated with practice. Second, an overview of planning education pathways and how planning education programs contribute to professional competence development is presented together with a selection of professional competencies frameworks. The third and final part examines different stages of professional competency assessment.

Status and Professionalization of the Planning Field

Recognition of planning as a standalone field and its professionalization started comparatively late at the beginning of the 20th century, when the first degree programs solely for planning as well as requisite professional societies were established. Until then, planning topics were covered within landscape, surveying, engineering and architecture education. Opinions are divided on exactly what establishes an independent profession: the designation of a study field, a set of core competencies, a professional body, or a combination thereof. Using another approach, Hoch (2012) linked the achievement of independent occupational status for planning to the point in time when labor statistics start counts of urban and regional planning professionals.

Present day narratives portray planning professionals holistically: as place-makers who help to shape the built environment, the socio-economic milieu as well as resident communities, to become healthier, and more sustainable, resilient places. This means planners "work on the spatial distribution of things and activities in human settlements" (Fischler, 2012). They perform a variety of tasks including, but not restricted to, analyses of existing conditions and devising strategies, plans and designs for future transformations and change. Planners work across spatial scales from the site and neighborhood via the city and metropolitan region to countries and even continents. Planning requires collaboration with affected stakeholders and allied professionals such as engineers, natural scientists, architects and public health officials in order to address problems in an integrated, interdisciplinary manner. Competencies for planning therefore can be seen as context-dependent and diverse (Alexander, 2001). Additionally, and not unlike in other fields, competency requirements tend to change with career progression whereby early career professionals are more likely to rely on specific technical knowledge and skills whereas individuals in advanced career stages often require more leadership and management skills, e.g., Guzzetta and Bollens (2003).

Knowledge areas, skills and values for baseline and advanced professional competencies are traditionally determined by either national governments together with professional bodies and stakeholders such as academics or a subset of these. Qualified (also known as chartered or certified) status in professional occupations signifies that an individual has achieved a predetermined level of professional competence. The status can be awarded by a professional body or statutory registration board (Lester, 2009). Professional bodies or registration boards also monitor ethical behavior (prescribed in codes of practice) and continued professional development (CPD) of members and registered practitioners. To ensure that future practitioners have suitable competencies, most professional bodies conduct regular reviews to update their competency frameworks. These frameworks, in turn, shape professional education programs, certification and CPD requirements.

Depending on the level of regulation associated with a profession, the implications of achieving certified status differ. Broadly, three levels of professional regulation can be distinguished. First, there are regulated professions for which certification is a pre-condition to legally practice. Regulated professions are those for which governments consider it necessary to protect the public as far as possible from serious harm incurred through incompetence or professional misconduct; they usually include health care professions, architects, air traffic controllers or selected specialist engineers but *rarely urban and city planners*.[2] As professional regulation is typically linked to nation states, requirements and regulation differ and qualifications are not necessarily and automatically transferable across national boundaries. Individuals relocating to another country and wishing to practice in a regulated profession have to have their qualifications recognized by the relevant national regulatory body. Administration of professional regulation is facilitated either via state-run processes or self-regulation (Randall, 2000) by a professional organization which has been granted the power of monitoring standards and qualifications by government.

A second type are self-organized[3] professions, for which in the absence of legal restrictions, professional bodies impose requirements to police qualifications for practitioners. Planning in the UK, Canada, Australia, New Zealand and the United States, for example, falls into this category. In contrast to regulated professions, individuals lacking formal qualifications such as a subject-specific (accredited) higher education degree and membership in a professional association are not barred to work as planners. However, entering self-employment will be difficult to impossible and most employers expect planners, especially for higher level posts, to hold professional qualifications and professional body memberships. Self-organization can thus create a *de facto* requirement for qualifications. Even if a shortage of certified professionals would facilitate employment of individuals without formal qualification, at the very least those who are certified generally enjoy better pay and career prospects.

The third level, unregulated professions, is one in which professionalization via a governing body and monitoring of standards is either entirely absent or only weakly established. Options of voluntary registration in an association may exist but bear relatively little benefits to those doing so. The planning profession in Sweden and Finland, for example, falls into this category.

It is worth noting that in some nations, planning is considered a specialization of architecture or engineering and professional recognition and regulation is *indirect* via the professional bodies and boards assessing these related professions. This is the case for example in Germany and Switzerland. Whether indirect regulation weakens or strengthens professional standards and standing must be assessed case by case. Moreover, even if the profession is not regulated, titles may still be protected. For instance, professional titles such as Chartered Town Planner, MRTPI (Member of the Royal Town Planning Institute), Stadtplaner (in Germany) or AICP (American Institute of Certified Planners) are awarded by professional bodies and can only be used by those awarded membership.

Throughout the 20th century, planning as a field evolved and its professionalization strengthened, supported by growing numbers of university-based planning education programs (e.g., Stiftel, et al. 2009; Frank, et al. 2014) that contribute to the development of skills and knowledge at levels commensurate for professional practice. However, the recognition of planning as a distinct discipline is neither secure nor universal (Rodwin and Sanyal, 2000; Geppert and Cotella, 2010; Kunzmann, 2015). Professional status and regulation remain very uneven across nations as illustrated by a study by the European Council of Spatial Planners. The results revealed that in 34 European Union countries (28 member and six candidate[4] and affiliated nations[5]) four countries had no regulation for planning professionals, and a further 12 had only indirect regulation via architecture or engineering. The remaining 18 states feature various levels of professional (self-)organization and regulation (ECTP-CEU, 2013, Table 4.9).

Educating for Professional Competence

Competencies for planning are typically acquired via postsecondary education at ISCED-97[6] level 5a and higher (ILO, 2012); that is, planners are expected to have at minimum a bachelor's degree. In many countries a master's in planning is mandatory for professional practice and for professional body membership. Doctoral degrees in planning are usually only required for academic positions and their primary purpose is to develop research and increasingly pedagogical skills. Hence, bachelor's and master's degrees are the main vehicles to develop professional competence.

Bachelor's degrees normally are three to four years for full-time study or longer if part-time.[7] Programs may include mandatory practice and work-based learning periods of several weeks up to 12 months. Full-time master's degrees are between one year (12 months) and two years in duration and may include up to one semester of mandatory internships. Dual degree programs such as a joint master's in planning and engineering or similar tend to require three years full-time or a longer period for part-time study. The majority of planning programs are residential, although opportunities for distance and online study are growing.

The diversity in the status, level of professionalization and regulation associated with the planning profession in different countries is mirrored by an equally complex education landscape and expectations for practice. Curricula and delivery formats respond to different professional ideologies and national regulations as well as university traditions. Drawing on underlying ideologies Rodríguez-Bachiller (1988) identified three archetypes. The first of these conceives of planning as a specialization of another profession such as architecture or engineering. As a result planning is taught as a specialization in either the bachelor's and/or master's of the "parent" discipline. A second archetype conceives of planning as a supplementary specialism. Here, planning education is offered as a postgraduate degree generally without much (if any) restriction in respect of the subject studied at undergraduate level. Bringing individuals with different backgrounds together is often seen as a way to foster interdisciplinary capabilities albeit this should not be taken for granted (Wagner, et al. 2014). The third archetype conceptualizes planning as an independent discipline, which translates into the expectation of planners acquiring both an undergraduate and a more specialist master's qualification in planning. The ideology aligns with the model promoted by Perloff (1957) of educating a generalist planner with a specialization (such as transport, historic conservation, urban design, urban regeneration etc.) and is one favored by many professional bodies. Although in the past these ideologies and associated education pathways reflected distinct nation-specific professional milieus, Frank et al. (2014, 83–84) observed a growing pluralism in education pathways for planners as a result of higher education reforms in Europe (EHEA, 1999) and globalization trends.

Professional Competency Development and Assessment

Competency in planning is typically developed and assessed over different stages: as part of (accredited) education programs, as part of professional certification and increasingly as part of life-long-learning in the form of CPD.

Education Program Accreditation: Approaches and Models

Alignment and compliance with professional competency frameworks are frequently enforced through some level of program accreditation which has proven effective in ensuring that curricula deliver the knowledge and skills needed in practice (Dawkins, 2016). The UK-based

Royal Town Planning Institute (RTPI) for example, started accrediting education programs in the 1930s. In the United States, accreditation of planning programs through the Planning Accreditation Board (PAB) began in 1984, while in Germany the state level approval of study programs was replaced by accreditation through external agencies following higher education sector reforms from 2004 (Frank, et al. 2012).

Overall, accreditation can be defined as the act of granting recognition, especially to an educational institution or program for providing a suitable or required standard. Accreditation should not be confused with quality assurance (QA), which by contrast, tends to focus on either accountability or improvement (Westerheijden, et al. 2007; Billing, 2004; European Association for Quality Assurance in Higher Education, 2010). QA and (professionally oriented, specialized) accreditation may be combined into a single process or may be divided into separate and distinct processes and criteria administered by different agents. Separate approaches can potentially lead to conflicts as QA may for instance emphasize transferable skills and global citizenship whereas professional or "specialized" accreditation as a form of consumer protection tends to prioritize professionally relevant skills and knowledge (Brennan and Williams, 2004; Frank, et al. 2012).

For planning education, different models of accreditation (and derivative variations) can be distinguished depending on the stakeholders in charge of accreditation, stakeholders involved in developing guidance, and the implications of results (Table 2.1). There is no right or wrong; rather each model implies a different quality perspective and is shaped by the external conditions and higher education framework within which it is situated. They have been labelled as:

- Professional practice-based (e.g., UK, Canada, New Zealand, Australia);
- State-determined/academic (e.g., Poland, Slovakia);
- Moderated agency (e.g., Germany, France, US) (Frank et al. 2012).

The professional practice-based model is ultimately market-driven and closely tied to professional competency frameworks. The model is typical for countries where professional bodies self-regulate access to the profession and therefore seek to exert maximum influence on the shape and content of planning curricula to ensure graduates are well prepared for practice. An accreditation process is typically employed in addition to institutionally-led QA reviews. Criteria of institutional quality and professional competency reviews may lead to conflicting demands on educators. Frequency and terms of re-accreditation can vary significantly by country and accrediting body. In the UK, for example, there are annual reviews by a panel which discusses improvements and changes in dialogue with program providers and without heavy bureaucratic burden. On the one hand, this approach affords flexibility to shape program content around local concerns and academic expertise, but on the other it is likely to lead to a more heterogeneous and less well-defined professional profile. Other countries have less flexible routines and longer periods between accreditation cycles. Theoretically programs can be offered without accreditation, but there is significant value from an institutional marketing perspective as many professional bodies require an accredited degree as a prerequisite for future professional body membership.

The state-determined accreditation model, as in Poland or Slovakia, is expert-driven with input from academics to determine subject-specific criteria. This model combines assessment for educational quality and professional relevance—however, there tends to be greater emphasis on science and principles than trending professional topics. Under this model, without accreditation, programs are not allowed to run and programs that fail accreditation will be closed. With a universal nation-wide approach, the competency profile for students completing a planning

Table 2.1 Accreditation models for planning (based on Frank, et al. 2012)

	Professional practice-based; market-driven;	State-determined, centralized, academic	Moderated agency
Typology based on country	United Kingdom	Poland	Germany
Initial program validation, i.e., students can be admitted to a program following . . .	a) Validation of program by higher education institution is required based on academic quality and marketability. b) However, professional accreditation is separate and optional to admit students, albeit desirable for branding.	Validation of program by state accreditation committee against subject-specific guidance is required as prerequisite to admit students. Institution has choice between technical or non-technical profile.	Validation of program by independent agency (for relevant degrees) – may be linked to funding. Institution may be able to select between different accreditation agencies and thus can steer profile/branding.
Failure to maintain professional /subject-specific accreditation	Reduced market value, ultimately withdrawal of program as non-attractive to market.	If not remedied, program closure.	If not remedied, program closure.
Frequency	a) Revalidation of programs every 4–6 years for institutional academic review. b) Annually for professional accreditation maintenance.	Cycle length 1–8 years.	Cycle length 5–7 years.
Who bears costs	a) Institutional subscription. b) Departmental fees to professional body.	State	Department/Higher Education Institution per accreditation visit.
Guidelines for planning curricula	a) Optional Quality Assurance Association (QAA) subject benchmark for bachelor's degrees. b) RTPI learning outcomes.	State provided curriculum framework.	Accreditation board for Studies in Architecture and Planning (developed by professional associations, academics).
Variant of model can be found in the following countries	Canada, Australia, New Zealand	Slovakia	US (through PAB), France (through Association pour la Promotion de l'Enseignement et de la Recherche en Aménagement et Urbanisme/ APERAU, an international association of francophone planning schools with members from Europe, Africa, Asia and Canada)*

*Other planning schools and associations have also developed guidelines for planning education, e.g., Association of European Schools of Planning (AESOP) and Association of Schools of Planning in Indonesia (ASPI) but are not involved in accreditation in the same way as APERAU (see Demazière, 2015).

degree will be fairly homogeneous and predictable. However as professional bodies have no formal influence over curricula there is a risk that graduates may not be as well prepared for professional practice as one might hope, especially if professional practice changes rapidly.

In the moderated agency model, programs must typically pass a QA review prior to any formal start of a program. Subject-specific accreditation, however, is a specialist service that is on a practical level outsourced to a set of agencies, such as the German ASIIN,[8] US-based PAB or APERAU (Demazière, 2015). Programs pay for the costs of being accredited. Unlike in the UK or Australia, professional bodies are not directly involved in the accreditation though they are invited to consult on subject-specific accreditation criteria. In Germany where there are several competing specialist accreditation services, program leadership and institutions can select between accrediting agencies as well as the guidelines to be used (Frank et al. 2012).

Although the competency frameworks of different professional bodies, associations or specialist agencies take on different formats, a comparison mapping shows reassuringly a considerable overlap in what is to be covered for the planning field. One classical structure distinguishes: (i) *general planning knowledge* (planning theory/history/law/ethics), (ii) *skills* (research and practical skills), and (iii) *values*; while another separates *general knowledge* further into: (a) planning foundations (including both theory and history), (b) context (economic and social processes), (c) cultural and social aspects of planning; and *skills* into (a) methods, and (b) planning practice skills, respectively. A third approach distinguishes between functional and enabling competencies (CIP, 2010). Functional competencies relate to planning and its tools:

- Human settlement (including transport systems and housing etc.);
- History and principles of community planning (including planning theories);
- Government, law and policy;
- Plan and policy considerations (including environmental issues, sustainability, diversity, inclusiveness, knowledge integration, economics, finance);
- Plan and policy making (including planning approaches, developing visions, strategic information collection and analysis);
- Plan and policy implementation (including evaluation, finance, project management, decision-making, risk management); and
- Developments in planning and policy (including emerging trends).

The traditional steering of competency development has been through the designation of core subject areas and minimum credit hours to be spent on studying a particular skill or area of knowledge as well as establishing an environment conducive to subject-specific knowledge acquisition. The latter includes teaching spaces, library and human resources and frequently a threshold percentage of faculty teaching on a program with membership in professional planning bodies. Over the last few decades, this input model has been increasingly replaced by an outcomes model articulated as learning outcomes (LO) which provides educators with greater flexibility in how to achieve learning objectives.

To further illustrate the criteria and approaches employed in program accreditation, excerpts from guidance by two prominent accreditation bodies are contrasted. The first is the guidance for initial planning education by the RTPI (2015), which accredits programs in the UK and Northern Ireland but also further afield (e.g. South Africa). It lists 13 LOs associated with spatial planning qualifications and six further LOs pertaining to specialist degrees at master level. Schools seeking accreditation need to cross-reference LOs against courses (called modules in UK) and rate the level of learning as either "introductory",

Table 2.2 RTPI indicative learning outcomes matrix (adapted from RTPI, 2015, Appendix 3)

Spatial learning outcome	\multicolumn{4}{l}{*In module* [add name] *students gain an introductory/assessed/consolidated ability to* (add columns as needed)}
	core	core	elective	elective

1. Explain and demonstrate how spatial planning operates within the context of institutional and legal frameworks.
2. Generate integrated and well-substantiated responses to spatial planning challenges.
3. Reflect on the arguments for and against spatial planning and particular theoretical approaches, and assess what can be learnt from experience of spatial planning in different contexts and spatial scales.
4. Demonstrate how efficient resource management helps to deliver effective spatial planning.
5. Explain the political and ethical nature of spatial planning and reflect on how planners work effectively within democratic decision-making structures.
6. Explain the contribution that planning can make to the built and natural environment and in particular recognize the implications of climate change.
7. Debate the concept of rights and the legal and practical implications of representing these rights in planning the decision-making process.
8. Evaluate different development strategies and the practical application of development finance; assess the implications for generating added value for the community.
9. Explain the principles of equality and equality of opportunity in relation to spatial planning in order to positively promote the involvement of different communities, and evaluate the importance and effectiveness of community engagement in the planning process.
10. Evaluate the principles and processes of design for creating high quality places and enhancing the public realm for the benefit of all in society.
11. Demonstrate effective research, analytical, evaluative and appraisal skills and the ability to reach appropriate, evidence-based decisions.
12. Recognize the role of communication skills in the planning process and the importance of working in an inter-disciplinary context, and be able to demonstrate negotiation, mediation, advocacy and leadership skills.
13. Distinguish the characteristics of a professional, including the importance of upholding the highest standards of ethical behavior and a commitment to lifelong learning and critical reflection, so as to maintain and develop professional competence.

(continued)

Table 2.2 (continued)

Specialist learning outcomes –	*In module* [add name] *students gain an introductory/assessed/consolidated ability to* (add columns as needed)			
	core	core	elective	elective
1 Engage in theoretical, practical and ethical debate at the forefront of the area of the specialism in the context of spatial planning.				
2 Evaluate the social, economic, environmental and political context for the area of specialism.				
3 Evaluate the distinctive contribution of the specialism to the making of place and the mediation of space.				
4 Demonstrate the relationship within a spatial planning context of the particular area of specialism to other specialist areas of expertise.				
5 Demonstrate the type and quality of skills that would be expected of a graduate from this specialism undertaking the practice experience period of the assessment of professional competency (APC).				
6 Assess the contribution of the specialism to the mitigation of, and adaptation to, climate change.				

"assessed" or "consolidated" (Table 2.2). There is no requirement that LOs must be covered in core modules, nor must the school cover all learning outcomes exhaustively and to the highest level. In contrast, the Planning Accreditation Board (PAB) responsible for accrediting planning programs in the USA (Table 2.3, following) requires that *all* specified LOs are covered in core courses. However, the PAB guidance refrains from guidance on specialism other than stipulating that sufficient credit hours need to be associated with it.

The inclusion, emphasis or omission of certain topics and skills give insights into the different contexts that shape planning policy and approaches in different world regions. In Australia, New Zealand and Canada, for instance, accreditation policies make explicit reference to planning with/for native cultures. The 2015 RTPI guidance asks that students be able to ". . . recognize the implications of climate change" while no reference to knowledge regarding climate or other natural hazards is made in US-based PAB guidance.

The German professionally oriented guidelines stipulate that students "recognize interdisciplinary correlations and the limits of one's own professional competence, specifically involve other disciplines (e.g. experts) and manage problems in a structured, self-directed and cooperative way, in interdisciplinary teams using scientific methods" (ASAP, 2014, 4). The guidance further acknowledges that teaching of interdisciplinary skills requires tailored pedagogies such as projects with different student groups or stakeholders. Similar emphasis on interdisciplinary working and approaches with a requirement to include several elements of interdisciplinary teaching in planning curricula are noted by Fischler (2012, 145) in APERAU's accreditation guidance. The RTPI guidance likewise mentions the role of communication skills for interdisciplinary work (LO 12), while PAB policy does not explicitly incorporate the development of interdisciplinary working.

Table 2.3 Excerpt from PAB standards, 14 April 2012: "The program shall offer a curriculum that teaches students the essential knowledge, skills and values central to the planning profession. These required components ... are [ordinarily] included in core courses required of all students".

1.	*General planning knowledge*	
a)	Purpose and Meaning of Planning	Appreciation of why planning is undertaken by communities, cities, regions and nations, and the impact planning is expected to have.
b)	Planning Theory	Appreciation of the behaviors and structures available to bring about sound planning outcomes.
c)	Planning Law	Appreciation of the legal and institutional contexts within which planning occurs.
d)	Human Settlements and History of Planning	Understanding of the growth and development of places over time and across space.
e)	The Future	Understanding of the relationships between past, present and future in planning domains, as well as the potential for methods of design, analysis and intervention to influence the future.
f)	Global Dimensions of Planning	Appreciation of interactions, flows of people and materials, cultures, and differing approaches to planning across world regions.
2.	*Planning skills*	
a)	Research	Tools for assembling and analyzing ideas and information from prior practice and scholarship, and from primary and secondary sources.
b)	Written, Oral and Graphic Communication	Ability to prepare clear, accurate and compelling text, graphics and maps for use in documents and presentations.
c)	Quantitative and Qualitative Methods	Data collection, analysis and modeling tools for forecasting, policy analysis, and design of projects and plans.
d)	Plan Creation and Implementation	Integrative tools useful for sound plan formulation, adoption, and implementation and enforcement.
e)	Planning Process Methods	Tools for stakeholder involvement, community engagement, and working with diverse communities.
f)	Leadership	Tools for attention, formation, strategic decision-making, team building, and organizational/community motivation.
3.	*Values and ethics*	
a)	Professional Ethics and Responsibility	Appreciation of key issues of planning ethics and related questions of the ethics of public decision-making, research, and client representation (including principles of the AICP Code of Ethics).
b)	Governance and Participation	Appreciation of the roles of officials, stakeholders and community members in planned change.
c)	Sustainability and Environmental Quality	Appreciation of natural resource and pollution control factors in planning, and understanding of how to create sustainable futures.
d)	Growth and Development	Appreciation of economic, social and cultural factors in urban and regional growth and change.
e)	Social Justice	Appreciation of equity concerns in planning.

Although not necessarily captured in specified learning outcomes, accreditation guidance from the RTPI, US-based PAB, APERAU, Australia's Planning Institute (PIA), New Zealand and the German-based ASAP all require curricula to facilitate students' familiarization with planning practice and the profession by including guest lectures from practitioners, field trips, work experience and placements. Scholars from around the globe have independently argued for embedding experiential learning (projects, service or work-based learning) in planning education as such learning supports the development of competencies complementary to knowledge and skills learned in the classroom (e.g. Baldwin and Rosier, 2017; Frank, 2010). However, while some policies recommend work placements prior to a course of study (ASAP, 2014, 9), and endorse extracurricular as well as work experience formally embedded and assessed as part of the curriculum, accreditation policies reviewed here do not require an inclusion of periods of work experience as is the case for example for study programs in the health care fields.

Program accreditation in the field of planning—regardless of the model—remains largely national-based. With increasing globalization and labor mobility, there is a growing need to consider transnational concepts of professionalization and its regulation (Evetts, 1998). Some professional bodies such as the Royal Institution of Chartered Surveyors (RICS) have started to adjust in order not to lose influence in competition with emerging international organizations. In the planning field, however, professional bodies and accreditation boards continue to shy away from international accreditation due to the national nature of professional milieus. To date and to the best of our knowledge, only the RTPI as a professional body has embraced its latent international reach (associated with the Commonwealth nations) and begun to accredit programs internationally (Table 2.4). The moderated agency model may be best suited for international accreditation and at a limited and voluntary level APERAU conducts accreditation for its francophone institutional members in Northern Africa and Quebec, for example. The Association of European Schools of Planning (AESOP) started to award a quality label to its member schools (although this is not equivalent to accreditation).

Table 2.4 Selected professional bodies and agencies conducting national / international program accreditation

Organization	National accreditation	International accreditation
Royal Town Planning Institute (RTPI)	Yes (UK, Northern Ireland)	Yes
Planning Institute of Australia (PIA)	Yes	Currently not
New Zealand	Yes	Currently not
Canadian Institute of Planners (CIP)	Yes	Currently not
Association of the accreditation of courses of Study in Architecture and Planning (ASAP)	Yes	Currently not
Association pour la Promotion de l'Enseignement et de la Recherche en Aménagement et Urbanisme (APERAU)	France (member schools only)	Francophone member schools in Africa, Canada, Belgium
Planning Accreditation Board (PAB)	Yes: US and Canada	Currently not

Assessment of Professional Competence for Certification

University studies and an (accredited) degree are often only the initial step on the path to fully qualified professional status and/or certified membership in a professional body. Professional bodies or governments may examine and assess an individual's professional competence as a condition for certification. Post-degree stages of establishing professional competence can include periods of practice, examinations, or establishing through reflective self-evaluation, a panel interview and/or log-books that the high quality knowledge expected has been gained and standards of conduct as set out by the profession are observed.

In the US, certification of professional competences is undertaken by AICP on behalf of the American Planning Association (APA). Following a period of building professional competences through a combination of higher education studies plus work experience in professional planning, individuals can take a multiple-choice exam (170 questions in five major topic areas) to qualify. A lack of educational achievement and degree level/type can be compensated for by additional work experience. So, for example, an accredited planning degree and two years' experience equates to the same pre-exam professional competence as a degree in a non-planning field with four years of professional planning experience.

The RTPI has abandoned the entry exam in lieu of an assessment of professional competency (APC) process that runs alongside professional practice following strict initial education requirements. Applicants for chartered membership must have completed either a spatial planning degree at undergraduate level and a specialist master's degree (both accredited by the RTPI) or a combined master's to be eligible for an initial licentiate membership. Following a minimum period of two years in professional planning practice, licentiates can apply for APC review. In response to an increasing diversity of education pathways and international mobility of professionals, the institute has recently begun to establish alternative pathways to membership and membership classes for those interested in membership but lacking the required educational background.[9] Professional bodies in planning in Australia, New Zealand and Canada likewise offer nuanced categories, often setting different standards and expectations for different levels of membership such as Student planner to Candidate/Licentiate planner, Associate planner, professionally qualified (full member), or academic members.

Maintaining Professional Competence: Continued Professional Development

Planners, like other professions, need to stay abreast of innovations in the field and changes in legislation that will affect their work. Professionals that are for example not familiar with newest government policies will be unable to serve clients at the highest level of professional expertise. Thus, a number of established professional bodies such as AICP or the RTPI have begun to review their members' engagement in continued professional development, setting out increasingly stringent requirements as a condition for retaining certification.

Variations in the philosophy around CPD can be gleaned from the guidance and advice for members (Table 2.5). For one, there are differences in the approaches of enforcing adherence. Those that fall into the more regimented end of the spectrum state that certified members will lose their status if they fail to engage sufficiently within a set timeframe and "will be obliged to seek recertification in order to regain the . . . credential" (AICP). While all professional bodies set a minimum time commitment, there is divergence in terms of prescribing subject areas or requiring reflection and planning. The RTPI has embedded continued professional development of their members in its code of conduct of professional standards and provides extensive

Table 2.5 CPD requirements of selected professional bodies in the planning field

Professional body	CPD requirements
American Planning Association (APA) www.planning.org/	32 hours (from certified providers) over 2 years with at least 1.5 hours dedicated to professional ethics and to planning law.
Royal Town Planning Institute www.rtpi.org.uk	50 hours over 2 years; plus a reflective log and personal development plan.
Planning Institute of Australia www.planning.org.au/	30–60 points (depending on membership level) over 2 years covering 3 of 6 defined practice areas; personal development plan submitted in advance; biannual code of conduct quiz.
New Zealand Planning Institute www.planning.org.nz/	10–25 points per year depending on membership level.
Canadian Institute of Planners www.cip-icu.ca	Specifics of requirements are devolved to provincial branches (i.e. the Alberta Professional Planners Institute, the Ontario Professional Planners Institute, etc.); 18 learning units (ca. 18 hrs) per annum of which at least 50% need to be "structured".

advice and guidance on documenting and choosing CPD in a manner that also fosters structured career development.[10] In addition to conducting CPD, the RTPI therefore asks members also to produce a professional development plan. Planning Institute of Australia's CPD policy is mindful of planners' access to CPD and offers, similarly to the New Zealand planning institute, online resources, differentiating requirements between different membership levels.[11] In Germany planners can carry the title of city planner only by being registered in the relevant category in the professional body for architects. Again all registered members have a professional duty to engage in continued learning but specific requirements are more obscure and differ by provincial sections.

Concluding Observations

Professionalization in planning has been comparatively slow and has been shaped by national professional milieus. The status attributed to the profession in different countries varies significantly. This is most visible through the level of professional regulation that dictates access to practice. Implications of qualified professional status range from a) representing a license to practice, or b) being customarily regarded as necessary to work in the profession, to c) providing a wider and better range of work and career progression (Lester, 2009). As the main vehicle to acquire professional competency in planning is through completing a degree in planning, or at least one in a related profession such as engineering or architecture with a specialization in planning, difficulties in accessing planning education in some geographic regions has been and continues to be a major obstacle to global professional development (Frank, et al. 2014; Levy, et al. 2011).

In many countries an accredited planning degree is a pre-condition for professional body membership. Program accreditation is a kind of quality certification which may be mandatory or optional. In cases where accreditation includes a strong subject specificity, it signals to prospective students and employers that a program's curriculum is delivering substantial or indeed prescribed levels of professionally relevant competencies and instills professional values as set out in frameworks and standards promoted by professional bodies, QA agencies, institutional quality targets, or governments for planners.

In the rare cases where planning is a regulated profession, the accreditation of an education program will be a necessity in order to ensure graduates will be able to enter the profession. In other circumstances, professional, subject-specific accreditation is desirable from a marketing point of view. The close alignment of learning outcomes with professional expectations ensures fitness for purpose and graduate employability. In a competitive higher education environment, institutions, particularly those that aspire to increase international ranking and student intake, tend to encourage accreditation as long-term gains are expected to outweigh costs associated with accreditation. Depending on the model and approach to QA and professional accreditation, conflicts around education goals can arise, e.g. around generic competencies and professionally deemed relevant ones. Overly prescriptive accreditation may reduce educators' flexibility in terms of the curriculum content, perpetuate conservative approaches entertained in practitioner circles and may stifle innovation (Healey, 1985; Wisniewska, 2011).

Such worries can however be countered by regular revisions of competency frameworks and the involvement of multiple stakeholder groups in formulating accreditation guidance. Today's professional bodies and accreditation agencies are well aware of the need to constantly update their frameworks. In fact, professional competency development represents a staged and ongoing process. Post degree, individuals seeking professional certification typically will need to pass further assessments of their competencies through exams and supervised periods of work experiences and they actively have to maintain currency of knowledge through CPD.

One enduring feature of the planning field is the persistence of nationally differentiated professional milieus and education practices. For good or bad, this context-specificity countervails global trends of streamlining professional practice. The difficulty of establishing an internationally recognized quality certification through program accreditation has been of concern to the planning education community for over a decade (Harrison, 2003; Levy, et al. 2011; Frank, et al. 2012). A program accreditation model administered through an independent agency with input of criteria that are shaped by a forum of practitioners and academics (moderated agency) may be the most promising way forward.

Notes

1 Minor subgroup 216 (ILO, 2012, p. 121).
2 Turkey is one of few countries where planning is a regulated profession.
3 Note: self-organized is not the same as self-regulated.
4 Turkey, Iceland and Serbia.
5 Norway, Liechtenstein and Switzerland.
6 ISCED – the International Standard Classification of Education was developed by the UNESCO Institute for Statistics (UIS) to facilitate comparisons of education statistics and indicators cross-nationally.
7 One exception is Spain where architects and planners need to complete a five-year undergraduate and one-year master's degree as minimum prerequisite for practice (Frank, et al. 2014).
8 ASIIN offers subject specific accreditation of programs in engineering, architecture and other science fields. www.asiin.de/en/about-us.html
9 www.rtpi.org.uk/membership/join/which-class-is-right-for-me/
10 www.rtpi.org.uk/media/1796460/cpd_practice_advice.pdf
11 www.planning.org.au/certification

References

Akkreditierungsverbund für Studiengänge der Architektur und Planung (ASAP). (2014). Criteria for the Accreditation of Courses of Study in Urban Planning/Spatial planning. Retrieved from www.asap-akkreditierung.de/dateien/dokumente/de/manual_urban-_spatial_planning_english_version-2014_.pdf

Alexander, E. R. (2001). What do planners need to know? *Journal of Planning Education and Research*, 20(3), 376–380. doi:10.1177/0739456x0102000309

American Institute of Certified Planners (AICP). (2013). *Information for the AICP Comprehensive Planning Examination*. Chicago: American Planning Association.

Baldwin, C., & Rosier, J. (2017). Growing future planners: A framework for integrating experiential learning into tertiary planning programs. *Journal of Planning Education and Research*, 37(1), 43–55. doi: 10.1177/0739456x16634864

Billing, D. (2004). International comparisons and trends in external quality assurance of higher education: Commonality or diversity? *Higher Education*, 47(1), 113–137. doi:10.1023/b:high.0000009804.31230.5e

Brennan, J., & Williams, R. (2004). Accreditation and related regulatory matters in the United Kingdom. In S. Schwarz & D. F. Westerheijden (Eds.), *Accreditation and Evaluation in the European Higher Education Area* (pp. 465–490). Dordrecht: Kluwer Academic Publishers.

Canadian Institute of Planners National Membership Standards Committee (CIP). (2010). *Accreditation of Academic Planning Programs for the Planning Profession in Canada*. Ottawa: Canadian Institute of Planners.

Caves, R., & Wagner, F. (2018). Are planning programs delivering what planning students need? Perspectives on planning education from practitioners. In A. I. Frank & C. Silver (Eds.), *Urban Planning Education* (pp. 323–335). Cham: Springer International Publishing.

Dalton, L. C. (2001). Weaving the fabric of planning as education. *Journal of Planning Education and Research*, 20, 423–436.

Dawkins, C. J. (2016). Preparing planners: The role of graduate planning education. *Journal of Planning Education and Research* 36(4), 414–426. doi:10.1177/0739456X15627193

Demazière, C. (2015). University curricula in urban and regional planning in France: A promoted and recognized quality. In I. Mironowicz (Ed.), *Excellence in Planning Education: Local, European & Global Perspective* (pp. 18–23). Leuven: AESOP.

European Association for Quality Assurance in Higher Education (ENQA). (2010). *ENQA 10 years (2000–2010): A Decade of European Co-operation in Quality Assurance in Higher Education*. Helsinki: ENQA. Retrieved from www.enqa.eu/wp-content/uploads/2013/06/ENQA-10th-Anniversary-publication.pdf

European Council of Spatial Planners (ECTP-CEU). (2013). *ECTP-CEU Study on the Recognition of Planning Qualifications in Europe*. Retrieved from www.ectp-ceu.eu/images/stories/PDF-docs/Amended%20 ECTP-CEU%20Study%20Draft%20(2012-11-21)%20-%20FINAL%20REPORT%20No%20App.pdf

European Higher Education Area (EHEA). (1999). *Bologna Declaration*. Retrieved from www.eurashe.eu/library/bologna_1999_bologna-declaration-pdf/

Evetts, J. (1998). Professionalism beyond the nation-state: international systems of professional regulation in Europe. *International Journal of Sociology and Social Policy*, 18(11/12), 47–64. doi:10.1108/01443339810788579

Fischler, R. (2012). Teaching spatial planners: Knowledge, skills, competencies and attitudes–Accreditation standards in the US and Canada. In B. Scholl (Ed.), *Higher Education in Spatial Planning: Positions and Reflections* (pp. 140–151). Zürich: vdf Hochschulverlag AG/ETH Press.

Frank, A. (2010). Making a case for complementarity of student learning from year-long work-based placements in town planning. *Learning and Teaching in Higher Education*, 4(2), 21–45.

Frank, A. (2015). Planning as a Self-Organized Profession. In I. Mironowicz (Ed.), *Excellence in Planning Education: Local, European and Global Perspective* (pp. 26–31). Leuven: AESOP.

Frank, A., Kurth, D., & Mironowicz, I. (2012) Accreditation and quality assurance for professional degree programmes: Comparing approaches in three European countries. *Quality in Higher Education* 18 (1), 75–95.

Frank, A., Mironowicz, I., Lourenco, J., Finka, M., Franchini, T., Ache, P., Scholl, B., Grams, A. (2014). Educating planners in Europe: A review of 21st century study programmes, *Progress in Planning*, 91, 30–94.

Geppert, A., & Cotella, G. (Eds.). (2010). *Quality Issues in a Changing European Higher Education Area*. Leuven: AESOP.

Guzzetta, J. D., & Bollens, S. A. (2003). Urban planners' skills and competencies: Are we different from other professions? Does context matter? Do we evolve? *Journal of Planning Education and Research*, 23(1), 96–106. doi:10.1177/0739456x03255426

Harrison, P. (2003). Towards the international accreditation of education in planning. *Newsletter of the Commonwealth Association of Planners, CAP News*, 9, 5–7.

Healey, P. (1985). The professionalisation of planning in Britain: its form and consequences. *Town Planning Review*, 56(4), 492–507. doi:10.3828/tpr.56.4.q595g78914432w46

Hoch, C. (2012). A report on urban planning education in the United States. In B. Scholl (Ed.), *HESP – Higher education in spatial planning – Positions and reflections* (pp. 128–137). Zürich: vdf Hochschulverlag AG/ETH Press.

International Labour Organization (ILO). (2012). *International Standard Classification of Occupations: ISCO – 08, Structure, Group Definitions and Correspondence Tables* (Vol. 1). Geneva: ILO.

Kerr, S., Von Glinow, M. A., & Schriesheim, J. (1977). Issues in the study of "professionals" in organizations: The case of scientists and engineers. *Organizational Behavior and Human Performance*, 18(2), 329–345. doi:10.1016/0030-5073(77)90034-4

Kunzmann, K. R. (2015). Challenges of planning education in times of globalization. In I. Mironowicz (Ed.), *Excellence in Planning Education: Local, European & Global Perspective* (Vol. 3, pp. 58–73). Leuven: AESOP.

Lester, S. (2009). Routes to qualified status: practices and trends among UK professional bodies. *Studies in Higher Education*, 34(2), 223–236. doi:10.1080/03075070802528296

Levy, C., Mattingly, M., & Wakely, P. (2011). *Commonwealth Capacity Building for Planning: Review of Planning Education Across the Commonwealth*. Edinburgh: Commonwealth Association of Planners.

Perloff, H. S. (1957). *Education for Planning: City, State and Regional*. Baltimore: Resources for the Future/The Johns Hopkins University Press.

Planning Accreditation Board. (2012). PAB Accreditation Standards and Criteria, Approved April 14, 2012. Retrieved from www.planningaccreditationboard.org/index.php?s=file_download&id=112

Randall, G. E. (2000). Understanding Professional Self Regulation. Retrieved from www.paramedicsofmanitoba.ca/uploaded/web/pdf/Understanding%20Professional%20Self-Regulation.pdf

Rodríguez-Bachiller, A. (1988). *Town planning education: An international survey*. Aldershot: Avebury.

Rodwin, L., & Sanyal, B. (Eds.). (2000). *The Profession of City Planning: Changes, Images, and Challenges, 1950–2000*. New Brunswick, NJ: Center for Urban Policy Research.

Royal Town Planning Institute (RTPI). (2015). Guide to RTPI Accreditation. Retrieved from www.rtpi.org.uk/media/1593916/rtpi_guide_to_accreditation_december_2015.pdf

Stiftel, B., Demerutis, J., Frank, A. I., Harper, T., Inkoom, D. K. B., Lee, L., et al. (2009). Chapter 10: Planning education. In UN-Habitat (Ed.), *Planning sustainable cities. UN-Habitat global report on human settlements* (pp. 185–198). London: Earthscan.

Wagner, T., Baum, L., & Newbill, P. (2014). From rhetoric to real world: fostering higher order thinking through transdisciplinary collaboration. *Innovations in Education and Teaching International*, 51(6), 664–673. doi:10.1080/14703297.2013.796726

Westerheijden, D. F., Stensaker, B., & Rosa, M. J. (Eds.). (2007). *Quality assurance in higher education: Trends in regulation, translation and transformation* (Vol. 20). Dortrecht: Springer Science & Business Media.

Wisniewska, M. (2011). Occupational knowledge: The role of business in creating and socially codifying new ideas. *Transactions*, 8(1), 5–24. doi:10.11120/tran.2011.08010005

PART 2

Pillars of Planning Education

3
PLANNING HISTORY

Robert Freestone

Introduction

The past is an integral part of planning and should be embedded in planning education. This is not universally the case despite the historical orientation of early planning instruction. Where explicitly integrated into curricula it is testimony to critical and often innovative approaches reflective of diverse contexts, needs, opportunities, philosophies and research agendas. This chapter briefly surveys different models for teaching history to planners and sets that within its own historical context. A guiding theme is that historical understanding is not static but is always evolving. The scope is slanted to the English-speaking world but acknowledges the global thrust of this book. I do not try to cover all the interdependencies including planning history writings, the history of planning education, and studies of planning educators; other recent contributions provide portals into this wider literature (Hein, 2018; Frank & Silver, 2018).

There are several main sections. First is a consideration of the rationale for planning history teaching (and research). Second is a brief survey of the development of planning history teaching from the early twentieth century. Third is a description of approaches to planning history pedagogy framed within a typology. Finally come some reflections criss-crossing the surveyed courses pointing to the vitality and integrity of planning history in the tertiary curriculum. But challenges still remain in firmly embedding it in future curricula. The chapter draws from a review of the literature, a survey of curricula and researcher-teachers in the field,[1] and my own experience teaching planning history to undergraduate students since the early 1990s.

Why Planning History?

In 1981 Anthony Sutcliffe posed the question "Why Planning History?" which he answered by asserting that both academic and professional planning have an inherent historical basis (Sutcliffe, 1981). Although some planners have been formally trained in history, ties to mainstream history are not systematically close with teaching and research agendas driven primarily by specific intellectual, professional and policy contexts. Mandelbaum (1985) observed the upsurge of interest in planning history from the 1980s as "rooted in a search for professional identity and direction". This socialising function still has legitimacy.

But there are other rationales for teaching planning history, here condensed to a set of five. First is the promotion of a critical approach to learning. Teitz (1989) expands the case: "The history of planning thought . . . needs to be taught . . . in ways that enable students to tell the difference between ideology and analysis". Second is as an antidote to present-mindedness. Third is to convey the societal and institutional complexity, rather than mono-directional continuity, of thought and action through time. An early reflective practitioner, Feiss (1945), stressed the value of gaining an informed understanding of the many forces making places and delivering special character. Fourth is the applied value. Hall (2014) may have defended his historical sensibility because he found "the subject intriguing", but set about solving contemporary problems through historical framing and knowledge (Freestone, 2014). Finally there is the case for history as a core analytical method (Abbott & Adler, 1989). Fischler (2006) neatly brings together some of these rationales:

> Teaching history to planners . . . means enabling students to hear the voices of their predecessors and be inspired (or dismayed) by their deeds as they act in the world today. It means giving prospective practitioners a feel for the profession they are about to join and an understanding of that profession's identity, values, and evolving character. It means making them understand that problems are not given but socially constructed . . . It means giving them a sense that cities can be improved, albeit very gradually, and damaged, sometimes dramatically. It means making them realize that they can be instrumental in fostering change but that change comes slowly, under popular pressure. It means giving them a sense of modesty as well as a sense of identity, a sense of caution as well as a sense of ambition. It means giving them knowledge but also making them think critically.

Planning History in Evolving Planning Curricula

The teaching of planning history can be set against the broader evolution of planning education, its character shaped by identifiable phases, captured by Davoudi and Pendlebury (2010) as formation (nineteenth century–1940s), consolidation (1950–1960s), fragmentation (1970s), reconstitution (1990s) and maturation (2000s–). Within this sequence, the 1940s is a crucial decade—when the formative years segued into an expansionist phase with many degree programs worldwide featuring obligatory history courses surveying the development of the field. In the post-war years history was often taught with a "peremptory nod" (Sutcliffe, 1977). Planning history underwent a revival from the 1970s at a time of challenges to planning's legitimacy underscored by the emergence of an international planning history research network.

The culture of history instruction was imported early from cognate disciplines like architecture and landscape architecture being dominated by histories of town and precinct development. The treatment is evident in Stübben's *Der Städtebau* (2014) with an "historical review" inserted to provide "an approximate idea of the development of city building in historical times" and "a certain basis for the consideration of modern problems of city building in connection and comparison with earlier creations".

The first tertiary instruction in Britain was in the Department of Civic Design at the University of Liverpool. The initial prospectus in 1909 detailed a core evening course taught jointly by the first Lever Professor Stanley Adshead and Patrick Abercrombie, namely "Outlines of Town Planning (The Development of the City and the Influences Affecting its Growth)". The flavour is revealed by Adshead's (1910) definition of a city as "the greatest of works of art" embodying "the traditions and history of the past". In the United States, the first course at

Harvard University the same year was a speciality in the landscape architecture degree entitled "The Principles of City Planning" taught by James Sturgis Pray with Frederick Law Olmsted Jr. (Pray, 1917). This also channelled an historicist approach to learning with the early accent on "presenting the determinants of city form through the use of historical examples" (Alofsin, 2002). Pray travelled extensively through Europe in 1911–1912 gathering resources to form the basis of a university library collection (Pray & Kimball, 1913). In 1913 the University of Illinois appointed Charles Mulford Robinson as Professor of Civic Design with the first students undertaking detailed studies of Urbana-Champaign (Silver, 2018).

Historic content satiated the lectures and exhibitions staged in several countries by biologist turned sociologist Patrick Geddes (Meller, 1990). French urbanist Marcel Poëte promulgated a similar brand of evolutionary urban history with a strong emphasis on urban form (Calabi, 1996). Instruction at L'Institut d'urbanisme de Paris strongly emphasised history up to the 1960s although Poëte's successor, Pierre Lavedan, brought a more "scientific" approach (Darin, 1998).

The 1920s and 1930s saw planning education expanding its footprint. Harvard offered the first substantive program from 1929, by which time there were over 30 institutions offering some city planning instruction (Adams & Hodge, 1965). MIT had offered an introductory course in planning principles from 1922 but initiated a five-year undergraduate degree in 1932 with the history and principles of city planning taught in year three (Adams, 1949). On the other side of the Atlantic, at University College London, history was formally recognised in the postgraduate curriculum with a notable emphasis on ancient, classical, mediaeval, baroque and early modern precedents (Collins, 2015).

American planning schools developed programs in diverse ways (Feiss, 1938) but by midcentury there was an emergent consensus on curriculum requirements with professional bodies also entering the picture. Three key subject areas were identified: Social Science, Physical Planning and Design, and Theory and Philosophy, including the history of planning and "general principles of city and regional planning as they have been developed in modern times" (Adams, 1954). At Harvard, lectures on the history of civic design by Joseph Hudnut, foundation Dean of the new Graduate School of Design (1936), were a staple for planning students (Gaus, 1943) but were contested ideologically by Walter Gropius who felt history as an introductory course stifled modern ideas and creativity (Pearlman, 2000).

In the British Commonwealth an influential course was "Outlines of Town and Country Planning" co-taught by Gordon Stephenson and Josephine Reynolds at the University of Liverpool. This offered "a brief historical sketch of the varieties and forms of urban and rural development, viewed in relation to geographical and social conditions, in classical, mediaeval, Renaissance and modern times; including recent development under town and country planning legislation in England" (Liverpool School of Architecture, 1948). Although Stephenson had overhauled the program influenced by American curricula in anticipating the recommendations of the Schuster Committee (1950), the treatment of planning history provided continuity with the "old" curriculum (Batey, 1985). Historical instruction of some kind but notably through surveys of developments from the nineteenth century settled comfortably into planning curricula worldwide.

The 1950s and 1960s as decades of consolidation meant few radical developments in planning education. By the 1970s change was afoot. The rise of the environmental movement, challenges to the "industrial-military complex" and a growing disenchantment with the cultural and design tenets of modernism converged to change the institutional climate for planning education. From within a notable turn to the social sciences was also evident.

In the late 1970s Hebbert conducted a survey amongst British educators that recorded a marked shift in attitudes towards history and its importance for practice. The most popular approach was "to open a critical and reflective perspective on the present" (Booth, 1986). The formation of the Planning History Group in 1974, metamorphosing into the International Planning History Society (IPHS) from 1993, was a supportive factor leveraging a closer relationship between teaching and research. A late 1980s update reported that despite the challenges of neo-liberal Thatcherism, history had actually captured a mainstream slot. What had changed was its delivery in a variety of permutations rather than one singular planning history course and with an overall focus on evolution of public policy (Booth, 1986). Birch (1981) conducted a comparable survey of over 80 American planning schools. Over 80% of Master's programs required history content but less than one third mandated a semester-length course. Coverage was declared to be "minimal" and attributed to faculty indifference, student antipathy, lack of curriculum space, and absence of good textbooks. A renewed enthusiasm for planning history evident at this time was soon tapped by formation of the Society for American City and Regional Planning History in 1986. A survey of Japanese planning departments in the same decade showed 19 offering planning history courses with an emphasis on planning after the Industrial Revolution (Nishimura, 1986).

From the 1990s the turn to a more critical and innovative history became emphatic within more flexible disciplinary, educational and professional milieu. Sandercock (1998) was a bellwether of these trends in questioning the dominant "great men" paradigm of planning history, its alignment with modernist rationality, and its silences on issues of gender, race and social justice. More recently, as other worthy topics come into planning's ambit, and traditional approaches to delivering curricula have been challenged, planning history has felt the squeeze. In the UK the introduction of an accredited one-year postgraduate course proved particularly constraining (Davoudi & Pendlebury, 2010).

History remains visible but not ubiquitous in diverse planning curricula. A 2006 teaching forum in the *Journal of Planning History* remains an insightful look into the state of the art. It reveals great variation in how planning educators "approach the challenges to teaching such a broad topic within the limited space that professional planning programs offer" (Silver, 2006), variously highlighting that the value of history lies in understanding complexity, interrogating texts, connections with urban history, links with theory and practice, and showcasing social equity concerns.

A Typology of Planning History Courses

Many planning students still graduate studying little or no history. The extent and depth of instruction is not readily ascertained at face value because a reconnaissance on course titles alone – with history not mentioned – under-enumerates what is on offer.[2] My admittedly limited survey draws from contacts through the IPHS network. Far from definitive, it nevertheless illustrates at least six approaches (Table 3.1).

Standalone: Dedicated full courses are flagships for planning history instruction. They tend to provide the best vehicle for dealing with both broader conceptual themes and intensive investigation around particular issues. They expose students to the historical emergence, development and denouement of planning ideas within a wider appreciation of cities, encompassing economic, cultural, political and technological parameters. In so doing they help cultivate historical skills and sensibility, thus enhancing learning and critical thought.

The two main formats are chronological and thematic, though they are invariably interlinked. The former typically explores an unfurling story over time across a sequence of episodes, e.g. industrial city, garden city, city beautiful, functional city, neo-traditional city, sustainable city, and so on, and their expression in different types of environment: metropolitan areas, city

Table 3.1 A Typology of Planning History Courses

Type	Characteristics
Standalone	Course dedicated to planning history, offering chronological and/or thematic overview focused on physical planning and urban policy in Anglo-American tradition
Urbanisme	Course dedicated to the history of urbanism, injecting broader consideration of the interplay of social life and urban form in the European tradition
History and theory	Course mixing history with theory, usually offered as an introduction to the field of planning
Thematic history	Course offering a specialised treatment of planning history through a disciplinary or topical lens
City history	Course examining broader influences and trends through an intensive study of a particular place
Distributed	Courses with some historical content which aggregate to a broader coverage

centres, the inner city, urban regeneration, suburbia, and new towns. The primary focus is unapologetically on the modern era; ancient planning as a substantive focus largely drops out. There are exceptions; the undergraduate program at Pretoria is notable for two complementary courses taught by Mark Oranje on "Planning and Settlement Histories" before and since the Industrial Revolution. The second thematic approach can break from this evolutionary framework to explore diverse topics, most of which would not be out of place in a theory course. For example, Joe Nasr's "Issues in Planning History, Thought and Practice" at Toronto ranged across "some of the most crucial issues facing cities today" including urban sprawl, food systems, power, social inclusion and environmental justice.

At Pennsylvania, which has resisted pressures to combine history and theory, the mixed approach is followed:

> Our history course, which is offered as two slightly smaller (30–40 student each) classes, looks at the history of modern (post 1870) urban planning ideas and practice from both a chronological perspective, and from a thematic perspective. This "matrix" approach is a little harder to execute than either a purely chronological OR thematic approach, but it seems to pay dividends with students. Some students learn best when material is presented chronologically; others when it is presented through the lens of a common thematic knowledge/theory/action base. It also helps students with non-traditional interests or backgrounds NOT to feel marginalized by the general male and white weight of a purely chronological approach.[3]

Urbanisme: This type is informed by the distinction between a "city planning" approach based on rationality in theory, method and intervention versus an "urbanistic" paradigm grounded more societally in architecture, urban morphology and project-based action (Hebbert, 2006). It picks up courses outside the Anglophone world that feature a more fluid and inter-disciplinary approach to the urban condition, less filtered through physicalist content and formal professional requirements. Formal "planning" instruction often enters as a specialism in the senior years of a more wide-ranging degree grounded in either design or social science. This has been referred to as a "bifurcated" model (Rodríguez-Bachiller, 1986). For example, in Portugal, urban planning is not a separate, autonomous discipline in any of the Architecture schools but the main undergraduate disciplines include study of historical developments and plan genealogy with stronger emphasis at the Master's and Doctoral level. In France planning is almost exclusively postgraduate. At the Ecole d'urbanisme de Paris introductory history courses are categorised as either "Histoire de la ville et genèse de l'urbanisme" (longitudinal survey) and "Histoires d'urbanisme" (study of key planning documents).

History and theory: John Friedmann argued that one of the best ways to introduce students to planning "and to socialize them to the mysteries of our field, is to give them a strong dose of theory and history" (Friedmann, 2011). History and theory as the two most distinctively academic contributions in planning education have been linked since at least the 1940s when history *was* theory, but over time, with the infusion of social science perspectives into mainstream planning education, these understandings were reconstructed through a succession of conceptual and methodological revolutions, such as systems analysis, Marxism and communicative planning (Hall, 2014).

The mutual benefit of linking history and theory has been well articulated, again by Fischler (2012) who holds that planning curricula should include:

> at least one course in planning history and theory, in order to introduce students to the field and profession they are about to enter, its origins and its evolution over time, its normative theories and descriptive theories. Such a course gives students models with which to frame their thinking and their actions (from theoretical concepts with which to put a name on their ideals to design precedents for use in actual plans), puts their individual work in historical perspective, and can, in so doing, instill in them both pride and humility.

Elsewhere he has written that history can help practitioners appreciate "why they do what they do by highlighting the contingent nature and historical origins of planning institutions and practices" (Fischler, 2000). Rahder (2000) similarly argued that "by situating theory within a critical historical framework, planning students are better able to understand the emergence and decline of specific planning concepts, values, and norms". Students are encouraged to contextualise and analyse particular discourses rather than be imprisoned by any one universal theoretical approach. In these terms, Fainstein and Campbell (2012) frame "the historical roots of planning" as a theoretical debate with simplistic heroic narratives ripe for critique.

While history may invigorate theory, the inverse relationship struggles – planning history as a research field remains predominantly empirical (Ward, Freestone, & Silver, 2011). How history fares against theory in combination courses has also been problematical (Birch, 1981). The weight given to the two fractions depends on many factors, notably the research interests and seniority of the instructor. At Harvard the leading urban social scientist Neil Brenner delivers his "History and Theory of Urban Interventions" as "a high-intensity introduction" to the continual transformation of planning under capitalist urbanization. At McGill Raphaël Fischler's "History and Theory of Planning" focuses on "the ways in which historical actors, especially professionals and their critics, thought and acted in the face of urban problems, for better or for worse" (see also Fischler, 2006).

Thematic history: Various adjectival history courses overlap and complement instruction in general planning history. These can be both specialist professional histories (e.g. transportation and social planning) as well as offerings from cognate disciplines (e.g. architecture, human geography, urban studies, heritage, urban history, landscape and environmental studies). An example of the former is Malo André Hutson's "Theory, History, and Practice of Community Development" at the University of California, Berkeley, and of the latter Ian Morley's "Patterns in Urban History and Development" at the Chinese University of Hong Kong. A recent trend in China has been to teach history in courses which present linkages with practice to better engage students. At Zhejiang University, for instance, Shulan Fu coordinates "Comparative Studies of Urban Development in China and Foreign Countries" with inputs from diverse specialists.

City history: These courses focus on particular national and place histories. The host city effectively becomes a laboratory for exploring a succession of planning ideas from different eras. At Toronto, Richard White's "Introduction to Planning History: Toronto and Its Region" exemplifies the type. The intention is to develop both local knowledge and broader understandings including "the limits of planning as a force shaping urban development" and "the intractability of certain urban problems, and the challenges that present-day planners and policy makers". This course type is relatively uncommon; instead the preferred model is to inject local applications via fieldtrips and assessments.

Distributed: Fischler (2006) argues that "introducing history in planning courses that are not explicitly devoted to the past is a good idea". This approach soaks up a large residue of planning curricula which do not otherwise appear to offer formal instruction in planning history. Historical content is often incorporated into "introduction to planning" modules and instructors frequently refer to history content scattered across the program. This diffuse model is not always convincing if there is no real coordination or ownership of the coverage. The educational rationale is stronger where there is evidence of formal integration. For example at TU Delft, the Faculty of Architecture and the Built Environment offers a course series called Grondslagen (Foundations) in the bachelor's degree that brings together teachers from different chairs and departments of the faculty, specifically the chair of History of Architecture and Urban Planning with teachers from the Urbanism, Landscape and Architecture departments.

Discussion

There is clearly considerable diversity in rationale, approach, content, and assessment. Teaching approaches today are shaped by many factors, but particularly the demands, protocols and characteristics of specific institutional settings. The key parameters shaping content and delivery include:

- Different national cultures
- Undergraduate versus postgraduate instruction
- Length of degrees
- Generalist versus specialised teaching
- Introductory versus senior units
- Compulsory versus elective courses
- Staff seniority and expertise including research agendas
- Professional accreditation requirements

Some of these will be self-explanatory and impact on the teaching of everything. An overarching consideration is the particularistic planning culture within which planning education sits (Sanyal, 2005). The level and length of degree is an important driver. Five pedagogic attributes of planning history instruction are discussed in turn.

Accreditation standards: With relatively close relationships between peak professional bodies and tertiary education providers developed through the professionalization of planning since the early twentieth century, accreditation policies have been a significant shaper of course content and ways of teaching planning history (Table 3.2).

Foci: Standalone courses are not cookie-cutter stereotypes drawing from a singular vision of planning history. A variety of permutations connect historical learning to wider themes and tasks. Some representative examples can be noted. At Newcastle upon Tyne under Zan Gunn it is basic information skills on note taking, sourcing information, and essay writing. At Boise State, Amanda Johnson Ashley provokes students by asking how can (and perhaps should) the history of place and of people "inform the investments we make in our communities today?" At Tokyo, Naoto Nakajima's "Planning History" takes a strong biographical turn in focusing

Table 3.2 Selected Professional Accreditation Requirements for Planning History

Country	Agency	Guidelines
United States	Planning Accreditation Board *Draft 2, dated 23 August 2016*	*General Planning Knowledge*: "The comprehension, representation, and use of ideas and information in the planning field, including appropriate perspectives from history, social science, and the design professions . . . [including] Human Settlements and History of Planning: understanding of the growth and development of places over time and across space"
Canada	Canadian Institute of Planners	"History of planning in Canada and other countries" is a core "functional competency"
Australia	Planning Institute of Australia *Accreditation policy for the recognition of Australian planning qualifications; Revised Draft for Consultation Purposes, April 2016*	*Performance Outcomes* for "Plan Making, Land use Allocation and Management, and Urban Design" includes "Knowledge of relevant aspects of the history of planning in Australia and elsewhere and of different planning approaches in their historical and comparative context"
New Zealand	New Zealand Planning Institute *Learning for a Better Future: Tertiary Education Policy and Accreditation Procedures, 2016*	*Content of Planning Programs* includes (a) Planning Foundations: "Thematic courses in planning including philosophy, policy, history, values, ethics, theory, and critical reflection of planning to provide students an overview of the nature and purpose of planning; planning history; contemporary debates and trends; planning theory; and planning at different spatial scales"
China	National Ministry of Education: Cheng-xiang-gui-hua (Urban and Rural Planning) Branch; Guideline for undergraduate course, 2013	"Cheng Shi Jian She Shi (Urban Construction History)" is listed as an obligatory course

mainly on the thoughts and works of planners and urbanists with a strong applied perspective. At Columbia, Clara Irazábal motivates students to become informed and "reflective practitioners" (Schön, 1987) as well as procuring a working knowledge of ideas and cases from the Global South.[4] At Portland State, Sy Adler, who has taught history and theory for over three decades, has evolved his approach into a "history, theory, and implementation course" with students having to "adopt a plan" to comprehensively analyse and communicate its strengths and weaknesses. At Tongji in Shanghai, Hou Li harnesses her history course as a platform to explore the boundaries of present knowledge given that Chinese historical research in this area is relatively sparse.

Critical approaches: While the tendency to hagiography may have been characteristic of old-style planning history, a critical approach is now almost *de jure*. Feiss (1949) recognised the importance of this long ago: "In retrospect there can be neither too much blame nor too much praise", he wrote, "It is now up to us to decide how to be influenced by our own past". This opens up the need to involve students in appreciating the strengths and weaknesses of different approaches to planning history (Freestone, 2000). Even the coverage and conclusions of an esteemed planning historian like Peter Hall are no longer uncontested (Stein, 1995).

Texts: Over three decades ago Booth (1986) observed that planning history reading lists were shifting away from classic texts like Mumford's *The City in History* (1961) and Rosenau's *The Ideal City* (1959) to more recent and specialised sources, and authors like Peter Hall, Gordon Cherry, and Anthony Sutcliffe. This trend has continued although several modern texts are popular including Hall (2014); Hall & Tewdwr-Jones, 2011; LeGates & Stout, 2015, and Taylor (1998). Fainstein and DeFilippis (2015, and earlier editions) is a ready-made set of incrementally evolving readings for American "history and theory" courses. Where textbooks are nominated, they predictably have connections related to the country, the institution, the course type, and the instructor. The major trend, especially for "standalone" courses is towards readers and bespoke reading lists.

In longitudinal perspective, planning history teaching has been linked to the research interests of lecturers to produce some classic texts. This connection dates to the early years of the planning movement. Adshead's *Town Planning and Town Development* (1923) draws from lectures at Liverpool and London when he was "still teaching himself his subject" (Wright, 1982) while his successor at both institutions, Abercrombie, produced his own book *Town & Country Planning* (first published in 1933) also drawing from his lectures and dedicating two chapters to "historic examples" both ancient and modern. The same synergies are evident more recently. Peter Hall's two most famous books emerged respectively out of his teaching at the Universities of Reading and California, Berkeley, namely *Urban and Regional Planning* (1974, first edition) and *Cities of Tomorrow* (1988, first edition). The genesis of Leonie Sandercock's pathbreaking *Making the Invisible Visible* (1998) was a graduate seminar in planning history at UCLA. She recalls that in the 1990s "desire for the recognition of difference was really strong" and her students challenged conventional texts which said nothing "about my people and my place in this city".[5]

Primary sources: A feature that stands out in some courses is the importance attached to exposing students to primary historical sources. Hise (2006) writes that students tend to find history courses "more meaningful" and they "learn content better" when teaching is linked to primary source analysis; original texts can have a strong "emotional impact". For Peterson (2006), these primary materials are "the bread and butter of historical analysis". David Gordon and Sue Cumming's "An Intellectual History of Urban and Regional Planning" at Queens University in Canada is structured around discussion of diverse precinct, city, metropolitan, regional, social, economic development and urban renewal plans from the late nineteenth century to the present, both national and international. Historic films, many now available on YouTube, are also an important element of some courses in capturing the contemporary context, promotion and reception of planning ideas and proposals. Fieldtrips also enable students to better "internalize information and ideas" by relating them to "real urban environments" (Fischler, 2006). They stand out as a distinctive component of many courses, be they walking tours or bus trips in the local area or further afield.

Assessments: The usual array of tests, examinations, research essays and presentations are employed with a philosophy of continuous engagement invariably stressed. A very common task nuanced across different variants is for students to prepare a major assignment on an historic event, plan, community or personality. Group work is common. Other written assignments are often constructed to simulate real world tasks to underline the relevance of planning history. Students of Kristen Larsen at Florida have to write and present a major book review as an historical study. At the University of Massachusetts, an original task is preparation of a graphic project to convey a visual strategy for communicating an historical/theoretical theme relevant to current and future planning. Blogs and digital storytelling are testimony to the creative utilisation of social media and digital technologies.

Conclusions

Birch (1981) questioned whether planning schools truly appreciated the value of historical study. The question might still be asked. The survey reported here suggests robust and creative engagement but involves "true believers" rather than sceptics. A more comprehensive and systematic survey may be timely because challenges clearly remain.

The historical evolution of planning curricula has been characterised as a "layer-cake approach" in incorporating new content. Like planning practice, education possesses a remarkably "absorptive" quality (Perloff, 1957). But the accumulation of content inevitably leads to a "thinning out" (Rodríguez-Bachiller, 1986). Given the primary vocational orientation of planning degrees, and their compression particularly at the postgraduate level, planning history can be seen as a luxury compromising other core content. Few programs employ specialist planning historians, so responsibility often defaults to junior members of staff. Planning history not being a dominant research interest makes it further vulnerable (Ellis, Murtaugh, & Copeland, 2010). These pressures play out in professional settings wherein students are nonetheless almost completely dependent on universities for historical instruction (Dawkins, 2016).

Planning history's problem in the modern curricula still lies in demonstrating its relevance. A recent analysis of US planning programs by Dawkins (2016) shows that of all the knowledge taught in postgraduate programs, the history of planning is the most underutilized in practice. Student pushback to historical content and the value of historical instruction has been long evident in many programs and one indicator of this comes in final year theses and dissertations wherein historical topics are not that popular because they are seen as bereft of vocational benefit. The case for planning history has thus to be constantly reiterated. John Landis has put it well: "If we are to succeed in making planning a truly global and robust enterprise, these types of general knowledge courses (provided they include diverse ideological, political, cultural, and geographic perspectives) are all the more important".[6]

Logistical challenges arise even when planning history is fairly firmly ensconced in curricula. The course types surveyed in this chapter all rise to that challenge but there remain historiographical, educational and programming issues. Finding the time and space to inject history into curricula is one of them. Caroline Miller reports a familiar problem: "The time available . . . to teach planning history is quite short and as such the students are whisked over quite an extensive period very quickly. There is clearly enough content . . . but there is not sufficient room in the curriculum".[7]

As for all courses, there are constant imperatives to maintain the relevance and up-to-dateness of planning history instruction, adapt best practice learning and teaching strategies, and ensure that the subject is not treated as just another deadening rite of passage. With such essentials and a creative, engaged spirit in place, the future of the past will hopefully be assured. Certainly, the potential to truly internationalise instruction through global scholarly and institutional networks is remarkably largely untapped.

Notes

1 I gratefully acknowledge feedback from my respondents (in alphabetical order): Daniel Abramson (University of Washington), Arturo Almandoz (Catholic University of Chile), Marco Amati (RMIT), Philip Booth (Sheffield), Jim Cohen (Maryland), Robert Fairbanks (University of Texas at Arlington), Raphael Fischler (McGill), Shulan Fu (Zhejiang University), Christine Garnaut (University of South Australia), John Gold (Oxford Brookes), David Gordon (Queens), Jill Grant (Dalhousie), Zan Gunn (Newcastle), Michael Hebbert (UCL), Richard Hu (Canberra), Peter Larkham (Birmingham City), John Landis (Penn), Hou Li (Tongji), Duanfung Lu (Sydney), Alan Mabin (South Africa), Madalena Cunha Matos (Technical University of Lisbon), Caroline Miller (Massey), Ian Morley (Chinese University of Hong Kong), Naoto Nakajima (Tokyo), Joe Nasr (Ryerson), David Nichols (Melbourne), Mark Oranje (Pretoria), Clément Orillard (Ecole d'urbanisme de Paris), John Pendlebury (Newcastle), Leonie Sandercock (UBC), Dirk Schubert (HafenCity), Christopher Silver (Florida), Florian Urban (Glasgow School of Art), Dominic Vitiello (Penn), Stephen Ward (Oxford Brookes) and Richard White (Toronto). The research for this chapter was conducted primarily in late 2016 and early 2017. My thanks also to Frances Pranoto and Julia Karlsen at UNSW for assembling some of the data.
2 The term "course" is used to denote a single semester/term-length study unit leading to itemised academic credit. Actual terminology differs across jurisdictions, e.g., subjects, units, papers. Note that quotations in this section are from course outlines unless otherwise indicated.
3 John Landis, 12 July 2014. Quoted with permission.
4 Clara Irazábal, 24 July 2014.
5 Skype interview with Leonie Sandercock, 25 April 2016. Quoted with permission.
6 John Landis, 12 July 2014. Quoted with permission.
7 Caroline Miller, Personal Communication, 13 January 2017. Quoted with permission.

References

Abbott, C., & Adler, S. (1989). Historical Analysis as a Planning Tool. *Journal of the American Planning Association, 55*(4), 467–473. doi:10.1080/01944368908975435
Adams, F. J. (1949). The Planning Schools: I. Massachusetts Institute of Technology. *Town Planning Review, 20*(2), 144. doi:10.3828/tpr.20.2.6k2l44x564133012
Adams, F. J. (1954). *Urban Planning Education in the United States*. Cincinnati: Alfred Bettman Foundation.
Adams, F. J., & Hodge, G. (1965). City Planning Instruction in the United States: The Pioneering Days, 1900–1930. *Journal of the American Institute of Planners, 31*(1), 43–51. doi:10.1080/01944366508978473
Adshead, S. D. (1910). An Introduction to the Study of Civic Design. *Town Planning Review, 1*(1), 3. doi:10.3828/tpr.1.1.k25421150511g571
Alofsin, A. (2002). *The Struggle for Modernism: Architecture, Landscape Architecture and City Planning at Harvard*. New York: W. W. Norton.
Batey, P. W. J. (1985). Postgraduate Planning Education in Britain: Its Purpose, Content and Organisation. *Town Planning Review, 56*(4), 407–420. doi:10.3828/tpr.56.4.62830317m6647x13
Birch, E. L. (1981). Planners–Lets Not Bury our History. *Planning History Bulletin, 3*(1), 12–15.
Booth, P. (1986). The Teaching of Planning History in Great Britain. *Planning History Bulletin, 8*(1), 21–27.
Calabi, D. (1996). Marcel Poete: Pioneer of 'l'urbanisme' and Defender of 'l'histoire des villes'. *Planning Perspectives, 11*(4), 413–436. doi:10.1080/026654396364835

Collins, M. P. (2015). The Development of Town Planning Education at University College London 1914–1969: The Contributions of Professors S. D. Adshead, L. P. Abercrombie, and W. G. Holford. *Planning Perspectives*, *31*(2), 283–298. doi:10.1080/02665433.2015.1094401

Darin, M. (1998). The Study of Urban Form in France. *Urban Morphology*, *2*(2), 63–76.

Davoudi, S., & Pendlebury, J. (2010). Centenary paper: The Evolution of Planning as an Academic Discipline. *Town Planning Review*, *81*(6), 613–646. doi:10.3828/tpr.2010.24

Dawkins, C. J. (2016). Preparing Planners: The Role of Graduate Planning Education. *Journal of Planning Education and Research*, *36*(4), 414–426. doi:10.1177/0739456x15627193

Ellis, G., Murtaugh, B., & Copeland, L. (2010). *The Future of the Planning Academy*. Belfast: Queen's University Belfast and the Royal Town Planning Institute.

Fainstein, S. S., & Campbell, S. D. (2012). Introduction: The Structure and Debates of Planning Theory. In S. S. Fainstein & S. D. Campbell (Eds.), *Readings in Planning Theory* (Third ed., pp. 1–20). Malden: WileyBlackwell.

Fainstein, S. S., & DeFilippis, J. (Eds.). (2015). *Readings in Planning Theory* (Fourth ed.). Malden: WileyBlackwell.

Feiss, C. (1938). *Status of Planning Instruction in Institutions of Higher Education*. Paper presented at the Proceedings of the National Conference on Planning, Minneapolis.

Feiss, C. (1945). History and the Modern Planner. *Journal of the American Institute of Planners*, *11*(2), 38–38. doi:10.1080/01944364508978546

Feiss, C. (1949). The Debt of Twentieth Century Planners to Nineteenth Century Pioneers. *American Journal of Economics and Sociology*, *9*(1), 35–43.

Fischler, R. (2000). Linking Planning Theory and History: The Case of Development Control. *Journal of Planning Education and Research*, *19*(3), 233–241. doi:10.1177/0739456x0001900302

Fischler, R. (2006). Teaching History to Planners. *Journal of Planning History*, *5*(4), 280–288. doi:10.1177/1538513206293711

Fischler, R. (2012). Teaching Spatial Planners: Knowledge, Skills, Competencies and Attitudes– Accreditation Standards in the US and Canada. In B. Scholl (Ed.), *Higher Education in Spatial Planning: Positions and Reflections* (pp. 140–148). Zurich: ETH Press.

Freestone, R. (2000). Learning from Planning's Histories. In R. Freestone (Ed.), *Urban Planning in a Changing World* (pp. 1–19). London: E&FN Spon.

Freestone, R. (2014). Peter Hall's Planning History. *Planning Perspectives*, *30*(1), 11–15. doi:10.1080/02665433.2014.965724

Friedmann, J. (2011). *Insurgencies: Essays in Planning Theory*. London: Routledge.

Gaus, J. M. (1943). *The Education of Planners, with Special Reference to the Graduate School of Design of Harvard University*. Cambridge, Massachusetts: Graduate School of Design.

Hall, P. (2014). *Cities of Tomorrow: An Intellectual History of Urban Planning and Design since 1890*. Chichester: Wiley Blackwell.

Hall, P., & Tewdwr-Jones, M. (2011). *Urban and Regional Planning* (Fifth ed.). Abingdon: Routledge.

Hebbert, M. (2006). Town Planning versus Urbanismo. *Planning Perspectives*, *21*(3), 233–251.

Hein, C. (Ed.) (2018). *The Routledge Handbook of Planning History*. Abingdon: Routledge.

Hise, G. (2006). Teaching Planners History. *Journal of Planning History*, *5*(4), 271–279.

LeGates, R., & Stout, F. (2015). *The City Reader* (Sixth ed.). New York: Longman.

Liverpool School of Architecture. (1948). *Prospectus for the session 1948–49*. Liverpool: Department of Civic Design, University of Liverpool.

Mandelbaum, S. J. (1985). Historians and Planners: The Construction of Pasts and Futures. *Journal of the American Planning Association*, *51*(2), 185–188. doi:10.1080/01944368508976209

Meller, H. (1990). *Patrick Geddes: Social Evolutionist and Town Planner*. Abingdon: Routledge.

Nishimura, I. (1986). On the Teaching of Planning History in Japan. *Planning History Bulletin*, *8*(2), 31–34.

Pearlman, J. (2000). Joseph Hudnut and the Unlikely Beginnings of Post-Modern Urbanism at the Harvard Bauhaus. *Planning Perspectives*, *15*(3), 201–239. doi:10.1080/026654300407445

Perloff, H. S. (1957). *Education for Planning: City, State and Regional*. Baltimore: Resources for the Future/ The Johns Hopkins University Press.

Peterson, S. J. (2006). Priming the Historian in All Planners. *Journal of Planning History*, *5*(4), 289–300.

Pray, J. S. (1917). The Department of Landscape Architecture at Harvard University. *Landscape Architecture*, January, 53–70.

Pray, J. S., & Kimball, T. (1913). *City Planning : A Comprehensive Analysis of the Subject Arranged for the Classification of Books, Plans, Photographs, Notes and Other Collected Material with Alphabetic Subject Index*. Cambridge, Massachusetts: Harvard University Press.

Rahder, B. L. (2000). Pedagogy under Duress: Teaching Planning Theory as History. *Planning History*, 22(1), 27–32.

Rodríguez-Bachiller, A. (1986). Planning Education in Europe. *Planning History Bulletin*, 8(2), 22–30.

Sandercock, L. (Ed.) (1998). *Making the Invisible Visible: A Multicultural Planning History*. Los Angeles: University of California Press.

Sanyal, B. (Ed.) (2005). *Comparative Planning Cultures*. New York: Routledge.

Schön, D. (1987). *Educating the Reflective Practitioner*. San Francisco: Jossey-Bass.

Silver, C. (2006). From the Editor. *Journal of Planning History*, 5(4), 269–270. doi:10.1177/1538513206294605

Silver, C. (2018). The Origins of Planning Education: Overview. In Frank A. I. and Silver C. (Eds.), *Urban Planning Education: Beginnings, Global Movement and Future Prospects* (pp. 11–25). Cham: Elsevier.

Frank, A. I. and Silver C. (Eds.) (2018). *Urban Planning Education: Beginnings, Global Movement and Future Prospects*. Cham: Elsevier.

Stein, J. M. (Ed.) (1995). *Classic Readings in Urban Planning : An Introduction*. New York: McGraw-Hill.

Stübben, J. (2014). *Der Städtebau: Reprint der 1. Auflage von 1890*. Wiesbaden: Vieweg+Teubner Verlag.

Sutcliffe, A. (1977). *The History of Modern Town Planning: A Bibliographic Guide*. Birmingham: University of Birmingham.

Sutcliffe, A. (1981). Why Planning History? *Built Environment*, 7(2), 64–67.

Taylor, N. (1998). *Urban Planning Theory since 1945*. London: Sage.

Teitz, M. B. (1989). The Uses and Misuses of History. *Journal of the American Planning Association*, 55(1), 81–82. doi:10.1080/01944368908975406

Ward, S., Freestone, R., & Silver, C. (2011). The 'new' planning history: Reflections, issues and directions. *Town Planning Review*, 82(3), 231–262. doi:10.3828/tpr.2011.16

Wright, M. (1982). *Lord Leverhulme's Unknown Venture: The Lever Chair and the Beginnings of Town and Regional Planning, 1908–48*. London: Hutchinson Benham.

4
TEACHING PLANNING THEORY IN CHINA

Kang Cao, Qinshi Li, Xiaolan Li, and Li Zheng

Introduction

This chapter discusses the teaching of planning theory by using a case study: specifically, the teaching of planning theory in Chinese universities. Undergraduate and graduate programs in the field of urban planning are offered in Chinese universities. As of 2017, the National Steering Committee of Urban and Rural Planning Education (NSCURPE) has estimated that 186 universities in China have established undergraduate programs in urban planning (or similar titles) (NSCURPE, 2017). Of this total, 58 offer a first-level authorized Master's in Urban Planning programs and 13 offer a first-level authorized Doctorate in Urban Planning programs. However, this statistical result excludes a few related graduate programs, such as human geography, which may share a similar training direction with urban planning.

In general, planning theory education is simultaneously offered in undergraduate and graduate programs. However, the perception of "planning theory" in undergraduate programs in urban planning is understood as the basic knowledge and theories related to urban planning practices. That is, the educational objective of this undergraduate program is to train planners toward designing and planning institutions. Tang (2014) identified two types of courses in the curriculum of this undergraduate program, namely, the theoretical and practical courses. He further explained that such courses as Introduction to Urban Planning, Principles of Urban Planning, Urban Economics, Urban Geography, Urban Master Plan Theory, Urban Transportation Planning, Urban System Planning, and Architecture Theory, and so forth, are regarded as basic theoretical courses in urban planning. Similarly, Huang (2004) argued that contemporary planning theory actually covers various areas, such as engineering technology, economics, sociology, ecology, and cultural study. In this sense, what is taught in China in the undergraduate program in urban planning is substantive planning theory or "theory in planning."

Procedural planning theory or "theory of planning" is generally taught in graduate programs. Consequently, this chapter primarily studies the actuality of the Chinese planning theory education at the graduate level, including course titles and types, textbooks and teaching materials, and teaching contents and methods. Our case studies investigated the instructors and students from four urban planning colleges and schools through interviews. We analyzed the aim of establishing the courses and course content based on the instructors' backgrounds, teaching methods, and grading methods. The purpose of this analysis is to unveil the current situation of graduate-level planning theory education in China.

Methods

We learn the status quo of the graduate-level planning theory education through three methods, namely, literature review, internet retrieval, and individual interviews. In particular, we attempt to outline a brief overview of the existing circumstances of graduate-level planning theory education through the first two methods. We mainly review journal articles and papers of conference proceedings. However, the related literature on Chinese planning theory education is limited, although the discussion on urban planning theory and urban planning education keeps intensifying (Zhang and Wang, 2012). The internet data, mainly the program details and course lists of the Master's in Urban Planning programs, come from the webpages, online information, and downloadable content of various colleges and schools from the websites of Chinese universities. In total only 26 sets of materials are available for analysis relative to the 58 graduate programs in urban planning because the program details either remain private on a few college and school websites (i.e., may only be downloaded through the intranet) or are too brief to be analyzed.

Our case study is conducted through interviews. We interview the instructors who teach planning theory courses and the students who attend these courses. For the instructors, we ask questions related to their main[1] focus and purpose in teaching planning theory, contents they introduce in each lecture, pedagogical approaches that they apply, and how the students participate in learning and understanding what is taught, etc. For the students, we inquire what they learn from the courses, what impresses them the most, and their thoughts on assignments and their participation in class, and so on.

Overview of Current Chinese Planning Theory Education

Internet retrieval enables us to learn that the official websites of the 58 universities that offer first-level authorized Master's in Urban Planning program do not indicate whether these institutions offer planning theory courses. Accordingly, we analyzed the program overviews and curriculum of urban planning in a few universities[2] and determined that 26 of these institutions offer planning theory courses, while two universities do not. This finding at least indicates that planning theory has received a certain level of attention in the urban planning education of graduates. However, the Chinese planning theory education is undeniably lagging behind, particularly when compared with the well-developed practice- and application-oriented Chinese planning education.

A general view of the related literature on planning theory education indicates that the current planning education research concentrates less on theoretical introduction and more on issues of imparting knowledge of planning technology and methods to students. It also focuses less on pure theoretical courses but more on the practice- or application-oriented courses. This is because, as Zhang and Wang (2012) observed, urban planning education has focused more on the teaching of practical planning techniques but ignored the instruction of planning theory and research methods. This situation undoubtedly hinders the development of urban planning theory education. Tang (2014) also found that most studies on Chinese urban planning education so far have focused on providing comments on the general situation of planning education locally and overseas but have been limited on the teaching of urban planning theory.

Meanwhile, the discrepancy in understanding what planning theory is has led most studies that focus on planning theory education to mainly involve theories related to planning or "theory in planning" rather than "theory of planning." Accordingly, the latter cannot be used as reference in this chapter.

Course Title and Type

The internet retrieval result of the websites of the colleges and schools that offer graduate programs in urban planning identifies three types of planning theory course titles, namely: Modern Urban Planning Theory, Urban (and Rural) Planning Theory and Method, and Urban Planning Theory and Practice (see Figure 4.1). The statistics showed that the most commonly used title is "Modern Urban Planning Theory," which is used by approximately one-third of all the schools and colleges counted. However, approximately two-fifths of these institutions name the "planning theory course" either "Planning Theory and Method" or "Planning Theory and Practice," thereby indicating a strong practical tendency in planning theory education.

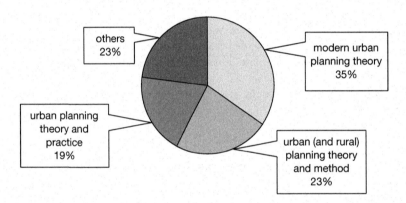

Figure 4.1 Titles of Planning Theory Courses in China

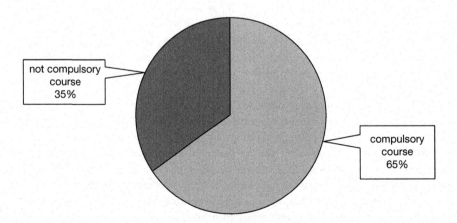

Figure 4.2 The Status of Planning Theory Courses in the Curriculum of Urban Planning Program
(*Source:* the websites of related city planning colleges and schools)

Approximately two-thirds of the colleges and schools make planning theory course a "compulsory course" in the curriculum of the Urban Planning program, while the rest make it optional (see Figure 4.2). This result implies that planning theory education is regarded by most colleges and schools that offer Urban Planning programs as fundamental for graduate students. In most cases when a planning theory course is not compulsory, it is offered as a basic degree course that is also essential. For example, students of the School of Architecture and Urban Planning of Southeast University are required to take either one of the two degree courses, namely, a planning theory course (Modern Urban Planning Theory) or a planning method course (Urban Planning Research Methodology).

Textbooks and Bibliography

No unified teaching materials or textbooks are used in the teaching of Chinese planning theory. The selection of teaching materials and bibliography generally depends on what is taught in class. The references can be journal articles, monographs, reports, and texts of the planning projects, among others.

Huang (2004) identified two problems that exist in current planning theory education and textbooks. The first problem is the lack of introduction to the social context and mechanism that generate Western planning theories, ideas, thoughts, and methods; these theories consistently form a necessary component of the introduction section of every planning theory course. The introduction of theory should be based on the analysis of the context and development process of theories, he argues, rather than merely making a list of occurrences and results. Moreover, he emphasized the importance of considering the different conditions of every country or region. The second problem is the lack of effort to propose creative solutions to the emerging problems in the Chinese urbanization process. Consequently, he argued that Chinese urban planning education lacks the critical spirit and courage, which is rooted in Western culture, to propose a new theory in terms of actual social and urban problems. This lack is directly reflected in the content of the textbooks, which, according to Huang, avoids exposing the actual problems in planning practice and rarely inspires theoretical innovation.

Zhang and Wang (2012) determined that a few Chinese universities have already listed *Readings in Planning Theory* (Fainstein and DeFilippis, 2016) and *City Reader* (LeGates and Stout, 2015) as important bibliographies in planning theory courses. They also suggested that published journal articles that discuss urban planning theory and are closely related to Chinese planning practices can be introduced as teaching/reading materials in China's urban planning theory education.

Content

We experienced difficulty in making an outline of the content taught in graduate-level planning theory courses in various departments, colleges, and schools of different universities. The simple reason is the lack of syllabus and teaching files that can be downloaded from the websites of the related colleges and schools of these universities. Consequently, we had to learn the content of the lectures through the interviews, which will be discussed in the following section.

Teaching Methods

At present, it is acknowledged that the teaching of planning theory generally involves a one-way behavior, that is, from the instructor to students. However, instructors are currently attempting to apply multiple methods of teaching. These methods include self-learning web query (Jin, 2012), case analysis (Xing and Zhao, 2015), spiral case study (Li, 2013), participatory teaching, heuristic teaching, and discussion-based teaching (Tang, 2014), and so on. The purpose of these new methods is to enable students to completely participate in the learning process. For instance, Jin (2012) explained that self-learning web query is a good preview method to enable students to understand what will be taught in advance. Xing and Zhao (2015) referred to case analysis as a comprehensive learning process that comprises a series of activities (e.g., survey, reading, thinking, analysis, discussion, and communication) between the instructors and students.

In addition, the case analysis method is highlighted in the literature and by the interviewees due to the highly practice-oriented planning theory education in China. However, the method of analyzing cases varies. Li (2013) interpreted spiral case study as a three-stage process, that is, "theory and model–practical application–query and innovation." The students can, according to him, understand the process of "from rationale to reality," subsequently abstracting theory from practice, thereby triggering their sense of initiative.

Case Studies of Four Chinese Universities

Zhejiang University (ZJU), Renmin University of China (RUC), Nanjing University (NU), and Tongji University (TU) are selected as case studies in the current research (see Table 4.1). The personal interviews indicated that colleges and schools have considerable discretion on the establishment of planning theory courses. Simultaneously, course contents and teaching methods are substantially related to the educational backgrounds and research fields of instructors.

Purpose

The syllabus of the Urban Planning Theory and Method course offered by DRUP of ZJU indicates that this course aims to: (1) review and explain the theoretical issues related to planning; (2) clarify the different values and rationalities involved in the planning process, and understand the scientificity and sociality of planning and their influence and differentiation between "theory

Table 4.1 Details of the Planning Theory Courses of Four Universities in China

Course Title	Schools, Colleges, or Departments	Instructors
Urban Planning Theory and Method	Department of Regional and Urban Planning (DRUP) of the College of Civic Engineering and Architecture, Zhejiang University	Prof. Chen Hua, Prof. Wangming Li, Prof. Dandong Ge, and Dr Donghui Wang
Western Urban Planning Theory	Department of Urban Planning and Management (DUPM) of the School of Public Administration and Policy, Renmin University of China	Prof. Lei Zhang
Urban Planning Theory and Practice	Department of Urban Planning (DUP) of the School of Architecture and Urban Planning, Nanjing University	Prof. Jingxiang Zhang and Prof. Tao Yu
Rationale of Modern Urban Planning	DUP of the School of Architecture and Urban Planning, Tongji University	Prof. Zilai Tang and Prof. Hok-Lin Leung

(*Sources*: Websites of the related colleges and schools, and personal interview)

of planning" and "theory in planning"; and (3) classify theories related to urban planning. Evidently, the lecturer has focused on a few dialectical concepts (e.g., scientificity vs. sociality and "theory of planning" vs. "theory in planning") in the study of planning theory.

The titles and contents of the courses provided by DRUP of ZJU, DUP of NU, and DUP of TU indicate that the graduate-level planning theory education in China ultimately aims to teach students practice-oriented Chinese planning theory based on the understanding of the development, nature, and issues of Western planning theory. Simultaneously, the perceptions of colleges, schools, and departments toward Chinese planning theory differ from one another, thereby leading to a variety of planning theory education modes in China.

Instructors and Contents

Instructors of urban planning theory should possess strong theoretical research ability and the skill of combining theory and practice. Our findings demonstrated that the instructors from the four universities are renowned professors with distinctive research abilities and achievements in planning practices. The interviews indicated that the planning theory education in most universities is closely related to planning practices. Virtually no university would instruct planning theory solely at the theoretical level. The contents of the planning theory courses offered by the four universities can be typically divided into two components: (1) introduction of the basic theories; and (2) analysis of planning theory application based on case studies. When providing instruction on basic theories or theories of planning, lecturers from the four universities would provide students with the widespread traditional (or classical) planning theories developed in the Western context and their own understanding of the nature and value of planning. However, the four cases presented a few variances in teaching activities due to the different educational backgrounds of the lecturers. For example, the learning experiences in Europe of the lead planning theory instructor of DRUP of ZJU have led him to substantially focus on European planning theories; the instructor from DUPM of RUC introduces numerous planning theories developed in the US context because of his American educational experiences. The main textbook employed by RUC is *Readings in Planning Theory*, edited by Susan S. Fainstein and Scott Campbell, and the publications of John Friedmann.

The application of the planning theory education varies depending on the teaching staff capability. Our case studies involve two situations: (1) one single instructor completely assumes the teaching responsibility; and (2) several instructors collaborate in teaching. The staffing situation has a direct influence on the educational result because the teaching contents are substantively decided by the planning practice experiences of the instructors. Consequently, notable variations can be observed in the application of the planning theory education among the four universities.

DRUP of ZJU: The Master's course titled Urban Planning Theory and Method offered by DRUP of ZJU lasts for eight weeks at four hours per week. The teaching team comprises one lead instructor and three co-instructors. The lead instructor is responsible for teaching the theories of planning, which includes: (1) values in urban planning; (2) scientific methods and logical processes in urban planning; and (3) rationality, notions, and forms of urban planning. The three co-instructors teach the following topics based on their respective professional strengths: (1) urbanization theory (using the massive economy of Zhejiang as an example); (2) basic theories and research of ecological planning, urban regulatory detailed planning, types of historic cities, and special planning (using the Yuquan and Zhijiang campuses of ZJU as examples); and (3) theories, methods, and cases of rural planning (using the teaching of rural planning as an example). In the lectures, the instructor initially provides an overall analysis and assessment of current rural planning and construction based on a review of the Chinese rural development. Thereafter, he proposes the necessary strategies and practices. During the lectures, sections of free discussion are designed and students are encouraged to present their own viewpoints.

DUPM of RUC: The Western Urban Planning Theory course offered by DUPM of RUC is the only course in our case studies that is taught by a single instructor. This course lasts for eight weeks at four hours per week. In the first two weeks, the instructor provides a brief introduction on planning theory, including the following topics: (1) what is planning theory, why planning theory is necessary, and whether planning theory is useful; and (2) values in planning theory and its social functions. Subsequently, the instructor uses the introduction of the theory's development background (including the philosophical and socioeconomic backgrounds, and so forth) as basis to reflect on the changes that occur in the theory's development process and the associated planning practices (e.g., industry development strategies, sustainable development, collaborative planning, etc.). He reviews the classical theories by taking planning in the USA as an example. The succeeding six weeks is designed as participatory teaching.

DUP of NU: The Urban Planning Theories and Practices course offered by DUP of NU lasts for 18 weeks. Two lecturers collaborate to teach, with each lecturer responsible for nine weeks of teaching. The first lecturer mainly introduces the urban planning education system and China's registered planner system, thereby enabling the students to develop a clear understanding of the interrelationship between academic education and professional career. Thereafter, the lecturer reviews the history of Western planning thoughts based on which he/she further introduces the following topics: (1) urban planning from the perspectives of property and development rights; (2) transition of industry parks; (3) Chinese strategic planning; (4) space governance; (5) overall transition of the Chinese urban and rural planning; (6) big events marketing; and (7) urban growth coalition, among others. Note that the course contents are closely related to planning practices. For example, the post-disaster reconstruction planning of the Wenchuan[3] earthquake area is used as a topic in teaching this course. Meanwhile, the teaching technique of the second lecturer is also a type of participatory teaching. The instructor first provides a few topics as options. Thereafter, each team of students selects one topic and completes a report for presentation and discussion.

DUP of TU: The Modern Urban Planning Theory course offered by DUP of TU lasts for 18 weeks with two instructors teaching. The lead instructor teaches for 14 weeks and his main responsibility is to introduce modern Western urban planning theories, current popular theories, and methods. In particular, his teaching contents include: (1) urban economic theories; (2) theories and methods of urban spatial structure; (3) theories and methods of urban policy analysis; (4) Western urban construction history and theories, including new town construction from the 1950s to the 1960s, urban renewal between the 1960s and the 1970s, and urban renaissance and urban regeneration since the 1980s; (5) enterprise relational evaluation methods of a regional urban system; (6) evaluation criteria and methods of worldwide urban systems in the context of economic globalization; and (7) the development strategies of Shanghai to become a global city. The other instructor spends five to eight weeks analyzing the philosophy of urban planning, including the main contents and thoughts of the book titled *Old Concepts and New Situations: Human-centered Urbanization* (Leung, 2016).

Course Requirements and Assignments

In terms of the dialectical, critical, dynamic, and uncertain features of theories, instructors experience difficulty in teaching planning theory using the traditional method, in which students passively acquire knowledge. Therefore, three of the universities (not DUP of TU) employ a two-way teaching method, in which students can interact with instructors and learn proactively. In addition, the participation of students directly influences the grades they will obtain. We will discuss this in the following section.

DUPM of RUC: In the eight-week course, the instructor introduces the theories in the first two weeks and the students should complete a team project in the next six weeks. The students are divided into six groups, with each group being asked to select one chapter (or one theoretical school) from *Readings in Planning Theory* as their topic. They are required to translate three pages of the chapter related to their selected topic and conduct their own additional literature research. The slides that they will make and present will be based on their understanding of the topics that they selected. From the third week onwards, the instructor initially provides a brief overview of one topic/theoretical school at the beginning of each lecture. Thereafter, the team of this topic/theoretical school is expected to make a 30–45 minute presentation followed by an open discussion on their topic/theoretical school. The grades are given based on the group presentation and individual written paper.

DUP of NU: The group presentation in DUP of NU is similar to that in DUPM of RUC. However, the differences lie in the students' opportunity to participate in the grading of the presentations. That is, the final mark of one group is decided by the average score given by the instructor and other groups in DUP of NU. Inside the group the students are graded by the group leader based on the actual load and quality of their work. This grading mechanism sparks a heated debate between the groups, thereby immensely promoting discussion and participation in the activity. Moreover, the inner group scoring immensely motivates member participation and effectively prevents "free riders."

DRUP of ZJU: The two-way teaching method is loosely applied in the class by the instructors. Students are encouraged to speak in class. However, the speaking is not mandatory, neither does it relates to the final grading. Sometimes the instructors may assign a topic or issue to the students for them to make a presentation, but this assignment is not regular.

Comparing Approaches to Theory

One of the current authors once attended the Planning Theory and Contemporary Practice course offered by the School of Global Studies, Social Science and Planning of the Royal Melbourne Institution of Technology (RMIT) with Prof. Jean Hillier as the lead instructor, and the Urban and Planning Theory course offered by the School of Design of the University of Pennsylvania (UPenn) with Prof. John Landis as the lead instructor. The following differences were identified when the two courses were compared with the planning theory courses in China.

1. The two courses only have one instructor, whereas three of the four universities in our Chinese case studies have at least two instructors who collaborate in teaching.
2. Teaching assistants (TAs) are available in the universities in Australia and the US. TAs assist the instructor in the class discussion (i.e., structured discussion in RMIT, and recitation in UPenn). In contrast, the TA system has not been established in China and the instructor directly organizes the discussion.
3. The organization of each lecture is different. The discussion in RMIT and UPenn is organized just after the instruction in each lecture, and the discussion centers on the topics taught and the related readings. In other words, teaching and discussion are intertwined with the lecture. In contrast, the instruction and discussion in China are not organized together. That is, the instructors normally complete their teaching first followed by separate

discussions. Meanwhile, the topics for discussion are often new topics provided by the instructors rather than the ones taught in the lectures.

4 In terms of grading, RMIT and UPenn often give more assignments to students than Chinese universities do.[4] In the Chinese cases, DRUP of ZJU decides the grades of students through a single exam. DUPM of RUC and DUP of NJ assess students through class discussions and written papers. DUP of TJ only considers the students' written papers.

5 In terms of the teaching contents, instructors in China typically spend one-fourth or less time in teaching planning theories but spend more time in elaborating the "Chinese planning theories"[5] (Cao and Hillier, 2013) through case studies. By comparison, the elaboration on planning theory in RMIT and UPenn takes up at least half of the teaching time. In particular, teaching in RMIT combines theories with their practical applications, while UPenn focuses on the "theories of urban growth, development & structure" and "planning theory." These methods involve extensive discussions on global and American urban development (and urban shrinking as well).

6 According to Klosterman (2011), despite the absence of a fixed textbook for planning theory courses in the US, *Planning Theory for Practitioners* (Brooks, 2002), *Readings in Planning Theory* (Fainstein and DeFilippis, 2016) and *Cities of Tomorrow* (Hall, 2002) are the most frequently required texts. Similarly, no fixed textbook is used in China but universities specify the reading materials completely differently.

Conclusion

Two conclusions can be drawn from the discussion. First, if planning theory is understood as procedural planning theory and substantive planning theory, then the procedural planning theory education is mainly embodied in the teaching of case studies. The analysis of the interviews, syllabi, and teaching materials indicated that the graduate-level education on planning theory in China is highly practice-oriented, which can be reflected by the course titles and course organization. Put another way, Chinese planning theorists have yet to establish Chinese planning theory in the abstract. Therefore, planning theory education has to be built upon various analyses of planning practices. Moreover, planning theory courses in China highlight the introduction of the origins of planning theories. However, the planning theories that are taught in Chinese universities are those developed in Europe and North America instead of domestic planning theory. As a matter of fact, Chinese planning theory is still in its developing phase but it should already be discussed in the academe. This situation is by and large overlooked in planning theory education in China. Furthermore, substantive planning theory or urban theory is not separated from the instruction of planning theory but combined with case studies. This situation demonstrates an unsystematic understanding toward planning theory in the academe.

Second, planning theory education in China presents a highly inconsistent situation that is reflected in the choices of textbooks and teaching materials and the organization of teaching contents. In this regard, Zhang and Wang (2012) explained that Chinese planning theory education is still in its beginning stages and the completion of planning theory courses largely depends on the development of Chinese planning theory itself. Given this situation, they do not think that unified textbooks are necessary in Chinese planning theory education but advocate for constructing the urban planning theory (education) framework with the adoption of the principles of learning from the classical works, as well as a discussion of the diverse planning and urban theories.

Zhang and Wang (2012) reviewed planning theory education in North America and argued that China will take time to improve the situation of planning theory education. Initially, planning theory education was also ignored in North America and only a few universities offered the associated courses. North America has spent a few decades aiming to change the situation and has eventually attracted the attention of universities toward planning theory education. The development of planning theory education in China is also expected to undergo the same process. As planning theory researchers and educators, our purpose is to think of what we can contribute to promote this process, which is precisely the aim of the current study.

Acknowledgements

The authors would like to express their sincere thanks to Prof. Chen Hua, Dr Dandong Ge, and Dr Donghui Wang at Zhejiang University, Prof. Lei Zhang at Renmin University, Dr Chen Chen, Yuan Lu, Jia Geng, Yue Wang at Tongji University, Yibo Qiao in Nanjing University, Dr Zhuoran Shan at Huazhong University of Science and Technology, Prof. Jean Hillier at RMIT, and Prof. John Landis at University of Pennsylvania for their comments and help.

Funding

This chapter is funded by the Natural Science Foundation of China (51678517), the High Education Pedagogical Reform Research Project of Zhejiang Province (jg2015002), the Graduate Education Research Project of Zhejiang University (20170307), and the Textbook Writing Project, Core Course Construction Project, and Pedagogical Reform Project of the College of Civil Engineering and Architecture at Zhejiang University.

Notes

1 All the instructors we interviewed are male.
2 Only 28 out of the 58 universities provide open online information on the overview of the urban planning program and curriculum.
3 Wenchuan is a city in Sichuan Province. It suffered from a massive earthquake in 2008.
4 RMIT gives three assignments and UPenn gives four.
5 Chinese planning theory here is interpreted as the working procedures, principles, and norms developed from the planning practices.

References

Brooks, M. P. (2002). *Planning Theory for Practitioners*. London and New York: Routledge.
Cao, K., & Hillier, J. (2013). Planning Theory in China and Chinese Planning Theory: Guest Editorial Introduction. *Planning Theory*, *12*(4), 331–334. doi:10.1177/1473095213493983
Fainstein, S. S. and DeFilippis, J. (2016). *Readings in Planning Theory*, 4th edition. Oxford: Wiley-Blackwell.
Hall, P. (2002). *Cities of Tomorrow: An Intellectual History of Urban Planning and Design in the Twentieth Century*, 3rd edition. Oxford: Wiley-Blackwell.
Huang, T.-Q. (2004). A View on the Multiple-subject of Theoretical Education for Urban Planning Specialty in China. *Planners*, *20*(4), 19–20.
Jin, C.-N. (2012). Study of the Modern Urban Planning Theory Teaching Methods. *Science and Technology Innovation Herald*, *32*, 139.
Klosterman, R. E. (2011). Planning Theory Education. *Journal of Planning Education and Research*, *31*(3), 319–331. doi:10.1177/0739456x11413601
LeGates, R. T. and Stout, F. (2015). *The City Reader*, 6th edition. London and New York: Routledge.
Leung, H. (2016). *Old Concepts and New Situations: Human-centered Urbanization*. Beijing: SDX Joint Publishing Company.
Li, F. (2013). A Reform of Three-stage Teaching Method of 'Spiral Case Study' Based on Cultivating Creative Thought: Case Study of Pedagogical Reform of 'Urban Form and Planning Theory' Course. *Forestry Education in China*, *31*(5), 64–67.

National Steering Committee of Urban and Rural Planning Education in China (NSCURPE). (2017). Labor Division of the Committee Members. Retrieved from www.nsc-urpec.org/index.php?classid=5923

Tang, C.-C. (2014). Reform Path of Seminar Style Teaching of Theoretical Courses in Urban Planning. *Journal of Changsha University of Science and Technology (Social Science), 29*(5), 115–119.

Xing, X.-N., & Zhao, Z.-F. (2015). Construction of 'Theory + Practice' at University Teaching Model – A Case Study of Urban Planning. *Popular Science & Technology, 17*(12), 112–113.

Zhang, L., & Wang, Z.-C. (2012). From Diversity to Norm: Experiences of Planning Education in North America. *Urban Planning Forum, 2*, 67–72.

5
PLANNING LAW

Richard K. Norton

What is "Planning Law" and Why Teach It?

An important distinction to draw when contemplating "planning law" is the difference between what planning law is and how that body of law relates to the practice of planning. Planning law would not be recognized as a subfield or distinct body of law in most law schools. In the U.S., for example, to the extent that there is a coherent body of law that might be called planning law, it exists as an amalgam of constitutional law, administrative law, and state and local government law more broadly, along with land use control law more particularly (e.g., zoning, subdivision control, growth management) and a variety of specialty topics thrown in for good measure (e.g., law of property, contracts, torts, housing policy, environmental protection, and real estate development). In other words, like the urban and regional planning profession itself, the body of planning law encompasses a broad, interdisciplinary, and highly integrated cross-section of more traditional and circumscribed academic and professional legal doctrines and practice areas.

The relationship between planning *law* as law and the discipline and practice of *planning* stems from the role that the planning profession plays in society. For purposes here, "the planning profession" is defined as a governmental function, a public endeavor aimed at providing public services and managing private land use for the benefit of the larger community. It encompasses the process of engaging a variety of public visioning, goal setting, analysis, prediction, and policy adoption activities (i.e., plan making) and linking them to governmental action. Examples of such action include the regulation of private land use, tax policy-making designed to encourage or discourage private commercial activities, public spending on things like education campaigns, the siting of public facilities like transit stations and community parks, and the provision of other public goods like water and roadway infrastructure.

Thus planning students and practicing planners do not need to know as much law as do law students and practicing lawyers, but they do need to understand some basic legal rules, principles, and institutional structures that speak directly to planning practice. They need a good sense of the logic of legal reasoning and methods of legal analysis, and the ways in which lawyers, legal academics, and (especially) judges justify specific legal decisions and broader legal doctrines. They need to have a solid grasp of the legal justifications for planners' authority and responsibility. And perhaps more importantly, they need to have a good sense of where they can get themselves into trouble, either for failing to do things they ought to do, or for doing things they surely ought *not* to do.

In the U.S., the entity that accredits professional urban and regional planning programs—the Planning Accreditation Board (PAB)—requires that graduate-level planning programs provide basic instruction on "planning law," which it defines as "legal and institutional contexts within which planning occurs."[1] A quick review of 15 U.S. planning programs generally considered to be among the top programs in the country suggests that about three-fourths of them meet this requirement by including, as a core program requirement, a course dedicated specifically to some version of planning law. Most of these courses, especially those taught by the planning program itself rather than through a companion law-school course, do not focus on planning law *per se*. Rather, they provide some version of planning law and its institutional aspects, such as "planning institutions and law," "legal environment of planning," "law and the quality of urban life," "law and plan making," and so on.

The purpose of this chapter is to present an overview of the core legal and institutional principles, procedures, and related knowledge that courses such as these should convey to planning students, not merely to ensure compliance with accreditation bodies such as the PAB, but more importantly to ensure that graduates of planning programs are well prepared to effectively, efficiently, and *legally* execute their roles and responsibilities as practicing, professional urban planners. For the sake of explicating key concepts, this chapter focuses primarily on the U.S. system. Even so, much of what is presented here is universal across countries and legal systems because many of the issues addressed speak to universal debates: about how to structure interactions between government and individuals, how to enable government to act without giving it the power to be abusive, and how to balance the promotion of a larger public welfare with the protection of individual rights.

The remainder of the chapter presents an overview of some theory and methods for teaching planning law, including thoughts on pedagogical approaches and key literatures for doing so. Throughout the chapter, the term "planning law" is used to encompass more broadly a survey of planning law and its institutional aspects as just discussed, rather than a collection of basic legal rules.

Theory and Methods

Planning systems differ across countries in terms of what exactly "planning" encompasses. All public planning endeavors involve undertaking a variety of planning-related activities, and all involve engaging governmental employees in one form or another to undertake those activities, such that planning law always necessarily encompasses enabling laws that create governmental planning authorities and authorize governmental agents to exercise those authorities.

In countries that effectively authorize plans as legally enforceable policies, "planning" (or "planning systems" or "planning instruments") generally encompasses both those plan/policy-making activities along with legally significant plan implementation activities (e.g., discretionary review and approval of development proposals). This is not the case in the U.S., strictly speaking. There "planning" usually encompasses only the *non*-enforceable analysis and policy-making actions that governments take. The legally enforceable actions taken to implement the plan are generally referred to as the specific legal actions involved themselves, such as zoning control, subdivision regulation, and so on. This is somewhat ironic in that the administration of these activities, even in the U.S., typically involves planners to some extent, and planning law even as conceived and taught in the U.S. focuses predominantly on the legally significant actions undertaken by governments to implement their plans.

Suffice it to say that an important part of teaching planning law in any country is to convey to students the fact that all governmental planning programs and agents require organic enabling laws to exist, laws that inevitably provide definition, scope, and limitations on those programs and agents. It is similarly important to provide the historical context for those enabling laws as much as possible because that context can help to explain much of contemporary practice. Beyond those organic provisions, most of what planning law as a body of knowledge speaks to—including in the U.S.—covers the implementation of planning schemes through legally significant action, particularly where governments interact with markets and especially where governments regulate the use of private property in one way or another. The focus of this chapter, accordingly, is on planning law in those contexts.

Initial Challenges

There are several challenges in teaching planning law that should be recognized right away. First, legal reasoning is not patently obvious to many. Something about the logic of the law, the process of discerning the appropriate and applicable rule, and then taking account of the exceptions to the rule—and sometimes even the exceptions to the exceptions to the rule—can be befuddling, as can distinguishing between the "what" of rules and the "how," "when," and "by whom" those rules are actually applied. Similarly, as noted, learning planning law surely requires learning some basic sets of legal rules ("black letter" law), but also much more. More subtly, planners do indeed need to learn the "who, when, how, and why" of public planning activities within the larger context of institutional structures and societal pressures.

This challenge is best confronted by not merely covering the rules of planning and planning implementation themselves but by emphasizing the principles underlying those rules and the explanations for them. It helps to keep straight various notice and related procedural requirements by understanding why, for example, such requirements for adopting an amendment to a zoning code are much broader and more permissive than they are for granting a variance (i.e., the former is a legislative action—making a law of broad applicability, subject to checks and balances through the political process—while the latter is a quasi-judicial action—applying the law to a particular individual, with a heightened potential for governmental bias and abuse).

Second, given the broad nature of planning activities, including especially the implementation of plans through legally significant actions like the administration of a zoning code, planners regularly engage in a wide variety of activities that arguably look like the practice of law (e.g., interpreting local ordinances). They need to be able to engage in these fuzzy boundary law-like activities to do their jobs and to ensure efficient and effective governmental function. The difficulty, however, is that while anyone (including lawyers) can effectively practice planning without a planning license (whether they do so credibly or not), in most if not all countries it is sanctionable for planners to practice law without a law license. While planners need to engage in law-practice-like activities, going too far into the actual practice of law could yield real problems for community and planner alike. The solution here is to educate students on the limits of their efforts through instruction on professional responsibility and a workable understanding of what the "practice of law" means.

Recognizing these challenges, there are three broad kinds of knowledge that an introductory planning law course for planning students should convey: foundational knowledge of planning law, applicable knowledge in planning law, and technical skills for legally informed planning practice, each of which has attributes that are more procedural or more substantive in nature. The remainder of this section steps through these topics in turn.

Foundational Knowledge of Planning Law

A key distinction common in the law is that between its procedural aspects, such as the requirement that adequate notice and opportunity for comment be provided when a locality considers a zoning variance request, and its substantive aspects, such as consideration of whether it would be fair to the landowner and/or her neighbors to grant that variance (i.e., based on some criteria other than whether the appropriate procedures were followed). While the boundaries are a bit fuzzy, this distinction is helpful for contemplating foundational aspects of planning law.

Procedural

From a procedural perspective, students of planning law should be taught the process of legal reasoning and various law-making and administration procedures.

The logic of **legal reasoning** is much the same as that of planning, except it is just different enough to be confusing for many planning students. At its core, legal reasoning is more prominently argumentative and normative. Beyond merely resolving disputes (or in order to resolve them), the law is all about determining through argument the appropriate rules that ought to be established to maintain a peaceful and flourishing society—rules that carry with them the potential for state-imposed sanction—and then applying those rules to individual cases. The forum for decision-making is not the lab or city hall but the court-room, facts are not established through scientific study or original analysis but are "found" by a jury or the "court" (i.e., the judge presiding over a case) using intricate rules of evidence, and the "theory" of a case or law is not a potential explanation for some natural or social phenomenon, as commonly understood by planners, but rather an argument for why a particular rule should be adopted as the law of the land or why that particular rule should be applied to a particular case, as commonly understood by lawyers. The abilities to discern which facts are material, which rules are applicable, and how facts should be applied to law (or how a court would likely apply fact to law) are perhaps the most difficult for planning students to master.

In addition to legal reasoning, planners need to understand the legally significant processes governments engage to make, adopt, and administer their plans or planning instruments. Most prominently, they should learn conceptual differences between **legislative, quasi-legislative, administrative, and quasi-judicial processes**. In a nutshell, legislative processes are those engaged to make laws (e.g., zoning codes adopted to implement a master plan), while quasi-legislative procedures (author's term) are those used to develop and adopt a master plan, especially where that plan is adopted by an appointed planning commission as a policy guiding document rather than by an elected body as enforceable policy or law. Similarly, administrative procedures are those engaged to execute those laws (e.g., the process specified in an ordinance to conduct and act on a site plan review), while quasi-judicial processes are those engaged by administrative appellate bodies (typically the "zoning board of appeals" in the U.S.) as an initial check on that decision. In the U.S., at least, key differences across these kinds of actions include, for example, the type of notice required for impending action (e.g., broad newspaper publication versus individual notice), the type of hearing required, whether "findings of fact" or other evidentiary requirements are specified, and what kinds of communication can take place outside of formal hearings.

Substantive

In addition to knowing how legal reasoning works and what procedures ought to be followed, planning students should understand some key foundational aspects of the law that are more substantive, again in keeping with the notion that truly understanding complex rules requires understanding the history and principles underlying those rules. The topics most important for students to survey include the following.

The philosophical and historical origins of legal rules: Following from the use of deductive logic to apply fact to law in order to determine what the appropriate legal outcome of a dispute should be (or likely will be), and given that law is inherently normative in that it dictates what members of society ought or ought not to do, it is helpful to understand where those laws (or norms or rules) come from in the first place. Legislatures, administrative agencies, and courts do not generate such rules out of thin air. They draw rules out of norms and expectations that hark back ultimately to principals of moral philosophy about how we ought to treat one another (e.g., Kantian notions about human reason and the duty not to cause harm), principles of political philosophy about how we ought to structure government and what government's role should be vis-à-vis private property rights (e.g., natural law theories about the role of private property in political society), and historical understandings and expectations about the abilities and failings of different governmental actors and what roles they can or should play. Planning students should be, at the very least, introduced to these foundational principals, historical events, and general expectations.

Bodies or types of law: "The law" actually consists of a complex array of laws coming from different sources, serving different purposes, and sometimes simply enjoying different labels. In so-called common-law countries, for example, *common law* is the body of judge-made law that developed over time through the accretion of precedential cases. *Constitutional law* speaks to law generated by the citizenry through a ratified constitution that, in general, both constitutes government and then constrains its exercise of authority. *Statutory law* is positive law (i.e., not judge-made common law) generated by legislatures, historically as either the codification of common law doctrine or a forward-looking attempt to address social or other problems not well addressed by case-specific, after-the-fact common law-making. An *ordinance*, at least in the U.S., is the term used to refer to statutory law made by a local legislative body—such as the city council—rather than the state or federal legislature. *Administrative rules* are law made by an administrative agency acting under authorities duly granted by a legislature. Finally, aside from common law, *case law* is judge-made law that establishes constitutional doctrine or that fills the gaps, providing explication of ambiguous statutory laws or administrative rules.

Along another dimension, and again using the U.S. as an example, *national law* (often referred to as *federal law* in the U.S.) is constitutional, statutory, or administrative law generated by a national governmental entity; *state law* is common, constitutional, statutory, or administrative law generated by a state governmental entity (i.e., judge-, legislature-, or agency-made law), and *local law* (often *municipal law*) is statutory or administrative law generated by a locality (legislature or agency). Similarly, law can be grouped or categorized into different bodies or doctrines according to the kinds of legal issues addressed, such as property, contracts, torts, and so on. Planning law implicates all of these different kinds and bodies of law, and students need to understand the similarities and differences between them.

Sources of governmental authority to engage in planning, and constraints on those authorities: Public planning requires *constitutional and statutory enabling laws* that create public planning entities and grant those entities authority to plan and to implement their plans. Planning law in the U.S., for example, is primarily state and local government law (there is no formal national planning system in the U.S., unlike other countries). States are the plenary authorities, and they enjoy two authorities in particular that speak to the implementation of plans through the control of private land use: the *police power* (the power to regulate for the purpose of protecting public health, safety, morals, and the general welfare), and the power of *eminent domain* (the power to compel the involuntary transfer of title in real property from a private landowner to the state).[2]

Drawing from those powers, the states create and then generally enable their local units of government to engage in planning and plan implementation activities (as well as the condemnation of private property under certain circumstances). While those bodies of law vary across the states in many ways, they are nonetheless quite similar in their larger contours.[3] Planning students should understand the historical origins of relevant enabling laws, and they need to understand (initially through coursework, then thoroughly through professional practice) the specifics of the enabling laws for the state(s) (or other relevant jurisdictions) within which they practice.

The primary constraints on planning authorities, again looking to the U.S. for illustration, are *structural* and *constitutional constraints*. The entire U.S. system of government was structured by design both to enable governments to function and to constrain their potential for abuse, through doctrines like *federalism* (i.e., the allocation of powers across different levels of government—state, national, and local) and *separation of powers* (i.e., the existence of a tri-part system—legislative, executive, and judiciary), where each has unique authorities and each provides a check on the powers of the other. In addition, selected amendments to the U.S. Constitution, and corresponding provisions in the several state constitutions, constrain planning actions by providing extra-ordinary protections for citizens as against governmental abuse—such as the right to due process of law (these specific protections are discussed more below). The practice of planning in all of its permutations functions entirely within this intricate set of authorities and constraints, which planning students correspondingly need to learn. Three attributes of this system that are especially important include the following.

Structural systems and authorities unique to planning law: Public planning is conducted as a governmental function that involves multiple governmental actors whose roles are not limited to planning, such as mayors, city managers, city attorneys, functional boards such as housing commissions, and so on. It also typically involves specialized actors and specialized processes unique to planning and plan implementation, including most notably special governmental boards like planning commissions and zoning boards of appeals, specially trained agents like professional planners, and unique and highly prescribed processes for the adoption of community plans and policies, enactment of local ordinances, and administration of those plans, policies, and ordinances. These actors and systems are, clearly, especially relevant to the practice of urban planning, and planning students should thoroughly understand them.

Private property: At its core, urban planning speaks to governmental interaction with markets, various private and public-interest associations, and other institutions to influence the use of land for both public and private purposes, and in most countries that function implicates public management of the use of privately owned real property. To fully understand the roles, reach, and limits of public planning in any given country, planning students need to have a profound understanding of the meanings, roles, reach, and limits of private property ownership in that country—meanings that vary across countries. Especially where planning is conducted within some form of representative government representing pluralistic goals and values, and thus where any planning action will bring to the table citizens with substantially different views on what the rights and responsibilities of property ownership entails, planners need to understand the competing notions of private property rights and responsibilities prevalent in their systems in both a comprehensive and critical way.

Unique social attributes confronting planning law: Finally, while much of planning entails the public management of private land use, often the motivations underlying those public management efforts implicate concerns regarding not so much the attributes of the land itself as two social dimensions implicated by the use of that land-as-private-property: first, who will actually enjoy the economic wealth potentially derived from use of the land, and second who—that is, what kinds of people—will actually own or use the land. In most countries, real property is one of the largest assets—if not *the* largest asset—that a person or family owns. To that extent, any restriction on the use of land that confronts a property owner's reasonable (i.e., socially-derived and recognized) expectations of what she should be able to do with her land will likely be perceived as an attempt to confiscate wealth from her, and key planning law doctrines accordingly speak to that concern.

Similarly, while an axiom of zoning law in the U.S. is that land is organized and regulated by use rather than by ownership, many of the protections built into processes for administering zoning codes (e.g., prohibitions on exclusionary zoning) and much of the litigation that has arisen from zoning disputes over time (e.g., constitutional doctrine regarding the use of covenants and restrictions on title) are much more about organizing social relationships than land use *per se*. In the U.S., those concerns implicate questions of social class, ethnicity, and especially race—that is, especially black-white racial relationships, given the history of slavery in the U.S. and its persistent aftermath. In other countries, they might speak uniquely to any number of relationships such as class, race, religion, ethnicity, national origin, and so on. Lest practicing planners stumble unwittingly into (unnecessarily) tense and contentious public disputes over past or proposed planning actions, planning students need to understand the historical origins, evolution, and continuing pitfalls of these ongoing social interactions as they play themselves out through land use regulation and other legally significant plan implementation efforts.

Applicable Knowledge in Planning Law

All of the foundational knowledge of planning law discussed above is broadly universal across counties, and providing a solid grasp of that knowledge should be a primary objective of any good planning law course. That knowledge will give students the depth of understanding and critical thinking skills that will carry them through their careers, recognizing that much of the specific law they will need to know in practice will come through practice within the particular jurisdiction where they work. Nonetheless, a good planning law course should also introduce students to the kinds of specific legal knowledge they will need to use in practice, and indeed any given planning law course will likely dedicate much of the content of the course to those kinds of specifics. Because that law is jurisdiction-specific, it is more difficult to summarize generically here. Again using the U.S. for illustrative purposes, this section highlights some of the key legal principles and processes that planning students should learn, organized first by substantive and then procedural knowledge.

Substantive

In addition to knowing the basics of the organic powers and laws that enable planning and plan-implementation activities in a jurisdiction, planning students should have at least introductory knowledge of bodies of law that are implicated by the exercise of those authorities, particularly with regard to the regulation of land use. These include especially **property law** (e.g., different kinds of title interest, forms of conveyance), the **law of contracts** (e.g., the formation of a contract and creation of title interests, such as through an options contract), and background common law doctrines like **nuisance** and **trespass**. One dimension that should be addressed in particular, combining doctrines of all of these bodies of law, is the **"private" control of land use**, such as through covenants and restrictions (property law) that constrain future uses of land (and possibly owners of land) through title conveyance, and private litigation through nuisance and trespass that do the same. Beyond that, most of what students need to learn, and much of what a typical planning law course will spend time on, are the specifics of the primary legal mechanisms used to implement the plan.

Procedural

Planning in many ways is all about process, and planning law is no less so. The foundational underpinnings of procedural considerations in planning law were noted above. The specifics of the procedural requirements to be followed for plan making, and for the legally significant actions taken to implement plans, for any given jurisdiction are found in the statutes that enable planning and local ordinances in that jurisdiction. They include, for example, the requirements specified for creating specialized planning bodies (e.g., formation of a planning commission) and the operation of those bodies in general, along with specific procedures for taking certain kinds of actions. Most of these procedural aspects will be addressed in conjunction with the particular action when covered by the planning law course, such as the process for adopting a master plan, the processes for adopting and amending zoning codes, the process for considering special use permits, the processes for reviewing and acting on preliminary and final subdivision plats, and so on.

Another key procedural aspect of planning law—one that could be considered foundational but that plays itself out regularly in practice—is the back-and-forth interaction that takes place between landowners and planners when some new development project is contemplated. While the requirements and procedures applicable may seem extensive (if not onerous) in theory, in practice there is necessarily substantial room for interpretation and discretion in the administration of planning actions. Indeed, much of the process of planning in these contexts is the **discretionary interpretation**, **negotiation**, and imposition of **exactions** that takes place as a developer firms up a proposal and the government prepares to act on that proposal.

How many residential-like facilities can a building contain, for example, before it is considered a residential use rather than a commercial use, or perhaps an accessory dwelling rather than just an accessory use? How many traffic-flow improvements like new turning lanes can a government request in response to a rezoning request before those requested improvements become unreasonable demands? At what point does the requirement that a developer pay into school improvement funds or wetland mitigation banks become the unlawful imposition of a new "tax" rather than merely a school impact or stormwater mitigation fee? How many requirements can government impose before its actions amount to a regulatory taking, or possibly an "unconstitutional condition"? These nuanced and complicated considerations, like legal reasoning more broadly, are also quite challenging concepts for planning law students to understand. But they are the bread-and-butter of planning practice, and they need to be well understood.

Technical Skills, Pedagogy, and Literatures

Technical Skills for Practicing the Legal Aspects of Planning

There is a substantial amount of law that planning students need to become familiar with—if not fully learn—through a planning law course. More substantively, they need to learn the key rules, principles, actors, processes, and historical evolution of planning law as presented above. More procedurally, they need understand the do's and don'ts of plan making and administration processes—and especially of the discretionary administration of legally significant implementation actions as they play themselves out through consultation, interpretation, and negotiation.

In terms of technical skills required to actually practice the legal aspects of planning, students need to develop the ability to deploy accurately **statutory interpretation**, knowing, for example, where to look for and how to read definitions, applicable rules, qualifications to those rules, and exceptions, as well as the proper meaning of provisions like lists (e.g., are they illustrative or exclusive?). They also need to learn how to **read cases**, interpreting and placing into a broader context their key legal holdings, especially for cases that speak to fundamental interpretations of statutory enabling laws and constitutional protections. At the same time, they need to recognize when the time has come to consult an attorney in doing any of these things, lest they cross the line and become liable for practicing law without a license, as described above. Finally, as with planning practice more broadly, they need to develop robust professional writing, meeting facilitation, and other communication skills.

Pedagogy

The primary pedagogical method employed in law schools, especially for courses designed to teach doctrinal law, is the case method. Under the case method, students read a series of cases (or excerpts from cases, along with notes provided by case-book authors), and then deconstruct those cases through Socratic dialogue in class with the professor to distill out the key issues, rules, and holdings provided by each case. While conveying those key issues, rules, and holdings more narrowly, this method is designed more broadly to teach law students to think like lawyers, engaging the legal reasoning skills described earlier.

This method works well enough when it is used consistently across multiple courses and terms, as happens in law school. It is not very efficient for a single planning law course being taught in an urban planning program, however, especially given the wide array of substantive and procedural topics typically addressed in such a course. The better approach is to develop an integrated array of lectures, problem sets, hypothetical in-class problems and exercises, and even written assignments (e.g., legal/policy analytical memos) that introduce students to topical material and then help them work and rework that material from different vantage points.

Literatures

Following from that pedagogical approach, while there are legal casebooks available for land use law courses and that might be used for a planning law course (Gitelman et al., 2004; Mandelker et al., 2011), those texts are designed for the case-based method just described and, as such, are difficult to use for non-case-based instruction. Other options are to rely on so-called hornbooks or other restatements or treatises on the law, such as Jurgensmeyer and Roberts' (2013) hornbook on *Land Use Planning and Development Regulation Law* or Mandelker's (2003) treatise on *Land Use Law*. These kinds of texts are very useful for providing clear statements on the rules, although they can be dry reading (especially for non-law students). Depending on their focus, they may also be somewhat less helpful in providing the historical origins of governmental action more broadly, or review of the historical origins and social issues pressing upon but not (yet) directly affecting planning law more specifically. Beyond more law-school or lawyer-oriented texts, there may also be available texts that are designed specifically for use in planning-program based planning law courses, such as Jourdan and Strauss (2016).

Finally, beyond an appropriate hornbook or text that provides a basic platform for a planning law course, especially in terms of canvasing legal rules and doctrine, it may be helpful to augment that text with articles or readings drawn from articles or books that speak to particular aspects of the law. These might include, for example, historically significant developments in planning law theory (Haar, 1955; DiMento, 1980; Babcock and Siemon 1985); academic work aimed specifically at planning-law related history and topics (Meck, 1996; Jacobs and Paulsen, 2009; Norton, 2011; Hirt, 2014); practitioner-oriented works that help to illustrate contemporary disputes, doctrine, or innovation, e.g. Merriam et al. (1999); Elliott (2008); or Giaimo and Lucero (2009); state- or jurisdiction-specific treatises that help to illustrate application of planning law within the planning law students' own jurisdiction (e.g., Fisher et al. 2016); or treaties not written specifically for planning audiences but highly relevant to them—especially on topics like property rights and responsibilities (e.g., Epstein, 1985; Glendon, 1991; Siegan, 1997; Freyfogle, 2007). In addition, depending on the larger context of material covered by a given planning law course, such a course might incorporate comparative works that both highlight variation in doctrine across countries and that help to illustrate the scope, reach, and limits of doctrine within the country of study by comparison with others (e.g., Alterman 2011; Norton and Bieri, 2014).

Notes

1 PAB Accreditation Standards and Criteria, March 3, 2017, Sec. 4A. Available at: www.planningaccreditationboard.org/
2 The federal government in the U.S. does not enjoy the police power; it has only the powers granted to it by the U.S. Constitution. The primary authority that the federal government exercises, which often looks like police-power regulation in practice, is the authority granted to it by Article I, Sec. 8 Par. 3 to regulate commerce "among the several States" (commonly referred to as the Commerce Clause). The federal government also enjoys the power of eminent domain by implication because exercise of that power is constrained by the Takings Clause of the Fifth Amendment to the U.S. Constitution ("... nor shall private property be taken for public use, without just compensation").
3 The U.S. Bureau of Commerce published the model Standard Zoning Enabling Act and Standard City Planning Enabling Act in the mid 1920s in an effort to encourage the states to enact their own planning and zoning enabling laws.

References

Alterman, R. (2011). *Takings International: A Comparative Perspective on Land Use Regulation and Compensation Rights*. Chicago: American Bar Association.
Babcock, R. F., & Siemon, C. L. (1985). *The Zoning Game Revisited*. Cambridge, MA: Lincoln Institute of Land Policy.
DiMento, J. F. (1980). *The Consistency Doctrine and the Limits of Planning*. Cambridge, MA: Oelgeschlager, Gunn & Hain.
Elliott, D. L. (2008). *A Better Way to Zone: Ten Principles to Create More Livable Cities*. Washington, DC: Island Press.
Epstein, R. A. (1985). *Takings: Private Property and the Power of Eminent Domain*. Cambridge, MA: Harvard University Press.
Fisher, G. A., Galvin, J. F., Greene, A. M., Need, G. K., Rosati, C. A., & Estey, S. R. (2016). *Michigan Zoning, Planning, and Land Use*. Ann Arbor, MI: Institute for Continuing Legal Education.
Freyfogle, E. T. (2007). *On Private Property: Finding Common Ground on the Ownership of Land*. Boston: Beacon Press.
Giaimo, M. S., & Lucero, L. A. (Eds.). (2009). *Religious Land Uses, Zoning, and the Courts*. Chicago: American Bar Association.
Gitelman, M., Nolon, J. R., Salkin, P. E., & Wright, R. R. (2004). *Land Use: Cases and Materials* (6th ed.). St. Paul, MN: Thompson/West Publishing.
Glendon, M. A. (1991). *Rights Talk: The Impoverishment of Political Discourse*. New York: The Free Press.
Haar, C. M. (1955). The Master Plan: An Impermanent Constitution. *Law and Contemporary Problems*, *20*(3), 353. doi:10.2307/1190476
Hirt, S. A. (2014). *Zoned in the USA: The Origins and Implications of American Land-Use Regulation*. Ithaca, NY: Cornell University Press.

Jacobs, H. M., & Paulsen, K. (2009). Property Rights: The Neglected Theme of 20th-Century American Planning. *Journal of the American Planning Association, 75*(2), 134–143. doi:10.1080/01944360802619721

Jourdan, D., & Strauss, E. (2016). *Planning for Wicked Problems: A Planner's Guide to Land Use Law.* New York, NY: Routledge.

Jurgensmeyer, J. C., & Roberts, T. E. (2013). *Land Use Planning and Development Regulation Law* (3rd ed.). St. Paul, MN: Thompson/West Publishing.

Mandelker, D. R. (2003). *Land Use Law* (3rd ed.). Newark, NJ: LexisNexis.

Mandelker, D. R., Brown, C. N., Meck, S., Merriam, D. H., Salsich, J., Peter W., Stroud, N. E., & Tappendorf, J. A. (2011). *Planning and Control of Land Development: Cases and Materials* (8th ed.). New Providence, NJ: LexisNexis.

Meck, S. (1996). Model Planning and Zoning Enabling Legislation: A Short History. In *Modernizing State Planning Statutes: The Growing Smart Working Papers, Volume 1.* Chicago, IL: American Planning Association.

Merriam, D. H., & Frank, R. M. (1999). *The Takings Issue: Constitutional Limits on Land-Use Control and Environmental Regulation.* Washington, DC: Island Press.

Norton, R. K. (2011). Who decides, how, and why? Planning for the judicial review of local legislative zoning decisions. *The Urban Lawyer, 43*(4), 1085–1105.

Norton, R. K., & Bieri, D. S. (2014). Planning, Law, and Property Rights: A US–European Cross-national Contemplation. *International Planning Studies, 19* (3–4), 379–397. doi:10.1080/13563475.2014.965249

Siegan, B. H. (1997). *Property and Freedom: The Constitution, the Courts, and Land-Use Regulation.* New Brunswick, NJ: Transaction Press.

PART 3

Pedagogy

6
DESIGNING CORE CURRICULA

Jessica L. H. Doyle and Bruce Stiftel

Introduction

While there are a modest number of widely used archetypes, the design of professional planning curricula is controversial. Core curricula, in particular, respond to national (or international) accreditation requirements, professional milieu, university administrative settings, and faculty orientations. The debates among these varying perspectives may be characterized as: design versus policy, theory versus practice, and generalist approach versus specialization.

The design-versus-policy tension in planning education dates to the period between the world wars when the applicability of the social sciences to planning began to contest the historic origins of planning as an extension of architecture and engineering. Tensions between theory and practice emerged as city planning programs moved to establish academic legitimacy in the mid-20th century. Within each, alternative visions emphasize such theoretic areas as economics, geography, or ecology, and such practice dimensions as quantitative analysis, communication, or ethics. As the scope of city and regional planning grew from its land-use origins to encompass transportation, housing, environment and natural resources, neighborhood and community development, and economic development, the core focus on land use expanded to what is sometimes the full range of domestic urban policy. Finally, always there is a balancing among efficiency, environmental quality, and equity.

There are national patterns to the resolution of these tensions which establish a context for differentiation within individual schools. Even in countries with national accreditation that lays out curricular learning objectives, schools make their own choices based on the disciplinary mix in their organizational homes, the training of their faculty, and the input of their employers and alumni.

The core usually takes on importance as the prescribed learning path that all students must complete. Specialties may come and go; electives are often tolerated even by those who question their worth, as long as sufficient voluntary enrollment is achieved. But the core defines what a graduate must know and as such is often hotly debated. In answering the question, "What is the core curriculum?" the institution and the faculty must be able to say what they find most important about planning and what planners must know.

The purpose of this chapter is to discuss the process of forming—re-forming, and refining—the core curriculum of a given planning program. It will begin by articulating why a core is necessary, from both practical and theoretical perspectives, and examining the driving factors behind the conception of a core. It will then look at the history of core curriculum design in planning, the contextual factors that shape individual core curricula, and how "archetypical" core curricula are created, as well as the differences between the most common core designs. It will conclude by discussing the future of the core curriculum, inextricable as it is from the future of planning itself.

Why a Core?

A complex craft such as planning demands on the job training, or *practice*. To listen to mid-career and senior professionals reflect on their educations and work, one sometimes gets the impression that experience of practice looms larger than takeaways from school. Given how much of planning practice is contextually sensitive, site-specific, and vulnerable to changes in public opinion, it can be tempting to conclude that learning planning is not nearly as important as actually doing it—that the planning classroom is at best a rite of passage for would-be practitioners not yet sensitive to the profession's customs and languages, and at worst a conduit for dangerously out-of-date ideas.

Yet this cynical take on planning education is not endorsed by the people seemingly most likely to endorse it—namely, practicing planners themselves, when you look at detailed survey and interview data. A survey of members of the American Planning Association (APA) found that, of 28 listed skills taught in planning programs, members used an average of 16 in their practice (Dawkins, 2016). On a less formal note, planning schools contemplating changes to their curricula will sometimes receive passionate responses from alumni—an indication that, while practitioners may not be consciously considering their education on a daily basis, they care deeply about it when roused.

The planning education does seem to offer the bricks to build a useful and meaningful future planning practice. Every program will have a core curriculum that functions as the clay. But what is the "core curriculum"? How does it get created, and then changed? How do planning teachers decide what to teach all their students, who may be coming from wildly different backgrounds and may have little to no knowledge of formal planning processes, and what to leave out? How sensitive should curriculum design be to the demands of students' future employers, which is to say local (and national) planning cultures? And how should ideas about what to learn—and how to learn—inform the curriculum?

The core curriculum ends up being at once driven by both top-down and bottom-up input. Accreditation standards, national, international, or professional quality assurance processes, and institutional frameworks often set boundaries within which the curricular development process must navigate. Perspectives of professional leaders, employers, alumni, and students interact with such top-down directives, mediated by the experience and views of the faculty. Once set, agreed-upon standards, publicized and widely understood, assist faculty in course design and current and future students as they investigate what they need from their planning education. Ultimately, the core helps planners articulate what they expect to accomplish with their profession and by achieving the credential of a planning degree.

History of the Core

> The question of what, if anything, is the core of planning knowledge has been asked forever ... A smattering of economics, statistics, and GIS can scarcely be enough substance to turn a college graduate into a professional planner.
>
> *(Friedmann, 1994)*

Table 6.1 Subjects Common in North American Planning Schools' Core Curricula (Friedmann, 1996)

Introduction to Planning
Theory and Practice of Planning
Urban Form and Theory
Physical Planning/Built Environment
Legal Aspects of Planning
Economics for Planners
Qualitative Methods and Computers
Planning and Policy Analysis
Issues in Practice
Core Studio Analysis

The core curriculum that developed in planning schools after World War II derived largely from an idea of planning as rational, comprehensive decision-making that is value-sensitive but politically neutral, drawing from expertise grounded in social science analysis, particularly quantitative modeling (Friedmann, 1994, citing Perloff, 1957 and Alexander, 1992). Friedmann's (1996) survey of the core curricula at North American planning schools highlighted a series of courses whose subjects were broadly the same, even if the course titles and local emphases differed. Those subjects are listed in Table 6.1.

Friedmann was identifying the core curriculum in order to critique it. He proposed that the "substantive domain" of planning could be derived from studying the intersections of six socio-spatial processes: urbanization, economic growth and change, city-building, cultural differentiation and change, the transformation of nature, and urban politics and empowerment. While planners should share some common information about history and methods, he argued, they should be trained to specialize to cope with problems at one of the intersections of those processes, developing a precise and useful vocabulary and using collaborations to build on each other's skill-sets.

There have been changes to the standard North American core curriculum since Friedmann's survey, though almost no schools have gone so far as to implement Friedmann's recommendation of adding a third year to the master's degree program. (More fashionable is a six-semester program that gives the student a joint degree, such as a master's in planning combined with a separate but related field such as public health, environmental studies, or public policy.) Studios and workshops have become more prominent, schools are more likely to require internships, and quantitative methods courses have expanded to include technological advances, such as the widespread adaptation of GIS (Edwards & Bates, 2011).

The common American core curriculum is worth dwelling on because it has proven so influential internationally. In both Canada and Europe, planning education expanded after World War II: although Great Britain's first planning school opened in 1909, Turkey did not have an independent planning program established until 1961, Austria until 1970, Greece and Italy until the 1980s (Frank et al., 2014). Similarly, the Town Planning Institute of Canada was founded in 1919, but formal planning schools did not begin opening until 1947, the first being an interdisciplinary program at McGill University (Lovlin & Seasons, 2014). Postgraduate planning education could thus be seen as part and parcel of widespread adoption of American-backed economic theory and cultural influence in the aftermath of World War II. This is not to imply that planning core curriculum design is not sensitive to national and local contexts, as will be discussed later, only that as postgraduate planning education became widespread the American model spread with it.

The Canadian core, as tracked by Lovlin and Seasons (2014), largely mirrored the (mostly) American one described by Friedmann (1996), including planning history and theory, legal aspects, quantitative methods, and the inclusion of a studio component. Planning in India and Hong Kong has been strongly influenced by their former colonizer, the British; in Taiwan, by the American model; schools in all three places have been shaped accordingly (Kunzmann, 2015). Throughout Asia, including Japan and the Republic of Korea, planning education descended primarily from architectural education, and in recent years has been expanding to include geography (Kunzmann, 2015).

In China, meanwhile, of the eight planning schools active by 1959, all were shuttered by 1969 as a result of the Cultural Revolution (Tian, 2016). The national Urban Planning Society formed in 1985, but there was no accreditation body for planning schools until 1998 (Huang, 2012). As China's economy began to expand rapidly in the 1990s, professional planning education programs expanded with it, "sprout[ing] like bamboo shoots after a spring rain": from 63 planning schools in 2001 to almost 200 in 2013 (Tian, 2016). With this rapid expansion has come a disconnect between the national accrediting body, whose standards emphasize architecture, and some of the planning programs based in schools of civil engineering, geography, or even forestry and agriculture, to the point that as of 2009 some 59 planning schools did not have accreditation because their programs could not meet the architectural studio requirements (Huang, 2012).

As is evident from looking at Chinese planning, the domain of planning thought has expanded. "In some national contexts," report Frank et al. (2014), "planning has moved almost exclusively into the realm of the social, behavioural, political, economic or environmental sciences." A similar shift has been happening in Africa, where, as in India and Hong Kong, both academic and planning cultures were often originally developed in the shadow of a European colonial power. African academic planning programs can now largely be divided into those with a technical or design focus, usually associated with architectural or engineering schools; those which have shifted to emphasize policy, management, and administration; and those most focused on geography, environmental sciences, and regional studies (Watson & Odendaal, 2012). In European schools, the core curriculum has expanded to include such issues as sustainability, resiliency, food provision, and health (Frank et al., 2014). The core, however broadly recognizable, can thus be modified to meet specific needs.

The Core and National Planning Cultures

> Planning cultures are not only deeply rooted in the historical context, cultural traditions, and natural situations of a country . . . they are also closely rooted to the political culture and regulatory system of that country. That makes it hard, or even impossible, to simply transfer any urban planning approach and planning education curricula from one country to another.
>
> *(Chinese planner quoted in Kunzmann, 2015)*

Given the spatial nature of planning study, core planning curricula are inevitably shaped by the geographic, economic, and legal contexts of their home institutions and national cultures; it would be a strange and unsuccessful planning school that refused to take such contexts into account. For example, Faludi (2010) has described the post-World War II difference between German and Dutch conceptions of planning, which was seen as a primarily land-use-based instrument for balancing human settlement and open space, and the French take, which emphasized regional economic development.

It should be noted that part of the national and local planning context will be shaped by, and subject to, other local political concerns: that planners will vary in their ability and willingness, so often encouraged in the rationalist planning model, to separate their own prejudices and passions from their planning work. An example would be the Jerusalem planner who told Bollens (2004), "We tried to be scholars, but we are all Israelis. And, I don't think you can be objective."

Greenlee, Edwards, and Anthony (2015) give another example of how the local context might affect the competencies needed by planners. Surveying practitioners in both growing and declining communities, they found, like Ozawa and Seltzer (1999), that a high premium was placed on communication throughout, but entry-level planners in declining communities were being asked to perform at higher levels in such areas as evaluation, grant-writing, and data analysis.

Finally, the local context will include the institution in which the planning school resides, whether it is primarily research- or teaching-focused, technical or policy-focused, local or national in scope. Some heads of British planning schools noted that they were subject to the demands not just of the accrediting body, the Royal Town Planning Institute (RTPI), but of their universities and departments, whose chiefs were not necessarily planning experts (Ellis, Murtaugh, & Copeland, 2010).

Thus, there is not, and never will be, *one* core. Any given institution teaching planning will shape its core in part as a response to the local environment, including the particular needs of the audiences it serves—students, alumni, employers. As Edwards and Bates (2011), reviewing the process of core curriculum revision for the Master of Urban Planning degree at the University of Illinois Urbana-Champaign (UIUC), put it: "Each school's core is evolving and inevitably a reflection of the uniqueness of the department and the students and faculty who define it." The UIUC core curriculum revision, for example, included consideration of the requirements of the (US) Planning Accreditation Board; the employment trends among the students, many of whom would not go on to enter jobs traditionally defined as "planning"; the length of the program and the existing coursework; and changes in the makeup of the faculty over time.

Ingredients of the Core

The most recent standard published by the Planning Accreditation Board (2017) divides the core curriculum into three broad areas: General Planning Knowledge, Planning Skills, and Values and Ethics. Table 6.2 shows the sub-categories of information and skills under each of these areas.

The Association of European Schools of Planning's (AESOP) outline of a core curriculum (1995) is organized along similar lines, though it includes an emphasis on knowledge of cultural and legal differences within Europe, and adds "integrating aesthetic and design dimensions" as a required skill.

More recently there have been calls for expanding the core by including less frequently featured pedagogical or methodological approaches, such as experiential learning (Baldwin & Rosier, 2017) or qualitative methods (Eizenberg & Shilon, 2016). Interestingly, there seems to exist very little pressure to *reduce* the core, even though the articulation of any core implies trade-offs. Describing the re-evaluation of the core curriculum at UIUC, Edwards and Bates (2011) note wryly, "We could not simply add classes to cover all the desired material, since the program is already a full two years."

Globally, it is probably useful to recognize a small number of world regions that share internal similarities and external differences. The Anglophone countries of North America,

Table 6.2 Sub-categories of the Three Main Curriculum Areas (from Required Skills, Knowledge, and Values of the Profession, Planning Accreditation Board, 2017)

General Planning Knowledge	• Purpose and Meaning of Planning
	• Planning Theory
	• Planning Law
	• Human Settlements and History of Planning
	• The Future
	• Global Dimensions of Planning
Planning Skills	• Research
	• Written, Oral, and Graphic Communication
	• Quantitative and Qualitative Methods
	• Plan Creation and Implementation
	• Planning Process Methods
	• Leadership
Values and Ethics	• Professional Ethics and Responsibility
	• Equity, Diversity, and Social Justice
	• Governance and Participation
	• Sustainability and Environmental Quality
	• Growth and Development
	• Health and Built Environment

the UK, Australia, and New Zealand share a greater than average attention to policy-oriented planning. The Mediterranean region, Latin America, and East Asia emphasize design more than other regions. Eastern Europe is an eclectic planning region still searching for a clear framework of planning in the aftermath of communism. Africa and south and southeast Asia are diverse planning regions reflecting the interplay of multiple colonial legacies and professional corps educated in many countries.

Different Approaches to the Core

One of the most common approaches to the core is to train, as Perloff (1957) put it, "generalists with a specialty." For a new planning program, a generalist core has several advantages. One is its relative respectability: it would be hard to put together a generalist core that would strike conservative critics as too radical or outré. A second is that it allows the program to train a wide variety of prospective students, including, as is often the case, those with little or no previous planning education or training. A third is that it has been tested, to some degree, and proven useful. Dalton (2007), surveying APA members—many of whom, having graduated from planning schools, had followed generalist curricula—found that fully 70% said that their planning educations influenced their identities as planners "a lot." A later survey by Dawkins (2016) asked planning school graduates what knowledges they used in their professions. The respondents were asked about eight different types of generalist knowledge (listed in Table 6.3). None of the eight was utilized by less than 59% of respondents, suggesting that general planning knowledges retain their practical utility.

Perhaps the greatest disadvantage of the generalist core is that it revolves around the question of *what* planners do rather than *how* they do it, when there is a body of research suggesting that the *how* is just as important—perhaps even more so. The two papers by Ozawa and Seltzer (1999; Seltzer & Ozawa, 2002) emphasize communication as a necessary

Table 6.3 Surveyed APA Members Indicating Use of General Planning Knowledges in Their Job (from Dawkins, 2016)

Type of General Planning Knowledge	Percent of Respondents Saying They Used that Knowledge in Their Planning Jobs
Understanding the rationale for and purposes of planning	90%
Understanding of the planning process and connections between planning and implementation	84%
Understanding of the ethical dimensions of urban planning, including awareness of the American Institute of Certified Planners (AICP) Code of Ethics	65%
Understanding of the legal context within which planning occurs	86%
Understanding of the history of the planning profession	59%
Understanding of basic economic theory and its application to planning	76%
Understanding of the political context within which planning occurs	73%
Understanding of environmental processes and the interactions between the built environment, human activity, and environmental change	81%

planning skill. Alexander's (2001) response to the first of those papers, while critical of Ozawa and Seltzer's framework, suggests that "the competent planner is a well-rounded person equipped with a blend of communicative, analytic, and synthesizing skills . . . If they need any deeper specialization or management skills, those can come later."

A second disadvantage of the generalist core, hinted at by Alexander, is that it can seem relatively closed-ended: teach the body of general knowledge, test the student on it via the AICP exam or a similar certification process, and declare the end goal attained. Dalton's (2007) call for lifelong learning structures, including for planners who enter mid-career with less (or no) formal planning education, was not directly meant as a critique of the generalist core but could, if adopted more thoroughly, imply changes in the structure of planning teaching and therefore the core.

An alternative design is to structure the core around a particular idea or framework—one (or more) of Friedmann's six socio-spatial processes, for example. Chapin (2003) held out GIS methods as an essential framework for structuring the core curriculum. Bina, Balula, Varanda, and Fokdal (2016) lay out a framework for embedding sustainability into an urban planning master's program; in an approach similar to Friedmann's, they conceptualize sustainability teaching around three "orientations" of design, policy, and management. Ashley and Vos (2015) propose civic capacity as the focus of the core, operationalized by integrated university-community work.

Conclusion: The Future of the Core

For all the diverse approaches to core instruction around the globe, planning school core curricula archetypes are widely evident and frequently line up with the expectations of national planning systems. An easy observation is that the strongest foundations for practice demand some exposure to each of the archetypical fields: design *and* policy, theory *and* practice, generalist *with* specialty, efficiency, environment *and* equity.

At the same time, today's urban challenges demand attention. Planning curricula have to be responsive to rapid urbanization, shrinking cities, climate change, informality, big data, and rising inequality, and they must do so with attention to global policy demands of sustainable development, resilience and inclusive governance. We can expect the top-down pressures from accreditors and quality assurance processes to push for coverage of more and more of this very wide range of knowledge, skills, and values.

As in the past, the demands on classroom time far exceed available hours, suggesting that different national systems and specific schools will continue to find new individualized patterns of core content and delivery. Yet, with planning school associations covering almost all the world, and growth of internet communication technologies making the world effectively smaller, higher incidence of cross-fertilization across schools and regions can be expected. The pace of change will be faster and the propagation of good practices more likely.

References

Alexander, E. R. (1992). A Transaction Cost Theory of Planning. *Journal of the American Planning Association*, *58*(2), 190–200.

Alexander, E. R. (2001). What Do Planners Need to Know? *Journal of Planning Education and Research*, *20*(3), 376–380. doi:10.1177/0739456x0102000309

Ashley, A. J., & Vos, J. (2015). The Department as a Third Sector Planner: Implementing Civic Capacity through the Planning Core Curriculum. *Journal of Planning Education and Research*, *35*(4), 501–514. doi:10.1177/0739456x15591281

Association of European Schools of Planning (AESOP). (1995). *Core Requirements for a High Quality European Planning Education*. Retrieved from www.aesop-planning.eu/en_GB/core-curriculum

Baldwin, C., & Rosier, J. (2017). Growing Future Planners: A Framework for Integrating Experiential Learning into Tertiary Planning Programs. *Journal of Planning Education and Research*, *37*(1), 43–55. doi:10.1177/0739456x16634864

Bina, O., Balula, L., Varanda, M., & Fokdal, J. (2016). Urban Studies and the Challenge of Embedding Sustainability: A Review of International Master Programmes. *Journal of Cleaner Production*, *137*, 330–346.

Bollens, S. A. (2004). Urban Planning and the Intergroup Conflict: Confronting a Fractured Public Interest. In B. Stiftel & V. Watson (Eds.), *Dialogues in Urban and Regional Planning 1* (pp. 209–246). New York: Routledge.

Chapin, T. S. (2003). Revolutionizing the Core: GIS in the Planning Curriculum. *Environment and Planning B: Planning and Design*, *30*(4), 565–573. doi:10.1068/b12993

Dalton, L. C. (2007). Preparing Planners for the Breadth of Practice. *Journal of the American Planning Association*, *73*(1), 35–48. doi:10.1080/01944360708976135

Dawkins, C. J. (2016). Preparing Planners: The Role of Graduate Planning Education. *Journal of Planning Education and Research*, *36*(4), 414–426. doi:10.1177/0739456x15627193

Edwards, M. M., & Bates, L. K. (2011). Planning's Core Curriculum: Knowledge, Practice, and Implementation. *Journal of Planning Education and Research*, *31*(2), 172–183.

Eizenberg, E., & Shilon, M. (2016). Pedagogy for the New Planner: Refining the Qualitative Toolbox. *Environment and Planning B*, *43*(6), 1118–1135.

Ellis, G., Murtaugh, B., & Copeland, L. (2010). *The Future of the Planning Academy*. Belfast: Queen's University Belfast and the Royal Town Planning Institute.

Faludi, A. (2010). Centenary Paper: European Spatial Planning: Past, Present and Future. *The Town Planning Review*, *81*(1), 1–22.

Frank, A., Mironowicz, I., Lourenco, J., Franchini, T., Ache, P., Finka, M., . . . Grams, A. (2014). Educating Planners in Europe: A Review of 21st Century Study Programmes. *Progress in Planning*, *91*, 30–94.

Friedmann, J. (1994). Planning Education for the Late Twentieth Century: An Initial Inquiry. *Journal of Planning Education and Research*, *14*(1), 55–64. doi:10.1177/0739456X9401400106

Friedmann, J. (1996). The Core Curriculum in Planning Revisited. *Journal of Planning Education and Research, 15*, 89–104.

Greenlee, A. J., Edwards, M. M., & Anthony, J. (2015). Planning Skills: An Examination of Supply and Local Government Demand. *Journal of Planning Education and Research, 35*(2), 161–173.

Huang, K.-t. (2012). *Remaking Chinese Planning as a Profession: Growing Demand and Challenges.* Ph.D, University of Washington.

Kunzmann, K. R. (2015). The State of the Art of Planning and Planning Education in Asia. *disP – The Planning Review, 51*(4), 42–51.

Lovlin, T., & Seasons, M. (2014). A History of the Core Curriculum of Planning Education in Canada. *Canadian Journal of Urban Research, 23*(1 (Supplement)), 98–115.

Ozawa, C. P., & Seltzer, E. (1999). Taking Our Bearings: Mapping a Relationship Among Planning Practice, Theory, and Education. *Journal of Planning Education and Research, 18*, 257–266.

Perloff, H. (1957). *Education for Planning: City, State, and Regional.* Baltimore: Johns Hopkins Press.

Planning Accreditation Board. (2017). PAB Accreditation Standards and Criteria. Retrieved from www.planningaccreditationboard.org/index.php?s=file_download&id=500

Seltzer, E., & Ozawa, C. P. (2002). Clear Signals: Moving on to Planning's Promise. *Journal of Planning Education and Research, 22*, 77–86.

Tian, L. (2016). Behind the Growth: Planning Education in China during Rapid Urbanization. *Journal of Planning Education and Research, 36*(4), 465–475.

Watson, V., & Odendaal, N. (2012). Changing Planning Education in Africa: The Role of the Association of African Planning Schools. *Journal of Planning Education and Research, 33*(1), 96–107.

7
PLANNING TECHNOLOGY

Jennifer Minner, Jennifer Evans-Cowley, and Nader Afzalan

Overview

The uses of information and communication technologies (ICT) and planning support systems (PSS) are expanding and diversifying in planning practice. The availability of technology is transforming the ways in which planning education can be delivered, as well as the pedagogical methods available to planning educators to prepare the next generation of practitioners (Evans-Cowley, 2018; Gaber, 2007). Meanwhile, these changes also have important implications for the content of planning curricula and pedagogical methods. There is an increasing array of opportunities to integrate technology into innovative practice. While some planning educators, professional planners, and students of the field are able to easily use technology effectively and creatively, others may be uncertain about the effective use of technological methods and tools and how they fit within their practices (Hughes & Ooms, 2004).

The aim of this chapter is to provide readers with an overview of five areas of technological innovation, gleaned from recent literature, roundtable discussions, interviews, and a national survey of educators. The first path includes innovations in the ways planning courses are made accessible, from fully online degree programs to Massive Open Online Courses (MOOCs) (Evans-Cowley, et al. 2014). A second area of innovation involves new ways educators can organize their classes, facilitate learning in the classroom, and communicate with students. This path entails strategies such as "the flipped classroom" (Enfield, 2013; Herreid & Schiller, 2013), and the use of social media, among other methods to facilitate communication with and between students. A third area includes the planning support technologies, broadly defined, that educators teach students to use, in order to build upon planners' analytical capabilities and their ability to facilitate participatory processes in planning. A fourth area includes new forms of analysis based on a growing number of sources of existing data – from open government data, to remote sensing, to call data from mobile phones. A fifth area of proposed innovation involves the ways educators can facilitate critical thinking about technology and help to nurture current and future generations of professionals not only to respond to technological change, but to shape it through critique and the creation of new tools (Drennon, 2005; Drummond & French, 2008) and methods.

Research on Planning Education and Technology

There is limited published research on planning education, and a dire deficit in published research on the many areas of technological change and its implications for planning educators. Even so, the existing literature reflects a remarkable variety of technologies used to enhance planning education.

In a conference paper, Riggs, Steins, and Brasuell (2016) share the outcomes of an effort to redesign two quantitative methods courses at Cal Poly San Luis Obispo. This pilot project involved the use of online Planetizen courses to enable a more "self-organizing" course in which students could complete parts of the curriculum at their own pace. The results were enhanced learning outcomes, such as increased technical proficiency in performing economic and geographic information system (GIS)-based analyses, as well as the use of Photoshop and SketchUp. This pilot project illustrates both the potential for new delivery of courses (via the online resource Planetizen) and also the use of new forms of delivery in finding new ways of organizing university courses.

There is also evidence that faculty are experimenting with a variety of technological means to engage students in learning planning concepts. This includes the use of digital games, including 3D online gaming engine Second Life (Evans-Cowley & Hollander, 2010), NextCampus to evaluate alternatives in university expansion (Poplin, 2012), SimCity to facilitate learning about urban form and planning history (Minnery & Searle, 2014; Adams, 1998; Gaber, 2007), and Tygron, a serious gaming engine to explore water management options and spatial planning (Zhou et al., 2016). Minecraft is another type of tool that is being used with youth for public engagement (de Andrade et al., 2016; Mather & Robinson, 2016; Stauskis, 2014).

Robinson (2016) notes the rapid expansion of civic technologies in planning practice and encourages planning educators to consider preparation for planning students to utilize a growing number of local government tools and open datasets. She writes:

> Perhaps the time has come to review local government open data catalogues to evaluate the extent to which the data sets provided are relevant and useful to local planning efforts. If there is a desire to more actively use civic technology tools in planning practice, then these tools need planning-related open data as an input . . . In planning education it is time to consider how many student planners are exposed to, let alone conversant in, open data efforts.
>
> *(Robinson, 2016, p. 10)*

Similarly, the expanding number of social media and web-based tools offer planners the opportunity for crowdsourced data collection efforts and new opportunities for public input and collaborative planning (Seltzer and Mahmoudi, 2012; Goodspeed et al., 2012; Johnson & Sieber, 2012; Hanzl, 2007; Hollander, 2011; Afzalan & Muller, 2014). While it is clear that social media and online tools for visualization and deliberation can be used by planning professionals, it is less clear how these tools are being used by educators.

Planning support systems (PSS) also have the potential to extend planners' capacities by offering robust ways to collect and analyze data and to communicate with the public (Petzer et al., 2015). Scenario planning similarly has the potential to enhance both participation and analysis in planning processes (Holway et. al., 2012). Yet there are few studies of the incorporation of scenario planning tools or PSS in planning curricula (Goodspeed, 2013). There is a longer track record of GIS education and participatory mapping as a tool for planning education

(Esnard & MacDougall, 1997; Sletto et al., 2010), which is often a prerequisite skill-set for the use of scenario planning tools.

Beyond the incorporation of existing planning support and civic technologies, some planning educators have ventured into the creation of new tools to aid community partners and community-based projects. Minner (2015) describes how a freely available scenario planning tool called Envision Tomorrow was modified by faculty and students at the University of Texas at Austin, in conjunction with Fregonese Associates, a planning consulting firm, and local government agencies, in a larger-scale regional planning process. The educational outcomes for the public have been compared to other regional planning processes using scenario planning tools (Goodspeed, 2013). Minner et al. (2015) also describe how an online participatory web tool was created to survey historic resources for planning purposes. Faculty and student researchers at the University of Texas at Austin and Cornell University (Mueller et al., 2018) have also created a new tool to prioritize transit corridors for affordable housing preservation and a curriculum associated with it that can be used by planning educators (Minner & Micklow, 2016; Fregonese Associates, 2016).

In addition to the entrepreneurial and creative aspects of technology, educators also have a responsibility to teach students to think critically about the use of technology. Writing of the communicative implications of a technology as basic as the spreadsheet, Urey (2002, p. 417)) has cautioned:

> As computing and communications applications become a part of more and more of how we do planning, we need to explore ways to learn ourselves and teach our students how to anticipate when a technological choice may lead to systematically distorted information and how to create transformative strategies to address such situations.

Senbel and Church (2011) provide an example of research that included student-participation to assess visualization media, from 3D modeling, to an energy consumption model, to the production of documentary films. The outcome was a research project that engaged students in assessing the communicative value of various media and the level of empowerment in directly involving public participants in urban design. The example provides both a critique of the effectiveness of some visual media in empowering neighborhood residents and student engagement in assessment and use of technology.

Within planning literature and in tandem with the research methods described in the next section, we see at least five areas in which technology is influencing or has the potential to influence planning education: 1) changes in means of access and delivery of planning education courses; 2) the organization of university-based learning and use of technologies to enhance faculty-student communication; 3) the pedagogy related to the use of planning support technologies; 4) new data sources and sensing tools for existing data; and 5) the expansion of planning education to include the creation and modification of new technological tools and critical thinking about the use and role of technology in the future of planning practice.

Research Methods

This chapter is derived from intersecting research projects that bring together investigations of educator practices with technology. Methods include the triangulation of results from two roundtable discussions among planning educators at the Association of Collegiate Schools of Planning conferences (Minner et al., 2014; Goodspeed et al., 2015),[1] individual interviews with planning educators, and a national survey of planning educators.[2] The survey was designed to gather information about the ways in which planning educators incorporate planning support technologies into urban and regional planning courses.

Five Areas of Innovation in Planning Education

The following sections provide a brief discussion of the five areas of innovation in planning education. These areas have implications for planning educators, department administrators, students, and governmental and non-profit organizations that have an interest in advancing knowledge of planning among citizens.

Access and Delivery of Planning Education

Access to planning education has been broadened by the availability of technology. A number of universities and organizations have created freely available online planning content. The American Planning Association (APA)'s Chapters and Divisions record their webcast series and make the hundreds of webcasts available to anyone who is interested. APA's "Using GIS to Improve Planning Decisions" has been viewed more than 12,000 times (APA, 2016). Strong Towns has a series of videos that explain key concepts in planning (Strong Towns, 2016). Florida Atlantic University has created a YouTube channel including an array of videos about planning, much like American University of Beirut, Texas A&M University, and the University of Michigan (American University of Beirut, 2016; Florida Atlantic University, 2016; Texas A&M University, 2016; and University of Michigan, 2016). UN-Habitat, The World Bank, the US National Oceanic and Atmospheric Administration and the US Federal Emergency Management Agency all offer online education materials that can be incorporated into planning courses (FEMA, 2016; NOAA, 2014; The World Bank, 2014; United Nations, 2016). Companies and organizations are offering tutorial videos, for example on how to use CommunityViz software (Placeways, 2016).

This expansion of content related to planning has the potential to enrich planning education in multiple ways. Planning educators may use these sources to supplement courses, as well as to deliver them. Freely available course materials can be accessed by students to supplement university courses or deepen their studies in concentrations of their choice. Non-profits and government agencies can further both professional and the general public's knowledge through educational content in the form of online videos and podcasts. For example, the APA offers a podcast series (APA, 2016). And Streetsblog is a popular blog that offers ongoing articles and video related to transportation planning (Streetsblog, 2016).

Organization of Courses and Use of Technology for Communication

Technological tools designed to enhance education have opened new possibilities for course communication. For example, most universities offer course management systems with an expanding number of online applications that students and faculty can access. Some campuses offer video-editing and recording studios that faculty (and students) can use to create their own media to enhance courses. This relates to a larger trend in which students increasingly access content outside of the classroom, allowing class time to be used for discussion and team work – known as a flipped classroom (O'Flaherty & Phillips, 2015). For example, in a Development and Globalization course at Temple University, Professor Sweet uses class time for participants to play games, hold discussion, and tackle course problems. Outside of class students complete lecture and reading materials and post questions about the materials reviewed (Sweet, 2016). Innovation is also happening with the use of social media to enhance lectures. For example, Professor Riggs at Cal Poly San Luis Obispo encourages students to use Twitter to ask questions (Riggs, 2014).

Assignments have been reimagined with the availability of digital platforms. At the Ohio State University, students in a workshop worked with the APA to identify ways for the organization to amplify its use of social media. Students contributed to Wikipedia and Yelp about locations that have been identified as APA Best Places Award winners. At Cornell University, culminating projects for planning courses have included the creation of blogs and blog posts, recording of podcasts, and creation of "clickbait" that can be used as vehicles for sharing their growing knowledge of planning with the public.[3] In addition, faculty can encourage students to create online data visualizations and web maps that require them to hone their analytical and mapping skills, while broadcasting the fruits of their labor, whether it is classroom or community-based.

Innovations in Incorporating Planning Support Technologies

A third area of innovation comprises the use of Planning Support Technologies (PST) in planning curricula. As mentioned above, a national survey of educators was conducted to understand how educators incorporate planning support technologies into their courses. In this survey, researchers used the broadest possible definition of planning support technologies, which included, but was not limited to web and desktop GIS, scenario planning tools, spatial statistical and social network analysis tools, urban design and visualization tools, and transportation models. Note that we switch here from the term planning support system (or PSS) to PST to indicate that the list may be broader than traditional definitions of PSS (Pelzer, et al., 2015).

For the survey, planning educators (N=699) were selected from a membership list from the Association of Collegiate Schools of Planning (ACSP) to receive an invitation to participate in the survey online. Educators were selected from the list based on two criteria: 1) they self-identified as having an expertise or area of research in spatial or physical planning, land use planning and policy, urban design, transportation, and other subareas that are likely to use GIS and other participatory and analytical technologies; and 2) educators who identified their main topic of interest to be geographic information systems, spatial analysis or other methodologies related to the use of technology. A total of 167 educators responded to the survey (24%).

Survey responses provide a sense of a broad sweep of technologies incorporated into educators' classes. The most popular tool was Desktop GIS (84%). The next most common tools incorporated were Web-based GIS tools (46%) and Urban Design/Visualization Tools (46%). Nearly a third (31%) indicated that they incorporated scenario planning tools, and 28% indicated Social Media. Transportation Models were incorporated by 26%. A relatively high proportion (28%) indicated that they use other types of PST. Social Network analysis tools, such as Gephi were used by 5%. Educators were encouraged to describe the PST that they incorporate.

Educators indicated a variety of reasons for incorporating PST. The most common was to prepare students for workplaces where they may employ the tools (87% of those who indicated the incorporation of one or more PST). Other responses suggest that educators see the value of PST as tools of learning, rather than simply a technology aimed at future employment. For example, 84% indicated that they incorporated the technologies to enhance the learning process and 50% indicated that they were used to reinforce plan-making methods. Over a third (36%) indicated that they incorporated PST to respond to student demand and interest.

Educators were also asked to select from a list of topics within their courses. The most common topics were: technology to enhance planning analysis (78%), for data collection (73%) and for data visualization (69%). "Thinking critically" was indicated by 60%, and 51% indicated "technology to visualize the built environment, future scenarios." Just under half of the respondents (49%) indicated that they incorporated the topic of participatory planning and collaborative decision-making, suggesting that the connection between analytical and visualization capabilities and technology is much more commonly discussed than the communicative or participatory value of PST. Perhaps reflecting a pool of respondents oriented toward the technical aspects of PST, a smaller, but still substantial proportion indicated topics such as open source versus proprietary tools (26% of respondents); scripting/computer programming (20%); and designing/creating technological tools (19%).

Survey respondents also shared successes related to the incorporating of PST. Many of the responses touched upon the ways in which learning a PST empowered students with new skills. A common thread focused on the impacts of community-based projects that applied PST and then were presented back to clients or community partners. Educators wrote about how impressed clients or community partners were with both visualization and analytical aspects of community-based projects that incorporated PST. In response to another closed-ended question, more than one-third of respondents (38%) indicated that students in their courses have applied PST to create a plan or other product for a client or community partner.[4]

Educators also expressed a relatively high level of satisfaction with student outcomes related to their ability to learn PST and their grasp of substantive planning concepts and theory in classes where PST were incorporated. Despite the overall level of satisfaction, educators reported a variety of barriers in incorporating PST in their classes. The most common barrier was the limited amount of time for preparation (57%) and lack of instructional support, such as TAs (39%). Funding for software and hardware was also a barrier for some educators, 28% and 24% respectively. Only 15% reported that there were no significant barriers.[5]

Survey respondents were also asked to select from a list of potential resources that would be most effective in encouraging the adoption of PST into the curriculum of the program or department where they teach. The greatest proportion (56%) selected "online tutorials available by tool providers or other educators." Other common selections included more teaching assistants to support this activity (50%) and hiring additional faculty with expertise in this area (34%). These responses suggest demand for additional curricular resources for educators, as well as workforce development needs among graduate students and faculty in the interest of addressing curricular needs.

Faculty responses to the national survey also included discussion of concerns and complications in the experience of educators with student learning. For example one respondent wrote:

> Far, far too often students spend time visualizing and representing things without really understanding what it is they are representing. At the first question of "why have you done this" the student then becomes panic stricken and can't explain the choices they made and keep deferring to showing images rather than explaining content.

While learning new tools can be empowering, students must have ample opportunities to understand underlying analytical processes and assumptions and to learn how to find the best match between a planning task or research question at hand and available tools and methods. This requires carefully framing and exploring the use of technological tools and their appropriateness. Similarly another survey respondent wrote:

> [Students] invest a lot of time acquiring tool competence, but then find that it does not answer many of the planning questions. The best metaphor for learning these is how we learn to cook. There is a developmental learning curve and you first need to learn the basics of cooking (planning) before you start using sophisticated tools. So the best support tools are ones that are quick and easy to learn, but that offer important conceptual and practical gains (like a good knife in the kitchen).

While the survey respondents had varied experiences with the use and instruction of PST, most of them found PST instruction valuable. Planning instructors found PST useful for augmenting students' understanding of the course content and techniques as well as their learning about the technology itself.

Using the Expanding Universe of Data: Data Mining, Crowdsensing, Citizen Science

Many of the methods planning students have principally learned are based on limited data availability. Open government initiatives and portals offer the potential for new insights into local, state, and federal government practices. New sources from distributed sensors, remote sensing, social media, and mobile records provide far more detailed data at multiple scales. "Crowdsensing" is one term used to describe the use of readily available social media to "understand the dynamic patterns of the city and the experiences of its citizens at a quasi-real-time rate" (Pereira et al., 2011). With the rise of growing volumes of available data, there are now opportunities to teach courses and content around data visualization, simulation, data mining, and machine learning (French et al., 2017; Schweitzer, 2014).

Comments from the national educator survey indicated that some faculty were already incorporating the necessary data scraping skills to empower students in this area. One educator wrote:

> Teaching students how to program in Python, scrape data from websites, pull data from open data APIs, and create web maps from the data after doing data cleaning and analysis, to planning students with no programming experience, has been challenging and immensely rewarding.

In another example from Columbia University, students were able to understand the fashion industry's need for physical proximity through the mapping of FourSquare check-ins (Williams et al., 2016). Another classroom assignment at Ohio State University focused students on developing infographics on a city's history, economics, and demographics. Students came to understand that data visualization is about making an argument (Kenitzer, 2016). An expansion of this assignment could involve assigning the creation of a photo collage of a city's history that draws from available online images.

Furthermore, these new data sources and methods are not limited to mining existing online data. Citizen science provides models of the co-production of information by interested citizens in the interest of science (Bowser and Shanley, 2013). This is a natural fit where planning intersects with natural resources and environmental management (Gouveia & Fonseca, 2008), but it can also be expanded to the engagement of citizens in the production of data related to the humanities and social sciences (Minner et al,, 2015).

Critical Thinking and Creative Shaping of Technology

Various methods, techniques, and activities can encourage a deeper appreciation for the intersections and complexities of technology and planning. In our fifth area of innovation, we encourage more attention to pedagogy that encourages students to think critically about the role of technology and its use in understanding communities and planning with citizens. Planning as a field should should be thinking critically about how all forms of technology are used in urban planning and governance (Townsend, 2013). The classroom is a valuable space for delving into the exploration of the strengths and weaknesses of technological tools and trends.

In response to critiques of the oversights and shortcomings of existing technology, students should further be encouraged to imagine and create new tools and methods (Frank, 2007), particularly those that might fulfill community needs (Drummond and French, 2008). In addition, two competitions organized by the Technology Division of the APA encouraged direct participation of students in the creation of new online tools. At conferences in Seattle and Phoenix, students and emerging professionals pitched ideas for new online tools, some of them in conceptual phases, and others already operational. In 2015, the winning app ChipIn got its start in a planning course at Ohio State University, when students had an exercise to create a concept. The students liked their idea enough, they then took it with them into a technology and planning course where they created a conceptual plan for the app. This then led to independent work on the part of the students to further develop the app for entry into the apps competition. The following year, two additional student and emerging professional teams won. The winning team created a new tool already in beta stages to support public engagement in the development process. A second winning team proposed an online tool to advance disability rights through an app to share of data about the accessibility of built environment. Based on the authors' correspondence with the contests' participants, the events helped students practice entrepreneurial aspects of planning and design collaboratively. Because of the success of this program, APA-registered Planning Student Organization (PSO) organized another competition on Smart Cities at the APA national conference 2017 in New York City. The event took place at the conference event Tech Zone, featuring students' Smart Cities projects.

Another support for the convergence of tool development and planning practice and education is the Consortium for Scenario Planning. The Consortium provides opportunities for professional planners and educators to meet with scenario planning tool developers via monthly online meetings and an annual symposium.[6] The network provides opportunities for these groups to collaborate. An online resource page includes a library of syllabi and lab assignments developed by planning educators.

Conclusion: The Power of Planning Education and Technology

In this scan of technology and planning education, we find important takeaways for educators, students, practitioners, and the organizations that support planning and planning education. The first takeaway is how education can build on emerging areas of innovation. We examined five areas of innovation: 1) expansion in the means of delivery and access to planning courses; 2) new means of organizing university-based learning using technology; 3) the incorporation of PST in the classroom as both content and method for teaching new technical skills and reinforcing planning concepts; and 4) use of a growing number of data sources from open government portals, to sensors, social media data. We also propose the advancement of a fifth area of innovation, in critical thinking about the use and role of technology in planning practice and the creation of new technological tools.

In these five areas of innovation, we see two important continua. The first continuum involves the scale of innovation, from the actions of individual students and educators, to the organizations that partner with them and the university departments that support them. This continuum expands beyond the university to national and international planning organizations that shape opportunities for collaboration, which can in turn, advance technology and its use in planning.

A second continuum is that of student empowerment in understanding, using, and shaping technology. At the most basic level, students can learn about technology and its use in planning. They can further learn to operative PST in responsible ways, and use them to advance analysis and participation. At the top of this conceptual ladder of technological empowerment, as inspired by Arnstein (1969) and Senbel and Church (2011), students can learn to shape and create technology to advance planning as a field. Thus, planning education has the power not only to inculcate students with technical, analytical, and communicative skills and to foster critical thinking, but it can generate a culture of creativity and entrepreneurship with technology that will deepen and expand planning theory and practice.

Acknowledgements

We would like to acknowledge and thank the collaborators on the National Survey of Planning Educators and ACSP roundtables: Robert Goodspeed, Thomas Hilde, and Robert Paterson, as well as the research assistants for the survey: Zeynep Goksel and Apoorva Kumar.

Notes

1 The first roundtable in 2014 encouraged educators to share thoughts on the following: How can land use planning and other plan-making courses incorporate these technologies? How do they aid, or hinder, the learning process? What are strategies for classroom adoption and experimentation in the context of different course configurations, e.g. introductory land use and environmental planning classes, studios, and online offerings? How can educators strike a balance between teaching the use of particular tools versus teaching essential concepts and critical thinking? A second roundtable in 2015 was similarly focused on teaching with scenario planning tools and on geodesign and urban informatics, and encouraged additional sharing among faculty.
2 Principal investigators on this survey research were Jennifer Minner, Nader Afzalan, Thomas Hilde, Robert Paterson and Robert Goodspeed.
3 The Buzzfeed Quiz "Which Utopian Vision Of The City Are You?!" www.buzzfeed.com/ehabebeid/quiz-which-utopian-vision-of-the-city-are-you-1waxq, is an example of "clickbait" as part of a classroom exercise. Clickbait and podcasts were examples of digital media created by students in the undergraduate, core class Promise and Pitfalls of Contemporary Planning. More information http://blogs.cornell.edu/crp2000/
4 A total of 59% indicated that students in their courses have applied planning support technology to a real world site (with or without a community partner or client).
5 The largest groups of educators reported being mostly satisfied (27%) to somewhat satisfied (24%) with the level of departmental support provided by their institution. A total of 26% of educators reported that they were somewhat to mostly dissatisfied with the level of institutional support. Five percent were completely satisfied and 16% were neither satisfied nor dissatisfied or didn't know (2%).
6 See the Consortium for Scenario Planning website at http://scenarioplanning.io/

References

Adams, P. C. (1998). Teaching and Learning with SimCity 2000. *Journal of Geography, 97*(2), 47–55. doi:10.1080/00221349808978827
Afzalan, N., & Muller, B. (2014). The Role of Social Media in Green Infrastructure Planning: A Case Study of Neighborhood Participation in Park Siting. *Journal of Urban Technology, 21*(3), 67–83. doi:10.1080/10630732.2014.940701
American Planning Association (APA) (Producer). (2016). Planning Webcast Series. [YouTube channel] Retrieved from www.youtube.com/user/PlanningWebcast
American Planning Association (APA) (2016). Podcasts. Retrieved from www.planning.org/multimedia/podcasts/
Arnstein, S. R. (1969). A Ladder Of Citizen Participation. *Journal of the American Institute of Planners, 35*(4), 216–224. doi:10.1080/01944366908977225
Beirut, A. U. o. (Producer). (2016, December 1). American University of Beirut. [YouTube channel] Retrieved from www.youtube.com/user/AUBatLebanon
Bowser, A., & Shanley, L. (2013). *New Visions in Citizen Science*. Retrieved from Washington, D. C.: www.wilsoncenter.org/sites/default/files/NewVisionsInCitizenScience.pdf

de Andrade, B. A., de Sena, Í. S., & Moura, A. C. M. (2016). Tirolcraft: The Quest of Children to Playing the Role of Planners at a Heritage Protected Town. In *Digital Heritage. Progress in Cultural Heritage: Documentation, Preservation, and Protection* (pp. 825–835): Springer International Publishing.

Drennon, C. (2005). Teaching Geographic Information Systems in a Problem-Based Learning Environment. *Journal of Geography in Higher Education, 29*(3), 385–402. doi:10.1080/03098260500290934

Drummond, W. J., & French, S. P. (2008). The Future of GIS in Planning: Converging Technologies and Diverging Interests. *Journal of the American Planning Association, 74*(2), 161–174. doi:10.1080/01944360801982146

Enfield, J. (2013). Looking at the Impact of the Flipped Classroom Model of Instruction on Undergraduate Multimedia Students at CSUN. *TechTrends, 57*(6), 14–27. doi:10.1007/s11528-013-0698-1

Esnard, A.-M., & MacDougall, E. B. (1997). Common Ground for Integrating Planning Theory and GIS Topics. *Journal of Planning Education and Research, 17*(1), 55–62. doi:10.1177/0739456x9701700106

Evans-Cowley, J. S. (2018). Planning Education with and through Technologies. In *Urban Planning Education* (pp. 293–306). Springer International Publishing.

Evans-Cowley, J., & Hollander, H. (2010). The New Generation of Public Participation: Internet-based Participation Tools. *Planning Practice and Research, 25*(3), 397–408.

Evans-Cowley, J. S., Sanchez, T. W., Afzalan, N., Lizcano, A. S., Kenitzer, Z., & Evans, T. (2014). Learning About E-Planning. *International Journal of E-Planning Research, 3*(3), 53–76. doi:10.4018/ijepr.2014070104

Federal Emergency Management Agency (FEMA). (2016). Distance Learning. Retrieved from https://training.fema.gov/is/

Florida Atlantic University. (2016). School of Urban & Regional Planning. Retrieved from www.youtube.com/user/fausurp

Frank, A. I. (2007). Entrepreneurship and enterprise skills: A missing element of planning education? *Planning Practice and Research, 22*(4), 635–648. doi:10.1080/02697450701770142

Fregonese Associates. (2016). Corridor Housing Preservation Tool on Envision Tomorrow Website. Retrieved from http://envisiontomorrow.org/corridor-housing-preservation-tool

French, S. P., Barchers, C., & Zhang, W. (2017). How Should Urban Planners Be Trained to Handle Big Data? In P. V. Thakuriah, N. Tilahun, & M. Zellner (Eds.), *Seeing Cities Through Big Data* (pp. 209–217). Springer International Publishing.

Gaber, J. (2007). Simulating Planning: SimCity as a Pedagogical Tool. *Journal of Planning Education and Research, 27*, 113–121. doi:10.1177/0739456X07305791

Goodspeed, R. (2013). *Planning Support Systems for Spatial Planning Through Social Learning.* Dissertation, Massachusetts Institute of Technology, Cambridge, Massachusetts. Retrieved from http://web.mit.edu/uis/theses/RGoodspeed_Dissertation_5-20-13.pdf

Goodspeed, R., Afzalan, N., Hilde, T. W., & Minner, J. (2015). *Teaching the New Technology: Scenario Planning Tools, Geodesign, and Urban Informatics.* Roundtable at the Association of Collegiate Schools of Planning, Houston, Texas.

Goodspeed, R., Spanring, C., & Reardon, T. (2012). *Crowdsourcing as Data Sharing: A Regional Web-based Real Estate Development Database.* Paper presented at the Proceedings of the 6th International Conference on Theory and Practice of Electronic Governance - ICEGOV '12. doi:10.1145/2463728.2463819

Gouveia, C., & Fonseca, A. (2008). New Approaches to Environmental Monitoring: The Use of ICT to Explore Volunteered Geographic Information. *GeoJournal, 72*(3–4), 185–197. doi:10.1007/s10708-008-9183-3

Hanzl, M. (2007). Information technology as a Tool for Public Participation in Urban Planning: A Review of Experiments and Potentials. *Design Studies, 28*(3), 289–307. doi:10.1016/j.destud.2007.02.003

Herreid, C. F., & Schiller, N. A. (2013). Case Studies and the Flipped Classroom. *Journal of College Science Teaching, 42*(5), 62–66.

Hollander, J. B. (2011). Approaching an Ideal: Using Technology to Apply Collaborative Rationality to Urban Planning Processes. *Planning Practice and Research, 26*(5), 587–596. doi:10.1080/02697459.2011.627001

Holway, J., Gabbe, C. J., Hebbert, F., Lally, J., Matthews, R., & Quay, R. (2012). *Opening Access to Scenario Planning Tools.* Retrieved from Cambridge, Massachusetts: www.lincolninst.edu/sites/default/files/pubfiles/opening-access-to-scenario-planning-tools-full-v2.pdf

Hughes, J. E., & Ooms, A. (2004). Content-Focused Technology Inquiry Groups. *Journal of Research on Technology in Education, 36*(4), 397–411. doi:10.1080/15391523.2004.10782422

Johnson, P. A., & Sieber, R. E. (2012). Situating the Adoption of VGI by Government. In *Crowdsourcing Geographic Knowledge* (pp. 65–81). Springer Netherlands.

Kenitzer, Z. (2016, December 1). Personal correspondence.
Mather, L. W., & Robinson, P. (2016). Civic Crafting in Urban Planning Public Consultation. *International Journal of E-Planning Research, 5*(3), 42–58. doi:10.4018/ijepr.2016070104
Minner, J., Hilde, T. W., Paterson, R., & Afzalan, N. (2014). *Plan-making Pedagogy and Technology: Forum to Share Curricular Experiments*. Roundtable at the Association for Collegiate Schools of Planning, Philadelphia, PA.
Minner, J., Holleran, M., Roberts, A., & Conrad, J. (2015). Capturing Volunteered Historical Information: Lessons from Development of a Local Government Crowdsourcing Tool. *International Journal of E-Planning Research, 4*(1), 19–41. doi:10.4018/ijepr.2015010102
Minner, J., & Micklow, A. (2016). *Lessons from Technology: From a National Survey of Educators to Participant Observations from Curriculum Development for a New Equity App*. Paper presented at the Association of Collegiate Schools of Planning, Portland, Oregon.
Minner, J. S. (2015). Recoding Embedded Assumptions: Adaptation of an Open Source Tool to Support Sustainability, Transparency and Participatory Governance. In S. Geertman, J. Ferreira Jr., R. Goodspeed, & J. Stillwell (Eds.), *Planning Support Systems and Smart Cities* (pp. 409–425). Springer International Publishing.
Minnery, J., & Searle, G. (2014). Toying with the City? Using the Computer Game SimCity™4 in Planning Education. *Planning Practice & Research, 29*(1), 41–55. doi:10.1080/02697459.2013.829335
Mueller, E. J., Hilde, T. W., & Torrado, M. J. (2018). Methods for Countering Spatial Inequality: Incorporating Strategic Opportunities for Housing Preservation into Transit-Oriented Development Planning. *Landscape and Urban Planning*. doi:10.1016/j.landurbplan.2018.01.003
National Oceanic and Atmospheric Administration (NOAA). (2014). Coastal and Marine Spatial Planning. Retrieved from www.msp.noaa.gov/news.html
O'Flaherty, J., & Phillips, C. (2015). The Use if Flipped Classrooms in Higher Education: A Scoping Review. *The Internet and Higher Education, 25*, 85–95. doi:10.1016/j.iheduc.2015.02.002
Pelzer, P., Arciniegas, G., Geertman, S., & Lenferink, S. (2015). Planning Support Systems and Task-Technology Fit: A Comparative Case Study. *Applied Spatial Analysis and Policy, 8*(2), 155–175. doi:10.1007/s12061-015-9135-5
Pereira, F. C., Vaccari, A., Giardin, F., Chiu, C., & Ratti, C. (2011). Crowdsensing in the Web: Analyzing the Citizen Experience in the Urban Space. In M. Foth, L. Forlano, C. Satchell, & M. Gibbs (Eds.), *From Social Butterfly to Engaged Citizen: Urban Informatics, Social Media, Ubiquitous Computing, and Mobile Technology to Support Citizen Engagement* (pp. 353–374). Cambridge, Massachusetts: The MIT Press.
Placeways. (2016). CommunityViz Video Tutorials. Retrieved from http://placeways.com/communityviz/videotutorials.html
Poplin, A. (2012). Playful Public Participation in Urban Planning: A Case Study for Online Serious Games. *Computers, Environment and Urban Systems, 36*(3), 195–206. doi:10.1016/j.compenvurbsys.2011.10.003
Riggs, W. (2014, September 15). Email correspondence with Jennifer Evans-Cowley.
Riggs, W., Steins, C., & Brasuell, J. (2016). *Teaching Quantitative Methods in a Self-Organized Learning Environment*. Paper presented at the Association for Collegiate Schools of Planning, Portland, Oregon.
Robinson, P. (2016). *Urban Planning: Is There an App for That?* Paper presented at the Association of Collegiate Schools of Planning, Portland, Oregon.
Schweitzer, L. (2014). Planning and Social Media: A Case Study of Public Transit and Stigma on Twitter. *Journal of the American Planning Association, 80*(3), 218–238. doi:10.1080/01944363.2014.980439
Seltzer, E., & Mahmoudi, D. (2012). Citizen Participation, Open Innovation, and Crowdsourcing. *Journal of Planning Literature, 28*(1), 3–18. doi:10.1177/0885412212469112
Senbel, M., & Church, S. P. (2011). Design Empowerment: The Limits of Accessible Visualization Media in Neighborhood Densification. *Journal of Planning Education and Research, 31*(4), 423–437. doi:10.1177/0739456x11417830
Sletto, B., Muñoz, S., Strange, S. M., Donoso, R. E., & Thomen, M. (2010). "El Rincón de los Olvidados": Participatory GIS, Experiential Learning and Critical Pedagogy in Santo Domingo, Dominican Republic. *Journal of Latin American Geography, 9*(3), 111–135. doi:10.1353/lag.2010.0022
Stauskis, G. (2014). Development of Methods and Practices of Virtual Reality as a Tool for Participatory Urban Planning: A Case Study of Vilnius City as an Example for Improving Environmental, Social and Energy Sustainability. *Energy, Sustainability and Society, 4*(1), 7. doi:10.1186/2192-0567-4-7
Streetsblog. (2016). Streetsblog NYC. Retrieved from www.streetsblog.org
Strong Towns (Producer). (2016). Strong Towns. [YouTube channel] Retrieved from www.youtube.com/user/strongtowns

Sweet, E. (2016, December 5). Email correspondence with Jennifer Evans-Cowley.

Texas A&M University (Producer). (2016, December 1). Urban Planning. [YouTube channel]. Retrieved from www.youtube.com/channel/UCCjUEsSQsqob_lpg77h29Zw

Townsend, A. M. (2013). *Smart Cities: Big Data, Civic Hackers, and the Quest for a New Utopia*. New York: WW Norton & Company.

United Nations. (2016). Launch of UN-Habitat's new free online resource – the Global Urban Lectures [Press release]. Retrieved from http://unhabitat.org/launch-of-the-global-urban-lectures-a-new-free-online-resource-by-un-habitat/

University of Michigan (Producer). (2016). University of Michigan, Taubman College. [YouTube channel] Retrieved from www.youtube.com/user/UMTaubmanCollege

Urey, G. (2002). A Critical Look at the Use of Computing Technologies in Planning Education. *Journal of Planning Education and Research*, *21*(4), 406–418. doi:10.1177/0739456x0202100405

VoiceThread. (2016). VoiceThread. Retrieved from http://voicethread.com/

Williams, K., Claridge, T., & Carroll, A. (2016). *Multimodal Transportation Planning Curriculum for Urban Planning Programs*. Retrieved from http://dx.doi.org/10.15760/trec.128

World Bank, The (Producer). (2014). Sustainable Urban Land Use Planning. [E-learning course] Retrieved from http://wbi.worldbank.org/wbi/news/2010/11/23/e-learning-course-sustainable-urban-land-use-planning

Zhou, Q., Bekebrede, G., Mayer, I., Warmerdam, J., & Knepflé, M. (2016). The Climate Game: Connecting Water Management and Spatial Planning through Simulation Gaming? In J. Edelenbos, N. Bressers, & P. Scholten (Eds.), *Water Governance as Connective Capacity* (pp. 109–127). London: Routledge.

8
ROLE OF STUDIOS AND WORKSHOPS[1]

Judith Grant Long

Introduction

Studio courses offer an enviably wide scope of instructional possibility. A quick survey of recent course offerings reveals that our planning studios engage an impressive array of issues, subjects, theories, geographies, and media. This widening scope is an important evolution from normative plan-making informed by comprehensive rationality.

Many innovations have been born of this broadened scope. Recent scholarship on planning studios describes an equally notable range of approaches that include new ideas about the role of planners and planning. Mirroring some of the transformations evident in contemporary planning practice, our studios are increasingly likely to be aligned with university outreach programs, with advocacy and service learning, or with experiential or project-based approaches.

At the same time as the potential of the studio is expanding, however, its use as a pedagogical approach in planning programs is diminishing. Evidence suggests that studio courses occupy a smaller proportion of classroom hours when compared to other more traditional pedagogies such as lecture and seminar. As an example, in the U.S., the role of studio pedagogy has fluctuated over the past century: Studio courses dominated the curriculum of our most venerable programs during the first half of the 20th century, only to be eliminated from many programs during the 1960s and 1970s. Studios then found their way back into planning curricula during the 1980s and 1990s, though most often as single courses intended to serve as capstone experiences in the final semester. In other countries, particularly those borne of western planning traditions, the role of studio is also that of a one-time capstone experience.

Is this current state of the studio—where studio courses play a comparatively small role in contemporary planning curricula—a good thing? Is a single capstone studio course the right amount of studio, or should we be looking for more ways to employ this unique learning approach? Meaningful answers to this question should rely, ideally, on a solid and broadly shared knowledge of studio pedagogy, including its goals (e.g., professional socialization, learning by doing), its unique instructional characteristics (e.g., engaging experts, a highly iterative and intense work pattern), and how it compares to other course formats. Teachers should have a sense of what subject matter is best taught in the studio setting, as well as the potential contributions of studio to the broader professional planning curriculum, including its weight in the curriculum (e.g., expressed as a percentage of total program hours), its placement in the curricular time frame (e.g., core or capstone), and its particular educational outcomes (e.g., synthesis).

Yet such broad and thorough understanding of studio pedagogy is harder to acquire than it should be. The existing literature on planning studios is relatively small and also somewhat out of date, having remained essentially dormant over a decade when many of the central concerns of planning have changed. There is also a sizeable knowledge gap between the practice and theory of studio instruction. For example, seasoned studio instructors, including this author—who are often trained in studio and/or have professional planning experience—can talk at length about what makes a good studio problem, a good client, or a good exercise, but may find it difficult to clearly articulate the educational theory that underlies studio-based learning without doing some extra homework. For the many faculty members who do not teach studio, but who nevertheless participate in curriculum planning decisions, there are no primers that summarize the value of studio pedagogy in planning education. Nor are there primers that prepare our students for what is often a brand new type of learning experience.

This chapter will revisit the role of studio courses in educating planners. Its primary questions are: What are the origins of studio pedagogy? What is the unique value of studio pedagogy in educating planners? It will first trace the emergence of studio courses in planning curricula, starting with the first city planning course offered at Harvard in 1909, and discuss trends over the past century, including an overview of the role of studios in other countries. It finds that studio courses may have reached a stable state, where planning students are typically required to take one studio course, often positioned as a capstone at the end of their study path, with the option to take one more as an elective. That studios are not more intensively used—despite their importance as a space for synthetic and experiential learning—is in part a result of an increasingly crowded planning curriculum, where students seeks exposure to a broadening array of substantive concerns and analytical technologies. Pragmatically, the cost and complexity of mounting studios have also lessened their influence, despite their appeal in recruiting students to specific programs, and to the profession.

The Origins and Objectives of Studio Courses

Early use of the word "studio" emphasized a location for the production of art, and it was the medieval guild system that first linked production to "pedagogy" through the apprenticeship system. This emerging studio pedagogy involved students learning under the direct tutelage of master practitioners, through example as much as through guidance, typically involving ongoing commitments of several years. The studio system eventually found more widespread legitimacy as an epistemology of practice in formal education circles through the professionalization of training architects. By the 19th century, the greatest architects in Europe were training disciples using the "studio" or "atelier" system, led by the Ecole des Beaux Arts in Paris (Chafee, 1977). This studio model of the European architectural education system strongly influenced the organization of architectural schools in the U.S., and subsequently, the city planning and landscape architecture programs that began to sprout from within these schools in the early 20th century.

Generally speaking, studio courses share a set of common characteristics, whether intended for the training of architects or planners. They begin with an open-ended problem, often taking account of current issues in the "real world" with "real clients," and giving students some choice in their direction within the scope of the problem. Then follow a series of structured conversations including the "desk crit," and the "review" or "jury." The desk crit (diminutive form of "criticism") is an extended and loosely structured interaction between the student and the instructor. The review or jury is a formal presentation and discussion of student work, where the instructor mediates the interaction between students and outside experts. Throughout a studio course, student work usually happens within a highly iterative and often intense working pattern, where problems are revisited repeatedly in a generative process leading to a final product.

Other variations on the studio include the workshop and the practicum. A "workshop" involves small groups working together to develop a set of skills or to discuss a specialized topic (or topics), but may or may not involve creative problem-solving, iterative expressions, or a final presentation of a finished product. A "practicum" is by definition a work experience component that is often required as part of a program of study, with examples in the fields of medicine, psychology, and law. Practica differ from "internships" in the degree of control the host educational institution has over their content and delivery, although these lines are routinely blurred.

Studios lay claim to a distinct set of learning objectives. Most often the unique qualities of studios are described as a synthetic learning experience, with "learning by doing" offered in a context of professional socialization with high levels of peer-led collaboration (Heumann & Wetmore, 1984; Long, 2012; Nemeth & Long, 2012). There are also a number of planning scholars who describe the potential of studio courses in addressing more narrowly defined goals. Although this is not a comprehensive list, some exemplars of the form include the following: Abramson (2005), Sletto (2012), and Klopp et al. (2014) on the potential of studio in engaging international planning issues; Forsyth et al. (2000), Hoyt (2005), Sletto (2010), Porter et al. (2015), and Levkoe et al. (2018) on community service learning; Grant and Manuel (1995) and Balassiano and West (2012) on peer-based learning in studio; Baum (1997), Kotval (2003) and Higgins et al. (2009) on experiential learning and teaching practice; Arefi and Triantafillou (2005) and Anselin et al. (2011) on planning and the design disciplines; Higgins and Morgan (2000) on creativity in planning; and on the role of technology, Thomas and Hollander (2010) on virtual studios, and Alizadeh et al. (2016) on online diaries as a means of engaging reflective learning among students taking studio courses for the first time.

The Changing Role of Studio Courses in American Planning Schools

Studio pedagogy dominated the early days of U.S.-based planning education; as late as the 1950s studios accounted for half or more of total course hours in the nearly 20 planning programs housed in prestigious universities (Adams, 1954). As evidence of this period of studio domination, Adams (1954, as reported in Heumann and Wetmore, 1984) provides what may be the first set of descriptive statistics on studio pedagogy in planning, based on his 1954 survey of all 18 planning master's degree programs in the U.S. (Table 8.1). Adams found that all graduate planning programs were offering a very similar student experience, centered on a sequence of three semester-long studio "workshop" courses that were required in the first three semesters of typically a four-semester program, although some were organized into six terms of varying duration. The subject matter of these workshop sequences was also similar across programs, encompassing higher degrees of complexity and larger scales as the student progressed through the program, beginning with site plans, then onward to district plans, and culminating with the comprehensive plan.

Table 8.1 Surveying the Evolution of Required Studio Courses, 1955–2011

	1955	1965	1975	1984	2011
	1 2 3 4 5 6	1 2 3 4 5 6	1 2 3 4 5 6	1 2 3 4 5 6	1 2 3 4 5 6
Harvard	■ ■ ■ ☐ - -	■ ■ ■ ☐ - -			- - ■ ■ ◊
MIT	■ ■ ■ ☐ - -	■ ■ ■ ☐ - -	☐ ☐ ☐ ☐ - -	● ☐ ☐ ☐ - -	☐ ☐ ◊ - -
Cornell	☐ ■ ■ ☐ - -	☐ ■ ■ ☐ - -	☐ ☐ ☐ ☐ - -	☐ ☐ ☐ ☐ - -	☐ ☐ ◊ - -
Berkeley	■ ■ ■ ☐ - -	■ ☐ ☐ ☐ - -	☐ ☐ ☐ ☐ - -	☐ ☐ ◊ ☐ - -	☐ ☐ ☐ ☐ - -
North Carolina	■ ■ ■ ☐ - -	■ ■ ☐ ☐ - -	☐ ☐ ◊ ◊ - -	☐ ☐ ☐ ◊ - -	☐ ☐ ◊ - -
Pennsylvania				● ☐ ☐ ☐ - -	☐ ● ☐ ◊ - -
Illinois (U-C)	■ ■ ■ ☐ - -	■ ■ ■ ☐ - -	☐ ☐ ◊ ☐ - -	☐ ☐ ◊ ☐ - -	● ☐ ☐ ◊ - -
Michigan State	■ ■ ■ ■ ☐ ☐	■ ■ ■ ☐ ☐ ☐	■ ■ ■ ☐ ☐ ☐	☐ ☐ ■ ■ ◊	☐ ☐ ◊ - -
Georgia Tech	■ ■ ■ ■ ☐ ☐	■ ■ ■ ☐ ☐ ☐	■ ■ ■ ☐ ☐ ☐	☐ ☐ ■ ■ ◊	☐ ☐ ☐ ◊ - -
Oklahoma	☐ ☐ ■ ■ - -	☐ ☐ ■ ■ - -	☐ ☐ ■ ■ - -	☐ ☐ ■ ■ - -	☐ ☐ ◊ ☐ - -

Source: Data for 1955, 1965, 1975, and 1984 are from Heumann and Westmore (1984). Data for 2011 are based on surveys of individual programs by the author. Data for Pennsylvania from 1955 through 1975 were missing from the 1984 study.

Note:

■ denotes a sequence of required studio(s)
☐ no studio required in that semester
● single required studio course
◊ studio required, but choice among offerings, and in some cases, choice among semesters.
- studio not on offer in 5th and 6th semesters
A blank cell means the studio program is not on offer.

Starting in the 1960s, the second phase of planning studio history was characterized by a movement away from "planning seen as a design profession to planning seen as a branch of applied social science" (Forester, 1983). Planning education, in response, became a mission of "training generalists with a specialty" based in a "core curriculum that would form the foundation for more specialized training in planning and for the continuing process of learning which should take place on the job" (Perloff, 1957). The impact on studio courses was "the fission of the planning workshop into separate parts reflecting, and perhaps leading, the separation of the profession into distinct and self-contained sub-parts" representing the functional areas of concern to planners at that time, such as housing, transportation, economy, etc. (Heumann and Wetmore, 1984). For studio courses, this meant that specialized topics and specialized clients—often aligned along areas of concentration—began replacing the practitioner as the point of "real world" contact and medium of comprehensive synthesis.

There were other factors driving the changing role of studio courses after 1960. Criticisms of a relentlessly rational approach and of the all-importance of the comprehensive plan applied to the use of studios as well. Meanwhile, studio courses were being "squeezed out" by the need to introduce areas of concentration in response to market demands for depth in a functional concern of planning, and for increased analytic methods training. At some schools, a new version of the introductory workshop or studio attempted to integrate multiple subjects, notably planning theory, into the first semester of education, often taught by teams of faculty members and practitioners, and making heavy use of case study instruction and group work approaches (Heumann and Wetmore, 1984).

Pragmatic concerns also affected the declining popularity of studios during this period. Compared to lectures and seminars, studios present additional expenses, such as travel costs or special materials for building models, plotting large maps, and preparing professional-quality reports. Studios also required dedicated classroom space for accommodating the work of the students, sometimes with specialized equipment, including drafting tables and room to store working materials. For many new planning programs created during this era, dedicated studio spaces were simply not part of the plan.

Beginning in the 1980s, a number of published articles advocated for renewed emphasis on studio pedagogy. Forester (1983), Jacobs (1983), Lang (1983), Chatterjee (1986), Kreditor (1990), and Dagenhart and Sawicki (1992) argued that regardless of labels "we need to find a way to restore them to their proper place in our curricula" (Chatterjee, 1986). During the 1990s, articles by Christensen (1993), Wachs (1994), Baum (1995, 1997), Friedmann (1996), and more broadly, Birch (2001) and Dalton (2001), among others, advocated for teaching practice, albeit with a broader framework than that used earlier in the century. These authors argue for a recalibration of practice-based learning, and further, that such courses ought to be taught by practitioners or by academic faculty trained to facilitate experiential learning. While not explicitly advocating for studio courses, these authors suggest that experience-based learning—including studios and internships—is the most appropriate approach to teaching practice.

Studio Courses Today

An analysis of the role of planning studios conducted in 2009—exactly 100 years after the first course in city planning was offered at Harvard—confirms that most planning programs now require their students to participate in some form of studio-based learning (Table 8.2). In most cases, these studio courses represent a comparatively small portion of total program hours and are timed as requirements in the second year of the program as capstone courses tailored to areas of concentration and student interests (Table 8.1). These findings are based on an analysis of U.S.-based graduate planning programs, appearing in the 2009 edition of the ACSP *Guide to Undergraduate and Graduate Education in Urban and Regional Planning*.[2]

Among the programs in the 2009 ACSP Guide, 84 percent require studio courses as part of their core curriculum, when studio is defined broadly to include its curricular cousins the "workshop," "practicum," and "client-based" course formats (Table 8.2). In these programs,

Table 8.2 Studio Courses in U.S.-Based Graduate Planning Programs, 2009

	Programs/Hours	Percentage
Accredited graduate programs in North America	72 programs	100
At least one studio course required	62 programs	84
More than 10 percent of program hours in studio	38 programs	53
More than 20 percent of program hours in studio	7 programs	10
Average percentage of program hours in studio	6.8 hours	10
Required studios taken in second year of program	n/a	76

Source: 2009 ACSP *Guide to Undergraduate and Graduate Education in Urban and Regional Planning*, 15th edition.

Note: Studio is defined as including workshop, practicum, and client-based courses. Seventy-two programs provided breakdowns of their program hours in the 2009 ACSP guide. Ten programs without these figures were not included. Undergraduate programs were not included. The number of required studio courses is an estimate based on actual program data in combination with estimates based on studio course hours relative to typical course loads in a given program.

the average student experience would include 10 percent of total program hours in studio courses. These required studios were often offered during the second year of two-year programs. The range of required program hours spent in studio courses ranged from more than 25 percent (in self-described "studio-based" programs) to zero percent (in "policy" programs).[3]

What do these figures tell us about the recent role of studios? Certainly, the fact that most programs require at least some time spent in studio courses can be viewed as widespread confidence in the value of studio pedagogy. Moreover, the snapshot data from 2009 suggest that on average, a little bit of studio is about right for most graduate programs, given that the faculty of each individual program make curricular decisions that best serve their educational goals. Importantly, there is no requirement for one size to fit all; there are some programs that value studio highly and others that choose to focus on other approaches to the exclusion of studio. The import of studio also varies within programs, as individual faculty often have different opinions on the matter of how much time should be spent in studio.

Table 8.1 is based on the longitudinal data provided in Heumann and Wetmore's 1984 study, extended from 1955 to 2011. A subsequent analysis by Long (2012) considered the same ten programs in 2011 based on curriculum information, syllabus reviews, and follow-up interviews with program faculty. This study found the role of the studio course in 2011 is quite different from the preceding periods. The most visibly dramatic change is the shift in timing of required studio courses to later stages of programs, as is the case in eight of the ten programs. Pragmatically, it can be argued that students in their second year of a program may be better equipped to take advantage of the learning approach offered by studios. In addition, these capstone courses can offer opportunities for collaboration with other disciplines. At Harvard, for example, students in their third or fourth semester of the planning program can take studio courses in any department of the school, including architecture and landscape architecture.

Another change evident in studio course offerings in 2011 is the high degree of choice in subject matter. This is in part due to the need for multiple sections: since studio courses typically feature low instructor-to-student ratios—estimated to average approximately 1:15 among these ten programs for example—most programs have to offer more than one section to serve the number of students who need the course to graduate. Moreover, since there are few economies of scale in delivering studio courses, most programs make a virtue of necessity by finding positive synergies with their teaching and research specializations, as well as community outreach objectives or other agendas. As examples, Cornell, Georgia Tech, and the University of North Carolina–Chapel Hill offer a wide range of studio choices, often changing each year, that are tied to their broader research missions, and are featured on their websites as demonstrations of program breadth and as showcases for outreach activities that undoubtedly appeal to prospective students.

It is interesting to find that, even within this small sample, programs are making a significant effort to engage their full-time faculty as instructors in required studios, rather than relying heavily on outsourcing to part-time or contract practitioner faculty. Both Georgia Tech and University of Illinois-Chicago (UIC) have an impressively high ratio of full-time faculty teaching in their required studios. The current UIC program integrates plan-making into its core curriculum at both the beginning (via a required common workshop) and end (via choice of capstone studio), in what may be the only visible effort among these ten programs to keep elements of the old and the new. Moreover, full-time faculty members at UIC are encouraged to teach in these courses, whether or not they have studio experience, as a means of strengthening the program mission.

It bears mention that studio courses are an expensive and complex undertaking as compared to lectures and seminars. Studio courses can rarely be replicated; each new studio course usually brings a new site or client, or both. Studio instructors are expensive, especially high-profile practitioners. They are paid more than typical adjunct faculty, in part because of the higher workload associated with creating a one-time course, but also due to the personal and often intense teaching approach, and the opportunity cost of time taken away from their practice. Many programs seek to leverage connections with alumni or others who might be willing to sponsor the studio, which may include donating some or all of their instructional salary if the project coincides with their professional or personal interests.

Travel costs are also significant, given that visiting the site is often considered a critical part of the studio experience. Depending on location, travel costs can exceed the cost of the instructor and overhead. Travel to international and some domestic destinations can easily exceed $25,000 for a studio with 12 students. In some programs, these extra costs are borne in full or in part by participating students, while in others they are included in program fees, or most ideally paid by a client or sponsor. While international studios can help provide a more globalized education, it is not realistic to expect that all programs will be able to offer international studio experiences to their students. Finally, while there have been some cost savings due to computing advances that have shrunk the student workstation and the need for physical models, the cost of providing and supporting these technologies has also increased across all types of course offerings.

Of course, any assessment of studio courses would benefit from a better understanding of how they are delivered in countries outside of the U.S., and specifically whether there are lessons to be learned from different approaches. (This is a different concern from the important question of how to deliver a more globalized curriculum using studio courses that focus on issues in international settings.) As the histories of planning as a profession and a discipline emerged along a similar timeline in the U.S., Great Britain, and to a lesser extent Canada, it is not surprising to find that the popularity of studio courses has moved in tandem with the broad trends described herein (Gurran et al., 2008; Long, 2012). In short, most students take one or two studio courses as a capstone experience, with differing degrees of emphasis between programs.

In other countries, the hegemony of westernized planning curricula appears intact, including the role of studio courses. In Australia and New Zealand, where planning emerged as a profession in the mid-20th century, studio courses are common, but are by no means universal elements of planning curricula. In both countries, however, significant efforts are underway to improve and re-frame studio offerings based on changing preferences in higher education that advocate more attention to experiential and field-based learning. While the outcomes of these initiatives are not yet clear, they are echoed in the activities of their national planning associations (Gurran et al., 2008; Higgins et al., 2009; Baldwin and Rosier, 2017).

In China and India, the history of planning education also reflects some aspects of these western influences, with similar boom and bust periods for studio courses, though the timing of these cycles is dictated by their distinct political and economic contexts. Chinese planners are tasked with educating their rapidly growing professional ranks in response to rapid urbanization, and there is great attention to the best path forward. With English language articles describing the Chinese approach to education planners beginning to emerge, we learn that here too the import of the studio is declining and shifting to the end of the study path, declining from one-fourth to one-sixth of program hours in one detailed case study (Hou, 2018). Similar planning education explorations are underway in India, also in response to urgent urban issues and the need for well-prepared professionals. However, the role that studio will play in any reformulation going forward is not yet clear (Kranthi and Valliappan, 2016).

Elsewhere, the dominance of western planning curricula and colonial planning traditions are being called into question. Planning educators in Africa, Latin America, and South America are charting a course forward that rejects colonial traditions in favor of new approaches that reflect local culture and traditions; see, for example, Sletto (2012) on the Dominican Republic or Ondendaal (2012) on Africa. While not focused exclusively on studio, Frank and Silver (2018) present an excellent edited volume comparing urban planning education in countries including Korea, Estonia, Poland, and Bangladesh. In all of these countries, studio courses may have an important role to play as an instrument of a more context-responsive curriculum.

Conclusion

Over the past century, the role and influence of studio courses in US-based planning programs has diminished. Today, most planning students have to take a studio course to graduate, but typically only one. The average student spends about ten percent of his or her total program hours in a required studio, where the course is positioned as a capstone course in the second year, and students are able to choose among different topics to develop their specific interests. Meanwhile, more full-time faculty are teaching these required studio courses, which is good news because it can be argued that the attention of full-time academic faculty to studio teaching makes all the difference given their unique capacity to integrate both intellectual and practical concerns. Certainly the literature suggests that many innovations are coming from full-time faculty, although of course this is a premise based on self-selection: academics are far more likely to submit articles on educational topics to scholarly journals than are practitioner-instructors, and as a general rule submittals are borne of successes, rather than failures, in the classroom.

This history also informs the question of how much time planning students should spend in studio. Faculty constantly recalibrate course offerings to meet an ever-changing scope of subject matter, in concert with increasing demands from students for curricular flexibility. Without further study of the role of studio courses in contemporary planning programs, it is difficult to gauge whether one studio course is enough. Since ideally teachers would match the education required to the best means of delivering it, then thinking about the role of studios in more detail may lead to discovering a greater range of uses for studio. Historically, studio courses taught plan-making exclusively, but today, most students can choose from a range of studio topics that may or may not include plan-making. These offerings often align with program specializations and areas of concentrations, but there is evidence of experimentation in studio topic and format (e.g., the role of technology). Future research on studio pedagogy might examine the potential and challenges of expanding studio courses to accommodate subject areas beyond those traditionally associated with studios.

Notes

1 This essay is in part abridged from "The State of the Studio: Revisiting the Potential of Studio Pedagogy in US-based Planning Programs" (Long, 2012).
2 In 2009, the 15th edition of the ACSP *Guide to Undergraduate and Graduate Education in Urban and Regional Planning* included curriculum details from 89 of 120 PAB-accredited planning programs. (Not all programs choose to participate in the guide listings.) Of the graduate programs listed, 62 of 72 required a studio (84 percent). Only schools based in the U.S. were included in this study. In these programs, studio courses accounted for approximately 10 percent of total program hours, on average; the rough equivalent of one or two standard courses. In terms of intensity of studio requirements in individual programs, the range is wide: 38 programs require more than 10 percent of program hours spent in studio-type courses, 17 require 15 percent or more; seven require 20 percent or more; and four require 25 percent or more of total program hours in required studios. Only 16 percent of planning programs require no studio courses at all.
3 A limitation of this analysis is the absence of data on elective studios, largely because it is much harder to track these data across even a small sample of ten programs let alone the population of graduate programs in the U.S. Another is the relatively small sample of programs surveyed in detail in 2011, yet this too is

present in the preexisting longitudinal data provided by Heumann and Wetmore. Nonetheless, these ten programs continue to represent a fair cross section of planning programs, and the trends witnessed here are—at least anecdotally—in keeping with the experiences related to the author by colleagues during presentations of this paper at conferences.

References

Abramson, D. B. (2005). The "Studio Abroad" as a Mode of Transcultural Engagement in Urban Planning Education. *Journal of Planning Education and Research*, 25(1), 89–102. doi:10.1177/0739456x04271475

Adams, F. J. (1954). *Urban planning education in the United States*. Cinicinnati: Alfred Bettman Foundation.

Alizadeh, T., Tomerini, D., & Colbran, S. (2016). Teaching Planning Studios: An Online Assessment Task to Enhance the First Year Experience. *Journal of Planning Education and Research*, 37(2), 234–245. doi:10.1177/0739456x16647162

Anselin, L., Nasar, J. L., & Talen, E. (2011). Where Do Planners Belong? Assessing the Relationship between Planning and Design in American Universities. *Journal of Planning Education and Research*, 31(2), 196–207. doi:10.1177/0739456x11402356

Arefi, M., & Triantafillou, M. (2005). Reflections on the Pedagogy of Place in Planning and Urban Design. *Journal of Planning Education and Research*, 25(1), 75–88. doi:10.1177/0739456x04270195

Association of Collegiate Schools of Planning (ACSP). (2009). *Guide to Undergraduate and Graduate Education in Urban and Regional Planning*. Retrieved from www.acsp.org/resource/collection/6CFCF359-2FDA-4EA0-AEFA-D7901C55E19C/2014_20th_Edition_ACSP_Guide.pdf

Balassiano, K., & West, D. (2012). Seeking the Studio Experience Outside of the Studio Course. *Journal of Planning Education and Research*, 32(4), 465–475. doi:10.1177/0739456x12454458

Baldwin, C., & Rosier, J. (2017). Growing Future Planners: A Framework for Integrating Experiential Learning into Tertiary Planning Programs. *Journal of Planning Education and Research*, 37(1), 43–55. doi:10.1177/0739456x16634864

Baum, H. S. (1995). A Further Case for Practitioner Faculty. *Journal of Planning Education and Research*, 14(3), 214–216. doi:10.1177/0739456x9501400310

Baum, H. S. (1997). Teaching Practice. *Journal of Planning Education and Research*, 17(1), 21–29. doi:10.1177/0739456x9701700103

Birch, E. L. (2001). Practitioners and the Art of Planning. *Journal of Planning Education and Research*, 20(4), 407–422. doi:10.1177/0739456x0102000403

Chafee, R. (1977). Essays: The Architecture of the Ecole des Beaux-Arts. In A. Drexler (Ed.), *The Architecture of the Ecole des Beaux-Arts*. New York: Museum of Modern Art.

Chatterjee, J. (1986). ACSP Presidential Address. *Journal of Planning Education and Research*, Autumn, 3–8.

Christensen, K. S. (1993). Teaching Savvy. *Journal of Planning Education and Research*, 12(3), 202–212. doi:10.1177/0739456x9301200304

Dagenhart, R., & Sawicki, D. (1992). Architecture and Planning: The Divergence of Two Fields. *Journal of Planning Education and Research*, 12(1), 1–16. doi:10.1177/0739456x9201200102

Dalton, L. C. (2001). Weaving the Fabric of Planning as Education. *Journal of Planning Education and Research*, 20(4), 423–436. doi:10.1177/0739456x0102000404

Forester, J. (1983). The Coming Design Challenge. *Journal of Planning Education and Research*, 3(1), 57–59. doi:10.1177/0739456x8300300111

Forsyth, A., Lu, H., & McGirr, P. (2000). Service Learning in an Urban Context: Implications for Planning and Design Education. *Journal of Architectural and Planning Research*, 17(3), 236–259.

Frank, A. I. & Silver, C. (Eds.). (2018). *Urban Planning Education: Beginnings, Global Movement and Future Prospects*. Cham: Springer International Publishing.

Friedmann, J. (1996). The Core Curriculum in Planning Revisited. *Journal of Planning Education and Research*, 15(2), 89–104. doi:10.1177/0739456x9601500202

Grant, J., & Manuel, P. (1995). Using a Peer Resource Learning Model in Planning Education. *Journal of Planning Education and Research*, 15(1), 51–57. doi:10.1177/0739456x9501500104

Gurran, N., Norman, B., & Gleeson, B. (2008). *Planning Education Discussion Paper* (January). Canberra: Planning Institute of Australia.

Heumann, L. F., & Wetmore, L. B. (1984). A Partial History of Planning Workshops: The Experience of Ten Schools from 1955 to 1984. *Journal of Planning Education and Research*, 4(2), 120–130. doi:10.1177/0739456x8400400207

Higgins, M., Aitken-Rose, E., & Dixon, J. (2009). The Pedagogy of the Planning Studio: A View from Down Under. *Journal for Education in the Built Environment*, 4(1), 8–30. doi:10.11120/jebe.2009.04010008

Higgins, M., & Morgan, J. (2000). The Role of Creativity in Planning: The "Creative Practitioner". *Planning Practice and Research*, 15(1–2), 117–127. doi:10.1080/713691881

Hou, L. (2018). Six Decades of Planning Education in China: Those Planned and Unplanned. In *Urban Planning Education* (pp. 81–99). Cham: Springer International Publishing.

Hoyt, L. M. (2005). A Core Commitment to Service-Learning: Bridging Theory and Practice. In M. C. Hardin, R. Eribes, & C. C. Poster (Eds.), *From the Studio to the Streets: Service-Learning in Planning and Architecture* (pp. 17–32). Sterling, VA: Stylus Publishing.

Jacobs, A. B. (1983). Thoughts on City Planning Practice and Education When No One Loves Us. *Journal of Planning Education and Research*, 3(1), 60. doi:10.1177/0739456x8300300112

Klopp, J., Chanin, J., Ngau, P., & Sclar, E. (2014). Globalisation and the Urban Studio: Evaluating an Inter-University Studio Collaboration in Nairobi. *International Development Planning Review*, 36(2), 205–226. doi:10.3828/idpr.2014.13

Kotval, Z. (2003). Teaching Experiential Learning in the Urban Planning Curriculum. *Journal of Geography in Higher Education*, 27(3), 297–308. doi:10.1080/0309826032000145061

Kranthi, N., & Valliappan, A. L. (2016). Need for a Shift in Pedagogy for Teaching Fundamentals of Planning Education. In *Urban and Regional Planning Education* (pp. 107–114). Springer Singapore.

Kreditor, A. (1990). The Neglect of Urban Design in the American Academic Succession. *Journal of Planning Education and Research*, 9(3), 155–163. doi:10.1177/0739456x9000900301

Lang, J. (1983). Teaching Planning to City Planning Students. An Argument for the Studio/Workshop Approach. *Journal of Planning Education and Research*, 2(2), 122–129. doi:10.1177/0739456x8300200208

Levkoe, C. Z., Friendly, A., & Daniere, A. (2018). Community Service-Learning in Graduate Planning Education. *Journal of Planning Education and Research*. doi:10.1177/0739456x18754318

Long, J. G. (2012). State of the Studio. *Journal of Planning Education and Research*, 32(4), 431–448. doi:10.1177/0739456x12457685

Nemeth, J., & Long, J. G. (2012). Assessing Learning Outcomes in U.S. Planning Studio Courses. *Journal of Planning Education and Research*, 32(4), 476–490. doi:10.1177/0739456x12453740

Odendaal, N. (2012). Reality Check: Planning Education in the African Urban Century. *Cities*, 29(3), 174–182. doi:10.1016/j.cities.2011.10.001

Perloff, H. S. (1957). *Education for Planning: City, State, and Regional*. Baltimore, MD: Johns Hopkins University Press.

Porter, L. et al. (2015). Partnerships of learning for planning education: Who is learning what from whom? *Planning Theory & Practice*, 16(3), 409–434. doi:10.1080/14649357.2015.1060688

Sletto, B. (2010). Educating Reflective Practitioners: Learning to Embrace the Unexpected through Service Learning. *Journal of Planning Education and Research*, 29(4), 403–415. doi:10.1177/0739456x10362771

Sletto, B. (2012). Insurgent Planning and Its Interlocutors. *Journal of Planning Education and Research*, 33(2), 228–240. doi:10.1177/0739456x12467375

Thomas, D., & Hollander, J. B. (2010). The City at Play: Second Life and the Virtual Urban Planning Studio. *Learning, Media and Technology*, 35(2), 227–242. doi:10.1080/17439884.2010.494433

Wachs, M. (1994). Comments. *Journal of Planning Education and Research*, 13(4), 290–296. doi:10.1177/0739456x9401300406

9
GENDER

Dory Reeves

Introduction

This chapter examines how the topic of gender is dealt with in the education of planners in the US, UK (England, Scotland, Wales and Northern Ireland), Australia and Aotearoa New Zealand, with an emphasis on course content.

Planning has a responsibility to ensure that, as both a discipline and a profession, it plays its role in bringing about gender equality. Research in the field of urban planning has demonstrated that there is a positive relationship between the spatial planning and design of cities and gender equality (UN-Habitat, 2009) and "that sex and gender bias can be socially harmful and expensive" (Schiebinger et al., 2011–2015, cited in Reeves & Zombori, 2016).

The Women and Aging Survey sponsored by the American Planning Association (APA) (Micklow, Kancilia & Warner, 2015) shows that planning programmes in the US are giving more attention to planning for aging than planning for women. While academic scholarship has been aware of the differing needs of women, planning practice has been slow to respond. We know from the research that conventional forms of land use regulation limit employment opportunities for women and as a result inhibit gender equality and women's empowerment.

The Sustainable Development Goals (SDGs) and the New Urban Agenda, agreed upon at Habitat III in October 2016 (UN, 2016) underline the gendered nature of environments, governance, the resources allocated and the need for this to be fully understood if society is to tackle gender inequality and achieve women's empowerment. The Huairou Commission, which came out of the 4th World Conference on Women in Beijing in 1995 and which focuses on "grassroots women leaders" in policy-making, has been instrumental in ensuring that the New Urban Agenda has a strong emphasis on women and gender equality.

The unanimous ratification of the SDGs by the United Nations (UN) on 25 September 2015 (UN, 2015), including Goal 5 (gender equality and empowerment of women and girls) and Goal 11 (inclusive, safe, resilient and sustainable cities and human settlements) has ensured that gender equality will remain on the global agenda.

Structure

The chapter provides an overview of the accreditation guidelines as they relate to gender in each of the geographic areas. It then introduces some examples of how gender is taught before concluding with an assessment of how planning programmes need to look to the future. Appendix 1 contains acknowledgments of scholars whose observations contributed to this chapter; Appendix 2 provides a timeline of landmark events in the incorporation of gender studies into planning; and Appendix 3 is a list of key readings.

Pedagogy, Core, and Specialisms

The chapter sits within the pedagogy section. Students specialize in an aspect of planning when they have covered the basics in the core curricula. It is therefore assumed that an up-to-date programme would include as part of its core an introduction to the importance of understanding planning from a gender perspective, as well as awareness of: the limitations of the traditional history of planning; feminist critiques of planning; the shifts that result from approaching planning through a gender-focused lens; and the implications of non-binary approaches to gender on planning practices.

The role of a gender and planning specialization is to build on the core courses and provide a base level of expertise to enable students of planning to gain an understanding of gender and planning so that they can appreciate how to further develop their expertise and engage the services of an expert where appropriate. Hoard (2015) defines the expert as someone with an "understanding regarding the cause and effect relationship between policies, actions and or activities and gender inequalities and who has been formally requested to provide his or her knowledge and services" (Hoard, 2015, 168). A specialization is one of many components of the overall curricula. However if gender bias and discrimination is not tackled throughout the curricula then the impact of a gender specialization will be limited. Initiatives such as the UK's Athena SWAN Charter have helped universities approach gender equality more holistically, in terms of the representation of women and men, progression of students into academia, journey through career milestones and working environment for all staff (Equality Challenge Unit, ECU, 2016).

The APA recognizes that conventional forms of land use regulation constrain mobility and limit employment opportunities for women, reinforce outdated family structures as the norm and provide inadequate support systems (Micklow et al., 2015). Today gender specialists agree that a consideration of gender should be mainstreamed or integrated into every aspect of planning education in addition to having a gender specialization. Gender needs to be taught as a core topic and then offered as a specialization. A gender specialization on its own will further marginalize and side stream a consideration of gender equality and women's empowerment.

If a reason for the integration of gender in education across the built and natural environment professions was needed, one need look no further than the record of the full hearing for the Restroom Gender Parity in Federal Buildings Act, in Washington, D.C. (Committee of Oversight and Reform, 2010). In her presentation, Professor Kathryn Anthony stated:

> Much of our built environment—including that owned by the federal government—was constructed in a different era, one where women were not as prevalent in the public realm and in the workforce as we are today. Until recently, most architects, contractors, engineers, building code officials, and clients were not concerned about this issue. They rarely contacted women about their restroom needs, women were rarely employed in these male-dominated professions, nor were they in a position to effect change.
>
> *(Anthony, 2010)*

Sources of Information

Each geographic area has a different means of recording gender education in planning. In the US, the American *Guide to Graduate and Undergraduate Education in Urban and Regional Planning* is an invaluable record and source (Association of Collegiate Schools of Planning, ACSP, 2016). In the UK, the Royal Town Planning Institute (RTPI) online resource on research in planning schools provides some information on research but not teaching (RTPI, 2016). Neither the Planning Institute of Australia (PIA) or the New Zealand Planning Institute (NZPI) maintains a record of research and teaching of faculty. The chapter draws on the academic literature, the websites of the professional institutes; and interviews and email correspondence with teachers of gender and planning, acknowledged in Appendix 1.

Global Context

According to the most recent global survey of planning education, published in 2009, 550 universities worldwide offered urban planning degrees, with more than half located in just ten countries (Stiftel et al., 2008). Unfortunately, this study has failed to collect information on which programmes teach gender and planning. In 2014 a large-scale study of planners in the US revealed that many planners do not know what it means to plan for women and this indicates that they may be insufficiently prepared for the profession. By contrast, we do know that 35 per cent of programmes worldwide taught social equity (Micklow et al., 2015).

We also have an indication that the level of understanding of gender issues amongst graduates needs to be higher. In a recent study of what makes early career planning professionals effective, Reeves (2016a) asked managers and early career planners to what extent an understanding of and ability to address gender equality and women's empowerment makes early career planners effective. The results revealed that managers ranked this profession specific attribute higher than did early career planners and could see its relevance. Related to this, membership studies carried out by the professional institutes show that planning has a better gender balance than the other built environment professions such as engineering and architecture but, at senior and decision-making levels, there is still a gender imbalance.

Current Guidelines—Where Does Gender Fit?

United States

Gender equity is not mentioned explicitly as a required element of courses in the US or as part of the aspirational principles in the code of ethics and professional conduct of the American Institute of Certified Planners (AICP, 2016).

Despite diversity, equality and inclusivity being recognized as essential to planning, we are seeing a decline in the number of faculty qualified in this area. In 2000, 87 faculty members (13 per cent), both male and female, affiliated to 46 programs or schools identified gender studies as part of their research or teaching (ACSP, 2000). Fourteen years later, out of the 73 universities running accredited planning programmes in the 2014 edition of the *Guide to Graduate and Undergraduate Education in Urban and Regional Planning*, only 28 faculty members were listed (both male and female) in 19 institutions, researching or teaching gender (ACSP, 2014). Table 9.1 lists the 19 ACSP-accredited institutions currently offering a specialization that explicitly references gender issues.

Table 9.1 ACSP-Accredited Institutions Offering a Specialization that Explicitly References Gender

University Name	Specialization
Arizona State University	Gender studies and planning
Cornell University	Gender (professor emerita)
California Polytechnic State University	Gender
Cal State-Northridge	Housing and gender in planning
Florida State University	Gender and the city
Harvard University	Gender and planning
Miami University, Ohio	Gender and sexuality
Pratt Institute (New York)	Gender and planning
Rutgers, The State University of New Jersey	Gender issues in Africa; Race gender and class in planning: Social, family and gender policies
State University of New York (SUNY) Albany	Gender studies
University of Buffalo SUNY	Race, class and gender
University of California, Berkeley	Gender studies and planning
University of Illinois (UI) at Chicago	Gender and planning; Gender studies and planning
UI at Urbana-Champaign	Gender issues in international planning
University of Massachusetts-Amherst	Ethnicity, race, gender and class in planning
University of New Mexico	Gender and planning
University of Southern Maine	Race and gender
University of Virginia	Gender studies and planning
Wayne State University	Gender studies and planning

On checking the institutional web pages of the 28 faculty members, only half teach courses to undergraduate or postgraduate students. Some are Professor Emerita and many research as opposed to teach in the topic of gender.

In terms of the broader curricula, the pool of women available for tenured positions has steadily increased. Many attribute part of this success to the APA Planning and Women Division, founded by Jacqueline Leavitt in 1979. Following on from this in the 1990s, the Faculty Women's Interest Group (FWIG) affiliated to the ACSP held a series of significant workshop events before the ACSP conferences. These were organized by Nancey Green Leigh, who invited Catherine Ross and Sandi Rosenbloom to discuss issues of the day. APA surveys have shown an increase in the percentage of women members over the past 30 years, although there has been little change in membership among non-white planners, whether male or female. The Sloane Report (2013) on Undergraduate Education in Urban Planning drew attention to the gender imbalance in the student population. Teaching about gender makes planning more relevant and should encourage more women into planning, and yet the study made no reference to the lack of gender in the course content.

A 2014 US study found that planners in general are more likely to plan for aging than for women and since women live longer than men, attention to aging can indirectly increase sensitivity to gender. Thus, planning for aging provides planners with an agenda to move toward more gender-sensitive planning (Micklow et al., 2015).

In a discussion at the genderSTE (2016) conference in Madrid, followed by email communication, Professor of Planning, Ayse Yonder provided an example for examining gender by describing the programme at the Pratt Institute in New York. Gender issues are introduced in year 1 of the planning programme, through a seminar and studio course teaching the fundamentals of planning. Her teaching is informed by activist work with grassroots women's organizations, including the National Congress of Neighbourhood Women which links to the international network of grassroots organizations—the Huairou Commission (2017). The seminar- and studio-based course provides a broad overview of planning practice today within its political context, with special attention to community-based and participatory planning and planning for sustainable development. The topics covered in the seminar include land use planning and zoning, environment and open space, economic development, transportation, housing, infrastructure and municipal services, preservation planning, and inter-governmental relations. The studio helps students relate the readings to practice, working for a community organization on a current planning issue identified by the client. This "learning-by-doing" approach also seeks to encourage collaborative teamwork. An example is the exploration of challenges and opportunities involved in the legalization of basement dwelling units in Jackson Heights (Yonder, Narciso, Osorio, 2017).

United Kingdom

Women make up only 36 per cent of Chartered Members and 35 per cent of all members of the RTPI, although the institute reported that nearly half of all new members in 2015 were women (RTPI, 2016). Using the RTPI's own figures, the percentage of women members increased by just 8 per cent in the last 16 years. In 1993 women made up 18 per cent of corporate members; by 2000 this had increased to 28 per cent and by 2016 it was 36 per cent (Table 9.2).

A key concern amongst some senior female academics contributing to this chapter is that gender will not have the coverage that it does now when the current generation of teachers retires. The recognition that gender must form a core part of the curricula will ensure that this issue is addressed. Emerita Professor Clara Greed, a recognized expert in the field of gender and planning, concluded in 2014 that the situation varies widely and the delivery of gender and planning is not even and consistent (Greed and Johnson, 2014).

There are examples of gender being taught as part of electives. For instance, email correspondence with Professor Emerita Marion Roberts, University of Westminster, in October 2016 confirmed that she teaches gender issues in an elective course entitled Public Realm. This encourages thought about gender issues in the design project, which takes up half the module's assessment. Other examples of teaching practice which all programmes would benefit from also come from the University of Westminster. In email correspondence, both Dr. Suzy Nelson and Professor Johan Woltjer stated that the Master's in Urban and Regional Planning (MAURP) covers social planning/social inclusion/social sustainability in Planning Theory and Practice 1 and 2 and throughout the MAURP course. Gender is specifically covered in the Master's course Planning Theory and Practice 2 where the focus is on the infrastructure for everyday life.

At Heriot Watt University in Scotland, planning courses which cover gender issues are led by academics of both sexes and addressed either as a specific topic, throughout the course

Table 9.2 Women Corporate Members of the RTPI, 1993–2016

Year	Percentage of women corporate members	Average annual increase
1993	18	
2000	28	10% over 7 years
2016	36	8% over 16 years

Source: RTPI

or, as in the case of the Sustainable Design, in relation to "the protected characteristics" of women as covered in UK equalities and human rights legislation. In the Planning Theories course, while one class is specifically dedicated to feminist perspectives and the city, students are encouraged to use feminist and other theories in critiquing city planning/development throughout the course. Students explore what a feminist perspective is, whether gender is a fundamental axis of urban analysis, whether women as a group have different perceptions of and experiences in the city from men, feminist perspectives on the city, gendered cities and how gendered spaces are produced and reproduced. Both undergraduate and postgraduate variants of the Governance and Participation module look at the impact of traditional systems of patriarchy in the built environment, how the planning system can discriminate against women, the role of equalities and human rights legislation and gender mainstreaming in countering this and intersectionality. Links are made to the Athena SWAN initiative in the School, which promotes gender equality among students and staff. Another module, Social Sustainability covers gender and performativity, gendered spaces, gender and the city, feminist theory, and intersectionality. In the Technical Networks course, gender issues are covered through the application of planning theories around city networks, and highlight the lack of representation of women as scientists or artists in the naming of those systems as well as through approaches which go beyond gender dichotomies in planning. In postgraduate Urban Design Theory, the student-led presentations and seminars include Dolores Hayden's (1984) *Redesigning the American Dream* as one of the set readings in the introductory Property Development and Planning course. The female academic leading the course addresses gender issues by including male and female authors, figures and guest speakers in all of her classes and as part of equality and diversity issues (Netto, 2017).

Australia

The accreditation policy for Australian Planning Schools was updated in 2015 (PIA, 2015) and September 2016 (PIA, 2016a). Six main areas of "supportive" knowledge are highlighted including social. Performance indicators include: "Recognition of social and cultural diversity and the capacity to assess the equity, health and social inclusion aspects of urban and regional plans and practices" (PIA, 2016a, 26). Under professional and ethical practice, the following performance indicator makes reference to children and older people but not women: "Knowledge of the diversity of populations served, including the cultures of ethnic groups in Australia, other groups with special needs, including children and older people, and a capacity to engage meaningfully with diverse groups" (PIA, 2016a, 13).

The code of ethics does refer to gender and members are required to "Uphold and promote the elimination of discrimination on the grounds of race, creed, gender, age, location, social status or disability" (PIA, 2014).

Where gender is taught it is integrated into the programmes in both core and specializations. For example, at Southern Cross University, gender is integrated into discussions in lectures, workshops and studios across various units. In email correspondence, Dr. Ruth Potts from Southern Cross stated that she is not aware of any university that teaches gender studies in planning explicitly, but has observed discussions of gender, race and religion issues in planning more broadly in university programmes and this enables students to reflect on gender/race/religious issues in a variety of contexts. For example, in the Urban Design unit the discussion centred around how urban design can be inclusive or exclusive and what this means for different groups in society, including women, indigenous communities, and those from different religions. Where planning is co-taught with geography, there appears to be more likelihood that gender is covered.

New Zealand

In New Zealand there are five programmes accredited by the NZPI at the Universities of Auckland, Lincoln, Massey, Otago and Waikato. The NZPI Constitution states that: "A planner shall ensure that special attention is paid to the interrelatedness of decisions and the environment, social, cultural and economic consequences of planning actions" (NZPI, 2015). That's the closest you'll get to a reference to gender. The Tertiary Education and Accreditation Procedures (NZPI, 2016) replaced the previous version (NZPI, 2011) and set out what accredited planning programmes must address. Social equity is used as a catch all phrase. Gender equality is not mentioned explicitly, nor is age or disability. For instance, under planning methods, programmes need to demonstrate that they cover:

> analysing and managing the built and natural environment through techniques and tools for environmental evaluation, impact assessment and urban design; policy development and analysis; planning and monitoring systems; principles of sustainability; and planning for a multi-ethnic, multicultural society and social equity.
>
> *(NZPI, 2016, 8).*

Under contextual issues, graduates must have an "understanding of a range of socio economic and equity issues" (NZPI, 2016, 9). A conclusion amongst teachers with an interest in gender in New Zealand is that it has been edged out of the planning programmes; that it should be a core feature of programmes and should be more of a priority in the NZPI guidelines.

Auckland University did have a long-standing core course, Gender and Ethics, run by Tricia Austin, which was discontinued in the last review in 2014 on the expectation that gender issues would be integrated into all aspects of the programmes. Examples are the new core courses at postgraduate and undergraduate level on Social Theories and Planning which incorporate gender. Each of the two assignments involves investigating an issue using a different lens, including gender (Reeves, 2016b).

Correspondence with Emma Fergusson (2016) established that at Massey University gender and planning is not a specific focus, although it is integrated into a number of papers and consideration is being given to developing new material for a future course which will have more of a focus on gender.

In an email Associate Professor Hamish Rennie (2016) stated that the planning programme at Waikato University, where he started his career, comes from a strong social geography focus and is noted for its emphasis on feminist planning and gender issues both masculinist and feminist. The planning programme at Lincoln University is recognized as having a more traditional land based and environmental management focus and the idea that there are gendered perspectives and practices in everything is perhaps acknowledged but not emphasized.

Correspondence and conversations with Professor Claire Freeman at Otago University established that the focus in their one year postgraduate planning programme is on social justice and difference with a different "identity group" highlighted each year. As a consequence gender is not a consistent part of the curricula.

Networks

In addition to professional bodies that accredit planning programmes and establish guidelines for the teaching or coverage of gender equality issues, Universities offering planning programmes also connect through networks such as the Global Planning Education Association Network

(GPEAN), Association of Collegiate Schools of Planning (ACSP) or the Australia and New Zealand Association of Planning Schools (ANZAPS).

The GPEAN Shanghai Statement confirmed that GPEAN was set up to improve the quality and visibility of planning education but makes no reference to the content of planning education or the way in which it should be delivered and so omits any reference to gender and gender equality (GPEAN, 2001).

Most planning Schools in the US belong to the ACSP and women faculty have a support group called the Faculty Women's Interest Group (FWIG, 2017). In the UK, the Women in Planning group, led by Charlotte Morphet, is active and an associated grass roots organisation for architecture/art activists called Urbanistas (2016) provides support.

In Australia, there is an active Women's Planning Network which tends to focus more on women in the profession (PIA, 2016b). In New Zealand a new organisation Women in Urbanism brings together practitioners and users of the city who want to make cities more gender sensitive (Women in Urbanism, 2017).

The Association of European Schools of Planning (AESOP) charter, which dates back to 1995 and sets out the requirements for a high quality European planning education, mentions society but not equality, gender or any other sectoral grouping. AESOP's core requirements for a quality planning education also date back to 1995 and are still used to assess applicants for full membership. The following knowledge requirement and the overall lack of gender neutral language dates the document, undermining its overall credibility: "... developments in the natural and man-made (economic and social) environment and knowledge of the impact of men's exploitation, i.e. possibilities for sustainable development" (AESOP, 1995).

AESOP is organized into Thematic Groups, and although there is not a specific gender group, the Ethics, Values & Planning group held its first seminar in February 2016: "New Spaces of Inequality", which discussed economic, social, formal and substantive issues "up to gender and intergenerational inequality—and in the context of the contemporary European city". To what extent does urban inequality constitute a moral problem; when does it become a concern for urban policies and governance and how do we qualify, investigate and tackle the inequalities relevant to urban planning? (Bastiaanssen, 2015).

Conclusion: Why an Explicit Consideration of Gender Is Needed in Planning Education

This review of gender and planning provides a basis for a continuing conversation, which all planning programmes need to have, about where and how to place a consideration of gender within the taught curricula. This is particularly the case given Habitat III, the New Urban Agenda, and the prominence of gender in the agenda. The evidence shows that the topic of gender and planning is too reliant on individuals and when these individuals move on or retire, the concern is that this part of the curricula becomes a void. The most recent reviews of planning education by the accrediting bodies in the US, UK, Australia and New Zealand, have reinforced the generic language of social equity which means that gender is no longer explicit. There appears to have been a decline in the explicit mention of gender and feminism in planning education and we cannot infer from this that it has been appropriately integrated into the curricula.

Planning programmes need to integrate gender in its broadest sense into the entire planning curricula. Gender needs to be integrated into the core curricula and specializations should then be developed from the core. All planners need to understand how the decisions they will make in practice affect gender equality and women's empowerment. Acknowledging Petra Doan's comment that the "Heterosexist bias runs deep within the field of planning and is interwoven in many of its basic assumptions" (Doan, 2011), educators supported by professional institutes need to equip the next generation of professionals to work with grass roots groups effectively.

We need planners who understand the equity gap and the gendered nature of the gap and how to address it through planning and other legislation as well as through non-statutory advocacy approaches. We need professionals who know what genuine participative approaches to planning look like and how to bring them about by working with grassroots groups.

A consideration of gender should be mainstreamed and integrated into every aspect of planning education as well as being offered as a specialization. The curricula needs to acknowledge the non-binary gender world. Material needs to be introduced early in the programme; be integrated, so that students see the connection between gender equality, theory and practice; involve links with locally based groups; and finally, involve learning by doing. A gender specialization on its own is welcome but not sufficient.

References

American Institute of Certified Planners (AICP). (2016, April 1). Code of Ethics and Professional Conduct. Retrieved from www.planning.org/ethics/ethicscode.htm

Anthony, K. (2010). *Presentation to Committee of Oversight for the Restroom Gender Parity in Federal Buildings Act*. Washington, D.C. Retrieved from http://oversight.house.gov/hearing/h-r-4869-the-restroom-gender-parity-in-federal-buildings-act.

Association of Collegiate Schools of Planning (ACSP). (2000). *Guide to Undergraduate and Graduate Education in Urban and Regional Planning*. Retrieved from www.acsp.org/resource/collection/6CFCF359-2FDA-4EA0-AEFA-D7901C55E19C/2014_20th_Edition_ACSP_Guide.pdf

Association of Collegiate Schools of Planning (ACSP). (2014). *Guide to Undergraduate and Graduate Education in Urban and Regional Planning*. Retrieved from www.acsp.org/resource/collection/6CFCF359-2FDA-4EA0-AEFA-D7901C55E19C/2014_20th_Edition_ACSP_Guide.pdf

Association of Collegiate Schools of Planning (ACSP). (2016). *Guide to Undergraduate and Graduate Education in Urban and Regional Planning*. Retrieved from www.acsp.org/resource/collection/6CFCF359-2FDA-4EA0-AEFA-D7901C55E19C/2014_20th_Edition_ACSP_Guide.pdf

Association of European Schools of Planning (AESOP). (1995). Charter. Retrieved from www.aesop-planning.eu/en_GB/core-curriculum

Australia and New Zealand Association of Planning Schools (ANZAPS). (2016). Home Page. Retrieved from http://anzaps.net

Bastiaanssen, J. (2015). New Spaces of In-Equality. Aesop Thematic Group: Ethics, Values and Planning, Aesop. Retrieved from www.aesop-planning.eu/blogs/posts/en_GB/research-ethics-in-planning/2015/12/16/readabout/seminar-new-spaces-of-inequality

Doan, P. L. (2011). Queerying Identity: Planning and the Tyranny of Gender. In P. L. Doan (Ed.), *Queerying Planning: Challenging Heteronormative Assumptions and Reframing Planning Practice* (pp. 89–106). London: Routledge.

Equality Challenge Unit (ECU). (2016). ECU Athena Swan Charter. Retrieved from www.ecu.ac.uk/equality-charters/athena-swan

Faculty Women's Interest Group (FWIG). (2017). Home. Retrieved from www.fwig.org

Fergusson, E. (2016, October 12). Personal correspondence.

Freeman, C. (2016). Personal correspondence.

genderSTE. (2016, October). Paper presented at the Engendering Habitat III, Madrid.

Global Planning Education Association Network (GPEAN). (2001, July 14). Shanghai Statement. Retrieved from www.gpean.org/inner/shanghai.htm

Gorman-Murray, A. (2011). Queerying Planning in Australia: The Problems and Possibilities of Multiscalar Governance fFor LGBT Minorities. In P. L. Doan (Ed.), *Queerying Planning: Challenging Heteronormative Assumptions and Reframing Planning Practice* (pp. 129–144). Farnham: Routledge.

Greed, C., & Johnson, D. (2014). *Planning in the UK: An Introduction*. London: Palgrave Macmillan.

Huairou Commission. (2017). Home Page. Retrieved from http://huairou.org

Hayden, D. (1984). *Redesigning the American Dream*. New Haven, Connecticut: Yale University Press.
Hoard, S. (2015). *Gender Expertise in Public Policy: Towards a Theory of Policy Success*. Basingstoke: Palgrave Macmillan UK.
Micklow, A., Kancilia, E., & Warner, M. (2015). *The Need to Plan for Women*. Retrieved from https://planning-org-uploaded-media.s3.amazonaws.com/legacy_resources/divisions/planningandwomen/pdf/nov2015issuebrief.pdf
National Congress of Neighborhood Women. Home Page. Retrieved from http://neighborhoodwomen.org/national-congress-of-neighborhood-women
Nelson, S. & Woltjer, J. (2016). Personal correspondence.
Netto, G. (2017). Personal communication.
New Zealand Planning Institute (NZPI). (2011). *Education Policy and Accreditation Procedures*. Auckland: NZPI.
New Zealand Planning Institute (NZPI). (2015). *Constitution*. Retrieved from www.planning.org.nz/Attachment?Action=Download&Attachment_id=3715
New Zealand Planning Institute (NZPI). (2016). *Learning for a Better Future*. Retrieved from www.planning.org.nz/Attachment?Action=Download&Attachment_id=1872
Parker, B. (2012). Gender, Cities and Planning. In R. Weber & R. Crane (Eds.), *The Oxford Handbook of Urban Planning* (pp. 609–633). Oxford: Oxford University Press.
Planning Institute of Australia (PIA). (2014). Code of Ethics and Professional Conduct. Retrieved from www.planning.org.au/oldmembershipinformation/code-of-conduct/code-of-conduct
Planning Institute of Australia (PIA). (2015). Accreditation policy for the recognition of Australian Planning Qualification.
Planning Institute of Australia (PIA). (2016a, September 29). Accreditation policy for the recognition of Australian Planning Qualification. Retrieved from www.planning.org.au/becomeaplanner/course-accreditation-process
Planning Institute of Australia (PIA). (2016b). Women's Planning Network. Retrieved from www.planning.org.au/viccontent/womens-planning-network-2
Potts, R. (2016). Personal correspondence.
Queensland Government. (2009). *Gender Analysis Toolkit parts 1–3*. Retrieved from www.communities.qld.gov.au/communityservices/women/about-office-women/gender-analysis/gender-analysis-toolkit-resource
Reeves, D. (2016a). *Management Skills for Effective Planners*. London: Palgrave Macmillan.
Reeves, D. (2016b). Social Theory and Planning BUrbPlan Course. Auckland, New Zealand: University of Auckland.
Reeves, D., & Zombori, E. (2016). Engendering Cities: International Dimensions from Aotearoa, New Zealand. *Town Planning Review*, *87*(5), 567–587. doi:10.3828/tpr.2016.37
Rennie, H. (2016). Personal correspondence.
Royal Town Planning Institute (RTPI). (2016). Planning Schools Research Directory. Retrieved from www.rtpi.org.uk/knowledge/research/planning-research-exchange/planning-schools-research-directory/
Schiebinger et al. (2011). What Is Gendered Innovations? European Union & Stanford University. Retrieved from http://genderedinnovations.stanford.edu/what-is-gendered-innovations.html
Sloane Report (2013). Assessing the State of Undergraduate Education in Urban Planning, Report of the Undergraduate Task Force to the Association of Collegiate Schools of Planning, ACSP. Retrieved from http://c.ymcdn.com/sites/www.acsp.org/resource/resmgr/Docs/Initiatives/ACSP_Sloane_Rpt_2013.pdf?hhSearchTerms=%22Guide+to+Graduate+and+Undergraduate+Education+in+Urban+and+Regional+Planning%22
Stiftel, B., Forsyth, A., Dalton, L., & Steiner, F. (2008). Assessing Planning School Performance. *Journal of Planning Education and Research*, *28*(3), 323–335. doi:10.1177/0739456x08325174
UN-Habitat. (2009). *Planning Sustainable Cities: Global Report on Human Settlements*. Nairobi: UN-Habitat.
United Nations (UN). (2015). *2030 Agenda for Sustainable Development*. Retrieved from www.un.org/sustainabledevelopment/sustainable-development-goals/
United Nations (UN). (2016, October 17–20). *New Urban Agenda*. Paper presented at the United Nations Conference on Housing and Sustainable Urban Development (Habitat III), Quito, Ecuador.
Urbanistas. Home Page. Retrieved from http://urbanistasuk.wordpress.com/about-us
Women in Urbanism. (2017). Retrieved from http://twitter.com/womeninurbanism
Yonder, A., Narciso, M., & Osorio, J. (2017). *Pedagogy Built on Working with Communities: A First Semester Core Course at Pratt Institute in New York*. Paper presented at the AESOP Conference: Spaces of Dialog for Places of Dignity, Lisbon.

Appendix 1: Acknowledgements

US

Professor Ayse Yonder, Pratt Institute, New York

UK: England

Emerita Professor Clara Greed, University of the West of England
Dr. Suzy Nelson, University of Westminster
Prof Marion Roberts, University of Westminster
Johan Woltjet, University of Westminster

UK: Scotland

Dr. Gina Netto, Heriot Watt University

Australia

Dr. Caryl Bosman, Griffiths University
Dr. Ruth Potts, Southern Cross University

New Zealand

Professor Claire Freeman, Otago University
Emma Fergusson, Massey University
Associate Professor Hamish Rennie, Lincoln University

Appendix 2: Timeline of Events

Table 9.3 Timeline of Events

Dates	United States	United Kingdom	Australia	New Zealand
1900	First wave feminism emphasis on built environment	First wave feminism emphasis on housing		
	1909 First planning legislation enacted at state level	1909 First planning legislation; 1909 Liverpool University started first planning programme		
	1928 First planning course at Harvard	1918 Women could become planners as a result of the 1919 Sex Disqualification Act. However on marriage women had to give up their job until after 1945 when the marriage bar was lifted.	1928 First planning legislation	1926 First planning legislation

Dates	United States	United Kingdom	Australia	New Zealand
1950				
	1964 Civil Rights Act; 1972 The Equal Employment Opportunity Act; 1969 The Stonewall Rebellion			1968 Helen Tobin first women graduate
	Emergence of intersectional theory first applied to race *1970s emergence of planners for equal opportunities* 1979 Women and Planning division of APA held its first meeting		1984 Sex Discrimination Act	1970s women and planning network group called WANDS set up
	1980 Special issue of *Signs* on women, gender and the city 1980s Emergence of queer theory	1980s emergence of women and/in planning groups in England, Scotland, Wales and N. Ireland. 1982 Greater London Council women's committee published 'Changing Places'. 1980s RTPI published Planning for Choice and Equal Opportunities. 1983: First women and planning conference in Scotland.		
	1990s In addition to women, focus on gendered socio spatial issues 1990s also saw a focus on diversity 1990s The Faculty Women's Interest Group ran a series of annual workshops prior to the ACSP conferences on gender issues of the day, organized by Nancey Green Leigh.	1990s emergence of mainstreaming gender theory and practice 1992 RTPI required colleges to give particular attention to giving students an appreciation of equal opportunities and diversity issues. 1993 Human Rights Act; 1997 Article 2 Treaty of Amsterdam confirms equality between women and men		1993 Human Rights Act; 2001 Human Rights Amendment Act

(continued)

Table 9.3 (continued)

Dates	United States	United Kingdom	Australia	New Zealand
		1995: RTPI Practice Advice Note Planning for Women 1998 Northern Ireland Good Friday Agreement and Scotland Act – introduction of Equality Impact Assessments (EQIAs)		
2000	2001 Publication of *Progressive Planning* Special Issue on Queers and Planning	2005 ECU Athena SWAN Charter established for science in higher education		
	2002 First article to be published by *Journal of Planning Education and Research* with an explicit queer agenda: Michael Frisch entitled 'The heterosexist project of planning' 2010 Gays and Lesbians in Planning Division (GALIP) of the American Planning Association (APA)	2012 EU genderSTE Project launched 2015 extension of the ECU Athena SWAN Charter to the humanities and arts. Recognizes work undertaken to address gender equality broadly.	2010 The Local Government Amendment (Planning and Reporting) "recommended that particular groups" needs to be considered in the formulation of new strategic plans – and one of these is "people of diverse sexualities (NSWDLG 2009)." (cited in Gorman-Murray, 2011, p. 143)	
2016	Habitat III and the New Urban Agenda	Habitat III and the New Urban Agenda	Habitat III and the New Urban Agenda	Habitat III and the New Urban Agenda
2017				Women in Urbanism established in Auckland Aotearoa New Zealand

Appendix 3: Key Readings

Core Material

Brenda Parker's review in the *Oxford Handbook of Planning* provides one of the most comprehensive reviews of the scholarly literature on gender and planning. It is an invaluable source for those working in this area and is particularly useful when it comes to the history of planning (Parker, 2012).

Overviews

Fincher, R., & Iveson, K. (2008). *Planning and Diversity in the City: Redistribution, Recognition and Encounter.* Basingstroke: Palgrave Macmillan.

Greed, C. H. (2003). *Women and Planning: Creating Gendered Realities.* London: Taylor & Francis.

Parker, B. (2012). Gender, Cities and Planning. In R. Weber & R. Crane (Eds.), *The Oxford Handbook of Urban Planning* (pp. 609–633). Oxford: Oxford University Press.

Reeves, D. (2007). *Planning for Diversity: Policy and Planning in a World of Difference.* London: Routledge.

Toolkits

Blank Noise. Home. Retrieved from www.blanknoise.org

Col-lectiu Punt 6. (2015). *Women Working: Urban Assessment Guide from a Gender Perspective.* Retrieved from https://issuu.com/punt6/docs/ww_issuu_simple

genderSTE. (2016, October). Paper presented at the Engendering Habitat III, Madrid.

Phadke, S., Khan, S., & Ranade, S. (2011). *Why Loiter?: Women and Risk on Mumbai Streets.* Delhi: Penguin Books India.

Queensland Government. (2009). *Gender Analysis Toolkit Parts 1–3.* Retrieved from www.communities.qld.gov.au/communityservices/women/about-office-women/gender-analysis/gender-analysis-toolkit-resource

Royal Town Planning Institute (RTPI). (2003). *Gender Equality and Plan Making: The Gender Mainstreaming Toolkit.* Retrieved from www.rtpi.org.uk/media/6338/GenderEquality-PlanMaking.pdf

Simpson, J. (2009). *Everyone Belongs: A Toolkit for Intersectionality.* Retrieved from www.criaw-icref.ca/sites/criaw/files/Everyone_Belongs_e.pdf

Theory

Bondi, L. (2005). Gender and the Reality of Cities: Embodied Identities, Social Relations and Performativities. In Institute of Geography Online Paper Series. Retrieved from http://hdl.handle.net/1842/822

Bondi, L., & Rose, D. (2003). Constructing Gender, Constructing the Urban: A Review of Anglo-American Feminist Urban Geography. *Gender, Place & Culture, 10*(3), 229–245. doi:10.1080/0966369032000114000

Fainstein, S. S. (2005). Feminism and Planning: Theoretical Issues. In S. S. Fainstein & L. Servon (Eds.), *Gender and Planning: A Reader* (pp. 120–140). New Brunswick, New Jersey: Rutgers University Press.

Meller, H. (1990). Planning Theory and Women's Role in the City. *Urban History, 17*, 85–98. doi:10.1017/S096392680001436X

Roberts, M., & Sánchez de Madariaga, I. (Eds.). (2016). *Fair Shared Cities: The Impact of Gender Planning in Europe.* New York: Taylor & Francis.

Whitzman, C., Legacy, C., Andrew, C., Klodawsky, F., Shaw, M., & Viswanath, K. (Eds.). (2013). *Building Inclusive Cities: Women's Safety and the Right to the City.* London: Routledge.

Place-specific

Greed, C., & Johnson, D. (2014). *Planning in the UK: An Introduction.* London: Palgrave Macmillan.

Reeves, D., & Zombori, E. (2016). Engendering Cities: International Dimensions from Aotearoa, New Zealand. *Town Planning Review, 87*(5), 567–587. doi:10.3828/tpr.2016.37

UN-Habitat (2014) Gender and Urban Planning. Nairobi: UN-Habitat.

Intersectional Thought and Planning

Forsyth, A. (2011). Queerying Planning Practice: Understanding Non-Conformist Assumptions. In P. L. Doan (Ed.), *Queerying Planning: Challenging Heteronormative Assumptions and Reframing Planning Practice* (pp. 21–52). London: Routledge.

Frisch, M. (2002). Planning as a Heterosexist Project. *Journal of Planning Education and Research, 21*(3), 254–266. doi:10.1177/0739456x0202100303

Lauria, M., & Knopp, L. (1985). Toward an Analysis of the Role of Gay Communities in the Urban Renaissance. *Urban Geography, 6*(2), 152–169. doi:10.2747/0272-3638.6.2.152

Whitten, C., & Thompson, S. (2005). *When Cultures Collide: Planning for The Public Spatial Needs of Muslim Women in Sydney.* Paper presented at the State of Australian Cities National Conference.

PART 4

Planning Skills

10
WRITTEN, ORAL, AND GRAPHIC COMMUNICATION

Hemalata C. Dandekar

Planners need to be able to communicate fluently and effectively with a variety of audiences and be able to do so in written, oral, and graphic forms. They also need to understand the context in which the communication is to occur, and with whom, and judiciously select the form and content to best reach desired audiences. This communicative task has increased in complexity as technology has caused a proliferation of modes, styles, and forms of communications and expanded the venues in which it can occur. The proliferation of cellular phones, hand held devices, and other ways to connect, and the increased capacity of fiber optic infrastructure to receive and deliver messages and information around the world has greatly expanded communication possibilities and expectations in planning practice. The combination of increasing globalization of local economies and new communication technologies has meant that, even more so than in the past, planning practitioners must have excellent communication skills to reach desired constituency or community to gain input into and support for their plans. Communication skills are arguably the single most important skill planners need in practice (Forsyth, 2008; McLoughlin, 2012).

Although most experienced planning practitioners acknowledge that good communication skills are crucial to successful practice, most academic planning programs have traditionally given less weight to the art and the craft of honing good communication skills than to other "core" planning skills. This core has included the ability to systematically select and use quantitative and qualitative data, analyze it in three and four dimensions, and use it to frame policy and action in conformance with legal and codified processes of governance. This emphasis has deepened the profession's use of scientific and social sciences-based tools and made them standard practice. An emphasis on substantive skills, theory, and analytical tools to parse verifiable data has dominated core pedagogy in most planning schools and institutions—both those concerned primarily with training future practitioners and those offering doctoral degrees. More often than not, planning problems are formulated in academia through a lens developed within the social sciences, focusing on empirical research aimed at building theory.

But planning practice includes process, in consensus building, policy formulation, and promoting action through cost-effective practical testing and methods. In practice, planners' pragmatism and the need to achieve action and have impact has them select methods which glean from existing secondary sources, or if these are not available, depend on qualitative, observational primary sources and even anecdotal information (American Planning Association, 2018). Both collecting and disseminating information requires extremely good oral, written, and graphic communication skills. Important though the scientific, quantifiable sources of information are, when people and political considerations are involved at the heart of framing policy and exercising leadership, it is good communication skills that enable, influence, and impact policy decisions and actions. So, given that communication is not foregrounded in the academic training of planners, where does the planner learn the skills to do this critical task? From informal, anecdotal conversations with experienced planners it appears that although the skills of effective communication are recognized and greatly valued on the job, they are also mostly learned on the job.

Changing Environments for Planning Communication

In the past few decades the environment in which planning occurs and the issues which planning addresses have been transformed by forces that have emerged, to a greater or lesser degree, in planning systems around the world. These include:

1   The ubiquitous *growth of information technology*, which has placed unprecedented access to information and ability in the hands of more people. It has connected people and communities both proximate and remote. The capabilities, uses, and impacts of twenty-first century digital technologies have constantly evolved, decreased in cost, and reduced the friction of distance for more and more people. They have made remote places, spaces, customs, and practices familiar in local contexts. Knowledge and information about best practices, proclivities, and experiences in a global, societal, framework have given impacted communities more opportunities to scrutinize traditional local planning measures and their impacts.
2   The *increase in the diversity of resident populations*, a result of globalized, integrated economies and the migration of people across nation-states combined with the proliferation in use of social media which the internet has enabled, have revolutionized the awareness about planning and its impacts on a broader community. The way planners must ply their trade has had to change as their audiences have expanded and diversified. They have been required to expand their selection of tools with which to communicate, the language they use to communicate with, their written and graphic approaches, and the means with which to best reach out to different demographic groups and constituencies. For effective communication in these interactions they have had to internalize new sensitivities and approaches to deal with a population, differentiated as never before by articulated sensitivities of race, language, culture, ethnicity, sexual preference and often quite conscious of the politics of gendered and racialized spaces and places.
3   Just as information retrieval and dissemination has become easier, the new modes facilitating communications have made creating, adding, revising, and disseminating written, graphic, and oral communications far easier, but also *increased the potential for missteps and errors*. Thus on the one hand they have reduced the tyranny of time and space, but on the other they have made a planner's communicative task more difficult. Technology is enabling exchanges over great distance, across continents, to cities and rural places in remote corners of the world. Communication, critique, and discussion can occur seamlessly face-to-face on the web. Electronic mail and digital files can speed across space and communicate to large numbers of people, with the click of a mouse on a home computer in the middle of the night. But therein lies the paradox. With this ease and facility has come the vulnerability and potential to make equally quick, inadvertent, and far-reaching mistakes and errors in judgment, easy to amplify but difficult to erase.

4   The planning profession has acknowledged that successful planning practitioners leaven their analysis, grounded in technical rationality, with a communicative process that takes the pulse of the moment and the human social context (Center for Community Health and Development at the University of Kansas, 2017). It has *accepted the political context* in which a planner must be effective, and learned to acknowledge that planning occurs in politically charged contexts and that technical knowledge, to have the largest impact on the public good, must be interpreted and communicated with an acute awareness of this fact.

5   Another key element in evolving planning practice has been the acknowledgement that successful *practice must embrace the emotive, qualitative, and subjective understanding* of human relationships that influence decisions, and to recognize that consideration of these can transcend consideration of the more rational, systematic, and methodologically sound options that scientific methods have yielded. And therefore, to cede that at critical moments, voice-to-voice oral communication and personal face-to-face contacts are still essential and may be crucial to success. Good communication in planning involves rational substantive analysis, use of technically sophisticated gadgets, tools, and means of dissemination, but also an acute understanding and grasp of the qualitative, subjective, emotional, political, and economic aspects of the context and moment of decision.

6   In current planning practice *public input as a source of information* has become as central to planners, particularly in the public sector, as census information, secondary sources of information, and the inventory of physical context and structured surveys of attitudes and perceptions. In recognition of this, planners have embraced the techniques of conducting focus groups, visioning, hosting open houses and large public meetings, and sponsoring a variety of public input events in which communicating with, and collecting input from, community involves a range of techniques in written, oral, and graphic forms.

But even in this new age of limitless venues and technologies with which to connect and communicate, some of the basics of effective communication—in written, oral, or graphic form—remain constant. The requirements for effectiveness in planning communication continues to be the need to pay close attention to accuracy, detail, voice, style and form, timing, and process and also the need to be aware of audience, intent, and the strategic and political context. Without this attention, professional communication in planning has the potential to fall short of achieving the desired end of thoughtfully envisioned policy and action that shapes societal change for the public good.

Selecting and Learning Communications Methods

Effective planning practice requires the professional not just to integrate theory and analysis but to synchronize this with a planning process externally governed, generally political, and outside his or her control. In this endeavor the planner's ability to communicate views, analyses, and ideas convincingly and in a timely way is crucial to success. Sophisticated conceptual models and complex analytic skills alone are insufficient and at times counter-productive if they are not interpreted and presented to make them accessible to the audience. To be effective, the planner has to extrapolate the essentials and communicate them convincingly to the client and interested constituents as and when needed to sway decisions.

The planner has to decide what to communicate, and how, be it results of a survey or focus group, content analysis of local publications, site reconnaissance, interviews of key figures in the community, or findings from large public meetings. Making good choices from the wide range of available tools, techniques, and data sources and choosing the right mode to communicate them can make a significant difference to outcomes. Practical methods for researching, analyzing, and presenting planning problems and possible solutions are essential to successful practice, as are the skills needed for choosing the form oral, written, graphic or a combination, and effective means, indirect or face-to-face, to communicate them (Dandekar, 2003, 2019).

Oral Communication[1]

A planner needs to be able to speak effectively in many settings: working in large or small groups, conducting field interviews, participating as a consultant to a subcommittee, speaking to a city council or a public gathering. Having good oral communication skills enhances a planner's ability to inform, convince, or persuade. An oral presentation usually has a primary function or goal, which can include: to *inform* constituencies without an expectation of impact or action; to *actuate* and persuade an audience to take a particular action; or, to *convince* the audience to a particular point of view.

Improving oral communication skills is largely dependent on three components:

Preparation, which includes analysis of oneself as a speaker; the occasion for making an oral presentation; the purpose of the presentation; an analysis of the audience; making sure the message can be stated in the time allocated; the place where the speech is to be given; the mode of delivery; development of an outline; and advance familiarity with any visual aids.

Organization, which includes developing a substantive progression from introduction to discussion of the core issue(s) and to conclusions that underscore the key "takeaways" of the presentation.

Delivery, which includes paying attention to the use of voice, action, and gestures, and making eye contact so that the message is communicated directly to audience members. The speaker must project enthusiasm as appropriate to the subject, and find the right balance between accessibility and technical credibility.

A certain amount of mental, physical, and emotional stress is normal when speaking in public. Storey suggests some strategies for coping: outlining the talk but rehearsing it several times, to oneself or before a friend or colleague; arriving early to become familiar with the venue and getting to know other speakers on the program; making sure any audio-visual equipment is functioning properly. Breathing deeply before the talk or taking a brief brisk walk outside can help reduce muscle tension and calm nerves.

In preparing and delivering a speech or lecture, it is important to:

- Know the time allocation and keep to it. This includes being ready to take stock of the audience's reactions and change course if the audience appears to be distracted, tired, fidgety, or bored.
- Speak for no more than 60 or 70 percent of the allocated time, by noting a time line in your outline for various sections of the presentation and staying on that informal schedule. Practice the talk ahead of time using the outline, to test if time limits set for each part of the speech can be met, and add or delete material as necessary.
- Have some idea of the characteristics of the audience, including their educational level, familiarity with and position(s) on the topic being discussed, economic status and political views. Similarly, learn what you can about the size and age range of the audience, and their expectations for the speech.

Planners' oral communication is largely extemporaneous. However, careful preparation is essential for this seemingly more "informal" mode of delivery: generally a word or sentence outline helps to give structure to the content and helps to limit the amount of material to be presented in a given time. The extemporaneous style of speaking offers many advantages, including a direct connection with the audience with the use of voice and gestures, the ability to focus attention on the audience and maintaining good eye contact, and a more effective use of charts, drawings, maps, overhead projectors and other audio-visual material. It is also easier to make on-the-spot adjustments with ideas and words and respond to audience reactions.

On more formal occasions a planner may need to deliver a speech that is fully written out. Maintaining eye contact with both the text and the audience is difficult unless teleprompters are available. Gestures are also limited. But a manuscript speech may be essential in situations in which great accuracy is needed; when detailed, statistical data is required; or issues of legality are involved.

Effective oral communication is also enabled by appropriate body language that communicates ease and physical comfort. Effective body language attracts the attention of listeners and helps them maintain an interest in the speaker, rendering the oral communication more attractive and interesting, as well as enhancing the speaker's message. Energetic bodily action can help to make and underscore transitions within a speech, integrate the speech, and make the voice vigorous and alert.

Direct eye contact with the audience is the single most important element of an effective oral communication. If a speaker looks directly into the eyes of individuals in an audience, those people feel a greater interest in the speaker and want to continue to look at the speaker. This improves the chances of having the audience listen to and understand the speaker's message, while letting the speaker know whether the audience is attentive and receptive.

Similarly, visual aids can clarify and add to the speaker's intent. In addition, audiences generally pay more attention and retain more knowledge afterwards from an oral presentation with visual supplements. Handling and pointing to visual aids has the speaker moving about and helps develop poise and ease tension for both speaker and the audience. Charts, diagrams, maps, graphs, flip charts, overhead projectors, slides, PowerPoint presentations, and video recordings are some of the important aids that planners use. They are particularly useful in explaining difficult or technical subjects.

Two types of interactions that planners engage in require particular attention to primarily oral modes of communication, albeit in conjunction with and complemented by written and graphic modes. These involve communications when working in groups or teams and when leading public forums.

Communicating in Groups. Planners rarely work alone but often as members of teams of specialists with diverse professional backgrounds and varied experience. In facilitating group work as a leader, a planner asserts influence in setting the agenda to give a sense of direction, facilitating the setting of appropriate goals, assigning tasks, directing problem-solving, turning individual decisions into group decisions, clarifying options and the consequences of options, promoting informality, encouraging participation, overcoming group resistance, brainstorming, and prioritizing alternatives and options.

Communicating in Venues of Public Participation. Public participation is now a widely embraced means to achieve better-informed public policy which relates to community values in determining goals, objectives, and policies. It is challenging because often, at the early stages of a planning process, it can mean requesting input when no concrete alternatives or options exist. It requires the planner to exercise good listening and interpretative skills.

Participation by leaders of civic groups, lay community members potentially impacted by policy changes, and special-interest groups must be reached with appropriate forms of communication. These now include social media, online announcements, newsletters and mail (both digital and in paper form). Depending on the audience the message may need to be translated into multiple languages. In garnering this participation the planner must skillfully present information in oral and written form, illustrated clearly with graphs and charts that are uncluttered, visually attractive, and decipherable by someone with no formal training. Finally, the message must be sensitive and tailored to the audience that is the focus of the communication.

Written Communication[2]

Writing is a primary means of communication and record keeping, used to inform, query, and persuade the many players in the planning process. As in oral communication, clarity regarding the audience to be addressed is a key consideration in framing any and all forms of written communication. The intent of the communication, to inform, query, or persuade, also needs to be clearly understood. Before writing a communication a planner needs to understand the *purpose* and the *audience*; determine the *tone*, the *format*, and the *length*; determine if *graphic illustrations, data tables or graphs* are needed; and assess the *completeness* and *accuracy* of information available and the statements that can be based on them, as well as the *style* and *language* to be used. And each written communication needs to be correct in terms of *grammar, spelling*, and *word usage*.

What constitutes good writing varies greatly in different contexts. The most universal and ubiquitous forms of written communications that planners use are described here.

Memos and Letters. Generally a communication within an organization takes the form of a memo, while a letter is generally used as communication from a member of the organization to an outsider. Memos and letters have distinct and different forms of address, closure, and signature, which are largely matters of convention. The format, language, and style are all part of the total effect and effectiveness of memos and letters. The body of the memo is organized like any good document, with an *introduction* (perhaps some history of the issue), a main section with a *discussion* of the issue, and a concluding sentence or paragraph with the *action* to be taken or the *question* asked.

Letters are usually for communication to individuals *outside* the organization. Some typical uses for letters are formal commendations and awards; notifications (for example, that a zoning change review was pending); requests for specific information; expressions of gratitude; and invitations. Letters can serve as a means of documenting a regulatory decision or a complaint. They are likely to be produced in court trials and sent to boards and commissions as evidence. Letters do not include graphics, tables, or long analyses of data. If these are needed, a cover letter is used, which refers to separate enclosures such as a map or diagram of a site and the specifics of the project being planned. Letters are generally no longer than two pages; assume that longer letters will not be read in their entirety unless they contain information extremely crucial to the recipient.

Reports. Planners are likely to write reports at every stage of a project and at every level of detail and completeness. Examples of reports include plan, zoning, or site plan reviews; studies and analysis of their results; summaries and analysis of small group or public participation proceedings; and plans. When writing a report a planner must be clear about the purpose, the types of information to be included, the data, graphics, or other supporting materials that will be used, and which conclusion or set of recommendations are to be stressed. The text must lead the reader through the arguments so that the conclusions or recommendations seem the natural and obvious outcome.

The basic sections of a report are: the *title*, which should be completely descriptive without being too lengthy; the *introduction*, which is a short summary of the purpose of the report and may include some background information, dates, locations, and the persons responsible and convey a good overview of what the report addresses; the *background* as a more lengthy history and some technical detail may be appropriate for some reports; the *body*, which contains all information and analysis including the methodology, data collected, and data analysis; *data, tables, charts, and graphics*, which are part of the body but should be self-contained and understandable and have a title; *illustrations, including maps and plans*; the conclusions to be drawn from the last two categories should be summarized in the text so the reader understands how they substantiate the key arguments; the *summary*, which reiterates the major points of the report; and a *conclusion*, which draws the *important findings* of the report into a *concise statement*. An *executive summary* at the beginning is short, one or two pages, and is often carefully read, serving to guide the reader to the methods, data, analysis, and key findings. It should be formatted for easy reading, with bullets and bold emphasis highlighting important points. Materials that are bulky, detailed and supplementary are often included as *appendices*.

Ordinances. Planning processes at times conclude with implementation steps, which require the adoption of ordinances or other legislation, the drawing up of regulations or policy documents, and the passage of resolutions to initiate them. These documents are legalistic in nature and require special care in precision and clarity of the language. Formats for ordinances are generally standardized within a unit of government. An ordinance has a descriptive *title* and the language is formal. A number of conventions are followed. A common example is that "shall" is used to indicate a requirement while "will" or "may" indicate optional choices. Ordinances, as legal documents, state the essentials of the law or code and contain a list of definitions.

If a planner is assigned to help with the drafting of an ordinance through a committee process they must be scrupulous in tracking proposed changes and draft versions. One convention for this is to use strikeout font to show deletions and bold to show new text as changes are made. Most governmental entities appoint an attorney or counsel to review the ordinance for compliance with the law.

Resolutions. Ordinances are commonly adopted by a resolution, which is prepared in conjunction with it and also drafted, and modified through negotiation, discussion, and a vote on the final form. They articulate the intent of the ordinance and the policies behind it. Their common format has a series of *Whereas* statements of intent followed by one or more *Resolved* lines that have the force of law. If the purpose is to adopt an ordinance, this is stated in the Resolved line while the Whereas statements, written in expansive language, cite larger goals than the issue specifically dealt with by the ordinance but explain the rationale for the ordinance.

Minutes. Planners often serve as the facilitators or coordinators for small or large groups engaged in a planning issue. These include specially appointed or convened committees. Minutes are the official record of actions taken by a body and name the individuals present, the date of the meeting, and the actions taken. The main conclusions and the main arguments for and against an action are summarized. Conclusions are reported succinctly in a neutral tone. Minutes should not be lengthy and should be formatted for quick review, using bullets and short paragraphs.

Announcements. Meetings to which the public or a general population is invited often require an announcement which typically includes a descriptive title, a brief paragraph description of the purpose and agenda of the meeting, the date, time and place, and location with address and room number, a telephone number of the person who can answer questions about the meeting. The announcement usually stipulates if there is an opportunity for the public to speak, and if written comments can be sent ahead of time.

Grant Proposals. Planners in governmental or nonprofit agencies may also write and submit grant proposals to foundations or other governmental agencies. This calls for persuasive writing, which differs from the expository writing used in most documents, requires a more fluid and eloquent style and the careful marshaling of arguments, especially in the portion that seeks to justify the award to the agency or group. In writing proposals it is important to adhere to the rules the reader or evaluator has set and to meet the set expectations and requirements.

Graphic Communication[3]

Graphics are a powerful tool with which planners communicate their plans, ideas, and information. Communicating directly with graphics opens up new ways of understanding spatial relationships for both the individual making the drawing and the observer. They offer an alternative language, to complement written and oral communications. In planning graphics are mostly used as a means to interpret and amplify a message. They do some things particularly well. Graphics help planners synthesize, organize, and condense complex situational information and relationships into a pictorial representation that is quickly grasped and understood. They are useful in overcoming barriers of language, class, education, and interest. In a rapidly globalizing environment, as urban populations grow ever more diverse, graphics can help communicate across different population groups and reach people who do not read or read well. They offer another perspective on a problem or an idea.

Graphic and non-graphic information should be balanced to complement each other creatively to enhance communication. Graphic communication is a craft. It can be learned and adapted and is not to be confused with "decorating" pages of reports and incorporating graphics on purely artistic or aesthetic grounds, which have little planning value. Graphics in planning require thoughtful transformation of information into visuals that an audience can grasp without misinterpretation.

Graphics needs to be adapted to the type and stage of a project. Urban design and physical planning projects naturally make use of graphics. However, a social policy report might benefit from a logo, photo image, or coloring, not only to enhance readability but to support identification and communicate human dimensions more effectively. Three-dimensional visualizations of new developments can be instrumental in assisting in decision-making, winning a project, or supporting an argument. A flip chart, sketches, and hand-drawn charts may be useful during an impromptu brainstorming session, while well-designed overheads or slides can effectively support an official presentation.

Objectives of Graphical Communication

Graphics are used in planning to achieve five broad objectives: For illustration and documentation; analysis and visualization; communication of concepts and ideas; persuasion through emotional engagement; and for identity building.

For *illustration and documentation* many different graphic media are used. For example, photographs or a video recording may be used to document the dilapidated conditions at a local housing estate. The images of broken windows and doors, missing stair rails and evidence of water leakage presented in a planning meeting will substantiate the need for repairs and investments. Improvements made can be illustrated with before and after pictures in a report to a housing authority. Sketches, line drawings, and annotations on maps can also serve the same function. An asset map can illustrate in two dimensions conditions on a site or a neighborhood. Aerial photographs or land use maps from different years are very effective to communicate urban growth and extent of sprawl or for comparing development patterns between different cities.

Graphics are also used for *data analysis and visualization* as large data can often be better understood when rendered into graphs and diagrams. Patterns and trends are much more easily detected. Scatter plots can indicate linear relationship between x and y and the outliers are clearly identifiable while these may be more difficult to identify in a table format. Much of the data that planners use is spatial, and linked to a geographic location. For example, traffic counts on city roads can be easily visualized on interactive maps, heavy traffic streets shown with dark, heavy lines and bright colors, less traffic with thinner lines and lighter colors.

Visual thinking, or visualization, is helpful in making decisions. Simulation software is used to provide different perspectives on data and to help display multivariate data for exploratory analysis of relationships and trends. Graphics are also used to communicate ideas, to the public, to investors, or to share with project team members. A drawing or perspective sketch of the landscaping of the new park communicates the ideas of the designer and architect to the planning board and to the public audience. In essence, the graphic depiction allows the designer to present the future experience of a space. Different design schemes can be presented to the audience and comparisons and feedback solicited. A range of techniques can be used from quick sketches to collages and computer-aided renderings.

Planners use images to convey a certain viewpoint and *persuade* the public of the importance of policy and action. Photographs and documentary films are especially powerful tools for evoking emotional reactions and are used to garner public support. For example photographs of wildlife strangled by barbed wire fences could be used to elicit support for a policy to ban such fencing, or photographs of deformed fish and waterfowl to campaign for a costly water purification program.

Planners use graphics for *marketing and to build identity*. Cities are increasingly marketing themselves as places with certain characteristics, and competing with each other for events, developments, and the right mix of residents to maintain a healthy and livable environment. Part of this marketing strategy is building identity, which often relies on unified street signage, color coded district markers, logos on websites, city plans, tourist brochures, and other publicity.

For effective graphic communication, the graphic content must fit the purpose, use, and setting. Asking the following questions may help in selecting graphics for a particular project:

- What is the objective of the particular task for which you are considering the graphic?
- Are you trying to present and discuss ideas, report on a survey, or facilitate decision-making? Who is the audience and who are the decision-makers? Some audiences are more receptive to graphic communications in the form of slides, maps, or drawings than others. It may be essential to use certain types of graphics to reach some audiences whereas others will find them too simplistic. Graphics must be carefully considered in light of one's expected audience.
- What is to be presented—data, ideas, and visions?
- Are the graphics to show facts based on numbers? If so, diagrams or charts may be most useful. If they are to show spatial distribution of a problem or policy, maps may be the graphic of choice.
- What is the setting? Is it a formal meeting or presentation in a large room? If communicating to a large audience, slides or overheads will be best. In small, less formal group, a few sketches and pinned-up diagrams on a wall may be sufficient, direct and more effective. Graphics have a wide variety of uses and methods of application. Different approaches are appropriate depending on the specific type of written information to be supported visually.

Conclusion

Oral, written, and graphic communication skills are key to successful planning practice. In the planning academy, hands-on-instruction in their use has received less attention than the attainment of other skills, and they have largely been learned on the job. Familiarity with, and deliberative design of, the various occasions in which oral, written, or graphic communications occur in the routine practice of planning will empower planners to be successful practitioners.

Notes

1 Adapted and summarized from Storey (2003).
2 This section has been adapted from Armentrout (2003).
3 This section has been adapted from Frank (2003).

References

American Planning Association. (2018). What Skills Do Planners Need? Retrieved from www.planning.org/choosingplanning/skills/

Armentrout, V. (2003). Written Communications. In H. C. Dandekar (Ed.), *The Planner's Use of Information*(2nd ed.). Planners Press (American Planning Association).

Center for Community Health and Development at the University of Kansas. (2017). Community Tool Box. Retrieved from http://ctb.ku.edu/en/table-of-contents

Dandekar, H. C. (Ed.). (2003). *The Planner's Use of Information* (2nd ed.). Planners Press (American Planning Association).

Dandekar, H. C. (Ed.). (2019). *The Planner's Use of Information* (3rd ed.). Routledge.

Forsyth, A. (2008, August 31). Defining the Planning Skill Set: Resources for Students. Retrieved from www.planetizen.com/node/34807

Frank, A. (2003). Graphic Communications. In H. C. Dandekar (Ed.), *The Planner's Use of Information* (2nd ed.). Planners Press (American Planning Association).

McLoughlin, M. (2012). *Employability Skills for Planners: A Scoping Report into the Changing Requirements of Planning Employers.* Retrieved from www.heacademy.ac.uk/system/files/employability_skills_for_planners.pdf

Storey, A. W. (2003). Speaking Skills for Presentations. In H. C. Dandekar (Ed.), *The Planner's Use of Information* (2nd ed.). Planners Press (American Planning Association).

11
RESEARCH DESIGN AND PRACTICE

David Hsu

Introduction

Designing research is considered a fundamental skill for scholarship. This topic is important enough in all of the social sciences, including planning, to be almost always taught to doctoral students in the first year (and also to undergraduates and master's-level students engaged in research). It is a critical first step for students to learn how to become independent scholars. This chapter explores how research design in planning differs from the broader social sciences, and what this implies for how and what planners teach.

Much of what has been written about research design in the social sciences is often quite formal and structured in tone, and often starts with epistemological foundations: how research and discovery are related to hypotheses, theories of knowledge, and the nature of truth. For example, Creswell (2013, 5) states: "although philosophical ideas remain largely hidden in research . . . they still influence the practice of research and need to be identified." Similarly, du Toit (2016, 63–64) states:

> Methodological paradigms are philosophies that permeate various facets of a study, albeit in very indirect or subtle ways . . . Although a paradigm addresses various aspects of scientific research, ranging from why we do research, what makes 'good' research, to what is considered ethical, paradigms are primarily about the nature of reality (ontology) and the grounds of knowledge (epistemology). Different paradigms have very different ontologies and epistemologies, and consequently very different requirements in terms of research design.

Epistemology, as the study of knowledge, is closely related to concerns about the nature of truth (Blackburn, 2016). Why start with philosophy? These philosophical foundations are needed to ground what can be said based on observations, and sometimes standard texts on research design argue that particular methods and procedures can or cannot be applied to certain kinds of data (see, for example, Labaree, 2016). Furthermore, as a recent textbook on research design in planning states, "the reason for interest in research design is that it underpins the *trustworthiness* of the claims that a researcher makes in a particular study" (Farthing, 2016, 2, my italics).

However, while these statements are reasonable and representative of the research design literature in both planning and the social sciences, there remains a key difference between them. Trust is not the same thing as truth, and establishing one does not necessarily lead to the other, in either direction. This distinction is especially relevant with regard to research design in new and unfamiliar surroundings, countries, or cultures. The key elements of the arguments that this chapter will develop are based on the following propositions:

1 Because planning research seeks to inform practice, which guides how cities are actually built, it must be crafted in a way to gain the attention and trust of the appropriate audience for research;
2 The special term 'craft' that is often used in the teaching of research design, implies tacit knowledge, which is rooted in 'soft' skills such as experience, understanding of context, and personal or reputational trust; and
3 These soft skills are something that might be taught via informal advising and research supervision, but they are rarely addressed concretely within a formal curriculum, or specifically with regards to research design.

Research Design in Planning Versus in the Social Sciences

Planning teachers often rely on a number of standard texts used throughout the social sciences on research design (for example, Creswell, 2013; Hakim, 2000; Yin, 2003). Yet, even within social sciences, planning as a discipline is both motivated and structured differently than other disciplines. Many authors have noted the diverse intellectual origins of the planning discipline and its engagement with many different research paradigms (Healey, 1991; Forsyth, 2012), while others have argued that planning is slowly developing a more cohesive disciplinary identity (Goldstein and Carmin, 2006). There are also two recent research design textbooks specifically focused on planning but at opposite ends of the weight scale: as mentioned in the beginning, Farthing (2016) is a slim but thorough and useful guide for students, and Silva et al. (2016) is a large edited handbook full of discussions about different aspects of research and perspectives from different countries.

However, inherent differences between practice and knowledge sometimes lead to a note of pessimism about the effectiveness of planning research. A pervasive sentiment throughout the literature on planning research is that it is often disconnected from how planning is practiced and how cities actually get built (Forester, 1988; Flyvbjerg, 2002, 2004; Krizek, Forsyth and Slotterback, 2009; Webster, 2016). This disconnect stems from the nature of planning as an action-oriented discipline situated within complex, dynamic, and *real* geographies that are not within the complete control of anyone, let alone urban planners and researchers. In addition, since planning is usually about a prospective and unknowable future, any act—of writing, predicting, exhorting, or advocating—about possible futures can be hazardous in hindsight. These are just occupational hazards associated with practicing and researching in the real world.

Since the building of cities happens in the real world, with others outside the communities of planning practitioners or researchers, planning research that can speak to and gain the trust of decision makers is especially valuable. While these decision makers are sometimes planners, they are just as likely to be politicians, other city bureaucrats, real estate developers, community groups, or practicing other disciplines like architecture, the law, or engineering: in short, every one else in the city. Identifying and gaining the trust of this audience therefore requires craft, a special term that deserves more exploration.

Craft and Tacit Knowledge in Research Design

In addition to some of the standard texts mentioned above that all focus on procedure and grounding for research approaches, there are a number of books that describe research as a 'craft'. The word 'craft' has positive associations with skill; membership within a community; refining products over time; and because physical craft often leads to intellectual growth, as Sennett (2008, ix) puts it, "making is thinking."

Similarly, three excellent books about research design written by senior scholars in diverse fields all take the theme of 'craft' in their titles (Wildavsky, 1993; Alford, 1998; Booth, Colomb and Williams, 2003). The word 'craft' in the titles of these three books may also be a way of paying respect to the classic sociological essay 'On intellectual craftsmanship' by C. Wright Mills (which all three books mention prominently). In this essay, Mills describes his own experiences thus:

> I am going to try candidly to report how I became interested in a topic I happen to be studying, and how I am going about studying it . . . Only by conversations in which experienced thinkers exchange information about their actual, informal ways of working can 'method' ever really be imparted to the beginning student. I know of no other way in which to begin such conversations, and thus to begin what I think needs to be done, than to set forth a brief but explicit statement of one man's working habits . . . I must repeat that I do not intend to write about method in any formal sense, nor, under the guise of methodology, to take up a statesman-like pose concerning the proper course for social science.
>
> (Mills, 1980, 63)

Mills' emphasis on informal conversation and habits is strongly reminiscent of writings on tacit knowledge, that is, knowledge that cannot be explicitly articulated or easily transferred to others. This idea, widely attributed to Michael Polanyi (2009), argues that to acquire such knowledge requires personal experience; to develop such knowledge requires experience in relevant contexts; and to transfer such knowledge requires close interaction and trust. Similarly, Gilbert Ryle (1945) asserted that:

> philosophers have not done justice to the distinction, which is quite familiar to all of us, between knowing that something is the case and knowing how to do things . . . I want to turn the tables and to prove that knowledge-how cannot be defined in terms of knowledge-that, and further, that knowledge-how is a concept logically prior to the concept of knowledge-that.
>
> (Ryle, 1945, 4–5)

Thus planners, both in the academic environment and in practice, are faced with the questions of how to design research in such a way as to facilitate the transfer of the knowledge to be gained from it. A common preamble in academic writing is to spell out the intellectual merit or contribution of the work, usually to a body of literature or debate. The established academic may be addressing peers within the university; the hired consultant has to address an outside audience; the brand-new practitioner has to transfer knowledge to potential listeners both inside and outside her new place of work; and all of these planners will be, to some degree, aware of the question of how to disseminate their work to the larger world.

The intended audiences, and the roles scholars play, are also subject to levels of trust—or the lack thereof—in relationships between planners and their research 'subjects.' Mutual understanding can be slow to develop and require painstaking effort, driven by humility and open-mindedness; this, too, must be accounted for in designing and evaluating a potential research project, either formally in the research timeline or informally in the researcher's own mind.

There are previous examples in planning literature of research design that requires active participation and immersion on the part of the researcher. Throgmorton (1996) and Flyvbjerg (2002) have shown how planners can engage in the public sphere, either through persuasive storytelling or active participation in political power-relations, in situations ranging from Chicago's electric system to downtown planning in Denmark. Planning is a field that particularly valorizes real-world experience, but our accounts of research design usually leave our prior experiences out. Yet deep contextual understanding is needed where planners and planning scholars want their research to have an impact, including ways of understanding how policy is made by people, groups, agencies, and processes.

Furthermore, relying on personal experience invariably depends on the individual researcher and how society perceives him or her. Healey (1991), for example, mentions that her background as a planning official enabled her to gain acceptance by the planners she was studying, while, in contrast, Campbell (2016, 26) discusses how being a young, female academic researcher from outside government denied her this kind of immediate acceptance and forced her to ask questions as an outsider (though still successfully). Building professional relationships with decision makers is good, and further developing empathy and trust is helpful, but Healey (1991, 450) also points out that the "potential for empathy and trust, however, carrie[s] with it certain ethical and methodological obligations," such as maintaining scholarly goals, independence, and rigor.

In addition, while the future is and always will be unknowable, researchers need to develop theories of action about how our research will make a difference, and this often depends on understanding particular places and policy situations as thoroughly as possible. This is why planning theorists are often drawn to the policy literature that explores how policies are developed and implemented (Stone, 2002; Sabatier and Weible, 2014). However, discussions of theories, methods, and how they fit together often leave out the deep contextual knowledge that planners respect.

Moreover, for a discipline focused on the built environment, many discussions of planning research and research design are curiously a-spatial and geographically dislocated. This is worth exploring more, since the connection between experience and learning is quite deep in theoretical texts, ranging from the writings of educational philosophers such as John Dewey (1938); to ample work in psychology that points to the formative nature of prior experiences, framing, and anchoring in human decision-making (Kahneman, Slovic and Tversky, 1982; Kahneman, 2011); to the experience of place (Hiss, 1990).

Meanwhile, planning researchers' roles may change over time. Like many design processes, the design of research is often iterative. An interesting strain of commentary in the planning literature has been on the various roles that planning scholars assume because of existing institutional, political, or academic cultures (Breheny, 1989; Healey, 1991; Forsyth, 2012; Siemiatycki, 2012). These articles classify the various ways in which planners engage in research that is meant to result in action or social change, in terms of motivations; the nature of the work; degree of collaboration with practitioners or policy makers; and their status as insiders, outsiders, advocates, or opponents. How researchers view their current roles, and how this changes over the course of doing research, should inform how they in turn teach students to anticipate the kinds of changes in their research that will come with further experience.

Teaching Soft Skills in Unfamiliar Places

Therefore, how should students gain this experience? How should planning teachers teach students to dig into, and commit to, particular contexts? How should they develop trust in those contexts? These are important factors when teaching research design in new and unfamiliar places, or preparing students to undertake research in other countries and cultures. Whether the dominant planning tradition comes from a hegemonic (Stiftel and Mukhopadhyay, 2007) or more heterodox planning culture, all planners must first recognize that learning in another place effectively requires commitment, skill, work, and time, that is, all things that go to help build experience. Planning students should travel; learn languages; immerse themselves in the cultures that they want to study through reading, collaboration, and observation; and reflect on these experiences as pro-actively as possible.

The only way to develop deep contextual knowledge is through experience. One could object: "How are we to teach students to do effective research design if they can only learn through experience?" A fair point; but without experience, planning professionals have even less of a chance to realize the desired impact of research without understanding particular places and people better. So, in addition to the ideas, theories, and methods that planning teachers regularly prepare students with, it is necessary to get students into the field and the contexts in which they want to do research as soon as possible. Either the planning professor, drawing from prior experience, should lead the students; or the students themselves should take the lead in going out and acquiring relevant experience.

All of this, of course, implies an ability to understand how the research context might be distinctive or unique compared to other research that has been done before. Many books on international research in planning make the point that planning is carried out in national contexts that differ in their histories, international relations, political structure and systems, population density, legal systems, existing built environments, aspirations and cultures, administrative systems, and physical size and space (Levy, Hirt and Jessen, 2011). Planning cultures themselves are differently situated within each country (Sanyal, 2005). Challenges with cross-national research can include simply addressing similar concepts across different cultures (Booth, 2016; Farthing, 2016).

All of these factors still point to the need for greater experience and engagement as soon as possible. It would also help to allow students to work and study in parallel or in syncopation, so their work and study can inform one another. Exposing students to real problems and policy situations earlier in their educations could have a substantial impact in the problems that they later choose to study. However, that does place a greater burden on planning teachers to make sure not only that their students, especially students relatively new to planning, not only understand the long-term consequences of choices in research design but the care that needs to be taken in interacting with their audience, who might be nervous, distrustful, or openly resistant to change—or, on the other hand, eager to push change through for their own reasons.

Therefore, to do planning research, perhaps planning teachers should discuss whether a higher bar is required to do research in new and unfamiliar places, or what kind of linguistic and cultural training might be required to execute research successfully. Even in cases where the cultural and political background are familiar, students may still need to be persuaded to drop their preconceptions and go into the new situation with an open mind. For either the new or experienced planning researcher, feeling inexperienced, unprepared, and uncertain—"stupid" (Schwartz, 2008)—should be reasonable and even predictable when beginning research.

A challenge of talking about research design that obscures this initial uncertainty is that good research design is often positively biased. Successful research projects appear to be, or are presented as, 'just-so' stories, like the stories for children by Kipling (1902) that often attribute mythical outcomes to magical beings or unlikely chains of coincidental events. As literature, the arc of these stories is "to answer the kinds of questions children ask, in ways that satisfy their taste for primitive and poetic justice" (Karlin, 2015). But one of the occupational hazards of planning is being engaged with the future in a complicated environment. Instead of telling students 'just-so' stories, experienced planners should expect the role of planners and their research to change continuously as cities do.

The topic of research design should have a special resonance for planning scholars because, like designing and planning cities, designing the process of research often begins with a deliberate intention that can only be realized when situated in reality. Planners often think about how the existing environment, agency, processes, resources, institutions, policies, power, and people all interact to shape planning outcomes. Reflecting on the act of planning inevitably leads us to classic normative questions such as: What is a good city? Who is the good city for? How do plans change cities? Similarly, thinking about research as an activity naturally leads to similar questions, such as: What is good research? Who defines what good research is? What kind of plans result in good research, and vice versa, how does good research lead to good planning? These normative questions are of course unresolvable, but they should inform both the teaching of the subject of research design and the design of research itself. Thinking about what good research is, what it can do, and prospectively planning the research conduct is subject to many of the same constraints as the planning of cities themselves. But every planning scholar, whether experienced or still a student, needs to locate this activity—and its potential impact—among real places and people.

Acknowledgments

Thank you to Subhrajit Guhathakurta, and to the first-year doctoral students in my spring 2017 seminar at MIT, for reading and providing feedback on previous versions of this manuscript. The errors within are of course mine alone.

References

Alford, R. R. (1998) *The craft of inquiry: Theories, methods, evidence*. Oxford: Oxford University Press.
Blackburn, S. (ed.) (2016) 'Epistemology', *The Oxford dictionary of philosophy*. 2nd revised ed. Available at: www.oxfordreference.com/view/10.1093/acref/9780199541430.001.0001/acref-9780199541430-e-1113 (Accessed: 6 June 2017).
Booth, P. (2016) 'What can we learn from France? Some reflections on the methodologies of cross-national research', in Silva, E. A. et al. (eds) *The Routledge handbook of planning research methods*. New York and London: Routledge, pp. 84–96.
Booth, W. C., Colomb, G. G. and Williams, J. M. (2003) *The craft of research*. Chicago: University of Chicago Press.
Breheny, M. (1989) 'Chalkface to coalface: A review of the academic—Practice interface—Jul 23, 2016', *Environment and Planning B: Planning and Design*, 16, pp. 451–468.
Campbell, H. (2016) 'It takes more than looking to make a difference: the challenge for planning research', in Silva, E. A. et al. (eds) *The Routledge handbook of planning research methods*. New York and London: Routledge, pp. 24–32.
Creswell, J. W. (2013) *Research design: Qualitative, quantitative, and mixed methods approaches*. 4th ed. Thousand Oaks: SAGE Publications, Inc.
Dewey, J. (1938) *Education and experience*. New York: Simon and Schuster.
du Toit, J. (2016) 'Research Design', in Silva, E. A. et al. (eds) *The Routledge handbook of planning research methods*. New York and London: Routledge, pp. 61–73.
Farthing, S. M. (2016) *Research design in urban planning: A student's guide*. Los Angeles: SAGE.
Flyvbjerg, B. (2002) 'Bringing power to planning research: One researcher's praxis story', *Journal of Planning Education and Research*, 21(4), pp. 353–366. doi:10.1177/0739456X0202100401.
Flyvbjerg, B. (2004) 'Phronetic planning research: Theoretical and methodological reflections', *Planning Theory & Practice*, 5(3), pp. 283–306. doi:10.1080/1464935042000250195.
Forester, J. (1988) *Planning in the face of power*. Berkeley: University of California Press.

Forsyth, A. (2012) 'Commentary: Alternative Cultures in Planning Research—From Extending Scientific Frontiers to Exploring Enduring Questions', *Journal of Planning Education and Research*, 32(2), pp. 160–168. doi:10.1177/0739456X12442217.

Goldstein, H. A. and Carmin, J. (2006) 'Compact, Diffuse, or Would-be Discipline? Assessing Cohesion in Planning Scholarship, 1963–2002', *Journal of Planning Education and Research*, 26(1), pp. 66–79. doi: 10.1177/0739456X05282353.

Hakim, C. (2000) *Research design: Successful designs for social and economic research*. 2nd ed. London and New York: Routledge (Social research today).

Healey, P. (1991) 'Researching planning practice', *Town Planning Review*, 62(4), pp. 447–459. doi:10.3828/tpr.62.4.0165405746487668.

Hiss, T. (1990) *The experience of place*. New York: Vintage Books.

Kahneman, D. (2011) *Thinking, fast and slow*. New York: Farrar, Straus and Giroux.

Kahneman, D., Slovic, P. and Tversky, A. (eds) (1982) *Judgement under uncertainty: Heuristics and biases*. Cambridge: Cambridge University Press.

Karlin, D. (2015) 'Kipling and the origins of the "Just-So" stories', *OUPblog*, 23 December. Available at: http://blog.oup.com/2015/12/kipling-stories-names/ (Accessed: 13 December 2016).

Kipling, R. (1902) *Just so stories*. Random House.

Krizek, K., Forsyth, A. and Slotterback, C. S. (2009) 'Is there a role for evidence-based practice in urban planning and policy?' *Planning Theory & Practice*, 10(4), pp. 459–478. doi:10.1080/14649350903417241.

Labaree, R. V. (2016) *Research guides: Organizing your social sciences research paper: Types of research designs*. Available at: http://libguides.usc.edu/writingguide/researchdesigns (Accessed: 1 December 2016).

Levy, J., Hirt, S. and Jessen, J. (2011) 'Planning in Other Nations', in *Contemporary urban planning*. 9th ed. London: Pearson Education, pp. 373–415.

Mills, C. W. (1980) 'On intellectual craftsmanship (1952)', *Society*, 17(2), pp. 63–70. doi:10.1007/BF02700062.

Polanyi, M. (2009) *The tacit dimension*. Chicago: University of Chicago Press.

Ryle, G. (1945) 'Knowing How and Knowing That: The Presidential Address', *Proceedings of the Aristotelian Society*, 46, pp. 1–16.

Sabatier, P. and Weible, C. (2014) *Theories of the policy process*. Boulder: Westview Press. Available at: https://books.google.com/books?hl=en&lr=&id=MzkGAwAAQBAJ&oi=fnd&pg=PR5&dq=theories+of+the+policy+process&ots=wPTTKdnp-q&sig=T4KarGoLmUVwazsYWAdQ4ZsaBnQ (Accessed: 8 June 2017).

Sanyal, B. (ed.) (2005) *Comparative planning cultures*. New York: Routledge.

Schwartz, M. A. (2008) 'The importance of stupidity in scientific research', *Journal of Cell Science*, 121(11), pp. 1771–1771. doi:10.1242/jcs.033340.

Sennett, R. (2008) *The craftsman*. New Haven: Yale University Press.

Siemiatycki, M. (2012) 'The role of the planning scholar research, conflict, and social change', *Journal of Planning Education and Research*, 32(2), pp. 147–159. doi:10.1177/0739456X12440729.

Silva, E. A. et al. (eds) (2016) *The Routledge handbook of planning research Methods*. New York and London: Routledge.

Stiftel, B. and Mukhopadhyay, C. (2007) 'Thoughts on Anglo-American hegemony in planning scholarship: Do we read each other's work?', *The Town Planning Review*, 78(5), pp. 545–572.

Stone, D. A. (2002) *Policy paradox: The art of political decision making*. New York: Norton. Available at: http://library.wur.nl/WebQuery/clc/1850664 (Accessed: 8 June 2017).

Throgmorton, J. A. (1996) *Planning as persuasive storytelling: The rhetorical construction of Chicago's electric future*. Chicago: University of Chicago Press.

Webster, C. (2016) 'Refutation and the knowledge base of planning', in Silva, E. A. et al. (eds) *The Routledge handbook of planning research methods*. New York and London: Routledge, pp. 107–120.

Wildavsky, A. B. (1993) *Craftways: On the organization of scholarly work*. New Jersey: Transaction Publishers.

Yin, R. K. (2003) *Case study research: Design and methods*. Thousand Oaks: SAGE.

12
QUANTITATIVE METHODS

William J. Drummond

Introduction

In the initial decades of the development of city planning as a distinct profession, its methods were most closely related to the design professions, in particular, architecture. But after World War II, planning methods became increasingly based upon quantitative analysis. One of the major catalysts was the publication of the first edition of Stuart Chapin's *Urban Land Use Planning* (Chapin 1957) textbook. Chapin's book re-directed land use planning from primarily a design activity to a fully quantitative analytical activity based upon methods borrowed from economics (input-output analysis) and demography (cohort component models).

The publication of *Urban Planning Analysis: Methods and Models* (Krueckeberg and Silvers 1974) elevated quantitative methods to a distinct component of the planning curriculum and provided a basic outline that still defines a majority of the core of planning-related quantitative methods. A contemporary teacher of planning methods who browses the contents of *Urban Planning Analysis* will be struck by the continued relevance of nearly every chapter, and the subsequent dearth of important new additions to the basic body of quantitative methods. It is true that the means of implementing the methods has changed dramatically. In terms of hardware we have moved from slide rule to mainframe computer to calculator to microcomputer to smartphone to virtual machines. In terms of software we now use both commercial and freely available open-source spreadsheets, database management systems, statistical software, and geographic information systems (GIS). But the fundamental quantitative methods have remained surprisingly constant, as can be seen in more recent methods textbooks such as those by Klosterman (1990); Klosterman et al. (2018); Wang and vom Hofe (2007); Patton, Sawicki, and Clark (2012); and Jepson and Weitz (2016).

Quantitative methods have become a standard component of the planning curriculum for three major reasons. First, these methods help us understand how and why cities grow and decline, flourish and languish. Population changes, for example, are determined by factors of fertility, mortality, and migration. An increase or decrease in basic employment will have a multiplicative effect on total employment. The shopping or commuting trips between any two areas will decline as the distance between them increases. Moreover, the process of developing models forces us to decide which factors are more important and which are less important, and the need to measure those factors forces us to define exactly what we mean by concepts such as employment or trips.

Second, quantitative methods provide us with procedures to forecast the values of important variables around which we build plans for the future. A 2050 traditional land use plan for a city with ten million persons will be much different than a plan for a population of five million. In addition, many forecasting methods can vary the values of input variables to provide sensitivity analysis for decision making under uncertainty. Yet, despite the historical importance of forecasting in planning, there is currently a major re-thinking of the value of forecasting (Klosterman 2013, Hopkins and Zapata 2007), which may in the future replace many forecast-based plans with scenario-based ones.

Third, quantitative methods allow us to track our progress in meeting important global and local goals. The sets of UN Millennial Development Goals and now Sustainable Development Goals each have one or more quantitative indicators that are tracked over time at the global, regional, and national levels. These indicators help us understand such major developments as the dramatic fall in global poverty.

Before addressing quantitative methods themselves, we must briefly consider several dimensions of the teaching environment, including pedagogical approaches, computer hardware, and recommended software. Across higher education there is currently extensive experimentation with modes of delivery beyond the traditional in-class lecture and out-of-class assigned reading. Some of the major innovations being tested include flipped classrooms, blended learning, and online offering of courses and degrees. Flipped classrooms have students absorb traditional lecture material, usually online, out of class, while homework, problem-solving, and small group learning are moved to scheduled class times. Blended learning combines face-to-face instruction with online materials. Online courses and degrees deliver lectures and PowerPoint slides across the Internet. Unfortunately, there is no online set of planning quantitative method lectures, although there are a number of special topic videos, PowerPoint presentations, and summaries of lecture notes. At some point in the future there may be a freely available integrated set of online methods materials, perhaps associated with one of the more recent methods textbooks. Until that happens, methods instructors will be largely limited to the more traditional modes of instruction.

There is no single textbook that covers all the methods and models included in this chapter. The major choices include Klosterman (1990); Wang and vom Hofe (2007); Patton, Sawicki, and Clark (2012); and Jepson and Weitz (2016). Klosterman (1990) covers trend extrapolation, population methods, and economic methods in good depth. Wang and vom Hofe (2007) also treat population and economic methods in depth, and adds basic statistics, land suitability analysis, and transportation methods. Patton, Sawicki, and Clark (2012) emphasize quick, basic, back-of-the-envelope methods of planning and policy analysis rather than the detailed quantitative analysis, but the case studies are especially valuable. Jepson and Weitz (2016) cover the broadest range of methods and helpfully place them in the context of developing a comprehensive plan, but the level of detail on traditional quantitative methods is not sufficient to allow students to fully understand them and implement them. Of these four methods textbooks, Wang and vom Hofe (2007) come closest to covering almost all of the recommended material in sufficient depth for a graduate course in quantitative methods. For a much deeper treatment of population models there is the recent Smith, Tayman, and Swanson (2016) or the older but still serviceable Smith, Tayman, and Swanson (2001). For more extensive discussion of economic development methods see Leigh and Blakely (2016) or McLean (1992).

Over the last decade the computing hardware environment has been changing so rapidly that it is difficult to predict how we will be conducting quantitative analysis even a few years into the future. For equipping a quantitative methods computer lab, completely serviceable desktop and laptop microcomputers are now available for less than $200, but given the fundamental prices of individual physical computer components it is hard to imagine system prices continuing to fall much below $150. Still, even the least expensive desktops and laptops have more than enough processing power and storage for teaching quantitative methods. Tablets and smartphones now provide an alternative hardware environment to traditional microcomputers. Such devices could be feasible for teaching quantitative methods, but they would need to be supplemented with external monitors, mice, and keyboards.

For quantitative methods the most important computing hardware trend is virtualization, which involves large server computers hosting any number of individual virtual computers or individual applications. Virtualization can be provided across the Internet by services such as Amazon Web Services, or local servers running virtualization software packages such as Citrix, VMware, or Hyper-V. Virtual machines can be accessed by very basic thin-client hardware, including smartphones and tablets, allowing inexpensive client hardware to run even the most sophisticated software. Economies of scale and fierce competition by virtualization providers make it likely that virtual computer costs will continue to fall into the indefinite future.

For software, the methods teacher has two fundamental options: open-source or commercial. Open-source has the great advantage of zero purchase cost, but the disadvantages of more difficult installation, less polished documentation, and a greater investment of instructor time. LibreOffice, for example, includes a word processor, spreadsheet, presentation program, and basic database management program. R is a very powerful open-source statistics package, although it has a command-line interface rather than the graphical menu interfaces offered by most commercial statistical software packages. Google offers Docs, Sheets, and Slides, which are free Web-based word processing, spreadsheet, and presentation programs. Free and open-source software also has the advantage of accompanying the student into planning practice. Different government units and companies will have purchased different commercial packages, but free or open-source software will still be available for a smooth transition into planning practice.

The remainder of the chapter is constructed around one overview table and four tables showing related groups of quantitative methods. The tables and associated discussion assume that the instructor has been tasked with teaching basic planning methods in either: (1) a one-month short course; (2) a two-month half semester course; (3) a three-month shorter semester course; or (4) a four-month full semester course. The rows of Table 12.1 describe these four options, which can also be interpreted as signaling the overall priority of different methods. The variation in course lengths give the option of including, in a typical four-month semester, quantitative methods plus some amount of qualitative methods, geographic information systems, or both.

One note of caution: although Table 12.1 draws a distinction between groups of "basic" and "advanced" methods, there is a large and growing body of evidence that more complex quantitative methods are no more accurate than simpler ones. After surveying the evidence in the business forecasting literature, Green and Armstrong (2015, p. 1684) conclude "Remarkably, no matter what type of forecasting method is used, complexity harms accuracy." Klosterman (2012, p. 3) reaches a similar conclusion regarding planning models: "It may seem that complex models will be able to project the future more accurately than simple models. However, an extensive body of research demonstrates convincingly that complex forecasting models are no more accurate than simpler models." Of course, the tradeoffs between basic and more advanced methods also include factors such as transparency, data requirements, and ability to incorporate the effects of policy changes. For the teacher of quantitative methods, the basic lesson of this surprising finding is that it is important for students to understand that more complicated methods are not necessarily more desirable than simpler ones, and in many cases simpler methods will be preferable.

Table 12.1 Quantitative Methods Course Options

Course Type	Course Length	Contact Hours	Types of Methods Included	Explanation
Short Course	4 weeks	12	Foundational methods, Basic analytical methods, Basic statistical methods	Focus on absolutely crucial methods
Half Semester	8 weeks	24	Methods listed above plus Basic database methods and Gravity models	Could be paired with half semester of qualitative methods or GIS
Shorter Semester	12 weeks	36	Methods listed above plus Advanced statistical methods and Discounting methods	Reserves one month for survey of GIS or survey of qualitative methods
Full Semester	16 weeks	48	Methods listed above plus Advanced database methods and Advanced analytical methods	Covers full range of planning-related quantitative methods, except for GIS

The following four tables each list the course length options across the columns and individual methods or groups of methods across the rows. An "X" in the body of the table indicates that a particular method is recommended for inclusion in the course of a particular length. The text accompanying the tables briefly explains the methods and discusses why they have been included or excluded from the different course options. The number of methods included for each course option is somewhat ambitious although not unreasonable. But, as a general principle, teachers should cover fewer methods with sufficient depth rather than survey a larger number of methods at a more superficial level.

Foundational Methods

Table 12.2 presents the set of foundational, cross-cutting methods that any planner in any substantive area should be equipped to apply. The table is divided into four sections, the first three of which should be taught in every quantitative methods course, no matter how long or short. These include basic methods of mathematical literacy, forecasting methods (since planning is about the future), and end-value methods (since planning is also about achieving values such as sustainability and justice). The fourth section (discounting methods dealing with the time-value of money) is especially important in countries of the Global South where increases in income (and sometimes inflation) may be rapid compared to the rest of the world. However, these economic concepts and their application are significantly more complex than the other foundational methods, so they have not been included in the short course. Each of the four sets of methods will now be discussed in detail.

The basic methods address issues relating to the quantitative framing and interpretation of raw numeric values. An estimate of the raw number of persons in an area living in extreme poverty is valuable, but when that estimate is converted to a percentage it can be compared to percentages from nearby areas, areas at a similar stage of development, or earlier and forecast future values from the same area. The dynamics of fertility rates, mortality rates, and migration rates will determine whether population in a local area, a country, or the world increases, stabilizes, or falls. Percent changes over time provide important indicators of whether conditions

Table 12.2 Foundational Methods

Method or Method Group	Short Course	Half Semester	Shorter Semester	Full Semester
Basic Methods				
Percents and proportions	X	X	X	X
Ratios and rates	X	X	X	X
Percent changes over time	X	X	X	X
Forecasting Methods				
Trend extrapolation	X	X	X	X
Constant share methods	X	X	X	X
Scenario planning	X	X	X	X
End-value methods				
UN development goals	X	X	X	X
Ecological footprint	X	X	X	X
Poverty measures	X	X	X	X
Gini coefficient			X	X
Discounting Methods				
Time-value of money			X	X
Net present value			X	X
Corrections for inflation			X	X
Annualization of changes over time			X	X

are improving or deteriorating, and how quickly they are improving or deteriorating. Because students come to planning from an extremely wide variety of academic backgrounds, it is important to teach even such basic concepts as the equivalency of 50% with the proportion 0.5, and that rates of change over time are calculated with a denominator of the measure at the beginning of the time period.

Thinking about the future is fundamental for planning (Myers and Kitsuse 2000, Wachs 2001) and one of the fundamental quantitative skills that help us to think about the future is forecasting. Given a time series of historic data, trend extrapolation methods fit different kinds of curves to the past data, then extend the curves into the future to generate forecasts. These methods are very easy to implement using graphic capabilities of modern spreadsheets. Constant share methods compare a target area to a larger reference area for which there may be existing projections. A city's future population can be projected by a constant share method that assumes the city's current share of population will continue into the future. Or, given city-level data for both a current and prior year plus national data for the same years plus a future year projection, a constant growth share model can forecast future city population by assuming that the city's share of projected national growth will be constant.

Trend extrapolation and constant share models can be understood as business-as-usual models. They assume that whatever past factors have been at work influencing variables such as population or employment, those same factors will continue into the future with the same relative strength, and that no new factors will emerge. For planners, these models have a major shortcoming since the fundamental purpose of our profession is to influence the future and change it for the better. But neither type of model allows us to incorporate the policy levers that would enable us to estimate whether action A or action B or no action whatsoever (business as usual) will produce a better outcome. Despite this major shortcoming, these models are still valuable as a motivation for action since they can help us understand what we can expect in the future if we simply allow past trends to continue. For example, most climate scientists agree that if past trends of atmospheric carbon emissions continue, by 2100 sea level will rise between 0.5 and 1 meter (IPCC 2014). This, in itself, is valuable and important information.

The table also includes a third category of forecasting method: scenario planning (Hopkins and Zapata 2007, Klosterman 2013). These methods may or may not be considered as forecasting methods, and may or may not be considered as quantitative methods. However, scenario planning is emerging as an important counterpoint to traditional forecast-based planning. It emphasizes public participation for the envisioning of possible and/or desirable futures, then working backward from the future to the present. Scenario planning can be especially fruitful for longer time periods as the uncertainty inherent in all forecasts becomes larger and larger over time.

The planning profession's goals include end-values such as environmental protection, social justice, and economic growth and efficiency (Campbell 1996). In the global context, in 2000 the United Nations identified eight Millennium Development Goals (MDGs, United Nations Statistics Division 2017a), superseded by the 17 Sustainable Development Goals (SDGs) adopted in 2015 (United Nations Statistics Division 2017b). Each goal has one or more quantitative indicators that can be downloaded as a full dataset (for the MDGs) or either by country or by indicator (for the SDGs).

With both the MDGs and SDGs there is a problem of over-abundance of multiple goals and hundreds of different indicators. But clearly two of the most important planning end-values are sustainability and social justice. One way to approach sustainability that is applicable at the global, national, and local scales is through ecological footprints (Wackernagel and Rees 1996). The method uses hectares of arable land as the basic metric and compares the supply of land (weighted by productivity) to the demand for land. An area's ecological footprint is the amount of land required for both productive uses and the absorption of waste products across a very broad range of human activities. The World Wildlife Fund has sponsored a series of reports that calculates ecological footprints at the global and national scales (World Wildlife Fund 2016). At present, globally we are using more than 1.5 times the earth's biocapacity each year, with more than half of our demand due to greenhouse gases. Ecological footprint calculations for different countries can serve to highlight the vast differences in use of the planet's biocapacity between more affluent areas and less affluent areas. The ecological footprint method does have weaknesses. It assumes that each unit of demand for land is equal in importance with no priority given, for example to food systems. It also leaves the impression that cities are bad for the planet because their ecological footprints are so much larger than their physical footprints, when, in reality, higher densities of population in cities creates less environmental impact than lower densities in suburbs or rural areas (Glaeser 2011).

For social justice, the Gini coefficient is the most common measure of income (or wealth) inequality. Ranging from a low of 0.0 to a high of 1.0, it provides a unit-less single summary measure that can be used to track inequality over time or compare different areas. It is also scalable since it can be calculated for the global, national, regional, and even local levels of geography. The Gini coefficient does, however, have serious drawbacks. It requires a frequency distribution of the amount (or percentage) of income across all low-to-high income groupings, or individual-level microdata. The calculations, although not inherently complex, are tedious, and there is no intuitive interpretation of Gini values. Finally, the coefficient is most sensitive to differences across the middle range of incomes, and least sensitive at the high and low ends of the income distribution.

When instructional time is limited, the alternative to the Gini coefficient is a set of poverty measures. The headcount index (or poverty rate) measures the incidence of poverty. It is the proportion of the population with income below a designated national or international poverty line. The weakness of the headcount index is that it does not distinguish between people substantially below the poverty line and people who are slightly below the line. The poverty gap measures the depth of poverty and is the mean shortfall below the poverty line (counting persons above the line as having zero shortfall) divided by the poverty line.

The final set of basic methods deals with the time-value of money. These are important methods since sustainability requires consideration of intergenerational equity and the tradeoff between present-generation investments and future-generation benefits. To address climate change, for example, the current generation must decide how much to spend now to stabilize the climate and prevent future generations from incurring substantial and widespread costs. The question becomes more complex if we assume that the future will be richer than the present, and that the benefits of a stable climate will last for many, many generations. Other applications include corrections for inflation and conversion of multiyear rates of changes to annual changes. From a pedagogical perspective, the core ideas of the time-value of money, discounting, and net present value can be difficult concepts for planning students and must be taught together as a unit, making it impossible to include them in the two shorter recommended curricula.

Database Methods

Database methods (Table 12.3) are not one of the traditional components of quantitative planning methods. Yet, over the long run planning-related data is too complex to be easily accommodated in spreadsheets. Planning data often falls into three dimensions: (1) geographic place; (2) time period (monthly, quarterly, annual); and (3) variable measured (population, employment, income, etc.). Further complexity is added with variables such as population that can be subdivided by age, gender, race, and ethnicity; and employment, which can be tabulated by industry, occupation, size of firm, or a number of additional dimensions. It may not be worthwhile to design a full database structure for a single analysis or project, but over the long run a well-structured planning database will save considerable time and effort.

From a pedagogical perspective, however, database material is "lumpy" in that it is difficult, if not impossible, to cover the material in a limited way in a compact period of time. For this reason, database methods have been excluded from the one-month short course. The half

Table 12.3 Database Methods

Method or Method Group	Short Course	Half Semester	Shorter Semester	Full Semester
Planning data dimensions: place, time, and variable		X	X	X
Table structure of columns-variables and rows-entities		X	X	X
Long vs. wide vs. intermediate tables		X	X	X
Queries or filters		X	X	X
Unique identifiers (keys)		X	X	X
Joining tables		X	X	X
SQL – Structured query language				X
Data normalization				X

semester and shorter semester recommendations culminate in the topic of joined tables, which is necessary for organizing all but the simplest individual tables. The prior topics address the basic elements of database management, and are all necessary for understanding how tables are joined using primary keys (in a table in which each key is a unique identifier) and foreign keys (in a table in which the keys may or may not be unique).

Basic database material is most easily learned in a graphic, interactive environment (query by example), but structured query language (SQL), as an advanced topic, provides a command-line interface to allow direct programming of database operations. Data normalization, the second advanced topic, provides students with the tools to render complex, real-world information environments into a series of rectangular tables with minimal duplication of information.

Instructors have available a wide range of database software. Commercial products, such as Microsoft Access, are easy to learn and use, especially with the well-developed query-by-example interface. Open-source products, such as MySQL (now owned by Oracle) and Base (a component of the LibreOffice suite) are free, but more difficult to install and teach.

Statistical Methods

Statistical methods (Table 12.4) have long been a core component of planning methods (Krueckeberg and Silvers, 1974, pp. 62–192), and given sufficient space in the curriculum they can justify a full semester-long course with textbooks such as Meier, Brudney, and Bohte (2015) or Healey (2015). If, however, statistical methods must be integrated into a single semester along with other quantitative methods, two statistical topics are important enough that they should be covered in even a short, one-month course: descriptive statistics and linear regression. The former includes topic areas such as measures of central tendency, measures of dispersion, and frequency tables. The latter builds upon trend extrapolation to give students a basic understanding of bivariate linear regression.

It is, of course, difficult to teach regression without an understanding of inferential statistics, but many planners will need to generate basic predictions of variable Y based upon the values of variable X, and bivariate regression allows such predictions to be done in a systematic, reproducible manner. Given additional weeks in the semester, it is possible to give a basic treatment of probability, inferential statistics, and hypothesis testing, culminating in discussion of multiple regression models. Basic statistical analysis can be accomplished in a spreadsheet environment, but more advanced topics benefit from a full statistical package such as the R open-source command-line-driven package or a commercial package like IBM-SPSS, which has an excellent menu interface.

Table 12.4 Statistical Methods

Method or Method Group	Short Course	Half Semester	Shorter Semester	Full Semester
Descriptive statistics	X	X	X	X
Bivariate regression	X	X	X	X
Probability			X	X
Inferential statistics			X	X
Hypothesis testing			X	X
Multiple regression			X	X

Analytical Methods

Analytical methods (Table 12.5) are a set of non-statistical approaches that are used primarily to analyze fundamental, cross-cutting variables such as population, employment, and transportation. The recommended population model for the full semester is the classic cohort component model. This model divides the population into cohorts by age and also, when data is available, by gender, race, and ethnicity. It addresses changes in population by calculating or applying, for each cohort, mortality rates, migration rates, and birth or fertility rates, usually based upon historic data. Although cohort component models are attractive in that they directly account for all three components of change (births, deaths, and migration), the data requirements are substantial and the interactions between the three components add a high degree of complexity. This is why they are recommended only for the full semester course.

The three shorter curricula recommend teaching the Hamilton-Perry method rather than the full cohort component model. This is a simplified model that only requires population divided into age cohorts for two past periods. Given that data, the model calculates cohort change ratios to describe how the population in any one group changes from the earlier period to the later period. If population by gender is available, the method calculates child/woman ratios to compare the number of children in younger cohorts to the number of women at risk of giving birth. If data on gender is not available, full population can be substituted. The Hamilton-Perry method has the advantages of more modest data requirements, simpler calculations, and comparable accuracy to full cohort component methods. However, the cohort change ratios combine the effects of mortality and migration in a single number, so it is very difficult to incorporate future expected changes in either of those components.

The second cross-cutting area that a majority of planners must address is the economy. Here planners have adopted a variety of methods ranging from simple *ad hoc* methods to complex input-output models. At the basic end of the scale are location quotients, usually calculated as the ratio of a local percentage employment in an industry to a larger, often national, reference area percentage employment in that industry. Location quotients may be easy to calculate, but they are very useful as analytic tools that can identify the industries with a high concentration (and importance) in the local economy. They also allow comparisons to be made across time, space, and industry-to-industry. Location quotients are not limited to employment but can be calculated from many economic and non-economic variables as well.

Economic base multipliers depend on the characterization of employment into two categories: basic or export employment, which sells goods or services to customers outside the region; and non-basic or service employment, whose markets are within the region. The economic base multiplier is the ratio of total employment to basic employment, and allows the analyst to forecast changes in total employment that result from the opening or closing of a manufacturing

Table 12.5 Analytical Methods

Method or Method Group	Short Course	Half Semester	Shorter Semester	Full Semester
Hamilton-Perry models	X	X	X	X
Location quotients	X	X	X	X
Economic base multipliers	X	X	X	X
Gravity models		X	X	X
Cohort component models				X
Shift-share models				X
Input-output models				X

plant, for example. The division of employment into two sectors is much neater in theory than in practice, but one common approach is to assign industries with location quotients above 1.0 to the basic sector.

At a moderate level of complexity are shift-share methods. These models use local and national industry employment data from two time periods to understand changes in employment as related to the national economy, the national industry, and the local industry. The most complex economic models commonly used by planners are input-output models, which track the purchases (inputs) and sales (outputs) of each industry from and to every other industry. They help planners identify for any one industry closely related industries and enable planners to estimate how growth or decline in any one industry affects both specific industries and the economy as a whole. Unfortunately, the data requirements for producing input-output models are massive, and planners are mostly consumers and appliers of these models rather than producers of them.

The final method listed in Table 12.5 is the gravity model, which attempts to quantify how interactions between areas decrease as the distance between areas increases. For each pair of areas, a gravity model of commuting, for example, includes a push factor of workers or population by residence, a pull factor of jobs by employment location, and a friction factor of distance or travel time between the areas. Results from a travel survey can be used to estimate the relative strength of each of those factors, and the model can then predict an expected spatial distribution of population, for example, based upon a given distribution of employment.

Analytical methods are important enough to comprise the largest single component of the recommended one-month short course. All planners should be familiar with these basic methods of population and economic analysis, and, as the amount of instructional time increases, the more complex models as well.

Conclusion

In the half-century since quantitative methods were incorporated into the planning curriculum, the basic body of methods has not changed dramatically. But enormous improvements in computing hardware, software, and connectivity have increased the ease of applying the methods by orders of magnitude, and lowered costs have extended these capabilities across the globe. What might we expect from the next generation of more diverse, more international, planning methods teachers? Certainly there will be some new additions to the basic suite of quantitative methods, and new textbooks will be written to incorporate those methods. But perhaps the definitive, next-generation methods textbook will not be a textbook at all, but a free library of Internet videos in the style of the Khan Academy. The availability of such a library would free teachers to use limited computer lab time for non-lecture activities such as personalized instruction, small group discussion, and repeated hands-on practice. Classes taught this way would reduce student anxiety, enhance learning outcomes, and add to the enjoyment of both student and teacher.

References

Campbell, S. (1996). Green cities, growing cities, just cities? Urban planning and the contradictions of sustainable development. *Journal of the American Planning Association, 62*(3), 296–312. doi: 10.1080/01944369608975696

Chapin, F. S. (1957). *Urban land use planning* (10th ed.). New York: Harper.

Glaeser, E. L. (2011). *Triumph of the city: How our greatest invention makes us richer, smarter, greener, healthier, and happier.* New York: Penguin Press.

Green, K. C., & Armstrong, J. S. (2015). Simple versus complex forecasting: The evidence. *Journal of Business Research, 68*(8), 1678–1685. doi: 10.1016/j.jbusres.2015.03.026

Healey, J. F. (2015). *Statistics: A tool for social research* (10th ed.). Belmont, CA: Wadsworth.

Hopkins, L. D., & Zapata, M. (2007). *Engaging the future: Forecasts, scenarios, plans, and projects.* Cambridge, MA: Lincoln Institute of Land Policy.

IPCC Core Writing Team. (2014). IPCC, 2014: Climate Change 2014: Synthesis Report. Contribution of Working Groups I, II and III to the Fifth Assessment Report of the Intergovernmental Panel on Climate Change. Geneva, Switzerland.

Jepson, E. J., & Weitz, J. (2016). *Fundamentals of plan making: Methods and techniques.* New York: Routledge.

Klosterman, R. E. (1990). *Community analysis and planning techniques.* Savage, MD: Rowman & Littlefield.

Klosterman, R. E. (2012). Simple and complex models. *Environment and Planning B-Planning & Design, 39*(1), 1–6. doi: 10.1068/b38155

Klosterman, R. E. (2013). Lessons learned about planning forecasting, participation, and technology. *Journal of the American Planning Association, 79*(2), 161–169. doi: 10.1080/01944363.2013.882647

Klosterman, R. E., Brooks, K., Drucker, J., Feser, E., and Renski, H. (2018). *Planning support methods: Urban and regional analysis and projection.* Lanham, MD: Rowman and Littlefield.

Krueckeberg, D. A., & Silvers, A. L. (1974). *Urban planning analysis: Methods and models.* New York: Wiley.

Leigh, N. G., & Blakely, E. J. (2016). *Planning local economic development: Theory and practice* (6th ed.). Los Angeles: Sage.

McLean, M. (1992). *Understanding your economy: Using analysis to guide local strategic planning* (2nd ed.). Chicago, IL: Planners Press, American Planning Association.

Meier, K. J., Brudney, J. L., & Bohte, J. (2015). *Applied statistics for public administration* (9th ed.). Belmont, CA: Wadsworth Publishing.

Myers, D., & Kitsuse, A. (2000). Constructing the future in planning: A survey of theories and tools. *Journal of Planning Education and Research, 19*(3), 221–231. doi: 10.1177/0739456x0001900301

Patton, C. V., Sawicki, D. S., & Clark, J. (2012). *Basic methods of policy analysis and planning* (3rd ed.). Upper Saddle River, NJ: Pearson.

Smith, S. K., Tayman, J., & Swanson, D. A. (2001). *State and local population projections: Methodology and analysis.* New York: Kluwer Academic/Plenum Publishers.

Smith, S. K., Tayman, J., & Swanson, D. A. (2016). *A practitioner's guide to state and local population projections.* New York: Springer.

United Nations Statistics Division. (2017a). Official list of MDG indicators. Retrieved 10/15/2017, from http://mdgs.un.org/unsd/mdg/Host.aspx?Content=Indicators/OfficialList.htm

United Nations Statistics Division. (2017b). Global indicator framework for the Sustainable Development Goals and targets of the 2030 Agenda for Sustainable Development Retrieved 10/15/2017, from https://unstats.un.org/sdgs/indicators/Global%20Indicator%20Framework_A.RES.71.313%20Annex.pdf

Wachs, M. (2001). Forecasting versus envisioning – A new window on the future. *Journal of the American Planning Association, 67*(4), 367–372. doi: 10.1080/01944360108976245

Wackernagel, M., & Rees, W. E. (1996). *Our ecological footprint: Reducing human impact on the earth.* Gabriola Island, BC; Philadelphia, PA: New Society Publishers.

Wang, X., & vom Hofe, R. (2007). *Research methods in urban and regional planning.* Beijing/New York: Tsinghua University Press/Springer.

World Wildlife Fund. (2016). *Living planet report 2016: Risk and resilience in a new era* (N. Oerlemans Ed.). Gland, Switzerland: World Wildlife Fund.

13
QUALITATIVE METHODS

Sai Balakrishnan and Ann Forsyth

Justification for Teaching Qualitative Methods

Why learn qualitative methods as part of a planning program? Partly because many qualitative approaches bear close resemblance to ordinary activities—interviewing is like a conversation, field audits involve looking around—and so they can be misunderstood as easy to pick up and requiring little in the way of preparation or monitoring. This oversimplifies qualitative academic research and professional investigation. Like other methods they require systematic research designs, data collection methods, sampling strategies, and analytical techniques. They are used to produce a number of important types of practice outputs from evaluations and inventories to case studies and scenarios. They can fill a gap in areas where other data are scarce, such as parts of the developing world. Because many of them involve interacting with living people, or providing rich data about them, they raise specific ethical concerns, however. This chapter explains how qualitative methods are used in planning practice and research, examines qualitative research design from conceptualization to outputs, confronts challenges such as access and ethics, and discusses how such methods can be incorporated into the curriculum.

We discuss two types of systematic qualitative methods—formal research and practical investigations (Forsyth, 2016). Formal research, or research type 1, builds on prior studies, is reviewed by peers, and is made public, in order to contribute to knowledge in a field. Practical investigations, research type 2, respond to a specific, concrete question, collect data in an organized way, and may draw on previous studies. However, the ultimate aim is to solve a problem rather than contributing to general knowledge. Examples include background case or precedent studies, site audits, policy histories, or photographic inventories. Practicing planners may use formal research but they are more likely to conduct investigations. Both, however, need to be systematic.

Why Methods Are Generally Useful

Qualitative methods have been the base for many classic intellectual contributions to planning—from Kevin Lynch to Judith Tendler (see Table 13.1). The strengths of qualitative methods are twofold.

Table 13.1 Selected Influential Works Based on Qualitative Research

Study	Core Question/Contribution	Example Methods
Whyte, *Street Corner Society* (1943)	Organizational analysis of a neighborhood	Participant observation. (Appendix on methods)
Jacobs, *Death and Life of Great American Cities* (1961)	"how cities work in real life . . . to learn what principles of planning . . . and rebuilding can promote social and economic vitality in cities" (p. 1)	Interviews with key informants, field observations, participant observation, document review (mentioned in passing throughout the book)
Lynch, *Image of the City* (1960)	"consider the visual quality of the American city by studying the mental image of that city which is held by its citizens" (p. 2)	Field reconnaissance, semi-structured interviews, drawing mental maps, photographic recognition, field trips (Chapter 2 and Appendix B)
Tendler, *Good Government in the Tropics* (1997)	Challenges the prevailing wisdom that governments in developing countries are rent-seeking and inefficient	Case study: selects good performing local governments in different sectors (healthcare, emergency response), interviews with street-level bureaucrats
Gans, *The Urban Villagers* (1962)	Critique of urban renewal through an ethnography of the rich social life in the West End, an Italian-American neighborhood in Boston, just prior to its demolition	Ethnography: Gans lived in the West End for nine months
Peattie, *A View from the Barrio* (1970)	Ethnography of a barrio inhabitated by rural migrants of low socioeconomic status in Venezuela	Participant observation, interviews, collection of life histories
Roy, *City Requiem, Calcutta* (2003)	A postcolonial urban theory of Calcutta (Kolkata), represented as a "requiem," i.e. "a satire on the very trope of the dying city, and as a critique of the icon of the chaotic Third World metropolis, always in trouble, always needing remedy" (p. 7)	Feminist ethnography, with research methodology spelled out in detail in appendix

Sources: Developed by authors from the texts cited.

Question type: Such methods have long been held to have strengths in answering questions about how and why phenomena occur, as opposed to questions about how much. They can help unpack complex processes, make sense of puzzles, and understand the meanings individuals or groups give to a social problem. For example why do the poor in certain developing countries continue to move out to informal settlements with insecure tenure despite being given secure public housing by the government?

Data availability: Qualitative data collection is suited for contexts without existing data, where existing data is not available, or where data is of uncertain quality and needs to be checked and triangulated.

Methods Overview: Theory and Approaches

Qualitative research design, like other research design more generally, involves an interplay between the research goals and ultimate output; data collection, sampling, and analysis; and testing and improving the validity of the findings. This section first outlines the main types of outputs or products that qualitative research and investigation create from histories to evaluations. It then explores how get to those products including collecting or finding data, choosing what to examine (sampling), and what you do with the data to make it into an output (analysis) (see Figure 13.1).

Outputs

Qualitative outputs include many of the core kinds of research and investigation products in urban planning with a variety of such outputs (Table 13.2). Studies often combine qualitative and quantitative components in what are called mixed methods designs. One characteristic is that they are more than either a single analysis or a description of a more complex situation or case. Instead they combine various data sources and analysis methods to answer larger questions such as how a situation came about, why something is successful or not, or how the future may develop. Many activities that bear a resemblance to one of these outputs do not hit the mark. For example, a precedent study may be merely a description of a successful project; to be a case study it would need to analyse more, such as how it came about and why the project was deemed successful. Just describing a content analysis of newspaper articles may indicate interesting patterns of public awareness about a planning initiative; to constitute an evaluation the findings would need to be assessed against goals or objectives.

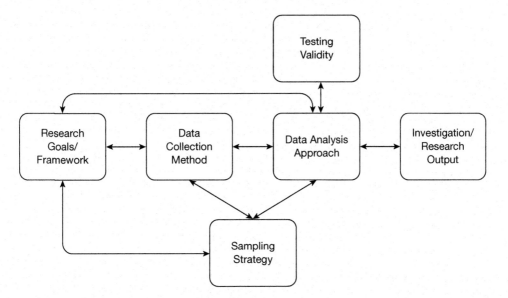

Figure 13.1 Relationship Between Qualitative Methods and Output

Table 13.2 Common Qualitative Outputs

Output	Time Period	Description	Example
History	Retrospective (long past)	Understanding how the current situation came to be, suggesting turning points and possible interventions	Policy history, neighborhood history, environmental history
Evaluation	Retrospective	Determines whether, why, and how well particular goals or outcomes were achieved. For feedback and to improve outcomes	Process evaluation, output or impact evaluation, outcome (long-term effects) evaluation
Inventory or Review	Contemporary	Compile, synthesize, and assess the range/character of what exists. Systematic understanding of the main issues in some domain	Policy inventory, regulation inventory, public perception scan, literature review
Case Study	Contemporary	Investigate contemporary phenomena, in real world context. Typically uses theory and triangulated data/analysis to deal with having more variables of interest than cases. To understand a situation in some depth; beyond mere description	Case study of policy implementation. Can be part of other outputs and other outputs can be parts of cases
Assessment or Critique	Contemporary	Assess relative to a standard. Often quantitative but can be qualitative (including participatory). Raises awareness and identifies changes	Health impact assessment, community needs assessment
Policy Analysis	Prospective	Examines which of alternative policy approaches will achieve a given set of goals. Often quantitative but can be qualitative	Political/stakeholder analysis of potential regulatory change options
Scenario	Prospective	Structured account of plausible future—often includes qualitative (vision/story, prediction) and quantitative (forecast, projection) components. To either identify a preferred scenario or prepare for possible futures	Regional climate change scenarios

Sources: Developed by the authors drawing on Yin, 1984; Thomas, 2011; Landis, 2014; Gaber & Gaber, 2007

Data Collection

To get to these products planners need to obtain data. They may compile data from existing sources, observe people and places, ask questions, and engage in collaborative methods. These are described in Table 13.3. The first categories—compiling, observing, and asking—can be done

Table 13.3 Qualitative Data Collection Methods

Category	Possible Method	Example or Explanation
Compiling	Archival and local history review	Review of reports, regulations, plans, maps, minutes, databases, organizational records, oral histories
	Media review	Systematic examination of local media: Newspapers, blogs, newsletters, photo collections
	Plan and policy inventory or review	Systematic analysis of prior work either currently in place (inventory) or over time (review)
	Literature review	Review of academic and professional studies
Observing People and Places	Locating physical traces	Identifying evidence of use such as remnants of historic buildings or evidence of desire paths
	Windshield survey	Drive-around observations using a checklist
	Site reconnaissance	Like a windshield survey but on foot
	Site audit	Observation using a highly structured tool like a walkability checklist
	Photographic site survey	Photography of an area using a specific protocol of what will be photographed
	Neighborhood atmosphere photography	Photography to communicate qualitative aspects of place
	Tomography	Multiple photographs on a theme to show range and variation
	Time lapse photography	By speeding up action shows how spaces are used
	Participant and semi-structured observations	Observations in organizations, events, and spaces—with a range of levels of intrusiveness
Asking Questions	Unstructured interviews	Free form questions, for example in a scoping meeting or correspondence
	Semi-structured interviews	Using an interview guide and questions that allow longer answers
	Focus groups, group interviews	Like semi-structured interviews but with interaction in a group
	Questionnaires and structured interviews	In person, over the phone, on paper, and online for a more structured set of answers; includes diaries
	Interactive tours	Visiting and discussing a place
	Creating image	Day-with-a-camera (photovoice) where locals take photographs and note their significance, drawing mental maps
	Reacting to images	Visual preference surveys selecting the best one from a matched pair, voting with dots on preferred images
	Social media responses	Reactions to a blog post
	Interacting with temporary installations	Responding to temporary street furnishings or signage

(continued)

Table 13.3 (continued)

Category	Possible Method	Example or Explanation
Collaborative Problem Identification and Solutions	Participatory online activities	Participatory geographic information systems; online prioritizing exercises
	Making maps and models	Annotating a neighborhood map with key assets and problem areas
	Prioritizing workshops	Identifying strengths, weaknesses, opportunities, and threats (SWOT); conducting a future search, prioritizing health impacts in a workshop
	Developing and prioritizing indicators	Community-developed sustainability indicators

Sources: Adapted from Forsyth, Salomon, & Smead, 2017; Nick Wates Associates, 2016; Gaber & Gaber, 2007; Hancock & Minkler, 2012; Participation Compass, 2016; U.S. CDC, 2015; University of Kansas, 2015

by professionals, activists, civic leaders, or local residents/workers, alone or in combination. The final category—engaging—needs to involve multiple groups.

Many students see the survey as the default data collection method, but as can be seen in the table there is a rich array of potential approaches, many better than surveys for particular purposes. Compiling existing data and conducting observations (with the exception of participant observations) also typically allow planners to obtain data with a lower burden to local participants than some of the interview, survey, and engagement techniques. This can be helpful in situations where locals suffer from participation fatigue from too many engagement processes and also to triangulate the results of such processes.

A key issue is how to be systematic in data collection—for example using instruments such as protocols, audit tools, contact summary forms, interview guides, and checklists to structure information input so that it is of good quality and can be compared with other information. This also allows researchers to keep track of provenance, to check quality and allow others to build on their work. Too often planners skip this vital step.

Sampling and Selection

A second issue is what examples to study. The basic idea is to find data of various sorts—cases, sites, interviews, observations, etc.—that can answer the research question in a substantial way that is still efficient in terms of time and other resources. Sometimes it may be possible to conduct a census, examining all possible instances, e.g. every signalized intersection in a small town. However, even then there is a decision about how to, potentially, select comparisons, e.g. similar but non-signalized intersections.

In the qualitative realm there are a variety of sampling approaches depending on the features needed (see Table 13.4). While multiple cases are useful for comparison, many important qualitative studies include a single case—for example *The Urban Villagers* (Gans, 1962). However, even within a single case there may be sampling decisions to be made, e.g. which people to interview, what days to observe a site.

As can be seen in the table, it is possible to randomly sample for qualitative research—this is most likely to be done when the qualitative investigation is fairly straightforward so that a large

Table 13.4 Qualitative Sampling and Selection Approaches

Apart from the samples where the underlying idea is "random," all others can be seen as purposeful samples, identifying information-rich cases (Palinkas et al. 2015).

Underlying Idea	Type of Sampling	Description
Richness	Information rich/intense	Rich data, but case is not extreme; can overlap other strategies
	Criterion	Cases met some criteria to assure quality, comparability. However, apart from the random samples, many of the others in this list may be seen as conforming to specific criteria
Theory	Confirming or disconfirming	Looking for exceptions to better evaluate theory
	Theory based	Using an example (case) related to a theory in order to evaluate/critique theory
	Key/critical case	Information rich; theory can be used to apply to wider range of cases
Uniqueness and Variation	Extreme case	Learning from extremes including best/worst cases
	Outlier case	Interesting because of departure form norm
	Typical case	Looks at the normal/average
	Homogenous	Provides focus
	Maximum variation	Demonstrates range
Access	Convenience/local knowledge	Convenient, easy access—saves time and money
	Opportunistic	Takes advantage of an opportunity that comes along
	Snowball or chain	Uses informants to recommend information-rich sources
Hybrid	Quota	Whatever the approach, make sure that a certain quote of people/items are from a particular group
	Random purposeful	Creates a universe that does not represent the entire population but randomly samples from a list created using other methods. Adds credibility but not generalizable
	Stratified purposeful	Illustrates subgroups; stratifies the identified cases and selects from each strata. Enhances variation in the sample though not full maximum variation
Generalizable	Census	Looking at every example
	Simple random sample	Every person/item has an equal chance of being selected; representative
	Stratified random	People/items are divided into important categories and then sampled; ensures important categories are represented
	Cluster	Universe is divided into small groups/areas (like blocks) that are randomly sampled; it is also possible to randomly sample from the sample. Makes it logistically easier to reach people

Sources: The list draws on Miles & Huberman, 1994, p. 28, and a very similar list in Palinkas et al., 2015, Table 1. It also reflects Thomas, 2011; Forsyth et al., 2012.

number of data points can be collected, and the universe of items to study is well known. For example, one might randomly sample street segments in a neighborhood to assess using an audit tool. For sampling methods examining fewer cases and focused on characteristics such as richness and uniqueness, sampling is often somewhat iterative, requiring some initial investigation to see if something is indeed interesting enough and fulfills other sampling criteria (Miles & Huberman, 1994). Sampling can also be a multistage process in that the researcher may select a case study using one method, then also need to select data sources within it such as specific people to interview, sites to observe, or media reports to analyze using another (Miles & Huberman, 1994).

This is obviously a tricky issue that deserves fuller treatment than is possible here. The main point is that sampling should be well thought out and even if a researcher decides on an opportunistic or convenience approach she does this for good reasons rather than as a default.

Analysis

Analysis is what links data to outputs. This is crucially important but is often not well specified in discussions of qualitative research. Basically it involves a number of strategies to (a) code and sort data, (b) identify findings, and (c) test the findings. These are often not discrete events. Table 13.5 provides a big picture view of approaches to analysis.

Most analyses start with some kind of data reduction. These methods can generally be made more systematic with instruments, e.g. a checklist of codes to speed identifying concepts. Some analyses stop at this stage but many go on to identify patterns or themes, compare and contrast concepts, or locate trends. There are literally scores of such techniques—Table 13.5 summarizes a number that are in common use, or potentially helpful, in the planning context. Some lines cluster together similar techniques that could be used separately.

As can be seen form the listing above, going beyond data reduction techniques can open up a wide range of analyses that can make qualitative outputs much richer. These different methods can also be used to cross-check or triangulate each other, much as is done with different data sources. This is an area where qualitative investigations in planning could be more self-conscious and reflective.

Table 13.5 Selected Analytical Approaches in Applied Qualitative Research

Approach to Findings	Type of Analysis	Description
Data Reduction/ Initial Conclusions	Coding/constant comparison	After reading the dataset, chunk data into smaller parts, and assign a code; codes can be preexisting or emerge from data (LO). Related to classical content analysis, below (LO).
	Marginal comments and reflective notes (MH)	Noting interesting elements and then writing brief reflective notes. Can identify new directions and interpret data. Simple to do digitally.
	Memoing, interim cases (MH)	Writing more structured descriptions and reflections; can include developing propositions or conclusions that come from the data, refining variables, etc.

Approach to Findings	Type of Analysis	Description
Identify Patterns and Themes	Content analyses (GG)	Identifies patterns in content by identifying words and concepts (including parts of images); includes numbers of mentions (word count); word contexts (keywords-in-context); or coded themes (classical content analysis) (LO). Looks at intensity, trends, meanings, and patterns/connections (GG).
	Meta-analysis (GG)	Brings together material from multiple reports/results/texts to identify themes, gaps.
	Literature review (B)	Comes in many forms (B), e.g. – Systematic search and review—best evidence synthesis – Mapping review—maps out literature to identify gaps – Critical review—assesses quality of sources – Integrative review—full understanding, theoretical and empirical – Scoping review—preliminary assessment Has narrative, tabular, and possibly graphical outputs
Compare and Contrast	Analytical matrix or scatterplot (MH)	Compare/critique cases/examples in terms of two or more variables. Creates a text table or text scatterplot. Can be ordered by theme, time period, role, scale, etc.
	Classification	Can be a classification/taxonomy used in the situation being studied or developed by the researcher.
Understand Possible Causality/Trends	Time series, timeline	What really follows? What happens at the same time? When were turning points?
	Decision tree	Helps identify and understand processes.
	Conceptual model, flow chart	What is connected and how? Identifies connections; can propose causal pathways.

Sources: Draws on Gaber & Gaber, 2007(GG); Booth, Colomb, & Williams, 2003 (B); Miles & Huberman, 1994 (MH); Leech & Onwuegbuzie, 2007 (LO)

Qualitative Challenges

Qualitative research differs in some key ways from quantitative methods, thus giving rise to specific challenges. One of the main strengths of qualitative research is the ability of researchers to get "close to the data" and to derive an "insider perspective" on the planning phenomenon (Gaber & Gaber, 2007). In many circumstances, these "thick descriptions" of cases and processes are possible because the researcher spends time in the natural (as opposed to controlled laboratory) setting and develops a rapport with her participants (Gaber & Gaber, 2007; Lincoln & Guba, 1985). These naturalistic observations and interviews raise ethical questions of the researcher's relationship and obligations to her participants.

Qualitative research also poses a different set of access challenges that are distinct from the more objective data that qualitative researchers work with: for instance, what are the ethical and pragmatic considerations that should guide a planner's entry into, and exit from, her research site? Since qualitative research generally involves an analysis of the meanings, experiences, and perspectives of specific research contexts, it requires a cultural sensitivity on the part of qualitative researchers so that they do not impose their own biases on the interpretation of their findings.

Finally, as qualitative research methods are used to understand processes, the standards of rigor generally used for quantitative research may not always be appropriate for qualitative work (this however depends on the sampling strategy). This does not mean that anything goes in terms of qualitative research, but only that a distinct set of standards are needed to evaluate the rigor of qualitative work. To ensure standards of rigor, it is imperative that qualitative researchers go through the same degrees of intensive methodological/technical training as quantitative researchers do. In the university setting, this means allocating adequate funds for qualitative research methods classes and ensuring that these courses receive the same support and resources that quantitative courses do.

Keeping in mind these key differences, this section outlines challenges that are specific to qualitative research. These are ethics, access, interpretation, and standards of rigor.

Ethics

Academic research ethics frequently revolve around three issues—justice, beneficence, and respect—first outlined in the 1979 Belmont Report commissioned by the U.S. Department of Health and Human Services. In an interesting report on ethics in research, the Australian government adds research merit to the list of issues (Australian Government National Health and Mental Research Council, 2015). While many of the research ethical problems have involved quantitative medical research, there are still implications for qualitative work, including more practical investigations.

Justice: This involves being fair about who is included and in the actual recruitment process so that no group is burdened by inclusion, exploitation is avoided, and that there is fair access to the benefits of research. For qualitative methods, an implication is to have a defensible sampling logic that is also clearly stated (Australian Government National Health and Mental Research Council, 2015).

Beneficence: A concept encompassing having the benefits to the individual or community outweigh the harm/discomfort of the research. It also involves minimizing harms, outlining harms to participants, and suspending research if risks outweigh the benefits. The qualitative issues involve the potential for rich data to identify research participants who may want to remain anonymous. There is also the possibility of emotional distress.

Respect: The idea of having regard for the intrinsic value of people and communities, along with issues of privacy, confidentiality, and cultural sensitivities. It also includes the capacity to make one's own decisions, and empowerment or protection where capacities are diminished, such as people with some disabiities. In qualitative research informed consent is important; but respect is also key in practice settings (Australian Government National Health and Mental Research Council, 2015).

Research merit and integrity: This entails whether research has a public benefit, and is well designed and conducted and thus is a worthwhile use of people's time. For qualitative work, developing a well-crafted and systematic research approach is key.

Access

Access is often understood as entry, but access in qualitative research is often part of a more enduring relationship, an ongoing process of negotiation (Feldman, Bell, & Berger, 2004). This is even the case for methods that do not involve direct contact with people, such as using archives or observing in public spaces. Qualitative research for planners can take place within varied settings: public sector agencies, private firms, community organizations, or neighborhoods. The terms of access for each of these settings varies. Broadly, negotiating access can be broken down into some key issues: gaining entry, building rapport/trust, and giving back.

Gaining entry: For qualitative researchers, gaining entry often means identifying the gatekeepers to a research setting. For instance, researching large organizations raises the question of where in the organizational hierarchy should researchers start? Should they start with the high-level managers or with the clerical staff? High-level gatekeepers may be helpful in opening doors to the entire organization, but they can also bias the research by directing researchers towards the least sensitive or discontent networks within the organization. Researchers should also guard against "elite bias," i.e. overweighing data from the more powerful and/or articulate individuals/groups and underrepresenting data from others.

To avoid the elite or articulate individual bias, it may be necessary for researchers to change their sampling strategy from a random to a stratified sample to ensure that the perspectives of underrepresented groups are adequately represented. For instance, in her research on the impacts of accelerated urban change on the lives and livelihoods of marginalized groups in India, Balakrishnan (2013) had identified the household as the unit of analysis, but realized that the male heads of households who controlled land titles and decision-making view urban change in markedly different ways than women and the older generations. It was necessary then to actively seek out women and seniors as part of the sampling strategy.

Entry can be complex, even with document sources, as many planning documents are held by government agencies, private firms, or even the collections of private individuals, and gaining permission to use them can be time consuming. While some observations in public spaces can be done without permission, it may necessary to obtain a formal permit or informal permission to conduct surveys or observations in such areas.

Building rapport/trust: Once the researcher has gained access, her identity can become a key variable in determining the quality of her engagement with participants. For instance, the researchers' social similarity or difference will affect her interactions. Being seen as an insider to the community can give the researcher access to information that would not be privy to someone that the participants do not feel as comfortable with. On the other hand, being a non-partisan outsider has advantages in certain contexts, like in high-conflict situations. The insider/outsider status however is not a clear cut binary, and a more nuanced way of thinking about insider/outsider perspectives distinguishes between different situations. In short, being an outsider may have advantages particularly in divisive/conflict ridden contexts, or it may enable the researcher to identify issues that someone who is too much of an insider may not because they do not have a critical distance from the site.

Giving back: Qualitative research commonly involves entering participants' everyday lives, and certain fields like anthropology have engaged deeply with the ethical question of how researchers can give back to participants. Much of planning research holds the view that research with tangible policy outcomes will have long-term positive effects and that is a justifiable way of giving back to the research site. Others, feminist ethnographers for instance, argue that "giving voice" to research participants—particularly to the marginalized, the excluded, the suppressed—and having their stories and perspectives counter dominant narratives gives ethical meaning and justification to research (Roy, 2003), Those from the tradition of participatory action research go a step beyond "giving voice." They argue that any knowledge is "deeply implicated in the operations of power" (Baker et al., 2004) and giving back means a new research methodology that is premised on the principle of equal power and the co-production of knowledge (Sandercock, 2004; Tandon, 2002).[1]

Researchers should also be highly sensitive to the costs they impose on respondents when the latter give up their time to participate in the research in the form of interviews, etc. The high degree of distrust and cynicism by communities, particularly those where their time and inputs are elicited time and time again, but without giving them anything back in terms of direct or tangible benefits, is referred to as participation or survey fatigue. In a telling example, a community member who had gone through rounds and rounds of participation without receiving any perceived benefits retorted to the researcher, "You can't eat participation, can you?" (Cornwall, 2008). Any qualitative research requires researchers to be reflective and aware of the unequal power dynamics that exist between researcher and participant, and the frequent misalignment of costs and benefits of research.

Interpretation

Since qualitative research often deals with the rich and complex experiences of individuals and groups, a key question that arises is the interpretation of these observations and interviews. Even less obtrusive data sources such as documents and observations raise issues of interpretation. How can we make sure that planners are not imposing their own assumptions and biases onto a particular context, and that they are interpreting the findings in a culturally competent way? Culture can be defined as the "shared traditions, beliefs, customs, history, folklore, and institutions of a group of people." To be culturally competent is to have knowledge about a particular culture, to be aware of and open to different worldviews. It also involves being sensitive, that is not assigning values to the differences. But cultural competence goes a step beyond awareness and sensitivity and also includes operationalizing awareness/sensitivity in research design (Center for Community Health and Development at the University of Kansas, 2017). Planners can prepare themselves to be culturally competent first, by acquiring fluent language skills, and second, by cultivating a deep knowledge of the particular research context.

Language skills: Being fluent in the dominant language of the research setting is crucial for a number of reasons. It helps to establish the credibility of the planner, especially if the planner is an outsider. It is a key "access" instrument in helping to foster rapport between the researcher and respondents (Feldman et al., 2004). To be able to grasp the meaning of what respondents say, researchers must be fluent not just in the language, but in the idioms, jokes, and other terms/phrases that are in popular use.

Knowledge of the particular research context: For researchers who are outsiders to a research setting, sustained and engaged grounded knowledge of the locale is needed so they grasp the conditions under which individuals and groups act and make their decisions.

For example, Kathryn Edin looked at low-income unwed fatherhood, which is considered one of the biggest social problems in inner-city United States (Edin & Nelson, 2013). Living for two years in Camden, New Jersey, Edin understood that young men choose fatherhood as a way of giving their lives meaning. Instead of dealing drugs on the street, they were home diapering their babies; in other words, they were choosing babies over guns. In her work on indigenous groups in the midst of rapid urban change in contemporary India, Balakrishnan (2013) was surprised to find that young men were eager to give up their sole and marginal plots of land, which was the source of subsistence agriculture, for large-scale urban developments. This counterintuitive finding can be explained if we understand that for these young men, an urban future, however uncertain and fraught with risk, was still a hopeful pathway out of the caste-ridden oppressions of agrarian life. A deep knowledge of the research context then moves us away from biased, judgmental evaluations (of poor young men making poor choices) towards framing more contextually situated planning programs that respond to real life contexts under which people make their decisions.

Good qualitative research, however, can be enhanced with the help of translators, who serve as "cultural brokers" between the planner and her respondents. An example of a fine ethnography conducted by an outsider is Katherine Boo's *Behind the Beautiful Forevers* (2012) on Mumbai's waste economy. Boo worked with a team of Mumbai translators over a period of three years, and she is insistent that her translators are "co-investigators" and together they were able to piece together a story of a complex setting.

Standards of Rigor

In the 2000s, the U.S. National Science Foundation convened qualitative researchers to organize workshops on standards of rigor for qualitative research methods (Lamont & White, 2009; Ragin, Nagel, & White, 2004). While qualitative researchers agree that the standards of rigor for qualitative research are distinct from those for quantitative, they also concur that qualitative research cannot be idiosyncratic. There has to be a collective set of standards against which the quality and the "truth value" of qualitative research is evaluated (Forsyth et al., 2012; Lytle, 2009; Miles & Huberman, 1994).

Confirmability: Research and investigation should be conducted with explicit methods and awareness of potential sources of bias (Miles & Huberman, 1994).

Reliability or repeatability: Researchers have an effect on the researched, and conversely, the researched have an effect on the researcher. Some would argue that research is never fully "objective" because the researcher always brings her positionality into her data collection and analysis. This brings up the question of reliability: would a different researcher come up with broadly similar findings? Reliability is commonly used by quantitative researchers to judge how closely the data collected and analyzed approximates the social world, and it is done through repeat measurements. If multiple researchers conduct the same research at different times, will they arrive at the same conclusions; if the same people are asked the same questions at different times will their answers be similar (assuming the questions are about some fairly stable characteristic)? While quantitative methods can more easily be tested for reliability, it is still a useful concept in qualitative research. Investigators can help reliability by clearly documenting their methods, assumptions, and their position in relation to what is being studied (e.g. insider or outsider status). Triangulating the researchers' interpretation of her data can also help in identifying researcher bias.

Validity or truthfulness: In qualitative research, validity is a strength as qualitative research is typically close to the subject of study and less prone than quantitative research to using proxy variables (such as age for health status). Technically there are many forms of validity (Lytle, 2009) but they fall broadly into two categories—accurate data and truthful interpretation. Descriptive validity is the "factual accuracy of the [researchers'] account – that is, they are not making up or distorting the things they saw and heard" (Maxwell, 2012). For interviews, a tape recording of adequate quality helps determine the accuracy of the researchers' account. But accuracy includes both what is included by the researcher in her accounts as well as what is omitted. A tape recording, for instance, will not capture the body language of the respondents; similarly, a verbatim interview transcript will not include the tone, stress and pitch of the respondents. But these sorts of "evidence," like the tape recording, are helpful when other researchers and/or methods come up with different accounts of the same place, people, phenomenon.

Interpretative validity relates to how does the researcher interpret her data from the perspective of her participants. There is "in-principle access to data that would unequivocally address threats to interpretative validity," but there are some common checks that researchers use to ensure the validity of their findings, including triangulation, carefully evaluating inconsistencies, and obtaining feedback from participants (dealt with later in this section).[2]

Perhaps the most important technique in planning is triangulation, or the use of three or more independent measures to cross-check validity. This can be applied to both data collection and analysis. For example, when investigating how well the planning development review process is working, a planner may interview people who have recently gone through the process, track the number of days taken at each stage by recent applications, and hold a focus group with planning and permitting staff. The focus group might be facilitated by an independent outsider to further triangulate researchers. The planner could then triangulate analysis of the focus group by doing general reading and making marginal notes, coding themes (a form of content analysis), and creating a decision tree or timeline.

Often the triangulated methods converge on a common interpretation, but they can also diverge or identify inconsistencies. Inconsistencies are particularly instructive as they can propmpt researchers to revise their analysis or help identify researcher bias. When sampling, the outlier or the exception case is a qualitative researchers' best friend. These outliers can guard researchers against their self-selecting biases. The researcher can also be more deliberate about these extreme cases, and make them a part of her sampling technique (see more on sampling above). A case in point is Judith Tendler's *Good Government in the Tropics* (1997) where Tendler actively looked for and focused on cases in Brazil where public sector planners were public spirited and committed to ensuring the provision of public goods to their citizens as a way of challenging conventional wisdom that planners/bureaucrats in developing countries are corrupt and inefficient. Tendler used her "good performing" cases in detail both to understand the institutional conditions that enabled good performance and to see how these background conditions can be replicated in other settings that may not have them.

Transferability to other contexts: Another common standard for quantitative research is that of generalizability: how can the findings from a specific sample be generalized to a larger population? For qualitative research a more relevant concept may be transferability, though we use the term interchangeably with generalizability. While the insights from any qualitative research should tell us about how planning works beyond the specifics of that particular place, the scale of such transferability varies depending on the type of qualitative output.

The standard of generalizability can be operationalized in the form of the comparative case method. Planners can draw instructive conclusions from researching two similar places/phenomena within the same context that yield different outcomes, or two different places/phenomena in different contexts that yield the same outcome. A simple way of thinking about the comparative case is why do the same seeds planted in the same soil yield different outcomes, or why do two seeds planted in different soils yield the same outcome. For instance, within the same city (thus keeping urban policy and politics constant), why was the sanitation infrastructure in informal settlement A well maintained, and why was it poorly maintained in informal settlement B? Such a comparison helps planners in understanding the enabling and disabling conditions that make certain outcomes possible in certain places and not in others, and to think about how these conditions can be approximated to lead to desired outcomes in varied contexts.

Utility or usefulness: in practical settings such as planning, will the findings make a difference? Are they clear and useful enough? Although primarily a form of triangulation to improve validity, getting feedback from participants, also called member checking, can ensure that the work is both accurate and useful. Researchers can encourage feedback from participants on the summary of findings, on the causal relationship, and on research predictions. This can be a time-consuming step, and has to be deliberately factored into the research schedule. In participatory action research, this step is not just about verifying the validity of research conclusions, but an integral step in the process of arriving at these conclusions with the participants as equal collaborators.

Qualitative Methods Course Design and Curriculum Placement

Qualitative methods are a key part of the planning toolkit for academic research and practical investigation and problem solving. Too often, however, they are seen as easy to pick up and not warranting special treatment in the curriculum. This exacerbates the sense that they are not very systematic and less important than quantitative methods and means planning students and graduate planners may not be fully aware of their potential.

Given this situation, there is not a standard way in which they are taught. Table 13.6 provides an overview of how such methods may be placed in the curriculum. There is no perfect position,

Table 13.6 Qualitative Methods in the Curriculum

Qualitative Methods Placement	Pro	Con
Stand-alone required course	Allows systematic treatment and substantial exercises over a semester	A full-semester course takes up a lot of space in the curriculum
Stand-alone module (6–8 weeks in semester or 1–2 weeks intensive)	Allows systematic treatment and takes less time than a full-semester course	Provides less time for sustained practice with methods unless integrated with other courses
Within a research course	Places in context	May be oriented toward research type 1 rather than investigations; may have to compete with other methods
Part of a workshop or studio	Integrates with practice	Methods taught may be determined by the specific project in the workshop, biasing content
Scattered throughout the curriculum	Integrated into many contexts/ bodies of knowledge	Difficult to coordinate; may miss coverage of key topics

but too often qualitative methods are taught within a studio or workshop, or scattered across the curriculum, and without a very strong curriculum framework may lack systematic treatment.

Qualitative methods at their best have been the basis for some of the most important works of planning scholarship and are a key part of the urban planning practice toolkit. Making sure they are taught in a consistent and comprehensive way should be a key aim of all planning curricula.

Notes

1 See for instance the Indigenous Community Planning curriculum at the University of British Columbia that is based on participatory action research: https://scarp.ubc.ca/indigenous-community-planning-concentration-mcrp. Also see the work of Participatory Research in Asia (PRIA): pria.org.
2 Adapted from Miles and Huberman (1994).

References

Australian Government National Health and Mental Research Council. (2015). *National statement on ethical conduct in human research, Section 1: Values and principles of ethical conduct*. Retrieved from www.nhmrc.gov.au/book/section-1-values-and-principles-ethical-conduct

Baker, J., Lynch, K., Cantillon, S., & Walsh, J. (2004). *Equality: From theory to action* (1st ed.). New York: Palgrave Macmillan.

Balakrishnan, S. (2013). *Land conflicts and cooperatives along Pune's highways: Managing India's agrarian to urban transition*. (PhD), Harvard University.

Boo, K. (2012). *Behind the beautiful forevers: Life, death, and hope in a Mumbai undercity*. New York: Random House.

Booth, W. C., Colomb, G. G., & Williams, J. M. (2003). *The craft of research* (2nd ed.). Chicago and London: University of Chicago Press.

Center for Community Health and Development at the University of Kansas. (2017). Community Tool Box. Retrieved from http://ctb.ku.edu/en/table-of-contents

Cornwall, A. (2008). Unpacking "Participation": models, meanings and practices. *Community Development Journal*, 43(3), 269–283. doi:10.1093/cdj/bsn010

Edin, K., & Nelson, T. J. (2013). *Doing the best I can: Fatherhood in the inner city*. Berkeley, California: University of California Press.

Feldman, M. S., Bell, J., & Berger, M. T. (2004). *Gaining access: A practical and theoretical guide for qualitative researchers*. Walnut Creek, California: AltaMira Press.

Forsyth, A. (2016). Investigating Research. *Planning Theory & Practice*, 17(3), 467–471.

Forsyth, A., Agrawal, A., & Krizek, K. (2012). Simple, inexpensive approach to sampling for pedestrian and bicycle surveys. *Transportation Research Record* 2299, 22–30.

Forsyth, A., Salomon, E., & Smead. L. (2017) *Creating healthy heighborhoods: Evidence-based planning and design strategies*. Chicago, Illinois: APA Planners Press/New York: Routledge.

Forsyth, A., Van Riper, D., Larson, N., Wall, M., & Neumark-Sztainer, D. (2012). Creating a replicable, valid cross-platform buffering technique: The sausage network buffer for measuring food and physical activity built environments. *International Journal of Health Geographics*, 11(1), 14. doi:10.1186/1476-072x-11-14

Gaber, J., & Gaber, S. L. (2007). *Qualitative analysis for planning and policy: Beyond the numbers*. Chicago, Illinois: American Planning Association.

Gans, H. J. (1962). *The urban villagers: Group and class in the life of Italian-Americans*. New York: Free Press of Glencoe.

Hancock, T. & Minkler, M. (2012). Community health assessment or healthy community assessment: Whose community? Whose health? Whose assessment? In M. Minkler (ed.), *Community organizing and community building for health* (pp. 138–157). Piscataway, New Jersey: Rutgers University Press.

Jacobs, J. (1961). *The death and life of great American cities*. New York: Random House.

Lamont, M., & White, P. (2009). *Workshop on interdisciplinary standards for systematic qualitative research*. Washington, D.C. Retrieved from www.nsf.gov/sbe/ses/soc/ISSQR_workshop_rpt.pdf.

Landis, J. (2014). Presentation to Association of Collegiate Schools of Planning Doctoral Student Workshop, Cambridge, MA.

Leech, N. L., & Onwuegbuzie, A. J. (2007). Sampling designs in qualitative research: Making the sampling process more public. *The Qualitative Report*, 12(2), 238–254.

Lincoln, Y. S., & Guba, E. G. (1985). *Naturalistic inquiry*. Newbury Park, California: Sage Publications.

Lynch, K. (1960). *The image of the city*. Cambridge, Massachussetts: The MIT Press.

Lytle, L. A. (2009). Measuring the Food Environment: State of the Science. *American Journal of Preventive Medicine*, 36(4), S134–S144. doi:10.1016/j.amepre.2009.01.018

Maxwell, J. A. (2012). *Qualitative research design: An interactive approach* (3rd ed.). Thousand Oaks, California: Sage Publications.

Miles, M. B., & Huberman, A. M. (1994). *Qualitative data analysis: An expanded sourcebook* (2nd ed.). Thousand Oaks, California: Sage Publications.

Nick Wates Associates (2016). Community Planning. Retrieved from http://communityplanning.net/

Palinkas, L. A., Horwitz, S. M., Green, C. A., Wisdom, J. P., Duan, N., & Eaton Hoagwood, K. (2015). Purposeful sampling for qualitative data collection and analysis in mixed method implementation research. *Administration and Policy in Mental Health and Mental Health Services Research*, 42(5), 533–544

Peattie, L. (1970). *The view from the barrio*. Ann Arbor, Michigan: University of Michigan Press.

Ragin, C., Nagel, J., & White, P. (2004). *Workshop on scientific foundations of qualitative research*. Retrieved from www.nsf.gov/pubs/2004/nsf04219/nsf04219.pdf.

Roy, A. (2003). *City requiem, Calcutta: Gender and the politics of poverty* (Vol. 10). Minneapolis, Minnesota: University of Minnesota Press.

Sandercock, L. (2004). Commentary: Indigenous planning and the burden of colonialism. *Planning Theory & Practice*, 5(1), 118–124. doi:10.1080/1464935042000204240

Tandon, R. (2002). *Participatory research: Revisiting the roots*. New Delhi: Mosaic Books.

Tendler, J. (1997). *Good government in the Tropics*. Baltimore, Maryland: Johns Hopkins University Press.

Thomas, G. (2011). *How to do your case study: A guide for students and researchers*. Thousand Oaks, California: Sage Publications.

Whyte, W. F. (1943). *Street corner society: The social structure of an Italian slum*. Chicago, Illinois: University of Chicago Press.

Yin, R. (1984). *Case study research and applications: Design and methods*. Thousand Oaks, California: Sage Publications.

14
SPATIAL ANALYSIS

Subhrajit Guhathakurta

Introduction

The location of people and activities in a place is of primary concern for planning given that accessibility to urban services is a critical aspect of residents' quality of life. People will generally seek out homes in locations that are close to destinations that are desirable, such as workplaces, parks, and recreation areas, and further from places that are undesirable, such as polluted or crime infested parts of the city. Similarly, businesses would want to locate in places that provide good access to its facilities for their workers, clients, and goods. However, access is not just about proximity. The infrastructure connecting different parts of the city can make places further away easier to access than the ones close-by. For example, central business districts of many cities are well connected through multiple modes of travel such as automobiles, trains, and buses to most parts of the city. Traveling from a suburb to central city by transit can often be more convenient than going to another less distant suburb. Therefore, an important part of spatial analysis is understanding the characteristics of networks.

While individual households make location and travel choices that optimize their private utility, the combined impact of such individual choices can often diverge from the social optimum. Several examples of such social costs of combined individual choices were discussed by Thomas C. Schelling in his book *Micromotives and Macrobehavior* (1978, 2006). The most famous of these examples was the thought experiment and simulation showing that even mild preferences for certain types of neighbors held by several households can lead to segregated neighborhoods over time. We come across many common examples of social costs of our individual choices everyday – such as costs of congestion on highways or the long lines at the Starbucks counter. Spatial analysis can help in designing policies that mitigate such costs by showing where such congestion can happen and how the excess demand can be redirected to less congested points.

The principal concerns of spatial analysis in urban and regional planning are, therefore, not just about spatial configurations of activities in a place, but about accessibility to various life-sustaining and life-affirming services, which inherently have important equity implications. While spatial analysis has wide application across many disciplines, the importance of various techniques and their nuances tend to vary by the type of problem being addressed. Yet, the fundamental aspects of spatial analytical techniques, which are often based on statistical methods, are similar across disciplines. This chapter does not delve into a review of the methods used in spatial analysis, but shows how spatial analysis is used in problems that commonly concern urban planners. The focus is on developing a framework for teaching spatial analysis for urban and regional planning in the global context, hence the examples will all be in this domain.

Objectives

The most fundamental concept in understanding spatial problems is the concept of spatial heterogeneity. As shown in Figure 14.1, spatial heterogeneity is the basis for discussing locational attributes and is key to understanding accessibility of places and other forms of spatial relationships. The method for conducting such analysis depends on the questions being asked. A principal objective of this chapter is to show how spatial heterogeneity is discussed and measured for different types of urban and regional analysis.

Spatial heterogeneity is especially important in examining questions of equity and vulnerability, which are discussed separately in later sections. The measures of equity essentially involve the delineation of different groups of people or households, their locations, and their options for enjoying various urban amenities or being burdened by disamenities. Plans and public investments are expected to ensure a reasonably equitable distribution of both burdens and benefits. An additional objective of this chapter is to highlight some of the common methods for undertaking the three different forms of analysis – spatial clustering, network analysis, and site suitability analysis – highlighted in Figure 14.1. Understanding these three types of spatial methods will help in analyzing the majority of the spatial problems in urban and regional analysis. Finally, this chapter will provide some guidance for designing a course on spatial analysis for urban and regional planners in the global context.

Equity

Almost all urban investments and policy decisions have an equity component. The choice of building a new highway, a new senior facility, or for adopting an inclusive housing ordinance, among other examples, all have consequences that affect communities and individuals

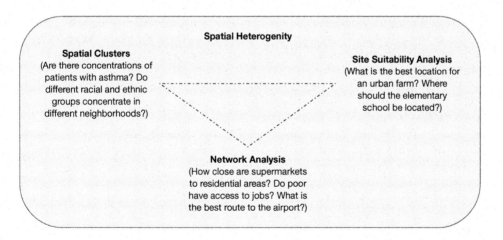

Figure 14.1 Common Methods of Spatial Analysis in Urban and Regional Planning

differentially. It is important to test how the costs and benefits of these policies or investments will be shared before implementing the plan or program. To examine how the new initiative affects equity, it is also critical to analyze the current status of the community to ensure that the burdens do not fall on those who are already the most disadvantaged, while the benefits mostly accrue to those who may not need them as much.

A decision to develop a new park in a city can illustrate how spatial heterogeneity plays a role in analyzing equity. Parks are important community assets since they provide several benefits including more recreational opportunities, better public health, cleaner air, and higher land values. Several standards are available for guidance regarding the size and ideal locations for neighborhood parks (e.g., Moeller, 1965). Ideally, neighborhood parks should be located within walking distance of each home. Several guidelines suggest that they should be about four acres for every 4000 persons. The first step in planning the new park is to determine whether there are areas within the city where households do not have access to a park that meets the minimum requirements within walking distance. That is, to ascertain the extent of spatial heterogeneity in park access in the city.

The task of determining the spatial heterogeneity in park access involves obtaining data on:

1 the current distribution of neighborhood parks (as defined);
2 the current distribution of housing units (points);
3 the distribution of households by demographic and socioeconomic characteristics by neighborhood (polygons); and
4 the street network for the city.

The analysis can be conducted by completing four steps. First, a network-based buffer is created around each housing unit. The network-based buffers create a virtual boundary around each housing unit where the edges are formed by connecting points on the street network that are within walking distance (say, 0.25 miles) from those units. Second, the demographic and socioeconomic information are overlaid on this set of buffers to identify housing units that are mostly described by areas with concentrations of different groups of people characterized by income, race, ethnicity, and other pertinent attributes. Third, we can overlay the neighborhood park map to determine the number and locations of housing units, characterized by demographic and socioeconomic attributes, whose buffers do not touch or intersect a park. Finally, based on the third step, a map can be created that shows the differential access to neighborhood parks for different groups of people. To improve equity in park access, the new park should be developed in the area where most people have low park access, and therefore will have the greatest benefit from this investment.

The entire analysis for determining whether neighborhood park access is equitable can be easily conducted with the help of a Geographic Information System (GIS; see, for example, Wolch, Wilson, & Fehrenbach, 2005). GIS are designed particularly for managing and analyzing spatial information that relates to places on the Earth's surface. GIS is the software platform (such as ArcGIS or QGIS), which incorporates a set of tools for storing, managing, updating, manipulating, and analyzing *geographically referenced* information. While this chapter will refer to several GIS operations as they relate to spatial analysis for urban planning, it cannot offer a comprehensive introduction to GIS. The reader is referred to the large volume of information on introductory GIS techniques and courses available online for gaining a better understanding of GIS fundamentals.

The general method for describing spatial heterogeneity in park access can be applied to many other urban features, which either create an amenity, or a disamenity, to households nearby. A similar approach can be used for assessing the equity in the distribution of landfills, generators of pollutants, and access to transit and jobs among other similar facilities.

Vulnerability

Vulnerability is a concept that expands the discussions about equity to include capabilities of individuals and groups to deal with an exposure to particular hazards. Consider the situation where there is spatial heterogeneity in the city's microclimate as it relates to the variation in temperature triggered by urban heat island (UHI) effects. Areas that are densely built-up are usually hotter due to the radiation of heat from materials such as asphalt and concrete that store sun's radiation during the day and release it at night, keeping the ambient temperatures warmer than the surrounding areas. The older adults and the sick are especially sensitive to the excessive heat and are affected to a greater extent than other healthier and younger persons. In addition, if these older adults are also poor, then they may not be able to enjoy the relief offered by an air-conditioned space. In other words, the aged poor are especially vulnerable to urban heat if they live in areas with high heat island effects and face greater exposure, since they have higher sensitivity to heat. In addition, they also suffer due to low adaptive capacity to mitigate the effects of heat as they lack resources for altering their immediate environment.

The example above illustrates the generalized model for measuring vulnerability, which is presented as follows:

Vulnerability = Exposure + Sensitivity - Adaptive Capacity

The concept of vulnerability is becoming the key to understanding resiliency of different communities to myriad environmental hazards such as coastal flooding, hurricanes, sea-level rise, and other adverse conditions triggered by the changing climate. This concept can also be applied to study the effects of unfavorable social conditions on particular groups of people. For example, children's vulnerability to crime ridden areas is higher because of their higher sensitivity and lower adaptive capacity. Spatial analysis is a critical tool for mapping vulnerability of different populations to specific hazards. Vulnerability mapping provides critical information for decision-makers for developing plans and policies that can mitigate these vulnerabilities and offer a means for prioritizing the most affected groups.

Similar to equity analysis, vulnerability mapping starts with a set of spatial datasets that are overlaid to determine the range of vulnerability scores to a particular hazard. Consider the example presented earlier about vulnerability to UHI effects. To generate a vulnerability map, we will need at least three datasets including: 1) a spatial distribution of nighttime temperatures (since UHI is especially a nighttime phenomenon); 2) a spatial distribution of adults who are 65 years and older; and 3) a spatial distribution of households in poverty (a proxy for low incomes). Depending on the specific objectives of the exercise, other datasets would also be useful – such as, the locations of health care centers and special shelters to provide relief from heat. An efficient way of conducting this analysis would be to create *raster* data files from all the datasets. The raster files should have the same *resolution* and grid coordinates to ensure that grid cells are perfectly aligned on all datasets. Assuming that a 1-mile square grid is adequate for the task, the vector data for each of the three datasets can be converted to raster by processes that are slightly different based on whether the original (vector) dataset contain points, polygons, or polylines.

The spatial distribution of temperatures can be converted into several ranges, say 10, and reclassified with higher numbers indicating higher temperatures. These reclassified numbers would be included in the grid attribute file. If the spatial distribution of older adults is provided by census tracts or neighborhoods (i.e., polygons), then a similar technique as the temperature profile can be used. That is, first create ranges for the number of such individuals in the tract and then attach that range-id or number to the grid cell that falls on the tracts. Make sure to use the same direction in range numbering as used previously, i.e., higher range numbers indicate greater values. Also, grid cells that intersect multiple polygons will have to use an algorithm to determine the final value to assume. This algorithm is typically based on the area of intersection and the final range value is the weighted sum of the separate values in the grid cell. If indeed the original vector dataset contain points, say each household in poverty is located by a point in the map, then the grids can simply aggregate these points and come up with a total for each grid.

The calculation of vulnerability to heat for each grid would involve an aggregation of all the raster values for that grid, which can also be individually weighted to reflect importance. Exposure, in this case, would be reflected by the index of heat (1 to 10), sensitivity would be represented by the ranges developed from the number of older adults, and adaptive capacity, or the lack thereof, would be reflected in the number of households in poverty. Additionally, the locations of shelters and health facilities can also be used to guide planning. This information will ensure that the locations of the most vulnerable individuals are targeted for development of additional shelters to reduce vulnerability to heat. Vulnerability analysis has been well documented for a variety of natural and man-made hazards including seal level rise, floods, earthquakes, and air pollution (Aubrecht, Özceylan, Steinnocher, & Freire, 2012; Copeland et al., 2010; Cova & Church, 1997; Dewan, 2013; Islam, Mitra, Dewan, & Akhter, 2016).

The analysis described above is the most intuitive method for mapping vulnerability but may not adequately capture the factors that contribute to *spatial clustering* effects. If indeed, neighborhoods or places exhibit similar characteristics when they are adjacent to each other, the underlying processes that are driving this clustering might also be related. In situations where spatial clustering effects are observed, special statistical tools are necessary to examine the spatial relationships among the proximal geographical locations. The next section presents some of the basic techniques of analyzing such spatial relationships.

Methods

Spatial Clustering

Geographic clustering is a phenomenon that follows Wald R. Tobler's first law of geography, which states "Everything is related to everything else, but near things are more related than distant things" (1970). The identification of clusters of events and activities as well as explaining why such clusters appear have been the subject of intensive research for about five decades. This section provides a brief outline of some of the tools that are routinely used in urban planning. Readers who are interested in more detailed study are directed to many excellent texts on the subject including, most recently, *Modern Spatial Econometrics in Practice*, authored by Luc Anselin and Sergio Rey (2014).

An important consideration in studying vulnerability is that of spatial dependencies. Spatial dependencies arise when nearby activities and impacts share similar conditions. Spatial dependencies can lead to areas with clusters of high and low incidences of the phenomenon being studied together with unique spots that are different from the adjoining areas (i.e., areas that exhibit a high incidence of the phenomenon surrounded by areas with low incidence, or vice-versa). To illustrate the methods for determining spatial clusters, we can take the previous example of spatial variation in heat island effects and ask whether clusters of *relatively* "hot" and "cold" areas exist. This question can be easily addressed by calculating the "Moran's I" index. Moran's I is an index showing how the values (temperature in this case) deviates from a random distribution of temperatures across the region and is derived in the following manner:

$$I = \frac{N}{W} \frac{\sum_i \sum_j w_{ij}(x_i - \bar{x})(x_j - \bar{x})}{\sum_i (x_i - \bar{x})^2}$$

Where N is the number of spatial units indexed by i and j; x is the measure of interest (temperature); $\bar{x}$ is the mean of x; w_{ij} is a matrix of spatial weights with zeroes on the diagonal; and W is the sum of all weights.

The Moran's I, as described above, is a *global* indicator of whether clusters of high and low exist in the spatially distributed data. Its values vary from +1 to −1, indicating complete segregation of data (+1) to complete homogeneity (0) to totally random distribution of high and low values (−1). However, this statistic is unable to show where the clusters of high and low values exist. For observing the location of these clusters several local indicators have been suggested including the local Moran's I, which is the basis for calculating the Local Indicators of Spatial Association (LISA) (Anselin, 1995).

LISA has become a popular technique to determine hot and cold spots within a region for any spatially distributed phenomenon. There are, however, several other methods for determining concentrations of particular features or attributes across space, such as Getis and Ord's (1992) statistics G_i and G_i^*. The attractiveness of LISA, as explained by Anselin (1995), is that it decomposes Moran's I measure into the individual contributions to that measure from each observation. Therefore, the sum of LISA scores over all locations is proportional to the corresponding global statistic.

The calculation of LISA is easily accomplished with the help of several software packages including the freely available GeoDa package developed by Luc Anselin (https://spatial.uchicago.edu/software) and from the geostatistical tools in ESRI's ArcMap. LISA is a univariate statistic requiring one variable of interest to be identified that varies across spatial units. The computation also asks how the adjacent spatial units should be delineated and their weights. For example, Figure 14.2 shows the clusters of high and low affordability for housing in Atlanta metro by census tracts. In this figure, the high-high clusters are census tracts where high proportion of households are paying more than 30% of their income for housing that are also surrounded by similar tracts. In contrast, the low-low clusters have mostly households that are bearing a lower burden for housing costs (less than 30% of their incomes), surrounded by similar other tracts. This spatial clustering technique using LISA has now become an essential component of courses on spatial analysis. The reader is directed to the extensive literature on geospatial analysis tools, techniques, and applications, including the volumes by Fischer & Getis, 2009; Wang, 2014; Nyerges, Couclelis, and McMaster, 2011; Fotheringham and Rogerson, 2008; and De Smith, Goodchild, and Longley, 2007.

Network Analysis

Networks are a group of objects that are connected through their interactions or relationships to each other. These objects can be people, places, computers, texts, or things. The connections between them are defined by measures of intensity, distance, frequency, or the strength of interactions. The connection can also have directionality. That is, connection between A → B

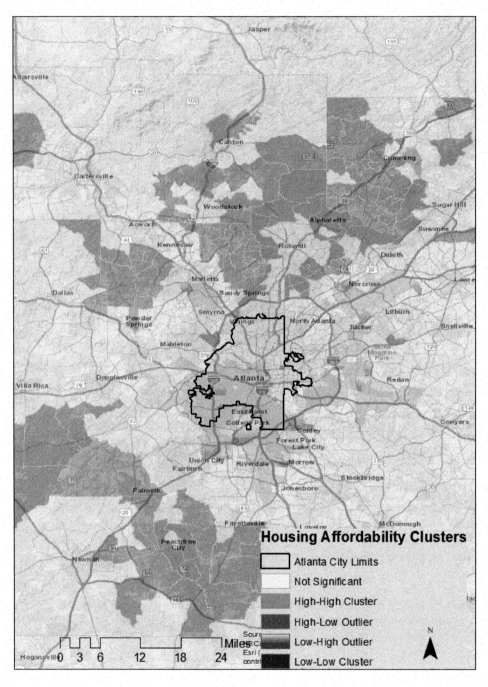

Figure 14.2 Sample LISA (Local Indicators of Spatial Association) Analysis of the Housing Market of Atlanta, Georgia (author's analysis)

does not necessarily suggest A ← B also exists. Networks are usually analyzed with the help of graph theory.

Not all networks have spatial attributes. Location or place may not be an important aspect of a computer network, but street networks are primarily spatial. Streets connect places that are fixed in space and defined by the Earth's geography. Streets are also characterized by distance, width, and directionality (one-way, two-way, etc.). To study street networks, we first derive the directional graph of this network. The directional graph represents the street network as a sequence of edges and nodes, where the streets form the edges and their points of connection to other streets (or an initial point) form the nodes. While the streets are characterized by distance, number of lanes, and direction of traffic, nodes often assume values of importance based on the intensity of activities occurring around them. Once the attributes of the directional graph, based on the street network, are derived, several network characteristics can be calculated including the shortest path between any two nodes, the most central (accessible) nodes, the redundancy (multiple travel options) and connectedness (efficiency) of the street network, among others.

Graph theory is an active branch of scholarship in mathematics and computational sciences, but planners are mostly concerned with the applications of this theory for particular purposes as discussed above. The conceptual basis of graphs are not difficult to convey to planning students and its applications are well known. Therefore, in planning programs network analysis is taught with the help of a software package such as Gephi, which is open source, or by using libraries in general purpose programing languages like Python (graph-tool, NetworkX) and R. In addition, GIS packages such as ESRI's ArcGIS also include many tools for network analysis including routing, shortest paths, and service area functions. Given that GIS is now part of the common core in planning programs, network analysis is mostly taught with the help of GIS software. For further reading on the topic, please refer to Porta, Crucitti, and Latora, 2006; Strogatz, 2001; Dorogovtsev and Mendes, 2002; Glückler, 2007; and Park and Yilmaz, 2010.

Site Suitability Analysis

Spatial heterogeneity is most commonly expressed in differences in density and the existence of clusters. As discussed earlier, Local Indicators of Spatial Association can show where clusters of high values surrounded by other high values (high-high) and low values surrounded by other low values (low-low) exist (as well as locations of high-low, and low-high clusters). These techniques are appropriate for univariate (with one variable or attribute) analysis. However, to select ideal locations for particular activities, such as schools, homes, and playgrounds, among others, we need to look at many more spatial factors. Site suitability analysis is the method of:

1 identifying the various characteristics of place and location that are suitable for an activity;
2 determining the benchmarks and criteria for combining these characteristics; and then
3 seeking out all locations that meet the combined criteria (suitability score) to locate the activity.

Site suitability analysis has been around for over five decades and popularized through Ian McHarg's celebrated book called *Design with Nature* (1969). Prior to the availability of computers, the method was simply a series of overlays of transparent paper, each containing information about a particular spatial attribute (slope, land use, vegetation, soil, etc.). Given that each attribute would be scaled from poor suitability to excellent suitability with the help of a color gradient (from light to dark), the best locations could easily be identified on the overlaid transparencies by noting the darkest areas. This method became the basis for the initial design of GIS. It also inspired other uses of this technique such as the Land Evaluation/Site Assessment (LESA) method adopted by the U.S. Department of Agriculture to evaluate the suitability of land parcels for agriculture, conservation, or development.

For an illustration of site suitability analysis, consider the example where a firm is seeking to identify the most suitable parcels of land for urban agriculture. The first step would be to list specific attributes that the ideal site should have, which could include particular type of soil, distance from highways, slope of land, drainage characteristics, a minimum size of parcel, among others. Each of the attributes are then measured along a standardized scale in the second step (e.g., with scores from 1 to 9, where 1 is least suitable and 9 is most suitable). Table 14.1 shows the scales based on some suitability criteria applied to each attribute. In the third step, the relative importance of each of the attributes is assigned as weights. If indeed soil quality is twice as important as being close to a highway, then soil quality would be weighed twice as much as highway access (making sure that the sum of all weights is 100%). Next, in Step Four, the composite score is calculated by aggregating the weighted total of all scores. The higher aggregate scores indicate the more suitable areas. There is, however, a final step that involves using other information, not included in the analysis, to remove parcels that are not suitable from the previous list.

Table 14.1 Suitability Criteria for an Urban Farm

Criteria for Weighted Overlay	Weight (%)	Range / Class		Suitability Score (scale 1–9)
Slope (%)	30	0–5 %		9
		5–15 %		5
		> 15 %		1
Land Cover (National Land Cover Database)	15	Open water	11	0
		Developed, open space	21	7
		Developed, low-intensity	22	7
		Developed, medium intensity	23	3
		Developed, high intensity	24	1
		Barren land	31	9
		Deciduous forest	41	3
		Evergreen forest	42	4
		Mixed forest	43	4
		Grassland/Herbaceous	71	9
		Pasture/Hay	81	9
		Woody Wetlands	90	1
Cost of land	35	< $500K per acre		9
		$500K–$1M/acre		4
		> $1M/acre		1
Distance from highway		< ½ mile		9
		½ mile – 1 mile		6
		1 mile – 3 miles		3
		> 3 miles		1
Distance from polluted sites		< ½ mile		1
		½ mile – 1 mile		3
		1 mile – 3 miles		5
		> 3 miles		9

Site suitability analysis is a common technique taught is intermediate level GIS courses. When this technique is introduced in the GIS software ArcGIS, the Spatial Analyst extension is commonly used since the process is simplified when the spatial layers are converted to a common raster-based layers. In addition, the entire process can be automated with the help of the Model Builder tool of ArcGIS. (The reader can find many books and other online materials to find more in-depth discussion of this technique together with examples, including the tutorials available in http://desktop.arcgis.com/en/arcmap/latest/extensions/spatial-analyst/tutorial/exercise-3-finding-a-site-for-a-new-school.htm.)

Structuring a Spatial Analysis Course

The topics discussed above can be packaged for an introductory course in spatial analysis but will require the students to have some familiarity with basic statistics and spatial planning. By completing such a course, a student should be able to:

- understand the characteristics and sources of spatial data;
- measure spatial heterogeneity and understand the factors driving it;
- recognize planning issues and problems that require spatial analysis;
- recognize and measure spatial equity and vulnerability;
- derive spatial clusters using Moran's I and LISA;
- conduct network analysis on transportation related data;
- use spatial analysis to conduct site suitability analysis; and
- become aware of multiple advanced tools that can support different aspects of spatial analysis.

Often the challenge in teaching spatial analysis is finding suitable sources of spatial data that the participants can relate to. This is especially true in places that have undeveloped data infrastructure due to low institutional capacity to maintain such an operation. Given that a significant part of the course is based on univariate data (only one variable), finding appropriate data that is suited to the context of the participants should not be a major challenge. Other datasets that can be used in this course could potentially be derived from ubiquitous sources such as OpenStreetMaps (e.g., street networks), satellite images (vegetation, soils, etc.) and aerial images (Google Earth).

To complete the course, a minimum of 20 sessions (of 1.5 contact hours or equivalent) would be required, together with substantial assigned tasks outside the contact hours. Therefore, assuming three contact hours per week, the entire course could be delivered in 10 weeks. While a more compressed schedule is also possible, it is not advisable to conduct this course under two weeks, especially for students who are unfamiliar with the tools introduced in the course. The 10-week course would potentially include the following schedule:

Week 1 – Introduction to spatial data

Week 2 – Planning problems requiring spatial analysis

Week 3 – Concept of spatial heterogeneity

Week 4 – Locating spatial clusters

Week 5 – Understanding and measuring spatial equity

Week 6 – Understanding and measuring vulnerability

Week 7 – Analyzing networks and their planning implications

Weeks 8 and 9 – Site suitability analysis

Week 10 – Advanced tools for spatial data analysis and wrap-up

The course module should offer hands-on exercises in class, preferably for each session. Ideally, the concepts and tools should be delivered through applications in a real and familiar context. Planning problems are contextual and the particularities of each context need to be discussed in order to demonstrate the potential of the tools together with their limitations. Assessments also need to include about five assignments that engage the students in topics of their interest using the tools introduced in the course.

Final Thoughts

Spatial analysis is a rapidly expanding domain of knowledge that is quickly becoming an essential component of several disciplines such as ecology, hydrology, geography, and planning, among others. The core concepts and tools of spatial analysis take on different forms based on the particular problems addressed by each discipline. The questions around spatial equity and vulnerability are central to planning problems, which can be analyzed with the help of clustering techniques and through network analysis. In addition, planning also deals with the specificity of each place and the suitability of that place for various activities. Site suitability analysis is designed to provide a template for assessing the right locations for a particular activity. A course that combines the principal objectives of planning together with the essential spatial tools for analyzing those objectives would provide a good introduction of spatial analysis in planning.

References

Anselin, L. (1995). Local Indicators of Spatial Association-LISA. *Geographical Analysis, 27*(2), 93–115. doi:10.1111/j.1538-4632.1995.tb00338.x

Anselin, L., & Rey, S. J. (2014). *Modern Spatial Econometrics in Practice: A Guide to GeoDa, GeoDaSpace and PySAL*. Chicago, Illinois: GeoDa Press LLC.

Aubrecht, C., Özceylan, D., Steinnocher, K., & Freire, S. (2012). Multi-level Geospatial Modeling of Human Exposure Patterns and Vulnerability Indicators. *Natural Hazards, 68*(1), 147–163. doi:10.1007/s11069-012-0389-9

Copeland, H. E., Tessman, S. A., Girvetz, E. H., Roberts, L., Enquist, C., Orabona, A., . . . Kiesecker, J. (2010). A Geospatial Assessment on the Distribution, Condition, and Vulnerability of Wyoming's Wetlands. *Ecological Indicators, 10*(4), 869–879. doi:10.1016/j.ecolind.2010.01.011

Cova, T. J., & Church, R. L. (1997). Modelling Community Evacuation Vulnerability using GIS. *International Journal of Geographical Information Science, 11*(8), 763–784. doi:10.1080/136588197242077

De Smith, M. J., Goodchild, M. F., & Longley, P. (2007). *Geospatial Analysis: A Comprehensive Guide to Principles, Techniques and Software Tools*. Leicester: Troubador Publishing.

Dewan, A. M. (2013). *Floods in a Megacity: Geospatial Techniques in Assessing Hazards, Risk, and Vulnerability*. Dordrecht: Springer Netherlands.

Dorogovtsev, S. N., & Mendes, J. F. F. (2002). Evolution of Networks. *Advances in Physics, 51*(4), 1079–1187. doi:10.1080/00018730110112519

Fischer, M. M., & Getis, A. (Eds.). (2009). *Handbook Of Applied Spatial Analysis: Software Tools, Methods And Applications*. Heidelberg: Springer Science & Business Media.

Fotheringham, A. S., & Rogerson, P. (Eds.). (2008). *The SAGE Handbook of Spatial Analysis*. London: SAGE Publications, Ltd.

Getis, A., & Ord, J. K. (1992). The Analysis of Spatial Association by Use of Distance Statistics. *Geographical Analysis, 24*(3), 189–206. doi:10.1111/j.1538-4632.1992.tb00261.x

Glückler, J. (2007). Economic Geography and the Evolution of Networks. *Journal of Economic Geography*, 7(5), 619–634. doi:10.1093/jeg/lbm023

Islam, M. A., Mitra, D., Dewan, A., & Akhter, S. H. (2016). Coastal Multi-Hazard Vulnerability Assessment along the Ganges Deltaic Coast of Bangladesh–A Geospatial Approach. *Ocean & Coastal Management*, 127, 1–15. doi:10.1016/j.ocecoaman.2016.03.012

McHarg, I. L., & American Museum of Natural History. (1969). *Design with Nature*. New York: Natural History Press.

Moeller, John (1965). Standards for Outdoor Recreational Areas. American Society of Planning Officials Report # 194. Chicago, IL.

Nyerges, T. L., Couclelis, H., & McMaster, R. (Eds.). (2011). *The SAGE Handbook of GIS and Society*. London: SAGE Publications, Inc.

Park, K., & Yilmaz, A. (2010). *A Social Network Analysis Approach to Analyze Road Networks*. Paper presented at the ASPRS Annual Conference, San Diego, California.

Porta, S., Crucitti, P., & Latora, V. (2006). The Network Analysis of Urban Streets: A Dual Approach. *Physica A: Statistical Mechanics and its Applications*, 369(2), 853–866. doi:10.1016/j.physa.2005.12.063

Schelling, T. C. (2006). *Micromotives and Macrobehavior* (2nd ed.). New York: W. W. Norton.

Strogatz, S. H. (2001). Exploring Complex Networks. *Nature*, 410(6825), 268–276. doi:10.1038/35065725

Tobler, W. R. (1970). A Computer Movie Simulating Urban Growth in the Detroit Region. *Economic Geography*, 46, 234. doi:10.2307/143141

Wang, F. (2014). *Quantitative Methods and Socio-Economic Applications in GIS* (2nd ed.). Boca Raton, Florida: CRC Press.

Wolch, J., Wilson, J. P., & Fehrenbach, J. (2005). Parks and Park Funding in Los Angeles: An Equity-Mapping Analysis. *Urban Geography*, 26(1), 4–35. doi:10.2747/0272-3638.26.1.4

15
LEADERSHIP

Michael Neuman

Planners are Natural Leaders[1]

Planners have a distinctive take on leadership, well suited for today's world. A strong planning culture induces leaders to be both collaborative and visionary. The profession of planning requires several leadership-oriented skills: a long-term horizon, a sense of the broader good, comprehensive consideration of the inter-relationship of complex and dynamic activities and their impacts, an inter-disciplinary perspective, and the ability to reconcile conflicting interests. This set of skills also characterizes a strong, positive planning culture (Neuman, 2007).

Other traits of planning leadership include being strategic, future-oriented, goal-directed, vision-creating, scenario-shaping, and consensus-seeking. In an increasingly interconnected world where multiple interests intersect and interact at multiple spatial and temporal scales, the simultaneous focus on places and processes sets the planning profession apart. Since planners are trained to see the interconnections among multiple types of factors and their impacts on place and people into the future, as well as to assess those impacts using multiple criteria, they are well equipped to understand and manage this level of complexity (Christensen, 1993, 1999).

This chapter sets out five general elements of planning leadership:

1 *Future orientation*: goals, objectives, strategies, and plans
2 *Situational awareness*: knowledge of place, context, and complexity
3 *Cultural awareness*: specifically (but not exclusively) of place cultures, organizational cultures, and interpersonal differences
4 *Communications*: listening, dialogue, understanding, evidence, and images
5 *Concern for the greater good*: public interest, commonwealth, and general welfare

Note that these elements are about people. Leaders lead people, and people run organizations. An ideal leader knows and can read the "mood" of the people in her charge, including that of constituents and others within her sphere of influence.

Typical scholarship about leadership and management delves deeply into decisions and actions. A leader is often seen as decisive, a "man of action." This perspective focuses on the leader as a person, rather than on the organization, its mission, performance, outcomes, and its members. Yet savvy and effective leaders know that mentoring and nurturing their subordinates—seeing junior staffers as leaders-in-training—is the surest path towards effective performance and good outcomes for the organization (Powell, 2012).

It is worth noting the difference between leadership and management. Management describes the day-to-day, periodic, and recurring functions of an organization. Managers organize and direct people to accomplish those functions. Thus, their essential role is controlling. Leadership has more to do with setting directions, communicating a vision, and inspiring people to achieve both personal and common goals. Therefore, leaders need to be motivational. As Kotter puts it, "Management controls people by pushing them in the right direction; leadership motivates them by satisfying basic human needs" (1999). Leadership and management are different sides of the same coin. A well-functioning group, organization, institution, project, or process needs both.

It is true that there are two sides (or more) to every story, including leadership (Beycioglu & Pashiardis, 2014). While there are different types of negative personality traits and disorders that impinge on leadership, guarding against and counteracting them can be abetted by strong organizational and leadership cultures, giving "power to the powerless." Blind faith in leadership, especially certain types and traits of it, can have deleterious consequences. Fortunately, the planning profession's style of leadership, by being collaborative, consensus-seeking, and participative, and by incorporating the traits indicated in this chapter, has the potential to neutralize the "dark side."

The following sections address the five elements of leadership listed above in turn, interweaving the decision and action components of leadership. This embedding of decision and action, often separate in the past, provides the context and scope by which to evaluate the quality of decisions and actions. By situating decision-making and action-taking in places, cultures, structures, and processes, we can better explicate criteria by which to evaluate the quality and efficacy of decisions. Making these criteria transparent not only encourages accountability but enables all members of an organization to better assess their own and their peers' decisions and actions, regardless of location in the chain of command. In this way, when decision and action criteria are transparent and widely shared within an organization, it turns all its members into leaders.

Future Orientation

Future orientation is the most definitive and perhaps the most instrumental of the leadership qualities of planners. Scenarios, plans, forecast, projects, designs, and images are among the tools employed to convey futures (Hopkins & Zapata, 2007). More recently, fixed images of the future of a place, such as a city plan, are becoming less consequential than a variety of representations used by actors, agents, and stakeholders that convey possibilities, illustrate consequences, and coalesce consensus. Images of the future motivate and inspire. This shift, from fixed form to malleable media, has led to a transformation of the planning profession into a more active and engaging process-orientation. This shift has been central to planners occupying roles of greater influence in public, private, and not-for-profit realms; and especially in forums and arenas composed of mixed realms.

Visual representation of a long-term vision in planning leadership has a long history. In many nations, starting in the 19th century, visionary planners occupied key roles in society and politics, from Haussmann in Paris and Cerdà in Barcelona to Burnham and Tugwell in America. From its earliest manifestations in the middle of the 19th century, urban planning traded on plans that contained visions of the future, usually conveyed in maps (Choay, 1969; Hall, 2014; Neuman, 2011).

Images of the future are the cornerstone of planning practice, central as they are to scenarios, plans, and projects. Images are also implied in forecasts. How planning cultures and images are created and used by individuals and institutions (that individuals also create and use) are [central to planning]

(Neuman, 2007).

Hopkins captured the visionary power of planning leadership in his phrase "engaging the future" (Hopkins & Zapata, 2007).

There is an implicit aspect of future orientation in the planner's leadership arsenal that is worth making explicit. In order to be able to plan for a better future, one must believe a better future exists. This aspect offers even more legitimacy and salience to planners today in the midst of many citizens' responses such as withdrawal and cynicism to a "post-truth," "post-political" world. Planners' visions counteract these responses with a positive message of hope and possibility of a better future. Planning for a better future must confer hope.

Situational Awareness

A seminal attribute of urban planning is its sensitivity to and sensibility about place, time, and context. This can be called *situational awareness*. When these three sensibilities come together, they endow a degree of savvy that comes from the immersion of "being there," of local knowledge situated in broader contexts (Christensen, 1993). In the twin arenas of politics and policy, city planning can exert leadership by using situational awareness and savvy (Forester, 1999; Hoch, 1994). Legitimate decisions (that are fair, balanced, and transparent), informed by an acute situational awareness, yield better results and are appreciated by time-strapped politicians and policy-makers.

Situational leadership is involved when a leader adjusts her style or approach in accordance with the needs of the situation and takes situational awareness to the next level. When a leader or leadership group analyses the decision/action arena in a manner analogous to the way a planner analyses a place, she is invoking situational awareness. The parallel phrase is "survey before lead," taken from Patrick Geddes's "survey before plan" (Geddes, 1915/1949, p. x).

Situational leadership requires knowledge of time and timing as well as of place and context. Knowing if, and when, to decide are two essential precursors to making any decision. Moreover, timing is an essential part of strategy, a precept that comes from military strategy and the waging of battles and campaigns. The criticality of timing as a leadership trait has been documented as far back as Lao Tzu in the *Tao Te Ching*: "when in action, watch the timing" (Lao Tzu, 2011).

Situational awareness and situational leadership also refer to organizational settings, including inter-organizational and institutional settings. Situational awareness entails knowing group dynamics, organizational and inter-organizational politics, and institutional cultures and traditions. In these challenging contexts, the leadership principle of "alignment"—aligning people and processes to goals and visions—is well suited to the planning leadership approach. By focusing on alignment of goals, values, and ethos, a leader allows the details of adapting to a procedure over time fall to her subordinates, trusting those subordinates to keep the proper alignment. Aligning goals and values in this way leads to empowerment of all members of an organization, as well as its constituents—in this instance, the planning public.

Cultural Awareness

"While the phenomenon of leadership is widely considered to be universal across cultures, the way in which it is operationalized is usually viewed as culturally specific" (Dorfman et al., 1997).

The term *culture* is contested in social sciences, especially in anthropology. Numerous definitions abound. One that serves our purposes defines culture as a:

> set of processes which are characteristic of human processes which involve acquisition and accumulation of information and its transmission by non-genetic means, mainly using learned symbols, from one human being to another, from one society to another and generation to generation
> *(Boyden, Miller, Newcombe, & O'Neill, 1981).*

There are several qualifiers of the word *culture* that specify its meaning in various settings. Here we distinguish leadership culture, organizational culture, planning culture, and place culture. A simplified view of leadership culture posits that it exists in an organizational setting, including inter-organizational networks and institutions, when there is widespread delegation and where accountability is devolved to the lowest level possible, so that individuals can exercise initiative without seeking permission from above. An attitude of confidence and accomplishment pervades, and members or employees are seen as peers and collaborators, regardless of which level or position they formally occupy. The pervasive quality in which these characteristics and behaviors are learned, passed along, and imbued in the organization so that they become customs and traditions is what makes a leadership *culture*.

Leadership culture is distinct from how leadership varies across cultures and across organizations. Much has been made of the difference between, say, Asian and "western" leadership approaches. Researchers have elaborated distinctions among "universal" and culturally-situated leadership styles (Dickson, Den Hartog, & Mitchelson, 2003).

Leaders establish and model cultural norms, whether in society or in individual organizations (Cremer, 2017). In urban planning, a city planning director able to demonstrate strong leadership can be instrumental in changing bureaucratic and governance cultures towards a long-term perspective in which public and common interests are balanced with individual and private interest. A good leader is a "cultural architect" and cultural gatekeeper whose influence can pervade. Culture is an umbrella term that casts its own meaning on a leader who knows his people.

We could also extend cultural awareness in leadership to a *culture of leadership*, which not only empowers employees or members, but also stakeholders outside the leader's or leadership group's immediate concern. An entire constituency or public can be aligned with and buy in to such a leader's or entity's vision. Within an organization this approach often leads to higher performance.

An organizational culture, simply put, refers to the culture that prevails in any organization. Organizations themselves exhibit distinct cultures compared to societies, groups, and other social entities. Different organizations, even in the same country/culture, can evince differences in organizational cultures. Organizational culture develops, evolves, and changes over time; in response to external changes (society, movements, fashions) and internal dynamics (leadership changes, training, success/failure). A leadership culture is a type of organizational culture. An architectural and design firm may have a creative culture, whereas an engineering firm may exhibit an efficiency culture. An organizational culture can embody multiple variations of culture based on the roles played by subordinate units. A branch office of a multi-national firm, for example, will be influenced both by organizational and the national cultures. There are many permutations and combinations of these factors, thereby requiring awareness, sensitivity, and cultural malleability.

"A planning culture forms the crucible in which planning activity occurs" (Neuman, 2007). Moreover, a planning culture defines the norms that guide planning and measures its efficacy. "A planning culture is a composite of social, political, institutional, and place cultures in which the multiple practices of planning occur" (Neuman, 2007). Moreover, planning culture can support planning activities and manifest the planning idea throughout society. Planning culture is distinguished from organizational culture while being related to the institutionalization of planning given its key role in mainstream organizations. A society exhibits a robust planning culture when urban planning is a daily topic of conversation across media, business, education, art, and entertainment—in short, in any aspect of social life.

A place culture is often an important antecedent to a planning culture. A place culture develops when residents closely identify with their hometown (or city, metropolis, or region). It is the inhabitants who recognize, enjoy, and cultivate qualities that make the place special. "The qualities that distinguish a special place and form a basis of the person-place relationship at the heart of a place culture can be readily identified by residents and visitors alike" (Neuman, 2007).

Communications

Effective communications is a cornerstone for planning practice. This is especially valid for problem solving in complex situations and environments where collaboration is central—that is, for just about every urban planning activity. Literatures analysing organizational failures and disaster responses often point to communications problems as the smoking gun to which a chain of causation is attributed (Hall, 1982, Vaughan, 2016).

Negotiations, consensus building, conflict resolution, and related approaches to contemporary planning processes all stress the importance of many aspects of communication (e.g. Forester, 1999; Susskind, 1987; Moore, 2014). Thoughtful mutual dialogue takes time to achieve. It requires trust, legitimacy, clear communication, and other prerequisites that are earned over time for careful deliberation to occur. Deliberation is essential to advance complex debate on policy, planning, and the futures of a place (Forester, 1999).

In planning and design professions, images of all kinds are core to their practices because images communicate key concepts visually. Images are central to meaning, clarity, and consensus; all three of which are important for effective communications. That is, communications that combines words with images is more complete in its story telling. Critically, the use of images (a map, a plan, a design, a scenario, for example) in planning helps to maintain and strengthen the institutionalized practices of planning. Images thus become tools in the planners' toolkit to shape and maintain power as exercised through the institutions in which planning occurs (Neuman, 2012, 1996).

Communication is embedded deeply into the "sinews" of individual behaviors, organizational behaviors, and interpersonal relations of all kinds. Moreover, language and communications are central to cultural identity. Communications affects motivation, knowledge, skills, agreements, understanding, risk, uncertainty, which is to say numerous important realms of action (Gudykunst, 1993).

The Greater Good

To focus on the greater good corresponds to the origin and enduring ethos of the city planning profession. It is a distinctive source of strength of the profession. By focusing on the greater good, planners are able to place a broader frame around and impart greater social meaning to individual interests that often conflict and thus splinter planning processes and their outcomes. Communities and their places from villages to city-regions suffer from the focus on individual interests, and often benefit from the planning focus on collective interests.

Focusing on the greater good places a premium on relational acuity that targets caring and nurturing of places and communities. The greater good, sometimes variously referred to as the public good, the public interest, the common good, common weal, commonwealth, and so on, has the further advantage of placing planning squarely back into the center of politics and policy (Meyerson & Banfield, 1955). The greater good provides an avenue by which to go beyond position-based and interest-based negotiations and deliberative planning processes.

Infrastructure and public or common lands were known previously as the "public trust." Another historical term for the material basis of public trust was commonwealth, wealth that was held in common, by the people who were its owners, through the *trust* placed by them in their *representatives* in government. In recent decades, there has been a steady, incremental, drip by drip erosion of the public trust with the privatization of many public lands and public works. This is but one consequence of neoliberalism.

Another facet of public trust is that it serves as glue holding messy democratic processes together. This aspect of trust is embedded in social and political capital that keeps people engaged meaningfully and constructively over the long periods of time needed to accomplish infrastructure planning and financing. This glue consists of two inter-related ingredients: trust and transparency, fairly applied. Without public trust, any process is on shaky ground, no matter how carefully constructed the process, how civil the proceedings, and how carefully selected the stakeholders. Interpersonal trust is insufficient. Polity-wide civic trust needs to be rekindled. The erosion of this facet of the public trust has been most damaging to our collective responsibility to plan and finance infrastructure, and to ensure its services and impacts are equitable. It is not incidental that good planning leadership abets the public trust. Inversely, focusing on the public trust and the public interest aids planning and positions it as a leadership profession.

To focus on the common good provides a means to address many seemingly intractable issues that have come to the fore as a by-product of neoliberalism. It also and importantly removes the focus on personal/private interests. In this way, the common good enables us to tap in to a broader purpose, providing a rationale for planning that embeds it deeply in the community.

Specific Forums and Arenas of Planning as Leadership

Many of the myriad predicaments and crises that contemporary societies and cities face, such as inequity, climate change, public health, infrastructure inadequacies, housing affordability, food security, "natural" disasters, pollution, and so on have urban roots and/or urban manifestations. Therefore, the urban planning and design professions are uniquely placed to make a difference in their resolution.

In this regard, designing and managing the forums and arenas where the definition, analysis, debate, and resolution of these issues take place is vital (Bryson & Crosby, 1993). This is a job for urban planning and design because the practices of planning and design bring together place and process, form and function, in ways that have been identified as process design and institutional design (Innes, 1995; Neuman, 1996). Designing and managing planning, policy, and political processes and the forums, arenas, and institutions in which they occur reveals planning's leadership role.

Five realms in which planning plays particularly strong leadership roles are in infrastructure, sustainability, place-based quality of life, public health, and design. These five are related. For example, the greatest contribution to urban sustainability is via infrastructure (Neuman, 2012). Also, active living and active transport, along with sustainable urban farming, are correlated with quality of life. This points to another aspect of planning leadership, which is to "connect the dots" in order to expand possibilities, enhance sustainability, and achieve efficiencies.

Infrastructure leads because it shapes urban development in the most direct and long-lasting ways. As the sums of money allocated to infrastructure dwarf other aspects of local and regional urban planning budgets, focusing on infrastructure offers a degree of leverage and impact not normally accorded to planners. Urban planners are beginning to recover protagonist roles in the development of infrastructure, as they did in the founding generations of the urban planning profession in the mid-late 19th century (Neuman, 2009, 2011). Infrastructure is a key element of the "greater good" aspect of planning leadership as argued above.

Sustainability leads because it is one of the most important concepts and practices that can safeguard planet Earth and its ecosystems and species, including humans. This confers legitimacy and urgency to planning. Sustainable practices share many qualities with urban planning. Both use approaches that are long-term, comprehensive, balanced, holistic, and integrated. Given these shared characteristics, implementing sustainability can easily be led by planners. Planners can lead sustainability efforts by responding to local needs and desires, which more removed levels of government or the private sector do not address adequately.

Place-based quality of life is arguably the biggest contribution to cities by the planning profession in recent decades. In this formulation, planners can exert leadership by highlighting the *place-based* aspect of quality of life, and by providing a broader set of criteria for quality of life assessments, expanding it beyond material well-being and consumption. By enhancing public, sustainable, and active transport, for example, and by promoting public health and local sustainability, planners can improve the overall quality of life. Planners lead other professions, such as public works, transport, and health, for example, by linking what they do into a coherent, placed-based plan.

Public health is closely related to place-based interventions, sustainability, and design. One could say that all urban planning has public health consequences. This was made explicit, for example, nearly a century ago in the legal justification for planning statutes in the United States—"to safeguard health, safety, and welfare"—encoded in the Department of Commerce's Standard Enabling Acts for planning and zoning (United States Department of Commerce, 1926, 1928). Public health undergirds all of planning, and moreover extends its reach to domains and professions previously not connected—active living, active transport, medicine, healthcare, schools, education, and sports, to name a few.

Design leadership refers in part to the creative aspect of planning, the ability to envision, create, and bring to life better places. It also refers to designing processes and institutions in which urban planning and design take place. In this latter way, planning bolsters governance and democracy by making policy making more transparent and participative. Planning has, since the 1960s, been at the forefront in advocacy, pluralism, and participation by citizens in their government because of its ethical stance in favor of expanding grassroots democracy and due to its ability to design and redesign processes of participation to enable it (Arnstein, 1969; Davidoff, 1965).

Teaching Leadership in Planning

While leadership *qualities* can seem to be innate, many if not most of the *skills* to apply leadership can be learned, practiced, and honed like any skill. Leadership is best understood as a way of being in the world, and a way of facing and addressing any situation. It starts with being a leader of one's own life. Most research on the topic boils down to one sentence: "Lead by example."

Teaching leadership is not as simple as something that could be taught in the traditional sense of teacher → student—a unidirectional flow of information and knowledge. Yet leading requires following. It is an interactive relationship. There can be no leader without followers. Like all interactive relations, it is an exchange relation, just like power relations. These relations imply and require a number of elements to be present. Among them is the mutual, ongoing evaluation of the leader by the followers and of the followers by the leader. This exchange relation involves the conferral of power, and of a certain degree of delegation. All this entails the exercise of judgment in active practice. Humans, consciously or not, continually judge others on many dimensions, including leadership. Most importantly, followers judge how successful a leader is in achieving the goals set by her and her community of followers. We admire and emulate success. Everyone likes and almost instinctively follows a leader because of demonstrated success. That is, leadership is expressed through actions deemed successful.[2] Fairness and caring are as essential to the leader-follower relation as success. Fair treatment and caring are personal dimensions that condition the extent to which a follower will follow, as the two form a critical part of the trust bond between leader and follower.

We cannot forget that leadership is a phenomenon conditioned by culture (Argyris, 2010; Schein, 2010). Leadership traits and skills vary culture to culture, and place to place. Moreover, the overall culture, whether of society, industry, profession, or organization, has its own leadership patterns. Thus, while leadership, including its scholarship, often focuses on the leader, the followers and the overall cultural context greatly influence the exchange relationship that defines leading and following.

A course on leadership would include several essential elements. First, the study of leaders in practice, whether successful or not, is an excellent pedagogical exercise. This is done by observing, and by reading case studies and research about leaders' actions as well as motivations. Students can also be assigned field observation exercises to follow a leader in action for a period of time (Healey, 1992). Reading exercises about leaders and leadership can include biographies and memoirs followed by some combination of written analysis and classroom discussion. Second, teachers can devise leadership exercises in the classroom and in the field. They can further challenge students themselves to create such exercises and games to conduct. Finally, teachers should think of themselves as leaders at all times and behave accordingly, because the followers are always watching, and taking notes. Teachers are leaders, in the classroom and outside of it. Urban planning teachers have a special responsibility because of the public trust imbued in planning, and the public interest served by planning.

Conclusion

In the realm of urban planning and its related disciplines, including urban governance, the common attributes ascribed to leaders, such as command, authority, and decisiveness, are not necessarily the most essential, given the complex arenas adjudicating multiple issues and interests. Rather, being attuned to the five general elements of planning leadership—future orientation, situational awareness, cultural awareness, communications, and a concern for the greater good—give planners an edge in leading policy and political processes intended to improve the public domain and citizens' lives.

Regardless of the common perception of leadership traits mentioned above, much of the leadership literature in recent decades has incorporated the empathic, interpersonal, and relational aspects of leadership (Anderson & Sun, 2015; Goleman, 2017). Moreover, gendered approaches to leadership have proliferated, suggesting that there exist differences in leadership styles and methods between women and men. However, the gender-based barriers are breaking down as many female leaders have emerged in practice. The scholarship surrounding these gendered and gender-aware practices have begun to emerge, even as leadership character traits that are stereotypically perceived as male are still seen more favorably in some arenas (Powell, 2012).

Thinking broadly about the intersection of planning and leadership in the ways put forth here suggests that leadership is a nuanced skill that can be learned, developed, and enhanced. Moreover, one size does not fit all. Instead, leadership is about mastering specific situations and their contexts, and bringing influence to bear on them so that resources and people can be marshalled to get things done.

Relational leadership approaches become critical, if not paramount, in a globalizing world where networked societies flourish and network-based social media have a massive impact (Castells, 2009, 2010). Added to this, increasing calls for openness, transparency, deliberation, and participation in government, which helps transform government to governance (Klijn & Koppenjan, 2015), also necessitate a relational approach to planning (Healey, 2006) and leadership.

Planning leads due to its unique ability to craft visions of and creative solutions for better futures. This quality endows planning with a positive outlook imbued with hope, which inspires citizens to action amid their indifferent or cynical responses to politics and business as usual. Planning as a leadership profession cannot underestimate or take for granted its ability to generate hope—the greatest leadership attribute of all.

Notes

1 Thanks to Professor Terry Lamb, Director of the Centre for Teaching Innovation, University of Westminster; Gil Dove, President of Gil Dove Associates; and Martin Meyerson, Gary Hack, Peter Hall, and Ed Blakely—planning leaders and mentors.
2 Leaders can lead using words, as great speeches attest. Leading through words and symbols can be inspiring, but if not supported by actions (by followers as much as leaders) then in the end, it can ring more hollow than inspiring.

References

Anderson, M. H., & Sun, P. Y. T. (2015). Reviewing Leadership Styles: Overlaps and the Need for a New "Full-Range" Theory. *International Journal of Management Reviews*, 19(1), 76–96. doi:10.1111/ijmr.12082

Argyris, C. (2010). *Organizational Traps: Leadership, Culture, Organizational Design*. Oxford: Oxford University Press.

Arnstein, S. R. (1969). A Ladder Of Citizen Participation. *Journal of the American Institute of Planners*, 35(4), 216–224. doi:10.1080/01944366908977225

Beycioglu, K., & Pashiardis, P. (2014). *Multidimensional Perspectives on Principal Leadership Effectiveness*. Hershey, Pennsylvania: IGI Global.

Boyden, S. V., Miller, S., Newcombe, K., & O'Neill, B. (1981). *The Ecology of a City and Its People: The Case of Hong Kong*. Canberra: Australian National University Press.

Bryson, J. M., & Crosby, B. C. (1993). Policy Planning and the Design and Use of Forums, Arenas, and Courts. *Environment and Planning B: Planning and Design*, 20(2), 175–194. doi:10.1068/b200175

Castells, M. (2009). *Communication Power*. Oxford: Oxford University Press.

Castells, M. (2010). *The Rise of the Network Society* (2nd ed.). Chichester: John Wiley & Sons.

Choay, F. (1969). *The Modern City: Planning in the 19th Century*. New York: G. Braziller.

Christensen, K. S. (1993). Teaching Savvy. *Journal of Planning Education and Research*, 12(3), 202–212. doi:10.1177/0739456x9301200304

Christensen, K. S. (1999). *Cities and Complexity: Making Intergovernmental Decisions* (Vol. 3). Newbury Park, California: Sage Publications.

Cremer, A. (2017, May 22). CEO says changing VW culture tougher than expected. *Reuters*. Retrieved from https://uk.reuters.com/article/uk-volkswagen-emissions-culture-idUKKBN18I2V2

Davidoff, P. (1965). Advocacy and Pluralism in Planning. *Journal of the American Institute of Planners*, 31(4), 331–338. doi:10.1080/01944366508978187

Dickson, M. W., Den Hartog, D. N., & Mitchelson, J. K. (2003). Research on Leadership in a Cross-cultural Context: Making Progress, and Raising New Questions. *The Leadership Quarterly*, 14(6), 729–768. doi:10.1016/j.leaqua.2003.09.002

Dorfman, P. W., Howell, J. P., Hibino, S., Lee, J. K., Tate, U., & Bautista, A. (1997). Leadership in Western and Asian countries: Commonalities and Differences in Effective Leadership Processes Across Cultures. *The Leadership Quarterly*, 8(3), 233–274. doi:10.1016/s1048-9843(97)90003-5

Forester, J. (1999). *The Deliberative Practitioner: Encouraging Participatory Planning Processes*. Cambridge, Massachusetts: The MIT Press.

Geddes, P. (1915/1949). *Cities in Evolution*. London: Williams & Norgate. (1949 edition edited by Jaqueline Tyrwhitt).

Goleman, D. (2017). *Leadership That Gets Results*. Cambridge, Massachusetts: Harvard Business Review Press.

Gudykunst, W. (1993). Toward a theory of effective interpersonal and intergroup communication: An anxiety/uncertainty management (AUM) perspective. In R. Wiseman, & J. Koester (Eds.), *Intercultural Communication Competence* (pp. 33–71). Thousand Oaks, California: Sage Publications,

Hall, P. (1982). *Great Planning Disasters*. Berkeley, California: University of California Press.

Hall, P. (2014). *Cities of Tomorrow: An Intellectual History of Urban Planning and Design since 1890*. Chichester: Wiley Blackwell.

Healey, P. (1992). A Planner's Day: Knowledge and Action in Communicative Practice. *Journal of the American Planning Association*, 58(1), 9–20. doi:10.1080/01944369208975531

Healey, P. (2006). *Urban Complexity and Spatial Strategies: Towards a Relational Planning for Our Times*. London: Taylor & Francis.

Hoch, C. J. (1994). *What Planners Do: Power, Politics, and Persuasion*. Chicago, Illinois: APA Planners Press.

Hopkins, L. D., & Zapata, M. A. (2007). *Engaging the Future: Forecasts, Scenarios, Plans, and Projects*. Cambridge, Massachusetts: Lincoln Institute of Land Policy.

Innes, J. E. (1995). Planning is Institutional Design. *Journal of Planning Education and Research*, 14(2), 140–143. doi:10.1177/0739456x9501400207

Klijn, E. H., & Koppenjan, J. (2015). *Governance Networks in the Public Sector*. London: Taylor & Francis.

Kotter, J. P. (1999). *John P. Kotter on what Leaders Really Do*. Boston, Massachusetts: Harvard Business School Press.

Lao Tzu. (2011). *The Tao Te Ching* (G.-F. Feng, J. English, & T. Lippe, Trans.). New York: Vintage Books.

Meyerson, M., & Banfield, E. C. (1955). *Politics, Planning, and the Public Interest: The Case of Public Housing in Chicago*. New York: The Free Press.

Moore, C. (2014). *The Mediation Process: Practical Strategies for Resolving Conflict*. San Francisco, California: Jossey-Bass.

Neuman, M. (1996). Images as institution builders: Metropolitan planning in Madrid. *European Planning Studies*, 4(3), 293–312. doi:10.1080/09654319608720347

Neuman, M. (2007). How Institutions and Individuals Use Plans: Planning Cultures and Images of Futures. In L. D. Hopkins & M. A. Zapata (Eds.), *Engaging the Future: Forecasts, Scenarios, Plans, and Projects* (pp. 155–174). Cambridge, Massachusetts: Lincoln Institute of Land Policy.

Neuman, M. (2009). Spatial Planning Leadership by Infrastructure: An American View. *International Planning Studies*, 14(2), 201–217. doi:10.1080/13563470903021241

Neuman, M. (2011). Centenary Paper: Ildefons Cerdà and the Future of Spatial Planning: The Network Urbanism of a City Planning Pioneer. *Town Planning Review*, 82(2), 117–144. doi:10.3828/tpr.2011.10

Neuman, M. (2012). Infrastructure Planning for Sustainable Cities. *Geographica Helvetica*, 66(2), 100–107. doi:10.5194/gh-66-100-2011

Powell, G. N. (2012). Six Ways of Seeing the Elephant: The Intersection of Sex, Gender, and Leadership. *Gender in Management: An International Journal*, 27(2), 119–141. doi:10.1108/17542411211214167

Schein, E. H. (2010). *Organizational Culture and Leadership* (4th ed.). San Francisco: John Wiley & Sons.

Susskind, L. (1987). *Breaking the Impasse: Consensual Approaches to Resolving Public Disputes*. New York: Basic Books.

United States Department of Commerce. (1926). Standard Zoning Enabling Act.

United States Department of Commerce. (1928). Standard City Planning Enabling Act.

Vaughan, D. (2016). *The Great Challenger Disaster*. Chicago, Illinois: University of Chicago Press.

PART 5A

Traditional Subjects of Specialization

16
LOCAL ECONOMIC DEVELOPMENT PLANNING

Nancey Green Leigh and Lynn M. Patterson

Introduction to Local Economic Development Planning

Economic development is a broad, multidisciplinary umbrella over a range of sub-disciplines in social and physical sciences such as economics, engineering, geography, political science, and sociology. Economic development planning is a core specialization area within city and regional planning, and it is a similarly broad umbrella over the other core specializations in the planning discipline. Traditionally, these core specializations have been environment, land use, housing and community development, transportation, and urban design. However, review of planning programs shows that the focus of core specializations can evolve to reflect progression of the public interest (for example, a core specialization that focuses on environment and health). They also evolve to address shifts in market failure and accompanying negative externalities.

Economic development *planning* can be distinguished by its spatial focus, along with that of market failure and inequality. In this chapter, we specifically focus on *local* economic development planning, in contrast to regional or international economic development planning. However, as noted below, the labels do not connote mutually exclusive categories; the distinction between the local and regional level is in the degree of "appliedness" of the planner's work. Local economic development planners are on the frontline of efforts to protect and advance local economies. There will always be a need for the local economic development planner because:

> Cities, towns, counties, and all local entities in a global economy have the challenge and opportunity of crafting their own economic destinies. This is true for the poorest as well as the wealthiest localities. In reality, the forces of nature, demography, technology, and industry are such that no local economy can ever count on an achieved position of stability and security.
>
> *(Leigh & Blakely, 2016)*

Defining Local Economic Development Planning

The intersection of economic development planning with other core specializations produces synergies and helps to shape the particular lens that planning brings to the definition, goals, and strategies of economic development (for example, specifying that development be sustainable).

So, too, do the core values of the planning profession. Specifically, the largest English-speaking professional planning organization, the American Planning Association (1992), states that the profession's purpose is to serve the public interest, and it includes stipulations that planners:

1. Strive to expand choice and opportunity for all persons, recognizing a special responsibility to plan for the needs of disadvantaged groups and persons;
2. Assist in the clarification of community goals, objectives and policies in plan-making;
3. Ensure that reports, records, and any other non-confidential information which is, or will be, available to decision makers is made available to the public in a convenient format and sufficiently in advance of any decision;
4. Strive to protect the integrity of the natural environment and the heritage of the built environment.

These core values help us to understand why planning's definition of economic development differs from that most widely used in the traditional field of economic development. In the latter definition, economic development is traditionally defined as wealth creation, obtained through job creation and increasing the tax base. Essentially, economic development is equated with economic growth.

The definition of economic development in planning is more complex than simple wealth creation. It internalizes the notion of serving the public interest, of addressing the needs of disadvantaged persons, and of environmental protection referenced in the core values above. Serving the public interest in economic development planning requires addressing market failures (as it does in the other core planning specialization areas). The assumption that perfect competition exists, often assumed in economic development practice outside planning, is explicitly rejected by economic development in the planning sphere. Rather, economic development planners acknowledge that modern market-based economies are characterized by a growing concentration of economic power and industry power that in turn contributes to rising inequality.

Economic development planning at the local level addresses market failure by using tools to strengthen market-based development. At the same time, it addresses the unintended consequences of market-based development such as displaced communities from gentrification, brownfields, jobs–housing imbalance, and inequality in its multiple forms.

While variations of the definition of economic development in planning exist, a widely published version, specifically targeting this chapter's focus on the local level, is below:

> Local economic development is achieved when a community's standard of living can be preserved and increased through a process of human and physical development that is based on principles of equity and sustainability.
>
> *(Leigh & Blakely, 2016)*

The definition is qualified by three criteria. That is, economic development:

1. establishes a minimum standard of living for all and increases the standard over time;
2. reduces inequality between demographic groups and spatially defined groups or economic and political units;
3. promotes and encourages sustainable resource use and production.

These are measurable criteria that local economies will need to track to more fully achieve economic development.

Local Economic Development Theory

There is considerable overlap between the theory that informs local economic development practice and regional economic development practice (the topic of Chapter 17). Further, both economic geographies are parts of larger national and international economies and affected by the forces of globalization. However, local economic development planning focuses predominantly on cities and towns that are administrative units with planning powers, and on neighborhoods or districts within these units.[1] In contrast, regional economic development geographies are larger, and while they may coincide with nations or states as administrative units, they have economic and cultural identifying characteristics which transcend administrative boundaries.

Regional (and Urban) Development theories inform the field of local economic development planning, particularly long-standing theories of central place (Christaller, 1966), agglomeration (Hoover, 1937), growth poles (Perroux, 1950), Marshallian districts (Marshall, 1895), and creative destruction (Schumpeter, 1976). More recent theory on regional innovation systems (Asheim & Gertler, 2006) and evolutionary economic geography (Martin & Sunley, 2014) is being applied to the local level (Katz & Wagner, 2014). A classic and still highly relevant theoretical question is whether local economic development planning should be focused on people or place prosperity (Bolton, 1992; Winnick, 1966). That cities are "growth machines" shaped by politics and, in particular, by land holding elites, is another influential theory originating with Molotch (Jonas & Wilson, 1999). Turning local economies into growth machines forces them to continually compete with other localities to the detriment of the majority of citizens. Inequality has been exacerbated as a result and has led to theories of Just Cities (Fainstein, 2010) and Just Growth (Benner & Pastor, 2013).

Developing the Local Economy Profile

In order for local economic development planners to understand how their local economies fit within larger economic, industrial, and international systems, they must have the skills to create and monitor a local economy's profile. A robust profile will include indicators of 12 major characteristics of the local economy: demographics, income, quality of life, infrastructure, environmental conditions, real estate, workforce, existing business, business climate, higher education/ research and development, markets, and development policies.

Combining the data collected for the profile with other data, and using economic development analytical methods, allows the local economic development planner to address five key questions:

1. What parts of the local economy are most valued by local residents and political leaders? How do the citizens see themselves compared with other communities?
2. What parts of the economy form the local economic base, accounting for the most substantial number of jobs and growth in wealth?
3. What parts of the local economy are growing most rapidly, forming jobs and generating opportunity? What can local leaders do about other parts that are declining?
4. How do changes multiply through the local economy? How does growth or decline in one part of the economy alter the other parts to which it sells or from which it buys?
5. What are the parts of the local economy that are most important because they are embedded in a strong and growing interdependent cluster of firms and related industries?

The answers to these questions can inform the strategies devised by planners, other local economic development practitioners, and community stakeholders. The strategies should explicitly state the local economy's development goals, as well as specify the sectors and groups that are their focus.

Local Economic Development Planning's Evolution

Local economic development planning and approaches have evolved over time, as has the broader economic development practice field. But the evolution has not always been harmonious. For example, economic development planners were early critics of the Business Attraction or "smoke stack chasing" that has dominated economic development practice, labeling it "competing your way to the bottom" (Bluestone & Harrison, 1982). This practice has evolved to focus on attracting corporate headquarters, advanced technology, and other types of firms. At the same time, there has also been a recognition of the value of existing businesses that led to economic development efforts focused on business retention and entrepreneurship strategies.

Technological advancements are a continuing factor in the evolution of local economies. More recently, developments in information and telecommunications infrastructure are changing where and how employees work. Many of these developments emanate from innovation centers in higher education and the private sector. E-commerce is similarly changing business models—everything from locations of supply chains to reducing the need for brick and mortar facilities to home based businesses and heavy demand for advanced telecommunications and workforces to service this industry is re-shaping infrastructure, building, and workforce needs.

Institutions of higher education have and will continue to significantly impact local economies. These institutions can be economic engines for communities – from procurement to job creation, student housing to student services, to expertise and commercialization and patenting. Indeed, there is a relatively recently formed sub-specialization within the economic development field that is focused on how universities can contribute to the economic development of the communities in which they are located.

When looking at the performance of the global, national, or even a regional economy, it is important to remember that these larger economies are all made of up smaller, local economies (Leigh & Blakely, 2016). These smaller economies are impacted by local demographics, markets, infrastructure, political climate, business decisions, and national economic (e.g., trade, intraregional cooperation, infrastructure) and social policies (e.g., education, health, migration.) Within these contexts, economic development planning seeks to shape and guide local economies to focus on long-term, sustainable, equitable, and resilient growth and holistic development for communities.

Thus, local economic development planning education is and will continue to evolve from skills and training focused on traditional business recruitment and development, to incorporating policies and processes that promote equity and sustainability. For example, these might include living wages, affordable housing, access to health care and quality education, reductions in racial, gender, and age inequalities and the responsible management and use of natural resources (Leigh & Blakely, 2016). These more comprehensive goals broaden the scope of education for local economic development planning.

Teaching Local Economic Development Planning

Developing a Curriculum

Courses in economic development planning cover theory, methods, and examination of practice. Economic development planning must be prepared for the unknown, such as changes in global and regional market forces, available capital, or business failures. Consequently, economic development planners require a strong foundation so they may be effective with what information they can gather and analyze. Economic development planners must have knowledge of the tools and programs of their field, as well as the capacity to analyze and apply them to their local economy. Analyzing case studies and best practices can be valuable pedagogical tools.

To understand how economic development planning is currently taught, the chapter authors analyzed the syllabi for 32 economic development planning courses (24 graduate and 8 undergraduate courses) found through an internet search of planning program websites and documents, to identify key themes, approaches, and content. The universities and courses analyzed are listed in Table 16.1. The geographic focus of nearly all of the course curricula was urban economic development, while slightly less than half also included rural communities.

Table 16.1 Economic Development Courses Analyzed and Their Respective Universities

	University	Course
Graduate	University of British Columbia (Canada)	Local Economic Development: Theory, Issues and Applications
	Cleveland State University	Economic Development Policy & Practice
	Columbia University	Local Economic Development Planning
	Georgia Institute of Technology	Local Economic Development Planning & Policy
	Georgia State University	Economic Development Policy
	Harvard University	Economic Development in Urban Planning
	Iowa State University	Economic Development Strategies
	Kansas State University	Rural Planning Seminar
	Massachusetts Institute of Technology	Economic Development Planning
	Massachusetts Institute of Technology	Introduction to Housing, Community, and Economic Development
	University of California, Los Angeles	Community Economic Development
	University of North Carolina, Chapel Hill	Economic Development Policy
	University of North Carolina, Greensboro	Community and Economic Development: Theory and Practice
	University of Illinois Urbana-Champaign	Economic Development Policy
	University of Florida	Economic Development Policy
	University of Illinois at Chicago	Economic Development Policy and Practice
	University of Michigan	Economic Development Planning
	University of Washington	Community Economic Development
	University of Wisconsin Milwaukee	Planning Local Economic Development
	University of Southern California	Local Economic Development: Theory and Finance
	University of Texas, Austin	Community and Regional Planning
	University of Texas, Dallas	Local Economic Development
	University of Texas, Panamerica	Introduction to Planning (Public Policy)
Undergraduate	Oregon State University	Rural Development Economics and Policy
	Saint Louis University	Urban Economic Development
	University of West Georgia	Sustainable Economic Development
	Washington University	Political Science
	Babes-Bolyai University (Romania)	Local Economic Development
	Comenius University (Slovakia)	Local Development, Urban Economics and Public Finance
	The Hebrew University of Jerusalem (Israel)	Issues in Urban Geography
	Western University (Canada)	Urban Economic Development and Policy

Table 16.2 Methods Covered in Economic Development Planning

Economic Profile	Industry/Business Analysis	Workforce Analysis
Economic Base	Cluster Analysis	Occupational Analysis
Location Quotient	Market Analysis	Labor Analysis
Shift-Share Analysis	Business Sector Analysis	
Economic Impact Analysis	Developmental Finance	
Cost/Benefit Analysis		
Multi-Criteria Analysis		

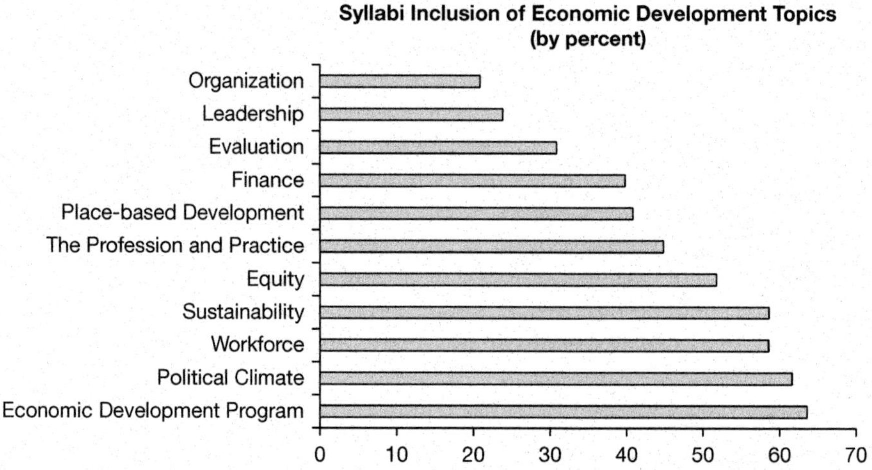

Syllabi Inclusion of Economic Development Topics (by percent)

- Organization: ~20
- Leadership: ~23
- Evaluation: ~30
- Finance: ~40
- Place-based Development: ~41
- The Profession and Practice: ~45
- Equity: ~52
- Sustainability: ~59
- Workforce: ~59
- Political Climate: ~62
- Economic Development Program: ~64

Figure 16.1 Most Common Topics Featured in Economic Development Courses

The methods covered in economic development planning courses fall into three categories, economic profile, industry/business analysis, and workforce analysis (see Table 16.2).

Figure 16.1 shows the most common topics included by percentage. Notably, while the traditional topic of economic development programs dominated (64%), the more recent focus on sustainability was covered almost as frequently.

The methods and topics listed in Table 16.1 could be considered to constitute the core content of economic development planning courses. Our review of syllabi found that courses are adopting a broader definition of economic development and continue to emphasize traditional methods. Additionally, we found there was a wide variety of smaller specialty topics that are reflective of economic development planning's broad umbrella as well as emerging issues. We have placed them into non-exclusive groups as follows:

- brownfield redevelopment, inner city revitalization and gentrification, suburban revitalization, urban sprawl, neighborhood planning, community and business improvement districts, anchor institutions, single industry towns, rural development;
- community organizing, living wages, community benefits agreements, citizen's role, immigrant and minority communities, gender, youth, social capital, migration;

- microenterprise, community development financial institutions, entrepreneurism, community development corporations, federal projects;
- tourism, entertainment, sports stadia, manufacturing, e-commerce, disaster recovery, technology and universities, diversity and creativity.

Notably, the emerging trends of automation, e-commerce, commercialization of technology, resiliency planning, and impacts of growing immigration/minority populations are only marginally represented in the economic development curriculum at this point, although they may have profound influences on the future of local economic development.

Analytical Methods[2]

Ideally, analytical methods are taught to students in a separate course that includes lab time and substantial opportunity to apply methods in problem solving. A wide range of categories that make up the local economy need to be analyzed for local economic development planning and implementation. Prior to conducting these analyses, substantial data needs to be gathered (detailed below). Doing so can be challenging because data is needed for small geographic areas, which is the least available of data. Historically, economic development planning relied on public sources of data. However, the information economy that has developed in the last 20 years is birthing new private sector firms that produce useful datasets from creative repackaging of public data as well mining the internet for new sources. Further, the future holds more promise for innovative datasets generated by monitoring sensors and geotagged data of goods and people moving through the economy.

Economic development analyses can be descriptive, predictive, or evaluative (Leigh & Blakely, 2016). Descriptive analyses provide insight into how a local economy is performing relative to its past, or to the present as measured against previously set development goals or reference economies such as the nation or a similar-sized competitor community. Descriptive analyses can be used to market the community to prospective firms, development projects, employers, employees, and new residents.

Predictive analyses make assessments of what the impacts of growth or development will be on the local economy, often taking the form of impact or causal analysis focused on fiscal, social, and economic conditions. However, impact analysis focused on building and land development associated with new economic development activities has dominated analytical activity, with fiscal analysis being a relative newcomer (practiced for the last three decades or so). Causal analysis has a longer-term perspective than fiscal analysis, and specifically focuses on forces that cause employment changes and can lead to changes in population, migration, income, and related phenomena (Isard et al., 2017).

Evaluative analysis is the least performed of the three forms that we discuss here because it can be expensive and politically sensitive. Evaluative analysis focuses on whether specific economic development goals have been met and what changes in economic development conditions have occurred. However, it is particularly important for assessing the unintended impacts of economic development such as whether new employment and businesses have caused widening inequality in a local economy.

Further Training and Professional Development

The broad occupational group of economic developers is made up of individuals with diverse educational backgrounds such as business, law, marketing, real estate, administration, among others. Individuals with these backgrounds are not necessarily trained in economic development in their academic studies. But once they find their way into the profession, there are multiple community and professional resources to help them acquire the specific skill sets and training needed to support local economic development practice. There may well be, however, an inherent delay in knowledge acquisition and likely efficacy when following this path.

Gaining this expertise within a planning program naturally lends itself to a more holistic view. This is because the general or core planning curriculum exposes students to theory and methods that inform economic development planning, and students also learn about other areas of planning that interact with economic development planning such as land use, transportation, and housing.

In addition to obtaining professional *planning* certifications after their university degrees, many economic development planners choose to acquire accreditation associated with the broader economic development field. The professional accreditation body in the United Kingdom, the Institute of Economic Development (IED), issues the Excellence in Economic Development for economic development organizations and offers continuing professional development courses for practitioners (www.ied.co.uk/). Economic Development Australia is the professional organization that offers accreditation of professionals through the ACEcD certification (www.edaustralia.com.au/). The International Economic Development Council (IEDC), based in Washington D.C., has a series of courses and an exam that experienced professionals may take for.

Each of these organizations has minimum experience requirements as well as specific course topics and ongoing continuing education programs they require for certification. Included in the topics are: business retention and expansion, credit analysis, real estate development and reuse, finance, marketing and attraction, strategic planning, small business development, neighborhood development, organizational management, technology-based development, and workforce development (Economic Development Australia; Institute of Economic Development, 2018; International Economic Development Council).

Conclusion

In the end, those who plan and practice local economic development planning must be simultaneously generalists and specialists. They must know general economic trends and markets while understanding the specific conditions and needs of their communities and industries. That is, they must be able to have conversations with business as well as with communities, and, compared to economic developers, they are better trained to engage with the latter.

Ideally, they will have a broad working knowledge in many subareas of local economic development, along with an awareness that these knowledge areas may operate with different sets of rules, regulations, partners, and networks. Local economic development planners need not be experts in each of these, but familiarity with these areas will help them to meet communities' specific and evolving needs through more equitable and resilient planning.

Notes

1 In the U.S. context, counties are also local administrative units; other countries can use different terminology.
2 This section draws from Chapter 6, Introduction to Analytical Methods for Local Economic Development Planning, in Leigh and Blakely (2016).

References

American Planning Association. (1992, May). *Ethical Principles in Planning*. Retrieved from www.planning.org/media/document/9121295/

Asheim, B. T., & Gertler, M. S. (2006). The Geography of Innovation: Regional Innovation Systems. In J. Fagerberg, D. C. Mowery, & R. R. Nelson (Eds.), *The Oxford Handbook of Innovation* (pp. 291–317). Oxford: Oxford University Press.

Benner, C., & Pastor, M. (2013). *Just Growth: Illusion and Prosperity in America's Metropolitan Regions*. Abingdon: Routledge.

Bluestone, B., & Harrison, B. (1982). *The Deindustrialization of America: Plant Closings, Community Abandonment, and the Dismantling of Basic Industry*. New York: Basic Books.

Bolton, R. (1992). "Place Prosperity vs People Prosperity" Revisited: An Old Issue with a New Angle. *Urban Studies, 29*(2), 185–203. doi:10.1080/00420989220080261

Christaller, W. (1966). *Central Places in Southern Germany* (C. W. Baskin, Trans.). Englewood Cliffs, New Jersey: Prentice-Hall.

Economic Development Australia. Accreditation. Retrieved from www.edaustralia.com.au/membership/accreditation-2/

Fainstein, S. S. (2010). *The Just City*. Ithaca: Cornell University Press.

Hoover, E. M. (1937). *Location Theory and the Shoe and Leather Industries*. Cambridge, Massachusetts: Harvard University Press.

Institute of Economic Development. (2018). *IED Accredited Courses and Qualifications*. Retrieved from https://ied.co.uk/skills_training/ied_accredited_courses_and_qualifications/

International Economic Development Council. *Certified Economic Developer Program*. Retrieved from www.iedconline.org/web-pages/professional-development/become-certified/

Isard, W., Azis, I. J., Drennan, M. P., Miller, R. E., Saltzman, S., & Thornbecke, E. (2017). *Methods of Interregional and Regional Analysis* (Reprint ed.). Abingdon: Routledge.

Jonas, A. E. G., & Wilson, D. (Eds.). (1999). *The Urban Growth Machine: Critical Perspectives, Two Decades Later*. Albany, New York: State University of New York Press.

Katz, B., & Wagner, J. (2014). *The Rise of Innovation Districts: A New Geography of Innovation in America*. Retrieved from Washington, D.C.: www.brookings.edu/wp-content/uploads/2016/07/InnovationDistricts1.pdf

Leigh, N. G., & Blakely, E. J. (2016). *Planning Local Economic Development* (6th ed.). Thousand Oaks, California: SAGE Publications.

Marshall, A. (1895). *Principles of Economics*. London: Macmillan and Co.

Martin, R., & Sunley, P. (2014). On the Notion of Regional Economic Resilience: Conceptualization and Explanation. *Journal of Economic Geography, 15*(1), 1–42. doi:10.1093/jeg/lbu015

Perroux, F. (1950). Economic Space: Theory and Applications. *The Quarterly Journal of Economics, 64*(1), 89. doi:10.2307/1881960

Schumpeter, J. A. (1976). *Capitalism, Socialism and Democracy*. London: George Allen & Unwin.

Winnick, L. (1966). Place Prosperity v. People Prosperity: Welfare Considerations in the Geographic Redistribution of Economic Activity. In Real Estate Research Program at the University of California Los Angeles (Ed.), *Essays in Urban Land Economics in Honor of the Sixty-fifth Birthday of Leo Grebler* (pp. 273–283). Los Angeles: Real Estate Research Program.

17
REGIONAL ECONOMIC DEVELOPMENT PLANNING

Edward M. Bergman and Edward Feser

Introduction

Economic development is a contested term, often confused with *economic growth* or *business development*, with which it shares some features. The latter two terms refer mainly to the scalar expansion and success of existing sectors or incumbent enterprises, whereas the former focuses on an economy's likelihood of evolving in a way better suited to a population's needs through interventions that might influence that evolution successfully. Economic development as a practice is common at the national, state, regional, provincial, city and neighborhood levels. Although the agents and strategies operational at different levels overlap somewhat, the measures and resources brought to bear differ markedly.

One broad but useful definition of *regional economic development*—which we modify slightly—describes it as the "[planned] application of economic processes and resources available to a region that result in the sustainable development of, and desired outcomes for, a region" (Stimson, Stough et al., 2006). This perspective dominates current North American, European and Australasian approaches to educating planners on the subject of regional economic development. This chapter discusses the origins and key features of the main regional economic development strategies common to practice in developed countries, covering the major topic areas for a course on regional economic development. The chapter refers the reader to the underlying research and literatures, and concludes with a discussion of educating current and future regional economic development planners.

Origins and History

Foundational to the emergence of regional economic development (hereafter, RED) as a planning topic was *Regional Development and Planning*, a 1964 collaboration between John Friedmann, then at the Massachusetts Institute of Technology, and William Alonso, then at Harvard.

Of the volume and its successor, Friedmann (2017) recalled that "it hadn't quite dawned on us that the world was already gearing up to the coming neo-liberal revolution, and that state-led planning would be one of its first victims". State-led refers to organized activity of a top-down, nation state apparatus that typically pursued "growth pole" strategies for regions that were considered by experts as ripe for socio-economic intervention, the favored approach within the unitary states of Latin America and much of Europe (Parr, 1999a, 1999b) well into the 20th century.

Meanwhile, the United States saw a renewed focus on the powers of local governments in the late 1960s and early 1970s that pushed the responsibility for economic development firmly down to city and state levels where property development had long been planned and where latent capacities for economic development (Hirsch, 1965) could be exploited. New capacities were further stimulated through a quarter century of intermittent cyclical punctuations of metropolitan regions and states and by the loss of intergovernmental aid in the mid-1970s, thereby encouraging local governments to offer many forms of support to existing business and startups as regional remedies (Goldstein and Bergman, 1986; Isserman, 1994). The former top-down, exogenously initiated, nation-led regional development so familiar to Friedmann and Alonso was being complemented and steadily supplanted by indigenously-led, bottom-up, regionally-competitive RED.

By the 1990s attention had begun to extend to how planners might best apply an experimental array of regional programs and policies, and to a greater appreciation for the dimensions of economic space and their effects on RED. The "new economic geography" (e.g., Fujita et al., 1999) highlights the fact that most international trade actually occurs *between regions* spread around the globe, often between industry branches within the same sectors. Moreover, much of this inter-regional trade is within global supply chains that link highly-specialized components of overall industrial production together. The singular role of spatial agglomeration thus gained renewed importance to RED planners (Feser, 1998). Concentrations of industry have always characterized US regions, more so than in Europe. However, global trade decimated previous low-tech concentrations of footwear, textiles and apparel, consumer electronics and other nondurable industries throughout the US; simultaneously, trade hyper-concentrated newly emergent knowledge industries (biotechnology, information technology, media, etc.) that are undergirded by the US innovation system and the skill-intensive branches of all sectors in new, rapidly evolving clusters. In advanced economies, the practice of RED therefore bifurcated along lines of approach most suited to either the most or the least-favored regions. As industrial technologies advanced ever more rapidly, their now-clarified *endogenous* origins (Romer, 1986, 1990, 1994; Lucas, 1988) added a vital new issue for RED: how to develop and exploit knowledge-based innovations within the more advanced regions, particularly among the swarms of new firms that populate successful innovative clusters.

RED in less advanced regions faces the classic trade-driven dilemmas associated with industrial decline, becoming similarly susceptibe to the processes underway in developing countries: what sectors or industries are possible to develop in an era of heavy global competition that could improve prosperity? The most traditional is to somehow attract (or locate) an "anchor" business, government installation, or other organization that does not depend heavily upon competitive advantages to a region in hopes of stimulating a growth pole. Two closely related concepts have recently been advanced to consider new competitive possibilities open to these regions. The first considers the nature of "product space", that is, the alternate sectors an active entrepreneur might independently identify and pursue (Hidalgo, Klinger et al., 2007), while the second focuses on the analytically-revealed "related diversification" potentials of technologically similar but absent sectors that might logically be pursued as part of a "smart specialization" approach to RED (Koen, Van Oort and Verburg, 2007). In either case, the presence of a substantial regional development body, initial development support, and some form of industry policy is invaluable (Goldstein and Bergman, 1986).

RED Strategy Rubrics

Although a robust literature on the theory, organizational apparatus, planning processes, and individual policy and planning tools undergirding regional economic development (hereafter RED), exists (Malizia and Feser, 1999; Stimson, Stough et al., 2006; Capello, 2009; Leigh and Clark, 2011; Ascani, Crescenzi et al., 2012; Dinc, 2016; Leigh and Blakely, 2016), there has been less written that synthesizes the main approaches to planning action from the perspective of broader strategy. This section groups development options and approaches into five broad rubrics that might be pursued as elements of a RED strategy, either singly or in combination.

In a few economically successful regions, a potent mix of infrastructure facilities, educational offerings, public- and business-serviced sites and structures, agglomeration advantages, efficient transportation, and taxes proportional to benefits has been built up over time. Regular indigenous business formation and expansion, as well as inward investment, are ensured by offering business investors a portfolio of local advantages that support productive and cost-effective operations. In those fortunate places, RED planning is a matter of cultivating the region's competitive business environment (CBE) by attending to these seemingly mundane but vitally important features with efficient public administration and sound regional planning.

For a majority of regions, the absence of one or more components of a thriving CBE calls for an expanded, active and engaged RED approach. Regions that possess only a rudimentary CBE must eventually remedy their worst shortcomings to make progress, while also undertaking one or more of the following general strategies as a means of mobilizing the attention of local citizens and external investors around potential development prospects:

- Acquiring/retaining direct investment in regional industries;
- Clustering the regional economy;
- Restructuring the regional industrial base;
- Stabilizing the regional economy; and
- Sustaining the regional economy.

Acquiring/Retaining Direct Investment in Regional Industries

Capital-deficient regions or those facing employment and population loss are understandably most interested in attracting external investment in local business and industry (Ilvento and Loveridge, 2000). The underlying reasons invariably need to be addressed, which may require long periods of sacrifice and further loss to eventually rectify. Meantime, efforts to attract new or replacement investment become an irresistible option.

To locate in marginal business environments, investors demand compensation in various forms, i.e., depressed wage levels, tax concessions and location subsidies (cash or in-kind), which appear generally to be of modest to equivocal effect (Buss, 2001; Luger and Bae, 2005; Bartik, 2011, 2014). Even with compensation, place-insensitive firms are always at risk of decamping to less expensive areas, either nearby or abroad. Moreover, such compensation strategies carry with them an opportunity cost—that of pursuing alternative strategies, such as improving the overall business environment or supporting labor migration to growing regions (Bartik, 2014).

Investment-seeking is not limited to the weakest regions, as strong regions also seek external capital infusions to maintain or improve their competitive positions. Such regions focus efforts on new or expanded investment by large firms or multi-nationals engaged in international trade, including foreign direct investors (FDI). Marketing efforts are directed to a broad spectrum of sectors and industries, including specialty retail, health and education services, headquarters, research labs, tourism, business fairs/conferencing, and transportation or logistics services.

Gaining investment in local business may also rely on various forms of entrepreneurship. The personal or business assets of residents provide initial sources of investment that could attract further external financing of growth once an enterprise has demonstrated market viability. Whether in the form of a new startup wholly unrelated to previous employment or a spin-off from a previous employer or knowledge-rich affiliation—such as a university or technology firm—entrepreneurs perform the valuable role of resource allocation within regional economies, thereby stimulating investment, new firms and potential growth sectors.

Indeed, opportunity-seeking entrepreneurs are seen as vital actors in economic development. They stimulate technological change (Ács and Varga, 2005; van der Zwan, Thurik et al., 2016), identify previously unseen development potentials (Hausmann and Rodrik, 2003), help diversify the existing industrial base (Content and Frenken, 2016), populate niches in supply-chain clusters (Feser and Bergman, 2000), exploit and incent the production of intellectual properties (Goldstein et al., 2013), and contribute to regional leadership and champions (Vecchio, 2003; Feldman, 2014). They are more active and effective in urban or metropolitan regions, perhaps building upon localization, urbanization and diversity effects, as well as a stronger entrepreneurial culture, particularly those from entrepreneurial families (Renski, 2011). But in all regions, less favored ones as well, there is evidence that entrepreneurial education can further stimulate the formation of new entrepreneurs (Lindh and Thorgren, 2016), as can role model observation (Ács, Desai et al., 2008; van der Zwan, Thurik et al., 2016), both of which are supportable with RED policies. Further impetus and support of entrepreneurial success may be possible in less favorable regions through the provision of one or more types of business incubators, suited to regional conditions (Bøllingtoft and Ulhøi, 2005).

Clustering the Regional Economy

Industrial or regional clusters are groupings of industries whose firms gain benefits from close proximity or other connections (Porter, 1990; Bergman and Feser, 1999; Delgado, Porter et al., 2015). They routinely result from advantage-seeking owners and entrepreneurs who recognize the agglomeration advantages of co-location and possible cooperation. Marshallian clusters consist of firms in the same or closely related industries that gain advantage from shared economies with other firms. Pools of skilled workers and occupations, business and public services, or transportation and facilities geared to specific industry needs are among the shared advantages that result from agglomerated densities of co-located firms (Feser, 2003; Trippl and Bergman, 2014).

A large body of literature now exists about how to stimulate and support clusters, much of which promotes various consultation services that advance the idea that cluster success depends upon regional interventions to coordinate and manage inter-firm relations as the means of recognizing and securing shared advantages (Feser, 2009). Industry targeting efforts using clusters as a framework often focus most intently on the intersection of industrial and occupational affinities, an idea originally proposed by Wilbur Thompson (Thompson and Thompson, 1985, 1987). Policies that promote cluster formation and development are most valuable in regions with relatively weak economies that lack the market incentives driving the formation of self-interested de facto clusters in more advanced regions. One role of the RED planner is to understand which of the most important elements of a CBE would benefit particular clusters and to design policies accordingly (Feser and Luger, 2003), while also offering guidance to regional industry attraction and entrepreneurial support efforts. But planners should be cautious in their analyses, as easily detectable clusters may be in industries past their prime (Bergman, 2008).

Restructuring the Regional Industrial Base

Regions display a distinctive mix of industry and enterprise types acquired over time, usually unplanned and in response to numerous historical influences. Faced with declining growth prospects, future losses of key businesses, or dissatisfaction with productivity and income from this mix, regions launch attempts to shift toward preferred industries. Transitional industries are likely to arise along a long ladder of related industries that lead from the current mix to the most desired industries of advanced economies (Hidalgo, Klinger et al., 2007). To encourage the growth of transitional industries, RED planners would want to support broad entrepreneurial and external investor entry.

The transfer of technologies and related capabilities of regional industries that are similar to those of preferred industries can help the region move higher on the development ladder. The concept of "related variety" has been widely adopted to argue that regions can branch out into new industries more easily if they are able to build upon capabilities similar to those found in one or more firms of the region (Koen, Van Oort and Verburg, 2007; Content and Frenken, 2016). New industries can also arise in quite unrelated sectors as well, which Boschma and Capone (2015) show is more likely to occur via entrepreneurs in market-oriented economies than in coordinated market economies of Europe and elsewhere that hew more closely to related variety forms of restructuring.

Restructuring a regional economy might also be guided by a concern for employment stability, particularly in cases of high regional unemployment elasticity during national economic downturns. In such cases, regions may attempt to select from among the possible or likely industries those having low business-cycle variations or that are inversely correlated during business cycles with major employers in the region. The so-called "portfolio" approach would favor industries that help dampen business-cycle impacts, but Lande (1994) shows this is likely to introduce a tradeoff between regional growth and stability, just as it does with stock portfolios.

Anchoring the Regional Economy

Stable regional employers, such as corporate headquarters, are important economic anchors in periods of cyclical turmoil and over longer periods, buffering regions from losses of employment and supply-chain purchases from local vendors. But the inexorable waves of corporate mergers and acquisitions can loosen even these anchors in a matter of months. RED planners therefore should be alert to the role of more spatially-bound anchors that resist periodic pressures and contribute steadily to regional prosperity. These include educational institutions, health service providers and non-profit organizations, essentially spatially immobile employers whose activities are either integral to the local economy or for which the location is either mandated or integral to their identity. Ultimately, "spatial immobility is the defining feature of an anchor institution" (Taylor and Luter, 2013).

Anchoring institutions may also extend beyond public universities and medical centers to public utilities, sports facilities, cultural and performing arts centers, public enterprises, and other social purpose institutions that offer desirable social and economic benefits. Prisons and military bases may capture the attention of RED planners as well. They are institutions sometimes sought, or settled for, by many least-favored regions desperate for infusions of any investment and stable employment (Besser and Hanson, 2013; Perdue and Sanchagrin, 2016). Rather than taking regional anchors and their beneficial functions for granted, RED planners should actively cultivate and engage anchors in regional economic development efforts.

Sustaining the Regional Economy

Even large and prosperous metropolitan regions able to leverage their present advantages can face problems of sustaining their economies. RED planners are now recognizing that global competition and disruptive innovations can swiftly unsettle economies in any region. These are the very forces that must be mastered to ensure future success, although such forces invariably favor the most prosperous regions.

Recent advances in research concerning regional growth now stress the importance of internal or endogenous factors that help prepare regions to advance knowledge and exploit competitive technologies (Roberts and Setterfield, 2010). The previously "unexplained residual" growth revealed in previous national growth models has been identified as the result of patterns of learning-by-doing that spill over and accumulate knowledge as a public good (Romer, 1986, 1990, 1994), which Lucas (1988) interpreted as the logical outcome of human interaction in close proximity.

The endogenous growth literature identifies human capital as the key reservoir and mobile transmitter of shared knowledge, which elevates the skill levels required in advancing firms. The vital, irreplaceable role of human capital in all aspects of endogenous growth processes requires its development as first priority, particularly where it is least abundant. Where it is least abundant is usually where it is least appreciated and vice versa, leading least-favored regions to pursue other more immediate measures rather than improving advanced education and training of residents. Labor supply policies include job training programs; primary, secondary and post-secondary education; early childhood education; summer educational programs for youth; and career support programs for both youth and adults. But the benefits also do not manifest themselves except over the longer run, as quality early education translates to stronger secondary education, post-secondary performance, and the overall attractiveness of a region for skilled workers, making the uncertainty of the investment a particular challenge for struggling regions.

Human capital investment is necessary, since a sizable, high quality human capital base serves as the foundation for sustained innovation. Skilled individuals conduct R&D while working closely with colleagues concerned with production, logistics, and other core functions, which permits firms to receive and incorporate findings from basic scientific fields into proprietary innovative advances at all levels. Regions that might benefit from a deeper skill base might increase efforts to increase their residential attractiveness to skilled workers.

A regional economy in which endogenous processes are well-embedded in clusters and related institutions could be described as a regional innovation system (RIS), a concept widely in use among European RED planners and policymakers (Cooke, Asheim et al., 2011). Regions fortunate to host educational and medical institutions have many additional reasons and numerous opportunities to support regional complexes of research and innovation, while less fortunate regions will need to leverage the knowledge base of their most advanced sectors and firms, including those engaged in trade with advanced firms elsewhere (Hausmann, Hwang et al., 2007; Cooke, Asheim et al., 2011), through "related variety" strategies (OECD, 2013) or by reducing barriers to RIS success (Isaksen, 2001).

Educating Regional Economic Development Planners

Learning to make sound diagnoses and execute good strategy means drawing upon the latest general theories and large-scale empirical research; applying the lessons found in a literature rich with case studies and broad findings; developing a deep understanding of local conditions, capacities and institutions; conducting sound quantitative analyses of the regional economy; and understanding that implementation matters. The centrality of context to good planning cannot be emphasized enough in a field that is prone to searching for simplified development models, broad macroeconomic solutions, general framework conditions, big pushes and quick hits (Easterly, 2006). Appreciating the institutional limits and potentials of RED and its context can be accomplished when students apply theories and methods to the actual circumstances of RED stakeholders in supervised projects and workshops.

Tendler and Amorim (1996) write about an instructive regional development success story in Brazil. The challenge was a highly agricultural region with little high value added activity in industry or services, little indigenous capacity to invest, and low entrepreneurial experience. Incomes lagged; jobs were few; poverty was high; innovation was a distant dream; local public sector capacity to address the economic weaknesses was limited.

One solution, in this instance, was to inject demand—in essence, to create a market—via public spending that would occur anyway: specifically, to direct public sector purchases to institutional furniture produced by local manufacturers in the region. (The natural resources of the region were particularly favorable for furniture manufacturing.) And to ensure that the furniture was of sufficient quality and quantity to meet the government's needs, the government also restructured the incentives facing an existing local business support agency—previously not known for its responsiveness and effectiveness in working with small firms and indigenous entrepreneurs—so the agency was sufficiently motivated to provide the right kinds of assistance to local producers. Careful attention to the marriage of demand-side and supply-side interventions was an especially important part of the story.

The result? Nascent firms suddenly had a market for their goods. Those local businesses now scrambling to meet that market got the kinds of technical support they needed. And a competitive furniture cluster comprised mostly of small and medium sized enterprises (SMEs) emerged, one key rung on a ladder to a more advanced industrialized economy.

The lesson is not that regional economic development is limited by inadequate demand, although it sometimes is. It is not that local businesses require technical support, although they sometimes do. It is not that regional linkages and import substitution opportunities must be cultivated, although they often should be, especially in lagging regions. It is that *well-informed strategy*—in the sense of an accurate diagnosis of a particular challenge or opportunity in a specific place, followed by the effective institutional execution of thoughtful and coordinated actions to counter the challenge or capture the opportunity—is a powerful driver of sustained economic development, however incremental and "small scale" it may appear on the face of it.

A growing body of research from several complementary perspectives highlights how important careful institutional design and process are to the likelihood of success of economic development strategies (Chang, 2003; Amsden, 2007; Rodrik, 2007; Block, 2008; Banerjee and Duflo, 2011). As Rodrik writes: "A first-best policy in the wrong institutional setting will do considerably less good than a second-best policy in an appropriate institutional setting . . . when it comes to industrial policy, specifying the process is more important than specifying the outcome" (2007, p. 111).

Regional economic development expertise is cultivated and imparted via multiple disciplines: planning, public policy, geography, economics and regional science. However, planning schools are particularly well-suited to training regional economic development practitioners skilled in developing and deploying good strategy (Feser, 2014). The teaching of regional development theory and economic and demographic analysis have long been planning education staples, and those subjects remain highly pertinent today.

Planning academics naturally focus on decision-making processes, strategic planning models and rubrics, institutional design, and methods of ensuring effective and diverse forms of stakeholder engagement. Although the full range of such concerns have received somewhat less focus in the research and instruction of economic development specializations in North American and European planning schools, that is easily changed and is well worth the challenge.

References

Ács, Z. J., Desai, S., & Hessels, J. (2008). Entrepreneurship, economic development and institutions. *Small Business Economics*, *31*(3), 219–234. doi:10.1007/s11187-008-9135-9

Ács, Z. J., & Varga, A. (2005). Entrepreneurship, agglomeration and technological change. *Small Business Economics*, *24*(3), 323–334. doi:10.1007/s11187-005-1998-4

Amsden, A. H. (2007). *Escape from Empire: The Developing World's Journey through Heaven and Hell*. Cambridge, Massachusetts: MIT Press.

Ascani, A., Crescenzi, R., & Iammarino, S. (2012). Economic institutions and the location strategies of european multinationals in their geographical neighbourhood. *SSRN Electronic Journal*. doi:10.2139/ssrn.2637486

Banerjee, A. V., & Duflo, E. (2011). *Poor Economics: A Radical Rethinking of the Way to Fight Global Poverty*. New York: PublicAffairs.

Bartik, T. J. (2011). *Investing in Kids: Early Childhood Programs and Local Economic Development*. Kalamazoo, Michigan: W.E. Upjohn Institute for Employment Research.

Bartik, T. J. (2014). *From Preschool to Prosperity: The Economic Payoff to Early Childhood Education*. Kalamazoo, Michigan: W.E. Upjohn Institute for Employment Research

Bergman, E. M. (2008). Cluster life-cycles: An emerging synthesis. In C. Karlsson (Ed.), *Handbook of Research on Cluster Theory* (pp. 114–132). Cheltenham: Edward Elgar Publishing.

Bergman, E. M., & Feser, E. J. (1999). *Industrial and Regional Clusters: Concepts and Comparative Applications*. Morganton, West Virginia: Regional Research Institute, West Virginia University.

Besser, T. L., & Hanson, M. M. (2013). Development of last resort: The impact of new state prisons on small town economies in the United States. In R. G. Phillips & T. L. Besser (Eds.), *Community Economic Development*. Abingdon: Routledge.

Block, F. (2008). Swimming against the current: The rise of a hidden developmental state in the United States. *Politics & Society*, *36*(2), 169–206. doi:10.1177/0032329208318731

Bøllingtoft, A., & Ulhøi, J. P. (2005). The networked business incubator—leveraging entrepreneurial agency? *Journal of Business Venturing*, *20*(2), 265–290. doi:10.1016/j.jbusvent.2003.12.005

Boschma, R., & Capone, G. (2015). Institutions and diversification: Related versus unrelated diversification in a varieties of capitalism framework. *Research Policy*, *44*(10), 1902–1914. doi:10.1016/j.respol.2015.06.013

Buss, T. F. (2001). The effect of state tax incentives on economic growth and firm location decisions: An overview of the literature. *Economic Development Quarterly*, *15*(1), 90–105. doi:10.1177/089124240101500108

Capello, R. (2009). Regional growth and local development theories: Conceptual evolution over fifty years of regional science. *Géographie, économie, société*, *11*(1), 9–21. doi:10.3166/ges.11.9-21

Chang, H.-J. (2003). *Kicking Away the Ladder: Development Strategy in Historical Perspective*. London: Anthem Press.

Content, J., & Frenken, K. (2016). Related variety and economic development: A literature review. *European Planning Studies*, *24*(12), 2097–2112. doi:10.1080/09654313.2016.1246517

Cooke, P., Asheim, B., Boschma, R., Martin, R., Schwartz, D., & Tödtling, F. (2011). *Handbook of Regional Innovation and Growth*. Cheltenham: Edward Elgar.

Delgado, M., Porter, M. E., & Stern, S. (2015). Defining clusters of related industries. *Journal of Economic Geography*, *16*(1), 1–38. doi:10.1093/jeg/lbv017

Dinc, M. (2016). *Introduction to Regional Economic Development: Major Theories and Basic Analytical Tools*. Cheltenham: Edward Elgar.

Easterly, W. (2006). *The White Man's Burden*. New York: Penguin Books.
Feldman, M. P. (2014). The character of innovative places: Entrepreneurial strategy, economic development, and prosperity. *Small Business Economics*, 43(1), 9–20. doi:10.1007/s11187-014-9574-4
Feser, E. (2009). Clusters and strategy in regional economic development. *Industry Clusters*, 3, 26–38.
Feser, E. (2014). Planning local economic development in the emerging world order. *Town Planning Review*, 85(1), 19–38. doi:10.3828/tpr.2014.4
Feser, E. J. (1998). Enterprises, External Economies, and Economic Development. *Journal of Planning Literature*, 12(3), 283–302. doi:10.1177/088541229801200302
Feser, E. J. (2003). What regions do rather than make: A proposed set of knowledge-based occupation clusters. *Urban Studies*, 40(10), 1937–1958. doi:10.1080/0042098032000116059
Feser, E. J., & Bergman, E. M. (2000). National industry cluster templates: A framework for applied regional cluster analysis. *Regional Studies*, 34(1), 1–19. doi:10.1080/00343400050005844
Feser, E. J., & Luger, M. I. (2003). Cluster analysis as a mode of inquiry: Its use in science and technology policymaking in North Carolina. *European Planning Studies*, 11(1), 11–24. doi:10.1080/09654310303664
Friedmann, J. (2017). Planning as a vocation: The journey so far. In B. Haselberger (Ed.), *Encounters in Planning Thought: 16 Autobiographical Essays by Key Thinkers in Spatial Planning* (pp. 15–34). London: Routledge.
Friedmann, J., & Alonso, W. (Eds.). (1964). *Regional Development and Planning: A Reader*. Cambridge, Massachusetts: MIT Press.
Fujita, M., Krugman, P., & Venables, A. J. (1999). *The Spatial Economy: Cities, Regions, and International Trade*. Cambridge, Massachusetts: MIT Press.
Fujita, M., & Thisse, J.-F. (2002). *Economics of Agglomeration: Cities, Industrial Location, and Regional Growth*. Cambridge: Cambridge University Press.
Goldstein, H. A., & Bergman, E. M. (1986). Institutional arrangements for state and local industrial policy. *Journal of the American Planning Association*, 52(3), 265–276. doi:10.1080/01944368608976433
Goldstein, H., Bergman, E. M., & Maier, G. (2013). University mission creep? Comparing EU and US faculty views of university involvement in regional economic development and commercialization. *Annals of Regional Science*, 50(2), 453–77.
Hausmann, R., & Rodrik, D. (2003). Economic development as self-discovery. *Journal of Development Economics*, 72(2), 603–633. doi:10.1016/s0304-3878(03)00124-x
Hausmann, R., Hwang, J., & Rodrik, D. (2007). What you export matters. *Journal of Economic Growth*, 12(1), 1–25. doi:10.1007/s10887-006-9009-4
Hidalgo, C. A., Klinger, B., Barabasi, A. L., & Hausmann, R. (2007). The product space conditions the development of nations. *Science*, 317(5837), 482–487. doi:10.1126/science.1144581
Hirsch, W. Z. (1965). Regional development planning: A reader by John Friedmann and William Alonso. *The American Economic Review*, 55(5), 1205–1207.
Ilvento, T., & Loveridge, S. (2000). *Factors Influencing Participation in BR&E Programs: A Study of Local Coordinators in Six States*. Retrieved from https://ageconsearch.umn.edu/record/15819?ln=en
Isaksen, A. (2001). Building regional innovation systems: Is endogenous industrial development possible in the global economy? *Canadian Journal of Regional Science*, 24(1), 101–120.
Isserman, A. M. (1994). State economic development policy and practice in the United States: A survey article. *International Regional Science Review*, 16(1–2), 49–100.
Koen, F., Van Oort, F., & Verburg, T. (2007). Related variety, unrelated variety and regional economic growth. *Regional Studies* 41, 685–97.
Lande, P. S. (1994). Regional industrial structure and economic growth and instability. *Journal of Regional Science*, 34(3), 343–360. doi:10.1111/j.1467-9787.1994.tb00871.x
Leigh, N. G., & Blakely, E. J. (2016). *Planning Local Economic Development* (Sixth ed.). Thousand Oaks, California: SAGE Publications.
Leigh, N. G., & Clark, J. (2011). North American perspectives on local and regional development. In A. Pike, A. Rodriguez-Pose, & J. Tomaney (Eds.), *Handbook of Local and Regional Development* (pp. 515–526). New York: Taylor & Francis.
Lindh, I., & Thorgren, S. (2016). Entrepreneurship education: The role of local business. *Entrepreneurship & Regional Development*, 28(5–6), 313–336. doi:10.1080/08985626.2015.1134678
Lucas, R. E. (1988). On the mechanics of economic development. *Journal of Monetary Economics*, 22(1), 3–42. doi:10.1016/0304-3932(88)90168-7
Luger, M. I., & Bae, S. (2005). The effectiveness of state business tax incentive programs: The case of North Carolina. *Economic Development Quarterly*, 19(4), 327–345. doi:10.1177/0891242405279684

Malizia, E. E., & Feser, E. J. (1999). *Understanding Local Economic Development*. New Brunswick, New Jersey: Center for Urban Policy Research.

Organisation for Economic Co-operation and Development (OECD). (2013). *Innovation-driven growth in regions: The role of smart specialisation*. Retrieved from www.oecd.org/sti/inno/smart-specialisation.pdf

Parr, J. B. (1999a). Growth-pole strategies in regional economic planning: A retrospective view (Part 1). *Urban Studies, 36*(7), 1195–1215. doi:10.1080/0042098993187

Parr, J. B. (1999b). Growth-pole strategies in regional economic planning: A retrospective view (Part 2). *Urban Studies, 36*(8), 1247–1268. doi:10.1080/0042098992971

Perdue, R. T., & Sanchagrin, K. (2016). Imprisoning Appalachia: The socio-economic impacts of prison development. *Journal of Appalachian Studies, 22*(2), 210. doi:10.5406/jappastud.22.2.0210

Porter, M. E. (1990). *The Competitive Advantage of Nations*. New York: Free Press.

Renski, H. (2011). External economies of localization, urbanization and industrial diversity and new firm survival. *Papers in Regional Science, 90*(3), 473–502. doi:10.1111/j.1435-5957.2010.00325.x

Roberts, M., & Setterfield, M. (2010). Endogenous regional growth: A critical survey. In M. Setterfield (Ed.), *Handbook of Alternative Theories of Economic Growth* (pp. 431–450). Cheltenham: Edward Elgar Publishing.

Rodrik, D. (2007). *One Economics, Many Recipes*. Princeton, New Jersey: Princeton University Press.

Romer, P. M. (1986). Increasing Returns and Long-Run Growth. *Journal of Political Economy, 94*(5), 1002–1037. doi:10.1086/261420

Romer, P. M. (1990). Endogenous Technological Change. *Journal of Political Economy, 98*(5, Part 2), S71–S102. doi:10.1086/261725

Romer, P. M. (1994). The Origins of Endogenous Growth. *Journal of Economic Perspectives, 8*(1), 3–22. doi:10.1257/jep.8.1.3

Stimson, R. J., Stough, R. R., & Roberts, B. H. (2006). *Regional Economic Development: Analysis and Planning Strategy*. Berlin: Springer Berlin Heidelberg.

Taylor, H. L., & Luter, G. (2013). *Anchor institutions: An interpretive review essay*. Buffalo, New York: University at Buffalo.

Tendler, J., & Amorim, M. A. (1996). Small firms and their helpers: Lessons on demand. *World Development, 24*(3), 407–426. doi:10.1016/0305-750x(95)00155-6

Thompson, W. R. (1965). *A Preface to Urban Economics*. Baltimore: Johns Hopkins Press.

Thompson, W. R., & Thompson, P. R. (1985). From industries to occupations: Rethinking local economic development, *Economic Development Commentary, 9*, 12–18.

Thompson, W. R., & Thompson, P. R. (1987). National industries and local occupational strengths: The cross-hairs of targeting. *Urban Studies, 24*(6), 547–560. doi:10.1080/00420988720080781

Trippl, M., & Bergman, E. M. (2014). Clusters, local districts, and innovative milieux. In M. M. Fischer & P. Nijkamp (Eds.), *Handbook of Regional Science* (Vol. 1, pp. 439–456). Berlin, Heidelberg: Springer.

van der Zwan, P., Thurik, R., Verheul, I., & Hessels, J. (2016). Factors influencing the entrepreneurial engagement of opportunity and necessity entrepreneurs. *Eurasian Business Review, 6*(3), 273–295. doi:10.1007/s40821-016-0065-1

Vecchio, R. P. (2003). Entrepreneurship and leadership: Common trends and common threads. *Human Resource Management Review, 13*(2), 303–327. doi:10.1016/s1053-4822(03)00019-6

18
PLANNING AT THE NATIONAL LEVEL

Daniel Galland and Frank Othengrafen

The Genesis of Planning at the National Level

Planning at the national level within diverse liberal capitalist nation-states has been subjected to substantial reorientations over the past three decades. A way to understand the nature of these reorientations is to trace how shifting political ideologies have gradually influenced national planning as a public sector function while readapting its role in catering to growth and development. In this chapter, we conceive the 'national' in terms of geographical and ideological scales. Geographically, planning is portrayed as it is practiced at the level of nation-states as territorially confined entities (Herod, 2011). At the same time, the 'national' is purported as a scale of ideology, meaning that nation-states are regarded "as they interrelate in a world-economy" (Taylor, 1981, p. 3). Political ideology is conceived as a driving force influencing government intervention insofar as it yields ad hoc planning policy and implementation. While this might have been evident at the time of the genesis and initial development of planning at the national level, the relationship between political ideology and the latter has been at times paradoxical (Alterman, 2001).

The driving forces that influence the substance and roles of planning at the national level are manifold and tend to differ over time. In Western European countries, the rationales behind planning at the national level have generally shifted from attaining equal development objectives via the reduction of inter-regional disparities within nation-states during the 1960s and 1970s, towards achieving sustainable development and infrastructure development objectives as well as accommodating growth pressures and other development needs from the late 1980s onwards (Alterman, 2001). Since then, neoliberalization processes have similarly favored economic growth agendas, which in turn have modified the capacities of government intervention in planning affairs. These major political and economic shifts have consequently altered the 'steering role' of national planning and, along with it, the provisions of diverse planning curricula in higher education institutions.

Frank et al. (2014) argue that planning education provision in Europe tends to shift as a result of several continental processes relating to integration policies (Williams, 1989), the Bologna process and reform (Frank, 2006), and general transformations resulting from higher education changes (Frank et al., 2014). To this we may add the impact that major driving forces such as global environmental change, economic restructuring, and migration have had on planning policy and practice, and thereby also on the character and content in planning knowledge and skills embedded in planning curricula (Pezzoli & Howe, 2001). The present contribution attempts to shed light on how national planning reorientations similarly influence the content and delivery of planning curricula. In doing so, this chapter asks the following questions:

- How has planning at the national level historically evolved?
- How have planning curricula essentially dealt with shifts in national planning policy?
- What does the particular shift from rational to communicative planning (and thereby from land-use towards strategic spatial planning) imply for planning education?
- At the same time, how are broader societal changes such as the influence of EU policy trends and the neoliberalization of planning reflected in planning curricula?
- What skills do planners need to acquire in more decentralized planning settings?

The chapter delves into the origins of national planning in terms of political ideology and synthesizes the first developments of planning education in the advent of rationalist thinking. The chapter then discusses the ideological reorientations of national planning after the 1980s. Lastly, it addresses the implications of these shifts as regards the fabric of planning education by alluding to illustrative examples concerning master's programs from Denmark and Germany.

Political Ideology and the Steering Role of National Planning

The emergence of planning as a distinctively modern policy domain at the national level is concomitant to the genesis of planning as a power of state intervention in the apex of rationalist thought during the first decades of the twentieth century. By emphasizing technical reason and social rationality, national planning relied on the decision that a set of institutional provisions should be established to direct, synchronize and control the policies and programs towards a new societal configuration. The purpose of planning was thereby to foster an imagined and structured social order in accordance with the general perception that planned societies were to benefit from (state) planning interventions in free and open societies characterized by escalating technological progress and rising population growth (Friedmann, 1987).

The first national planning experiments in liberal capitalist nation-states in Western Europe took shape during the interwar period as a means to deal with the increasing economic difficulties derived from the impact of the Great Depression of 1929. John Maynard Keynes's revolutionary ideas and predictions as regards the inability of capitalist market forces to mitigate the imbalances produced by economic growth were particularly relevant. Keynes's theories largely shaped the role ascribed to national planning during the three decades of reconstruction in the post-World War II era – the so-called 'Glorious Thirty' (*les Trente Glorieuses*) (Fourastié, 1979). Characterized by remarkable growth and prosperity in some Western European countries (mainly in France, Germany and the United Kingdom) as well as in the United States, this period largely paved the course of the world economy during those decades.

The emergence of national planning ran parallel to the rise of 'Keynesian welfarism', i.e. the interventionist position of capitalist states to secure full employment and economic growth through a congruent association between national economy, national state and national society (Jessop, 2000). A foundational idea that historically enabled planning to materialize and progress was the hypothesis that social practices could be developed, adjusted and comprehensively controlled by *the state* in centralized and hierarchical forms. These foundational premises further relied on the assumption that socio-economic processes could be managed *rationally* alongside the fulfillment of specified socio-spatial objectives. For example, some European governments sought to organize regional space via hierarchical settlement patterns, following Christaller's theory of central places (Christaller, 1966).

The original steering role of national planning was then linked to the achievement of socio-spatial aims such as reducing inter-regional disparities, fostering industrial development, and managing rapid economic growth and population redistribution. In terms of instruments and methods, planning at the national level as a public sector activity dealt with land-use allocation, urban growth management, infrastructure development, settlement improvements and sectoral policy co-ordination, amongst other key policy areas (Healey, Khakee, Motte, & Needham, 1997; Tewdwr-Jones, 2001). The 'Glorious Thirty' thereby also witnessed the emergence and gradual formation of spatial planning systems in several European nation-states alongside the rise of classical modernist institutions (Hajer, 2003) organized through formal and hierarchical top-down structures wherein national planning policies steered sub-national levels of planning administration (Tewdwr-Jones, 1997). The comprehensive feature of spatial planning systems was hence reflected in their coordinative, integrative and hierarchical character (Alexander, 1992). In part the role of national planning policy was to operationalize these systems (e.g. Galland, 2012b) and guide land-use and development decisions by catering to growth and development (Healey et al., 1997).

The Initial Link between National Planning and Planning Education

Planning education at the university level started in the early twentieth century with the emergence of a 'specialist' course in civic design at the University of Liverpool and a degree in town planning at the University of Karlsruhe in Germany (Stiftel, Demerutis, Frank, Inkoom, & Lee, 2009). Focusing on the physical layout and land-use dimensions of urban areas, and thereby on master planning, at the core of their curricula (Taylor, 2010), the first planning education endeavors held a post-professional character that signified an 'elitist' qualification for engineers and architects (Frank et al., 2014). Similarly, the birth of planning education in the United States by the late 1920s held a physical design orientation (Krueckeberg, 1985). The design emphasis of early planning education was gradually replaced by a social science foundation in several planning schools both in the US and the UK during the post-World War II era, which eventually led planning programs in these countries to cover a wide range of policy areas such as economic development, environmental resources management, infrastructure and transportation, and housing (Stiftel et al., 2009).

Planning education then shifted during the first decade of the 'Glorious Thirty', which witnessed a rise in the conception of planning as a rational enterprise that could be used to correct market failures. The rational decision-making process was conceived as a generic planning model to define and systematize core areas of knowledge in planning (Alexander, 1986; Banfield, 1959). Advanced by the Chicago School during the 1950s, the rational decision-making model theoretically reinforced the discipline with a scientific and objective methodological arsenal as it came to be characterized by its formal rationality (the planning process) whereby the means were clearly separated from the ends (i.e. substantial rationality, then defined as a social optimum) (Faludi, 1973). This distinction led to a perception that holistic social engineering was feasible through centralized planning – what Faludi (ibid.), building on the work of Banfield (1959) and Altshuler (1965) regarded as "rational comprehensive planning".

This objective view of knowledge stressed the procedural and synoptic view of planning. The planning process could then be applied to any problem where procedural decision-making was deemed appropriate. In 1957, Perloff suggested that prospective planners be trained as "generalists with a specialty" and in doing so, he proposed ". . . the idea of planning as an enlightenment discipline with an appropriate core curriculum" (cited in Friedmann, 1996, p. 89). As this idea became widely accepted in the United States, the core curriculum of planning centered on rational decision-making (ibid.). In Europe, the bulk of planning programs embraced "... a comprehensive and interdisciplinary approach to planning education incorporating policy, economic, geographic and social sciences as new components with urban design declining in importance" (Frank et al., 2014). Influenced by national planning reorientations since the 1980s, planning education in both continents has gradually undergone a series of structural adjustments. We now turn to address these shifts in the following section.

National Planning Reorientations: Shifting Political Ideology and the Strategic Turn

The rational-comprehensive mode of planning lost favor after the Oil Crisis in the 1970s. The downfall of Keynesian welfarism during the 1970s led to a neoliberal regime shift that focused on promoting international competitiveness and socio-technical innovation in open economies. While this reorientation entailed subduing social policy to economic policy in allowing for greater labor market flexibility (Jessop, 2002), it also replaced the interventionist, steering role of national planning with an 'enabling' function aimed at facilitating the competitive provision of services (Healey et al., 1997). In Western Europe, this essentially meant that different policy tasks and responsibilities were gradually transferred (vertically and horizontally) to an array of different state and non-state actors operating at different territorial scales (e.g. Galland, 2012a).

As widely discussed by a number of planning scholars since the 1990s, the planning domain moved away from its distinctively steering role and rational-comprehensive mode towards adopting a more *strategic* role via communicative rationality (Albrechts, Healey, & Kunzmann, 2003; Healey, Khakee, Motte, & Needham, 1999; Salet & Faludi, 2000). While this was most evident in planning at the scale of city regions, planning at the national level in several Western European nation-states shifted from a comprehensive to a strategic approach. From a strategic perspective, planning at the national level embraced a relational conception often endorsed by the spatial relations between territories driven by specific planning 'episodes' (Healey, 2004, 2006). The strategic role of spatial planning therefore entailed that planning supplemented its land-use focus with an emphasis on innovative place-making activities based on relational processes for decision-making (Healey, 2007). While hierarchical spatial planning systems seem to remain as a façade in different national contexts (Galland & Elinbaum, 2015), the focus on place qualities involves the formation of networks of multiple actors beyond public planning who influence spatial development. The strategic reorientation of national planning hence fostered new governance capacities in settings where territorial relationships have included rather complex urban and regional dynamics.

The resulting shift towards strategic spatial planning and its emphasis on relational thinking represented a changing planning era that demanded a renewed understanding concerning the future governance relationships and capacities between national and sub-national levels. At the same time, the shift similarly entailed a more relational perception of space (Graham & Healey, 1999). As put by Davoudi (2012), the conception of spatial and scalar order shifted away from the positivist tradition that sought to "tame space and create order" (p. 432), towards an interpretive tradition where both scale and space are now regarded "... as socially constructed with contingent boundaries which are constantly territorialized and open to political contestation" (pp. 432–433). In Europe, this transition towards spatial relationality can be exemplified through the impact of European Union policies on national policy making via regulations and directives that nation-states ought to implement into national laws (e.g. environmental regulations and directives such as the Bird and Habitat directive or the Environmental Impact Assessment directive); European discourses about spatial planning and territorial development, promoted by the EU, that affect national policies indirectly (e.g. the European Spatial Development Concept or the presentation of transnational macro-regions); and informal exchanges of national planning experts, ministers, and other 'policy entrepreneurs' in various Committees of the European Council (e.g. Peck & Theodore, 2010).

Altogether, the shifting scope of planning at the national level in several Western European countries (especially Germany, Denmark, The Netherlands, Ireland and Finland) was evidently driven by a combination of factors such as: the influence of European Union policies in planning practices (Frank et al., 2014); moving away from rational-comprehensive planning and hierarchical modes towards communicative and deliberative planning, decentralization and new governance arrangements (Stiftel, 2009; Stiftel et al., 2009); and the influence of broader societal shifts as a result of shifting political ideologies (e.g. Davoudi, Galland and Stead, 2019). In such contexts, what did such shifting planning rationalities, roles and governance arrangements imply for planning education? In other words, how was the neoliberalization of planning and the adoption of a strategic role reflected in planning curricula and in the skills that planners should acquire?

The Influence of National Planning on the Fabric of Planning Education

Multiple insightful analyses concerning the historical development and evolution of planning education in relation to planning knowledge, skills and pedagogies have been published over the past decades (Dalton, 2001; Frank, 2006; Frank, 2002; Friedmann, 1996; Shepherd & Cosgrif, 1998). These examinations have identified the evolving scope of learning objectives and their translation into skills and competencies. At the same time, several studies have embraced the question of how alternative pedagogical approaches pave the way towards the delivery of state-of-the-art planning knowledge and skills (Shepherd & Cosgrif, 1998).

The strategic role of national planning, the overall political ideology shift towards neoliberalism, and the continued innovations and challenges associated with institutional practices at different planning scales have influenced the kind of knowledge and skills that planners need. Applying Dalton's (2001) metaphor of planning education as a fabric to the context of planning programs in Northern European settings, we discuss how the distinctive strategic role associated with national level planning coupled with the paradigm shift from rational towards communicative action (in neoliberalizing and decentralizing contexts) have been woven into specific planning curricula over the past two decades. In accordance with Dalton's depiction (p. 423), the fabric of planning education is structured by: first, length and breadth of the fabric representing time and scope of the planning field, respectively; second, warp and woof, depicting respectively what planners need to know and how they learn and are taught; third, web of threads, entailing how pedagogy and the application of knowledge lead to effective practice; and finally, weavers, namely planning instructors, theorists, practitioners, civil society members and planning students themselves. In our analysis we make reference to this metaphor and its vocabulary to better illustrate how planning education is 'woven' as a complex and multifaceted fabric constituted by an array of elements each representing different kinds of knowledge, skills, pedagogies shaped by different institutional forces (ibid.).

Ideological reorientations have been evidently reflected in national planning policies since the mid-1990s and, as such, have reshaped the fabric of planning education within different European universities. If one considers that the core of planning programs is constituted by evolving knowledge and skills within physical planning and the social sciences, then the more relational and decentralized approach of planning adds new threads to the fabric of planning education through the inclusion of knowledge, skills and pedagogies concentrating on *inter alia* studies of communicative (micro-) practices (Forester, 1999; Hoch, 1994). As national planning policies throughout Europe became more concerned with 'relational visions' about how sub-national territories should develop, increasingly there has been a perceived need to incorporate 'pragmatist' content pertaining to deliberative processes and practices such as knowledge and skills regarding facilitation and mediation techniques to foster dialogue, moderate debate and mediate negotiation between stakeholders (e.g. Forester, 2006, 2008).

In the same light, another shift towards more strategic and relational national planning is the use of spatial imagery as first promoted by the EU through the European Spatial Development Perspective two decades ago (Committee for Spatial Development, 1999). Planning imagery combines words, images and visions in representing selected features of given territories (e.g. van Duinen, 2004; Zonneveld, 2005), which do not necessarily correspond with boundaries of political administration. Through spatial imagery, national policies express visions of desired futures through which the spatial structures of such unbounded territories should develop (Albrechts et al., 2003; Healey, 2007; van Duinen, 2004). While in this context national planning policy might imply greater flexibility, the less tangible tradeoff is that it also breeds uncertainty about how planning should be pursued at sub-national levels. In the context of the 'making' of twenty-first-century metropolitan regions, this essentially implies that students are to become aware of the inevitable tensions between planning and politics (see Galland and Harrison, 2020).

While the education of planners has not changed radically over the past thirty years, elements of the so-called communicative and strategic turns have clearly influenced the knowledge base as well as the skills and competencies associated with specific programs and single courses in both Europe and North America. At the same time, planning curricula continue to respond to the challenges and demands posed by neoliberal market economies through a stronger emphasis on real estate development courses, project management, formation of city regions, and so forth. This is also evident in relation to the introduction of new planning professorships within these particular fields in Western European settings. In what follows, we zoom into two specific master's programs from Denmark and Germany with the aim to illustrate how national planning reorientations have influenced the delivery of planning knowledge and skills.

Denmark

An illustrative example concerning the incorporation of knowledge, the application of skills and the development of competences concerning communicative practices, power and politics in planning is the master's specialization in urban planning at Aalborg University. Taught partly through problem-based learning pedagogy via student projects (cf. Graaff & Kolmos, 2003) and partly through lectures and seminars based on active-learning formats, the program devotes a full semester to the understanding of how power is exercised and how power relations are handled within the frame of urban and regional development contexts. In doing so, the program puts aside the naïve idea that planning is a value-neutral domain and instead portrays planning itself as one amongst many other forces affecting the governance of urban development.

More specifically, the Danish program suggests that besides the need to acquire knowledge concerning deliberative practices in handling planning processes within contexts characterized by conflicting interests (while attaining negotiation skills for the sake of catering to stakeholder mediation in the shaping of spatial development processes and outcomes), students similarly attain knowledge and skills regarding power and politics in planning. In this respect, classical planning knowledge centering on legalistic, regulatory and land-use dimensions is to be supplemented by: knowledge concerning the political and value-laden nature of planning; knowledge about the roles of planning practitioners in 'muddling through' power relations; research skills to examine power in the context of different planning practices.

An understanding of planning processes and their relation to politics and power is thereby illustrative of an expanded web of threads in the fabric of planning education, which entails how pedagogy and the application of new knowledge and skills lead to more effective (prospective) practice. This also shows how planning education must be shifted away from an exclusive focus on 'bounded territories', to include more flexible "soft spaces of governance" (Allmendinger & Haughton, 2009; Haughton, Allmendinger, Counsell, & Vigar, 2010), which supplement 'hard' regulatory spaces of planning. Soft spaces of governance emerge as arenas that bring different policy actors together to rework 'the real geographies of development', a new planning situation which in turn breeds further conflict and complexity. This reality demands weaving new knowledge and skills so students are carefully prepared to understand how stakeholder initiatives are framed amidst highly complex planning processes characterized by multiple and conflicting interests across policy sectors and administrative scales.

The fabric of planning education in this Danish master's specialization has then been restructured through an expansion of its warp and supplemented by the woof of additional planning pedagogies. The new web of threads is operationalized by the addition of active-learning formats and problem-based learning pedagogies that lead towards the development of deliberation competences and the application of other management skills aimed at handling planning processes influenced by power relations and dynamics. No less important is the fact that students themselves become key weavers in the process, alongside planning practitioners who are also actively involved in seminars and workshops. Besides in-classroom active-learning formats through seminars and workshops as well as fieldtrips and visits to government agencies, the students' knowledge and skillsets are expanded through project-organized learning (Graaff & Kolmos, 2003). By concentrating on contemporary and real-life planning issues that target, for instance, changes in national planning legislation and their spatial implications, the emphasis on problem analysis at the core of the learning process allows students to integrate knowledge and practice through self-organized collaboration and reflective processes in ways that better resemble practical realities (Shepherd & Cosgrif, 1998).

Germany

Since the 2000s full-fledged courses in and around European spatial planning have emerged. One of these programs, the European Master in Territorial Development (EuMiTD) was introduced at Leibniz Universität Hannover in 2014 to respond to the manifold impacts of the EU on national planning, namely: EU legislation; European discourses about spatial planning and territorial development; and the informal exchange of national experts, ministers and other policy actors. These interrelations between the European Union as a supranational organization and its member states is also affecting national planning policies, demanding new knowledge and skills so that students can enhance their abilities to act in international contexts and to use EU and national funding policies successfully.

Therefore, EuMiTD devotes the first two semesters to understanding how integrative and sustainable development of cities and regions can be achieved in a European context. This includes lectures and seminars focusing on the planning systems and practices of various EU member states. The different courses address spatial planning and territorial development from a comprehensive and integrated perspective, complemented by lectures and seminars on landscape planning and environmental global challenges (water protection, Environmental Impact Assessment, etc.), traffic planning, or land and tenure policy. Moreover, strong emphasis is put on EU regional and rural policies (including the European Regional Development Fund, European Territorial Co-operation, the European Social Fund, and the European Agricultural Fund for Rural Development), their spatial impacts, and their key achievements or failures.

This is achieved by active or experiential learning approaches (Baldwin & Rosier, 2017; Shepherd & Cosgrif, 1998; Warburton, 2003), which entail the combination of input lectures by the educator and independent, self-organized and often group-based work from the students, as well as the combination of theoretical and practical issues. Active learning includes involvement from practitioners – e.g., senior planning experts from public planning associations or senior consultants from public bodies with an expertise in allocating EU regional funds – in the courses, either as lecturers or through field trips. This knowledge is further deepened in student projects which are a central element in EuMiTD. The student projects – focusing, for example, on comparisons of national housing policies or of national and regional policies to reduce land development – are of particular relevance as they emphasize 'learning by doing', meaning that students, in a self-directed and self-organized process, identify problem situations, analyze them, design solutions and evaluate them (Graaff & Kolmos, 2003; Lang, 1983; Shepherd & Cosgrif, 1998).

Altogether, the increasing influence of the European Union on national policy making, and thus on national planning, has led to the introduction of new master programs such as EuMiTD, indicating that the fabric of planning education is broadened through an expansion of its warp. In similar fashion, this also includes an extension of its woof, with the aim to make students more familiar with appropriate public incentives and measures (from both the EU level and the national level) as well as with planning strategies or instruments from other European member states to support an integrated and sustainable spatial development. The new web of threads is operationalized by shifting pedagogies that enhance the students' competences to reflect critically on EU policies and the spatial (national, regional or local) impacts, and to apply successfully for European funding. Students similarly become key weavers in the process of acknowledging that EU policy instruments change the fabric of planning education.

Conclusion

Planning at the national level is a public policy domain subject to ideological and instrumental reorientations. By synthesizing some of these outstanding shifts in the context of liberal capitalist nation-states, the chapter has argued that changes in the rubric of national planning led to the expansion and adjustment of the fabric of planning education. This influence is most evident as regards: the adjustment of learning objectives pertaining to planning curricula, which are typically perceived in the addition of new planning knowledge, skillsets and pedagogies in the context of master's specializations; and the development of relatively specialized courses and master's programs relating to the new roles of national planning in catering to spatial development.

Historical paradigmatic shifts in planning have clearly widened the fabric of planning education, an example being the reorientation from urban design towards rational decision-making, and thereafter from rational-comprehensive planning and land-use planning towards communicative rationality and strategic spatial planning in the context of changing political ideologies. This is reflected not only in the more ample content of planning knowledge across planning curricula but also in that planning students become more actively engaged in developing and acquiring skills and competences through active-learning, project-organized and problem-based learning pedagogies, which better resemble practical realities and might therefore contribute to lead towards more effective planning practice.

By becoming the new weavers of the fabric of planning education alongside instructors and practicing planners themselves, planning students gain the capacity to progressively shape the pedagogies through which they learn. As shown by the Danish case, the latest paradigm shift in planning is revealed both in the content of planning curricula delivered in the master's specialization as well as in the means towards attaining new knowledge through project-organized and problem-based learning pedagogies – portrayed here as planning skills and competences themselves. Parallel to the influence of shifting political ideology and changing planning paradigms on planning curricula and their learning objectives, other more localized socio-political changes such as the so-called 'Europeanization of spatial planning' similarly affect the content and delivery of planning education. As shown by the German case, the influence of EU policies on national planning over the past two decades has created a need to develop more specialized planning knowledge and skills aimed at filling in new planning positions in the European job market.

As aptly noted by Frank (A. I. Frank, 2006), "[p]lanning education, its provision, and curricula not only change over time but differ by national context". Further explorations into individual contexts of planning at the national level thereby hold the intrinsic potential to identify multiple forms of knowledge, skills and competences currently being generated in localized settings and milieus. In this respect, the brief cases herein described might be suggestive of the need to map out and better understand how planning at the national level affects what prospective planners need to know, but more importantly how they ultimately learn.

References

Albrechts, L., Healey, P., & Kunzmann, K. (2003). Strategic spatial planning and regional governance in Europe. *Journal of the American Planning Association, 69*(2), 113–129.

Alexander, E. R. (1986). What and how? Planning definitions and process. In E. R. Alexander (Ed.), *Approaches to Planning. Introducing Current Planning Theories, Concepts, and Issues* (pp. 39–63). New York: Gordon and Breach Science Publishers.

Alexander, E. R. (1992). A transaction cost theory of planning. *Journal of American Planning Association, 58*(2), 190–200.

Allmendinger, P., & Haughton, G. (2009). Soft spaces, fuzzy boundaries, and metagovernance: The new spatial planning in the Thames Gateway. *Environment and Planning A, 41*(3), 617–633.

Alterman, R. (2001). National-level planning in democratic countries: A comparative perspective. In R. Alterman (Ed.), *National-Level Planning in Democratic Countries: An International Comparison of City and Regional Policy-Making* (pp. 1–42). Liverpool: Liverpool University Press.

Altshuler, A. (1965). The goals of comprehensive planning. *Journal of the American Planning Association, 31*(3), 186–195.

Baldwin, C., & Rosier, J. (2017). Growing future planners: A framework for integrating experiential learning into tertiary planning programs. *Journal of Planning Education and Research, 37*(1), 43–55.

Banfield, E. C. (1959). Ends and means in planning. *International Social Science Journal, 11*(3), 361–368.

Christaller, W. (1966). *Central Places in Southern Germany (Die Zentralen Orte in Süddeutschland)*. Englewood Cliffs, NJ: Prentice-Hall.

Committee for Spatial Development. (1999). *ESDP European Spatial Development Perspective. European Spatial Towards Balanced and Sustainable of the European Union*. Luxembourg.

Dalton, L. C. (2001). Weaving the fabric of planning as education. *Journal of Planning Education and Research, 20*(4), 423–436.

Davoudi, S. (2012). The legacy of positivism and the emergence of interpretive tradition in spatial planning. *Regional Studies, 46*(4), 429–441.

Davoudi, S., Galland, D., & Stead, D. (2019). Reinventing planning and planners: ideological decontestations and rhetorical appeals. *Planning Theory* (forthcoming).

Faludi, A. (1973). *Planning Theory*. Oxford: Pergamon Press.
Forester, J. (1999). *The Deliberative Practitioner: Encouraging Participatory Planning Processes*. Cambridge: MIT Press.
Forester, J. (2006). Making participation work when interests conflict: Moving from facilitating dialogue and moderating debate to mediating negotiations. *Journal of the American Planning Association*, 72(4), 447–456.
Forester, J. (2008). Editorial. *Planning Theory & Practice*, 9(3), 299–304.
Fourastié, J. (1979). *Les Trente Glorieuses ou la Révolution Invisible de 1946 à 1975*. Paris: Fayard.
Frank, A. I. (2006). Three decades of thought on planning education. *Journal of Planning Literature*, 21(1), 15–67.
Frank, A. I., Mironowicz, I., Lourenço, J., Franchini, T., Ache, P., Finka, M., . . . Grams, A. (2014). Educating planners in Europe: A review of 21st century study programmes. *Progress in Planning*, 91, 30–94.
Frank, N. (2002). Rethinking planning theory for a master's-level curriculum. *Journal of Planning Education and Research*, 21(3), 323–330.
Friedmann, J. (1987). *Planning in the Public Domain: From Knowledge to Action*. Princeton, New Jersey: Princeton University Press.
Friedmann, J. (1996). The core curriculum in planning revisited. *Journal of Planning Education and Research*, 15(2), 89–104.
Galland, D. (2012a). Is regional planning dead or just coping? The transformation of a state sociospatial project into growth-oriented strategies. *Environment and Planning C: Government and Policy*, 30(3), 536–552.
Galland, D. (2012b). Understanding the reorientations and roles of spatial planning: The case of national planning policy in Denmark. *European Planning Studies*, 20(8), 1359–1392.
Galland, D., & Elinbaum, P. (2015). Redefining territorial scales and the strategic role of spatial planning: Evidence from Denmark and Catalonia. *DisP - The Planning Review*, 51(4), 66–85.
Galland, D., & Harrison, J. (2020) Conceptualising metropolitan regions: How institutions, policies, spatial imaginaries, and planning are influencing metropolitan development. In K. Zimmermann, D. Galland, and J. Harrison (Eds.), *Metropolitan Regions, Planning and Governance* (pp. 1–32). Berlin: Springer.
Graaff, E. de, & Kolmos, A. (2003). Characteristics of problem-based learning. *International Journal of Engineering Education*, 19(5), 657–662.
Graham, S., & Healey, P. (1999). Relational concepts of space and place: Issues for planning theory and practice. *European Planning Studies*, 7(5), 623–646.
Hajer, M. (2003). Policy without polity? Policy analysis and the institutional void. *Policy Sciences*, 36(2), 175–195.
Haughton, G., Allmendinger, P., Counsell, D., & Vigar, G. (2010). *The New Spatial Planning. Territorial Management with Soft Spaces and Fuzzy Boundaries*. London: Routledge.
Healey, P. (2004). The treatment of space and place in the new strategic spatial planning in Europe. *International Journal of Urban and Regional Research*, 28(1), 45–67.
Healey, P. (2006). Transforming governance : challenges of institutional adaptation and a new politics of space. *European Planning Studies*, 14(3), 299–320.
Healey, P. (2007). Strategy-making in a relational world. In *Urban Complexity and Spatial Strategies* (pp. 171–200). London: Routledge.
Healey, P., Khakee, A., Motte, A., & Needham, B. (1997). *Making Strategic Spatial Plans: Innovation in Europe*. London: UCL Press.
Healey, P., Khakee, A., Motte, A., & Needham, B. (1999). European developments in strategic spatial planning. *European Planning Studies*, 7(3), 339–355.
Herod, A. (2011). The national. In *Scale* (pp. 167–211). New York: Routledge.
Hoch, C. J. (1994). *What Planners Do: Power Politics and Persuasion*. Chicago: APA Planners Press.
Jessop, B. (2000). The crisis of the national spatio-temporal fix and the tendential ecological dominance of globalizing capitalism. *International Journal of Urban and Regional Studies*, 24(2), 323–360.
Jessop, B. (2002). Liberalism, neoliberalism and urban governance: A state-theoretical perspective. *Antipode*, 34, 452–472.
Krueckeberg, D. A. (1985). The tuition of American planning. *Town Planning Review*, 56(4), 421–441.
Lang, J. (1983). Teaching planning to city planning students. An argument for the studio/workshop approach. *Journal of Planning Education and Research*, 2, 122–129.
Peck, J., & Theodore, N. (2010). Mobilizing policy: Models, methods, and mutations. *Geoforum*, 41(2), 169–174.

Pezzoli, K., & Howe, D. (2001). Planning pedagogy and globalization. *Journal of Planning Education and Research*, *20*(3), 365–375.

Salet, W., & Faludi, A. (2000). *The Revival of Strategic Spatial Planning*. (W. Salet & A. Faludi, Eds.). Amsterdam: Koninklijke Nederlandse Akademie van Wetenschappen.

Shepherd, A., & Cosgrif, B. (1998). Problem-based learning: A bridge between planning education and planning practice. *Journal of Planning Education and Research*, *17*, 348–357.

Stiftel, B. (2009). Planning the paths of planning schools. *Australian Planner*, *46*(1), 38–47.

Stiftel, B., Demerutis, J., Frank, A. I., Inkoom, D. K. B., & Lee, L. (2009). Chapter 10. Planning Education. *Planning Sustainable Cities. Global Report on Human Settlements 2009*. Earthscan: London.

Taylor, N. (2010). Urban Planning. In *Encyclopedia of Urban Studies* (pp. 904–908). Sage Publications.

Taylor, P. J. (1981). Geographical scales within the world-economy approach. *Review*, *5*(1), 3–11.

Tewdwr-Jones, M. (1997). Plans, policies and inter-governmental relations: Assessing the role of national planning guidance in England and Wales. *Urban Studies*, *34*(1), 141–162.

Tewdwr-Jones, M. (2001). Complexity and interdependency in a kaleidoscopic spatial planning landscape for Europe. In L. Albrechts, J. Alden, & A. da Rosa Pires (Eds.), *The Changing Institutional Landscape of Planning* (pp. 8–34). Aldershot: Ashgate.

van Duinen, L. (2004). *Planning Imagery. The Emergence and Development of New Planning Concepts in Dutch National Spatial Policy*. Amsterdam: University of Amsterdam.

Warburton, K. (2003). Deep learning and education for sustainability. *International Journal of Sustainability in Higher Education*, *4*(1), 44–56.

Williams, R. H. (1989). Internationalizing planning education, 1992 and the European ERASMUS Program. *Journal of Planning Education and Research*, *10*(1), 75–78.

Zonneveld, W. (2005). Multiple visioning: New ways of constructing transnational spatial visions. *Environment and Planning C: Government and Policy*, *23*(1), 41–62.

19
INTERNATIONAL COMPARATIVE PLANNING

Frank Othengrafen and Daniel Galland

Introduction

According to various authors (e.g., Alterman 2017a; Goldstein et al. 2006; Hoey et al. 2017; Stiftel et al. 2009), there is an 'increased focus on internationally oriented planning education' that stems mainly from globalized changes, such as financial and economic crises, climate change, or international migration flows, and 'from a number of changes in settings where planners practice' (Hoey et al. 2017, 223). As nations and regions are highly interdependent, planning schools and educators have to be aware that economic or political transformations or environmental catastrophes in other regions or countries 'can have profound effects on their home countries' cities and regions' (Goldstein et al. 2006, 349). At the same time, the planning profession in each country is bounded by its own national and local legal frameworks which are embedded in specific socio-cultural and political contexts (Alterman 2017a, 21). This might help explain why international comparative planning, while a recurrent theme in planning education and research, is frequently subject to an array of interpretations and only poorly grounded as regards theory and methodology (e.g., Baldwin & Rosier 2017; Faludi & Hamnett 1975; Hoey et al. 2017; Kantor & Savitch 2005; Masser 1984; Nadin & Stead 2013; Thomas et al. 1983).

It seems that the potential of international planning research and education is not fully exploited yet (Pezzoli & Howe 2001, 366) as there is still a 'great deal of confusion about both the nature and scope of comparative planning studies' (Masser 1984, 137). This is not only restricted to urban and regional planning but can also be observed in sociology and other social sciences for which Mills et al. (2006, 619) conclude that 'although comparative research flourishes [. . .], persistent methodological problems remain'. Of course, many planning programs – for example in the United States, Europe, and Australia – introduce comparative elements in their curricula, invite international guest researchers for specific areas, or 'utilize new technologies such as distance learning to increase international connections' (Goldstein et al. 2006, 349). However, the number of courses focusing on international comparative planning is certainly limited at least when compared with other courses such as planning theory, planning methods, and so forth (see, for example, Bornemann et al. 2017; Goldstein et al. 2006; Stiftel et al. 2009). At the same time, the conceptual and practical knowledge on teaching methods for comparative planning is fragmented and rudimentary. In this light, the following contribution aims to address the plurality of conceptual approaches and teaching methods that could be used by planning educators to systematically structure international comparisons concerning different planning systems, policies, and practices in order to best achieve their teaching goals, i.e. to prepare graduating planners with practical planning skills while contributing to develop their ability to find innovative solutions that can be adapted to their own contexts.

Reasons for Teaching International Comparative Planning

There are multiple reasons for teaching international comparative planning. Following the logic of sociologists Emile Durkheim and Max Weber, research and education should privilege comparison rather than the study of singular independent facts (cf. Nissen 1998; Ragin & Zaret 1983). 'Comparative sociology is not a particular branch of sociology; it is sociology itself in so far as it ceases to be purely descriptive and aspires to render account for facts' (Durkheim 1964, 139). Comparisons are thereby a fundamental teaching element or method in social sciences. This also includes the fields of urban studies as well as urban and regional planning, as comparisons contribute to move planning educators and practitioners 'beyond their "comfort zone" of their familiar national contexts [. . .] to learn how to transfer knowledge across national and continental borders in a manner that would fit local needs' (Alterman 2017b, 10; see also Booth 2015, 83–85; Kantor & Savitch 2005, 135). Teaching international comparative planning is thus, at least theoretically, valuable for various reasons (Baldwin & Rosier 2017; Faludi & Hamnett 1975; Goldsmith 1999; Goldstein et al. 2006; Hoey et al. 2017; Masser 1984; Pezzoli & Howe 2001; Stiftel et al. 2009):

- It ensures that future planners are attuned to globalization or internationalization processes.
- It strengthens the ability of planners to adapt and be sensitive to other cultures and views.
- It enables planners to build a repertoire of lessons from other contexts by understanding emerging problems in unfamiliar contexts and by acquiring and developing transferable skills.
- It allows planners to gain a better understanding of planning practices in specific situations and to improve planning practice at one place by adopting certain (successful) planning policies, strategies or instruments from other contexts.
- It enables planners to identify and understand effects of policy interventions in different contexts by detecting practical values and routines in different cities and regions.
- It ensures that planners reflect critically on their own behavior, routines, and attitudes on the basis of their knowledge of other contexts.

However, '[d]espite the recognition and heightened importance [. . .] placed on global planning education for all students', it seems that many planning schools face difficulties 'to offer robust international planning education' and to make use of the potentials offered by planning courses on international comparative planning (Hoey et al. 2017, 224). On the one hand, this is reflected in the limited number of programs offering adequate courses in this subject area. On the other hand, it further points out to the general gap between planning education and practice as (academic) planning programs often seem to be reluctant to incorporate new topics, methods, or approaches from planning practice in the curriculum (for example, Frank et al. 2014; Hoey et al. 2017). At the same time, it is clear that '[t]he complexity and uncertainty encountered in practice situations cannot be duplicated in a traditional classroom education' (Baldwin &

Rosier 2017, 43); this is especially true for international comparisons. Consequently, innovative teaching approaches should be introduced to facilitate educators to use international comparative approaches as a systematic 'tool' for their teaching. The following section thereby presents selected comparative approaches, both inferred from our own teaching experiences and from the practices of other (planning) educators and researchers (for example, Baldwin & Rosier 2017; Goldstein et al. 2006; Hoey et al. 2017; Shepherd & Cosgriff 1998).

How to Teach International Comparative Planning: Pedagogical Approaches

How to teach international comparative planning? Naturally, stays abroad or overseas field trips offer an excellent option to make experiences and to reflect on 'one's place in the world' (Goldsmith 1999, 194). But if this is not an integral part of a study program, it is difficult to integrate long-term and recurring stays abroad into the curriculum. Thus approaches are needed that can 'bring examples from outside our own countries into our classrooms [. . .]' (Stiftel 2009, 45–46). One option is to introduce or impart basic knowledge on planning systems via the classical teacher-centered mode. However, we perceive at least two shortcomings stemming from this teaching approach: First, these teaching formats are not based on principles of active learning while they also regard students as consumers that receive information passively. Second, educators mainly focus on theoretical comparisons of planning systems – including the legal framework of planning systems; the extent and type of planning at national and regional levels; constitutional provisions and administrative traditions; the locus of power: the maturity or completeness of the system; processes of making and reviewing plans; or regulations and permits etc. (see, for example, Nadin & Stead 2013; CEC 1997) – and not on specific cases or planning practices. In this respect, there are 'expressed concerns about the limited exposure students have to [. . .] experiences, practices, and contexts where planning professionals work' (Hoey et al. 2017, 225), which call for more innovative and effective ways of bringing international planning practice into the classroom. This includes more case-based or practice-based approaches as well as active or blended learning.

Case-based Learning as Integral Strategy

Case studies offer many advantages for teaching international comparative planning in classes. By focusing on concrete challenges and solutions in specific (local or regional) contexts they link theory to practice (Walsh & Allin 2012) and offer students insights 'into the deeply situated contexts where planning happens' (Hoey et al. 2017, 225). As cases are grounded in place and time with different actors and sometimes conflicting views involved, they can be 'experienced' and can touch students emotionally. Through this students might 'build a mental repertoire of past experiences' (Watson 2002, 184) which will probably increase their ability to retain what they have learned. Consequently, case-based learning might contribute to 'a better understanding of the nature of difference, and generating ideas and propositions which can more adequately inform practice' (Watson 2003, 396). Additionally, it will move students beyond 'dichotomous thinking' or 'reductionist reasoning' to comprehensive, systematic, and interdisciplinary reflections (Hoey et al., 2017, 226).

There are at least three different research approaches for case-based learning. *Individualizing comparisons* focus on detailed case studies that consider the contextual and historical factors to understand the specific situational constellations and decisions (Robinson 2011, 6–7).

The strength of this teaching approach is that it presents a broad range of case studies and experiences, including various policy approaches, instruments, and strategies, different governance arrangements etc. This openness stimulates students (implicitly or explicitly) to test hypotheses and causal relations that have been generated in other cases (Tilly 1984, 81). At the same time, the diversity and heterogeneity can also limit the potential of the case-study approach as teaching strategy, especially when the cases are only loosely coupled or purely descriptive, or do not follow a systemic and comprehensive conceptual framework.

Encompassing comparisons assume that different case studies of urban and regional planning can (indirectly) be related to each other by developments at a national or supranational level (Robinson 2011, 7; Tilly 1984, 126–127). In planning courses, educators can thus use the encompassing approach, for example, to analyze how globalization, neo-liberalism, migration flows, governance rescaling, or Europeanization processes affect planning systems and policies in different countries and at different scales (for example, Fainstein 2001; Waterhout et al. 2013; Galland & Elinbaum 2015). Within this common and overarching reference frame, a variety of topics can be addressed by students, meaning that the conceptual framework allows some flexibility in comparative teaching.

The *variation-finding approach* draws on specific theoretical propositions set by the educator, which are the starting points for students to compare different cases to find out and to establish principles of variation among cases (Tilly 1984). For instance, this can include debates around regime theory and governance (for example, DiGaetano & Strom, 2003; Kantor & Savitch, 2005) or can focus on different strategies and instruments to control local development (e.g., Elinbaum & Galland 2016; Thomas et al. 1983) or on aspects such as the institutionalization of planning, planning discourses, the relation between theory and practice, and so forth. Altogether, the theoretical foundation that characterizes the variation-finding approach allows for comprehensive and systematic case comparisons thereby enabling students to generate hypotheses (Robinson 2011, 10).

To sum up, the various case-based approaches offer the possibility to 'respond to planning practices in international contexts and to prepare students better for complex and dynamic planning environments through active learning approaches' (Hoey et al. 2017, 225). '[R]ather than through passive reception of knowledge' (Million & Parnell 2017, 78), case-based approaches recognize the potential for students to learn intentionally, to understand practices in different contexts, and to co-construct knowledge through a process of critical questioning and through their interactions with other students and the teacher.

Active Learning in Lectures and Seminars

Active or experiential learning is based on pedagogical approaches such as problem-solving, imaginative reconstruction, self-reflection, independent thinking, group work, and discussion (Hoey et al. 2017, 225; Warburton 2003, 45). It can further be described as 'a purposeful process of engaged, active learning in which the student constructs knowledge, skills, or values by means of direct experiences in authentic, real world contexts' (Kassem 2007, 2; in: Baldwin & Rosier 2017, 45) or in contexts that depict reality for teaching purposes. In doing so, active-learning approaches in the subject area of international comparative planning 'broaden students' learning experiences by placing them in a new context for learning' (Baldwin & Rosier 2017, 43).

In general, teachers can take a case-based and active-learning approach by using the following techniques (Warburton, 2003, see also Baldwin and Rosier 2017; Hoey et al. 2017; Shepherd & Cosgriff 1998):

- Developing the full potential of case-based and active or deep learning approaches requires a mix of imparting scientific knowledge and leaving space for experiential learning or knowledge (Biggs 1987). This also includes a combination of input lectures given by the educator and independent, self-organized and often group-based work from the students.
- The conceptual framework sets the frame for active or deep learning approaches and offers clear dimensions for the students on which they should concentrate (see also Baldwin & Rosier, 2017, 48). Additionally, active learning can be encouraged by emphasizing principles and concepts rather than accumulated facts (Hounsell, 1997). This means that it is the task of the educator to identify the relevant key concepts and to consider interpretations and implications of each concept.
- Involving students in the learning process intentionally can be stimulated by asking questions rather than providing a set of irrevocable answers. By doing so, 'students can be encouraged to clarify assumptions, choose analytic techniques and examine value judgements' (Warburton 2003, 49).
- The role of the educator is then *inter alia* to: (1) encourage the student's responsibility, (2) provide opportunities for learning to learn and self-regulation, (3) foster conversational interaction, (4) promote reflective enquiry, and (5) make sure that students consider the conceptual framework (see also Million & Parnell 2017, 78).

In operationalizing some of the above principles, we will introduce the illustrative example of teaching metropolitan planning from an international comparative perspective (referring to Elinbaum & Galland 2016) in the context of the two-year master's program specialization in Land Management at Aalborg University. During the period 2015 to 2017, this specialization included sessions in metropolitan planning taught by Daniel Galland within the frame of the course Spatial Planning and Governance. By making use of case-based and active-learning teaching formats, a module on international comparative planning can be taught through a combination of traditional lectures, group workshops, student presentations, and interactive plenary sessions – the latter three formats placing emphasis on the students' active involvement. While the frequency of use of these particular teaching methods and the degree of student participation might vary in function of the nature of the instructed subject, a three- or four-hour session concerning the teaching of metropolitan planning could be based on the following sequence:

First, the instructor delivers an ad hoc lecture using a variation-finding approach, where concepts are introduced as the point of departure for students to carry out subsequent comparisons concerning different contemporary metropolitan spatial plans. For the sake of operationalizing the comparisons, such concepts are framed as 'analytical variables' and 'analytical parameters', i.e. the actual themes and points of reference that the students will discuss when comparing plans.

The lecture is then followed by a workshop based on a specific comparative assignment comprised of a series of questions that build on both the introduced variables and selected readings assigned to the students before the session. The class is split into groups of four or five students; the role of the instructor is to facilitate interactive discussions. One of the perceived advantages of the workshop as a teaching method is that the students develop ownership of the problem or case.

In responding to the comparative assignment, a series of student group presentations follows with the aim to expose the other groups to the presenting group's thoughts and deliberations in relation to metropolitan planning contexts, contents, processes, outcomes, and implications. After every group presentation, the role of the instructor is to facilitate dialogue and to moderate class debates and discussions that might lead to either new questions or potential conclusions.

Finally, the instructor and students participate in a plenary session aimed at synthesizing the comparisons. The role of the instructor is to sum up relevant results as well as take-home lessons. Whenever possible, a supplementary teaching device is to make use of site visits both locally and internationally to illustrate particular linkages between in-class learning and actual on-site spatial outcomes. For instance, the students have been exposed to historical and contemporary urban and metropolitan planning interventions in Barcelona during study trips. Organized and led by the instructor, these trips include 'themed tours', group tutorials as well as visits to regional and municipal government agencies and academic institutions.

While a common feature spanning the above range of teaching methods is analytical reflection, active learning can additionally take place beyond the classroom by using online tools. The combination of case-based and online community learning is normally referred to in the higher education literature as blended learning (Savin-Baden 2007), which similarly combines the interaction amongst students and between them and the instructor albeit with the advantages of asynchronous learning (Lawless et al. 2000). This distance-learning approach gives the students the possibility to reflect prior to delivering a written response while enabling them to develop analytical and critical writing skills.

Problem-Based Learning in Student Projects

International comparative planning can also be part of hands-on experiential learning processes in student projects which are a central element in most planning faculties in North America and Western Europe (e.g., Edwards & Bates 2011). In student projects, a group of eight to ten students meet once or twice a week to work on context-specific planning challenges that can cover a wide range of issues (de Graaff & Kolmos 2003; Viswanathan et al. 2012, 389). The projects are of particular relevance as they emphasize 'learning by doing', meaning that students, in a self-directed and self-organized process, identify problem situations, analyze them, design solutions and evaluate them (e.g., Lang 1983; Shepherd & Cosgriff 1998).

Student projects are very useful to consider international comparative planning issues, as various experiences in the master program 'European Master in Territorial Development' (EuMiTD) at Leibniz Universität Hanover indicate. The EuMiTD is a two-year master program based on a transdisciplinary and international approach in the field of regional and urban development. This is achieved by (1) focusing on urban and regional, transport and environmental planning in a European context, (2) examining the impacts of EU regional policies and other sectoral policies on territorial development in the EU member states, and (3) combining various teaching formats such as lectures, seminars, student projects, and group discussions.[1]

The student projects are mandatory for the students and have varying topics. One of the current student projects focuses on a comparison of national housing policies in Europe – a representative central policy field in all EU member states. It is the aim of the project to compare the national housing policies in various EU member states, including their main principles, priorities, and strategies to provide decent, adequate, affordable, and healthy housing. As such a comparison or overview is largely absent, the student project is somehow problem-based (for example, de Graaff & Kolmos 2003, 658) and can, to a certain extent, contribute to the European dialogue on housing policies which is a goal of the German EU presidency in 2020. In this context, the project provides good conditions for learning on international comparative planning as students, in a first step, concentrate on conceptual classifications of European welfare state typologies and on different planning systems or families to be able to build a theoretical frame for their further analysis on housing policies. By doing so, they are, in a second step, able to choose four or five countries that differ from each other to focus on concrete issues such as the provision on social or affordable housing and the relation of supply-side and demand-side subsidies (variation-finding approach). The policy analysis in these countries is conducted independently by the students and includes (national) policy documents, scientific references and expert interviews (phone interviews) with planning officials in the ministries, national housing associations or with researchers in this field.

In this understanding, learning is based on the experiences of the students which increases their motivation to participate actively in the project. Additionally, the self-directed learning process – the students usually formulate their problem and develop adequate planning strategies independently – encourages activity-based learning, requiring activities such as research, interactive discussions, joint decision-making, and writing (project report). Because students are organizing their own work and sharing 'responsibility for choosing the right analytical tools and project outcomes' (Baldwin & Rosier 2017, 47), their student projects also strengthen group-based learning as the majority of the discussions and learning process take place in groups or teams (de Graaff & Kolmos 2003, 659). At the same time, the comparative approach ensures that students understand effects of policy interventions in different contexts so that they are able to adopt specific planning policies or strategies from other contexts. Offering students sufficient room for independent and self-reflective work in this project (including the freedom to focus on requested policy fields), ensures that they are highly motivated to participate actively in the project and it seems more likely that they retain what they have learned (Cornell et al. 2013; de Graaff and Kolmos 2003; Hoey et al. 2017; Warburton 2003). The role of the teacher is that of a 'cognitive coach' (Shepherd & Cosgriff 1998, 348) who facilitates the learning process by, among other actions, proposing ways for effective collaboration or the management of the project.

Conclusion

Teaching international comparative planning is a central task as it enables future planners (1) to build a repertoire of lessons from other situated contexts, (2) to reflect critically on their own behavior, routines, and attitudes on the basis of knowledge drawn from other situated contexts, and (3) to improve planning practice by adopting and adapting certain (successful) planning policies, strategies, or instruments from other situated contexts. This argument indicates that it becomes necessary for educators involved in teaching international comparative planning to focus on case-based or problem-based learning approaches to improve and consolidate the practical knowledge of future planners. Additionally, educators have to introduce active learning and group-based learning approaches that allow the varied comparison of international cases and solutions. The implementation of these pedagogical tools constitutes nonetheless a challenge for instructors given that cases or examples need be carefully and purposefully prepared before their analysis and subsequent debate in the classrooms.

Looking at our own involvements and considering other experiences (e.g., Hoey et al. 2017) we can summarize that variation-finding and encompassing approaches constitute suitable pedagogical means to teach international comparative planning via active and problem-based learning. We can further conclude that the mix of imparting scientific knowledge, on the one side, and providing opportunities for student-based, experiential or independent learning on the other, seems to be highly beneficial. The example of teaching metropolitan planning from an international comparative perspective shows that the combination of case-based approaches and different teaching formats such as traditional lectures, group workshops, student presentations, and interactive discussions, offers the potential for students to learn intentionally, to understand planning practices in different contexts, and to co-construct knowledge with regard to relevant (global) issues. At the same time, the comparative dimension can be further enhanced through web-based or e-learning approaches where academics or practitioners from selected metropolitan regions get virtually involved to provide first-hand experiences to the students.

Finally, student problem-based projects comprise another example where suitable pedagogical conditions are provided for learning on international comparative planning issues including, for example, comparisons of national housing policies, of regional planning strategies addressing climate change or of the impact of neo-liberalization on urban regeneration strategies in various cities. The self-directed and self-organized group work on these (globally-relevant) issues encourages activity-based learning and enables students to critically reflect on certain planning aspects from a comparative perspective. It is especially here that we have observed how teaching international comparative planning not only enhances the students' competences in critical thinking and adaptive learning but also improves students' intercultural skills and their perspective transformations, i.e. the 'process' of becoming aware of different worldviews and being willing to change and adapt personal ideologies.

Note

1 For further information see www.landschaft.uni-hannover.de/msc_eumitd.html

References

Alterman, R. (2017a). A Giant Contribution to Global Planning Education. Klaus Kunzmann and the Founding of AESOP. *disP – The Planning Review, 53*(2), 21–23. doi:10.1080/02513625.2017.1340535

Alterman, R. (2017b). From a Minor to a Major Profession: Can Planning and Planning Theory Meet the Challenges of Globalisation? *Transactions of the Association of European Schools of Planning, 1*(1), 1–17. doi:10.24306/TrAESOP.2017.01.001

Baldwin, C., & Rosier, J. (2017). Growing Future Planners: A Framework for Integrating Experiential Learning into Tertiary Planning Programs. *Journal of Planning Education and Research, 37*(1), 43–55.

Berting, J. (1979). What Is the Use of International Comparative Research? In J. Berting, F. Geyer, & R. Jurkovich (Eds.), *Problems in international comparative research in the social sciences* (pp. 159–177). Oxford: Pergamon Press.

Biggs, J. (1987). *Studying Australian Student Approaches to Learning*. Hawthorn: Australian Council for Educational Research. Retrieved from https://files.eric.ed.gov/fulltext/ED308201.pdf

Booth, P. (2015). What Can we Learn from France? Some Reflections on the Methodologies of Cross-National Research. In E. A. Silva, P. Healey, N. Harris, & P. van den Broeck (Eds.), *The Routledge Handbook of Planning Research Methods* (pp. 84–96). New York and Abingdon: Routledge.

Bornemann, L., Gerloff, S., Konieczek-Woger, M., Timm, M., & Wilke, H. (2017). *Stadtplanung Heute – Stadtplanung Morgen, Eine Berufsfeldanalyse*. Berlin: Arbeitshefte des Instituts für Stadt- und Regionalplanung der Technischen Universität Berlin 81.

Brenner, N. (2001). World City Theory, Globalization and the Comparative-Historical Method. *Urban Affairs Review, 37*, 124–147.

Commission of the European Communities (CEC). (1997). *The EU Compendium of Spatial Planning Systems and Policies*. Luxembourg: Office for Official Publications of the European Communities.

Cornell, R. M., Johnson, C. B., & Schwartz Jr., W. C. (2013). Enhancing Student Experiential Learning With Structured Interviews. *Journal of Education for Business, 88*(3), 136–146.

De Graaff, E., & Kolmos, A. (2003). Characteristics of Problem-Based Learning. *International Journal of Engineering Education, 19*(5), 657–662.

DiGaetano, A., & Strom, E. (2003). Comparative Urban Governance: An Integrated Approach. *Urban Affairs Review, 38*, 356–395.

Durkheim, E. (1964). *The Rules of Sociological Method*. New York: The Free Press.

Edwards, M. M., & Bates, L. K. (2011). Planning's Core Curriculum: Knowledge, Practice, and Implementation. *Journal of Planning Education & Research*, *31*, 172–183.

Elinbaum, P., & Galland, D. (2016). Analysing Contemporary Metropolitan Spatial Plans in Europe Through Their Institutional Context, Instrumental Content and Planning Process. *European Planning Studies*, *24*(1), 181–206.

Fainstein, S. S. (2001). *The City Builders: Property Development in New York and London*. Lawrence, Kansas: University of Kansas Press.

Faludi, A., & Hamnett, S. (1975). *The Study of Comparative Planning*. Conference paper. London: Centre for Environmental Studies.

Frank, A. I., Mironowicz, I., Lourenço, J., Franchini, T., Ache, P., Finka, M., . . . Grams, A. (2014). Educating Planners in Europe: A Review of 21st Century Study Programmes. *Progress in Planning*, *91*, 30–94.

Galland, D., & Elinbaum, P. (2015). Redefining Territorial Scales and the Strategic Role of Spatial Planning: Evidence from Denmark and Catalonia. *disP - The Planning Review*, *51*, 66–85.

Goldsmith, W. W. (1999). What's Under the Bed? City, Pasta, or Commie: Reflections on Teaching American Students in Italy. *Journal of Planning Education & Research*, *19*(2), 193–200.

Goldstein, H. A., Bollens, S., Feser, E., & Silver, C. (2006). An Experiment in the Internationalization of Planning Education: The NEURUS Program. *Journal of Planning Education & Research*, *25*, 349–363.

Hoey, L., Rumbach, A., & Shake, J. D. (2017). Bringing Practice to the Classroom: Using a Deliberative Learning and Case Study Approach to Teach International Planning. *Journal of Planning Education and Research*, *37*(2), 223–233.

Hounsell, D. (1997). Understanding Teaching and Teaching for Understanding. In F. Marton, D. Hounsell, & N. J. Entwistle (Eds.), *The Experience of Learning*. Edinburgh: Scottish Academic Press.

Kantor, P., & Savitch, H. V. (2005). How to Study Comparative Urban Development Politics: A Research Note. *International Journal of Urban & Regional Research*, *29*, 135–151.

Lang, J. (1983). Teaching Planning to City Planning Students. An Argument for the Studio/Workshop Approach. *Journal of Planning Education and Research*, *2*(2), 122–129.

Lawless, N., Allan, J., & O'Dwyer, M. (2000). Face-to-face or Distance Training: Two Different Approaches to Motivate SMEs to Learn. *Education & Training*, *42*, 308–316.

Masser, I. (1984). Cross National Comparative Planning Studies: A Review. *Town Planning Review*, *55*(2), 137–149.

McMichael, P. (1990). Incorporating Comparison within a World-Historical Perspective: An Alternative Comparative Method. *American Sociological Review*, *55*, 385–397.

Million, A., & Parnell, R. (2017). The Educative Planner. *disP - The Planning Review*, *53*(2), 78–79.

Mills, M., van de Bunt, G. G., & de Brujn, J. (2006). Comparative Research, Persistent Problems and Promising Solutions. *International Sociology*, *21*, 619–631.

Nadin, V., & Stead, D. (2013). Opening up the Compendium: An Evaluation of International Comparative Planning Research Methodologies. *European Planning Studies*, *21*(10), 1542–1561.

Nissen, S. (1998). The Case of Case Studies: On the Methodological Discussion in Comparative Political Science. *Quality & Quantity*, *32*(4), 399–418.

Pezzoli, K., & Howe, D. (2001). Planning Pedagogy and Globalization. *Journal of Planning Education and Research*, *20*, 365–375.

Ragin, C., & Zaret, D. (1983). Theory and Method in Comparative Research: Two Strategies. *Social Forces*, *61*(3), 731–754.

Robinson, J. (2011). Cities in a World of Cities: The Comparative Gesture. *International Journal of Urban and Regional Research*, *35*, 1–23.

Savin-Baden, M. (2007). *A Practical Guide to Problem Based Learning Online*. London: Routledge.

Shepherd, A., & Cosgriff, B. (1998). Problem-Based Learning: A Bridge Between Planning Education and Planning Practice. *Journal of Planning Education & Research*, *17*(4), 348–357.

Stiftel, B., Forsyth, A., Dalton, L., & Steiner, F. (2009). Assessing Planning School Performance: Multiple Paths, Multiple Measures. *Journal of Planning Education and Research*, *28*(3), 323–335.

Thomas, D., Minett, J., Hopkins, S., Hamnett, S. L., Faludi, A., & Barrell, D. (1983). *Flexibility and Commitment in Planning*. The Hague: Martinus Nijhoff.

Tilly, C. (1984). *Big Structures, Large Processes, Huge Comparisons*. New York: Russell Sage Foundation.

Viswanathan, L. (2012). Evaluating the Role of the Project Course in Professional Planning Education and Its Influence on Planning Policy and Practice. *Planning Practice & Research*, *27*, 387–403.

Walsh, C., & Allin, S. (2012). Strategic Spatial Planning: Responding to Diverse Territorial Development Challenges: Towards an Inductive Comparative Approach. *International Planning Studies*, *17*(4), 377–395.

Warburton, K. (2003). Deep Learning and Education for Sustainability. *International Journal of Sustainability in Higher Education*, *4*, 44–56.

Waterhout, B., Othengrafen, F., & Sykes, O. (2013). Neo-liberalization Processes and Spatial Planning in France, Germany, and the Netherlands: An Exploration. *Planning Practice & Research*, *28*(1), 141–159.

Watson, V. (2002). Do We Learn from Planning Practice? The Contribution of the Practice Movement to Planning Theory. *Journal of Planning Education & Research*, *22*, 178–187.

Watson, V. (2003). Conflicting Rationalities: Implications for Planning Theory and Ethics. *Planning Theory & Practice*, *4*(4), 395–407.

20
LAND USE PLANNING

Nicole Gurran

Land use planning is a form of public intervention for controlling change through the urban development process, in line with strategic spatial policy objectives. Described by the International Society of City and Regional Planners (ISOCARP 2001, p. xi) as "anticipating", "regulating" and "promoting", "changes in the use of land and buildings", knowledge of land use planning processes and development control techniques is a distinctive mark of professional expertise and competency. Even if the technical skills of plan making and development control are not used by all planners in practice, understanding the processes and operational techniques of land use planning is critical for implementing strategic spatial policy across all scales of urban governance and geography.

However, land use planning processes for plan making and techniques for development control differ between countries and often within them. These differences reflect historically evolved systems of law and bureaucratic administration, reflecting particular relationships between the state, the market, and private property, as well as land ownership arrangements and associated rights and obligations (Gurran, Gallent et al. 2016). These differences can make it difficult for students and early career practitioners to grasp the underlying principles and techniques which should form the framework for learning about land use planning. Thus the aim of this chapter is to set out the elements of a curriculum designed to educate future practitioners about the theoretical basis and normative objectives of land use planning, as well as key methods and processes.

The first section of the chapter sets out the theories and methods of land use planning. It explains the key arguments and rationales for justifying public intervention in the urban development process through land use regulation. It also articulates a set of normative principles for ensuring that these interventions promote socially fair and environmentally sustainable development, within a legal framework intended to balance private property rights with wider societal goals. Methods for balancing these public and private interests through strategic planning processes for allocating land to different uses, and by controlling the impacts of particular developments, are then explained. The third section of the chapter provides an overview of key texts and other literature for teaching, learning, and practicing land use planning, and section four illustrates a scaffold for course design.

Theory and Methods

From the very beginning, the notion of regulating development on private land through planning control has been contentious. In the early 20th century, modern town planning schemes in Britain were criticized for increasing development costs by imposing minimum requirements for street layouts, building set-backs, and open space, but it was argued that these costs were offset by the benefits of coordinated development (Aldridge 1909). In the US, land use zoning spread rapidly in the mid-1920s (Cullingworth and Caves 2014), enabling suburban homeowners to maintain social exclusivity by tightly dictating the style and density of new homes (Fischel 2004). By the 1970s and 1980s, planning policies designed to contain urban development and manage growth were being questioned for their effects on land supply and housing affordability pressures in the UK (Hall 1973, Cheshire and Leven 1986) and the US (Lillydahl and Singell 1987, Kushner 2002). By the 1990s, the global spread of neoliberal political ideas – which generally challenge government involvement in market processes and promote deregulation (Sager 2011) – helped cast land use planning as obstructing free market development and undermining economic competition. In the face of generalized and ideological opposition to the legitimacy of land use planning as encouraged by neoliberalism, it is important to consider the reasons why governments intervene in the private development process through legally codified rules and processes.

There are different ways to justify land use planning intervention in the private development process, but the so called "welfare economics" case is the most prevalent (Webster 1998). First advanced by English economist Arthur Cecil Pigou in the early 20th Century (Pigou 1914), "Pigouvian" welfare economics rests on five key arguments: 1) the need to manage "externalities" – the spillover effects arising from development; 2) the need to protect and provide public goods; 3) the need to promote social fairness in urban development; 4) the need to share information to coordinate decision making and urban investment; and 5) the potential problem of monopolies in the land market.

The primary justification for regulating the ways that privately owned land is developed and used arises from the problem of "externalities". Externalities are the impacts which arise from activities on one site but which have flow on effects for neighboring landholders and the broader community. Examples of circumstances in which externalities arise include the erection of a building which blocks sun or views from nearby properties or the public domain; the establishment of a factory which generates noise, waste and odour; or a new shopping centre which generates increased traffic congestion and demand for local parking spaces. As shown in these examples, externalities may be primarily negative, implying a need to minimize their impact or prevent the development occurring altogether. However, it is usually the case that development, even though generally intended to serve private interests (a home or business), can also bring positive benefits for local and regional communities – such as increases to the housing stock as well as new facilities and employment opportunities. Managing the costs and benefits arising from these processes is complex and requires a level of co-ordination which is usually difficult for private individuals to achieve in isolation.

Therefore, a clear land use plan, developed with public input, and setting out the rules governing future changes and the parameters for assessing particular development proposals, gives members of the community a degree of certainty and involvement about future changes.

Another way to think about the justification for planning in managing urban growth is to focus on the aspects which are not easily dealt with by the private market. For instance, planning processes ensure that the shared facilities on which private development depends – like road infrastructure or public space – are provided in efficient and equitable ways and deliver information to coordinate and guide the future decisions of many different actors and stakeholders. These coordinating functions serve to resolve potentially competing objectives for urban development – such as the need to provide land for industry, housing, and infrastructure, while preserving the environment. Finally, the problem of monopolies in land markets, which can stifle development, can be overcome through planning powers which ensure a variety of potential development sites and enable compulsory acquisition of private land if needed for a public purpose.

Towards Sustainable Land Use Planning

Urban land use planning has always aimed to coordinate development in ways which protect existing qualities of the built and natural environment, primarily by separating incompatible land uses. From the 1960s, however, wider concerns about the environmental degradation and atmospheric pollution began to permeate public consciousness. In 1983 the World Commission on Environment and Development (WCED), an independent commission assembled by the United Nations, presented the notion of "sustainable development", which it defined as: "development that meets the needs of the present without compromising the ability of future generations to meet their own needs" (WCED 1987; p. 27). Intrinsic to this notion is that human activities, including processes of land use change and urban development, do not threaten the systems on which life depends, now or in the future (Beatley and Manning 1997).

The objective of sustainable development is now enshrined within policy frameworks from the international through to the national, state, regional, and local level. It is given legal weight through national, state, and local planning legislation in many countries. For instance, the UK's *National Planning Policy Framework* (Department for Communities and Local Government (DCLG) 2012), establishes that the overall purpose of the planning system is to contribute to achieving sustainable development in making land use plans and in deciding particular development proposals. This framework is supported by the nation's *Sustainable Development Strategy Securing the Future*, which sets out five "guiding principles" for achieving sustainable development: that plans and development decisions should recognize "the planet's environmental limits"; ensure "a strong, healthy and just society"; achieve a "sustainable economy"; "promote "good governance"; and use "sound science responsibly" (DCLG 2012; p. 6).

These principles emphasize a balance between environmental, social, and economic objectives, while also referring to the need for strong and effective governance and decision-making processes which are informed by sound scientific evidence. In practice, this means that sustainability principles should inform decisions about the overall structure of a neighborhood, precinct, or city; the location of particular activities; and rules for the intensity and physical construction of buildings. This involves:

- respecting ecological limits in the siting of particular developments and in determining appropriate scale and impact, including cumulative impacts (the potential for many similar developments to occur in the area, adding increased pressures);
- the physical structure of new and existing urban areas, having regard to the accessibility of key activities (employment, services, recreation, housing), through strategies which enable

compatible mixed uses and the potential to reduce car dependency while maximizing public transit, walking, and cycling opportunities;
- the opportunities to promote locally sustainable "self-reliance" – decentralized power (eg. solar) and water sources, the reduction and local absorption of waste (eg. permeable surfaces to reduce water runoff; shared composting systems in buildings or neighborhoods), private or shared spaces to cultivate local food (eg. pocket or roof gardens);
- promoting or mandating more sustainable forms of design, construction, and ongoing use in the siting and design of individual buildings and in the selection of and sourcing of materials.

From these objectives arise a series of implementation techniques through the planning process of identifying appropriate locations for future activities, preparing legally enforceable plans, and articulating development controls to situate and manage the impact of specific development.

Legislation and Land Use

As mentioned above, land use planning systems have common elements and processes, even though the terminology for describing these processes, and the specific forms of plan making and development control tend to differ from place to place. Overall, land use planning systems depend on a source of legislative power, which establishes the arrangements for making and enforcing land use plans through development assessment and control. Depending on the division of responsibilities between different levels of government, land use planning legislation might emanate from a national level of government (the United Kingdom, New Zealand) or at the State/Provincial level (the US, Canada, Australia).

From this "enabling" legislation, specific plans for particular local areas or regions are able to be prepared, typically containing a mix of strategic objectives or goals, which are interpreted through spatial controls for the location of particular activities, as well as specific rules to control the physical scale and impact of developments. Land use planning in a statutory sense is about managing future changes, rather than stopping or changing land uses which are ongoing. Thus land use plans often remain dormant until a new activity or development needs permission to go ahead. For this reason the definition of development – the range of activities requiring consent to carry out change – becomes an important trigger for the planning system to come into operation.

In preparing land use plans and in considering particular development, authorities will need to consider whether they are required under planning law to consult with the wider public. There are often specific requirements to consult with neighboring landholders when planning laws are being made or varied and where there is a significant proposal under consideration. It is usually good practice to involve a wide range of potential stakeholders early in a strategic planning process, irrespective of legal obligations.

Although specific requirements vary widely by jurisdiction, the land use planning process involves a number of fairly predictable steps which can be divided into two primary phases. The process of forward, or "strategic" planning involves identifying objectives and spatial policies to achieve them, primarily through land use plans. The process of development "control" involves assessing particular proposals against these planning controls, and determining whether or not to approve, refuse, or require further modifications to the proposal.

Strategic planning processes are informed by research and consultation. Studies are needed to identify existing and likely future needs, given demographic trends (population growth and change), economic factors (income, labor market trends) and existing sites and development opportunities. Environmental constraints, as well as natural and cultural attributes, must be identified and considered in determining appropriate land uses and development controls. Local residents, indigenous land owners, businesses, developers and house builders, service providers, and public agencies, should all be consulted during this phase of the planning process. A set of overall objectives and guiding principles for the planning process can also be articulated at this time.

Existing and potential future land uses and activities within particular areas of the locality can then be considered, subject to considerations about environmental capacity, landscape characteristics, and the existing settlement pattern. Key sites for industry or housing might be situated within existing urban areas or on previously undeveloped rural land. Some land owners may benefit from potential increases in land value through this often highly contentious process. Under many planning systems, it is difficult to change a land use designation in ways that reduce development potential, and this may involve a need to pay compensation to affected owners. So it is important to balance the need for new development sites with the need to avoid an oversupply of land which might not be used for many years. Dispersed, ad hoc, and poorly serviced development is likely to result when there is an oversupply of potential building land, unless there are mechanisms to control the sequencing of infrastructure provision and subdivision release.

Once broad decisions about land use have been made, implementation mechanisms are needed. In many countries, land use zoning is used to define permissible activities. At a more detailed level, development standards can then be implemented to control the density, scale, and design of buildings. These controls might apply to particular locations or land use zones, for instance rules to avoid or to elevate buildings in flood prone areas, or to ensure that development is in keeping with a heritage conservation precinct. Controls might also apply to specific development types, such as separate dwellings on their own plot of land, or to apartments. There are many different ways in which such controls can be articulated, outlined further below.

At this point, a draft plan showing indicative land uses, and often particular development controls, will be formally exhibited subject to consultation requirements specified in the relevant planning law. During this period members of the public are usually able to make submissions in support or opposition of the plan and its provisions. Once all concerns are resolved, the plan can be made and will usually have the force of law. Note that planning authorities may be local or higher levels of government, or an independent panel or board, depending on the institutional arrangements defining each planning system. Once the plan is made, specific proposals for development can be considered by the planning authority against the criteria or rules contained in the land use plan along with any other relevant legislation or policy. Again there will often be a requirement that development proposals be publicly exhibited, with opportunity for members of the public to comment. Depending on the potential impact of the proposal, for instance on the natural environment or on local infrastructure, the development may also be referred to other government agencies for their comment or endorsement. If the proposal is likely to have a very high impact on the environment (as defined by thresholds in the relevant planning law), it will need to undergo a more detailed environmental impact assessment. Following this assessment, the planning authority will approve, refuse, or negotiate a modified development outcome, and specify conditions which must be satisfied as the project moves forward. Unhappy applicants and, in many jurisdictions, third parties are often able to seek a review of the outcome or lodge a formal appeal through the relevant court of law.

Finally, it is important to identify processes for reviewing and updating land use plans, in relation to expected outcomes or changed circumstances. However, in reviewing land use plans it is important to remember that implementation depends on the voluntary actions of private individuals and firms to initiate and complete a project, which in turn often depends on wider economic factors and demand for housing or new development.

Managing the Impact of Development

There are many different approaches and techniques for managing the impact of development within a given area through legally enforceable rules and decision-making processes. These approaches usually sit somewhere on a spectrum from rule-based control enshrined in land use zones or equivalent, and related local provisions, ordinances, or codes; to merit-based discretion exercised by decision makers in response to the specific circumstances of each case. In many systems a combination of approaches will apply, with rule-based controls applying to lower risk or pre-determined development types and merit-based discretion used to decide more complex or higher impact proposals.

We have already described land use zoning which assigns permissible uses to parcels of land. Zoning can operate in ways which are very inflexible – for instance, when only a very limited number of land uses are permitted. Alternatively, it is becoming more common for jurisdictions to enable mixed-use zones which allow many potentially compatible uses, such as commercial, retail, and higher density housing. However, under land use zoning systems it is important to be careful to ensure that the highest value uses do not "crowd out" other important or ongoing activities. This can occur, for example, in contexts where residential housing is a much more valuable land use than office space or agricultural activities.

Specific development controls or standards can regulate the configuration, appearance, density (concentration of development relative to the overall site), heights, building materials, landscaping requirements, or provisions for parking. Minimum allotment sizes are common development standards to manage land use change and density. For instance, large minimum allotment sizes for single detached dwellings impose very low density residential development, while controls which permit smaller sized allotments can enable more diverse housing types. Controls on site coverage and the ratio of total floor space within a building to the total area of the site ("floor space ratio") are also commonly used rules to manage the scale of housing or commercial development. Building heights, the number of stories or floors in a building, minimum building front, rear and side set-backs and other such criteria can also control the density and diversity of development. Other development controls regarding design issues such as height, building materials, or landscaping are intended to achieve objectives relating to urban design, heritage conservation, privacy or environmental conservation.

Strategic land use planning processes generally aim to coordinate and provide opportunities for a balance of development types needed to support a community, aiming for "self-containment" in employment opportunities, retail markets, services, educational facilities, and recreational areas. It can be difficult to ensure this mix over a particular timeframe, although it is common to require developers to contribute towards education, open space, affordable housing, or community facilities. When major new settlements or urban extensions are planned, a 'master planning' process can be used to allocate specific developments or buildings (as opposed to general classes of activities) on specific sites. Another approach is to include threshold requirements, for instance, by requiring the evidence that infrastructure and community facilities are able to be delivered in a timely way, before new subdivisions or housing developments can be approved.

Maintaining a distinction between settled and rural or natural areas is an important planning principle which is imposed in many countries. This separation protects scenic landscapes, preserves the viability of rural activity, and ensures the efficient and affordable provision of infrastructure and services. This can be achieved through land use zoning or through mapped designations of urban and rural land. In some jurisdictions, a firmer "urban growth boundary" is desired to signal that urban development will not proceed beyond the specified area. The 'green belt' system used in the UK also operates to contain urban growth within established settlements and to mark a separation between localities.

Specific variations in development, and in conditions of growth, have led to appropriate variations in land use planning tools. In rural and non-metropolitan areas, objectives typically include preserving and enabling traditional and emerging rural enterprises (which may include some industrial activities); offering some opportunities for rural residential lifestyles in certain areas; preserving scenic values including ridgelines; protecting environmental and water catchment values; and sometimes, identifying lands which may be converted for urban development in the future. In urban contexts, where land is needed to provide for the full range of activities – residential, commercial, recreation, industry, health and community, industry – it is important to monitor demand for, and availability of land for different uses. Where land is vacant – for instance, a "greenfield" site converted directly from agricultural to urban uses – the potential conflicts between existing and new land uses are minimized because there are no existing neighbors, although there may be complex environmental risks which need to be managed. Further, ensuring that greenfield land is developed in orderly ways (ideally contiguously from established urban areas), is challenging where there are many landowners, some of whom may be uninterested in selling their land. On "brownfield" sites – formerly used for industry or other urban purposes – challenges often relate to issues of site contamination and remediation.

When incrementally developing or redeveloping smaller sites within established commercial, residential, and mixed-use settings, complex issues around impacts for surrounding neighbors – such as overshadowing, privacy, view loss, protection of cultural heritage, and so on, arise. These context-based considerations come to life when allocating land uses, drafting land use planning controls, and assessing particular development proposals. Ideally, when allocating land uses through the strategic planning process, two fundamental questions should be resolved: are the range of anticipated or permissible land uses suitable for the site, and can any significant risks (e.g., to the environment, cultural heritage, or human health [in the case of potentially contaminated land]) be managed? If so, the framework for land use control can ensure that detailed consideration and mitigating efforts can be deferred until particular development proposals come forward.

Ethics in Plan Making

Any course on land use plan making and development control must acknowledge the ethical considerations arising in these processes. Since land use plans signal the different activities and developments that can occur on a site, individuals may stand to gain or lose financially from a particular planning designation applying to their own or to neighboring land. Similarly, the development approval process can result in a significant windfall for individuals. It is for these reasons that ethical considerations for professional planners, elected representatives, and any others involved in the plan making or development assessment process, arise.

There are some basic rules of ethical practice which planners can observe to ensure that these matters are decided objectively and in favour of the broad public interest. Critically, planners should ensure that all members of the public have an equal opportunity to engage in the plan making process and development determination process, in line with statutory exhibition and consultation requirements. Individuals involved in the decision-making process must declare any actual or potential conflicts of interest. Planning practitioners should also promote openness and transparency in their own work, by documenting meetings, site visits, telephone calls, and any undertakings or agreements. Practitioners should be aware of how to seek assistance within their organization or potentially from their professional association, if they experience inappropriate pressure from a member of the public, developer, or elected official.

Across all aspects of plan making and development assessment, it is important for planners to maintain a clear distinction between their professional opinion and duties in relation to existing plans and endorsed government policies, and personal or political views. At the organizational level, if strategic and land use plans are kept up to date, there will be less pressure to approve developments which are contrary to established policy and rules. Ensuring that planning controls and procedural requirements are clear and easy to understand also reduces the likelihood that these processes will be inadvertently or deliberately varied in a way that is unethical and contrary to the public interest.

Key Literature Contributions

Since land use planning systems differ between countries and often within them, literature on land use planning tends to be specific to a single country. Yet a comparative lens can be helpful for understanding the underlying principles, processes, and techniques which are common to land use planning systems throughout the world. For a practice oriented overview of land use planning systems in more than 135 countries, see the ISOCARP *International Manual of Planning Practice* (Ryser and Franchini 2015). *Fundamentals of Plan Making: Methods and Techniques* (Jepson and Weitz 2016) offers technical guidance on land use analysis and the preparation of land use maps, contextualized within the wider set of economic, housing, transportation, and environmental studies undertaken to inform comprehensive planning processes.

For learning and practicing land use planning in North America, *Planning in the USA, Policies, Issues and Processes* (Cullingworth and Caves 2014) includes a series of sections on land use regulation, including the relationship between comprehensive plans and techniques of zoning and subdivision regulations. For the UK, *Town and Country Planning in the UK* (Cullingworth, Nadin et al. 2014) provides detailed information on national and local (development) plans, the plan making process, as well as techniques and approaches to development control (now understood as development management). *Planning in the UK* (Greed with Johnson 2014) also offers an accessible introduction to the planning system and development control process, along with focused applications for specific sectors and settings (the countryside, urban regeneration and renewal, transportation and urban design).

Dutch Land-use Planning: The Principles and the Practice (Needham 2014) introduces Dutch spatial planning policy as well as the legal basis for land use plans and the development permitting process. For practitioners and students in Australia, *Australian Urban Land Use Planning* (Gurran 2011) provides an overview of the state planning systems as well as the national and local contexts for planning.

Teaching Land Use Planning and Course Design

Key learning objectives for land use planning curricula relate to a combination of core knowledge areas and skills. Core areas of knowledge center around the theoretical and technical aspects of land use planning theory, processes, and practices, as outlined above. Importantly this combines both wider knowledge of land use planning, processes, and practices with specific knowledge of the particular policy, legal, and practice arrangements for urban land use planning within a particular jurisdictions. Skills relevant to the planning process include the capacity to critically read and review technical studies about land characteristics and constraints, the ability to translate this material into land allocation and plan making processes, and the capacity to interpret development controls as they apply to specific proposals. Land use planning syllabi, readings learning materials, and assessment items should be organized accordingly.

A syllabus which is organized sequentially and grouped into thematic modules might progress as follows.

Module One: Land Use Planning Objectives and Principles

This module introduces theories about why government intervention in land use and development through statutory rules and processes is justified, the normative objectives that land use planning systems aim to achieve, and the guiding principles for efficient and fair land use planning processes. In this module, techniques for effective public involvement and for ethical considerations in professional plan making and development control, should also be established. Key readings as outlined above are used to inform and inspire class discussion or debate.

Module Two: Land Use Planning Systems and Processes

In this module students learn the key elements and processes which are common to land use planning systems in most countries of the world, and how to apply this knowledge to an operational understanding of the institutional arrangements and processes in the jurisdictions that they are likely to encounter in their own professional life. Class preparation or group learning exercises can involve investigating other jurisdictions, to answer a series of key questions such as: 1) What is the overarching source of power or legal authority for the planning system in this jurisdiction? 2) Which level/s of government are responsible for making plans and assessing/deciding development proposals? 3) What are the main techniques of development control?

Module Three: Making Land Use Plans

This module focuses on the ways in which information sources are assembled and used to prepare a new land use plan, or to critique an existing plan in relation to considerations such as: the location of land uses (avoiding or managing environmental constraints and land use conflict, and maximizing efficient infrastructure and transport arrangements); and the adequacy of land supply and development opportunities in relation to existing and forecast need (opportunities for housing, commercial, industrial, recreation, infrastructure etc.). It is often useful to apply this learning to a particular locality, and there may be opportunities to engage students in an existing land use planning process which is already underway. Drawing on actual materials – studies and forecasts – as well as existing and draft plans – can provide a practice oriented focus for this module. Site visits and field work are often an important part of understanding how environmental, social, and economic studies come to inform land use plan making in practice. Alternatively, students can critically review existing land use plans, and propose changes with reference to existing studies and recent patterns of development activity within the area.

Module Four: Development Control

In this module, students learn how to consider specific development proposals against the particular land use planning controls which apply. Often the best way to apply this learning is to consider actual development proposals and for students to identify the key issues which are likely to be raised, given the nature and scale of the development, as well as the specific characteristics of the site and surrounding locality. What is the likely extent of these impacts and are there ways in which they could be managed? Students also need to identify the specific planning rules applying to the development type and site, cognizant that the overlapping sets of rules articulated by different levels of government and or in different documents, might apply. Is the proposed development or activity legal on the site, and if so, what are the rules or criteria which need to be addressed before the proposal is able to be approved? Ideally, class materials will draw on documentation for "real" development proposals, and it may be useful to consider a variety of development types through group exercises and or field trips. Students can report either verbally or through a written assignment, on their consideration of the proposal in relation to the relevant controls.

Case Studies and "Problem-Based Learning"

Land use planning syllabi are easily adapted to a more "problem-based learning" or studio approach. There is now an abundance of material on local planning and development control available via government websites which can form the basis of case studies or simulation exercises. In most instances professional planners will welcome the opportunity to meet a group of students on site or come into the classroom to talk directly about the plan making and development control process from a practice oriented perspective. Students can also attend public meetings where planning or development proposals are being discussed. Interactive exercises in the class room can also involve role playing where students use case material relating to a particular planning or development proposal and debate key issues from different perspectives (eg. proponent/developer; neighbor/s; professional planner; local representative; environmental expert; architect and so on).

Finally, there is some interest in whether computer games which simulate aspects of land use planning, such as SimCity or Second Life, might be useful tools for teaching, learning, and group collaboration (Minnery and Searle 2014). Overall, the evidence is mixed (Gaber 2007, Terzano and Morckel 2017), with key criticisms relating to the fact that the simulations approximate, but do not accurately represent, real life planning scenarios which are bound by idiosyncratic laws, conventions, and site constraints (Hollander and Thomas 2009).

Land use planning, embedded within a particular statutory system and process, is one of the most powerful mechanisms for implementing strategic spatial policy. However, it is important to recognize the limits of the planning system and of land use plans which often reflect imperfect compromises made in response to environmental, economic, or political constraints, and which come into effect largely through market driven processes of private development. In situating land use planning within a wider educational curriculum, the challenge is for students to grasp these dynamics of urban and economic development, their intersections with the existing qualities of the built and natural environment, and the role of statutory planning processes in mediating change.

References

Aldridge, H. R. (1909). *The Case for Town Planning*. London: The National Planning and Town Planning Council.
Beatley, T., & Manning, K. (1997). *The Ecology of Place: Planning for Environment, Economy, and Community*. Washington, DC: Island Press.

Cheshire, P., & Leven, C. L. (1986). *On the Costs and Economic Consequences of the British Land Use Planning System*. Reading: Department of Economics, University of Reading.

Cullingworth, B., & Caves, R. (2014). *Planning in the USA, Policies, Issues and Processes*, Fourth Edition. Oxon: Routledge.

Cullingworth, B., Nadin, V., Hart, T., Davoudi, S., Pendlebury, J., Vigar, G., . . . Townshend, T. (Eds.). (2014). *Town and Country Planning in the UK*. London: Routledge.

Department for Communities and Local Government (DCLG) (2012). *National Planning Policy Framework*. London: Department for Communities and Local Government.

Fischel, W. A. (2004). An economic history of zoning and a cure for its exclusionary effects. *Urban Studies*, *41*(2), 317–340. doi:10.1080/0042098032000165271

Gaber, J. (2007). Simulating planning – SimCity as a pedagogical tool. *Journal of Planning Education and Research*, *27*(2), 113–121. doi:10.1177/0739456xo7305791

Greed, C., & Johnson, D. (2014). *Planning in the UK: An Introduction*. Surrey: Palgrave Macmillan.

Gurran, N. (2011). *Australian Urban Land Use Planning: Principles, Systems and Practice*. Sydney: Sydney University Press.

Gurran, N., Gallent, N., & Chiu, R. L. (2016). *Politics, Planning and Housing Supply in Australia, England and Hong Kong*. Oxon: Routledge.

Hall, P. G. (1973). *The Containment of Urban England: The Planning System: Objectives, Operations, Impacts*. London: Allen and Unwin.

Hollander, J. B., & Thomas, D. (2009). Commentary: Virtual planning second life and the online studio. *Journal of Planning Education and Research*, *29*(1), 108–113. doi:10.1177/0739456x09334142

International Society of City and Regional Planners (ISOCARP) (2001). *Manual of Planning Practice*. The Hague: ISOCARP.

Jepson, E. J., & Weitz, J. (2016). *Fundamentals of Plan Making: Methods and Techniques*. New York: Routledge.

Kushner, J. A. (2002). Smart growth, new urbanism and diversity: Progressive planning movements in America and their impact on poor and minority ethnic populations. *UCLA Journal of Environmental Law and Policy*, 45.

Lillydahl, J. H., & Singell, L. D. (1987). The effects of growth management on the housing market: A review of the theoretical and empirical evidence. *Journal of Urban Affairs*, *9*(1), 63–77. doi:10.1111/j.1467-9906.1987.tb00464.x

Minnery, J., & Searle, G. (2014). Toying with the city? Using the computer game SimCity™4 in planning education. *Planning Practice & Research*, *29*(1), 41–55. doi:10.1080/02697459.2013.829335

Needham, B. (2014). *Dutch Land-use Planning: The Principles and the Practice*. Dorchester: Ashgate.

Pigou, A. C. (1914). Some aspects of the housing problem. In S. B. Rowntree & A. C. Pigou (Eds.), *Lectures on Housing, The Warburton lectures for 1914*. Manchester: Sherratt and Hughes.

Ryser, J., & Franchini, T. (Eds.). (2015). *International Manual of Planning Practice*. The Hague, Netherlands: International Society of City and Regional Planners (ISOCARP)

Sager, T. (2011). Neo-liberal urban planning policies: A literature survey 1990–2010. *Progress in Planning*, 76, 147–199. doi:10.1016/j.progress.2011.09.001

Terzano, K., & Morckel, V. (2017). SimCity in the community planning classroom: Effects on student knowledge, interests, and perceptions of the discipline of planning. *Journal of Planning Education and Research*, *37*(1), 95–105. doi:10.1177/0739456x16628959

World Commission on Environment and Development (WCED). (1987). *Our common future*. Oxford: Oxford University Press.

Webster, C. J. (1998). Public choice, Pigouvian and Coasian planning theory. *Urban Studies*, *35*(1), 53–75. doi:10.1080/0042098985078

21
ENVIRONMENTAL PLANNING

Christian Zuidema and Gert de Roo

Introduction

Environmental planning finds its roots in attempts to protect humans and ecosystems from the adverse effects of human activities. In the early 20th century environmental planning began with a focus on nature protection and this became known as conservation planning. From the 1970s environmental planning became the label for policies countering the negative impact of human activities and economic development on our local and global environment. Many human activities result in undesired side-effects that are also called 'externalities'. These externalities can put pressure on health and hygiene qualities in human environments, such as deterioration in the quality of the water, air and soil and intrusions caused by noise, odour, safety risks, radiation, etc. These pressures can be quite serious. The World Health Organisation (2014) for example calculated that in 2012 approximately 3.7 million people died worldwide due to poor outdoor air quality alone. Human activities are not only putting pressure on the quality of our environment in the here and now. Global pollution, climate change, excessive resource consumption and the ongoing deterioration of biodiversity are also having long term impacts, suggesting our current global society is inherently unsustainable (for discussions see Global Footprint Network 2010). Environmental planning responds by addressing both localized environmental problems and global and long term impacts of human activities.

Environmental planning is nowadays a broad field of practice both regarding the activities conducted and the stakeholders involved. It is an interdisciplinary activity, involving processes of policy making, implementation and management, something also recognized in teaching environmental planning (e.g. Bosman & Dedekorkut-Howes 2014; Hurlimann 2009; Niebanck 1993). What makes environmental planning distinctive is its relation with spatial or land use planning. It is explicitly in understanding how we might better develop and use land and natural resources that environmental planning contributes to improved environmental conditions now and in the future. By doing this, environmental planning crosses many disciplinary boundaries. After all, whether we talk about housing, traffic management, economic development or energy policies, we will also have to talk about their environmental implications.

We begin this chapter by discussing environmental planning education and its main characteristics. After that, we trace the development of environmental policies from the 1970s onwards. Notably, we will discuss the shift away from rather centralized, generic and regulatory based environmental policies towards more strategic, situation specific and integrated forms of environmental planning. It is this shift that stands as a context in which we can we highlight core issues that have emerged over the years, and that environmental planning education benefits from engaging with.

Environmental Planning Education

Environmental issues have to some degree always played an important role in planning. Following the industrial revolution in mostly the 19th century, the availability of clean air and water, access to green space and the prevention of unacceptable risks were among the triggers for improved urban planning (Corburn 2012). Specific education on environmental planning, however, only evolved from the 1960s onwards in line with the swift development of environmental policies in many industrialized countries (Lim 1993).

Environmental planning never developed into a widely known and clearly defined educational discipline. As a result, there is also no readily available canon for environmental planning education (e.g. White & Mayo, 2005; Soule & Press 1998). Furthermore, environmental planning education has also gained rather modest academic attention (e.g. Bosman & Dedekorkut-Howes 2014; Hurlimann, 2009). Nevertheless, environmental planning is clearly visible within planning education. Environmental planning is often seen as being among the central disciplines within (land use) planning. In the USA the Association of Collegiate Schools of Planning, for example, identified environmental planning as one of the five primary areas of planning practice back in 2000 (White & Mayo 2005). Similarly, Sandercock (1997) recognizes planning to be based on five core literacies; next to technical, analytical, multi- or cross-cultural, and design she also highlights the ecological dimension as central. In the meantime, uptake of environmental planning is also very common, with for example 86% of planning programmes in the USA including environmental planning (White & Mayo 2005, but see Gunder 2006 for a contrasting picture in Australia and New Zealand).

A likely explanation for environmental planning not being a clearly defined educational discipline is its strong interdisciplinary focus (e.g. Bosman & Dedekorkut-Howes 2014; Hurlimann 2009; Niebanck 1993). This raises questions regarding the relationship between planning programmes and other forms of environmental education. Environmental planning depends on sound knowledge of our physical environment and of how environmental stress and pollution influence human health and wellbeing. The result is that environmental planning requires literacy on ecological processes (White & Mayo 2005; Bosman & Dedekorkut-Howes 2014), often requiring technical and specialist knowledge and skills (e.g. Vos 2000). On the one hand, if environmental planning is recognized as being a central part of planning, such knowledge and skills should be included in planning curricula. It is possible, however, that the curricula could become rather shallow, especially concerning more technical environmental knowledge and skills, as many other forms of knowledge and skills are taught (e.g. Soule & Press 1998).

On the other hand, as authors such as Susskind (2000) and Niebanck (1993) suggest, environmental planning relies on much more than planning education alone. Instead, other disciplines should be involved. Such involvement can, for example, be based on electives focusing on specific environmental expertise such as ecology, health and hygiene, climate change, sustainable transport, etc. It is up to distinct planning curricula to identify whether and which specific fields they target as additional to their own planning courses.

It is obviously up to planning curricula to decide how they aim to acquaint students with environmental planning. Such decisions should consider the degrees in which curricula target literacy, skills, and/or critical thinking on environmental issues. Based on a survey amongst Australian planning professionals, Hurlimann (2009) found that many environmental planners identify skills as the central target of environmental planning education. It is a finding that resonates with the research of White & Mayo (2005), and suggests that curricula should target environmental design, the use of geographical information systems, environmental impact assessments, environmental policy and law, site planning and negotiation skills (also Bosman & Dedekorkut-Howes 2014). The result is a planning education with distinct skills that can be applied in practice to cope with environmental challenges. Both Hurlimann (2009) and White & Mayo (2005) consider that literacy on aspects such as ecological concepts, environmental economics, environmental philosophy, environmental psychology and sustainability is just as crucial. Finally, environmental planning education also is identified as having a key normative dimension. Environmental literacy creates awareness and might also impact the behaviour of students as individual citizens and within future planning projects they are involved in (Portman & Teff-Seker, 2016). Environmental planning education might thus also provide a degree of normative guidance (Martin & Beatley 1993, Sherran 2008).

Normative guidance can be modest, in the sense that environmental planning education merely helps students become aware of the environmental ethics and related issues of social justice (e.g. Bosman & Dedekorkut-Howes 2014; Gunder 2006). Environmental ethics are then a trigger for creating a critical perspective (also Niebanck 1993) on planning and its role in the larger process of societal development by questioning our society's environmental impacts. Vos (2000) adds to this that environmental planning education simply has to prepare students for the conflicts and trade-offs that can emerge when trying to navigate the ecological, social and economic dimensions of sustainable development. Environmental justice is then a specific form of ethical thinking, where students explore the distributional environmental impacts of policy choices across various social groups. Stronger forms of normative guidance imply that environmental planning education assists students in translating a critical perspective into leadership for pursuing societal change (e.g. Niebank 1993). Either way, both literacy and skills seem crucial for planners to be able to engage with environmental issues.

Environmental planning within planning curricula can thus take many forms. What at least stands out is that it is necessarily interdisciplinary and involves raising awareness about the ecological context in which planning takes place. It is not first and foremost the teaching of practical skills that a curriculum should target, but mostly an ability to carry out informed critical thinking about society's environmental challenges.

Standards and Regulations

Somewhere during the 1960s a global sense of urgency rose over the adverse environmental impacts of economic growth. Books such as Rachel Carson's *Silent Spring* (1962), articles such as Garret Hardin's "Tragedy of the Commons" (1968) and reports such as *The Limits to Growth* (Meadows et al. 1972) helped to further fuel a growing social pressure to act against these impacts. Starting in the industrialized world and especially following the 1972 United Nations conference in Stockholm on the human environment, countries responded by swiftly developing environmental policies and supporting bureaucracies. Joined by the popularity of centralized policy schemes, this urgency triggered environmental planning to start with a reliance on centralized policy approaches (e.g. Andersen & Liefferink 1997; Jordan et al. 2005; Lowe & Ward 1998; Vig & Kraft 2013; Weidner et al. 2002). The result was a swift development of environmental standards and related permit systems, which every environmental planning curriculum is advised to discuss.

Environmental standards remain important ingredients in environmental planning up to today. They vary in their exact focus, ranging from attempts to prevent activities to promoting others. Prevention might include bans on using certain techniques such as landfills for waste or substances such as leaded fuels or certain chemicals. Targeting the reduction of pollution at its source is another example, such as through promoting the use of the best available technologies or technical measures such as filters, catalysts, silencers (e.g. Jänicke & Jörgens 2006). Environmental standards can furthermore set minimum quality levels regarding the amount of nuisance or pollution tolerated in an area or in the soil, water or air. To illustrate, they can dictate the maximum amount of noise that is officially tolerated in housing areas or office parks or dictate limits to concentrations of small particles tolerated in the air or maximum amounts of nitrates in surface water.

Environmental standards have some notable benefits that support their wide use. Since they are general policy guidelines, environmental standards can be applied uniformly and provide high levels of legal certainty to companies and citizens. In that respect environmental standards are often formulated as quantitative values. That makes them relatively easy to understand by implementing agencies and authorities. Also, because they are supported by permit and license systems and related financial or legal sanctions, environmental standards can also be rather effectively implemented. Nevertheless, relying on central government control and environmental standards also has important limitations. Societal stakeholders such as companies, consumers or private individuals are not actively involved in environmental planning other than through legislation (e.g. Jordan et al 2005). Also, there are important risks that centrally issued policies are ill-adapted to unique local circumstances and solution strategies (e.g. de Roo 2003; Zuidema 2016). Finally, a reliance on regulations and central governmental control is also criticized for being merely a form of damage control (e.g. Barrow 1995; Simonis 1988). As a result central government control and environmental standards are considered *only a part* of the puzzle of environmental planning (e.g. Jordan et al 2005; Lemos & Agrawal 2006). As a result, environmental planning has over the past decades expanded its use of instruments and approaches. Literacy on environmental standards, thus, is only a beginning for planning students.

From Reactive to Proactive

A good start in understanding how environmental planning is much more than merely the development and implementation of environmental standards is to recognize the difference between reactive and proactive environmental policies. Environmental standards often mean to merely set restrictions on development-oriented policies and societal decisions; i.e. they are essentially *reactive* policies (see also Andersen & Liefferink 1997; Barrow 1995; Butler & Oluoch-Kosura 2006; Jänicke & Jörgens 2006; Milbrath 1989; Walker and Meyers 2004). In being reactive, standards have some important drawbacks. As Simonis (1988), for example, explains:

> expenditures for environmental protection are made when damage to the natural environment has occurred. They are belated; they are repairs to the process of economic growth, signs of a post-fact policy that reacts to damages (and must react to them) but does not, or cannot, prevent them.

In other words, "reactive forms of environmental policy have been and are perhaps increasingly unable to respond effectively or efficiently to many of the negative impacts of economic development" (Gouldson & Roberts 2000: 4). In contrast, proactive approaches to the environment mean to move beyond what Barrow (1995) for example calls a "react and mend" approach and towards an "anticipate-and-avoid" approach (also Simonis 1988).

Proactive approaches can be connected to the rise of popularity of 'sustainable development'. Sustainable development is most specifically promoted through the report *Our Common Future* from the 1987 UN Brundtland commission, defining it as "development that meets the needs of the present without compromising the ability of future generations to meet their own needs" (World Commission on Environment and Development (WCED) 1987: 43). To meet those needs, sustainable development assumes that environmental protection and improvement should go together with economic and social development and vice versa. As such, sustainable development recognizes how environmental problems often touch upon a wide range of societal needs and interests that are in themselves considered desirable; i.e. economic growth, mobility, industrial production, energy consumption etc. Hence, as Briassoulis explains, environmental issues are often "complex and interrelated, defying treatment by means either of narrow, sectoral policies or of all-encompassing, super-policies" (2005: 2). Instead, coping with interrelated policies and issues requires coordination between various societal and sectoral interests (also Jordan & Lenschow 2010; Lafferty & Hovden 2003; Persson 2002).

The shift towards more proactive environmental policies has triggered the rise of alternative approaches to regulations and standards that nowadays form important parts of environmental planning. They are thus also among the approaches that planning curricula would ideally discuss. The first of these approaches rose in the 1980s and promotes more proactive environmental policies by improving the integration of environmental objectives in other policy decisions (e.g. Gouldson & Roberts 2000; Lafferty & Hovden 2003; Simonis 1988). It is supported by the "recognition that the environmental sector alone will not be able to secure environmental objectives, and that each sector must therefore take on board environmental policy objectives if these are to be achieved" (Lafferty & Hovden 2003: 1). The use of environmental impact assessments is a first step in doing so (Glasson et al. 2013; Wood 2003). Environmental impact assessments require that developments with potentially serious environmental impacts are assessed prior to development. Although they do not necessarily imply such developments cannot be pursued if such impacts are identified, they do promote awareness of these impacts and can help to at least partly prevent or mitigate them. After starting in the United States in 1970s, environmental impact assessments are nowadays used in over a hundred countries worldwide (Glasson et al. 2013) and are also identified as being among the key skills to teach in environmental planning education (e.g. Bosman & Dedekorkut-Howes 2014).

Environmental impact assessments address isolated plans and projects rather than the full range of government policies. Another approach, environmental policy integration, goes a step further in promoting the integration of environmental objectives into non-environmental policy fields (e.g. Jordan & Lenschow 2010; Lafferty & Hovden 2003; Persson 2002). Environmental policy integration seeks the development of cross-sectoral policy approaches in promoting environmental objectives. The idea is not only that non-environmental policy fields actively contribute to the promotion of environmental quality, but environmental policy integration is also considered important to correct or prevent coordination deficits and policy incoherencies (e.g. Andersen & Liefferink 1997; Jordan & Lenschow 2010). Environmental policy integration is seen as an important condition for coping with the 'complex and interrelated' problems just mentioned. As Briassoulis notes, it can help "bind together currently departmentalized, disparate and uncoordinated policies that fail to tackle contemporary, cross-cutting, complex socio-environmental problems, sometimes being among the forces producing these problems" (2005: 351). Nevertheless, environmental policy integration is especially focused on improving the coherency and cooperation of governmental policies and most notably the central state (e.g. Lafferty & Hovden 2003). Hence, it pays less attention to including non-governmental parties such as companies and civil society actors into the process of environmental planning.

The inclusion of non-governmental stakeholders in the process of developing and delivering environmental objectives can be linked to what Jordan et al (2005) describe as the emergence of 'new environmental policy instruments' (also Jänicke & Jörgens 2006; Lemos & Agrawal 2006; Mol et al. 2000; Vig & Kraft 2013). These are instruments that not only highlight the different ingredients that might be included in environmental planning education. They also highlight that environmental planners operate in a societal context where next to environmental literacy and skills, organisational and bargaining skills are also required.

A first group of new environmental policy instruments are 'market based instruments' that follow the rise of neoliberal tendencies in politics and governing. They include instruments such as eco-taxes, pollution charges, tradable permits and government subsidies (e.g. Jordan et al. 2005; Lemos & Agrawal 2006; Sonnenfeld & Mol 2002; Stavins 2003). Their aim is to 'internalize' environmental costs and benefits in market processes and thus to influence pro-environmental choices by consumers and producers. Market based instruments, thus, are regulations "that encourage behavior through market signals rather than through explicit directives regarding pollution control levels or methods" (Stavins 2003: 358).

A second group of new environmental policy instruments stimulates environmentally friendly behaviour through the (semi)voluntary action of companies and citizens. A wide range of informational devices are based on the argumentative power of the message portrayed. They include well-known examples such as eco-labels, sustainability labels or media campaigns (e.g. Siebert 1987). Finally there are 'voluntary agreements' that are typically made between governments and specific target groups such as the fishing industry, petrochemical industries or the agricultural sector (e.g. Mol et al. 2000; Sonnenfeld & Mol 2002). Voluntary agreements are statements of intent on taking environmental measures and can range from fully voluntary to legally binding contracts (e.g. Jordan et al. 2005).

New environmental policy instruments help to internalize environmental quality criteria in decision making within other policy sectors and societal activities. They help expand the scope of environmental planning beyond a sole reliance on government regulations. Still, these instruments often do rely on government funding and regulation to be effective. As Jordan et al. (2005) explain, they thus function under the "shadow of the law". Regulations are thus used to 'activate' pro-environmental behaviour in markets and the civil society. A well-known example of this is the notion of 'ecological modernization', where progressive standard setting and regulations are used to promote green innovation within the market and society (e.g. Buttel 2000; Jänicke 2008; Mol et al. 2009; Spaargaren & Mol 1992).

Local Environmental Planning

Promoting more socially inclusive, integrated and proactive forms of environmental planning is also relevant on a local level (e.g. Ericksen et al. 2o004; Evans et al. 2005; de Roo & Miller 2000; Pinderhughes 2004; Marcotullio et al. 2004). This is especially true for urban areas, which are concentrations of human economic and social activities and are therefore the main sites for industrial production and the consumption of resources. Not only does this result in a concentration of environmental pollution and stress in urban areas, it also makes urban areas crucial in pursuing global sustainability.

The interaction between environmental policy ambitions and spatial planning becomes highly explicit when we consider the local level. Coping with urban transportation, polluted soil, industrial emissions or energy consumption are just some examples showing a need to combine spatial and environmental choices. The interaction between environmental policies and spatial planning goes two ways, each of which highlights yet another ingredient that seems crucial within environmental planning education; this is where land use planning and environmental policies interact.

First of all, it is on the local level where the spatial consequences of (inter)national environmental policies and regulations become manifest. This is most explicitly so when we consider environmental stressors that have so called 'tapering effects' (e.g. de Roo 2003). Tapering effects imply that the level of pollution or environmental stress becomes less when distance to the source of pollution or stress increases (Figure 21.1). Good examples are noise from busy roads or railways, safety risks around fuel stations or odour from factories. The result is that physically separating environmentally intrusive functions ('sources') from environmentally sensitive functions ('exposure') becomes a planning tool. Based on the standards set and the height of the emissions at the source, distances can be calculated that need to be maintained. Based on such calculations, a buffer zone can be installed in order to ensure that sensitive functions, such as housing, would be outside of the zones with intolerable levels of exposure. The result is the development of *environmental zones* surrounding environmentally intrusive functions (e.g. Miller & de Roo 1996). Environmental zones make visible where new urban development runs into environmental problems or where intolerable levels of environmental stress overlap with sensitive land use functions.

Environmental standards are important triggers for local environmental planning. Nevertheless, there is also a need to look beyond environmental standards in local environmental planning. Environmental standards often mean to guarantee that certain exposure levels are not exceeded and therefore tend to apply generically; i.e., they are similar in different places. In the meantime, a wide range of local activities contribute to the existence of environmental problems. Hence, solving environmental problems has implications for such activities, ranging from mobility, industrial production, housing to energy consumption. The implications differ per area, fuelled by difference such as climate, topography or regarding economic development, the local job market and existing political or institutional capacities.

[...]

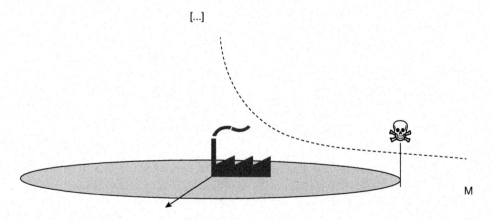

Figure 21.1 Environmental Stress with Tapering Effects

The result is that responding to environmental problems might require specific local circumstances to be taken into account.

Generic standards are not meant to respond specifically to local circumstances (e.g. de Roo 2003; Zuidema 2016). On the one hand, this implies that local circumstances can make meeting environmental standards difficult if not unrealistic. Local authorities have several possibilities to reduce the size of environmental zones. Examples are the installation of barriers against noise, the relocation of highly intrusive activities or road traffic that is diverted through new ring roads or parking routes. Nevertheless, this strategy might not always work. To illustrate: meeting noise quality standards might be feasible or even easy in a rural village or a suburban town. In a busy urban centre this can be quite different. Historical developments lead to a patchwork of urban land uses that are strongly interwoven in a small physical space. Changing such situations can be costly and time-consuming and might also be undesirable for reasons such as neighbourhood identity, aesthetics, culture, heritage, or even because polluting activities are considered crucial, for example with ports, key industries or airports. Under such complex urban conditions, the benefits of meeting environmental standards might not be considered to outweigh the financial and social costs (e.g. Borst et al. 1995; Oates 2001). Rather, there is a need for developing policy approaches that are tailor-made to the local circumstances where even deviations from generic standards might be required (e.g. Zuidema 2016).

Secondly, generic policies and standards provide minimal requirements, but are not necessarily triggers to pursue higher quality. Local planning is therefore important to proactively add value to pursuing higher quality. Ideally, environmental planning seeks to improve environmental quality as far as is considered realistic while taking other interests into account. The result is an attempt to continuously balance interests in the search of the most effective and efficient ways to promote environmental quality now and in the future. As each locality has different problems, priorities, and stakeholder interests, pursuing such balancing is problematic for central states or international organizations through the use of generic policies (Kersbergen & Van Waarden 2004; Rhodes 1997). Instead, the proximity of local authorities to local circumstances, stakeholder interests and the 'civil society' puts local authorities at an advantage over central government in terms of translating the interrelatedness of issues and interests in situ into integrated strategies (e.g. de Roo 2004; Dryzek 1987; Jordan 1999; Liefferink & Hajer 2002).

Local planning approaches can thus be important in solving local environmental issues and to add value to generic standards. Local authorities can for example try and reduce certain intrusive activities. Creating buffer zones, shifting to more renewable energy resources or the reduction of road traffic are excellent examples. At first sight, such local approaches seem most relevant for making contributions when environmental issues are local in origin and impact. Noise and odour nuisance, soil remediation and waste management are among the examples. Nevertheless, in being the prime areas worldwide of unsustainable consumption, local environmental planning is also crucial to pursue a serious reduction of urban ecological footprints; i.e. the amount of land and water required by these areas to sustain their current patterns of consumption and assimilate their wastes (Wackernagel & Rees, 1996). Hence, local tailor-made policies can also be important for other policies, including (inter)national issues such as air pollution, clean energy or climate adaptation. To illustrate, many towns and cities aim to pursue a modal shift away from cars to public transport or biking through building bike roads or installing low emission zones in (inner) cities where certain cars are no longer allowed or need to pay for access (e.g. Boogaard et al. 2012; Wolff 2014).

Generic and Specific

Many national governments have since the 1990s recognized the need for local action as complementary to generic polices and attempts to influence markets and behaviour through new environmental policy instruments (e.g. Buckingham & Theobald 2003; Evans et al. 2005; Heberle & Opp 2008; Haughton & Hunter 2004; Miller & de Roo 2004 & 2005; Moore & Scott 2005; Pinderhughes 2004; Rydin 2012; Selman 1996). This is also well-illustrated by the rise of Local Agenda 21 policies that followed the 1992 United Nations conference in Rio de Janeiro (Selman 1996). In the meantime, several national governments began to pursue deregulation and decentralization operations for increasing the 'regulatory room' for local environmental planning (e.g. van Tatenhove et al. 2000; Lemos & Agrawal 2006; Wätli 2004). Their idea is to reduce the impact of top-down policy imperatives that potentially constrain local authorities and stakeholders in setting their own priorities and targets. Instead, the idea is that environmental priorities and targets should be increasingly formulated at the local level.

For environmental planners it is crucial to understand that when shifting power and responsibilities in environmental planning to the local level, there are also risks involved (e.g. Connerly et al. 2010; De Vries 2000; Flynn 2000; Fleurke & Hulst 2006; Prud'homme 1994; Walberg et al. 2000). Decentralization means that the outcomes of governance become increasingly dependent on available local willingness and ability to perform decentralized tasks and responsibilities (e.g. de Roo 2004; Zuidema 2016). Willingness and ability are, however, not self-evident in a local realm.

When it comes to local ability, time, funding, competent staff and legal instruments are among the immediate resources needed. As Prud'homme (1994) explains, central governments can more easily invest in research and development, innovative projects and in attracting people with many different competencies and forms of expertise. This is more problematic for smaller units such as municipalities when it comes to environmental policies (e.g. Burström and Korhonen 2001; Flynn 2000; Walberg et al. 2000). When it comes to local willingness, risks relate notably to some key characteristics of environmental ambitions. For one, many environmental ambitions have a relatively 'weak profile' as compared to more development-oriented priorities (e.g. Zuidema 2016). Environmental benefits can, for example, be hard to express in financial terms (such as noise nuisance), are often invisible (as with safety risks), diffuse (as with air pollution), are highly subjective (odour) or focus on a long time horizon (e.g. sustainability). Economic growth, social development or, for example, financial costs are easier to envision and often relate to the short term. Local environmental planning seeks to balance environmental objectives with other local objectives; i.e. they are 'tradable'. Their 'weak profile', however, means that environmental objectives might be easily 'overruled' by other more powerful economic and social objectives (e.g. Eckersley 1992; Jordan 1999; Walberg et al. 2000).

Secondly, many environmental issues also manifest themselves as 'social dilemmas' (e.g. Lemos and Agrawal, 2006; Wätli, 2004). Social dilemmas are issues where the benefits of local investments in improved environmental conditions 'spill over' to adjacent jurisdictions, while the costs are confined to the local realm; e.g. air pollution, the depletion of the ozone layer, global warming, river pollution, etc. Without sufficient incentives local authorities might not be inclined to take action. They might even be inclined to accept the 'costs' of additional environmental pollution of which they only experience a modest share, in the face of the 'benefits' of additional growth which they can experience to the fullest. Instead, coordination between local authorities is desirable, where central governments can play a key role in organizing coordination, installing incentives and avoiding 'free riders'.

Increased reliance on local governance in environmental planning thus has important risks. Notably, there are risks that might create serious challenges to human health, ecosystem qualities and the pursuit of a more sustainable society. On the one hand, this highlights the need for environmental literacy among planning students so as to allow them to take a critical stance in evaluating policy choices that have environmental implications. That is not to say that planners should necessarily take a normative pro-environmental standpoint, but in the face of a possible lack of literacy and willingness among politicians and society, it is at least their task to make environmental consequences visible.

On the other hand, promoting local environmental governance might well amplify differences in environmental qualities between jurisdictions. Hence, there is an increased chance of an unequal distribution of environmental burdens. Notions of environmental justice (e.g. Bullard 2005; Schlosberg 2007) are then quick to arise, again putting a responsibility on planning curricula to help planning students in being able to recognize and articulate environmental justice issues.

Finally, planning students, especially those that seek employment in national institutes, also benefit from an awareness of the interaction between central, top-down and generic policies and local self-governance for pursuing tailor-made approaches. Certainly, degrees of local governance are important to implement generic policies under complex circumstances *and* to add value to such generic policies. But central governments can also play a role when it comes to developing locally based solution strategies to add value to generic standards (e.g. Zuidema 2016). Central governments are for example important to enable local authorities with legal tools and resources to attract the right staff and competences. Alternatively, a wide range of environmental planning methods is available for local authorities to develop environmental planning strategies (e.g. CEC 2007; de Roo et al. 2011). Supporting the use of such methods by central governments making these available or cheaper to use can further avoid each locality having to 'reinvent the wheel'.

Environmental Planning Under Construction

After over four decades, environmental planning has developed into a mature policy practice in much of the Western world. Much has changed since its initial rise through regulations that started in the 1970s. Environmental planning spread from industrialized countries to increasingly become a globally institutionalized practice. Environmental policy integration has helped develop a more coherent approach to environmental planning. Tasks and responsibilities have been shifted to a variety of societal stakeholders and market parties through the use of new policy instruments. Furthermore, decentralization and local initiative has supported the development of environmental planning practices well adapted to local circumstances and ambitions. Nevertheless, we also have to conclude environmental planning remains under construction.

We remain challenged by localised sites of pollution, while on a global scale, air pollution, the pollution of our oceans, excessive resource consumption and the deterioration of biodiversity are unprecedented. In the meantime, the acceptance of the severe urgency of climate change and especially clean energy is confronting society with an urgency similar to the environmental pollution of the 1970s. In the face of the risk of runaway climate change and the need to structurally adjust our socio-economic system towards a sustainable and zero-emission society, the challenge seems even bigger than before. Academics have also begun to understand that actually controlling the complex and unpredictable interrelations between economy, society, climate and ecology is unrealistic (e.g. Folke et al 2010). Instead, they are looking towards ways to improve the capacity of cities, regions, communities and ecosystems to better respond and adapt to unpredictable and possibly extreme change we might face. Highlighted with the notion of 'resilience', policies thus also focus on adapting to change rather than trying to control it (e.g. Berkes et al. 2003; Davoudi 2012; Folke et al 2010). For planning curricula it seems inescapable not to include such new developments as these will bring the kind of literacy and skills that prospective planners will need in their work.

What seems at least as important for planning curricula is to explain how governance has also for environmental issues become a mixture between state, market and civil society approaches. The rise of market based instruments, entrepreneurs seeking for green growth and the rise of citizen based initiatives on for example community energy or urban gardening are illustrating this changing governance landscape. Nevertheless, with environmental planning being focused on the protection of ecosystems and especially human health and safety, renewing environmental planning should be treated with care and prudence. Criteria such as legal security, social equity, minimal levels of protection against pollution and preventing risks are highly valued within the realm of environmental planning and are traditionally protected through government control. Central governments therefore remain important. They can provide the necessary pushes for new policy instruments to function under the "shadow of the law" (Jordan et al. 2005). They can provide the "smart regulations" to push or societies and economies to keep innovating (Jänicke and Jörgens 2006). And finally, they can provide the robust basis of policies to enable and stimulate local authorities to develop proactive and integrated approaches in a local realm (Zuidema 2016). Ambitious and proactive environmental planning, therefore, remains an unescapable reality for all levels of authority and society if we are to develop healthy, clean and sustainable areas and futures. It is this lesson that seems fundamental for planning curricula to convey to students. The environment needs their help.

References

Andersen, M. S., & Liefferink, D. (1997). *The innovation of EU environmental policy*. Oslo: Scandinavian University Press.
Barrow, C. J. (1995). *Developing the Environment: Problems and Management*. Harlow: Longman Scientific & Technical.
Berkes, F., Colding, J., & Folke, C. (Eds.). (2003). *Navigating Social-ecological Systems: Building Resilience for Complexity and Change*. Cambridge: Cambridge University Press.
Boogaard, H., Janssen, N. A. H., Fischer, P. H., Kos, G. P. A., Weijers, E. P., Cassee, F. R., . . . Hoek, G. (2012). Impact of low emission zones and local traffic policies on ambient air pollution concentrations. *Science of the Total Environment*, 435–436, 132–140. doi:10.1016/j.scitotenv.2012.06.089
Borst, H., de Roo, G., Voogd, H., & van der Werf, H. (1995). *Milieuzones in beweging*. Alphen aan den Rijn: Samson H.D. Teenjk WillinK.
Bosman, C., & Dedekorkut-Howes, A. (2014). Environmental planning education and the possibilities for studio pedagogy. In M. Imran, J. Ross, & I. Luxmore (Eds.), *Planning, Politics and People: Proceedings of the Australia and New Zealand Association of Planning Schools Conference*. Wellington: Massey University.
Briassoulis, H. (2005). Policy integration: Realistic expectation or elusive goal? In H. Briassoulis (Ed.), *Policy Integration for Complex Environmental Problems, The Example of Mediterranean Desertification*. Aldershot: Ashgate.
Buckingham, S., & Theobald, K. (2003). Building alliances for local environmental sustainability. In S. Buckingham, & K. Theobald, K. (Eds.), *Local Environmental Sustainability* (pp. 1–17). Cambridge: Elsevier.

Buckingham, S., & Theobald, K. (Eds.). (2003). *Local Environmental Sustainability*. Cambridge: Elsevier.
Bullard, R. D. (Ed.) (2005). *The Quest for Environmental Justice: Human Rights and the Politics of Pollution*. San Francisco, CA: Sierra Club Books.
Burström, F., & Korhonen, J. (2001). Municipalities and industrial ecology: Reconsidering municipal environmental management. *Sustainable Development*, 9(1), 36–46. doi:10.1002/sd.154
Butler, C. D., & Oluoch-Kosura, W. (2006). Linking Future Ecosystem Services and Future Human Wellbeing. *Ecology and Society*, 11(1). doi:10.5751/es-01602-110130
Buttel, F. H. (2000). Ecological modernization as social theory. *Geoforum*, 31(1), 57–65. doi:10.1016/s0016-7185(99)00044-5
Carson, R. (1962). *Silent Spring*. Middlesex: Penguin Books.
Corburn, J. (2012). Reconnecting urban planning and public health. In R. Weber & R. Crane (Eds.), *The Oxford Handbook of Urban Planning* (pp. 392–417). New York: Oxford University Press.
Commission of the European Communities (CEC). (2007). *Integrated environmental management, guidance in relation to the Thematic Strategy on the Urban Environment*. Retrieved from www.ccre.org/docs/guide_environment_mangement.pdf
Connerley, E., Eaton, K., & Smoke, P. J. (2010). *Making Decentralization Work: Democracy, Development, and Security*. Boulder, CO: Lynne Rienner Publishers.
Davoudi, S. (2012). Resilience: A bridging concept or a dead end? *Planning Theory & Practice*, 13(2), 299–307. doi:10.1080/14649357.2012.677124
de Roo, G. (2003). *Environmental Planning in the Netherlands: Too Good to be True: From Command-and-Control Planning to Shared Governance*. Aldershot: Ashgate.
de Roo, G. (2004). *Toekomst van het Milieubeleid: Over de regels en het spel van decentralisatie*. Assen: Van GorcumDutch.
de Roo, G., & Miller, D. (Eds.). (2000). *Compact Cities and Sustainable Urban Development: A Critical Assessment of Policies and Plans from an International Perspective*. Aldershot: Ashgate.
de Roo, G., Visser, J., & Zuidema, C. (2011). *Smart Methods for Environmental Externalities: Urban Planning, Environmental Health and Hygiene in the Netherlands*. Farnham: Ashgate.
De Vries, M. S. (2000). The rise and fall of decentralization: A comparative analysis of arguments and practices in European countries. *European Journal of Political Research*, 38(2), 193–224. doi:10.1111/1475-6765.00532
Dryzek, J. S. (1987). *Rational Ecology: Environment and Political Economy*. Oxford: Basil Blackwell.
Eckersley, R. (1992). *Environmentalism and Political Theory: Toward an Ecocentric Approach*. London: UCL Press.
Ericksen, N. J., Berke, P. R., Crawford, J. L., & Dixon, J. E. (2004). *Plan-making for Sustainability: The New Zealand Experience*. Aldershot: Ashgate.
Evans, B., Joas, M., Sundback, S., & Theobald, K. (2005). *Governing Sustainable Cities*. London: Earthscan.
Fleurke, F., & Hulst, R. (2006). A Contingency Approach to Decentralization. *Public Organization Review*, 6(1), 37–56. doi:10.1007/s11115-006-6902-4
Flynn, B. (2000). Is local truly better? Some reflections on sharing environmental policy between local governments and the EU. *European Environment*, 10(2), 75–84. doi:10.1002/(sici)1099-0976(200003/04)10:2<75::aid-eet216>3.0.co;2-3
Folke, C., Carpenter, S. R., Walker, B., Scheffer, M., Chapin, T., & Rockström, J. (2010). Resilience thinking: Integrating resilience, adaptability and transformability. *Ecology and Society*, 15(4). doi:10.5751/es-03610-150420
Glasson, J., Therivel, R., & Chadwick, A. (2013). *Introduction to Environmental Impact Assessment* (Third ed.). London: Routledge.
Global Footprint Network. (2010). *Ecological Footprint Atlas 2010*. Oakland, California: The Ecological Footprint, Global Office.
Gouldson, A., & Roberts, P. (2000). *Integrating Environment and Economy: Strategies for Local and Regional Government*. London: Earthscan.
Gunder, M. (2006). Sustainability: Planning's saving grace or road to perdition? *Journal of Planning Education and Research*, 26(2), 208–221. doi:10.1177/0739456x06289359
Hardin, G. J. (1968). The tragedy of the commons. *Science*, 162(3859), 1243–1248. doi:10.1126/science.162.3859.1243
Haughton, G., & Hunter, C. (2004). *Sustainable Cities*. London: Routledge.
Heberle, L. C., & Opp, S. M. (Eds.). (2008). *Local Sustainable Urban Development in a Globalized World*. Hampshire: Ashgate Press.

Hurlimann, A. C. (2009). Responding to environmental challenges: An initial assessment of higher education curricula needs by Australian planning professionals. *Environmental Education Research*, 15(6), 643–659. doi:10.1080/13504620903244159

Jänicke, M. (2008). Ecological modernisation: New perspectives. *Journal of Cleaner Production*, 16(5), 557–565. doi:10.1016/j.jclepro.2007.02.011

Jänicke, M., & Jörgens, H. (2006). New approaches to environmental governance. In K. Jacob & M. Jänicke (Eds.), *Environmental Governance in Global Perspective: New Approaches to Ecological and Political Modernisation*. Berlin: Freie Universität Berlin.

Jordan, A. (1999). *Subsidiarity and Environmental Policy: Which Level of Government Should Do What in the European Union?* Working Paper. CSERGE. Norwich.

Jordan, A., & Lenschow, A. (2010). Environmental policy integration: A state of the art review. *Environmental Policy and Governance*, 20(3), 147–158. doi:10.1002/eet.539

Jordan, A., Wurzel, R. K. W., & Zito, A. (2005). The rise of 'new' policy instruments in comparative perspective: Has governance eclipsed government? *Political Studies*, 53(3), 477–496. doi:10.1111/j.1467-9248.2005.00540.x

Kersbergen, K. V., & Waarden, F. V. (2004). 'Governance' as a bridge between disciplines: Cross-disciplinary inspiration regarding shifts in governance and problems of governability, accountability and legitimacy. *European Journal of Political Research*, 43(2), 143–171. doi:10.1111/j.1475-6765.2004.00149.x

Lafferty, W. M., & Hovden, E. (2003). Environmental policy integration: towards an analytical framework. *Environmental Politics*, 12(3), 1–22. doi:10.1080/09644010412331308254

Lemos, M. C., & Agrawal, A. (2006). Environmental governance. *Annual Review of Environment and Resources*, 31(1), 297–325. doi:10.1146/annurev.energy.31.042605.135621

Liefferink, D., & Andersen, M. S. (1998). Strategies of the 'green' member states in EU environmental policy-making. *Journal of European Public Policy*, 5(2), 254–270. doi:10.1080/135017698343974

Liefferink, D., & Hajer, J. v. T. (2002). The dynamics of European nature policy: The interplay of front stage and back stage by 2030. In W. Kuindersma (Ed.), *Bestuurlijke trends en het natuurbeleid*, Planbureaustudies No. 3. Wageningen: Natuurplanbureau.

Lim, G. C. (1993). Reforming education toward the global century. *Environment and Planning B: Planning and Design*, 20(5), 567–576. doi:10.1068/b200567

Lowe, P., & Ward, S. (Eds.). (1998). *British Environmental Policy and Europe: Politics and Policy in Transition*. London: Routledge.

Marcotullio, P. J., Sorensen, A., & Grant, J. (Eds.). (2004). *Towards Sustainable Cities: East Asian, North American and European Perspectives on Managing Urban Regions*. Aldershot: Ashgate.

Martin, E., & Beatley, T. (1993). Our relationship with the Earth: Environmental ethics in planning education. *Journal of Planning Education and Research*, 12(2), 117–126. doi:10.1177/0739456x9301200207

Meadows, D. H., Meadows, D. L., Panders, J., & Behrens, W. W. (1972). *The Limits to Growth: A report for the Club of Rome's Project on the Predicament of Mankind*. New York: Universal Books.

Milbrath, L. W. (1989). *Envisioning a Sustainable Society: Learning Our Way Out*. New York: State University of New York Press.

Miller, D., & de Roo, G. (Eds.). (2004). *Integrating City Planning and Environmental Improvement: Practicable Strategies for Sustainable Urban Development*. Aldershot: Ashgate.

Miller, D., & de Roo, G. (Eds.). (2005). *Urban Environmental Planning: Policies, Instruments and Methods in an International Perspective*. Aldershot: Ashgate.

Miller, D., & de Roo, G. (1996). Integrated environmental zoning: An innovative Dutch approach to measuring and managing environmental spillovers in urban regions. *Journal of the American Planning Association*, 62(3), 373–380. doi:10.1080/01944369608975701

Mol, A. P. J., Lauber, V., & Liefferink, D. (Eds.). (2000). *The Voluntary Approach to Environmental Policy: Joint Environmental Approach to Environmental Policy-making in Europe*. Oxford: Oxford University Press.

Mol, A. P. J., Sonnenfeld, D. A., & Spaargaren, G. (Eds.). (2009). *The Ecological Modernisation Reader: Environmental Reform in Theory and Practice*. London: Routledge.

Moore, N., & Scott, M. (2005). *Renewing Urban Communities: Environment, Citizenship and Sustainability in Ireland*. Aldershot: Ashgate.

Niebanck, P. (1993). The shape of environmental planning education. *Environment and Planning B: Planning and Design*, 20(5), 511–518. doi:10.1068/b200511

Oates, W. E. (2001). *A Reconsideration of Environmental Federalism*. Retrieved from: https://pdfs.semanticscholar.org/f209/8436fa6cab9d9458619b3ce4076b749d10f6.pdf

Persson, A. (2002). *Environmental Policy Integration, An Introduction*. Stockholm: Stockholm Environment Institute.

Pinderhughes, R. (2004). *Alternative Urban Futures: Planning for Sustainable Development in Cities throughout the World*. Lanham, ML: Rowman & Littlefield Publishers.

Portman, M. E., & Teff-Seker, Y. (2016). Community-level environmental projects as learning tools for planners: A case study of graduate planning students. *Environmental Education Research*, 23(3), 415–435. doi:10.1080/13504622.2015.1136597

Prud'homme, R. (1994). *On the Dangers of Decentralization*. Retrieved from http://documents.worldbank.org/curated/en/218141468739288067/On-the-dangers-of-decentralization

Rhodes, R. A. W. (1997). *Understanding Governance: Policy Networks, Governance, Reflexivity, and Accountability*. Buckingham: Open University Press.

Rydin, Y. (2012). *Governing for Sustainable Urban Development*. London: Earthscan.

Sandercock, L. (1997). The planner tamed. *Australian Planner*, 34(2), 90–95. doi:10.1080/07293682.1997.9657754

Schlosberg, D. (2007). *Defining Environmental Justice: Theories, Movements, and Nature*. Oxford: Oxford University Press.

Selman, P. H. (1996). *Local Sustainability: Managing and Planning Ecologically Sound Places*. New York: St. Martin's Press.

Sherran, K. (2008). Higher environmental education: core disciplines and the transition to sustainability the transition to sustainability. *Australasian Journal of Environmental Management*, 15(3), 190–196. doi:10.1080/14486563.2008.9725201

Siebert, H. (1987). *Economics of the Environment: Theory and Policy*. Berlin: Springer-Verlag.

Siebert, H. (1987). Policy instruments. In *Economics of the Environment* (pp. 119–139). Berlin: Springer-Verlag.

Simonis, U. E. (1988). International environmental problems and the role of legislators. In A. Vlavianos-Arvanitis (Ed.), *Biopolitics, the Bio-environment* (Vol. 1). Athens: Primera Conferencia Internacional del B.I.O.

Sonnenfeld, D. A., & Mol, A. P. J. (2002). Globalization and the transformation of environmental governance. *American Behavioral Scientist*, 45(9), 1318–1339. doi:10.1177/0002764202045009003

Sonnenfeld, D. A., & Mol, A. P. J. (2002). Globalization and the transformation of environmental governance: An introduction. *American Behavioral Scientist*, 45(9), 1417–1434.

Soule, M. E., & Press, D. (1998). What is environmental studies? *BioScience*, 48(5), 397–405. doi:10.2307/1313379

Spaargaren, G., & Mol, A. P. J. (1992). Sociology, environment, and modernity: Ecological modernization as a theory of social change. *Society & Natural Resources*, 5(4), 323–344. doi:10.1080/08941929209380797

Stavins, R. N. (2003). Experience with market-based environmental policy instruments. In K. Mäler & J. R. Vincent (Eds.), *Handbook of Environmental Economics, Economywide and International Environmental Issues* (pp. 355–435). Amsterdam: Elsevier.

Susskind, L. E. (2000). Environmental planning: The changing demands of effective practice. In L. Rodwin & B. Sanyal (Eds.), *The Profession of City Planning: Changes, Images and Challenges 1950–2000* (pp. 161–173). New Brunswick, NJ: Center for Urban Policy Research, Rutgers University.

van Tatenhove, J., Arts, B., & Leroy, P. (Eds.). (2000). *Political Modernisation and the Environment: The Renewal of Environmental Policy Arrangements*. Dordrecht: Kluwer Academic Publishers.

Vig, N. J., & Kraft, M. E. (2013). *Environmental Policy: New Directions for the Twenty-First Century* (Eighth ed.). New York: SAGE Publications.

Vos, J. (2000). Teaching environmental planning and policy by linking theory and praxis. *Journal of Public Affairs Education*, 6(2), 105–113.

Wackernagel, M., Rees, W. E. (1996). *Our Ecological Footprint: Reducing Human Impact on the Earth*. Gabriola Island, BC: New Society Publishing.

Walberg, H. J., Paik, S. J., Komukai, A., & Freeman, K. (2000). Decentralization: An international perspective. *Educational Horizons*, 78(3), 153–164.

Walker, B., & Meyers, J. A. (2004). Thresholds in ecological and social-ecological systems: A developing database. *Ecology and Society*, 9(2). doi:10.5751/es-00664-090203

Wätli, S. (2004). How multilevel structures affect environmental policy in industrialized countries. *European Journal of Political Research*, 43(4), 599–634. doi:10.1111/j.1475-6765.2004.00167.x

Weidner, H., Jänicke, M., & Jörgens, H. (Eds.). (2002). *Capacity Building in National Environmental Policy: A Comparative Study of 17 Countries*. Berlin: Springer-Verlag.

White, S. S., & Mayo, J. M. (2005). Environmental education in graduate professional degrees: The case of urban planning. *The Journal of Environmental Education*, 36(3), 31–38. doi:10.3200/joee.36.3.31-38

Wolff, H. (2014). Keep your clunker in the suburb: Low-emission zones and adoption of green vehicles. *The Economic Journal*, 124(578), F481–F512. doi:10.1111/ecoj.12091

Wood, C. (2003). *Environmental Impact Assessment: A comparative review* (Second ed.). Harlow: Pearson Education Ltd.

World Commission on Environment and Development (WCED). (1987). *Our Common Future*. Oxford: Oxford University Press.

World Health Organization. (2014). 7 million premature deaths annually linked to air pollution. Retrieved from: www.who.int/mediacentre/news/releases/2014/air-pollution/en/

World Health Organization. (2010). *Urban Planning, Environment and Health: From Evidence to Policy Action*. Retrieved from www.euro.who.int/en/health-topics/environment-and-health/Housing-and-health/publications/2010/urban-planning,-environment-and-health-from-evidence-to-policy-action

Zuidema, C. (2016). *Decentralization in Environmental Governance: A Post-contingency Approach*. Abingdon: Routledge.

22
TRANSPORTATION PLANNING

Andrea Broaddus and Robert Cervero

Introduction to Transportation Planning

Transportation is one of five main specializations in US planning education (Association of Collegiate Schools of Planning, ACSP, 2014).

Transportation planning is a modern term for the ancient practice, at least since the Roman Empire, of developing and organizing transportation infrastructure, networks, and services in support of the economic activities of complex societies. It is a future-oriented activity practiced at three scales:

1) the nation/state, which is concerned with flows between metropolitan regions using highways, heavy railways, water ports, and airports;
2) the metropolitan region, which focuses on flows between urban centers via highways, commuter rail, ferries, and bicycle networks; and
3) the municipal level, which is concerned with internal flows on arterial and local roads, and bicycle and pedestrian networks.

Graduates of planning programs with a transportation specialization may work at any level, although most commonly at the regional or local level. Either may be referred to as urban transportation planning.

Transportation planning requires a systems framework reflecting the two-way relationship between transportation networks and the places they serve. Urban transportation planning seeks to prepare for future growth in flows of people and goods as well as to shape where and by which mode growth occurs, through an awareness of the interaction between transportation and land use. The process of transportation planning begins with defining goals from which transportation policies, designs, and investments are derived. Increasingly, it is a collaborative process incorporating the input of many stakeholders, including governmental bodies, private businesses, and the public. Planners develop a range of alternative transportation solutions and project how they will affect flows, as well as externalities like impacts on the environment and residential communities.

Often forecasting methods such as travel demand models are used to evaluate alternative projects in terms of travel time savings, mode splits, and cost-benefit ratios. Two fundamental principles are applied in demand forecasting. First, travel is understood as a derived demand, that is, people do not desire to travel for its own sake, but for the purpose of accessing activities at specific destinations. As demand for the destination activity increases (e.g. a job, healthcare, education), elasticity of demand for travel decreases. Secondly, people are expected to choose a mode of travel and a route which minimizes their generalized cost of travel, that is, in terms of both monetary (out of pocket) and time cost.

Historically, transportation planning was conducted as a branch of civil engineering (Weiner, 1992). Transportation engineering focuses on infrastructure design and traffic flows of motorized vehicles, with little consideration of the overall patterns of economic activity, interactions with land use, social and economic context, or externalities. Transportation planning emerged as a specialization to address these gaps, and there is some overlap between the two fields. In the US, it was claimed as a specialty by the American Planning Association, but is often practiced by engineers. Several universities offer transportation joint degrees between planning and engineering departments. In Europe, meanwhile, there are also efforts to establish transportation planning as its own discipline distinct from engineering, but also from traditional spatial and town planning. For example, in the UK, transportation planning is not claimed as a specialization by the Royal Town Planning Association; rather, a separate Transport Planning Society (TPS) was formed and a new professional certification for transport specialists was established (Transport Planning Professional, or TPP) (Chartered Institution of Highways and Transportation, CIHP, 2016; TPS, 2016).

Trends in Transportation Planning

Three major factors are contributing growing demand for transportation planning: globalization, urbanization, and the rise of information-communication technologies (ICTs). Globalization has expanded networks of trade and reduced barriers to employment, increasing the volume and complexity of flows of information, people, and goods throughout the world. (Rodrigue, Comtois, & Slack, 2013) ICTs, rather than suppressing demand for travel, have created new sources for demand as services such as ride-sharing and online shopping change the nature, amount, and routes, of shipping flows. While some of these trips might replace drive-alone trips, decreased costs and increased convenience are expected to induce demand for a net increase in home delivery and personal transit (taxi-type) trips. Some argue that physical mobility has become even more important to full participation in the economy and society, despite the prevalence of ICTs (Bertolini, le Clerq, & Straatemeier, 2008).

Urbanization is increasing the density of urban areas. In doing so it places more pressure on urban transportation infrastructure and services and increases demand for public transportation, bicycling, and walking solutions. Yet simultaneously, urban regions are becoming larger geographically, spreading origins and destinations further apart. This larger geographic spread increases the costs of establishing or expanding public transit systems, while also making biking or walking impractical. Regions which have multiple employment centers struggle with a mismatch between the geometry of hub-and-spoke transit networks and the geography of commuting from suburb-to-suburb (Cervero, 2001). People living in far-flung suburban areas where commercial land uses are segregated from residential areas must make complex linked trips, or "trip chains", to accomplish daily activities. Both of these trends increase single-occupant auto travel.

Activities like commuting or shopping, which used to be accomplished within a local area, are increasingly replaced by longer trips to regional destinations. This change in the activity-space of households from the local to regional-scale is a mismatch with transportation networks designed to serve either the local (two-lane roads) or state or multi-state scale (interstate highways). There is a need to redefine transportation planning institutions in terms of both scales, to enable regional strategic capacity, and scope, to allow for private sector participation in service provision (Bertolini et al., 2008).

Traditionally, transportation planning has taken a "predict and provide" approach, seeking to predict where demand will grow, and provide appropriate infrastructure and services to accommodate this growth. This approach is no longer viable, due to increasing financial constraints and social resistance to the negative impacts of expanding urban transport infrastructure. In an era of rapid change, when even transportation technologies and services themselves are changing, it is increasingly difficult to predict future demand. Even where needs are clear, there is often a lack of material support, both financial and political, to provide for them. Mobility has become an essential condition for active participation in urban social and economic life, and as a consequence, the competing approach of "travel demand management" can be politically unpopular (Bertolini et al., 2008). For all these reasons, urban transportation planning is a discipline in transition.

Transport planning was dominated by the rational technical planning model for most of the twentieth century, but a paradigm shift has been underway in the US, Europe, Canada, and Australia for at least the past decade. State and local government transportation agencies in these countries have begun to change their policies, plans, and processes in similar ways. They have increasingly shifted their missions away from highway building to broader goals, including planning for a multi-modal transportation system, place-making, and system maintenance (Burke, Mateo-Babiano, & Pan, 2013; Schiller, Bruun, & Kenworthy, 2010; Zhou & Schweitzer, 2009). In the US, this shift first got underway with federal legislation that created Metropolitan Planning Organizations for regional-scale planning, linked transportation investments to conformity with air quality regulations, and required public involvement for all projects (Hanson & Giuliano, 2004).

A key aspect of this paradigm shift is a change of emphasis from "mobility" to "accessibility" planning (Cervero, 2001). This basically means the overarching goal of transportation has changed from improving the mobility of vehicles to improving the accessibility of key destinations. Where traditional planning prioritized the movement of vehicles, using cars as the basic unit of analysis, accessibility planning considers the movement of people. Activity patterns of people, and the level of access that they have to key destinations like workplaces, schools, and health care, are used as metrics in accessibility planning. Many factors affect accessibility, including the quality of public transit services, infrastructure for bicycling and walking, and the ability to telecommute (Litman, 2013). Much of the current research focuses on travel behavior, improving understanding of how people plan trips, which factors influence route and mode choice, and how to modify them to advance accessibility.

Today's transportation problems are too complex for a mono-disciplinary approach; interdisciplinary and integrated approaches are increasingly sought to address social and environmental concerns. Transportation agencies increasingly seek to collaborate and partner with other public policy sectors like environmental, economic development and public health agencies. Addressing emerging urban and regional-scale problems requires transportation planners to play a connecting and coordinating role among public agency staff like traffic engineers, urban designers, and neighborhood planners, but also among private parties like developers and transportation service providers. As private-sector mobility services (i.e. on-demand ride hailing, shared bicycles and scooters) gain market share, planners must also negotiate with operators in order to develop new regulations and data reporting requirements. As a result, transportation planning is an increasingly communication-oriented activity, reflecting the increased amount of

Table 22.1 A Paradigm Shift in Transportation Planning (with input from Banister, 2008, and Litman, 2013)

	Traditional approach	Sustainable approach
Definition of transportation	Mobility, physical travel	Accessibility, people's overall ability to reach destinations
Measured in terms of	Movement of vehicles	Movement of people
Scale designed for	National/state	Local
Overarching goal	Improve mobility of vehicles	Improve accessibility to key destinations
Modes of transportation planned for	Mainly automobiles	Multi-modal: public transit, bicycling, walking, and delivery services
Planning objectives	Maximize road and parking capacity, reduce congestion, increase travel speeds, reduce travel times	Optimize capacity for system efficiency, balance needs of all users, improve safety, slow traffic, improve travel time reliability
Planning methods	Traffic forecasting and modelling, economic evaluation	Visioning, scenario development and modeling, multi-criteria analysis accounting for environmental, social and equity concerns
Concept of streets	Facilities which should be engineered to maximize vehicle flows	Public places which should be managed to comfortably balance the needs of all users, including public transit, bicycling, and walking
Public involvement	Public hearings and comment periods towards end of process	Outreach and community engagement at beginning of process

time spent on collaboration, stakeholder engagement, and gaining public acceptance (Bertolini et al., 2008).

As a transitioning discipline, urban transportation planning is increasingly focused on delivering "sustainable transportation" that emphasizes environmental and financial sustainability as well as social equity. The sustainable transportation approach seeks to reduce emissions, largely by reducing private vehicle trips, and increase system efficiencies. It prioritizes policy measures and investments in infrastructure and services which reduce the number of trips, trip length, and mode used (Banister, 2008). Table 22.1 contrasts the traditional approach to the emerging one of sustainable transportation.

The Role of Transportation in Planning Education

The most basic function of transportation courses in a planning program is to familiarize students with the institutions, regulatory requirements, and processes of transportation planning. Across the world, transportation educators are expected to keep abreast of changing transportation policies and laws and train students accordingly. For example, in the US, federal transportation policy dictates both the factors that state and local officials must consider and the kinds of processes they must use in developing transportation plans (Handy, Weston, Song, & Lane, 2002).

Increasing complexity in transportation planning means the field is broadening in scope. It may be understood as an "interstitial field", meaning that transportation planners must increasingly overlap, mesh, and integrate with other disciplines such as land use planning, public health, and economic development to meet public objectives for the transportation system (Ferreira, Marsden, & Te Brömmelstroet, 2013). Transportation planning education therefore requires a multi-disciplinary approach to develop some knowledge of each, as well as their inter-dependencies. In the US, graduate courses in transportation planning taught at planning schools are often cross-listed by graduate schools of engineering, public policy, and geography. At universities that do not have a graduate school of planning, transportation courses covering much of the same material may be offered by these other schools (Zhou & Schweitzer, 2009) In the UK, Europe, and Australia, transportation planning education also takes place in both civil engineering and planning programs, but joint degrees are far less common than in the US.

To understand how transportation planning education is developed and delivered in different international contexts, we reviewed several recent studies on transportation planning course topics and pedagogical methods in the US, Europe, Australia, and China (Bertolini et al., 2008; Burke, Mateo-Babiano, et al., 2013; Ferreira et al., 2013; Handy et al., 2002; Krizek & Levinson, 2005; Zhou & Schweitzer, 2009) All of these studies emphasized the paradigm shift in transportation planning, described earlier, and the consequent need for an interdisciplinary approach to both teaching and practicing transportation planning, with an increased emphasis on integration with land use planning and communicative skills. Moreover, the studies agreed that transportation planning lacks a standard approach, or "canon", of theory, topics, and methods. The number and topics of courses offered, and whether they were offered by transportation planning departments, was highly variable.

Lack of consensus among academics and of guidance from planning program accrediting bodies and professional associations, help to explain the lack of a common approach among transportation planning courses (Burke, Mateo-Babiano, et al., 2013). For example, the UK Royal Town Planning Institute suggests transportation as an area of specialization without further guidance, as does the US Planning Accreditation Board. In contrast, the Planning Institute of Australia and the Chinese Urban Planning Education Authority have both codified some key aspects of what should be included in transportation planning courses. In Australia, the professional organization for planning (Planning Institute of Australia, PIA) sets guidelines for what knowledge and skills must be covered in transportation planning courses at accredited planning schools (PIA, 2015). The five core competencies it requires for certification as a transportation planning professional are listed in Table 22.2.

Table 22.2 Core Competencies of Transportation Planners as Defined by the Planning Institute of Australia (PIA 2015)

1 Knowledge of the relationship and integration between transport and land use.
2 Knowledge of the principles of transport planning and modelling.
3 Knowledge of various transport modes and their operation.
4 Capacity to critique plans and design proposals, according to sustainable transport planning principles, linking these with other forms of planning and urban change influences.
5 Capacity to produce transportation plans at a level demonstrating understanding of the main components of transport plan production and implementation.

Course Topics, Theory and Skills

Our literature review identified a range of specific knowledge and skills covered in transportation planning. A synopsis of course topics relating to institutions and processes, modal planning concepts, policy issues, and theory is provided in Table 22.3. A synopsis of course topics listed in each article relating to design, methods, professional development, and skills is given in Table 22.4.

Two of the studies were comprehensive analyses of transportation course syllabi in the US. The first conducted a curriculum analysis to compare planning requirements mandated by federal law with course offerings (Handy et al., 2002). Graduate transportation courses offered by 66 accredited schools of planning were investigated, as well as transportation courses offered by 62 non-planning departments affiliated with the Council of University Transportation Centers. Overall, two-thirds of the transportation planning courses were taught by planning faculty, 20% by engineering faculty, and 13% by faculty from other departments, including public policy and geography. Table 22.5 shows the most common topics of these courses.

Nineteen of the planning departments did not offer any courses in transportation planning. Of the 47 that did, an average of 2.6 transportation planning courses were offered. Transportation was offered as a concentration by 32 of the planning departments, six of which offered a joint degree with transportation engineering. Eight of the planning departments were strongly specialized in transportation, offering seven or more transportation courses. Of the 62 non-planning departments offering transportation planning courses, 45 were civil or environmental engineering departments, nine were public policy, and eight were interdisciplinary departments of transportation studies or transportation science. Fifteen of these departments offered one or fewer courses in transportation planning; the remaining 47 offered 3.8 transportation planning courses on average. Thirteen departments were strongly specialized in in transportation, offering seven or more courses, and four of them offered a joint degree in engineering and either urban planning or public policy. The authors noted that engineering departments were providing transportation planning courses in-house when they were not offered by the planning department, or the university did not have a planning department.

As part of their study, Handy et al. also conducted a survey of transportation professionals to assess how their education and training matched up with the knowledge and skills needed on the job. To reach transportation professionals, they invited over 1,000 members of the American Planning Association and 1,100 members of the Institute of Transportation Engineers to take the survey; 360 were completed. Of these, 44% had a master's degree in planning, 16% a master's degree in engineering, and 2% a joint master's degree, with the remainder in other fields or lacking a master's degree. Over three-quarters of respondents said their duties included analyzing project alternatives, conducting public involvement, developing long-range plans, and assessing the community impacts of transportation projects. About two-thirds said their duties included prioritizing projects and conducting policy analysis and development, and over half said they assessed environmental impacts of transportation projects. Fifty-nine percent said their jobs were "mostly planning", while 64% said they did "some engineering". The results emphasize the interdisciplinary nature of transportation planning, suggesting it is a combination of the fields of planning and engineering.

The professionals surveyed were asked to rate which transportation planning course topics were the most important on the job. The top five (in order) were: regional transportation planning, the transportation and land use (TLU) connection, public involvement, multi-modal integration, and travel demand forecasting. They were also asked to rate which skills covered in transportation planning courses were most needed on the job. The top

Table 22.3 Transportation Planning Course Topics Relating to Institutions and Processes, Modal Planning Concepts, Policy Issues, and Theory

Theme	Course topic	Handy et al. 2002 (US)	Krizek & Levinson 2005 (US)	Zhou & Schweitzer 2009 (US)	Burke et al. 2013 (Aust.)	Burke et al. 2013 (China)	Total
Institutions and planning processes	Regulation of land use, zoning, growth management / Land use planning	x	x		x	x	4
	Metropolitan planning procedures and processes / Regional governance & MPOs / Regional transportation planning	x	x	x			3
	Federal policy / Law & regulation	x	x	x			3
	History	x	x		x		3
	Transportation planning process / Infrastructure planning, budgeting, finance		x		x	x	3
	Neighborhood planning	x					1
Modal planning concepts	Transit planning and management / Transit network design	x	x	x	x	x	5
	Pedestrian & bicycle planning / Non-motorized travel	x	x	x	x		4
	Road and bridge design, road network design	x	x			x	3
	Multimodal integration / Intermodal planning	x		x	x		3
	Freight & logistics / Goods movement	x	x		x		3
	Highway, waterway, and aviation engineering	x					1
Policy issues	Transport and land use connection / Integration	x	x	x	x	x	5
	Intelligent transportation systems	x	x	x			3
	Environmental justice and equity / Equity	x	x	x			3
	Travel demand management	x	x		x		3
	Environmental sustainability issues / Energy & environment		x	x	x		3
	Travel behavior	x					1
	Safety	x					1
	Pricing		x				1
	Telecommunication and travel		x				1
	Environmental impacts			x			1
	Gender issues			x			1
	Health and physical activity			x			1
	Security			x			1
	Parking			x			1
Theory	Transportation economics	x			x		1
	Induced demand						1
	Social networks		x				1
	Planning theory		x		x		1
	Urban economics				x		1

Table 22.4 Transportation Planning Course Topics Relating to Design, Methods, Professional Development, and Skills

Theme	Course topic	Handy et al 2002 (US)	Krizek & Levinson 2005 (US)	Zhou & Schweitzer 2009 (US)	Burke et al. 20×3 (Aust.)	Burke et al. 20×3 (China)	Total
Design	Facility design (traffic calming, sidewalks, bike paths, etc)	x					2
	Urban design	x			x		2
	System design	x					1
	Site design (transport-oriented development/ TOD, etc)		x				1
Methods	Travel demand forecasting/ modeling	x		x	x	x	4
	Case studies	x	x	x			3
	Traffic impact analysis	x	x		x		3
	Transportation models		x		x	x	3
	System management	x	x				2
	Software applications (ie GIS, TransSIM, TransCAD)	x		x			2
	Travel survey questionnaire / diary				x	x	2
	Environmental impact analysis	x					1
	Statistical analysis	x					1
	Cost-benefit analysis	x					1
	Population forecasting	x					1
	Transportation control measures	x					1
	Land use models		x				1
	Performance measurement		x				1
	Project evaluation and assessment			x			1
	Accessibility modeling / measures				x		1
Professional development	Professional ethics	x		x	x		3
	Public speaking	x				x	2
	Meeting facilitation	x					1
Skills	Public involvement / Working with the public	x		x			2
	Data presentation	x				x	2
	Technical writing	x					1
	Writing for the public	x					1
	Data collection	x					1
	Budget preparation	x					1
	Basic statistics					x	1

Table 22.5 Most Common Transportation Course Offerings in the United States (adapted from Handy, 2002)

	Planning schools	Non-planning schools
Urban transportation planning overview	31%	27%
Transportation policy	12%	9%
Transportation and land use	11%	Not reported
Special topics, seminars, or studios	10%	Not reported
Transportation systems planning and analysis	7%	12%
Transportation finance and economics	5%	12%
Public transit planning	6%	11%

five (in order) were: public speaking, data presentation, working with the public, technical writing, and writing for the public. The authors then compared those topics rated as the highest importance with those rated as the least covered in their coursework. The top five of these high priority yet under-taught topics (in order) were: public involvement, bicycle and pedestrian planning, transit planning, regional transportation planning, and travel demand forecasting. In addition, high percentages of both planning and engineering graduates reported that these topics were insufficiently covered in their programs: the Americans with Disability Act, environmental justice, intelligent transportation systems, bicycle and pedestrian planning, urban design, and air quality conformity. Finally, respondents involved in hiring decisions were asked to rank the importance of various transportation planning topics for entry-level planners. The top five (in order) were: the TLU connection, regional transportation planning, public involvement, professional ethics, and land use planning.

The second comprehensive analysis of transportation course syllabi in the US was the Nationwide Survey of Transportation Planning Courses (Zhou & Schweitzer, 2009). The study found 72 planning departments and 209 engineering departments that offered transportation planning courses. From this population, a representative sample of 71 transportation programs at 47 universities were selected for the survey. The authors also conducted a literature review to trace the evolution of transportation planning courses over time, and found that some topics have become more widely taught in recent years. For example, nearly all course now include an overview of the federal legislation guiding transportation planning, planning for multiple modes, and training on engaging with the public.

Survey responses were received from 34 faculty, who submitted 40 course syllabi. The most prevalent topics covered in these courses were the TLU connection and travel demand forecasting (96%). Most of them covered metropolitan planning procedures and processes, environmental impacts and sustainability issues, transportation project evaluation and assessment, public involvement, multi-modal integration, intelligent transportation systems, and transit planning and management (75–89%). About half covered software applications in transportation planning, pedestrian and bicycle planning, safety, environmental justice and social equity (52–59%). The least reported topics were professional ethics (33%), gender (30%), health and physical activity (26%), and security (11%). The study did not report what textbooks and readings were assigned in these courses, but responding faculty were explicitly asked about their use of federal transportation agency websites. The majority (91%) reported using websites offered by US DOT to find policies, case studies, reports, and data. The Federal Highway Administration website was the most popular, followed by US DOT, the National Transportation Library, and the Transportation Planning Capacity Building Program.

A third study analyzing transportation course syllabi focused more narrowly on how the subfield of TLU interaction is taught in planning programs (Krizek & Levinson, 2005). The authors noted that coursework on TLU interaction was a gap revealed by Handy et al.'s study, yet it was one of the top five most desired areas of knowledge for entry-level planners (Handy et al., 2002). This subfield has been gaining importance as planning initiatives at the intersection of transportation and land use gain popularity in implementation, such as smart growth, transit oriented and infill development, reform of minimum parking requirements, and pedestrian friendly urban design. (Krizek & Levinson, 2005) Increasingly in practice, transportation planners are expected to understand how land use contributes to demand for travel, and land use planners are expected to have rudimentary knowledge of traffic patterns and travel behavior.

Twenty urban planning programs offer courses addressing integrated transportation and land use planning, including 15 with "transportation and land use" in the course title. Larger programs (as measured by both number of faculty and those that offered a PhD degree) were more likely to offer such a course. Of the six universities offering a joint transportation planning and engineering degree, only one offered a TLU course. The syllabi for these 15 courses were collected and examined for topics, readings, and skills. The top three topics covered were: transit oriented development, debates about high density versus sprawling development patterns, and understanding travel behavior. Other important topics included the jobs-housing balance, growth management and zoning, induced demand and pricing, and network design. Eleven courses contained theory topics drawn from urban and transportation economics, including bid rent, gravity models, utility theory, and cost-benefit analysis. As for pedagogical methods, the authors noted that many of the courses used case studies to introduce real world examples.

Only one study analyzing transportation planning course topics and syllabi outside the US was found (Burke, Mateo-Babiano, et al., 2013). The authors collected syllabi from transportation planning courses in Australia and China, and compared them to the courses discussed in Handy (2002) and Krizek and Levinson (2005). Transportation planning courses in the UK, US, and Australia tend to focus on a similar range of planning and policy issues, whereas the Chinese transport planning course included geometric road design and traffic engineering as major elements, as well as inter-urban transport systems engineering. Compared to the US, the Australian courses dealt less with transport economics, but more with pedestrian and bicycle planning and public transportation. The main reason for these differences in course content were differing requirements set by accreditation bodies in each country.

Burke, Mateo-Babiano, and Pan (2013) argued that planning theory should reintroduced into transport planning courses, in order to explore its implications for transportation planning processes and decision-making. Educators need to convey a richer understanding of planning theory, its contestation, and its application to transport planning. To this end, they suggested using an in-depth study of decision-making at a regional transportation planning agency as an introduction to four "planning styles": technical/bureaucratic, political influence, social movement, and collaborative (Innes & Gruber, 2005).

The authors also noted a tension in transport planning courses between breadth and depth of topics covered. Introductory classes on policy and planning context, or even more specialized classes on the transportation and land use connection, tend to be broad survey courses where educators try to fit in as many concepts and policy issues as possible, at the expense of a deep focus on any one issue. This could be addressed by prioritizing a smaller number of topics to address at depth, and giving students experiential learning opportunities.

Considering pedagogical methods, Burke et al. argued for modes of experiential learning such as studio, simulated consulting and situated learning exercises, as well as fieldwork and hands-on survey data collection and analysis. They also stressed the importance of guest lecturers as a way to expose students to people with different values and conflicting worldviews, and to help them understand power and political dynamics.

Challenges for Educators

As transportation planning is currently a field in transition, educators have a unique role to play in shaping its future and aiding transition to the sustainability paradigm. In particular, this entails training students in accessibility planning, rather than the traditional four-step model.

Transportation planning is an "interstitial" field where the emphasis on inter-disciplinarity is increasing. Coursework should prepare students for multidisciplinary problems and solutions, which may require creativity in class projects, exercises and pedagogical methods. Some schools have developed interdisciplinary graduate degrees in transportation, offering degrees composed of courses taught by faculty in planning, engineering, management, public policy and economics across several departments (Handy et al., 2002) For example, Massachusetts Institute of Technology's Center for Transportation Studies offers an interdepartmental Master of Science in transportation linking six departments, including planning.

The studies we reviewed identified transportation and land use interaction, bicycle, and pedestrian planning as emerging subfields. Students should be exposed to theories explaining how the transport system interacts with land uses, and how to mitigate traffic impacts of changing land uses. They should also be introduced to multi-modal planning, meaning planning infrastructure and services for transit, bicycles, and pedestrians. Programs offering a degree or specialization in transportation should offer specialized courses on these topics.

Public involvement requirements have made transportation planning increasingly visible to the public, and forced planners to become more skilled at communications and more responsive to public concerns. It is critical that educators provide opportunities to improve communication skills (e.g., technical writing, writing for the public, data presentation, public speaking, and interpersonal communication). Students must also be prepared to work in a politicized context by giving them a taste of political realities and what compromises may be needed to complete projects. Maintaining links with transportation professionals to keep abreast of the changing planning context and demands of the job can help with curriculum development, and serve as a source of guest speakers who can expose students to different viewpoints.

Equally important is teaching critical thinking, such that students understand both strengths and limitations of tools and techniques they use. For example, working graduates reported that key legislation and measures related to social equity and environmental justice were inadequately covered in their coursework. Students should be able to identify different perspectives from which a problem could be defined or a solution evaluated, and how their own attitudes and preferences influence their work.

The field of transportation is changing rapidly, with new vehicles (e.g., electric cars, bikes, and scooters), ICT-based services (e.g., telecommuting, ride-hailing, and online shopping and delivery), and technologies (e.g., automated vehicles). While more studies about these modes are being published every year, they are quickly outdated. A solid grounding in theory will best prepare students to deal with rapidly changing travel demand patterns and the changing role of the public sector. For example, bid rent and other location theory from urban economics is important to understand the transportation-land use connection. Behavioral and social networks theory aids understanding travel demand and preferences to improve services, while microeconomics theory provides measures for managing demand through pricing and incentives. Faculty need to identify appropriate theory and teach it effectively, in ways that students will be able to apply as an important tool on the job.

Further Reading

Givoni, Moshe and David Banister (eds.). (2010) *Integrated Transport: From Policy to Practice*. Oxon, UK: Routledge.
Hickman, Robin, et al. (2015) *Handbook on Transport and Development*. Cheltenham, UK: Edward Elgar.
Meyer, Michael and Eric Miller. (2001) *Urban Transportation Planning: A Decision Oriented Approach*. New York: McGraw-Hill.
Moore, Terry, Paul Thorsnes, and Bruce Appleyard. (2007) *The Transportation/Land Use Connection*. Chicago, IL: American Planning Association.
Suzuki, Hiroaki, Robert Cervero and Kanako Iuchi. (2013) *Transforming Cities with Transit*. Washington, DC: The World Bank.
Van Wee, Bert, Annema, Jan-Anne, and Banister, David. (eds.) (2013) *The Transport System and Transport Policy: An Introduction*. Cheltenham, UK: Edward Elgar.
Vuchic, Vukan. (2005) *Urban Transit: Operations, Planning and Economics*. Hoboken, NJ: John Wiley & Sons.
Walker, Jarrett. (2011) *Human Transit*. Washington, DC: Island Press.

References

Association of Collegiate Schools of Planning (ACSP). (2014). *Guide to Undergraduate and Graduate Education in Urban and Regional Planning*. Retrieved from www.acsp.org/resource/collection/6CFCF359-2FDA-4EA0-AEFA-D7901C55E19C/2014_20th_Edition_ACSP_Guide.pdf
Banister, D. (2008). The sustainable mobility paradigm. *Transport Policy*, 15(2), 73–80. doi:10.1016/j.tranpol.2007.10.005
Bertolini, L., le Clerq, F., & Straatemeier, T. (2008). Urban transportation planning in transition. *Transport Policy*, 15(2), 69–72. doi:10.1016/j.tranpol.2007.11.002
Burke, M., Mateo-Babiano, I., B., & Pan, H. (2013). Improving student learning in transport and land use planning in Australia and in China: Theory, concepts and ways forward. *Journal of the Eastern Asia Society for Transportation Studies*, 10, 1059–1075. doi:10.11175/easts.10.1059
Cervero, R. (2001). Transportation planning. In N. J. Smelser & P. B. Baltes (Eds.), *International Encyclopedia of the Social & Behavioral Sciences* (pp. 15873–15878). Oxford: Elsevier.
Chartered Institution of Highways and Transportation (CIHP). (2016). *Transport Planning Professional*. Retrieved from www.tpprofessional.org/en/tpp/about-tpp/index.cfm
Ferreira, A., Marsden, G., & Te Brömmelstroet, M. (2013). What curriculum for mobility and transport studies? A critical exploration. *Transport Reviews*, 33(5), 501–525. doi:10.1080/01441647.2013.827266
Handy, S., Weston, L., Song, J., & Lane, K. M. D. (2002). Education of transportation planning professionals. *Transportation Research Record: Journal of the Transportation Research Board*, 1812, 151–160.
Hanson, S., & Giuliano, G. (Eds.). (2004). *The Geography of Urban Transportation* (3rd ed.). New York: Guilford Press.
Innes, J. E., & Gruber, J. (2005). Planning styles in conflict: The metropolitan transportation commission. *Journal of the American Planning Association*, 71(2), 177–188. doi:10.1080/01944360508976691
Krizek, K., & Levinson, D. (2005). Teaching integrated land use-transportation planning: Topics, readings, and strategies. *Journal of Planning Education and Research*, 24(3), 304.
Litman, T. (2013). The new transportation planning paradigm. *ITE Journal*, 83(6), 20–24.
PIA. (2015). *Accreditation Policy for the Recognition of Australian Planning Qualifications*. Retrieved from Canberra, Australia: www.planning.org.au/documents/item/48
Rodrigue, J.-P., Comtois, C., & Slack, B. (2013). *The Geography of Transport Systems*. Oxon, UK: Routledge.
Schiller, P., Bruun, E., & Kenworthy, J. (2010). *An Introduction to Sustainable Transportation: Policy, Planning and Implementation*. London: Earthscan.
TPS. (2016). Transport Planning Society. Retrieved from https://tps.org.uk/society/our_history
Weiner, E. (1992). *Urban Transportation in the United States: An Historical Overview*. Washington, DC: USDOT Retrieved from http://ntl.bts.gov/DOCS/UTP.html
Zhou, J., & Schweitzer, L. (2009). Transportation planning education in the United States: Literature review, course survey, and findings. *Transportation Research Record: Journal of the Transportation Research Board*, 2109, 1–11.

23
HOUSING AND REAL ESTATE PLANNING

Katrin B. Anacker

Introduction

Traditionally, planning education and the planning profession, regardless of the country in which they were taught or practiced, had entailed land use and environmental planning on the one hand and urban and regional studies, including urban geography, urban economics, urban sociology, and urban politics, on the other (Alterman 1992; Dagenhart and Sawicki 1992). However, in the 1950s and 1960s planning educators and planners in the United States, Canada, Australia, New Zealand, the Netherlands, and France started including social planning in their curricula and activities. Interestingly, social planning may be considered to be nontraditional planning by planning educators and planners in the United Kingdom, Germany, and other countries (Alterman 1992; Alterman and MacRae 1983; Dagenhart and Sawicki 1992; Garr 1997; Kreditor 1990; Rodríguez-Bachiller 1988).[1] As Alterman illustrates, "A typical European planning student visiting many American planning schools will not discern at first sight that he or she is in a planning program as distinct from a program in political science, economics, or policy analysis" (Alterman 1992: 43). Indeed, while planning for housing is part of planning education and the planning profession in the United States, Canada, Australia, New Zealand, the Netherlands, France, and some Eastern European countries, this is typically not the case in the United Kingdom, Germany, and some other countries in continental Europe (Rodríguez-Bachiller 1988).

The *Guide to Undergraduate and Graduate Education in Urban and Regional Planning*, published by the Association of Collegiate Schools of Planning (ACSP; 2014), lists housing and community development as one of the five most common planning specializations and states as follows:

> Housing planners help develop strategies to increase the supply of affordable housing and expand home ownership among low income or disadvantaged groups. These planners often try to create incentives and remove constraints on private home builders or work with public or non-profit organizations to build housing units for low income families or senior citizens
>
> *(Association of Collegiate Schools of Planning 2014: iii)*

The importance of housing and community development is also visible in the number of scheduled tracks at the ACSP conference. For example, the 58th annual ACSP conference in Buffalo,

New York in October 2018 had 36 scheduled sessions in Track 5, Housing and Community Development, the second highest number of sessions per track (Association of Collegiate Schools of Planning 2018).

Interestingly, the *Core Curriculum of the Association of European Schools of Planning* does not emphasize housing and community development. Rather, it lists somewhat generic core curriculum requirements of planning education in terms of knowledge, practical competence, and attitude without discussing planning for housing. It then states,

> Next to these [,] any planning education should offer its students opportunities to specialise in particular fields of planning such as housing, infrastructure and transport, recreation, land development and building, design and international [,] i.e. [,] European affairs.
>
> *(Association of European Schools of Planning 1995: n.p.)*[2]

This chapter examines the activities of housing educators and planners, based on the description given by the ACSP. First, it focuses on disadvantaged groups; second, it discusses increasing the supply of affordable housing for disadvantaged households; third, it covers expanding homeownership for disadvantaged households; fourth, it explores creating incentives for and removing constraints of private home builders to build housing units for disadvantaged households; and finally, it describes working with public or nonprofit organizations to build housing units for disadvantaged households.

Focusing on Disadvantaged Groups

The three professional (i.e., nonacademic) planning associations in the United States, Europe, and Australia and New Zealand have ethics statements that focus on disadvantaged groups, which are of particular concern for housing planners. Interestingly, the tone of the three associations when addressing these groups is different. First, the American Planning Association (APA) has the following statement in its Ethical Principles in Planning, adopted by the APA Board in May 1992: "Planning Process Participants should [. . .], recognize[e] a special responsibility to plan for the needs of disadvantaged groups and persons [. . .]" as these groups may lack formal organization, resources, or influence (American Planning Association n.d.: n.p.).

The Royal Town Planning Institute (RTPI), which focuses on the United Kingdom and Ireland, has the following statement in its Code of Professional Conduct, last amended by the Board of Trustees in February 2016: "Members must not discriminate on grounds including but not limited to race, nationality, gender, sexual orientation, religion, disability or age. Members must seek to eliminate discrimination by others and promote equality of opportunity throughout their professional activities." (Royal Town Planning Institute 2016: 4).

Finally, the Planning Institute of Australia (PIA), which focuses on Australia and New Zealand, has the following statement in its Code of Professional Conduct, updated in January 2018: "Our Members will [. . .] not discriminate on the grounds of race, creed, gender, age, location, social status or disability" (Planning Institute of Australia 2018: n.p.). In sum, while the three associations focus on disadvantaged groups, the tone of the APA statement appears to be positive ("recognize a special responsibility to plan for"), whereas the tones of the RTPI and PIA statements appear to be negative ("must not discriminate"; "will not discriminate", respectively).

Increasing the Supply of Affordable Housing for Disadvantaged Households

Housing affordability for low-income and/or senior households, which are often renters, has been a concern for housing educators and planners in many countries for decades (Berry et al. 2011, Joint Center for Housing Studies of Harvard University 2017; Watson et al. 2017; Williams 2011). Housing affordability challenges may result in overcrowding or doubling up with family or friends or difficulties meeting expenses related to food, transportation to work, healthcare, and education, among others, possibly resulting in eviction and eventual homelessness (Desmond 2016; Watson et al. 2017).

Housing educators and planners typically focus on measuring housing affordability, which can be measured in multiple ways. First, it can be measured through the housing expenditure-to-income ratio, through which a household with housing costs higher than 30 percent of its income is assumed to be cost-burdened and that a household with housing costs higher than 50 percent of its income is assumed to be severely cost-burdened (Carliner and Marya 2016; Watson et al. 2017; U.S. Department of Housing and Urban Development n.d.a). Second, it can be measured through the housing wage, or the hourly wage required to rent a two-bedroom unit without paying more than 30 percent of a household's income on housing (National Low Income Housing Coalition 2018). Third, it can be measured through the residual income approach, which is the amount of income a household can spend on housing after accounting for other necessary expenditures of living (Stone 2006; 2009a; 2009b).

Housing educators and planners focus on the reasons for the housing affordability challenges of renters, differentiating between the *demand* and the *supply* sides. The absolute and relative increase in the *demand* for affordable housing in multiple countries over the past few years and decades may have been caused by several factors. First, there has been an absolute and relative increase of households in general, due to birth rates being higher than death rates and immigration rates being higher than emigration rates in most of the countries discussed in this chapter (Joint Center for Housing Studies of Harvard University 2014; Steffen et al. 2015). Second, there has been an absolute and relative increase of minority and senior households, which are disproportionately renters (Joint Center for Housing Studies of Harvard University 2017). Third, there has been an absolute and relative increase of renter households with relatively low incomes, especially during and after the Global Financial Crisis (Joint Center for Housing Studies of Harvard University 2017; National Low Income Housing Coalition 2018; Ronald and Lennartz 2020; Watson et al. 2017).

Many potential first-time borrowers have faced difficulties obtaining mortgages due to house prices that have rapidly increased over the past few years and decades versus real household incomes, which have decreased, stagnated, or only moderately increased (National Association of Home Builders 2016; Williams 2011). Another concern is access to a mortgage, as most lenders have become very careful when originating mortgages. For example, in the United States, borrowers with a relatively low credit score still have difficulties gaining access to a mortgage (Urban Institute Housing Finance Policy Center 2019).

Some argue that while there have been some government subsidies for eligible renter households, they have been insufficient. For example, in the United States, programs that are directly geared towards the housing affordability of renters have been Housing Choice Vouchers, HOPE VI, and the U.S. Department of Housing and Urban Development- Veterans Affairs Supportive Housing program (HUD-VASH), among others, although they only serve a fraction of eligible renter households and often come with long wait times (Schwartz 2015). In the United Kingdom, the Right to Buy program has facilitated homeownership for about two million sitting council tenants, although some argue that the program has failed to meet housing needs and it is unclear whether the proceeds have been reinvested in housing (Murie 2016).

The absolute and relative decrease in the *supply* of affordable housing may have been caused by several factors. First, a disproportionate number of affordable rental units have been torn down due to building age, code issues, and relatively little revenue to cover operating and maintenance cost for landlords. For example, in the United States, the loss rate for any rental unit was about 5.6 percent (1.9 million units demolished out of 34.8 million units) between 2001 and 2011, compared to the loss rate of 12.8 percent for units renting for less than $400, 6.7 percent for units renting between $400 and $600, and 3 percent for units renting above $800 per month (Joint Center for Housing Studies of Harvard University 2013).

Second, while there have been policies that support the production of (affordable) housing units, the number of produced units is insufficient. For example, the Low Income Housing Tax Credit (LIHTC) has produced about 3.05 million low-income units since its inception in 1987 (U.S. Department of Housing and Urban Development 2018), but there are still long wait times for affordable housing units (Desmond 2016; Schwartz 2015). Indeed, the median wait time of 320 public housing authorities (PHAs) who responded to a survey administered by the National Low Income Housing Coalition (NLIHC) is nine months, although 25 percent of responding PHAs had a wait time of at least 18 months (Aurand et al. 2016). The largest PHAs had a median wait time of 24 months, although 25 percent of them had wait times of at least 51 months (Aurand et al. 2016). Eleven percent of PHAs who responded to the survey had closed their wait lists (Aurand et al. 2016).

Third, some argue that there has been excessive local government land use regulation, resulting in exclusionary or inclusionary zoning, exemplified by specified features of a building, construction materials, the method of construction, assessing fees on development, or condemning substandard or uninhabitable buildings (Massey et al 2013; Somerville and Mayer 2013). These regulations may increase the quality of housing and thus the quality of life, but they may also decrease the quantity of affordable housing while increasing housing costs, resulting in housing affordability issues (McFate 1999).

Fourth, some argue that there has been excessive profit seeking by landlords, which may occur when profits exceed the "'reasonable return' formula [. . .] as market economics drive the price of housing out of reach for all but the wealthiest" (Gilderbloom 1981: 50/51). Regardless of whether profit seeking is excessive or not, the vast majority of actors in the private sector are unwilling to provide affordable housing without subsidies (Jakabovics et al 2014).

These and other factors have resulted in a scarcity of affordable rental housing. In the United States, only 62 affordable units are available per 100 very-low-income renters and only 38 affordable units are available per 100 extremely-low-income renters (Watson et al. 2017). However, not all affordable units are rented by renters with extremely low incomes.

Expanding Homeownership for Disadvantaged Households

In many countries, most housing educators and planners support homeownership based on the belief that it facilitates wealth building and may be utilized to meet future needs, such as attending college, establishing a business, or retiring (Ronald and Lennartz 2020).

In the United States, homeownership for households has been supported by several policies and programs. The Federal National Mortgage Association (FNMA), known as Fannie Mae, was established in 1938, and the Federal Home Loan Mortgage Corporation (FHLMC), known as Freddie Mac, was established in 1970 (Carr and Anacker 2014). These two government-sponsored enterprises are subject to annual affordable housing goals, which specify their purchases of mortgages for housing that is affordable to low-income and very-low-income households, as specified in the Federal Housing Enterprises Financial Safety and Soundness Act of 1992, amended by the Housing and Economic Recovery Act of 2008 (Carr and Anacker 2014). In terms of policies, the Federal Housing Administration (FHA) provides mortgage insurance for lenders of conventional mortgages for single-family, multifamily, and manufactured homes. Mortgages insured by the FHA require a downpayment of 3.5 percent instead of a conventional downpayment of 20 percent. In return, the borrower has to pay a mortgage insurance premium (U.S. Department of Housing and Urban Development n.d.b).

Somewhat recently, Secretary Ben Carson of the U.S. Department of the Housing and Urban Development worried about the relatively low homeownership rate of first-time homebuyers, many of them Millennials (i.e., people born between 1981 and 1996) (Pew Research Center 2010), stating, "In the 1920s, Hemingway's contemporaries were famously called 'the lost generation.' I worry that Millennials may become a lost generation for homeownership, excluded from the American Dream, pushed as an unintended by-product of the financial crisis of 2008." (Carson 2017: n.p.). In order to facilitate homeownership for first-time home buyers, the Housing Opportunity through Modernization Act of 2016 allowed the FHA to lower its required owner-occupancy standard from 50 to 35 percent for approved condominium developments under certain circumstances (Carson 2017). Also, Fannie Mae somewhat recently announced that it would reduce its debt-to-income ratio to facilitate homeownership (Carson 2017). The question of how many Millennials will actually become homebuyers due to these two policy changes remains.

While the Great Recession ended in June 2009, the labor market has needed a long time to recover, causing Millennials to defer decisions about homeownership, household formation, and children. In 2012, 36 percent of young adults ages 18 to 31 lived with their parents, 23 percent were married, 23 percent had other independent living arrangements, 7 percent lived alone, and 7 percent lived with other kin (Fry 2013). By contrast, in 1981 (1968), 31 (32) percent of young adults ages 18 to 31 lived with their parents, 43 (56) percent were married, 14 (6) percent had other independent living arrangements, 8 (3) percent lived alone, and 4 (4) percent lived with other kin (Fry 2013).

In the United Kingdom, homeownership for disadvantaged households has been supported by the Right to Buy program since 1980 through discounted pricing for buyers, resulting in homeownership opportunities for almost three million tenants (although Scotland and Wales left the program recently; Murie 2016). However, the possibility of Britain's exit from the European Union has added not only economic uncertainty but most likely negatively impacted the homeownership rate (Bingham 2016). In many countries in Eastern Europe, homeownership for disadvantaged households was made possible because the public (U.S. term) or social rental housing (European term) stock was dismantled due to political changes, resulting in very high homeownership rates (Memken and Niemeyer, 2018).

Creating Incentives for and Removing Constraints on Private Home Builders to Build Housing Units for Disadvantaged Households

In order to facilitate the construction of (affordable) housing units, many municipalities have relaxed zoning and regulations by providing density bonuses, resulting in the densification and the retrofitting of many inner cities and mature suburbs, and by allowing tiny or small homes, the conversion of nonresidential structures to affordable housing units, and alternative housing, such as Elder Cottage Housing Opportunity (ECHO) housing, Elder Cottages, Homecare Suites, and Accessory Dwelling Units (ADUs) (Anacker and Niedt, forthcoming).

Recently, some scholars have suggested "bending the cost curve," which will "enable developers to deliver additional affordable rental homes and help jurisdictions provide more housing choices meet the growing need for affordable rentals" (Jakabovics et al. 2014: 8). Suggestions are to promote cost-effectiveness through consolidation, coordination, and simplification; to remove barriers that reduce construction costs and delays; to facilitate a more efficient deal assembly and development timeline; to improve and align incentives; to improve the flexibility of existing sources of financing and create new financial products that better meet needs; and to support the development and dissemination of information and best practices (Jakabovics et al. 2014). Local case studies should be undertaken by researchers to see whether "bending the cost curve" is a feasible approach.

Working with Public or Nonprofit Organizations to Build Housing Units for Disadvantaged Households

Many public and nonprofit organizations have been involved in building housing units for disadvantaged households. For example, in the United States, (nonprofit) community development corporations (CDCs) focus on housing, commercial revitalization, and job training. While CDCs have been in business since the late 19th century, the modern CDC movement traces its origin to 1966, when Senator Robert F. Kennedy authorized the federal antipoverty program to fund CDCs in select neighborhoods. Currently, CDCs are funded through the Community Development Block Grant (CDGB) program (Keating 2012).

Recent discussions in the United States involve the elimination of the $3 billion CDBG program administered by the U.S. Department of Housing and Urban Development, based on the statement that the CDBG "is not well-targeted to the poorest populations and has not demonstrated results" (Quigley 2017: n.p.). Others state that in fiscal year 2016, the CDBG benefited 73,757 households, created or retained 17,545 jobs, and provided public service to 9.2 million Americans (Quigley 2017).

In the United States, some nonprofit organizations may be able to take advantage of the National Housing Trust Fund, which was established in 2008 but has only recently been funded to enable the production, rehabilitation, and preservation of affordable rental housing for eligible residents by an assessment of 0.042 percent of the business volume of government-sponsored strategies for solving housing affordability problems. The Fund requires units, regardless of whether they are owned or rented, to be affordable for at least 30 years. The Fund also encourages reducing costs by employing alternative land use strategies, utilizing new building materials or systems, and taking out low- or no-interest loans and tax credits (National Low Income Housing Coalition 2013). As the Fund is a somewhat recent policy tool, its impacts have not yet been analyzed by policy analysts.

Conclusion

While planning education is taught and the planning profession is practiced all over the world, there are few comparative approaches. Interestingly, Ertur (1990) provides three arguments for a comparative international approach to housing challenges. First, while there are vast differences in physical, socioeconomic, and cultural housing characteristics, there are also similarities. Second, there are differences in the conceptualization and interpretations of housing challenges among and within countries. Third, there have been an increasing number of students who are interested in international affairs. All of these arguments suggest that housing curricula should be adjusted.

Ertur (1990) also argues that cross-cultural and cross-settlement variations in housing result in various policy approaches to housing challenges. Finally, he suggests creating databases at various universities that contain local housing-related information, including housing finance, the housing stock, and housing characteristics. Quantitative analyses could focus on the similarities and differences in the housing landscape, while subsequent policy analyses could focus on action strategies. A networked database would allow planning educators and planning professionals to comparatively and ideally historically analyze housing challenges to design housing policies that are inspired by other countries.

Notes

1 Interestingly, Glasmeier and Kahn's (1989) survey classified nontraditional planners as individuals in fields other than land use planning, current land use planning, regional planning, comprehensive planning, environmental planning, physical planning, social planning, transportation planning, housing human services planning, redevelopment, and general planning.
2 *AESOP Planning Education Number 1: Towards a European Recognition for the Planning Profession* focuses on professional standards, quality assurance, accreditation, and the harmonization of planning education in times of the Bologna process (Geppert and Verhage 2008). *AESOP Planning Education Number 2: Quality Issues in a Changing European Higher Education Area* deals with the evolving landscape for European planning schools; planning between interdisciplinarity, sovereignty, and loss of identity; and the role of AESOP in the promotion of quality in planning education (Geppert and Cotella 2010). *AESOP Planning Education Number 3: Excellence in Planning Education: Local, European, and Global Perspective* focuses on the gradual demise of European diversity in planning, university curricula in urban and regional planning in France, managing planning schools in a time of external and internal strains in Italy, planners in the UK, the European dimension of planners, the Europeanization of planning education and the progression, planning with communities in Italy, the European dimension in planning programs, challenges of planning education in times of globalization, the effect of future trends on international cooperation in planning education in the case of Spain and Latin America, and reflections on the internationalization of urban planning education (Mironowicz 2015). In other words, none of the three documents, while important and interesting, discusses aspects of planning for housing. Unfortunately, the author was unable to access the *AESOP Directory of Planning Schools 2001*. In addition, AESOP does not publish its conference programs on its website.

Further Reading

Anacker, K. B., Carswell, A. T., Kirby, S. D. and Tremblay, K. R. (Eds.). (2018). *Introduction to housing*. Athens, Georgia: University of Georgia Press.
Anacker, K., Nguyen, M. T. and Varady, D. P. (Eds.). (2020). *The Routledge handbook of housing policy and planning*. New York: Routledge.
Bratt, R. G., Stone, M. E., and Hartman, C. (2006). *A right to housing: Foundation for a new social agenda*. Philadelphia, Pennsylvania: Temple University.
Bull, M., & Gross, A. (2018). *Housing in America*. New York: Routledge.
Carswell, A. T. (2012). *The encyclopedia of housing*. Los Angeles, California: SAGE.
Jones, C., and Watkins, C. (2009). *Housing markets and planning policy*. Ames: Wiley-Blackwell.
Molina, E. T. (2017). *Housing America: Issues and Debates*. New York: Routledge.
Schwartz, A. F. (2015). *Housing policy in the United States*. New York: Routledge.

Silverman, R. M., and Patterson, K. L. (Eds.). (2011). *Fair and affordable housing in the U.S.: Trends, outcomes, future directions*. Boston, Massachusetts: Brill.

Tighe, J. R., and Mueller, E. J. (Eds.). (2013). *The affordable housing reader*. New York: Routledge.

References

Alterman, R. (1992). A Transatlantic View of Planning Education and Professional Practice. *Journal of Planning Education and Research*, 12(1), 39–54. doi:10.1177/0739456x9201200105

Alterman, R., & MacRae, D. (1983). Planning and Policy Analysis Converging or Diverging Trends? *Journal of the American Planning Association*, 49(2), 200–215. doi:10.1080/01944368308977064

American Planning Association. (1992). Ethical Principles in Planning. Retrieved from www.planning.org/ethics/ethicalprinciples/

Anacker, K. B. & Niedt, C. (forthcoming). Classifying Regulatory Approaches of Jurisdictions for Accessory Dwelling Units: The Case of Long Island. *Journal of Planning Education and Research*.

Anacker, K. B., Carswell, A. T., Kirby, S., & Tremblay, K. R. (2018). *Introduction to housing*. Athens, Georgia: University of Georgia Press.

Association of Collegiate Schools of Planning (ACSP). (2014). *Guide to Undergraduate and Graduate Education in Urban and Regional Planning*. Retrieved from www.acsp.org/resource/collection/6CFCF359-2FDA-4EA0-AEFA-D7901C55E19C/2014_20th_Edition_ACSP_Guide.pdf

Association of Collegiate Schools of Planning (ACSP). (2018). *58th Annual ACSP Conference Program*. Retrieved from https://cdn.ymaws.com/www.acsp.org/resource/collection/1E387680-3D4A-4EFC-830E-97842B4C4A36/2018conferenceprogram_web_no.pdf

Association of European Schools of Planning (AESOP). (1995). *Core requirements for a high quality European planning education*. Porto, Portugal: Association of European Schools of Planning.

Aurand, A., Emmanuel, D., Yentel, D., Errico, E., Chapin, Z., Leong, G. M., & Rodrigues, K. (2016). *The long wait for a home*. Retrieved from http://nlihc.org/article/housing-spotlight-volume-6-issue-1

Berry, M., Dalton, T., & Nelson, A. (2011). The Impacts of the Global Financial Crisis on Housing and Mortgage Markets in Australia: A View from the Vulnerable. In R. Forrest & N.-M. Yip (Eds.), *Housing markets and the global financial crisis: The uneven impact on households* (pp. 131–149). Northampton: Edward Elgar.

Bingham, J. (2016, October 31). Britain Falls Behind Most of Europe for Home Ownership. *The Telegraph*.

Carliner, M., & Marya, E. (2016). *Rental housing: An international comparison*. Cambridge, Massachussets: Joint Center for Housing Studies of Harvard University. Retrieved from www.jchs.harvard.edu/research/publications/rental-housing-international-comparison

Carr, J. H., & Anacker, K. B. (2014). The Past and Current Politics of Housing Finance and the Future of Fannie Mae, Freddie Mac, and Homeownership in the United States. *Banking and Financial Services Policy Report*, 33(7), 1–10.

Carson, B. (2017). Remarks: National Housing Symposium. Washington, D.C.: U.S. Department of Housing and Urban Development.

Dagenhart, R., & Sawicki, D. (1992). Architecture and Planning: The Divergence of Two Fields. *Journal of Planning Education and Research*, 12(1), 1–16. doi:10.1177/0739456x9201200102

Desmond, M. (2016). *Evicted: Poverty and profit in the American city*. New York: Crown Publishers.

Ertur, O. S. (1990). A Comparative Approach to Housing Problems. In B. Sanyal (Ed.), *Breaking the boundaries: A one-world approach to planning education* (pp. 143–151). New York: Plenum Press.

Fry, R. (2013). *A Rising Share of Young Adults Live in Their Parents' Home: A Record 21.6 Million in 2012*. Washington, DC: Pew Research Center. Retrieved from www.pewsocialtrends.org/2013/08/01/a-rising-share-of-young-adults-live-in-their-parents-home/

Garr, D. (1997). How Much For Housing? Cautionary Indications on The State of Shelter Concerns in Planning Education. *Journal of Planning Education and Research*, 17(2), 178–181. doi:10.1177/0739456x9701700208

Geppert, A., & Cotella, G. (Eds.). (2010). *Quality issues in a changing European higher education area*. Leuven: AESOP.

Geppert, A., & Verhage, R. (Eds.). (2008). *Towards a European recognition for the planning profession* (Vol. 1). Leuven, Belgium: Association of European Schools of Planning.

Gilderbloom, J. I. (1981). Moderate Rent Control: Its Impact on the Quality and Quantity of the Housing Stock. *Urban Affairs Quarterly*, 17(2), 123–142. doi:10.1177/004208168101700201

Glasmeier, A., & Kahn, T. (1989). Planners in the '80s: Who We Are, Where We Work. *Journal of Planning Education and Research, 9*(1), 5–17. doi:10.1177/0739456x8900900101

Jakabovics, A., Ross, L. M., Simpson, M., & Spotts, M. (2014). *Bending the cost curve: Solutions to expand the supply of affordable rentals*. Washington, D.C.: Urban Land Institute.

Joint Center for Housing Studies of Harvard University. (2013). *The state of the nation's housing*. Cambridge, Massachusetts: Joint Center for Housing Studies of Harvard University. Retrieved from www.jchs.harvard.edu/sites/jchs.harvard.edu/files/son2013.pdf

Joint Center for Housing Studies of Harvard University. (2014). *The state of the nation's housing*. Cambridge, Massachusetts: Joint Center for Housing Studies of Harvard University.

Joint Center for Housing Studies of Harvard University. (2017). *America's rental housing: Evolving markets and needs*. Cambridge, Massachusetts: Joint Center for Housing Studies of Harvard University. Retrieved from www.jchs.harvard.edu/research/americas-rental-housing-2017

Keating, W. D. (2012). Community Development Corporations. In A. T. Carswell (Ed.), *The encyclopedia of housing* (pp. 68–70). Los Angeles, California: SAGE.

Kreditor, A. (1990). The Neglect of Urban Design in the American Academic Succession. *Journal of Planning Education and Research, 9*(3), 155–163. doi:10.1177/0739456x9000900301

Massey, D. S., Albright, L., Casciano, R., Derickson, E., & Kinsey, D. N. (2013). *Climbing Mount Laurel: The struggle for affordable housing and social mobility in an American suburb*. Princeton, New Jersey: Princeton University Press.

McFate, K. (1999). General Commentary. *Federal Reserve Bank of New York Economic Policy Review, 5*(3), 171–177.

Memken, J., & Niemeyer, S. (2018). Housing in Europe. In K. B. Anacker, A. T. Carswell, S. Kirby, & K. R. Tremblay (Eds.), *Introduction to housing* (pp. 396–408). Athens, Georgia: University of Georgia Press.

Mironowicz, I. (Ed.) (2015). *AESOP Planning Education Number 3: Excellence in Planning Education: Local, European, and Global Perspective*. Porto, Portugal: Association of European Schools of Planning.

Murie, A. (2016). *The Right to Buy?* Bristol: Policy Press.

National Association of Home Builders. (2016). *The NAHB/Wells Fargo Housing Opportunity Index (1991-current)*. Washington, D.C.: National Association of Home Builders.

National Low Income Housing Coalition. (2013). America's Affordable Housing Shortage, and How to End It. *Housing Spotlight, 3*.

National Low Income Housing Coalition. (2018). *Out of Reach 2018: The High Cost of Housing*. Washington, D.C.: National Low Income Housing Coalition. Retrieved from https://nlihc.org/sites/default/files/oor/OOR_2018.pdf

Pew Research Center. (2010). *Millennials: A Portrait of Generation Next*. Washington, D.C.: Pew Research Center. Retrieved from https://assets.pewresearch.org/wp-content/uploads/sites/3/2010/10/millennials-confident-connected-open-to-change.pdf

Planning Institute of Australia. (2018). *Code of Professional Conduct*. Kingston: Planning Institute of Australia. Retrieved from www.planning.org.au/documents/item/6014

Quigley, A. (2017). Why Trump's Budget Terrifies America's Mayors: New Survey Reveals Anxiety Over Potential Loss of Housing and Transportation Dollars. *Politico*. Retrieved from www.politico.com/magazine/story/2017/04/24/donald-trump-budget-mayors-215067

Rodríguez-Bachiller, A. (1988). *Town planning education: An international survey*. Aldershot: Ashgate Publishing Company.

Ronald, R., & Lennartz, C. (2020). Declining Homeownership in Liberal, English Speaking Countries. In K. B. Anacker, M. T. Nguyen, & D. P. Varady (Eds.), *The Routledge handbook of housing policy and planning* (pp. 117–125). New York: Routledge.

Royal Town Planning Institute (2016). *Code of Professional Conduct: As Last Amended by the Board of Trustees: Effective from 10 February 2016*. London: Royal Town Planning Institute. Retrieved from www.rtpi.org.uk/media/1736907/rtpi_code_of_professional_conduct_-_feb_2016.pdf

Schwartz, A. F. (2015). *Housing policy in the United States*. New York: Routledge.

Somerville, C. T., & Mayer, C. J. (2013). Government Regulation and Changes in the Affordable Housing Stock. *Economic Policy Review, 9*(2), 45–62.

Stone, M. E. (2006). What is Housing Affordability? The Case for the Residual Income Approach. *Housing Policy Debate, 17*(1), 151–184. doi:10.1080/10511482.2006.9521564

Stone, M. E. (2009a). *Renter Affordability in the City of Boston*. Boston, Massachusetts: Center for Social Policy.

Stone, M. E. (2009b). Unaffordable "Affordable" Housing: Challenging the US Department of Housing and Urban Development Area Median Income. *Progressive Planning, 180*(Summer), 36–39.

U. S. Department of Housing and Urban Development (HUD). (n.d.a). *Affordable Housing*. Retrieved from www.hud.gov/program_offices/comm_planning/affordablehousing/

U. S. Department of Housing and Urban Development (HUD). (n.d.b). *Let FHA Loans Help You*. Retrieved from www.hud.gov/buying/loans

U.S. Department of Housing and Urban Development (HUD). (2018). *Low-Income Housing Tax Credits*. Washington, D.C.: U.S. Department of Housing and Urban Development. Retrieved from www.huduser.gov/portal/datasets/lihtc.html

Urban Institute Housing Finance Policy Center. (2019). *Housing Finance at a Glance: A Monthly Chartbook*. Retrieved from www.urban.org/research/publication/housing-finance-glance-monthly-chartbook-march-2019/view/full_report

Watson, N. E., Steffen, B. L., Martin, M., & Vandenbroucke, D. A. (2017). *Worst Case Housing Needs: 2017 Report to Congress*. Washington, D.C.: U.S. Department of Housing and Urban Development. Retrieved from www.huduser.gov/portal/sites/default/files/pdf/Worst-Case-Housing-Needs.pdf

Williams, P. (2011). The Credit Crunch in the UK: Understanding the Impact on Housing Markets, Policies and Households. In R. Forrest & N.-M. Yip (Eds.), *Housing markets and the global financial crisis: The uneven impact on households* (pp. 41–56). Northampton: Edward Elgar Publishing.

24
URBAN DESIGN

Barbara Faga

Introduction

Sociopolitical power drives the design of cities. Penn's plan for Philadelphia (1683), McMillan's Washington DC Mall (1901), the New York City grid (1811), and Haussmann's plan for Paris (1853) all exemplify this principle. Without the power granted him by Napoléon III, how could Haussmann clear 12,000 buildings to build sewers, reservoirs, and aqueducts, install train tracks, and construct 137 km of boulevards while designing 27 new parks? Moreover, planners are generally held accountable for shaping development: "The fact is that no city, however arbitrary its form may appear to us, can be said to be *unplanned*" (Kostof 1991, p 52). *The City Shaped*, Kostof's study of the evolution of cities, reinforces the power of planning: "Power designs cities, and the rawest form of power is control over urban land." Legates (1998) further echoed the reality that power is what drives design throughout history: "City building has preoccupied kings and cardinals, mayors and burghers for thousands of years. But it was only in the modern period that urban planning became an accepted profession and a well-defined field of study."

Higher education has merged the arts of design, planning, and administration into a curriculum that can underwrite urban design practice. Power, influence, and a desire to protect the health and safety of cities fueled the formation of the urban planning profession in 1909. Architects, landscape architects, and, at times, even engineers refer to their services as *planning and urban design*, and urban designers, properly empowered, hold the keys to the character and direction of cities' evolution. Edward Bacon, mid-20th century preeminent planner, defined urban design as follows:

> The planners have traditionally considered the design of physical structures as a detail. Administrators almost invariably think in terms of specific projects and procedures rather than the underlying correlative relationships. What we need is the architect-planner-administrator, and if we ever get it we will then really have an urban designer
>
> (Progressive Architecture, *1956*)[1]

Gamble and Heyda (2016) further describe the complexities through case studies of fifteen U.S. redevelopment projects: "The discipline involves conceptualizing permanent constructions or landscape systems incorporating multiple buildings, blocks or spaces with connections to infrastructural systems."

Foundations of Urban Design

The struggle for control and power over city planning has a long history. The first vestiges of urban design were proclaimed by King Philip II of Spain in 1573 with his 148 *Ordinances* for design in the Americas:

> The main plaza is to be the starting point of the town: if the town is situated on the sea coast, it should be placed at the landing place of the port, but inland it should be at the center of the town . . . it should be square or rectangular . . . as this shape is best for fiestas
>
> *(Hack, 2018)*

In 1899, the Technical University of Berlin became the first recorded location for formal design lectures in education. Joseph Brix and Felix Genzmer began their "Städtebauliche Vorträge" lectures by defining the profession as "the progressive science of technology, health and economics" (Bodenschatz 2011, p 28). The lectures gained importance as Brix and Genzmer further explored urban design as a discipline encompassing the study of art, science, and engineering. Urban design was established as an international practice when global participants assembled for the Berlin 1910 International Urban Design Exhibition. When Berlin began offering urban design classes in 1908, universities also established their own schools (Bodenschatz 2011).

Thomas Adams, the British planner, described *civic design* at the Third National Conference on City Planning (Boston 1911) by challenging the attendees to:

> Plan the town, if you like; but in doing it do not forget that you have got to spread the people . . . Make wider roads, but do not narrow the tenements behind. Dignify the city, but not at the expense of the health of the home and the family life and the comfort of the average workman and citizen . . . If you do this, we all of us shall be rewarded by the betterment of our towns, the beautification of our streets, the improvement of our suburbs; we shall have made one step forward to still further elevating, improving, and dignifying the life of our citizens.[2]

The City Beautiful movement reached its zenith from 1890 to 1920, fostering the enhancement of cities for flâneurs with the addition of Olmsted and Vaux's Central Park plan (1858) and Chicago's Burnham Plan (1909) (Cullingworth and Caves, 2014). British designer Ebenezer Howard founded the modern town planning movement with Letchworth and Welwyn, the garden city suburbs of London, in the early 1900s as the ideal of community-based housing and safe development.[3] John Nolen, the Harvard-educated landscape architect and planner, designed Mariemont, the 1923 Utopian village garden city in the Cincinnati suburbs.[4] Clarence Stein's 1929 plan for Radburn, NJ, is considered "an exemplar of the (planning) profession's principles but also its design became a steady resource for practitioners" (Birch 1980, p 146). Each of these town plans is an early illustration of New Urbanism, with short, mixed-use blocks and a residential and retail community (Rogers 2001). By 1950, lawyers and engineers had wrested control of city building from the City Beautiful architects, landscape architects, and artists to form the City Efficient movement (Cullingworth and Caves 2014).

Urban design emerged as a form of study in the United States in 1956, at the Harvard-sponsored First Urban Design Conference. The intent of the conference was to gather and merge the work of architects, landscape architects, and urban planners into an accepted practice. Specialists including economists, ecologists, historic preservationists, lawyers, and engineers were asked to contribute their expertise to planning teams. But it was the urban designers who were charged with knowing enough about each of those professions to understand how they intersect to create cities. "Urban design is that part of city planning which deals with the physical form of the city," José Luis Sert famously asserted to attendees at this First Urban Design Conference.[5] Sert, the dean of Harvard's Graduate School of Design (GSD) from 1953 to 1969, described the new profession as "the most creative phase of city planning and that in which imagination and artistic capacities can play a more important part" (Krieger 2009). In *Urban Design* (2009), Krieger and Saunders outline the foundation and movement of urban design in practice and academia explaining that it is "the urban designers, not the planner, who has emerged as the place-centered professional with *urban design* often assuming a friendlier, more acceptable popular connotation then *planning*."

Lofty Goals, Quotidian Challenges

Universities frequently encounter the complicated task of educating planners for a profession that requires an often-dizzying set of skills. Planners are expected to know something about everything, ranging from administration to zoning, and to understand a language that is both quantitative and qualitative – all while keeping the community and politicians involved. At times, it appears that planning practice has devolved from the goal of ensuring health and safety by protecting the population from industrial uses and pollution, to a derided example of government inefficiency.

Critics disparage planning for not achieving its goal of making cities better, viewing it instead as separating cities into poorly developed islands of bureaucracy. Ben-Joseph (2005, p 115) summarizes the discussion as follows:

> The planning profession has generally been reluctant to champion physical design, largely because of an ideological commitment to social-science based disciplines as the foundation for urban planning education and practice. This has resulted in the marginalization of urban design and physical planning to the point that it all but disappeared from urban planning curricula. Physical planning tasks have been turned over to others following the formulas of local codes and regulations. This has not only created a one-dimensional approach to planning, but it has also rendered planning practices inadequately prepared to deal with current environmental and development trends.

Inadequate, one-dimensional and *marginalized* are damning and tough criticisms of the planning profession. Architects, planners, and urban designers have long agitated to take back the design of cities from social scientists, lawyers, and engineers. Sitte argued against symmetry as a monotonous protocol implemented by engineers, and advocated for the freeform design of public space (Collins 2006). Le Corbusier (1987) opposed Sitte's work, contrasting freeform design with his own ironically brutalist, concrete formal organization of buildings. The planning profession today can be viewed as a tentative alliance that combines "soft" and "brutal" principles along with design and social issues for maximum efficiency.

New York City has historically been the U.S. leader in shaping form and development. The city's 1915 zoning code and subsequent leadership improvements to performance-based design drew praise from Ada Louise Huxtable, a prominent architecture critic for the New York Times: "The city you see is to a great extent the city that zoning makes" (1971). Barnett (1974) described New York's innovative design regulations implemented since the 1960s, which legitimized urban design by implementing incentives including: (1) placement and scale of buildings to fit into existing neighborhoods; (2) bonusing for building plaza spaces, referred to as the *tower in the park* theory; (3) bonuses for building streetscape and open space; and (4) special districts that identify land use and design districts.[6] For example, special districts were created to guide specific design and land use in prominent areas of the city. The 1982 Special Midtown District (MiD) required that the Times Square Great White Way building facades include oversized illuminated signs, and protected historic theaters in the Theater SubDistrict from demolition.[7]

However, planning progress is not limited to big cities in the United States. Beaufort, South Carolina, won acclaim for its "localism," described as enabling urban design that is "rooted in participatory democracy, utiliz(ing) electronic media to structure and extend democratic debate." The results are "clear implementation strategies and regulations through the use of form-based or design coding." Online town halls to discuss the attributes of rezoning are a new trend that "is a clear advancement of design-based planning in the USA." Though very different in essence and in context, both Beaufort and New York illustrate the advancement of the intersection of planning and urban design (Walters 2011, p 216).

In a 1992 retrospective, McHarg described his 1969 *Design With Nature* as a look at conserving natural systems, and concluded that over the next 20 years "Events far exceeded predictions" (p v). Sustainability is described in relation to urban design as protection and preservation of the natural environmental infrastructure.[8] Palazzo and Steiner (2011) address environmental, sustainability and urban design issues by reinforcing the need for equal focus on ecology and density. Thompson and Steiner (1997) summarize: "Planning that strives for fitness between people and the landscape. . . is one of the promising ways to reestablish the form and content of the dialogue between human and natural processes" (p 30). The sprawl-versus-urbanism-versus-sustainable-environments debate added ecology and sustainability to the mix, and in 2011, the discourse broadened to become a *landscape urbanism* versus urban design discussion that appears to be ongoing (although many planners dismiss it a distraction).[9]

Educating Urban Designers

The debate over planning as *either* a design *or* a social-science profession was first discussed at the Columbia University on Planning in 1928.[10] Participants were petitioned to depart from educating planners as "masters of many subjects" and return to their foundations as masters of design (Krueckeberg 1985). Through the 1930s, U.S. planning schools were primarily housed within architecture colleges. In 1940, the University of North Carolina was the first to establish a planning school independent of a design overview, followed by the University of Chicago in 1949 (Hemmens 1988). The location of where planning, architecture, and urban design reside within academia is a long-standing dilemma, that some may classify as a feud (Anselin, Nasar and Talen 2011; Dagenhart and Sawicki 1992; Inam 2002). Others see the research emphasis at best as irrelevant and at worst as a threat to achieving excellence in professional education and practice" (Forsyth 2007).

Direct or Indirect Urban Design

Typically, students are offered two education paths that will determine what the graduate can do in the profession: (1) direct urban design, and (2) indirect urban design as a planner, often employed by the public sector, who convenes, reviews, and influences shape and form (Barnett, 1974).

"Qualifying as an urban designer without the design degree . . . (is) an issue," Antonin Nelessen (2017) says of his Rutgers graduate students with an urban design concentration. "(Urban design) is the vision that students want, and they are looking for ways to qualify themselves." Nelessen faults planners for zoning that "has produced the ugly stuff," as evidenced by the work of many New Urbanist architects. Students register early and quickly fill his *Introduction to Design* classes because they desire knowledge of design and the requisite supporting portfolio. While Nelessen clearly states that graduates will not qualify as professional urban designers, they do attain planning positions with design overview.

During the 1990s, the Atlanta, GA office of landscape architecture, urban design, and planning firm EDAW (now part of the engineering firm AECOM) often interviewed Georgia Tech School of Urban and Regional Planning (SCARP) graduates who presented their certificates in urban design as an entry to the design firm. Often, these candidates were operating under the illusion that they were proficient urban designers. When teamed with architects and landscape architects, however, they were dismayed to find they could not compete. Recently, Georgia Tech's College of Design (which houses SCARP) moved their urban design degree exclusively within their School of Architecture (Heath 2017). Denise Scott Brown noted that like most firms who employ urban designers, "We rarely hired people with urban design qualifications into our firm. I prefer to find architects who have both visual and verbal abilities and three or four years of architectural experience. Then I train them in urban design" (Brown 2009, p 82).

"Urban design should be at the center, as the critical intersection of the planning discipline to create the dimensional world we live in," says Jacinta McCann, AECOM's Design, Planning + Economics Director (2017). Exemplifying this principle, the Harvard GSD/AECOM China Project is in its third round of joint program partnering. Three 16-week semester studios examined Xiamen as a case study to research hyper-urbanization for *Common Frameworks: Rethinking the Developmental City in China* (Lee, 2013). McCann describes students who will grab images online to pull together representative 3-D views, and compile them into drawings. The result is a conceptual visioning plan that appears finished and comparable to a design development phase plan. While the product is helpful for students, McCann notes that "Clients expect to see urban designers draw; that is what they think they pay you to do."

Planning evolved throughout the 1950s from Sert's vision of planning as a physical plan to reside (perhaps more rationally) within the social sciences. Planning education continued to shift its focus from design and land use to social science and administrative policy through the 1980s. Social science emerged as the basis for planning, with schools offering a modicum of basic design instruction. Designers moved back to architecture and landscape architecture schools, separated and unrelated to planning. During this time, many schools dismissed zoning and design altogether as unrelated byproducts of the planning practice, with the result that planners educated over the second half of the last century are quick to express their lack of understanding or even interest in design, scale, and form. They do not understand site plans, read a scale nor do they know how many square feet are in an acre.

Lynch's *The Image of the City* (1960), with its vision of paths, nodes, landmarks, districts and edges, is the structural "glue" of planning, urban design practice and education. Many designers consider the lack of inclusion of Lynch in basic planning theory as a missed opportunity for planners to understand the physical design framework of the city.[11] While planning schools surrendered interest and involvement in the physical design of cities for the administration of government programs and social science, architects and landscape architects added *planning and urban design* to their business cards to sell full-service teams. In effect, planners relegated themselves to administrative desk jobs (Hemmens 1988).

Anselin, Nasar and Talen (2011) found that overall academia was satisfied with the planning/design disconnect, noting that "The administrative relationship between planning and architecture seems volatile" (p 196). Their survey of 181 planning professors concluded that planning faculty are "more satisfied professionally" in a non-design school rather than a design-related school (p 204).[12] The differences included: (1) design school faculty promotions are based on publishing in non-peer-reviewed journals and exhibitions, as opposed to planning faculty promotions primarily on juried articles; (2) differing views of the influence of the importance of design influence on social policy, and (3) designers being focused on building owners and developer clients, as opposed to planners' interest in solving societal issues. Their results appear to support the movement of education from design to social and administrative policy.

Planning Education Follows Practice

From 1990 through 2010, design returned to the forefront as *starchitecture* (often referred to as The Bilbao Effect after the lauded branch of the Frank Gehry designed Guggenheim art museum in that city). Robert A. M. Stern, FAIA, dean of the Yale School of Architecture, established a preeminent school of design, while heading his firm offering planning and urban design services to international clients. Emulating Burnham's City Beautiful movement of the prior century, cities began the clean-up of their overlooked yet still venerated historic public space, as evidenced by the restoration of New York's Bryant Park and Times Square, along with Chicago's Michigan Avenue.

The New Urbanists, including Professors Emily Talen and Randell Arendt, architect practitioner Andres Duany, and architect and former dean of the design school at the University of Miami, Elizabeth Plater-Zyberk, are acknowledged as leading the resurgence of urban design. New Urbanists placed blame squarely on planning practice and education for the lack of design and form enacted by conventional zoning and the subsequent resulting suburban monotony. Inam (2002) criticized the urban design profession as superficial, obsessed with design while lacking understanding of cities' socioeconomic issues. Denise Scott Brown criticized academia's attempt to educate planners (specifically the University of Pennsylvania) with the accusation that "The areas of questioning had to do with discovering how people actually lived and wanted to live in cities, as opposed to how planners felt they ought to live" (2009, p 72).

Despite such criticisms, design and planning practitioners remain the acknowledged global problem-solvers. In 2007, the Rockefeller Foundation convened 100 public and private sector urbanists for their 2007 Global Urban Summit at their Bellagio Center, and declared the 21st century the Century of the City.[13] The Foundation's goal was to "create approaches and the urgent agenda for harnessing the vast opportunities of urbanization for a better world." Focused on "solving 21st century urban challenges," the summit honored Jane Jacobs' prediction that "In order for a society to flourish there must be a flourishing city at its core" (Jacobs 1961).

Planetizen, the U.S. based planning website, hosts an online list of 64 schools offering graduate degrees in planning with an urban design specialization, as listed in Table 24.1. Undergraduate planning schools with an urban design specialization are listed in Table 24.2. Students with an undergraduate degree in professional design (architecture or landscape architecture) have an understandably stronger design capability compared to those without such experience. With computer graphics programs, students may imagine they become "instant designers" by mastering a few keystrokes and commands, yet they lack understanding of design fundamentals. Students who become familiar with design through graphics classes are made aware of the discrepancy in their urban design education when they participate in studios. Those holding a professional design degree understand the importance of researching precedents and comparable projects while envisioning spatial aspects. In studio, when planning students questioned the value of precedents, the student with an architect degree defended the research by explaining; "It is too hard to create something from nothing." The architects and landscape architects are familiar with the language and form of design, and with the construction process. Those without a similar background soon understand they are not equipped to be urban designers by replacing a professional four- or five-year design program with a few classes and credits.

McHarg's *Design With Nature* (1992) is central to understanding the basis of design using Geographic Information Systems (GIS). McHarg used his 1960–1970s layering drawing technique as the foundation of design long before GIS was a computerized basis for data. Graphics and GIS classes remain in high demand, and schools are beginning to specify them as required degree credits. Computer-Aided Design and Drafting (CADD), along with three-dimensional drawing software such as SketchUp and Rhino, are valuable tools for envisioning and understanding the planning process. Students without an undergraduate degree in architecture or landscape architecture learn how to build site plans using graphic software packages. Juan Ayala, who teaches extensive graphics and design classes to Rutgers graduate students, says "They learn to compose at the same time they produce site design, instead of using the programs to apply a pretty graphic at the end of the design process. They portray buildings and public space in graphic form using images of architectural and landscape form gathered from the internet," not exactly informed urban design, but a good skill to have for a practicing urban planner.

Table 24.1 Graduate Planning Schools with an Urban Design Specialization

Country	University	Program	Location
Australia	La Trobe University	Master of Spatial Planning, Management and Design	Bendigo VIC
Australia	University of New South Wales	Master of City Planning	Sydney NSW
Australia	University of Sydney	Master of Urban and Regional Planning	Sydney NSW
Canada	McGill University	Master of Urban Planning	Montréal QC
Sweden	Lulea University of Technology	Master of Science in Climate Sensitive Urban Planning and Building	Lulea
Sweden	Royal Institute of Technology	Master of Science in Urban Planning and Design	Stockholm
United Kingdom	London South Bank University	Master of Arts in Urban Planning Design	London
United Kingdom	University College London	Master of Science in Urban Design and City Planning	London
United Kingdom	University of Liverpool	Master of Civic Design in Town and Regional Planning	Liverpool
United Kingdom	University of Liverpool	Master of Arts in Town and Regional Planning	Liverpool
United Kingdom	University of Sheffield	Master of Arts in Urban Design and Planning	Sheffield
United States	Arizona State University	Master of Urban and Environmental Planning	Tempe AZ
United States	Auburn University	Master of Community Planning	Auburn AL
United States	Ball State University	Master of Urban and Regional Planning	Muncie IN
United States	Boston University	Master of City Planning	Boston MA
United States	California Polytechnic State University, San Luis Obispo	Master of City and Regional Planning	San Luis Obispo CA
United States	California State Polytechnic University, Pomona	Master of Urban and Regional Planning	Pomona CA
United States	Catholic University of America	Master of City and Regional Planning	Washington DC
United States	Clemson University	Master of City and Regional Planning	Clemson SC
United States	Cornell University	Master of Regional Planning	Ithaca NY
United States	Florida State University	Master of Science in Planning	Tallahassee FL
United States	Georgetown University	Master of Professional Studies in Urban & Regional Planning	Washington DC
United States	Georgia Institute of Technology	Master of City and Regional Planning	Atlanta GA

Country	University	Program	Location
Australia	La Trobe University	Master of Spatial Planning, Management and Design	Bendigo VIC
United States	Harvard University	Master in Urban Planning	Cambridge MA
United States	Hunter College, City University of New York	Master in Urban Planning	New York NY
United States	Iowa State University	Master of Community and Regional Planning	Ames IA
United States	Jackson State University	Master of Arts in Urban and Regional Planning	Jackson MS
United States	Kansas State University	Master of Regional and Community Planning	Manhattan KS
United States	Massachusetts Institute of Technology	Master in City Planning	Cambridge MA
United States	Michigan State University	Master in Urban and Regional Planning	East Lansing MI
United States	Morgan State University	Master of City and Regional Planning	Baltimore MD
United States	New Jersey Institute of Technology	Master of Infrastructure Planning	Newark NJ
United States	Northern Arizona University	Master of Science of Applied Geospatial Sciences – Emphasis in Planning	Flagstaff AZ
United States	Rutgers, The State University of New Jersey	Master of City and Regional Planning	New Brunswick NJ
United States	San José State University	Master of Urban Planning	San José CA
United States	Savannah State University	Master of Urban Studies and Planning	Savannah GA
United States	The Ohio State University	Master of City and Regional Planning	Columbus OH
United States	The University of Memphis	Master of City and Regional Planning	Memphis TN
United States	Tufts University	Master of Arts in Urban and Environmental Policy and Planning	Medford MA
United States	University at Buffalo, State University of New York	Master of Urban Planning	Buffalo NY
United States	University of Arizona	Master of Science in Planning	Tucson AZ
United States	University of California, Berkeley	Master of City Planning	Berkeley CA
United States	University of California, Irvine	Master of Urban and Regional Planning	Irvine CA
United States	University of California, Irvine	Master of Environmental Engineering	Irvine CA
United States	University of California, Los Angeles	Master of Urban and Regional Planning	Los Angeles CA
United States	University of Cincinnati	Master of Community Planning	Cincinnati OH
United States	University of Colorado Denver	Master of Urban and Regional Planning	Denver CO
United States	University of Florida	Master of Urban and Regional Planning	Gainesville FL
United States	University of Hawaii at Manoa	Master of Urban and Regional Planning	Honolulu HI
United States	University of Idaho	Master of Bioregional Planning and Community Design	Boise ID
United States	University of Michigan	Master of Urban Planning	Ann Arbor MI

(continued)

Table 24.1 (continued)

Australia	La Trobe University	Master of Spatial Planning, Management and Design	Bendigo VIC
United States	University of Minnesota	Master of Urban and Regional Planning	Minneapolis MN
United States	University of New Mexico	Master of Community and Regional Planning	Albuquerque NM
United States	University of New Orleans	Master of Urban and Regional Planning	New Orleans LA
United States	University of Oregon	Master of Community and Regional Planning	Eugene OR
United States	University of Pennsylvania	Master of City Planning	Philadelphia PA
United States	University of South Florida	Master of Urban and Regional Planning	Tampa FL
United States	University of Southern California	Master of Planning	Los Angeles CA
United States	University of Toledo	Master of Arts in Geography and Planning	Toledo OH
United States	University of Utah	Master of City and Metropolitan Planning	Salt Lake City UT
United States	University of Virginia	Master of Urban and Environmental Planning	Charlottesville VA
United States	University of Washington	Master of Urban Planning	Seattle WA
United States	University of Wisconsin – Milwaukee	Master of Urban Planning	Milwaukee WI
United States	Virginia Tech	Master of Urban and Regional Planning	Blacksburg VA

Table 24.2 Undergraduate Planning Schools with an Urban Design Specialization

United Kingdom	University College London	Bachelor of Science in Urban Planning, Design and Management	London
United States	Iowa State University	Bachelor of Science in Community and Regional Planning	Ames IA
United States	Rutgers, The State University of New Jersey	Bachelor of Science in Urban Planning and Design	New Brunswick NJ
United States	University of Missouri - Kansas City	Bachelor of Arts in Urban Planning and Design	Kansas City MO
United States	University of New Mexico	Bachelor of Arts in Environmental Planning and Design	Albuquerque NM
United States	University of Virginia	Bachelor of Urban and Environmental Planning	Charlottesville VA

Source: Planetizen school directory. www.planetizen.com/search-schools/?f[0]=sm_field_prog_degree%3AGraduate&f[1]=sm_field_prog_discipline%3AUrban%20Planning&f[2]=im_field_prog_specialization%3A30984

Lecture versus Studio versus Online Learning

Schools throughout the European Union, China, United States, and Australia are remarkably similar in their class list and syllabus approach to educating students in design concentrations. According to professors with multi-cultural experience, lectures on urban design policy and practice vary minimally by country and culture but delivery, however, may be different. Lecturers mention that students in Asia and the EU are more inclined to sit through a two-hour lecture on a specific design topic, while U.S. students prefer more interactive discussion.[14] EU professors report they adjust their teaching style while in the U.S. to include more time for interaction and shortened lectures, intimating students are more engaged by active participation.

Studios are the ballast of urban design education. Inam (2002) focused the pedagogical approach to studios on an equal mix of research, community outreach, and cross-cultural learning. Macdonald (2013) describes their benefits as "work(ing) together for extended periods in a dedicated work space," and "foster(ing) joint learning at the same time that (they) allow and encourage individual creative development and expression." Teamwork is the primary goal of studio. Students learn how to collaborate in an office-like setting to solve design problems for a real or fictional client. Professors differ as to whether it is best to work through an actual client, or consider studio as the last opportunity to imagine a solution without the realities of client, scope, and fee. Either option is an opportunity to design a framework and communicate solutions by producing a drawing, report, video, or presentation. Studios are the opportunity to work in a collegial atmosphere within a given time frame while benefiting from the comradery and cultural interaction with others.

This sample of courses available during the spring semester 2017 exemplifies the variety of studio choices:

- Harvard GSD, *Savannah: Rethinking the Multi-Scalar Capacity of the City Project*, "The studio's work is situated within a line of research of the GSD, 'Re-visiting Urban Grids,' and

must allow discussion of the tradition of the regular city and its current potential for the design of the city today."[15]
- University of Pennsylvania, *Paris Modern: Spiral City*, "The aim of the class will be to provide conceptual and pragmatic (visual, experiential) links between a number of texts, theories and films deploying various concepts of the modern in Paris, with a guided tour of the main places discussed."[16]
- Georgia Institute of Technology, *Tokyo Smart City Studio Project for a 2020 Olympics Site*, "The project aims to develop a smart and ecologically sound community as a pilot project to demonstrate how a smart city is designed, evaluated, and financed in Japan."[17]
- University of California, Berkeley, *Old Oak Common, London/Oakland*, "The studio will develop urban design plans for two sites. One is for Old Oak Common in West London. This is a brownfield site crisscrossed by railway lines and the location for a major transit hub with a new station for both Crossrail and the future High Speed 2 rail line serving London and the North. Old Oak Common is a real project currently being proposed by the Greater London Authority (GLA) with a detailed programme to build over 10,000 new housing units and employment for construction of five million square feet. Downtown Oakland could be a site for similar growth particularly if the I-980 freeway corridor is used as the path for the new Transbay line. The 250-acre site could connect Downtown Oakland with the currently isolated West Oakland and repair damage done by the now discredited 1960 era policies of urban renewal and urban freeways."[18]
- Rutgers University, *NEC FUTURE*, "To identify a dramatically different mix of design, land use and development along the 2040 North East Corridor (NEC) rail from Washington, DC to Boston and how it will impact future economic development. The Preferred Alternative for the NEC FUTURE Rail Investment Plan was released December 2016. This semester we will work with the U.S. Department of Transportation, Federal Railroad Administration (FRA) and their consultant AECOM on the Northeast Corridor vision plan. The Federal Railroad Administration recommends a vision to build a better Northeast Corridor over the next several decades and releases the Tier 1 Final Environmental Impact Statement (EIS) for NEC FUTURE."[19]

Online opportunities are available for advanced urban design education and certification upon graduation. Planetizen's online courses in urban design are the most-viewed courses offered, and include: *Software Tools, Neighborhoods and Transects, Connectivity and Design Interventions, Neighborhood Centers, Neighborhood Edges, Mix and Diversity, Proximity and Density*, and finally *Parking and Traffic*.[20] The series instructor offers what could be interpreted as an overstated goal: "With our knowledge about planning principles and the design of place in hand, these communication tools fundamentally change who can claim the role of urban designer." Coursera online offers *Designing Cities*, created by the University of Pennsylvania's PennDesign, estimated to have enrolled over 70,000 participants since 2013. Forty percent are experienced with city building, with the remainder interested in ancillary studies. Over 5,000 students have completed the peer-graded program.[21] Classes include *How Today's City Evolved: The Ideas That Shape Cities, Tools for Designing Cities, Making Cities Sustainable, Preserving Older Cities, Designing New Cities, Districts and Neighborhoods*, and *Visionary Cities*, each in 12-minute modules.[22] APA offers online classes and sponsors a newly created AICP Certified Urban Designer (AICP/CUD) specialty certification. Requirements include: (1) AICP certification; (2) eight years of urban design experience; and (3) three 500-word essays on personal project criteria, working across constituencies on urban design issues.[23]

Beijing, Cincinnati, Atlanta, Milan, and New Brunswick program comparisons

China's expansion of city regions has been well-documented by the United Nations (Laquian 2008) and the Rockefeller Foundation (Peirce 2008), as Asian nations looked to designers to address societal inequalities in cities and their rapid economic growth with efforts at community-building (Abramson 2006). In the 1940s, Tsinghua University was the first to establish *civic design* as a discipline. Their Master of Urban Planning (MUP) degree is in their School of Architecture. The Professional Master in Urban and Rural Planning (MURP) includes classes in GIS and new technologies. Along with MURP, urban design is part of the School of Architecture. Tang and Hack (2017) describe the long-standing joint MIT and Tsinghua studio themes as:

> the search for structural approaches to large-scale urban development; the recovery of urban ecologies as a force in shaping urban development; the transformation of obsolete industrial areas into mixed-use urban districts; and the integration of urbanization and agriculture on the edges of cities.

Established in 2009, the annual studios are credited with the impact on urban design education and local government policy by changing the status quo, quite a feat for the design studios.

The University of Cincinnati offers a certificate in urban design within their Bachelor of Urban Planning (BUP) five-year professional degree program, and a joint six-year combined Bachelor of Urban Planning/Master of Community Planning (BUP/MCP) option. Urban design classes include topics in place-making, design elements, urbanism, the contemporary city and fragmentation, inclusiveness, and urban transformation. Their *cooperative education* program represents a unique opportunity. Founded in 1906, the program augments classes with professional in-office practice every other semester (within a year-round schedule), offering five semesters as a working internship for the five-year program.[24] School of Planning Director Danilo Palazzo describes co-op as the *reality studio*, offering students in-office experience and job placement in high-profile offices including Sasaki and Design Collective. Palazzo, formerly with Politecnico di Milano, mentions that his "U.S. teaching style is completely different," noting that his two-hour lecture on Kevin Lynch is "popular in Milan and now shortened to 40 minutes" for his current students.

The Georgia Institute of Technology recently established a Master of Science in Urban Design (MSUD) as a one-year, three-semester program, relocating the degree to their School of Architecture. Formerly, urban design was a certificate offered through the SCARP. The new MSUD includes two planning classes (Growth Management Law and Principles of Real Estate Finance) along with studios and theory of design classes. It is described as having a threefold emphasis that includes planning:

> To build a culture of collaboration linking requisite knowledge and expertise across fields of architecture, planning, landscape, and engineering; to enable analysis of complex problem sets occupying nebulous zones beyond the limits of a single building, owner, or site; and to facilitate the design of integrated and implementable solutions, whether comprised of structures or systems; of policies, processes, or plans.[25]

The Master of Science degree in urban planning and policy design at the Politecnico di Milano is described as a twofold program. Combining urban management in housing, transport, and environment along with design, urbanism, and contemporary urban policies, its graduates are well-suited to employment in local government and private firms. The courses are taught in English and comparable to the U.S. programs. Their program is directed toward international students from the Middle East, Australia, China, and India, in addition to the EU. Masters classes for the two-year program include contemporary city social change and policies; infrastructure planning and design; land use ethics and the law; EU regional urban policy; economics of public issues; urban ethnography; housing and neighborhoods; digital cities and urban planning, urban and planning history; workshops/studios; and final thesis.

In addition to their Master of City and Regional Planning (MCRP) Rutgers University's Bloustein School of Planning and Public Policy offers a Bachelor of Science in Urban Planning and Design, described as four-year program uniting "all the built environment professions, including urban planning, landscape architecture, architecture, civil and municipal engineering, and focus(ing) on the design, quality, character and appearance of places."[26] Encompassing classes in transportation, graphics, communication, and studios, the degree includes nine credits of design classes. A streamlined path to a MCRP degree includes an urban design track with classes in planning and design, studios, and real estate finance. Students apply their sophomore year, and take their Graduate Record Examinations in the third year to complete the five-year program.

What is the Future?

Practitioners often believe that planning is the process of "muddling through" (Lindblom 1959) a "wicked problem" (Rittel and Webber 1973). Indeed, practice as "civic theater" is how Faga (2006) examines this dynamic and concludes in part that a more rational method may be to return to design as a problem-solving activity, as Rand described in his *Politics of Design* (1985). This chapter was prefaced by the idea that socio-politically, "planning is power;" planning practitioners wishing to exert the full influence of that power are increasingly driven to acknowledge the significance of design. And universities, attempting to empower students as they embark on their careers, are following suit.

Technology in Service of Design

Although education may not be changing as rapidly as practice, neither does it stand as still as we sometimes believe. It is clear that design as a critical component is enjoying a resurgence. This extends to issues of sustainability perhaps most famously pioneered by Patrick Geddes in his *Cities in Evolution* (1915), which examined the relationship between the countryside and the metropolis and pioneered civics as a new field of sociology. Fast forward several decades to the 1970s, when practitioners used pin bars to layer acetate drawings depicting natural and built systems as the foundations of design. In the 1980s, GIS became the technology that transposed these overlays into systems that let designers plan millions of acres. Higher education continues to offer the newest and best avenues to creative thinking with new software and design competitions. Space Syntax and City CAD added reality to the generation of planners who learned about city planning from SimCity. Students assemble teams of architects, landscape architects, planners, MBAs and urban designers to compete for the Urban Land Institute (ULI) Hines Urban Design Competition, HUD and other named competitions. The 2017 ULI winning team from the University of Texas was awarded their $50,000 annual prize, and a Rutgers team won the HUD 2017 Affordable Housing Competition award of $20,000.[27] Placemaking, live-projects, living labs, and a wealth of new books and online journals are on the increase. The paradigm shift is toward cultural and coastal resiliency studios in Florida, New Jersey, Mexico, Taiwan, and China (Watson 2002).

In 2009, GeoDesign was introduced at the Environmental Systems Research Institute (ESRI) as the "next new idea" basis for designing in 2D or 3D platforms. Almost 10 years after GeoDesign's advent, urban designers are empowered to produce their work with more information than ever before. The *Landscape and Urban Planning* online journal published an entire issue describing GeoDesign as "the topic of professional conferences to the focus of research centers to the premise for new classes at many institutions of higher learning and degrees at leading universities." Additionally:

> the aim and ability to extend the range of scales considered from the region and district (common in GIS) to the parcel and site, where most design decisions—decisions about the precise locations, materials and dimensions of elements in the built environment—are made. A potential significance of this advance is the way it can inform the well-recognized, but previously un- or under-integrated, cross-scale interactions that often occur with environmental change
>
> *(Steiner and Shearer 2016, pp 1–2)*

Steinitz (2016) describes GeoDesign as enabling the design and science professions to emphasize "systems thinking" as the "the complex of many interrelated systems" that ultimately enables (large-scale) design (p 23). Framed as an opportunity for scientists and designers to comingle their ideas and solutions, GeoDesign is considered the next-wave tool for solving large-scale design problems.

Now More than Ever, Design Is Power

As long as education remains open to good ideas (old and new), the practice of urban design will retain the power to change history. Urban designers will continue to wield their sociopolitical clout to make cities from Dubai to Sydney and Miami to Milan more resilient places. As Malcolm Gladwell wrote in *The Tipping Point* (2002), "Look at the world around you. It may seem like an immovable, implacable place. It is not. With the slightest push – in just the right place – it can be tipped." Urban planning and design education continue to be among our best levers for change on a global scale.

Notes

1 Edward Bacon (1910–2005) Executive Director of the Philadelphia City Planning Commission from 1949 to 1970 known for his "total vision of the city" as described by Alexander Garvin in his introduction to *Edward Bacon, Planning, Politics and the Building of Modern Philadelphia* (Garvin 2013).
2 Thomas Adams (1871–1940), leader of urban planning in the UK, Canada, and the U.S. http://urbanplanning.library.cornell.edu/DOCS/adams_t.htm
3 www.ourwelwyngardencity.org.uk/content/category/history-of-welwyn-garden-city/the_history_of_welwyn_garden_city
4 John Nolen (1869–1939) was the first American who self-identified as a city planner. A University of Pennsylvania Wharton School graduate, Nolen entered Harvard University at age 34 to become a landscape architect, http://tclf.org/pioneer/john-nolen (accessed September 6, 2014).
5 Held April 9 and 10, 1956 at the Harvard Graduate School of Design (GSD). Conference participants included Jane Jacobs, Edmund N. Bacon, Charles Abrams, Ladislas Segoe, Lewis Mumford, Garrett Eckbo and José Luis Sert among others (Progressive Architecture August 1956).
6 Bonusing refers to adding elements (such as square footage) beyond the existing zoning for additions included by the developer (such as public space or workforce housing) specified by the governing authority.
7 www1.nyc.gov/site/planning/zoning/districts-tools/special-purpose-districts-manhattan.page
8 http://sustainabledevelopment.un.org/content/documents/Agenda21.pdf

9 http://bettercities.net/article/street-fight-landscape-urbanism-versus-new-urbanism-14855
10 Conference on "Project of Research and Instruction in City and Regional Planning" held at Columbia University on May 28, 1928.
11 That Lynch is not required reading as a foundation of planning education is a missed opportunity to understand basic design.
12 The political context for this paper is the Arizona State University planning program move from the design school to geography.
13 www.rockefellerfoundation.org/report/century-of-the-city/
14 Danilo Palazzo and Vikas Mehta, personal communication, March 22, 2017
15 www.gsd.harvard.edu/course/savannah-rethinking-the-multi-scalar-capacity-of-the-city-project-spring-2017/
16 www.design.upenn.edu/sites/default/files/uploads/PennDesign%20-%20Spring%202017%20Elective%20Course%20Offerings_0.pdf
17 https://planning.gatech.edu/news/georgia-tech-kicks-tokyo-smart-city-studio-project-2020-olympic-site
18 https://ced.berkeley.edu/academics/city-regional-planning/courses/spring-2017-courses/
19 https://bloustein.rutgers.edu/ontrack-transit-oriented-development-for-north-brunswick/
20 www.planetizen.com/node/75724
21 Gary Hack PhD, FAICP personal communication, June 9, 2017
22 www.coursera.org/learn/designing-cities
23 www.planning.org/asc/urbandesign/
24 http://daap.uc.edu/academics/planning/b_urban_planning.html
25 https://arch.gatech.edu/master-science-urban-design
26 http://bloustein.rutgers.edu/wp-content/uploads/2015/03/EJBPPP-UPD-brochure.pdf
27 HUD awards 2017: www.huduser.gov/portal/pdredge/pdr-edge-featd-article-050117.html. ULI awards 2017: https://urbanland.uli.org/planning-design/university-texas-austin-team-wins-2017-uli-hines-student-competition/

References

Abramson, D. B. (2006). Urban Planning in China: Continuity and Change: What the future holds may surprise you. *Journal of the American Planning Association*, 72(2), 197–215. doi:10.1080/01944360608976739

Anselin, L., Nasar, J. L., & Talen, E. (2011). Where Do Planners Belong? Assessing the Relationship between Planning and Design in American Universities. *Journal of Planning Education and Research*, 31(2), 196–207. doi:10.1177/0739456x11402356

Barnett, J. (1974). *Urban Design as Public Policy: Practical Methods for Improving Cities*. Philadelphia, Pennsylvania: Architectural Record Books.

Ben-Joseph, E. (2005). *The Code of the City: Standards and the Hidden Language of Place Making*. Cambridge, Massachusetts: MIT Press.

Birch, E. L. (1980). Radburn and the American Planning Movement. *Journal of the American Planning Association*, 46(4), 424–431. doi:10.1080/01944368008977075

Bodenschatz, H. (2011). 100 Years and More of Urban Design at TU Berlin. In B. Bauerfeind & J. Fokdal (Eds.), *Bridging Urbanities: Reflections on Urban Design in Shanghai and Berlin*. Berlin: Lit Verlag.

Brown, D. S. (2009). Urban Design at Fifty: A Personal View. In A. Krieger & W. S. Saunders (Eds.), *Urban Design*. Minneapolis: University of Minnesota Press.

Collins, G. R. & Collins, C. C. (2006). *Camillo Sitte: The Birth of Modern City Planning*. Minneola, NY: Dover Publications.

Cullingworth, B., & Caves, R. W. (2014). *Planning in the USA: Policies, Issues, and Processes* (4th ed.) New York: Routledge.

Dagenhart, R., & Sawicki, D. (1992). Architecture and Planning: The Divergence of Two Fields. *Journal of Planning Education and Research*, 12(1), 1–16. doi:10.1177/0739456x9201200102

Faga, B. (2006). *Designing Public Consensus: The Civic Theater of Community Participation*. Hoboken, New Jersey: Wiley & Sons.

Forsyth, A. (2007). Innovation in Urban Design: Does Research Help? *Journal of Urban Design*, 12(3), 461–473. doi:10.1080/13574800701602569

Gamble, D., & Heyda, P. (2016). *Rebuilding the American City: Design and Strategy for the 21st Century Urban Core*. New York: Routledge.

Garvin, A. (2013). Foreword. In G. L. Heller, *Ed Bacon: Planning, Politics, and the Building of Modern Philadelphia*. Philadelphia, Pennsylvania: University of Pennsylvania Press.

Geddes, P. (1915). *Cities in Evolution: An Introduction to the Town Planning Movement and to the Study of Civics*. London: Williams.
Gladwell, M. (2002). *The Tipping Point*. Boston, Massachusetts: Back Bay Books.
Hack, G. (2018). *Site Planning; International Practice*. Cambridge, Massachusetts: MIT Press.
Heath, E. (2017, March 20). Personal communication.
Hemmens, G. C. (1988). Thirty Years of Planning Education. *Journal of Planning Education and Research*, 7(2), 85–91. doi:10.1177/0739456x8800700208
Huxtable, A. L. (1971, March 7). Thinking Man's Zoning. *The New York Times*, p. 22.
Inam, A. (2002). Meaningful Urban Design: Teleological/Catalytic/Relevant. *Journal of Urban Design*, 7(1), 35–58. doi:10.1080/13574800220129222
Inam, A. (2011). From Dichotomy to Dialectic: Practising Theory in Urban Design. *Journal of Urban Design*, 16(2), 257–277. doi:10.1080/13574809.2011.552835
Jacobs, J. (1961). *The Death and Life of Great American Cities*. New York, NY: Random House.
Kostof, S. (1991). *The City Shaped: Urban Patterns and Meanings Through History*. New York: Bulfinch Press.
Krieger, A. (2009). Where and How Does Urban Design Happen? In A. Krieger & W. S. Saunders (Eds.), *Urban Design*. Minneapolis: University of Minnesota Press.
Krieger, A., & Saunders, W. S. (Eds.). (2009). *Urban Design*. Minneapolis: University of Minnesota Press.
Krueckeberg, D. A. (1985). The Tuition of American Planning: From Dependency toward Self-reliance. *Town Planning Review*, 56(4), 421. doi:10.3828/tpr.56.4.x726267t33222277
Laquian, A. A. (2008). *The Planning and Governance of Asia's Mega-Urban Regions*. Paper presented at the United Nations Secretariat Expert Group Meeting on Population Distribution, Urbanization, Internal Migration and Development, New York. Retrieved from www.un.org/en/development/desa/population/events/pdf/expert/13/P04_Laquian.pdf
Le Corbusier. (1987). *The City of Tomorrow and Its Planning*. New York: Dover Publications.
Lee, C. C. M. (2013). *Common Frameworks: Rethinking the Developmental City in China, Part 1*. Cambridge, Massachusetts: Harvard University Graduate School of Design.
Legates, R. T., & Stout, F. (1998). *Modernism and Early Urban Planning, 1870–1940*. London: Routledge/Thoemmes Press.
Lindblom, C. E. (1959). The Science of "Muddling Though", *Public Administration Review*, 19(2), 79–88. doi:10.2307/973677
Lynch, K. (1960). *The Image of the City*. Cambridge, Massachusetts: Joint Center of Urban Studies, Massachusetts Institute of Technology and Harvard University.
Macdonald, E. (2013). Designing the Urban Design Studio. In M. Larice & E. Macdonald (Eds.), *The Urban Design Reader*. Abingdon: Routledge.
McCann, J. (2017, March 22). Personal communication.
McHarg, I. L. (1992). *Design With Nature*. Hoboken, New Jersey: Wiley.
Nelessen, A. (2017, March 29). Personal communication.
Palazzo, D., & Steiner, F. (2011). *Urban Ecological Design: A Process for Regenerative Places*. Washington, D. C.: Island Press.
Peirce, N. R., & Johnson, C. W. (2008). *The Century of the City*. Bellagio Center Italy: The Rockefeller Foundation.
Rand, P. (2000). *The Politics of Design*. New Haven CT: Yale University Press.
Rittel, H. W. J., and Webber, M. M. (1973). Dilemmas in a General Theory of Planning, *Policy Sciences*, 4(2), 155–169. doi.org/10.1007/BF01405730
Steiner, F. R., & Shearer, A. W. (2016). Geodesign—Changing the world, changing design. *Landscape and Urban Planning*, 156, 1–4. doi:10.1016/j.landurbplan.2016.11.006
Steinitz, C. (2016). On Change and Geodesign. *Landscape and Urban Planning*, 156, 23–25. doi:10.1016/j.landurbplan.2016.09.023
Tang, Y., & Hack, G. (2017). Transforming Urban Design Education at Tsinghua University. *Proceedings of the Institution of Civil Engineers – Urban Design and Planning*, 170(3), 107–120. doi:10.1680/jurdp.16.00007
Thompson, G. F., & Steiner, F. (1997). *Ecological Design and Planning*. New York: John Wiley & Sons.
Walters, D. (2011). Smart Cities, Smart Places, Smart Democracy: Form-Based Codes, Electronic Governance and the Role of Place in Making Smart Cities. *Intelligent Buildings International*, 3(3), 198–218. doi:10.1080/17508975.2011.586670
Watson, V. (2002). Do We Learn from Planning Practice? *Journal of Planning Education and Research*, 22(2), 178–187. doi:10.1177/0739456x02238446

PART 5B

Essential Subjects of Planning Sustainable Places

25
CLIMATE CHANGE

Ward Lyles and Mark Stevens

Introduction

Since the early 2000s, attention to planning for climate change has increased dramatically in practice and research, as evidenced in growing numbers of climate change plans, reports, and scholarly articles and books. Climate change mitigation—primarily focused on reducing greenhouse gas emissions—aligns with many, if not all, of the core themes of planning in recent decades, including increased sustainability, equity, livability, and resilience. Moreover, the potential impacts of climate change touch on nearly every aspect of planning, from transportation to housing to economic development to the natural environment. Likewise, the topic of climate change adaptation goes hand in hand with that of natural hazards and disasters, as well as planning for food systems, infrastructure, and natural areas (c.f. Blanco, Alberti et al. 2009, Berke and Lyles 2013).

Scholarly attention to challenges in teaching climate change is in its infancy. The causes and impacts of climate change affect essentially every aspect of planning so pervasively that climate change merits coverage, or at least acknowledgement, in all planning courses. Simultaneously, climate change merits its own course-level focus because of the importance of understanding the specific natural and human-influenced physical processes involved, the unavoidable intersection of global and local concerns, and the ongoing political contention about its existence, causes, impacts, and implications. Teaching climate change involves broad-scope, department-wide choices, such as where to situate climate change in a planning program, as well as more narrowly scoped choices specific to individual class periods, such as selection of readings and dealing with technical jargon. Some choices we identify in this chapter are common to teaching any planning topic, while other decisions are especially vexing or entirely unique to teaching climate change planning. Almost every choice involves tradeoffs between reasonable options. We have focused this chapter on fundamental choices we anticipate instructors will face for years to come, like the types of materials to use in teaching, rather than choices that will become irrelevant soon, like whether to use a specific resource recently made available.

In terms of organization, our chapter begins by briefly summarizing the only other scholarly writing on the topic of climate change pedagogy. We then explain four first-level decisions that we believe must be resolved at the outset of designing a course that addresses climate change planning. Next we walk through six additional considerations that present second-level decisions for instructors, organized from the most straightforward to the most perplexing. Then we focus in more detail on two emerging issues that need more attention in planning instruction in general, but are especially pertinent to climate change pedagogy: 1) promoting student engagement through active learning and 2) helping students cope with emotionally taxing issues that arise in a course. Finally, in the supplemental material we provide four vignettes of decisions we have made in our own teaching of climate change planning.

First-Level Decisions

To date the only article addressing climate change pedagogy in planning we are aware of is Hamin and Marcucci (2013). After highlighting the rise of climate change as an issue of practical and scholarly attention in planning, they provide a brief review of why climate change is important for planning. Hamin and Marcucci identify core pedagogy issues to consider in teaching climate change, including ensuring basic understanding of climate science, incorporating social-political and technical dimensions of planning for climate change, and ensuring climate change is understood as a contemporary and relevant challenge (2013). They also note the resonance of debate in climate planning about whether climate change should be planned for via stand-alone plans or 'mainstreamed' into more comprehensive planning efforts with debates about addressing climate change in curricula. That is, should schools offer stand-alone climate change planning courses or integrate climate change into broader-scope courses? Hamin and Marcucci recommend a combined approach.

In following Hamin and Marcucci's consideration of the pedagogical issues related to climate change, we propose that instructors consider four first-level decisions as the choices that must be made at the departmental and instructor-level well in advance of the actual beginning of a course. We anticipate that these choices will be more difficult to rethink and adjust on the fly as a course proceeds during a semester. The four first-level decisions are summarized in Table 25.1.

Student Participants: Instructors, in consultation with their department chairs or curriculum committees, must decide if the student participants in the course will be undergraduates, graduate students, or a mix thereof. A survey of more than 20 planning programs found that 72% of climate change courses were taught at the graduate level (Hamin and Marcucci 2013). Their survey was conducted in the early 2010s, however, and we suspect more planning programs offer courses with climate change content today. Instructors must recognize and adapt their courses to the huge variation in academic, professional, and personal maturity of students, such as the differences between the typical first-semester undergraduate student and the typical final-semester graduate student. In all likelihood, most planning programs' student populations vary widely in preparation to approach climate change planning. Climate change is subject to active misinformation campaigns (Oreskes and Conway 2011), probably more than almost any planning-related issue. Thus, instructors should take time at the beginning of the semester to get to know their students' backgrounds and identify how much background information on climate science needs presentation. This information can help the instructor on multiple levels, from customizing lectures and assignments, to providing supplementary materials for selected students, and balancing the composition of student groups.

Course Scope: Instructors must consider how climate change relates to the core subject matter of the course. Some courses will focus solely on climate change; others may include a climate change unit as one of multiple units. Still other courses will tackle even broader topics, such as planning theory or methods or planning for sustainability, and incorporate climate change throughout all aspects of the course. How climate change relates to the core subject matter of the course may be dictated by larger department-level curriculum considerations and be out of an instructor's control. Regardless of the instructor's autonomy to set the scope, instructors need to be explicit and transparent as to how and why they are approaching the scope of incorporation of climate change.

A closely related choice for instructors is whether their course will tackle climate change mitigation, climate change adaptation, or both mitigation and adaptation. Where and how mitigation and adaptation fit in a course depends greatly on the topic. For instance, in a course on environmental planning, mitigation may fit best in a module on planning for energy, while adaptation may fit best in a module on reducing risks from natural hazards. Hamin and Marcucci found that 40% of courses addressed mitigation and adaptation, 24% mitigation only, and 36% adaptation only (2013). As the climate connections to major disaster events like Hurricane Sandy receive more attention, policy makers may become increasingly concerned with local adaptation concerns.

Topic Scope: Few courses will be able to cover all aspects of climate change planning. Instead, instructors will have to balance topics such as climate science, climate policy and planning, and technical solutions. Hamin and Marcucci (2013) categorized a range of specific topics and provided some early evidence about which ones planning instructors choose to emphasize. Their categories, from most to least commonly covered in courses, include: climate science, policy/law/economics, mitigation topics and skills, adaptation topics and skills, and focus areas (health, development, species + habitat, food and water). The relative balance of coverage within a course will be a function of the course's place in the curriculum, the instructor's expertise, and student interest, among other factors. Here, too, instructors should acknowledge to students how and why they have weighted some topics more than other topics.

Geographic Scale: Instructors must consider the geographic scale at which they wish to focus. Planning curricula may have places for courses (or at least course modules) on global and/or national policy considerations, including tensions between the interests of the Global North and

Table 25.1 First-Level Decisions for Instructors

Category	Choice for Instructors
Student Participants	Undergraduate only (upper-level versus lower-level)
	Graduate only
	Mixed undergraduate and graduate
Course Scope	Stand-alone climate change course (mitigation, adaptation or both)
	Climate change unit in broader course
	Climate change fully integrated as organizing concept in broader course
Topic Scope	Climate science
	Law/policy/politics
	Mitigation specific topics and skills
	Adaptation specific topics and skills
	Focus areas such as health or development
Geographic Scope	Global
	National
	Regional/State
	Local
Physical Setting	Lecture hall
	Seminar room
	Studio
	Flexible space
	Online

the Global South. Likewise, there may be a need for courses or modules on state- or regional-level efforts to build capacity and commitment to address climate change through policy, infrastructure investments, and technical support for local governments. Finally, and probably most commonly in planning curricula, instructors may heavily emphasize local planning for climate change. Combining and linking teaching about climate change across these different levels, each of which is particularly dynamic at this period in history, can be challenging to say the least. There are also huge challenges communicating the temporal and spatial uncertainty of actual climate change impacts, a point to which we return in the next section.

Second-Level Considerations

We next examine second-level considerations that, for the most part, derive from the first-level decisions. We present these considerations in order from most straightforward to address to the most perplexing.

Selecting Course Materials: Knowledge of climate change and its impacts is evolving so rapidly as to render materials quickly out of date. Nonetheless, some mainstays for overviews of climate change issues include reports by the Intergovernmental Panel on Climate Change (IPCC) (www.ipcc.ch/) and the US National Climate Assessment (http://nca2014.globalchange.gov/). Instructors can also turn to libraries of case studies and reports from non-profit organizations, such as ICLEI (www.iclei.org/) and CAKE, the Climate Adaptation Knowledge Exchange (www.cakex.org/); academic entities, such as the Georgetown Climate Center (www.georgetownclimate.org/); and state repositories, such as State of California's Climate Change Portal (http://climatechange.ca.gov/). In their survey, Hamin and Marcucci found that 40% of planning for climate change courses had students read IPCC report(s), while 60% used case studies (2014). In addition to providing access to broadly applicable materials, instructors should strongly consider designing individual or group projects that allow students to dig more deeply into the wider range of resources available for a particular locality (e.g. city plans) or on a particular topic (e.g. agriculture).

Dealing with Jargon: Dealing with jargon is a challenge planning instructors are familiar with, whether they have taught theory (epistemology and ontology, anyone?), technical skills (consider multivariate regression and geospatial analysis), and substantive topics (keeping track of the subfield-specific alphabet soups of acronyms for policies, programs, and organizations). Still, in the context of the widely interdisciplinary field of climate change, dealing with jargon is especially challenging. Consider the basic term *mitigation* and how it repeatedly leads to confusion. In the environmental-sciences dominated field of climate change science, *mitigation* typically refers to greenhouse gas reductions, while *adaptation* refers to reducing negative impacts and leveraging positive impacts. Meanwhile, in the emergency management-dominated field of natural hazards, *mitigation* refers to long-term risk reduction, largely overlapping with the way *adaptation* is used in climate science. Thus, even one of the most basic terms in climate change planning might easily lead to confusion. Instructors can use the challenge of dealing with jargon as an opportunity to teach about the responsibility planners have to communicate clearly, especially with the general public and decision makers.

Local Context Dependence: Instructors must consider the local sociopolitical context in which a course is taught: teaching climate change planning in Europe will be quite different than in North America, which will be different than in Asia, and so on. Even within North America, the contexts vary widely. In heavily urbanized coastal cities, instruction may focus on how to be a cutting-edge global leader in long-term planning for climate change. In 'fly-over' country in the middle of North America, where the political climate might be very different, much of the instruction may focus on how to plan for climate change without ever using the words 'climate change.'

Hyper-politicization: Almost all of the work of planners is political, from infrastructure investments, to housing policy, to economic development incentives. Yet, compared to climate change, none of our other core planning topics has been subjected to such a systematic, coordinated, and persistent attack of basic knowledge and science (Oreskes & Conway, 2011). As instructors, we have to contend with the possibility that some of our students are climate change deniers, while others may major in topics such as petroleum engineering that may create for them deep cognitive dissonance. As such, we face the challenge of being sensitive to the potential diversity of students' views and deeply held beliefs, while not compromising our teaching of scientific consensus or the need for shifts in energy use and development patterns.

Extreme Uncertainty: Planning's long-standing theoretical and practical efforts to contend with uncertainty are reflected in more than a half-century debate about the role of comprehensive planning (c.f. Kent 1964, Kaiser and Godschalk 1995, Innes 1996). Where climate change differs from other planning topics is the extreme degree to which climate change is spatially and temporally uncertain. As a global phenomenon, climate change engages nearly every physical, social, economic, political and other system in the world, which makes many types of prediction inherently impossible. We, along with many peers who have written about the emergence of climate change planning (c.f. Blanco et al. 2009, Wheeler 2008, Boswell, Greve and Seale 2012), contend that planning theory and practices are especially well suited to the demands of climate change, in no small part because of attention to the process of planning as much as the substance of plans. We see the implication of the extreme uncertainty of climate change as closely tied to the need to train planners to communicate clearly (and without jargon), to engage the public early and often (even—or especially—in the face of hyper-politicization), and to never lose sight of the interplay of broadly applicable theories and practices and the unique characteristics of local contexts.

Diversity and Equity: Climate change is not and will not affect everyone similarly. Not only will impacts vary widely over space and time, those impacted will experience the impacts with pronounced differences in underlying vulnerability to impacts (IPCC 2014). The interplay between social vulnerability and environmental justice is increasingly visible (c.f. Bullard 1990, Cutter, Boruff, and Shirley 2003). Instructors must find space in their courses to engage the equity dimension of sustainability, including touching on how race, gender, physical ability or disability, age, and social status contribute to vulnerability.

Broad Pedagogy Approaches Well Suited to Teaching Climate Change Planning

One key task for instructors is to promote engagement with the work of climate change planning through active learning, including creating effective in-class activities, fostering discussion, and designing assignments and projects. A second key task is to provide students with the perspective, resources, and tools for coping with how emotionally taxing issues related to planning for climate change can be.

Promoting Engagement Through Active Learning: In the late 1990s, the National Academy of Science endorsed creating more active and engaged learning environments to foster deep understanding, problem solving skills, and the capacity for knowledge transfer (Bransford et al. 2000). Active learning consists of techniques such as peer discussion, peer-to-peer instruction, and collaborative testing, which support conceptual reasoning, quantitative problem solving, and higher-level problem solving (Crouch and Mazur 2001, Smith et al. 2009, Gilley and Clarkston 2014, Linton, Farmer, and Peterson 2014). Moreover, a meta-analysis of 225 pedagogical publications in the STEM disciplines found stronger student performance in active learning environments than in traditional learning environments centered on lecture, memorization, and mastery of text (Freeman et al. 2014). Active learning works especially well for closing the long-standing achievement gap for underrepresented groups, particularly for African-American and first-generation students (Eddy and Hogan 2014).

Active learning is especially well suited to the demands of training planning practitioners to work in the realm of climate change. Climate change planning requires collaborative, problem-oriented, and ongoing policy learning in messy situations emblematic of the concepts of 'wicked problems' (c.f. Rittel and Webber 1973, Goldstein and Butler 2010, Innes and Booher 2010, Berke and Lyles 2013). Active learning approaches provide settings for students to build the requisite knowledge, skills, and approaches to ongoing learning for climate change planning. Moreover, active learning experiences can help students test and refine leadership skills necessary to overcome the challenges of hyper-politicization and jargon. Prominent approaches to collaborative planning and decision making to foster sustainability and resilience, including consensus building, shared learning networks, overcoming disciplinary silos, and joint problem solving, are likewise supported and simulated in active learning environments (Godschalk, Brody, and Burby 2003, National Research Council 2011, Goldstein and Butler 2010, Innes and Booher 2010, Margerum 2011).

We have found Team Based Learning (TBL), a theoretically grounded and empirically tested system for implementing active, engaged learning environments for interdisciplinary teamwork, especially well suited to teaching climate change planning (Michaelsen, Knight and Fink 2002). Core principles of TBL include consistent, diverse teams; individual responsibility for initial concept acquisition through reading; dedication of class time to concept application and teamwork; and simulating concept application in professional work environments (Michaelsen, Knight and Fink 2002). At the outset of the semester, instructors create teams of students through a systematic and transparent process, akin to a manager assigning a team of planners to work together on a climate planning initiative. The TBL format, like professional planning offices, consists of interactions during scheduled team sessions (i.e. class time) with individual tasks to be completed between work sessions. The instructor functions as a guide on the side, rather than a traditional sage on the stage.

TBL is especially well suited to the challenge of teaching climate change planning because it provides opportunities for shared learning about emerging issues, collaboration between individuals with diverse backgrounds, and collective solving of real-world problems. Additionally, TBL helps students develop the skills essential for success as a professional planner, including working with the public and colleagues, considering multiple perspectives, thinking on one's feet, and completing projects in a timely manner with limited resources (Ozawa & Seltzer, 1999). Finally, TBL fosters critical self-reflection as students gain experience listening, speaking, and thinking in the context of collaborative learning.

Coping with Emotionally Taxing Issues: As behavioral economist Dan Ariely has deftly pointed out, if you wanted to design a problem to maximize human apathy, it would be climate change (Ariely 2013). The risks are easily perceived as temporally and spatially distant, while the costs of mitigation are current and the benefits do not necessarily accrue to those who pay the costs. Even for those motivated to learn about and work on climate change planning, the emotional demands can be huge. The negative impacts of climate change—from ecosystem alteration to species extinction to human suffering—are so widespread and pervasive that focusing attention on them can easily lead to anxiety, depression, and deep feelings of hopelessness. Both instructors and their students, being human, are vulnerable to such debilitating emotions. A core question, then, is how can instructors create an emotionally safe and beneficial environment for learning about climate change planning?

There are at least two promising lines of action instructors can take. The first deals with the emotional experience in the classroom. Creating a classroom climate that promotes trust, honesty, and collaboration, can create a community in which students (and instructors) shift from people who simply share space for a couple of hours a week to people who get to know and care about each other. In turn, the classroom can be a place to openly talk about not just facts and opinions, but also the feelings that condition how we interpret and use facts and opinions. As a starting point, the TBL approach, or similar team-focused teaching, can help create such a place.

But, as instructors, we can go farther. A recent edited volume, *Contemplative Approaches to Sustainability in Higher Education: Theory and Practice*, makes a provocative and persuasive argument that attending to the emotional dimensions of higher education must receive more attention if we want to engage, motivate, and even inspire students to work on 'wicked problems' like climate change planning (Eaton and Hughes 2016). Intentionally cultivating students' abilities to recognize and work with their emotions, and to maintain focused attention on a topic even in the face of deeply disturbing realties and possibilities, is part of our responsibility in educating students on topics like climate change.

The volume includes a wide range of contemplative techniques that instructors can incorporate into classes to foster these skills in students. The techniques include: instructors can directly acknowledge and discuss with students the emotional dimensions of the topic, right from the beginning of a course; instructors can lead students in brief mindfulness meditation exercises that calm the mind and body, or direct students to existing resources for doing so; students can be required to engage in journaling or reflective writing exercises, which can then be shared with peers or the instructor; instructors can help to lighten the overall classroom mood by taking advantage of the wide array of songs, videos, and other forms of art that poignantly bridge the divide between hope and despair. For many instructors, moving into this territory of pedagogic approaches will be uncomfortable for fear of opening up a Pandora's box of emotional discussions that cannot be undone or of seeming touchy-feely and unprofessional. Fortunately, the array of techniques is so broad and flexible that most instructors should be able to find multiple ways to productively engage the emotional context. Many instructors probably already do so and we hope more and more instructors feel comfortable sharing such approaches.

The second line of action for instructors relates to course content. As Baum (2015) has argued, planning scholarship overall exhibits a huge blind spot in considering emotion in planning. Given the extensive knowledge base in psychology, neuroscience, and related fields of the interplay between thought and emotion, the gap in attention to emotion is surprising and concerning. How can we work with communities on contentious issues affecting diverse populations while paying so little attention to emotion? In line with Baum's observations, we are not aware of any studies of the degree to which planning courses include content on emotion and more broadly, psychology and neuroscience. But we can attest that including a unit on basic psychological concepts, such as rewards and incentives, cognitive dissonance, social norms, modeling, and prompts, can be very eye-opening and empowering for students. Beyond recognizing their own thoughts and behaviors through these lenses, students can begin to see how they can more effectively communicate and achieve planning objectives.

Linking these psychological concepts to broader theories of political and social action from the Tragedy of the Commons (Hardin 2009) to *Community-Based Social Marketing* (McKenzie-Mohr 2011) can help students understand the realities of change: that effectively appealing to people's morals is a slow process, depending heavily on existing morals, social norms, and the messenger; that education requires carefully communicative messages and mediums; that incentives and punishments have to be closely linked to the behavior one desires to change; and that community-based solutions often depend on the close social ties typically only present in small groups (c.f. Gardner and Stern 1996). A student will likely much more deeply engage in designing an effective program to promote walking and biking to reduce greenhouse gases when the student can see the connection between planning initiatives (e.g. bicycle lanes, signage, bike share programs) and individual behaviors (e.g. avoiding busy roads and hills, needing information at the point of action, and perceptions of time and costs).

Conclusion

For instructors looking to incorporate climate change into their planning curricula, whether in a dedicated course or incorporated into existing courses, there is no one-size-fits-all approach. Not only will the local implications of climate change vary from location to location, but the student participants will vary widely between and within teaching settings.

Thus instructors need to think carefully not simply about what they are teaching, but how they teach it. Climate change planning requires consideration of so much more than technical solutions and thus requires creating a community of trust and openness in the classroom. Moreover, climate change planning is a demanding topic, intellectually and emotionally, for students and instructors alike. Instructors need to use pedagogy approaches that engage students on multiple levels, including active learning strategies like TBL and contemplative exercises that allow students to process their emotional reactions.

Finally, those considering the potential changes implied by teaching climate change on a planning curriculum would do well to revisit the inherent tensions between the three E's of sustainability (environment, economics, and equity) laid out by Scott Campbell more than two decades ago (1996). Campbell's article, alongside Agyeman's work on just sustainabilities (2003), Beatley's work on Biophilic cities (2011), and the work of numerous others who consider the intersections of humans and the natural environment in planning, provide important touchstones for planning teachers. This is the particular challenge of climate change: it requires instructors to recognize that their task is only partly to convey information, pass on technical skills, and help students refine their capacity for communication and collaboration. They are also, at bottom, charged with considering alongside students the deep ethical orientation of planning and its power to support a more sustainable future in the face of global climate change.

References

Agyeman, J. (2003). *Just Sustainabilities: Development in an Unequal World*. Cambridge, Massachusetts: MIT Press.
Ariely, D. (2013). Keynote Speech: University of North Carolina at Chapel Hill Doctoral Hooding Ceremony. Retrieved from https://gradschool.unc.edu/news/2013/arielyhooding.html#keynote
Baum, H. (2015). Planning with Half a Mind: Why Planners Resist Emotion. *Planning Theory & Practice*, 16(4), 498–516. doi:10.1080/14649357.2015.1071870
Beatley, T. (2011). Biophilic Cities: Integrating Nature into Urban Design and Planning. In *Biophilic Cities* (pp. 83–129). Washington, D.C.: Island Press/Center for Resource Economics.

Berke, P., & Lyles, W. (2013). Public Risks and the Challenges to Climate-Change Adaptation: A Proposed Framework for Planning in the Age of Uncertainty. *Cityscape, 15*(1), 181–208.

Blanco, H., Alberti, M., Forsyth, A., Krizek, K. J., Rodríguez, D. A., Talen, E., & Ellis, C. (2009). Hot, Congested, Crowded and Diverse: Emerging Research Agendas in Planning. *Progress in Planning, 71*(4), 153–205. doi:10.1016/j.progress.2009.03.001

Boswell, M. R., Greve, A. I., & Seale, T. L. (2012). *Local Climate Action Planning.* Washington, D.C.: Island Press/Center for Resource Economics.

Bransford, J. D., Brown, A. L., Cocking, R. R., Donovan, M. S., & Pellegrino, J. W. (Eds.). (2000). *How People Learn: Brain, Mind, Experience, and School.* Washington, D.C. : National Academy Press.

Bullard, R. D. (1990). *Dumping In Dixie: Race, Class, And Environmental Quality* (Third ed.). Abingdon: Taylor & Francis.

Campbell, S. (1996). Green Cities, Growing Cities, Just Cities?: Urban Planning and the Contradictions of Sustainable Development. *Journal of the American Planning Association, 62*(3), 296–312. doi:10.1080/01944369608975696

Crouch, C. H., & Mazur, E. (2001). Peer Instruction: Ten Years of Experience and Results. *American Journal of Physics, 69*(9), 970–977. doi:10.1119/1.1374249

Cutter, S. L., Boruff, B. J., & Shirley, W. L. (2003). Social Vulnerability to Environmental Hazards. *Social Science Quarterly, 84*(2), 242–261. doi:10.1111/1540-6237.8402002

Eaton, M., Hughes, H. J., & MacGregor, J. (2016). *Contemplative Approaches to Sustainability in Higher Education: Theory and Practice.* New York: Routledge.

Eddy, S. L., & Hogan, K. A. (2014). Getting Under the Hood: How and for Whom Does Increasing Course Structure Work? *CBE—Life Sciences Education, 13*(3), 453–468. doi:10.1187/cbe.14-03-0050

Freeman, S., Eddy, S. L., McDonough, M., Smith, M. K., Okoroafor, N., Jordt, H., & Wenderoth, M. P. (2014). Active Learning Increases Student Performance in Science, Engineering, and Mathematics. *Proceedings of the National Academy of Sciences, 111*(23), 8410–8415. doi:10.1073/pnas.1319030111

Gardner, G. T., & Stern, P. C. (1996). *Environmental Problems and Human Behavior.* Allyn & Bacon.

Gilley, B., & Clarkston, B. (2014). Research and Teaching: Collaborative Testing: Evidence of Learning in a Controlled In-Class Study of Undergraduate Students. *Journal of College Science Teaching, 43*(3). doi:10.2505/4/jcst14_043_03_83

Godschalk, D. R., Brody, S., & Burby, R. (2003). Public Participation in Natural Hazard Mitigation Policy Formation: Challenges for Comprehensive Planning. *Journal of Environmental Planning and Management, 46*(5), 733–754. doi:10.1080/0964056032000138463

Goldstein, B. E., & Butler, W. H. (2010). Expanding the Scope and Impact of Collaborative Planning. *Journal of the American Planning Association, 76*(2), 238–249. doi:10.1080/01944361003646463

Hamin, E., & Marcucci, D. (2013). Mainstreaming Climate in the Classroom: Teaching Climate Change Planning. *Planning Practice and Research, 28*(4), 470–488. doi:10.1080/02697459.2012.732327

Hardin, G. (2009). The Tragedy of the Commons. *Journal of Natural Resources Policy Research, 1*(3), 243–253. doi:10.1080/19390450903037302

Innes, J. E. (1996). Planning Through Consensus Building: A New View of the Comprehensive Planning Ideal. *Journal of the American Planning Association, 62*(4), 460–472. doi:10.1080/01944369608975712

Innes, J. E., & Booher, D. E. (2010). *Planning with Complexity: An Introduction to Collaborative Rationality for Public Policy.* New York: Taylor & Francis.

Intergovernmental Panel on Climate Change (IPCC). (2014). *Climate Change 2014–Impacts, Adaptation, and Vulnerability: Regional Aspects.* Cambridge: Cambridge University Press.

Kaiser, E., & Godschalk, D. (1995). Twentieth Century Land Use Planning: A Stalwart Family Tree. *Journal of the American Planning Association, 61*(3), 365–385. doi:10.1080/01944369508975648

Kent, T. J. (1964). *The Urban General Plan.* San Francisco: Chandler Publishing Company. (Second ed., 1991. Chicago, IL: Planners Press, American Planning Association.

Linton, D. L., Farmer, J. K., & Peterson, E. (2014). Is Peer Interaction Necessary for Optimal Active Learning? *CBE—Life Sciences Education, 13*(2), 243–252. doi:10.1187/cbe.13-10-0201

Margerum, R. D. (2011). *Beyond Consensus.* Cambridge, Massachusetts: The MIT Press.

McKenzie-Mohr, D. (2011). *Fostering Sustainable Behavior: An Introduction to Community-based Social Marketing.* Gabriola Island, British Columbia: New Society Publishers.

Michaelsen, L. K., Knight, A. B., & Fink, L. D. (Eds.). (2002). *Team-based Learning: A Transformative Use of Small Groups.* Westport, Connecticut: Praeger.

National Research Council. (2011). *Building Community Disaster Resilience Through Private-Public Collaboration.* Washington, D.C.: National Academy Press.

Oreskes, N., & Conway, E. M. (2011). Defeating the Merchants of Doubt. *Nature, 465*(7299), 686–687. doi:10.1038/465686a

Ozawa, C. P., & Seltzer, E. P. (1999). Taking Our Bearings: Mapping a Relationship Among Planning Practice, Theory, and Education. *Journal of Planning Education and Research, 18*(3), 257–266. doi:10.1177/0739456x9901800307

Rittel, H. W. J., & Webber, M. M. (1973). Dilemmas in a General Theory of Planning. *Policy Sciences, 4*(2), 155–169. doi:10.1007/bf01405730

Smith, M. K., Wood, W. B., Adams, W. K., Wieman, C. E., Knight, J. K., Guild, N., & Su, T. T. (2009). Why Peer Discussion Improves Student Performance on In-Class Concept Questions. *Developmental Biology, 331*(2), 416. doi:10.1016/j.ydbio.2009.05.104

Wheeler, S. M. (2008). State and Municipal Climate Change Plans: The First Generation. *Journal of the American Planning Association, 74*(4), 481–496. doi:10.1080/01944360802377973

26
WATER RESOURCES PLANNING

Caitlin Dyckman

Introduction

Since the 20th century, in developed countries, where human habitation has expanded water has been assumed to follow. This expectation is based on a sacrosanct, legally binding will-serve principle that constitutes one of the integral purposes of a city, particularly with public utility provision and the move from private to public water supply at the turn of the 20th century in the U.S. (Wilcox, 1910; Tarlock, 2010).[1] While generally invisible and assumed in developed countries, water is already our greatest resource issue. Our urban areas sprawl into contiguous megaregions, susceptible to increasingly longer and more intense droughts from climate change (Li, Endter-Wada & Li 2015), while reliant on crumbling and unsustainable infrastructure with high capital investment (Elmer & Leigland, 2014; Hanemann, 2006), on unsustainable large-scale water and energy provision projects (i.e., dams), and on tenuous legal rights to the captured water itself (Hanemann, Dyckman & Park, 2015; Dyckman, 2011). Thus the need to consider water management—a vast topic area that is conducted by several disciplines, including engineering, law, economics, hydrology, geography, and increasingly, planning.

And yet, planners have historically ignored this topic in the U.S., relegating it to the redundancies of delivery and infrastructure systems in the engineering discipline and the public utilities departments in city and county government—or to special districts responsible solely for water provision at local or regional scales. According to the American Planning Association's (APA) report on planners and water, "most planners do not routinely work with water service or utility professionals" (Cesanek, Elmer & Graeff, 2017, 13) and there is an institutional siloing (Dyckman, 2018; Dyckman, forthcoming). When and if planners have been involved in engaging with water management, they have done so through environmental planning measures that protect watersheds and through floodplain management or hazard mitigation, rather than direct involvement in utilities' water and wastewater decision-making (Cesanek et al., 2017). But as this chapter will illustrate, there are several ways in which planners are intending—and starting—to integrate water into their practice.

According to the APA, "many forward-thinking land use planners, urban designers, and architects are developing new planning practices in concern with local utilities, water engineers, and landscape architects. Yet most planners could benefit from more information about water" (Cesanek et al., 2017, 13). The biggest impediment to their involvement appears to be knowledge about the water resources management field (Cesanek et al., 2017).

History of Water Resource Management

How did the single most powerful resource in a city become the perceived purview of engineers? The irony is particularly rife, since the first planners were actually sanitary engineers who planned waste removal infrastructure and projected/estimated growth during the Sanitary Reform Movement of the 1850s in Chicago and New York City (Peterson, 1979; Platt, 2014). But for the past century, the engineering profession has dominated water provision, quality, and control, while attorneys and state agencies control allocation determinations.

The massive scale of the supply infrastructure necessitates sophisticated engineering (Hanemann, 2006), particularly as cities' water demand exceeds their watersheds' supply capacity. The dams on the Colorado River and the corresponding aqueducts are large-scale engineering efforts that demonstrate the capital output needed to sustain several of the largest cities in the U.S. (Hundley, 2001). The same has occurred with the Three Gorges dam in China. Once the construction investment is made, the infrastructure to convey water from source to city has impressive longevity (Hundley, 2001; Hanemann, 2006). Engineers have also met the distributional needs within cities, maintaining system redundancy to address leakage and removing waste/protecting public health through sanitary sewer and water treatment systems. The development of urban water systems has been large-scale and centralized since the building of ancient Rome, as "modern water infrastructure is still guided by its original blueprint of ancient Roman-style aqueducts and cloacae" (Sedlak, 2014, 238).

But this centralized engineering is increasingly fallible, through a combination of design flaws, deferred maintenance, and capacity exceedance. For instance, the combined sewer system approach has a tendency to release raw sewage into water bodies during rain events, and cities like Philadelphia and Atlanta have been legally forced to confront the externalities that neglect/deferred maintenance and rapid growth have manifested in their water systems. In the U.S.:

> planners, architects, landscape architects, and water professionals are now in transition from industrial-era infrastructure, often characterized as "gray infrastructure" or legacy systems, to post-industrial integrated systems, where the waste from one function serves as an input to another and where more holistic thinking about all systems occurs
> *(Cesanek et al., 2017, 13–14).*

With more extremity and variability in water's presence in our cities, decentralized solutions that involve the planning discipline are becoming more attractive (Mukheibir, Howe & Gallet, 2014).

And yet, while many American planning programs have at least one course devoted solely to water, few offer water-focused specializations (Elmer, Blanco & Hsu, 2016, 1). This is in contrast to the planning programs in other countries, particularly in Australia. There, four of the top universities have joined together for a master's in integrated water resources management,[2] and there is a Cooperative Research Centre for Water Sensitive Cities that was started in 2012 as an element of the Australian government's Cooperative Research Centre (CRC) Programme. The CRC for Water Sensitive Cities (2016) works with "60 PhD candidates from seven national and international universities and research organisations to generate the knowledge and on-ground solutions required to transform cities into liveable, resilient, sustainable, and productive places" (CRC for Water Sensitive Cities, 2016). Their focus has been predominately on water sensitive urban design.

While not a dedicated planning "duty," water policy and management—as well as water planning itself—are seeping into the profession. The results of the APA Planning Advisory Service (PAS) report on planners and water suggests that planners should both "intervene" and "intersect" with existing professions with water management authority (Cesanek et al., 2017, 7). These include: (1) roles in water supply itself (i.e., linkages between the water providers' water management plans—both quality and quantity—and local comprehensive plans; demand management through built form/zoning; protection of water supply areas/watersheds, etc.); (2) improved wastewater management through on-site treatment and service expansion locations; (3) stormwater management with green stormwater infrastructure; (4) more equitable water pricing; (5) stronger coordination with capital improvement strategies; and (6) understanding water rights and availability, among others (Cesanek et al., 2017). Thus, planners must be aware of the following fundamental concepts, which should be incorporated into a planning course/unit of study in water resources.

Theory, Principles and Methods of Water Resources Planning, Policy and Management to Include in a Planning Course on Planners' Roles in Water

How Water Eschews All Boundaries

Water, as a resource, eschews all boundaries, whether jurisdictional or disciplinary. This can mean that responsibility for water management and planning belongs to everyone and no one simultaneously. It is conceptually divided into quantity and quality, as well as by source (i.e., surface water or groundwater), but these distinctions are beginning to blur. In the United States alone, at least 24 different agencies at the federal level have some responsibility for water policy (Dyckman & Paulsen 2012; Western Water Policy Review Advisory Commission, 1998). And each state has allocation and planning authority, which may be shared or delegated to the regional/watershed and local levels.

This dispersed authority leads to fragmented water resources management, with water quality legally managed at the federal level (and implemented by states with federal oversight), water allocation legally managed at the state level, and the land uses that drive the demand and impact quality legally managed at the local level (Cosens & Stow, 2014). Water rights, law, and legal processes constrain the basis/allocation of water uses in the U.S. and in other countries (e.g., U.K., South Africa, Tanzania, etc.). There are four state water law structures in the U.S., with riparianism and regulated riparianism predominantly used in the East, and prior appropriation and the hybrid of riparian and prior appropriation used in the West.

Figure 26.1 gives a sense of the complexity of basic U.S. water allocation, with the arrows exposing the choice points and the connections in the intricate web of actors, institutions, and legal mechanisms that perpetually hangs over the physical supply infrastructure. But the figure is relatively simplified, since it would be visually chaotic to correspondingly depict the interrelationships and temporal aspects of these institutions and legal systems.

The forms of water planning are also differentiated, following the quantity/quality and scalar governance distinctions. There is water *quantity* planning, which is conducted at the federal (Army Corps of Engineers, Bureau of Reclamation), state (state resource or public health departments, generally), regional/watershed (special districts, county suppliers), and local (public utilities departments, planners) levels. There is also water *quality* planning, which is primarily conducted by stormwater engineers at the county or city level in the United States (see the federal Clean Water Act's Sections 319 and 208 and the federal Safe Drinking Water Act). Water quality planning tends to be more reactionary than anticipatory, responding to and remediating contamination rather than overtly preventing it. Finally, there is *watershed-based*

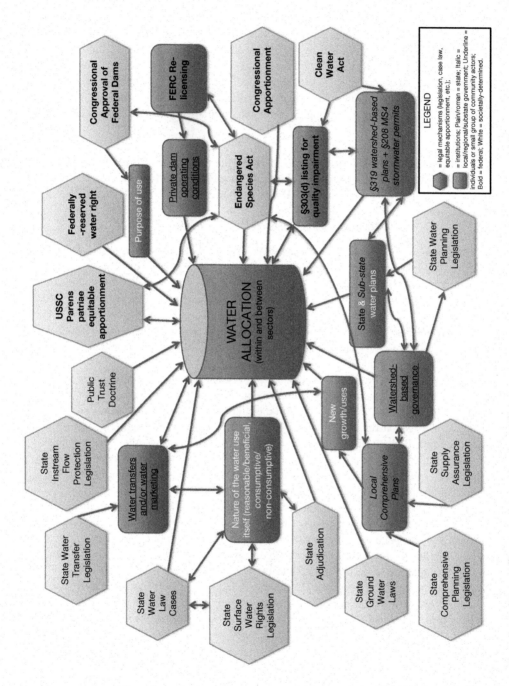

Figure 26.1 Water Allocation Institutions in the U.S.

planning through ad hoc, organic, or problem-shed collaborative watershed management processes (Innes & Booher, 2010; Ostrom & Cox, 2010; Sabatier et al., 2005; Freeman & Farber, 2005; Margerum, 2011).

Although a logical analog, water supply/availability and land uses have only recently been legally linked, and only in parts of the United States. With water shortage, cities have faced the fundamental dichotomy of "doling out water permits for new development with one hand and stopping people from watering their lawns with the other" (Barnett, 2007, 37). But there are five strategies at the state level to address supply constraint, including:

> (1) continuing unlimited growth accommodation; (2) capping growth; (3) shifting the burden of supply acquisition to local governments and developers; (4) adopting aggressive, technological, and managerial water conservation initiatives such as information provision, xeriscaping requirements, marginal cost pricing, desalinization and the use of greywater; and (5) constraining growth to match available and projected supplies.
> *(Tarlock, 2010, 35)*

Historically, urban planners were only tangentially involved in water provision in most states; they planned for and permitted the growth that water suppliers (and their engineers) delivered. But Tarlock's (2010) fifth strategy, known as an assured supply law (Davies, 2007, 2010; Bates, 2012; Klein & Kenney, 2009), has shifted the responsibility for determining whether there is sufficient water supply to support projected growth to local governments and their planners.

State legislation is also starting to expand planners' roles in state-level water planning by mandating that state and sub-state agencies plan for water on a macro-scale, while regional and local suppliers—as well as urban planners—correspondingly address projected growth and supply availability on a more micro-scale. State water plans can range in duration and typology, from single purpose plans to multiple objective plans, and to comprehensive/integrated water resources plans that address supply and demand management (Viessman, 2009, 46). Twenty-six states currently require comprehensive water planning at the state and sub-state levels (Kundell, DeMeo & Myszewski, 2000) and where the state comprehensive water planning legislation mandates sub-state planning, the local water plans must exhibit consistency with the broader state plan. It is important to note that these state water plans are separate from state drought plans (National Drought Mitigation Center, 2017; Steinemann & Cavalcanti, 2006). The majority of states have drought response—not mitigation—plans, although there is a clear need to more proactively drought-proof our cities using urban to rural water transfers between cities and farmers (Richter et al., 2013), and introducing water conservation measures in built form.

Water Conservation and Built Form Requirements

Strategies towards creating a more engaged role in water management and water planning include:

- Adding a water element to the general or comprehensive plan;
- Synthesizing information from land use and water supply plans;
- Introducing water conservation plans for each new development, or for the entire city, coupled with an ordinance prohibiting water waste;

- Shifting to a model of "watershed zoning," in which the carrying capacity of the watershed is established as a legal check on allowed growth to protect water quantity, quality, or both;
- Incorporating water conservation and treatment mechanisms into the built form, through price controls or non-price measures such as requiring greywater reuse; and
- Addressing water supply concerns through drought plans.

While not a comprehensive list since there are constantly emerging but not yet documented approaches, the majority of these strategies have already been implemented in various communities. In Pennsylvania, the Brandywine Conservancy has proposed "water based land use regulation" that includes, in its zoning code, a maximum water usage per unit in the area and enhanced stormwater recharge using transfer of development rights where water recharge or constraints prevent development. (Horner, n.d.).

Local governments can incorporate water conservation and quality/treatment mechanisms into built form, whether overtly or subtly. Water demand management takes two forms: water efficiency, which hardens demand through technology and engineering, effectively using less water for the same services; and water conservation, which promotes behavioral and service change to reduce demand (Brooks, 2005, 2). The water efficiency literature is an extensive and deep one, with engineers constantly improving efficiency through technologic advances for end uses (e.g., evapotranspiration controllers (ET controllers)), and delivery system efficiency (e.g., leak detection and audits, pressure reduction, etc.) (Haie & Keller, 2008; Satterfield & Bhardwaj, 2005; Tsai, Cohen & Vogel, 2011).

Water conservation is further subdivided into two kinds of approaches: price and non-price measures. Non-price water conservation strategies are a relatively newer and burgeoning area, particularly in growing municipal and residential sectors (Wentz and Gober, 2007; Kenney et al., 2008; St. Hilaire et al., 2008). This growth creates an imperative that planners be involved in water demand management, particularly non-price conservation through regulatory authority that only rests with the planners under the police power (Dyckman, forthcoming). In physical platting and the development approval process, planners can limit lot size, or restrict the amount of impervious surface on the lots, adopt a native planting ordinance that reduces water consumption, and prohibit pools. They can also encourage on-site water reuse. Arizona is regarded as a leader in encouraging local greywater reuse (Allen, Christian-Smith & Palaniappan, 2010). Planners can augment the international building codes to include dual piping for both potable and recycled water (aka "purple piping") in appropriate facilities and can mandate that each residence contain hot-water pipe insulation to assure that water remains hot in moving between the water heater and the faucet/showerhead, among other strategies (Dyckman, forthcoming). The Alliance for Water Efficiency (AWE) has partnered with the APA as part of a Water Task Force, and along with the Environmental Law Institute and the River Network, the AWE has created a Net Blue Ordinance Toolkit to help planners draft ordinances for "water neutral growth" that reflects the particular water issues in their community/watershed and includes some of the above measures (allianceforwaterefficiency.org, 2017).

Water Supply and Demand Forecasting

Water supply management is also dependent on long-range forecasting and assumptions about individual water use, both of which will vary by location and technology use. Planners should be able to understand the demand forecasting and estimations that the water purveyors are generating—especially in relation to individual water budgets by lot. And if they are responsible for forecasting that corresponds to their urban growth projections, they need to know the elements that should be present in a demand forecast. The best guide for this approach is Baumann, Boland & Hanemann's (1998) book, *Urban Water Demand Management and Planning*, which provides multiple demand-estimation equations and associated reasoning.

Any water supply plan, whether at the city, regional, or state level, should contain the physical characteristics of the geographic area, including the watershed boundaries and the physical water sources (groundwater and surface water), followed by the existing water supply and demand. This means identifying the suppliers and their reported demand, their physical capacity, and their supply constraints (physical and legal). A water budget can supplement this information by providing estimates of hydrologic inputs and outputs, precipitation, surface water consumption, ground water consumption, evapotranspiration, natural stream flow, and interbasin transfers (Richter, 2014). Water use forecasting models range from the very simple to the more sophisticated, and often make projections under multiple scenarios, such as abnormally wet years or droughts; some include predicted effects of climate change.

There is potential to overestimate or underestimate demand, based on the lack of nuance and individualization in the standard approaches. Water consumption numbers fluctuate by season, climate, use sector or class, relative wealth and life-stage of the consumer, behavior of adjacent users, and the lot characteristics, among other factors; meanwhile, projections often fail to account for water efficiency practices, whether generated by technology, prices, or behavioral change (Heberger, Donnelly & Cooley, 2016). Consequently, forecasting water demand increasingly relies on disaggregated approaches based on the lot size and household characteristics, the gold standard of which is the Irvine Ranch Water District's approach. Increasingly, scholars and water management practitioners are noting the value of fine-scale, parcel-level demand prediction and interventions, which are impacted primarily by the land use type, and built form features such as swimming pools (Wentz & Gober, 2007; Shandas & Parandvash, 2010; Irvine Ranch Water District, 2017). Planners will have to be sensitive to the unique water demands of their given jurisdiction, and the tools available to water-supply engineers and public-policy-makers. They may cooperate with or support their water district in these projections, or they may be solely responsible for them, depending on the assured supply laws in their state.

Flooding Mitigation and Green Stormwater Management

Water volume is clearly variable and relative over space and time, with both drought and flooding, which are influenced by human perceptions and alterations through engineering (Howe, 1979). Increased impervious surface in a watershed, which is now considered an environmental indicator in natural resources planning, exacerbates flooding potential through velocity and volume, and reduces downstream water quality (Leopold, 1968). According to Moglen and Kim (2007), "when imperviousness exceeds 10 to 15% of a watershed, various metrics of stream quality decline markedly" (161). The stream channel is eroded accordingly, and goes through different geomorphological changes, depending on the stage or degree of urbanization and the kinds of land uses in the watershed (Riley, 1998; Rosgen, 1994). Planners in coastal areas must address the compounding problem of flooding from both upstream and oceanfront sources, as the overall amount of urbanization in the watershed impacts the locations where the freshwater meets the ocean, and flooding is more likely to occur more frequently with climate change-induced accelerated sea level rise. The flooding is also exacerbated by coastal subsidence from groundwater pumping and impervious surface over coastal aquifers, which reduces the potential for and quality of groundwater recharge. If communities continue to build in floodplains after flooding events, planners perpetuate a cycle of "hazard-zone use, disaster, hazard control, more intensive use, larger disasters, and more elaborate (and expensive) hazard control" (Burby, 1998, 263).

Thus planners must be prepared to incorporate flood risk into land use planning decisions.Randolph (2012) has an excellent chapter entitled "Water and Land Use: Stream Flow, Flooding, and Runoff Pollution," which details how planners calculate peak discharge, flooding, and flood hazards within their communities. In fact, at least three chapters in his *Environmental Land Use Planning and Management* relate to water, illustrating its growing import in the planning discipline.

Potential planning strategies to mitigate flood risk include: hazard mitigation plans that are either incorporated into the local comprehensive plan, or are stand alone and consistent with the plan (Burby & May, 1997; Berke, Smith & Lyles, 2012); prohibiting growth in hazardous areas using zoning (Beatley, 2009; Godschalk et al., 1999); adopting a flood hazard zoning ordinance that sets additional standards for structures in hazard-prone areas (Beatley, 2009; Titus, 1998); and establishing a buy-out program or use of transfer of development rights to remove structures from the hazardous areas (Titus, 1998). Additionally, planners can focus on site design that realizes water conservation opportunities and consumption reduction, as well as controls excess water—or its quality—through on-site capture and treatment before the water reaches a larger water body, especially as nonpoint source pollution (i.e., runoff from impervious surfaces in a watershed) is the greatest source of water contamination in the U.S. (Fisher-Vanden and Olmstead, 2013, citing to the U.S. Environmental Protection Agency, 2005).

Planners have also started to incorporate the idea of green stormwater infrastructure (GSI), which is a subset of the broader green infrastructure (GI) concept, to address issues of flooding mitigation, stormwater management, and general water quality (Benedict & McMahon, 2006; Harrington & Hsu, 2018). GSI is a set of tools to control and purify stormwater runoff, whether on site or for the city as a whole. It comes in several forms, including engineering best management practices (BMPs) such as detention ponds, and low-impact development (LID) strategies that control runoff on site, including green roofs, rain gardens/on-site rainwater harvesting (via flow-through planters and rain barrels), stormwater tree trenching, stormwater bump outs, stormwater planters, and permeable pavement (City of Philadelphia, 2016). Planning researchers are modeling efforts to predict water quality and quantity, as well as control outcomes from these approaches so that practitioners can quickly determine the appropriate location and strategy, depending on objective (i.e., reducing flooding, improving water quality, etc.) (Zellner et al., 2016).

Equality of Access to Water

Although it is not a historical concern in the U.S., there is an important view of water as a human right that has been codified in other countries:

> While the international community first enshrined human rights in the Universal Declaration of Human Rights in 1948, the human right to water and sanitation remained primarily implied and amorphous until the United Nations Committee on Economic, Social and Cultural Rights adopted General Comment No. 15 in 2002
> *(Beail-Farkas, 2012, 765).*

Admittedly "largely theoretical for much of the world's population" (Beail-Farkas, 2012, 765), some countries have implemented legal and physical mechanisms to meet this UN declaration. For instance, in South Africa, with the end of Apartheid, the new government created both a human and an environmental right to water through the National Water Act of 1998 (NWA). The NWA redefines the public and the private water demarcations, prioritizing a public interest in water supply for domestic use and environmental sustainability (Davies & Day, 1998; Peckham & Rowntree, 2000). Built on expert water governance consultation from Australia, Chile, Mexico, Spain, and the United States, the NWA eliminates the perpetuity of water rights, now considered a national resource. Akin to the land reform process, the South African national government has the power to curtail privately held water rights, and has a constitutional obligation to assess and measure the amount of water needed for basic food, drinking and sanitation, as well as sufficient water to maintain environmental sustainability, producing ecosystem goods and services. This flow allocation is known as the Reserve, but does not yet have an absolute measure. Rather, it is tailored to the specific water source and the local demands, both present and projected (NWA, 1998). But the reality remains that in many developing countries, water access and provision falls to women, who spend a considerable portion of each day locating the water to support their households in areas without government-provided water supply infrastructure (UN-Habitat, 2003).

Access to quality water is also an acknowledged but unaddressed issue in the U.S., as its cities are realizing the cost of deferred maintenance, infrastructure replacement and provision (American Society of Civil Engineers, 2017). The Flint, Michigan example of a water utility switching sources and impacting an entire community to save short-term costs is unfortunately replicated throughout our country, as the Natural Resources Defense Council's seminal reports, "What's on Tap" (Olson, 2003) and "What's in Your Water" (Olson & Fedinick, 2016) show the prevalence of multiple contaminants (i.e., pathogens, carcinogens, perchlorates, arsenic, etc.) in city water supplies in 2003, and lead and copper contamination in 2016 (Olson, 2003; Olson & Fedinick, 2016). In fact, using the human right to water concept, the United Nations argued that the Flint residents' fundamental rights had been violated (Associated Press, 2016). There are other endocrine-disrupting contaminants, pharmaceuticals, poly- and perfluoroalkyls (PFAs) and personal care products that the U.S. EPA has yet to list (Kumar & Xagoraraki, 2010; Hu et al., 2016), which are compounding in our drinking water and can viably be removed if regulated and corresponding treatment infrastructure investments are made (Burkhardt-Holm, 2010; Vieno et al., 2007; Schröder et al., 2012).

But infrastructure quality and other unregulated contaminants are not the only emerging quality problems; there is also a concern about the impact of fracking (i.e., injecting fluid into shale beds to extract natural gas) on drinking water quality (Prud'homme, 2011). Planners and their local jurisdictions are just beginning, albeit variably, to address this water quality impact through "road restrictions . . . special land use permits for fracking sites and setbacks for compressor stations associated with fracking activity" (Loh & Osland, 2016, 229).

Additionally, equity manifests in concerns about water pricing when there are infrastructure system upgrades that can impact low income families, as water is such a fundamental need for survival. One solution is to use a life-line rate, a deeply discounted rate for a small amount of water use, when a water utility introduces an increasing block rate structure for water and wastewater pricing per household. In some American municipalities, a life-line rate is available for 500 cubic feet or less use per month.

In sum, planners can use regulatory authority that water providers lack to link water and land use planning. For instance, planners can consider the water resources and land uses within the entire watershed, identify asset areas and priorities for preservation and development at the watershed level, and work with other jurisdictions to achieve more coordinated development and water conservation plans. They can vertically and horizontally link watershed-based plans and/or water supply plans with comprehensive and hazard mitigation plans to improve water quality and supply assurance. They can also employ the transfer of development rights tool to move or reduce development in sensitive watersheds (e.g., the Long Island Pine Barrens, Lake

Tahoe basin) (Dyckman, forthcoming). They can coordinate with sewer and water authorities on provision/assured supply and equitable pricing, promote water conservation in built form, synchronize capital improvements in water and wastewater infrastructure with changing land uses, and anticipate both cumulative and secondary impacts of existing and future development in a floodplain. Finally, they can promote LID at the parcel and site level.

Towards More Resilient and Sustainable Water Management Planning

This more comprehensive, holistic view of both water quality and quantity management is concurrent with the realization that top-down, dominant agency strategies to address watershed management problems (aka common pool resources) have not been as effective in resolving non-point source pollution, aquatic species protection, etc. as initially hoped. Rather, water policy-makers and planners addressing water provision and water quality issues need a more malleable structure tailored to a problem-shed perspective that involves all of the stakeholders, if possible.

This is where the collaborative management structures enter the water policy landscape. Some of the universal characteristics of this newer form include: "face-to-face information exchange and problem solving among all the relevant stakeholders, usually under fairly strict civility guidelines and some form of consensus rule" (Sabatier et al., 2005, p. 5, citing Weber, 1998, 2003). Sabatier et al. (2005) characterize the collaborative variations that use processes such as social learning and adaptive management (Pahl-Wostl et al., 2007b) as collaborative superagencies (Connick & Innes 2003; Innes & Booher, 2010) and associated modular environmental regulation (Freeman & Farber, 2005); collaborative engagement processes (Margerum, 2011); and collaborative watershed partnerships (Born & Genskow, 2001; Ostrom & Cox 2010). The laws, policies, and plans that emerge from the collaborative processes have power to monitor, mandate, and deliver political and economic consequences, but nature always responds, so they must include an ecosystem perspective.

Researchers have engaged different aspects of commons management, trying to identify the necessary preconditions that support a successful avoidance of the tragedy of the commons with increasing environmental and global pressures over natural resources.

But these processes are challenging to measure. To attempt to predict and assess public involvement, an integral component of social learning (Pahl-Wostl et al., 2007a), the engineering field has introduced the concept of shared vision planning (Palmer et al., 2013), and the environmental economics field has embraced mediated modeling, each of which are tools to facilitate public involvement in multi-scalar learning and decision-making (van den Belt & Blake, 2015). However, more participation "does not always result in successful planning and decision making" (Palmer et al., 2013, 616), as is evidenced in the San Francisco Bay Delta's CALFED process (Hanemann & Dyckman, 2009) and any overburdened participatory and complex environmental problem solving process (Deppsich & Hasibovic, 2013). The quality, perception of and process through which the social learning occurs are equally as important as the inclusiveness (Margerum, 2011).

Contextual, Creative International Water Management Strategies

International examples suggest that more resilient water resources outcomes can be achieved, but that they are dependent on the national environmental, legal, social, and political contexts. For instance, South Africa established a system to effectuate the Reserve setting that is now being emulated in other countries. Through a consensus-based catchment-management level process, users determine an acceptable class for the river (e.g., the level of environmental degradation and economic utilization of the river system). The river is then classified for its ecological state, adding in the sociocultural issues and uses around the river, and it is scored from pristine to highly degraded. In a workshop with all of the users, there is debate about each section of the river, and whether it should be improved, as well as the water volume needed to maintain the chosen state. Those goals are translated into flows on a monthly basis (with flooding), and the Reserve's flow regime is calculated (Conca, 2006). If the human and ecological needs are ever in conflict on a very constrained catchment, then the fundamental priority is with human needs and the river can be classified at a lower environmental level.

In contrast, Australia has a more privatized system, retaining private water rights, and the government effectively buys back flows for the environment, particularly in the Murray Darling Basin. Like South Africa and the U.S. Colorado River, the Murray Darling Basin found itself in an environmental crisis in the early 1990s (Connell & Grafton, 2011). In addition to consistently low flows, rivers were contaminated with agricultural wastes from upstream irrigation and urban growth diversion. A Murray Darling Basin Commission ordered a water use audit, and based on those results, imposed a temporary and then a more permanent Cap (limited to diversions of 1993/1994 levels) on the volume of water diverted from the basin's rivers for consumption. The federal government now issues guidelines to determine environmental flows, and if the states and their communities seek to grow within the basin, they must institute conservation measures and transfer water via a water market (Turral et al., 2005).

American planning efforts haven't as effectually balanced water allocation between competing needs and users, particularly in preserving the environmental health of the water systems. In places of complex and significant water conflict, including the San Francisco Bay Delta, the Florida Everglades, the Klamath River basin, the Chesapeake Bay, the Great Lakes basin, the Colorado River, and the ACT-ACF rivers, the endangered species continue to experience decline. However, there are multiple management approaches in these areas, including modular environmental regulation (SF Bay Delta), collaborative management (FL Everglades), negotiations and resort to the legal system for water rights adjudication (the Klamath, the CO River), compacting (the Great Lakes Basin), and *parens patriae* suit for equitable apportionment from the U.S. Supreme Court (the ACF, *Florida v. Georgia*). Of these options, the compacting (Sherk, 2005; Dellapenna, 2005; Schlager & Heikkila, 2009), as well as the state comprehensive water planning to internally manage their water resources (Kundell et al., 2000; Moreau & Hatch, 2008; Dyckman, 2016) are the most viable.

Trickling Back In: A New Era in Planning Education

Planners are poised to connect the shaping of built form and the management of water quality and quantity, as well as conduct the facilitation needed for larger-scale watershed management and collaborative process approaches. Consequently, water resource management principles, particularly the policy and law noted in this chapter, are and should be incorporated into U.S. planning curricula. The primary components/most valuable parts of water resource study to incorporate into a general course on water or dispersed through other environmental courses are:

- a basic review of the hydrologic cycle and water budgets;
- water economics and valuation (supply, pricing, provision typology (public versus private), demand management/water conservation measures—especially in built form);
- water rights frameworks and environmental laws (particularly in the U.S.) and the distinction between surface and groundwater, as well as protection of environmental flows;
- the anticipated impacts of climate change on water rights and water supply, both locally and globally;

- water management and allocation policy, especially:
  - interstate river conflicts and compacting,
  - collaborative watershed management,
  - water transfers, and
  - water as a planning tool (water supply and planning requirements, the mechanics of comprehensive water planning at state and local levels, watershed-based planning);
- and emerging water policy issues, especially:
  - supply for megacities,
  - quality issues (endocrine-disrupting compounds, infrastructure failure or absence, etc.),
  - climate change, drought planning, and dam removal (or construction, depending on the country),
  - water manufacturing (deslination, gray water reuse and treatment, etc.); and
  - flooding and stormwater control (especially GSI).

To give students full exposure to water resources management principles in a planning curriculum would require at least three courses: (1) a discrete, stand-alone water policy and law course that is part of the core curriculum; (2) a course on hydrology for planners and others in the built form disciplines (i.e., landscape architects, engineers, etc.); and (3) environmental planning courses that include the following principles/concepts: low impact development, GI and GSI, water planning, river restoration (particularly in urban areas), watershed-scale planning with water zoning, and nonpoint source control.

The body of literature most useful for those at the intersection of water management and planning is expanding. Randolph's text is an excellent place to start, as well as Riley's *Restoring Streams in Cities* (1998), and Dunne and Leopold's (1978) classic, *Water in Environmental Planning*. Postel and Richter (2003) have an important book on protecting environmental flows, and more recently, Richter (2014) looked at the balance of international water management in *Chasing Water: A Guide for Moving from Scarcity to Sustainability*. Islam and Susskind (2013) offer a water diplomacy model to begin to conduct larger negotiations around water conflict, whether local or international.

An entire literature has emerged regarding the associated collaborative processes, as well as a separate but complementary local policy network literature, to procedurally document the character and outcomes of the watershed-based planning groups—particularly in relation to agricultural watershed management (Sabatier et al., 2005; Lubell & Fulton, 2007; Ostrom, 2010; Innes & Booher, 2010; Margerum, 2011). While their research shows decided difference in the watershed groups' composition, formalization, and water quality typology, the unifying component is the use of collaborative, place-based process to address watershed protection. This chapter has attempted to address the fundamental concepts in water resources management of which planners should be aware/have the opportunity to influence. But the field is vast, and there are inevitable relevant topical omissions, particularly as holistic water resources management is evolving quickly. All of the referenced material for this chapter could support a planning course in water resources management, but the following list of recommended readings enumerates the fundamental material for a syllabus.

Notes

1 The reverse is true in England, which is the only European country to be entirely privatized in its water and wastewater provision, with varying degrees of privatization in other European countries (Haarmeyer & Coy, 2002). China, Vietnam, South Korea, Argentina, Brazil, Chile, and Bolivia have embraced

water privatization, and the remainder of Asian and Latin American countries have variably followed (Haarmeyer & Coy, 2002).
2   Although accepted in Australia and by the international community (i.e., the World Bank, Global Water Partnership, U.S.A.I.D., etc.), integrated water resources management is extensively and viably criticized in the literature by renowned and leading water management and planning scholars (e.g., Blomquist & Schlager, 2005; Saravanan, McDonald & Mollinga, 2009; Islam & Susskind, 2013, etc.).

Recommended Readings

Barnett, Cynthia. 2007. *Florida and the Vanishing Water of the Eastern U.S.* Ann Arbor, MI: The University of Michigan Press.
Conca, Ken. 2006. *Governing Water: Contentious Transnational Politics and Global Institution Building.* Cambridge, MA: The MIT Press.
Doremus, Holly and A. Dan Tarlock. 2008. *Water War in the Klamath Basin.* Washington D.C.: Island Press.
Dunne, Thomas and Luna B. Leopold. 1978. *Water in Environmental Planning.* New York: W.H. Freeman and Company.
Elmer, Vicki and Adam Leigland. 2014. *Infrastructure Planning and Finance: A Smart and Sustainable Guide for Local Practitioners.* New York: Routledge Press.
Feldman, David Lewis. 2007. *Water Policy for Sustainable Development.* Baltimore, MD: The Johns Hopkins University Press.
Gleick, Peter. 2014. *The World's Water Volume 8: The Biennial Report on Freshwater Resources.* Washington, D.C.: Island Press.
Glennon, Robert. 2002. *Water Follies: Groundwater Pumping and the Fate of America's Fresh Waters.* Washington, D.C.: Island Press.
Hundley, Norris Jr. 2001. *The Great Thirst: Californians and Water: a History*, revised edition. Berkeley, CA: University of California Press.
Islam, Shafiqul and Lawrence Susskind. 2013. *Water Diplomacy: A Negotiated Approach to Managing Complex Water Networks.* New York: Resources For the Future Press.
Lassiter, Alison, ed. 2015. *Sustainable Water: Challenges and Solutions from California.* Berkeley, CA: University of California Press.
Postel, Sandra and Brian Richter. 2003. *Rivers for Life: Managing Water for People and Nature.* Washington, D.C.: Island Press.
Prud'Homme, Alex. 2011. *The Ripple Effect: The Fate of Freshwater In the Twenty-First Century.* New York: Scribner.
Randolph, John. 2012. *Environmental Land Use Planning and Management*, 2nd edition. Washington, D.C.: Island Press.
Reisner, Marc. 1993. *Cadillac Desert: The American West and Its Disappearing Water.* New York: Penguin Books.
Richter, Brian. 2014. *Chasing Water: A Guide for Moving from Scarcity to Sustainability.* Washington D.C.: Island Press.
Riley, Ann. 1998. *Restoring Streams in Cities: A Guide for Planners, Policy Makers, and Citizens.* Washington D.C.: Island Press.
Sabatier, Paul, Will Focht, Mark Lubell, Zev Trachtenberg, Arnold Vedlitz, and Marty Matlock (Eds.). 2005. *Swimming Upstream: Collaborative Approaches to Watershed Management.* Cambridge, MA: The MIT Press.
Sedlak, David. 2014. *Water 4.0: The Past, Present, and Future of the World's Most Vital Resource.* New Haven, CT: Yale University Press.

References

Allen, L., Christian-Smith, J., & Palaniappan, M. (2010). *Overview of Greywater Reuse: The Potential of Greywater Systems tTo Aid Sustainable Water Management.* Oakland, CA: Pacific Institute. Retrieved from www.pacinst.org/wp-content/uploads/sites/21/2013/02/greywater_overview3.pdf
Alliance for Water Efficiency. (2017). Retrieved from www.allianceforwaterefficiency.org/1Column.aspx?id=10025&terms=net+blue
American Society of Civil Engineers. (2017). Infrastructure Report Card. Retrieved from www.infrastructurereportcard.org/

Associated Press. (2016). UN experts: Human rights in Flint may have been violated. *Associated Press*. Retrieved from https://wtop.com/health-fitness/2016/05/un-experts-human-rights-in-flint-may-have-been-violated/

Barnett, C. 2007. *Florida and the Vanishing Water of the Eastern U.S.* Ann Arbor, MI: The University of Michigan Press.

Bates, S. (2012). Bridging the Governance Gap: Emerging Strategies to Integrate Water and Land Use Planning. *Natural Resources Journal*, 52(1), 61–97.

Baumann, D. D., Boland, J. J., & Hanemann, W. M. (1998). *Urban Water Demand Management and Planning*. New York: McGraw-Hill.

Beail-Farkas, L. (2012). The Human Right to Water and Sanitation: Context, Contours, and Enforcement Prospects. *Wisconsin International Law Journal*, 30, 762–801.

Beatley, T. (2009). *Planning for Coastal Resilience: Best Practices for Calamitous Times*. Washington, D.C.: Island Press.

Benedict, M. A., & McMahon, E. T. (2006). *Green Infrastructure: Linking Landscape and Communities*. Washington, D.C.: Island Press.

Berke, P., Smith, G., & Lyles, W. (2012). Planning for Resiliency: Evaluation of State Hazard Mitigation Plans under the Disaster Mitigation Act. *Natural Hazards Review*, 13(2), 139–149.

Blomquist, W., & Schlager, E. (2005). Political Pitfalls of Integrated Watershed Management. *Society & Natural Resources*, 18(2), 101–117. doi:10.1080/08941920590894435

Born, S. M., & Genskow, K. D. (2001). *Toward Understanding New Watershed Initiatives: A Report from the Madison Watershed Workshop, July 20–21, 2000, Madison, Wisconsin*. Paper presented at the Madison Watershed Workshop, Madison, Wisconsin.

Brooks, D. B. (2005). Beyond Greater Efficiency: The Concept of Water Soft Path. *Canadian Water Resources Journal*, 30(1), 83–92.

Burby, R. J. (1998). Policies for Sustainable Land Use. In R. J. Burby (Ed.), *Cooperating with Nature: Confronting Natural Hazards with Land-Use Planning for Sustainable Communities* (pp. 263–291). Washington, D.C.: Joseph Henry Press.

Burby, R. J., & May, P. J. (1997). *Making Governments Plan: State Experiments in Managing Land Use*. Baltimore, Maryland: The Johns Hopkins University Press.

Burkhardt-Holm, P. (2010). Endocrine Disruptors and Water Quality: A State-of-the-Art Review. *International Journal of Water Resources Development*, 26(3), 477–493.

Cahill, T. H. (2012). *Low Impact Development and Sustainable Stormwater Management*. Hoboken, New Jersey: John Wiley & Sons.

Cesanek, W., Elmer, V., & Graeff, J. (2017). *PAS Report 588: Planners and Water*. Chicago, IL: American Planning Association. Retrieved from www.planning.org/publications/report/9131532/

City of Philadelphia (2016). Retrieved from www.phila.gov/water/pages/default.aspx

Conca, K. 2006. *Governing Water: Contentious Transnational Politics and Global Institution Building*. Cambridge, MA: The MIT Press.

Connell, D., & Grafton, R. Q. (2011). Water reform in the Murray-Darling Basin. *Water Resources Research*, 47(12), 1–9.

Connick, S., & Innes, J. E. (2003). Outcomes of Collaborative Water Policy Making: Applying Complexity Thinking to Evaluation. *Journal of Environmental Planning and Management*, 46(2), 177–197.

Cosens, B. A., & Stow, C. A. (2014). *Resilience and Water Governance: Addressing Fragmentation and Uncertainty in Water Allocation and Water Quality Law*. (522). Retrieved from http://digitalcommons.unl.edu/usdeptcommercepub/522.

CRC for Water Sensitive Cities. (2016, April 11). About the CRCWSC. Retrieved from https://watersensitivecities.org.au/about-the-crcwsc/

Davies, B. R., & Day, J. A. (1998). *Vanishing Waters*. Cape Town: University of Cape Town Press.

Davies, L. L. (2007). Just a Big, "Hot Fuss"? Assessing the Value of Connecting Suburban Sprawl, Land Use, and Water Rights through Assured Supply Laws. *Ecology Law Quarterly*, 34(4), 1217–1295.

Davies, L. L. (2010). East Going West?: The Promise of Assured Supply Laws in Modern Real Estate Development, 43 J. Marshall L. Rev. 319 (2010). *The John Marshall Law Review*, 43(2), 2.

Dellapenna, J. W. (2005). Transboundary Water Allocation in the Twenty-First Century: Colloquium Article: Interstate Struggles Over Rivers: The Southeastern States and the Struggle Over the Hooch. *New York University Environmental Law Journal*, 12, 828–900.

Deppisch, S., & Hasibovic, S. (2013). Social-ecological Resilience Thinking as a Bridging Concept in Transdisciplinary Research on Climate-Change Adaptation. *Natural Hazards*, 67(1), 117–127.

Dyckman, C. S. (2011). Another Case of the Century—Comparing the Legacy and Potential Implications of Arizona v. California and the South Carolina v. North Carolina Proceedings. *Natural Resources Journal, 51*, 189.

Dyckman, C. S. (2016). Sustaining the Commons: The Coercive to Cooperative, Resilient, and Adaptive Nature of State Comprehensive Water Planning Legislation. *Journal of the American Planning Association, 82*(4), 327–349.

Dyckman, C. S. (2018). Planning without the Planners: South Carolina's Section 319 Local Watershed Planning Process. *Environmental Science & Policy, 89*, 126–141.

Dyckman, C. S. (forthcoming). Planners' Presence in Planning for Water Quality and Availability. In E. Deakin, *Transportation, Land Use and Environmental Planning: Integrating for Sustainability*. Amsterdam: Elsevier.

Dyckman, C. S., & Paulsen, K. (2012). Not in my Watershed! Will Increased Federal Supervision Really Bring Better Coordination between Land Use and Water Planning? *Journal of Planning Education and Research, 32*(1), 91–106.

Elmer, V., Blanco, H., & Hsu, D. (2016). *APA–ACSP Survey of ACSP Academic Planning Programs with Respect to Water*. Unpublished, available on request from vickielmer@aol.com.

Elmer, V. & Leigland, A. (2014). *Infrastructure Planning and Finance: A Smart and Sustainable Guide for Local Practitioners*. New York: Routledge.

Fisher-Vanden, K., & Olmstead, S. (2013). Moving Pollution Trading from Air to Water: Potential, Problems, and Prognosis. *The Journal of Economic Perspectives, 27*(1), 147–171.

Florida v. Georgia, No. 220142 (U.S. Supreme Court).

Freeman, J., & Farber, D. A. (2005). Modular Environmental Regulation. *Duke Law Journal, 54*(4), 795–912.

Godschalk, D. R., Beatley, T., Berke, P., Brower, D. J., & Kaiser, E. J. (1999). *Natural Hazard Mitigation: Recasting Disaster Policy and Planning*. Washington, D.C.: Island Press.

Haarmeyer, D., & Coy, D. G. (2002). An Overview of Private Sector Participation in the Global and US Water and Wastewater Sector. In P. Seidenstat, D. Haarmeyer, & S. Hakim (Eds.), *Reinventing Water and Wastewater Systems: Global Lessons for Improving Water Management* (pp. 7–27). New York: John Wiley & Sons.

Haie, N., & Keller, A. A. (2008). Effective Efficiency as a Tool for Sustainable Water Resources Management. *JAWRA Journal of the American Water Resources Association, 44*(4), 961–968.

Hanemann, W. M. (2006). The economic conception of water. In P. P. Rogers, M. R. Llamas, & L. Martinez-Cortina (Eds.), *Water Crisis: Myth or Reality?* (pp. 61–91). London: Taylor & Francis.

Hanemann, W. M., & Dyckman, C. (2009). The San Francisco Bay-Delta: A failure of decision-making capacity. *Environmental Science & Policy, 12*(6), 710–725.

Hanemann, W. M., Dyckman, C., & Park, D. (2015). California's Flawed Water Surface Right. In A. Lassiter (Ed.), *Sustainable Water: Challenges and Solutions from California* (pp. 52–82). Oakland, California: University of California Press.

Harrington, E., & Hsu, D. (2018). Roles for Government and Other Sectors in the Governance of Green Infrastructure in the U.S. *Environmental Science & Policy, 88*, 104–115.

Heberger, M., Donnelly, K., & Cooley, H. (2016). *A Community Guide for Evaluating Future Urban Water Demand*. Retrieved from http://pacinst.org/news/community-guide-evaluating-future-urban-water-demand/

Horner, W. (no date). Water Budgeting: Scientifically Linking Water Resources to Land Use Planning. Session 3Q. Chadds Ford, PA: Brandywine Conservancy.

Howe, C. W. (1979). *Natural Resource Economics: Issues, Analysis, and Policy*. New York: John Wiley & Sons.

Hu, X. C., Andrews, D. Q., Lindstrom, A. B., Bruton, T. A., Schaider, L. A., Grandjean, P., . . . Sunderland, E. M. (2016). Detection of Poly- and Perfluoroalkyl Substances (PFASs) in U.S. Drinking Water Linked to Industrial Sites, Military Fire Training Areas, and Wastewater Treatment Plants. *Environmental Science & Technology Letters, 3*(10), 344–350. doi:10.1021/acs.estlett.6b00260

Hundley, N. 2001. *The Great Thirst: Californians and Water: a History*, revised edition. Berkeley, CA: University of California Press.

Innes, J. E., & Booher, D. E. (2010). *Planning with Complexity: An Introduction to Collaborative Rationality for Public Policy*. London: Routledge.

Irvine Ranch Water District. (2017). Rates & Charges. Retrieved from www.irwd.com/rates-charges

Islam, S. & Susskind, L. 2013. *Water Diplomacy: A Negotiated Approach to Managing Complex Water Networks*. New York: Resources For the Future Press.

Kenney, D. S., Goemans, C., Klein, R., Lowrey, J., & Reidy, K. (2008). Residential Water Demand Management: Lessons from Aurora, Colorado. *JAWRA Journal of the American Water Resources Association*, *44*(1), 192–207. doi:10.1111/j.1752-1688.2007.00147.x

Klein, B., & Kenney, D. S. (2009). *The Land Use Planning, Water Resources and Climate Change Adaptation Connection: Challenges and Opportunities: A Review*. Boulder, CO: Natural Resources Law Center. Retrieved from https://scholar.law.colorado.edu/books_reports_studies/131/

Kumar, A., & Xagoraraki, I. (2010). Pharmaceuticals, Personal Care Products and Endocrine-Disrupting Chemicals in U.S. Surface and Finished Drinking Waters: A Proposed Ranking System. *Science of the Total Environment*, *408*, 5972–5989. doi:10.1016/j.scitotenv.2010.08.048

Kundell, J. E., DeMeo, T. A., & Myszewski, M. (2000). *Developing a Comprehensive State Water Management Plan: A Framework for Managing Georgia's Water Resources*. Atlanta, GA: Georgia State University. Retrieved from https://southeastaquatics.net/resources/pdfs/state%20water%20management%20plan%20review_kundell%20et%20al%202005.pdf

Leopold, L. B. (1968). *Hydrology for urban land planning: A guidebook on the hydrologic effects of urban land use*. U.S. Geological Survey Circular 554. Retrieved from https://pubs.usgs.gov/circ/1968/0554/report.pdf

Li, E., Endter-Wada, J., & Li, S. (2015). Characterizing and Contextualizing the Water Challenges of Megacities. *JAWRA Journal of the American Water Resources Association*, *51*(3), 589–613.

Loh, C. G., & Osland, A. C. (2016). Local Land Use Planning Responses to Hydraulic Fracturing. *Journal of the American Planning Association*, *82*(3), 222–235.

Lubell, M., & Fulton, A. (2007). Local Diffusion Networks Act as Pathways to Sustainable Agriculture in the Sacramento River Valley. *California Agriculture*, *61*(3), 131–137.

Margerum, R. D. (2011). *Beyond Consensus: Improving Collaborative Planning and Management*. Cambridge, Massachusetts: MIT Press.

Moglen, G. E., & Kim, S. (2007). Limiting Imperviousness: Are Threshold-Based Policies a Good Idea? *Journal of the American Planning Association*, *73*(2), 161–171.

Moreau, D. H., & Hatch, L. U. (2008). *Statutes Governing Water Allocation and Water Resource Planning in South Atlantic States*. Chapel Hill, NC: Water Resources Research Institute of the University of North Carolina. doi:10.1.1.174.6203

Mukheibir, P., Howe, C., & Gallet, D. (2014). What's Getting in the Way of a "One Water" Approach to Water Services Planning and Management? An Analysis of the Challenges and Barriers to An Integrated Approach To Water. *Water: Journal of the Australian Water Association 41*(3), 67–73.

National Drought Mitigation Center. (2017). National Drought Migration Center, University of Nebraska.

Olson, E. (2003). *What's on Tap: Grading Drinking Water in U.S. Cities*. New York: Natural Resources Defense Council. Retrieved from www.nrdc.org/sites/default/files/whatsontap.pdf

Olson, E., & Fedinick, K. P. (2016). *What's in Your Water? Flint and Beyond: Analysis of EPA Data Reveals Widespread Lead Crisis Potentially Affecting Millions of Americans*. New York: Natural Resources Defense Council. Retrieved from www.nrdc.org/sites/default/files/whats-in-your-water-flint-beyond-report.pdf

Ostrom, E. (2010). Polycentric Systems for Coping with Collective Action and Global Environmental Change. *Global Environmental Change*, *20*(4), 550–557.

Ostrom, E., & Cox, M. (2010). Moving beyond Panaceas: A Multi-Tiered Diagnostic Approach for Social-Ecological Analysis. *Environmental Conservation*, *37*(4), 451–463.

Pahl-Wostl, C., Craps, M., Dewulf, A., Mostert, E., Tabara, D., & Taillieu, T. (2007a). Social Learning and Water Resources Management. *Ecology and Society*, *12*(2).

Pahl-Wostl, C., Sendzimir, J., Jeffrey, P., Aerts, J., Berkamp, G., & Cross, K. (2007b). Managing Change toward Adaptive Water Management through Social Learning. *Ecology and Society*, *12*(2).

Palmer, R. N., Cardwell, H. E., Lorie, M. A., & Werick, W. (2013). Disciplined Planning, Structured Participation, and Collaborative Modeling—Applying Shared Vision Planning to Water Resources. *JAWRA Journal of the American Water Resources Association*, *49*(3), 614–628.

Peckham, B., & Rowntree, K. (2000). Law and Environment in South Africa. In R. Fox & K. Rowntree (Eds.), *The Geography of South Africa in a Changing World*. Oxford: Oxford University Press.

Peterson, J. A. (1979). The Impact of Sanitary Reform upon American Urban Planning, 1840–1890. *Journal of Social History*, *13*(1), 83–103.

Platt, R. H. (2014). *Land Use and Society : Geography, Law, and Public Policy* (Third ed.). Washington, D.C.: Island Press.

Prud'Homme, A. 2011. *The Ripple Effect: The Fate of Freshwater In the Twenty-First Century*. New York: Scribner.

Randolph, J. 2012. *Environmental Land Use Planning and Management*, 2nd edition. Washington, D.C.: Island Press.

Republic of South Africa. (1998). National Water Act (Act No. 36 of 1998). *Government Gazette*(19182).

Richter, B. D., Abell, D., Bacha, E., Brauman, K., Calos, S., Cohn, A., . . . Kaiser, S. (2013). Tapped Out: How Can Cities Secure their Water Future? *Water Policy, 15*(3), 335–363.

Riley, A. 1998. *Restoring Streams in Cities: A Guide for Planners, Policy Makers, and Citizens*. Washington D.C.: Island Press.

Rosgen, D. L. (1994). A Classification of Natural Rivers. *Catena, 22*, 169–199.

Rouse, D. C., & Bunster-Ossa, I. F. (2013). *Green Infrastructure: A Landscape Approach*. Planning Advisory Service Report Number 571. Chicago, IL: American Planning Association.

Sabatier, P., Focht, W., Lubell, M., Trachtenberg, Z., Vedlitz, A., & Matlock, M. (Eds.). 2005. *Swimming Upstream: Collaborative Approaches to Watershed Management*. Cambridge, MA: The MIT Press.

Saravanan, V. S., McDonald, G. T., & Mollinga, P. P. (2009). Critical review of Integrated Water Resources Management: Moving beyond Polarised Discourse. *Natural Resources Forum, 33*(1), 76–86. doi:10.1111/j.1477-8947.2009.01210.x

Satterfield, Z., & Bhardwaj, V. (2005). Water Meters. In *Water Encyclopedia* (pp. 347–341). Hoboken, NJ: John Wiley & Sons.

Schlager, E., & Heikkila, T. (2009). Resolving Water Conflicts: A Comparative Analysis of Interstate River Compacts. *Policy Studies Journal, 37*(3), 367–392.

Schröder, H. F., Tambosi, J. L., Sena, R. F., Moreira, R. F. P. M., José, H. J., & Pinnekamp, J. (2012). The Removal and Degradation of Pharmaceutical Compounds during Membrane Bioreactor Treatment. *Water Science and Technology, 65*(5), 833–839. doi:10.2166/wst.2012.828

Sedlak, D. 2014. *Water 4.0: The Past, Present, and Future of the World's Most Vital Resource*. New Haven, CT: Yale University Press.

Shandas, V., & Parandvash, G. H. (2010). Integrating Urban Form and Demographics in Water-Demand Management: An Empirical Case Study of Portland, Oregon. *Environment and Planning B: Planning and Design, 37*(1), 112–128.

Sherk, G. W. (2005). Transboundary Water Allocation in the Twenty-First Century: Colloquium Article: The Management of Interstate Water Conflicts in the Twenty-First Century: Is It Time to Call Uncle? *New York University Environmental Law Journal, 12*, 764–946.

St. Hilaire, R., Arnold, M. A., Wilkerson, D. C., Devitt, D. A., Hurd, B. H., Lesikar, B. J., . . . Zoldoske, D. F. (2008). Efficient Water Use in Residential Urban Landscapes. *HortScience, 43*(7), 2081–2092.

Steinemann, A. C., & Cavalcanti, L. F. N. (2006). Developing Multiple Indicators and Triggers for Drought Plans. *Journal of Water Resources Planning and Management, 132*(3), 164–174.

Tarlock, A. D. (2010). How Well Can Water Law Adapt to the Potential Stresses of Global Climate Change. *University of Denver Water Law Review, 14*, 1.

Titus, J. G. (1998). Rising Seas, Coastal Erosion, and the Takings Clause: How to Save Wetlands and Beaches without Hurting Property Owners. *Maryland Law Review, 57*, 1279.

Tsai, Y., Cohen, S., & Vogel, R. M. (2011). The impacts of Water Conservation Strategies on Water Use: Four Case Studies. *JAWRA Journal of the American Water Resources Association, 47*(4), 687–701.

Turral, H. N., Etchells, T., Malano, H. M. M., Wijedasa, H. A., Taylor, P., McMahon, T. A. M., & Austin, N. (2005). Water Trading at the Margin: The Evolution of Water Markets in the Murray-Darling Basin. *Water Resources Research, 41*(7). doi:10.1029/2004WR003463

UN-Habitat. (2003). *Water and Sanitation in the World's Cities: Local Action for Global Goals*. London: Earthscan Publications, Ltd.

United States Environmental Protection Agency. (2005). *Protecting Water Quality from Agricultural Runoff*. (EPA 841-F-05-001). Washington, D.C. Retrieved from www.epa.gov/nps/nonpoint-source-fact-sheets.

United States Environmental Protection Agency. (2009). *National Water Quality Inventory: Report to Congress*. Retrieved from Washington, D.C.:

van den Belt, M., & Blake, D. (2015). Investing in Natural Capital and Getting Returns: An Ecosystem Service Approach. *Business Strategy and the Environment, 24*(7), 667–677.

Vieno, N. M., Harkki, H., Tuhkanen, T., & Kronberg, L. (2007). Occurrence of Pharmaceuticals in River Water and Their Elimination in a Pilot-Scale Drinking Water Treatment Plant. *Environmental Science & Technology, 41*(14), 5077–5084.

Viessman Jr., W. (2009). A History of the United States Water Resources Planning and Development. In C. S. Russell & D. D. Baumann (Eds.), *The Evolution of Water Resource Planning and Decision Making* (pp. 14–82). Cheltenham: Edward Elgar Publishers.

Water Conservation Plan Guidelines, City of Chula Vista Growth Management Ordinance, Municipal Code Section 19.09.050C C.F.R. (2014), Adopted May 27, 2003.

Wentz, E. A., & Gober, P. (2007). Determinants of Small-Area Water Consumption for the City of Phoenix, Arizona. *Water Resources Management, 21*(11), 1849–1863.

Western Water Policy Review Advisory Commission. (1998). *Water in the West: Challenge for the Next Century.* Retrieved from https://azmemory.azlibrary.gov/digital/collection/p17220coll7/id/1565/

Wilcox, D. F. (1910). *Municipal Franchises: A Description of the Terms and Conditions Upon which Private Corporations Enjoy Special Privileges in the Streets of American Cities.* New York: McGraw-Hill Book Company.

Zellner, M., Massey, D., Minor, E., & Gonzalez-Meler, M. (2016). Exploring the Effects of Green Infrastructure Placement on Neighborhood-Level Flooding via Spatially Explicit Simulations. *Computers, Environment and Urban Systems, 59*, 116–128.

27
PLANNING THE JUST CITY

Rachel Garshick Kleit and Rebecca F. Kemper

Introduction

Social justice is an integral aspiration in the planning profession, as expressed in the codes of professional conduct across varied national contexts. The US's *AICP Code of Ethics and Professional Conduct* (2016) contains "aspirational principles" to guide planners' actions in the public interest. These principles focus on democratic participation, the rights of the individual and under-represented groups, the promotion of racial and economic integration, access to choice and opportunity, and the fairness of planning processes. Similarly, the Planning Institute of Australia's *Professional Code of Ethics* (2014) offers standards of conduct that support the elimination of discrimination and the inclusion of people who are disproportionately affected by planning processes, with special attention to aboriginal groups. In Britain, the Royal Town Planning Institute (2016) highlights five core principles, one of which focuses on non-discriminatory practice and equal opportunity. The Canadian Institute of Planners (2016) provides guidelines to the province-specific codes of conduct, defining working in the public interest as respect for diversity. Other internationally recognized ethical planning guidelines also focus on inclusive and participatory planning to balance urban development and human rights (UN-Habitat, 2015).

These variations demonstrate diversity of thought concerning ethical planning action that contribute to the idea of the socially just city. Thus, conceptions of the just city vary, and, in fact, may differ across country contexts or even within them (Marcuse, Connolly, Novy, Olivio, & Steil, 2009). Fainstein (2010) suggests that a just city is rooted in democratic principles, where diversity of thought and background are integral to inclusive planning process. Harvey (2003) suggests a just city is one where the inhabitants shape their environments without fear of displacement.

Yet planning rests at the intersection of different specializations, cultural histories and personal narratives (Fainstein, 2010; Rittel & Webber, 1973; Yiftachel, 1998). As in other interdisciplinary professions, planners need to be able to discuss actively ethical frameworks (Illingsworth, 2009). Furthermore, ongoing dialogue concerning ethical principles is necessary; dialogue, as opposed to debate or mere discussion, facilitates interpersonal knowledge and experiences that can combat preconceived notions and biases, especially in the classroom (Grice, Rebellino, & Stamper, 2017; Yang, 2016). Therefore, this chapter lays out a philosophy of teaching the socially just city based in the code of ethics for the American Institute of Certified Planners (AICP) and pedagogy of dialogue.

This chapter is designed to serve as a template for a seminar that leads students through a semester-long thought process, to help them consider the role of social structure in replicating societal inequity. Six main topics frame the course, beginning conceptually and ending with specific planning concerns and concrete actions. First is an explication of social justice perspectives that coexist within the Western democratic sphere. Second, the course sketches the historical context of social and economic inequity within an urbanizing world, noting planning's past responses. Third is a discussion of the experience of varied populations, with the goal of helping students to identify injustices and question their own implicit biases. Fourth is a unit teaching skills of measurement and interpretation needed to explain inequity. Fifth is a discussion of the market and urban systems' roles in perpetuating inequity, and a review of tools for altering these patterns, including the historical, legal, and social antecedents. Policy options or case studies of actions aimed at reducing social inequity demonstrate paths for progress. The course concludes with a discussion of equity planning, engagement, and societal diversity for students to incorporate into their own practice.

Dialogue as a Pedagogical Approach in Teaching Social Justice

Dialogue concerning ethical principles facilitates empathy and understanding for others as a mode of collaborative inquiry, which can include self-exploration (Burbules, 2000; Lapid, 2003). Bineham (2000) notes that dialogue creates new knowledge by asking participants to question whether they identify with the whole of the conversation, rather than just their own piece of it, and if they can commit to a larger view than their own personal position. Understanding positional knowledge limitations is made even more challenging considering increased income and spatial inequity, especially within the US urban context (Berube & Holmes, 2016); additional contributing barriers exist concerning the damaging effects of racial segregation to regional prosperity (Acs, Pendall, Trekson, & Khare, 2017), an aging white population in combination with an increasingly young population of people of color (Frey, 2014), and the federated and fragmented nature of US metropolitan regions (Conant & Myers, 2006). These barriers not only inhibit the understanding of those other than oneself, but also subsequently limit the ability of planners to facilitate social justice.

Defining Justice and the Just City

Western political perspectives on social justice are broader than those in the *AICP Code of Ethics* (American Planning Association, 2016), those offered as guidance to the international community through UN-Habitat (2015), or those in the more articulated Habitat-III's *New Urban Agenda* (United Nations, 2017). Learning varied perspectives allows students to respond to those in the public sphere who espouse alternative views in order to facilitate inclusive mutual goals within a community setting.

A particularly good compilation of primary reading on basic perspectives on justice is Clayton and Williams (2004). Fainstein's (2010) first two chapters of *The Just City* allow for a more direct tie to these varied perspectives on justice and planning. The addition of Sen's (2004) writing includes a human-rights perspective to which US students frequently have not had exposure. Young (2012) explains cogently the dynamics of institutionalized inequity.

Allowing space for these variations in conceptualization helps students apprehend their own implicit understandings of social justice while moving them towards the *Code of Ethics* as a framework for action. The starting place is the idea that justice is not the same as equality, nor is it the same as fairness or equity. Rather, conceptions of what individuals and groups deserve vary—what is fair depends upon who has "desert" (Clayton & Williams, 2004). Desert, in short, is the idea of having a right to the fruits of one's labor, or the results of a process. Three other basic themes are (1) balancing the rights of the individual with that of society; (2) whether justice concerns the process or outcome; and (3) the balance between cohesion and competition.

Understanding the trade-offs in these perspectives helps planners to guide future action toward equity and inclusion. In short, the planner is seeking to create a just process with equitable representation while creating spaces for inclusion and producing outcomes that enhance societal equity and personal opportunity. Tying these philosophical perspectives to action is crucial in a curriculum focused on the training of professionals. Carmon (2013) provides an especially cogent discussion of planning's societal mandate. Coupled with Fainstein and Fainstein's (2013) discussion of the need to restore just outcomes to planning, these articles offer the motivation for planners to focus on social justice. Additionally, using a community-development framework, planners can outline the essential role of communities and their assets in achieving these sorts of goals (DeFilippis & Saegert, 2012a; Sampson, 2012). Campbell's (2007) planner's triangle of the conflicts among economic, social equity, and environmental goals in planning broadens the scope of social justice concerns, making clear that such concerns are embedded in nearly every decision and recommendation that planners make. Thomas (2008) is especially eloquent about planning's normative emphasis on equity running counter to societal and political dynamics and the lack of widely accepted tools to achieve the goal of social equity.

Preparing Students to Address Inequities

The contemporary metropolitan experience is one of population diversity. Yet professional planners and planning students often come from the dominant race or ethnicity, with little knowledge or experience with those of other backgrounds or their experiences of the world. (This problem is especially visible in, though not limited to, the United States.) The danger, Thomas (2008) notes, is that when societal conflict occurs, planners either "negotiate difficult shoals of allegiance and reform, or . . . have become tools of the state used to create and legitimize situations of spatial control of oppressed racial, ethnic, or religious groups" (Thomas, 2008: 229). Explorations into normative theory and its impact upon framing of planning responsibilities is now integrated into many social justice planning courses exploring minority identities such as sexuality, gender, race/ethnicity, citizenship status, age, economic status, and ableism being recognized within the planning realm (S. Sen, Umemoto, Koh, & Zambonelli, 2017). Planning education has begun embracing multiculturalism's assertion that assimilationist assumptions for minorities loses the diversity of knowledge needed for understanding and addressing societal concerns (S. Sen et al., 2017; Tiryakian, 2003; UNESCO, 2003).

Yet, dialogue about difference is limited when participants are homogenous; with care instructors can avoid institutionalizing dominant perspectives within higher education settings (Kaufman, 2010; MacNevin & Berman, 2017). Exposure to the experiences of varied groups is essential in the training of planners to enhance social justice.

Exposure to that diversity of knowledge can also happen through readings. Doan's (2011) edited volume and Frisch's (2002) article provide insightful resources for challenging hetero normative assumptions of place. Garber (2012) focuses on the shape of feminist spaces. Howe (2013) clarifies the importance of planning for aging populations. Immigration trends are another important context for exploring inequity; urban housing costs have created suburban immigrant enclaves, distinct from the urban experience of previous generations (Singer, 2013). Mental health and disability are often omitted from discussions of diversity, yet often the mentally ill are the most visible on urban US street corners. Coming from the US legal arena, Failer's (2002) *Who Qualifies for Rights?* tells the story of the civil commitment of a homeless woman who was involuntarily treated for mental illness. In the end, the court ruled that despite her "unconventional" living situation, she had the right to live as she wished. This case allows students to have an in-depth conversation about issues of ability, the responsibilities of the state, and the rights of the individual.

Understanding and Measuring Patterns of Diversity: Social and Economic Inequity in the City

Planners must exhibit not only cultural competence, but also diagnose and support equity. They need tools to demonstrate the implications of metropolitan and local inequity. Traditionally, planners have used measures such as dissimilarity indices to document levels of racial segregation and social isolation (Massey & Denton, 1988). Many on-line sites contain the calculated indices that summarize a metropolitan area's level of segregation (Population Studies Center, 2017). More recently, in the United States, tools such as the Kirwan Institutes for the Study of Race and Ethnicity's Opportunity Mapping (Martin, 2015) create the opportunity for community conversation about residential segregation's impact on access to opportunity and regional prosperity. One example of how opportunity mapping has been used to argue for intervention is in the decade-long legal case *Thompson vs. HUD* in Baltimore, Maryland; the uneven distribution of opportunity throughout that region became the basis for the court-ordered solution (Lui, Knapp, & Knaap, 2014). Opportunity mapping later became central to HUD's Sustainable Communities Initiative under implementation of the 2013 program rules.

These sorts of measurement tools, however, are lacking without effective, localized narratives to clarify findings. Some resources on the intersection of planning and poverty are Teitz and Chapple (2013) and Andreotti and Mingione (2013). Briggs (2005a) provides a clear depiction of the problems of spatial, racial, and economic inequality. Conant and Myers (2006) provide a good overview of how inequality can define US regional problems and regional governance can address them. A. Sen (2012) outlines analysis of disadvantage, contrasting utilitarian notions of maximizing utility with a focus on human achievement, while the Opportunity Agenda (2017) provides guidance on framing narratives for action.

Inequity in the Domains of Planning

Social justice issues play out in a variety of planning arenas. What follows are some of those arenas, with some resources:

> *Housing.* Topics include the role of housing and neighborhoods in child outcomes (Galster & Santiago, 2017), incorporating problems of implicit bias within the housing market and the enforcement of the Fair Housing Act (Olinger, Capatosto, & McKay, 2016), the disparate impacts of the foreclosure crisis and solutions (Immergluck, 2012), and implications of financialization and household debt for spatial inequality (Walks, 2014).
>
> *Transportation.* A focus on mobility versus accessibility; the construction of free markets for service delivery; and a problematic use of revealed willingness to pay as an analysis tool for transportation service delivery, suggests that they reinforce existing societal inequities (Levine, 2013). Sanchez, Brenman, Ma, and Stolz (2007) lay out the legal framework for

transportation as a right and the dynamics of the racialized delivery of transportation services. Walker (2008) offers excellent guidance on how to shape public conversations around public transport and transportation equity. An award-winning documentary film follows the first application of the US Civil Rights Act to transportation (Bell, 2017).

Employment and Economic Development. Fitzgerald and Leigh (2002) offer an overview of traditional perspectives on economic development, as well as options for increasing the equity of local economic development policy. Understanding the basics of agglomeration economies allows for strategic thinking to accommodate "equity and justice in addition to economic efficiency" (Shefer & Frenkel, 2013: 198). Living wage laws may reconcile economic development and equity aims (Lester, 2012). Simon (2001) presents an excellent discussion of the role of third-sector organizations and property rights in insuring local benefit.

Parks, Service Delivery, and Environment. The differential access to green space has an impact on health. Wen, Zhang, Harris, Holt, and Croft (2013) document spatial disparities in the distribution of green space in the US, and Wright Wendel, Zarger, and Mihelcic (2012) provide a cogent discussion of norms regarding accessibility and usability.

Globalization and Immigration. The last five chapters of Fainstein's (2010) book provide analysis of varied approaches to inclusion and how those approaches contribute to a just city. Berry (2001) offers conceptual clarity on multiculturalism and the incorporation of immigrants into their new countries.

Health Care and Wellness. Acevedo-Garcia and Osypuk (2008) summarize the relationship between neighborhoods, health, and race, and offer policy options. A case example is Marinescu et al.'s (2013) work on supporting physical activity in public housing. A fun and cogent TEDx talk by Teresa Long (2010), MD, MPH, public health commissioner, shapes the community conversation.

Digital Equity. For a framework for a discussion of the social equity implications of our increasingly networked society, see (Gurstein, 2013). For an on-the-ground case study, see Boston's Broadband and Digital Equity Department (City of Boston, 2016).

What Can a Planner Do?

Some localities have created local equity plans using a disparate impact to analyze potential effects of policies. For two Washington State examples, see the Seattle Race and Social Justice Initiative's three-year plan and toolkit (City of Seattle, N.D.) and the King County Washington Equity and Social Justice Initiative's Strategic Plan (King County Washington, 2015). These on-the ground actions help students visualize what Krumholz (2012) discusses as equity-oriented planning practice.

Assignments emphasize the analysis of planning for social justice action. For example, students might create a Social Justice Rubric (or Toolkit) that a planner might use to evaluate an approach, process, plan, or policy. Here, students identify three to five decision criteria. A final paper asks them to select a program, plan, policy, or situation that is (or could be) working toward a socially just outcome. The paper asks students to describe the problem and the effort to address it, and then respond to some key questions: How is this effort creating a socially just city or region? What are the goals of the people who are involved, and why do they think what they are doing will increase socially just outcomes?

Expanding on other tools helps students define potential paths forward. Framing their citizen engagement training in terms of the socially just city is one possible route (Bratt & Reardon, 2013; DeFilippis & Saegert, 2012b). Focusing on social integration and exploring its challenges is another vital emphasis (Charles, 2005; Galster, 2013). Briggs' (2005b) edited volume contains key readings on smart growth, fair housing, and equitable development. More recent work (Dierwechter, 2014; Zapata & Bates, 2015) combines both equity planning theory and practice. A pedagogy of dialogue that allows for personal transformation combined with concrete tools to increase regional equity teaches new planners that the socially just city is not a merely an aspiration but an obtainable reality.

References

Acevedo-Garcia, D., & Osypuk, T. L. (2008). Impacts of Housing and Neighborhoods: Pathways, Racial/Ethnic Disparities, and Policy Direction. In J. Carr & N. K. Kutty (Eds.), *Segregation: The Rising Cost for America* (pp. 197–236). New York: Routledge.

Acs, G., Pendall, R., Trekson, M., & Khare, A. (2017). *The Cost of Segregation: National Trends and the Case of Chicago, 1990–2010*. Retrieved from Washington, DC: www.urban.org/sites/default/files/publication/89201/the_cost_of_segregation_final.pdf

American Planning Association. (2016, April 1). AICP Code of Ethics and Professional Conduct. Retrieved from www.planning.org/ethics/ethicscode.htm

Andreotti, A., & Mingione, E. (2013). The City as Local Welfare System. In N. Carmon & S. S. Fainstein (Eds.), *Policy, Planning, and People: Promoting Justice in Urban Development* (pp. 224–241). Philadelphia: University of Pennsylvania Press.

Bell, J. (Writer). (2017). *Free to Ride* [film]. M. Martin (Producer). Columbus, OH: Kirwan Institute for the Study of Race and Ethnicity, The Ohio State University.

Berry, J. W. (2001). A Psychology of Immigration. *Journal of Social Issues, 57*(3), 615–631. doi:10.1111/0022-4537.00231

Berube, A., & Holmes, N. (2016). *City and Metropolitan Inequality on the Rise, Driven by Declining Incomes*. Retrieved from Washington, DC: www.brookings.edu/research/city-and-metropolitan-inequality-on-the-rise-driven-by-declining-incomes/

Bineham, J. (2000). From Debate to Dialogue: Toward a Pedagogy of Nonpolarized Public Discourse. *Southern Communication Journal, 65*, 221.

Bratt, R. G., & Reardon, K. M. (2013). Beyond the Ladder: New Ideas about Resident Roles in Contemporary Community Development in the United States. In N. Carmon & S. S. Fainstein (Eds.), *Policy, Planning, and People: Promoting Justice in Urban Development* (pp. 356–381). Philadelphia: University of Pennsylvania Press.

Briggs, X. D. S. (2005a). More Pluribus, Less Unum? The Changing Geography of Race and Opportunity. In X. D. S. Briggs (Ed.), *The Geography of Opportunity* (pp. 17–41). Washington, DC: The Brookings Institution.

Briggs, X. D. S. (Ed.) (2005b). *The Geography of Opportunity*. Washington, DC: The Brookings Institution.

Burbules, N. (2000). The Limits of Dialogue as Critical Pedagogy. In P. Trifonas (Ed.), *Revolutionary Pedagogies: Cultural Politics, Education, and Discourse of Theory* (pp. 251–273). New York: Routledge.

Campbell, S. (2007). Green Cities, Growing Cities, Just Cities? Urban Planning and the Contradictions of Sustainable Development. *Journal of the American Planning Association, 62*(3), 296–312.

Canadian Institute of Planners. (2016, 2017). Codes of Professional Conduct. Retrieved from www.cip-icu.ca/Careers-in-Planning/Codes-of-Professional-Conduct

Carmon, N. (2013). The Profession of Planning and its Societal Mandate. In N. Carmon & S. S. Fainstein (Eds.), *Policy, Planning, and People: Promoting Justice in Urban Development* (pp. 13–31). Philadelphia: University of Pennsylvania Press.

Charles, C. Z. (2005). Can We Live Together? Racial Preferences and Neighborhood Outcomes. In X. d. S. Briggs (Ed.), *The Geography of Opportunity: Race and Housing Choice in Metropolitan America* (pp. 45–80). Washington, DC: Brookings Institution Press.

City of Boston. (2016). Broadband and Digital Equity. Retrieved from www.boston.gov/innovation-and-technology/broadband-and-digital-equity

City of Seattle. (N.D.). Race and Social Justice Initiative (RSIJ). Retrieved from www.seattle.gov/rsji/
Clayton, M., & Williams, A. (2004). *Social Justice*. Malden, MA: Wiley-Blackwell.
Conant, R. W., & Myers, D. J. (2006). *Toward a more Perfect Union: The Governance of Metropolitan America* (2nd ed.). Novato, CA: Chandler and Sharp.
DeFilippis, J., & Saegert, S. (2012a). Communities Develop: The Question Is How? In J. DeFilippis & S. Saegert (Eds.), *The Community Development Reader* (2nd ed., pp. 1–7). New York: Routledge.
DeFilippis, J., & Saegert, S. (2012b). *The Community Development Reader* (2nd ed.). New York: Routledge.
Dierwechter, Y. (2014). The Spaces that Smart Growth Makes: Sustainability, Segregation, and Residential Change across Greater Seattle. *Urban Geography*, *35*(5), 691–714. doi:10.1080/02723638.2014.916905
Doan, P. L. (Ed.) (2011). *Queerying Planning: Challenging Heteronormative Assumptions and Reframing Planning Practice*. Ashgate: Surrey.
Failer, J. (2002). *Who Qualifies for Rights?* Ithaca: Cornell University Press.
Fainstein, N., & Fainstein, S. S. (2013). Restoring Just Outcomes to Planning Concerns. In N. Carmon & S. S. Fainstein (Eds.), *Policy, Planning, and People: Promoting Justice in Urban Development* (pp. 32–53). Philadelphia: University of Pennsylvania Press.
Fainstein, S. S. (2010). *The Just City*. Ithaca: Cornell University Press.
Fitzgerald, J., & Leigh, N. G. (2002). *Economic Revitalization: Cases and Strategies for City and Suburb*. Thousand Oaks, CA: Sage Publications.
Frey, W. H. (2014). *Diversity Explosion: How New Racial Demographics are Remaking America*. Washington, DC: Brookings Institution Press.
Frisch, M. (2002). Planning as a Heterosexist Project. *Journal of Planning Education and Research*, *21*, 254–266.
Galster, G. C. (2013). Neighborhood Social Mix: Theory, Evidence, and Implications for Policy and Planning. In N. Carmon & S. S. Fainstein (Eds.), *Policy, Planning, and People: Promoting Justice in Urban Development* (pp. 307–336). Philadelphia: University of Pennsylvania Press.
Galster, G. C., & Santiago, A. M. (2017). Do Neighborhood Effects on Low-Income Minority Children Depend on Their Age? Evidence From a Public Housing Natural Experiment. *Housing Policy Debate*, *27*(4), 584–610. doi:10.1080/10511482.2016.1254098
Garber, J. (2012). Defining the Feminist Community: Place, Choice, and Urban Politics of Difference. In J. DeFilippis & S. Saegert (Eds.), *The Community Development Reader* (2nd ed., pp. 338–346). New York: Routledge.
Grice, K. M., Rebellino, R. L. R., & Stamper, C. N. (2017). Connecting across Borders by Reading without Walls: Using Non-Prose Narratives to Multiply Multicultural Class Content. *English Journal*, *107*(1), 48–53.
Gurstein, P. (2013). Social Equity in the Network Society: Implications for Communities. In N. Carmon & S. S. Fainstein (Eds.), *Policy, Planning, and People: Promoting Justice in Urban Development* (pp. 161–182). Philadelphia: University of Pennsylvania Press.
Harvey, D. (2003). The Right to the City. *International Journal of Urban and Regional Research*, *27*(4), 939–941. doi:10.1111/j.0309-1317.2003.00492.x
Howe, D. (2013). Planning for Aging Involves Planning for Life. In N. Carmon & S. S. Fainstein (Eds.), *Policy, Planning, and People: Promoting Justice in Urban Development* (pp. 262–282). Philadelphia: University of Pennsylvania Press.
Illingsworth, S. (2009). Ethics of Interdisciplinarity: Theory and Practice. In B. Chandramohan & S. J. Fallows (Eds.), *Interdisciplinary Learning and Teaching in Higher Education: Theory and Practice* (pp. 18–29). New York: Routledge.
Immergluck, D. (2012). Community Response to Foreclosure. In J. DeFilippis & S. Saegert (Eds.), *The Community Development Reader* (2nd ed., pp. 90–98). New York: Routledge.
Kaufman, J. J. (2010). The Practice of Dialogue in Critial Pedagogy. *Adult Education Quarterly*, *60*(5), 456–476.
King County Washington. (2015). Equity and Social Justice. Retrieved from www.kingcounty.gov/elected/executive/equity-social-justice.aspx
Kirwan Institute for the Study of Race and Ethnicity. (2015). Understanding Implicit Bias. Retrieved from http://kirwaninstitute.osu.edu/research/understanding-implicit-bias/
Krumholz, N. (2012). Toward an Equity-Oriented Planning Practice in the United States. In N. Carmon & S. S. Fainstein (Eds.), *Policy, Planning, and People: Promoting Justice in Urban Development* (pp. 123–140). Philadelphia: University of Pennsylvania Press.
Lapid, Y. (2003). Through Dialogue to Engaged Pluralism: The Unfinished Business of the Third Debate. *International Studies Review*, *5*(1), 128–131.

Lester, W. (2012). Labor Standards and Local Economic Development: Do Living Wage Provisions Harm Economic Growth? *Journal of Planning Education and Research*, *32*(3), 331–348.

Levine, J. (2013). Urban Transportation and Social Equity: Transportation-Planning Paradigms that Impeded Policy Reform. In N. Carmon & S. S. Fainstein (Eds.), *Policy, Planning, and People: Promoting Justice in Urban Development* (pp. 141–160). Philadelphia: University of Pennsylvania Press.

Long, T. (2010). One Vision. Retrieved from www.tedxcolumbus.com/speakers-performers/2010-whats-next-speakers-performers/teresa-long-m-d/

Lui, C., Knapp, E., & Knaap, G.-J. (2014). *Opportunity Mapping: A Conceptual Analysis and Application to the Baltimore Metropolitan Area*. Paper presented at the Association of Public Policy and Management (APPAM). www.appam.org/assets/1/7/Opportunity_Mapping_A_conceptual_Analysis_and_application_to_the_Baltimore_Metropolitan_Area.pdf

MacNevin, M., & Berman, R. (2017). The Black Baby Doll Doesn't Fit the Disconnect between Early Childhood Diversity Policy, Early Childhood Educator Practice, and Children's Play. *Early Child Development and Care*, *187*(5–6), 827–839.

Marcuse, P., Connolly, J., Novy, J., Olivio, I., & Steil, J. (Eds.). (2009). *Searching for the Just City: Debates in Urban Theory and Practice*. New York: Routledge.

Marinescu, L. G., Sharify, D., Krieger, J., Saelens, B. E., Calleja, J., & Aden, A. (2013). Be Active Together: Supporting Physical Activity in Public Housing Communities Through Women-Only Program. *Progress in Community Health Partnerships: Research, Education, and Action*, *7*(1), 57–66.

Martin, M. (2015). Opportunity Mapping Initiative and Project Listing. Retrieved from http://kirwaninstitute.osu.edu/researchandstrategicinitiatives/opportunity-communities/mapping/

Massey, D. S., & Denton, N. A. (1988). The Dimensions of Residential Segregation. *Social Forces*, *67*(2), 281–315.

Olinger, J., Capatosto, K., & McKay, M. A. (2016). *Challenging Race as Risk: How Implicit Bias Feeds into the Structural Racism that Keeps Housing in America Separate and Unequal–And What We Can Do about it*. Retrieved from Columbus, OH: http://kirwaninstitute.osu.edu/my-product/challenging-race-as-risk-implicit-bias-in-housing/

The Opportunity Agenda. (2017). Retrieved from https://opportunityagenda.org/

Planning Institute of Australia. (2014). Planning Institute of Australia Code of Professional Conduct. Retrieved from www.planning.org.au/membershipinformation/code-of-professional-conduct

Population Studies Center. (2017). New Racial Segregation Measures for States and Large Metropolitan Areas: Analysis of the 2005–2009 American Community Survey. Retrieved from www.psc.isr.umich.edu/dis/census/segregation.html

Rittel, H. W., & Webber, M. M. (1973). Dilemmas in a General Theory of Planning. *Policy Sciences*, *4*(2), 155–169.

Royal Town Planning Institute. (2016). RTPI Professional Standards: Code of Professional Conduct. Retrieved from www.rtpi.org.uk/membership/professional-standards/

Sampson, R. J. (2012). What Community Supplies. In J. DeFilippis & S. Saegert (Eds.), *The Community Development Reader* (2nd ed., pp. 308–318). New York: Routledge.

Sanchez, T., Brenman, M., Ma, J. S., & Stolz, R. H. (2007). *The Right to Transportation: Moving to Equity*. Chicago, IL: American Planning Association.

Sen, A. (2004). Elements of a Theory of Human Rights. *Philosophy & Public Affairs*, *32*(4), 315–356.

Sen, A. (2012). Development as Capability Expansion. In J. DeFilippis & S. Saegert (Eds.), *The Community Development Reader* (2nd ed., pp. 319–327). New York: Routledge.

Sen, S., Umemoto, K., Koh, A., & Zambonelli, V. (2017). Diversity and Social Justice in Planning Education: A Synthesis of Topics, Pedagogical Approaches, and Educational Goals in Planning Syllabi. *Journal of Planning Education and Research*, *37*(3), 347–357.

Shefer, D., & Frenkel, A. (2013). The Center-Periphery Dilemma: Spatial Inequality and Regional Development. In N. Carmon & S. S. Fainstein (Eds.), *Policy, Planning, and People: Promoting Justice in Urban Development* (pp. 183–202). Philadelphia: University of Pennsylvania Press.

Simon, W. H. (2001). *The Community Economic Development Movement: Law, Business, and the New Social Policy*. Durham: Duke University Press.

Singer, A. (2013). Contemporary Immigrant Gateways in Historical Perspective. *Daedelus*, *142*(3), 76–91.

Teitz, M. B., & Chapple, K. (2013). Planning and Poverty: An Uneasy Relationship. In N. Carmon & S. S. Fainstein (Eds.), *Policy, Planning, and People: Promoting Justice in Urban Development* (pp. 205–223). Philadelphia: University of Pennsylvania Press.

Thomas, J. M. (2008). The Minority-Race Planner and the Quest for a Just City. *Planning Theory, 7*(3), 227–247.

Tiryakian, E. A. (2003). Assessing Multiculturalism Theoretically: E Pluribus Unum, Sic et Non. *International Journal on Multicultural Societies, 5*(1), 20–39.

UN-Habitat. (2015). *International Guidelines on Urban and Regional Territorial Planning: Towards a Compendium of Inspiring Practices*. Retrieved from Nairobi: https://unhabitat.org/wp-content/uploads/2015/04/International%20Guidelines%20%20-%20Compendium%20Inspiring%20Practices.pdf

UNESCO. (2003). Multiculturalism and Political Integration in Modern Nation-States. *International Journal on Multicultural Societies, 5*(1).

United Nations. (2017). *New Urban Agenda*. Retrieved from http://habitat3.org/wp-content/uploads/NUA-English.pdf

Walker, J. (2008). Purpose-Driven Public Transport: Creating a Clear Conversation about Public Transport Goals. *Journal of Transport Geography, 16*(6), 436–442.

Walks, A. (2014). From Financialization to Sociospatial Polarization of the City? Evidence from Canada. *Economic Geography, 90*(1), 33–66.

Wen, M., Zhang, X., Harris, C. D., Holt, J. B., & Croft, J. B. (2013). Spatial Disparities in the Distribution of Parks and Green Spaces in the USA. *Annals of Behavioral Medicine, 45*(1), 18–27. doi:10.1007/s12160-012-9426-x

Wright Wendel, H. E., Zarger, R. K., & Mihelcic, J. R. (2012). Accessibility and Usability: Green Space Preferences, Perceptions, and Barriers in a Rapidly Urbanizing City in Latin America. *Landscape and Urban Planning, 107*(3), 272–282. doi:10.1016/J.LANDURBPLAN.2012.06.003

Yang, G. L. (2016, August 23). Glare of Disdain. *New York Times*. Retrieved from www.nytimes.com/interactive/2016/04/01/books/review/28sketchbook-yang.html

Yiftachel, O. (1998). Planning and Social Control: Exploring the Dark Side. *Journal of Planning Literature, 12*(4), 395–406.

Young, I. M. (2012). Five Faces of Oppression. In J. DeFilippis & S. Saegert (Eds.), *The Community Development Reader* (2nd ed., pp. 328–337). New York: Routledge.

Zapata, M. A., & Bates, L. K. (2015). Equity Planning Revisited. *Journal of Planning Education and Research, 35*(3), 245–248. doi:10.1177/0739456x15589967

28
FOOD SYSTEMS

Alfonso Morales and Rosalind Greenstein

Introduction

In planning and other professional fields new subjects for inquiry gain traction through research, teaching, policy and practice. These are often simultaneous and tumultuous. Witness food systems planning. In the late 1990s, Jerry Kaufman at the University of Wisconsin was teaching nascent food systems classes, delivering workshops, and assisting in the creation of food planning positions in local government. He and Pothukuchi published the seminal article "The Food System, A Stranger to the Planning Field" in 2000 (Pothukuchi & Kaufman, 2000). In 2004, he edited a *Journal of Planning Education and Research* special issue on the role of planning in community food systems in response to the rising public interest in the USA in food systems issues and the observed lack of attention given to the topic in the North American planning literature. The Call for Papers on community food systems generated significant interest, especially among educators in planning programs in the USA (Kaufman, 2004). As part of the special issue, Janet Hammer provided an assessment of the state of food systems education in planning programs in the USA at that time (Hammer, 2004).

Unsurprisingly, there was little pedagogical progress on food system planning. Upon contacting all accredited programs on the Association of Collegiate Schools of Planning (ACSP) website, Hammer found that only 13% of schools with planning programs were either currently offering a course on food systems, at one time had offered a course that focused on food systems, or had the subject of food systems embedded in a broader planning course (Hammer, 2004). Despite the many reasons to include food systems in planning (the inherent overlap between food systems and traditional planning areas such as land use, transportation systems, public health, economic development, and environmental concerns such as air and water quality), there had been little systematic attention by planning educators in the USA to the food system (Pothukuchi & Kaufman, 2000).

Food is a basic human need and the food supply chain relies on physical, political, and policy infrastructures inflected by and influencing urban and regional systems and planning. Public awareness of food systems in the USA has continued to escalate over the last decade, and the discussion of farm and food industry consolidation and globalization, natural resource depletion, obesity and metabolic disease, food security, urban agriculture, conventional versus alternative food production, and distribution and marketing have become part of the lexicon of many academic disciplines. This led us to conclude that the time was ripe for a reconsideration of the pedagogical place of the food system in planning (Greenstein, Jacobson, Coulson, & Morales, 2015). In that work we found that in the short span of a decade, the food system has come to occupy a prominent place in planning, and food systems pedagogical practice embraces virtually every planning sub discipline, mirroring the central, and ever differentiating, role of food in society.

What then is the state of the pedagogy of food system planning outside of the USA? This chapter reports on a similar investigation that we took of planning educators across the globe and finds a very different landscape. As USA based planning educators, this exercise has provided us with more questions about our own assumptions regarding planning practice, planning education, and pedagogy. Indeed, this research propels us to seek a deeper understanding of the state of the pedagogy of food system planning across the globe than the survey methods we used here can provide. Still, for the focus of this handbook, we engaged in a rigorous effort to gain an understanding of food systems pedagogy in the English-speaking world outside of the USA We did not ignore the non-English world, but time and resource constraints have limited our research, thus we provide what we have learned about the pedagogical practices described to us, and what we have learned about the assumption and congruence between pedagogical and professional practice. Clearly more work is needed, still, we offer this modest effort in hopes of motivating more interest in this important and timely topic.

Exploration into Identifying Current Food Systems Course Offerings

To determine the food systems planning offerings across the globe we contacted the organizations of planning educators in all regions.[1] We asked the contacts of each organization if they would help us in our research by posting a request for food system planning syllabi among their members. At this early stage in our work we discovered that while the term "food systems planning" has gained a meaningful measure of common understanding among planning academics in the USA, this was not true in other countries. One of our respondents from New Zealand asked us to clarify and define food systems planning. We sent out a second request that included this definition:

> For the purposes of this request we are defining **food system planning** as intentional and collective activities to develop and support healthy, sustainable local and regional food systems that rely on the planners' tools such as, needs assessment, data collection, collaborative planning processes, integration of land use, economic development, public health, transportation, and environmental planning.

In order to be included in our study the syllabus had to focus on the food system, as defined above and not on a more general topic such as social-ecological systems as a whole. We included a syllabus in this study if all or part of the course included the food system. In addition, we included courses that were "marketed" to planning students, even if the instructor was not a planner. Our international outreach yielded 15 responses and 10 usable syllabi. Because this work is exploratory we cannot identify the population or offer a response rate. What we hope our initial effort has done is to sensitize colleagues around the world about food systems in the same way that the term "land use" has relatively similar reference among professionals and academics around the world. However, our effort is nascent, and only generates avenues of exploration for planning practice, planning pedagogy, planning theory, and professional relationships

Table 28.1 Distribution of Syllabi Received by Country and Rank on Human Development Index

Country	Number Syllabi	Rank on HDI
Australia	2	2
Canada	3	9*
Colombia	1	97
Mexico	1	74
Netherlands	2	5
New Zealand	1	9*

Source: Jahan, Human Development Report 2015: Work for Human Development (United Nations Development Programme)

Note: * tie

between planning academics and similarly oriented academics (geographers, policy scholars, etc.) around the world.

Similar to Hammer and our previous investigation of USA planning schools, we found food systems education largely concentrated at the graduate level. Seven of the syllabi received were taught for graduate students and three were for undergraduates; one of the three undergraduate courses was targeted to fourth-year students. This reflects what we understand to be the focus of the membership organizations that we partnered with to distribute our request (Table 28.1).

Six of the syllabi were from English-speaking countries, two from Spanish-speaking countries, and two from the Netherlands. Though we reached out to organizations that serve all continents across the globe, our responses were highly limited. The reasons for this limited response are of keen interest to us, but addressing those issues are beyond the scope of this study. All of the countries represented by the syllabi submitted, however, rank either "very high" or "high" on the Human Development Index (Jahan, 2015).

Current Food Systems Course Assessment

Course syllabi were coded for a variety of features, including course structure, teaching method, whether or not the course is interdisciplinary, how students are asked to engage with the subject, the geographic scope of the course content, how the course addresses the human-ecological relationship, and whether or not the course takes a comprehensive perspective or takes a specific planning perspective (e.g., equity or transportation planning), or relates to an interdisciplinary problem of interest to planning, (e.g., food security analysis or sanitation/waste recovery). Because planning is a profession with a heavily applied focus, we assessed the ways in which practical applications were incorporated into the course. Examples of incorporating practical applications included: community engagement through projects, case studies, and program assessments. In addition, we assessed the scope of the engagement, from global food system assessments to very specific community projects. Furthermore, because planning is a profession with a reciprocal relationship to a number of related disciplines, we evaluated the ways in which food systems assessment is used to address concerns central to professions outside of planning, such as public health. Finally, to evaluate different pedagogical methods, we looked at the material presented, the ways in which professors chose to present the material, and how they assessed student learning.

We identified a variety of course structures and pedagogical practices. Here we simply enumerate this variety as even descriptive statistics are inappropriate for this small study population. The course structures identified included online, seminar, lecture only, lecture plus substantial student engagement through discussion sections. Primary teaching methods identified were assigned readings and films with discussion, lectures, tutorials, writing assignments, presentations, personal reflection journals, participatory projects, in-class debates, field trips and site visits, and guest lecturers. These seem to us representative of contemporary teaching practices we reported elsewhere.

Whether or not a planning course is interdisciplinary can be difficult to determine since the planning profession is inherently interdisciplinary. For this assessment criterion we reviewed syllabi to determine if courses were cross-listed with another department or if they had an obvious influence from another discipline based on title, description or course objectives.

In the assessment of how students were asked to engage the material, we considered student engagement with current events to be present if the instructor asked students to follow food news sites, blogs, or report on examples of food organizations and policies from the news. We defined personal reflection as students writing about or discussing their own involvement in the food system or their personal connection to classwork. We considered students to be engaged in the larger community if they took part in a participatory project, such as working at a local farm or working with a community hunger relief organization. We did not consider research projects to be participatory community engagement unless students had to actively interact with community members.

We evaluated courses for their geographic focus. We placed courses into three categories: Global, Local or Regional, and Global/Local. A course with a Global focus discussed a broad range of food systems topics that are applicable to the global food system as a whole, or explicitly looked at the global impact of certain national and/or regional food systems practices. Local or Regional courses focused on the food system for a specific city or region. Global/Local courses broadly addressed global food systems topics but also discussed or engaged the local food system directly.

We used four categories to characterize the human-ecological relationship: social, cultural, ecological, or mixed. Social courses focused on social issues related to the food system, such as public health, economics, food security, food justice and community planning. Any mention of ecological science is peripheral in the context of a social issue, for example using organic farming methods in urban agriculture systems to address social concerns, not environmental concerns. Cultural courses were similar to social courses, but added a strong focus on history of food traditions, cultural food identity, and cultural implications of global food policy. Ecological courses focused primarily on the ecological and environmental impacts of the food system. Mixed courses gave equal focus to social issues and environmental or ecological issues such as climate change, energy use, and environmental impacts of different farming and food systems.

We analyzed course objectives to determine the skills and competencies that students would have at course completion. Course objectives were categorized as: providing an understanding of the food system, providing tools to directly change the food system, or providing tools to change food system policies. Courses that promised understanding of the food system, without tools to change policy or practice, were coded as "providing understanding." Courses that promised understanding the food system along with providing tools to change practice and or policy, were coded as "providing tools." Courses that promised providing tools to change policy or practice, without mention of understanding the food system as whole, were also coded as "providing tools."

Pedagogical Assessment

The lecture format dominates among food systems courses. None of the courses were organized as lecture only, one was organized as an online course (including online lectures), six as "lecture plus," and three as seminars.

The most common teaching method combined lectures with readings and student preparation for discussion, colloquia, or tutorials, as would be expected from the dominance of the "lecture plus" format. We found only two courses with a project component; both of these were written projects with strong community involvement, in the spirit of the "planning studio" where there was an identified client. In one case the client was a part of the administrative state and in one case the client was part of a social movement. Writing, excluding final reports associated with a project, was incorporated in nine of the courses; two courses included assignments for students to create videos. In addition, two classes required that students keep food system journals. Three courses incorporated field trips or site visits. Lectures were included as a regular component of the course by seven instructors, and three included guest lecturers. Student presentations were also a common teaching method, required by six of the ten courses.

Keeping in mind that planning is inherently interdisciplinary, eight courses were identified as being cross-listed or heavily influenced by another discipline and met our criteria for interdisciplinarity. We understand the limitations to this indicator. For example, the size of the university and the presence of other departments (e.g., agriculture or public health) may influence whether or the degree to which a planning professor can cross-list a course. Such structural variation internationally in cross-listing classes, as well as variation in the ease or bureaucratic difficulty of the practice, would be important research to undertake to undergird such comparative thinking.

How students engage current events, personal reflection, and the larger community varies by course. Only one course asked students to follow food news or other current events related to food systems. Whether or not this indicates the maturation of the field is unclear. Often, rapidly evolving fields require following popular news sources, current events, and activists' websites, along with strictly peer-reviewed and published papers. In our USA study, we found 25% of syllabi analyzed included the course requirement of reading popular sources. At the time of that study we were agnostic on the utility of integrating food news as it relies on particular classroom-level pedagogical goals and practices. This is an example of the fundamental dilemma we faced in this research; our description of food syllabi is only part of the larger question of pedagogical practices.

Three courses incorporated personal reflection of readings or a student's role in the food system through writing and discussion. In our USA study we found 22% of syllabi analyzed articulated a course objective of changing a student's relationship to the food system. While two courses of our international study population did have a community project as a central component of the course, in both cases this was one large class project, not a course requirement that each student engage in a community-based project related to the local food system. This was a notable contrast to the 52% of courses analyzed in our USA study that had this requirement. We acknowledge the difficulties associated with interpreting this finding. While we contacted international organizations of planning educators, only four of the courses represented in our study population are from planning departments (including a combined department of geography and planning). The others come from environmental studies, agroecology, a department of environment and geography, and a department of agriculture, society, and environment. The distribution of departments is listed in Table 28.2.

In the USA, the value of community-based research or project assignments is a pedagogical approach recognized at the institutional level of planning education as the North American

Table 28.2 Academic Departments Represented in Study Population

Departmental Home of Course	Frequency
Community Planning and Development	1
Land Use Planning	1
Urban and Regional Planning	1
Geography and Planning	1
Agroecology	1
Environmental Studies	3
Agriculture, Society, and Environment	1
Environment and Geography	1

Planning Accreditation Board encourages student engagement in community-based planning activities. Furthermore, taken together, community engagement or service projects, site visits, and other experiential learning strategies are indicators of an emerging stance in planning education that we discuss below.

Half of the courses in our international study population looked at the global influence and organization of food systems, either because the focus was on the international forces that shape our current food system or because the local food system was explicitly understood within the context of the global system. Five courses focused specifically on the local food system. Frequently, these locally focused courses were looking at the local food system through multiple lenses.

We believe this concern for different geographies is one reason why food systems holds significant scholarly attraction. Global and local or larger and smaller scale activities are related, through systems of interwoven ideas and behavior. For instance, in the USA, Madison, Wisconsin has the nation's largest producer-only farmers' market, which is located in Capitol Square. Vendors' activities may be guided either by state law or city law depending on which sidewalk a farmer is selling her produce from. Sidewalks on one side of the square are regulated by the City of Madison while across the street on state-owned property state law governs. In this instance of administrative geographies dividing human activities, laws are codified and expected to hold, even if one legal regime or law might not govern the specific system of vending space allocation or the type of products sold legitimately from one side of a street to the next. It is these many entrees and implications, for instance of formal and informal institutional rules constitutive of some activity, that make food system research and teaching of great intellectual and practical interest.

Nine of the ten food systems planning courses explicitly acknowledged the multi-disciplinary aspect of the human-ecological relationship with respect to food systems, and these nine syllabi reflected the instructors' attempts to include that synthesis in their courses. Unlike our findings in the USA study, this study population showed no distinction between the social and political-economic relations, cultural relations, social impacts, and the combination of social and ecological considerations. That is, nearly all syllabi, from these very different countries, reflected what we called the mixed social and ecological considerations.

Six of the ten courses identified understanding the food system as one of their central student learning objectives. Examples of this generalized course objective include:

- "Deepening an analysis of the global food system, as a reflection of and driving force of colonialism and neo-liberal capitalism."
- "Identify the historical and current factors that shape the global food system."

- "Understand some of the main theories and concepts around the global food system through a systems-based approach."
- Develop "a deeper understanding of the [nation's] food and agriculture system, through an interdisciplinary lens."
- "To understand food and hunger politics in the context of environmental justice and social change."
- "Define the main aspects that make up contemporary food crises and their political repercussions."
- "The course aims to ground students in the core theoretical and policy debates on food security, with particular reference to the recent emergence of urban food security as a key research and development theme."

Three of the ten courses identified tools to change policy as one of the central learning objectives. Examples of these learning objectives include:

- "To develop analytical tools to criticize and develop alternatives to current food systems."
- "Be able to provide guidance on the above mentioned[2] conceptual issues and to apply these in actual challenges of strategic planning in city-regions."
- "Understand relationships between food production and consumption in [the country] and how food security can be further strengthened."

One of the ten courses identified tools to change planning practice as one of the central learning objectives. Examples of these include:

- "Apply current approaches to landscape design and planning—as taught in [our university]—to the domain of health and food."
- "Show a critical reflexive understanding of advanced theories and design concepts pertaining to healthy lifestyles and food in landscape design and planning."

This research is just the beginning of an exploration of what the pedagogy of food system planning looks like around the globe. Our initial responses indicate that professors across the globe are bringing food systems planning into the academy. They are doing this in planning departments, as well as in allied departments such as environmental studies and geography. While the term was unknown or confusing to some of our respondents, we were able to dispel the confusion once we defined the domain of interest. Certainly differences will remain in consumption patterns and the particulars of local and national political and policy processes make for unique circumstances. However, because food must be produced, processed, and distributed, such categories provide the rudiments of a common language and similarity in frameworks that will still be recognizable to those with different experiences in regions as varied as Bogotá, Chiapas, Cape Town, and Toronto. This foundation creates the possibility for two-way learning around a number of issues including problem definition, frameworks, theories of change, and pedagogy. For professors, the area of pedagogy may be a useful entry point to begin to explore congruencies in concepts and similarities of policy and practice. Examples of pedagogic issues raised in this study that may provide a useful starting point for such discussions and the eventual emergence of a shared language appropriate to many, though not all, food planning circumstances. In the following discussion, we take up the issue of professional practice and then we offer suggestions for further research.

Discussion

Half of our syllabi came from departments with programs that train professionals for practice with either technical or generalist skills applicable in creating social and/or physical change (e.g., planners and agroecologists). The other half came from departments with programs that train professionals with analytic and synthetic skills useful for deepening understanding and/or framing questions (e.g., environmental studies, environment and geography, agriculture, society, and environment).

For those of us training practitioners who will take up the challenge of participating in social change, it is important that we consider our theory of change, the roles that our students are likely to take in contributing to change, and help them to understand their own commitments within the context of limits and ambiguities of action (Murphy, 1981). Some of our students take up roles in the administrative state, others in private firms that have contractual relationships with and serve the administrative state. Increasingly, our students aspire for roles with "alternative" economic systems proffering organizational models and values distinct from those of late capitalism. These students are training for work at the center of or in alliance with social movements. Thus, we see students engaged in a number of professional programs, from law, to business, to planning, all of a similar mind—extending the organizational alternatives to those dominant in the food system. Frequently this means work in international spaces, for instance fostering networks of cooperatives in coffee cultivation and consumption. In short, our teaching reveals significant variation in students and in the demand from employers for people able to think outside the typical "market sector," and in terms of "social impact" and the "triple bottom line," even among for-profit private corporations. Despite their location with respect to loci of power, it is crucial for students to understand the relationships among and between these dominant institutional structures in order to develop effective strategies for change and identify allies.

This perspective was evident in a number of the syllabi. For example, by way of background, context, and motivation of the course, one instructor wrote:

> Through an analysis of the food system we will deepen our understanding of the nature, structure and impacts of the global economy; examine the many ways groups are using food as a strategy of resistance and basis for community action; and develop an awareness of the ways we participate in and resist global power relations through our everyday food choices.

Such a perspective provides the student with an understanding of the larger system, their position within that system, of the forces at work within the system, and ways that those who oppose these larger forces use food as a strategy in that opposition. However, the student still faces the challenge of translating that larger understanding into an application of the planners' tools in support of place-based (i.e., local or regional) intentional and collective activities to develop and support healthy and sustainable food systems.

We found a more traditional and technical planning approach in a landscape architecture course titled *Foodscapes, Urban Lifestyles, and Transitions*. Here the food system is defined more narrowly and the foodscape is understood as "places and spaces where food is produced, processed, acquired, distributed, consumed and the waste processed." The system is defined in such a way that state actors, including planners and landscape architects, have influence by structuring policies, programs, and infrastructure that structures residents' actions. Non-state actors, such as activists and the media, influence behavior by shaping residents' understanding of these practices.

Which approach should we planning professors be teaching? We wonder if the more generalized approach, that addresses understanding of forces and their impact on communities is part of the early stages of development of a new sub discipline within planning. While possible, the question demands further investigation. Let us turn to some broad research themes we believe warrant immediate attention.

First of all, we need to develop an understanding of the concepts and categories common to food system practices and the variation within these categories. Similar to Wittgenstein's (2010) language game, the idea or language game of food production has many recognizable permutations, beginning with the variety of ways production can be organized, each nested within a broader economic, social, and regulatory context. Furthermore, each of those has connections to biophysical processes as well as connections to processing, distribution, and other elements of the "supply chain." Indeed, contingent on scale even the notion of a supply chain may be problematic. However, it is clear that food moves through relationships, in the myriad ways they are conceived and organized, and students are increasingly interested in envisioning variations of this organization. One important means to achieving an understanding of these concepts and categories, and how they are applied, is through examining the products students produce in class.

Second, we need a clearer sense of what is being taught, how, and with respect to which kinds of different human problems. This has two parts: disciplinary considerations and pedagogical considerations. Similar pedagogical practice can be found in a variety of disciplines, yet we understand the various pedagogical practices deemed suitable for food systems as well as appropriate to local context. We also want to understand how food systems education is organized in higher education. This would include questions of disciplinary location, as well as the relative interest and importance of connecting course offerings across disciplines. A recent scan at the University of Wisconsin of courses offered over the prior three years found 90 courses with food systems content in seven schools and colleges (Business, Agriculture and Life Sciences, Humanities, Law, Letters and Sciences, Medicine and Public Health, and the Nelson Institute), spanning disciplines from philosophy to plant pathology and from folklore to law. How the course content is imparted relies in part on the instructor, the number of students, the level of the course, as well as class goals. Clearly, our recent work on food system pedagogy in planning can usefully be expanded to the teaching of food systems in universities. The challenges here are notable, but not insurmountable, the payoff, especially in understanding the learning outcomes being advanced could be significant.

Third, we need to understand the various ways food system teaching is fostering consciousness of community and connections. By this we mean the importance of history and of scale, as well as inquiry that seeks to make the invisible visible. Students are increasingly conscious of the historical roots of our contemporary political-economic dilemmas and their consequences for global problems such as climate change. They are very familiar with our interconnected world and the ramifications (good and bad) of practices originated or innovated in one place and adopted—either wholesale or with adaptation—in other places. By examining food within a system they come to understand the (absence of) expectations people associate with food and food systems and extend this understanding to other human needs that are commodified. Finally, many students who came to understand these connections and processes in the context of food systems are intervening in everything from resource considerations, to genetics, to health and socio-economic science, to law and regulation, to the stories we tell.

Conclusion

However modest our effort has been, we are among those who express hope, and even a cautious optimism for the way food systems teaching can foster pro-social values and broader human relationships and understanding. Yet we are clear about the challenges teachers of this material face. Further, though we are confident of the important payoff, we are not sure the resources are available to address the research needs we have identified. Still, this nascent effort may take root and bear fruit not only in pedagogical practice, but in advancing our more general interest in equitable, sustainable, and vibrant societies.

Notes

1 We began by contacting organizations listed on the Global Planning Educational Associations Network (GEPAN) website (www.gpean.org) on February 1, 2016. The organizations we contacted included: Association of African Planning Schools (AAPS); Association of Canadian University Planning Programs (ACUPP); Association of European Schools of Planning (AESOP); the Latin American Association of Schools of Urbanism and Planning (ALEUP); the Brazilian National Association of Postgraduate and Research in Urban and Regional Planning (ANPUR); the Australian and New Zealand Association of Planning Schools (ANZAPS); Association of the Advancement of Education and Research and Development Planning (APERAU), and the Asian Planning Schools Association (APSA). In addition we contacted the Commonwealth Association of Planners (CAP); the Irish Planning Institute (IPI); the Planning Institute of Australia (PIA); the Royal Town Planning Institute (RTPI); the Association of Planning Schools of Turkey (TUPOB), and the Association of Indonesian Planning Schools (ASPI).
2 The "above mentioned issues" are: in particular strategies to deal with complexity and uncertainty; a solid methodology of problem setting; dealing with dilemmas of contextualization of regulation and legislation.

References

Greenstein, R., Jacobson, A., Coulson, M., & Morales, A. (2015). Innovations in the Pedagogy of Food System Planning. *Journal of Planning Education and Research*, 35(4), 489–500. doi:10.1177/0739456x15586628

Hammer, J. (2004). Community Food Systems and Planning Curricula. *Journal of Planning Education and Research*, 23(4), 424–434. doi:10.1177/0739456x04264907

Jahan, S. (2015). Human Development Report 2015: Work for Human Development. United Nations Development Programme. Retrieved from http://hdr.undp.org/sites/default/files/2015_human_development_report.pdf.

Kaufman, J. L. (2004). Introduction. *Journal of Planning Education and Research*, 23(4), 335–340. doi:10.1177/0739456x04264897

Murphy, M. B. (1981). Context and Commitment: The Use of Political Economy and Democratic Theory in Teaching Public Administration. *Dialogue*, 3(4), 2–8.

Pothukuchi, K., & Kaufman, J. L. (2000). The Food System. *Journal of the American Planning Association*, 66(2), 113–124. doi:10.1080/01944360008976093

Wittgenstein, L. (2010). *Philosophical Investigations* (G. E. M. Anscombe, P. M. S. Hacker, & J. Schulte, Trans., 4th ed.). London: John Wiley & Sons.

INDEX

Note: References in *italics* are to figures, those in **bold** to tables; 'n' refers to chapter notes.:

Abercrombie, P. 32, 39
academic staff 4
accreditation and professional competence 5, 12–13, 15; assessment for certification 23; continued professional development 23–24, **24**; educating for professional competence 15; program accreditation 15–22, **17**; status and professionalization 13–14; concluding observations 24–25
Acevedo-Garcia, D. 327
ACSP *see* Association of Collegiate Schools of Planning
active learning in lectures and seminars 220–222, 299–300
Adams, F. J. 33, 92
Adams, T. 276
Adler, S. 39
administrative procedures 58
administrative rules 59
Adshead, S. D. 32, 39
AESOP *see* Association of European Schools of Planning
affordable housing 267–268
Africa 72, 97
Agyeman, J. 302
Alexander, E. R. 75
Allmendinger, P. 212
Alofsin, A. 33
Alonso, W. 196
Alterman, R. 218, 265
Altshuler, A. 208
American Institute of Certified Planners (AICP) 14, 23, **24**, 323, 324
American Planning Association (APA) 23, 70, 74, 101, 188, 254; Ethical Principles in Planning 266; online tools 85; Planning and Women Division 103; water resources 305, 306–307; web casts 81; Women and Aging Survey 100
Amorim, M. A. 202
Andreotti, A. 326
announcements 123
Anselin, L. *et al.* 166, 167, 280
Anthony, K. 101
ANZAPS (Australia and New Zealand Associationof Planning Schools) 107
Arendt, R. 280
Ariely, D. 300
Armstrong, J. S. 136
Arnstein, S. R. 84
Ashley, A. J. 38, 75
Association of Collegiate Schools of Planning (ACSP, US) 5, 80, 82; environmental planning 239; Faculty Women's Interest Group (FWIG) 103, 107; food systems 332; gender 102, **103**, 107; housing and community development 265; studio courses 94
Association of European Schools of Planning (AESOP) 22, 73, 107, 266, 271n2
Auckland University 106
Austin, T. 106
Australia 14; Economic Development Australia (ACEcD) 194; environmental planning 239, 240; gender: current guidelines 105; land use planning 234; Planning Institute (PIA) 22, **22**, 24, **24**, 102, 105, 257, 266, 323; studio courses 96; transportation planning 257, **257**; water resources 306, 315; Women's Planning Network 107
Australia and New Zealand Associationof Planning Schools (ANZAPS) 107

342

Index

Austria 71
autonomy 12
Ayala, J. 281

Bacon, E. 275
Baker, J. et al. 156
Balakrishnan, S. 155, 157
Baldwin, C. 218–219, 220, 223
Banfield, E. C. 208
Barnett, C. 309
Barnett, J. 278, 279
Barrow, C. J. 242
Bates, L. K. 73
Baum, H. 301
Baumann, D. D. et al. 311
Beail-Farkas, L. 312
Beatley, T. 302
Beaufort, South Carolina 278
Belmont Report (1979) 154
Ben-Joseph, E. 277
beneficence 154
Berry, J. W. 327
Bina, O. et al. 75
Bineham, J. 324
Birch, E. L. 34, 40, 277
Blakely, E. J. 135, 187, 188
blended learning 135
Bluestone, B. 190
Bodenschatz, H. 276
body language 121
Bollens, S. A. 73
Boo, K. 157
Booth, P. 34, 39
Boschma, R. 200
Boyden, S. V. et al. 177
Brenner, Neil 36
Briassoulis, H. 242–243
Briggs, X. D. S. 326
Brix, J. 276
Brown, D. S. 279, 281
Burby, R. J. 311
Burke, M. et al. **259**, **260**, 262–263

CADD (Computer-Aided Design and Drafting) 281
CAKE (Climate Adaptation Knowledge Exchange) 298
Cal Poly Dan Luis Obispo 81
Campbell, H. 130
Campbell, S. 302, 325
Campbell, S. D. 36
Canada 14, 71; core curriculum 72; planning history courses 35, 36, 37; Town Planning Institute 71
Canadian Institute of Planners (CIP) **22**, **24**, 323
Capone, G. 200
Carmon, N. 325
Carson, B. 269

Carson, R. 240
case-based learning 219–220; active learning in lectures and seminars 220–222; problem-based learning 236; *see also* planning theory in Chinese universities
case law 59, 63
Caves, R. 234
Cesanek, W. et al. 305
Chapin, F. S. 134
Chapin, T. S. 75
Chapple, K. 326
Chicago School 208
China 72; National Steering Committee of Urban and Rural Planning Education (NSCURPE) 44; studio courses 96; Tsinghua University studios 287; Urban Planning Education Authority 257; Urban Planning Society 72; water resources 306; *see also* planning theory in Chinese universities; planning theory in Chinese universities: case studies
Christaller, W. 208
Church, S. P. 80, 84
CIP *see* Canadian Institute of Planners
civic design 276
civil engineering 254
Clayton, M. 324
Climate Adaptation Knowledge Exchange (CAKE) 298
climate change 9, 295–296, 299; active learning 299–300; adaptation 295, 297, 298; broad pedagogy approaches 299–302; core pedagogy issues 296; course scope 296–297, 301; dealing with jargon 298; diversity and equity 299; emotionally taxing issues 300–301; extreme uncertainty 299; first-level decisions 296–298, **297**; geographic scale 297, 298; hyper-politicization 299; local context dependence 298–299; mitigation 295, 297, 298; political and social action 302; second-level considerations 298–299; selecting course materials 298; student participants 296; sustainability 300, 301, 302; Team Based Learning (TBL) 300; topic scope 297; conclusion 302
commitment 12, 118
common good 178–179
common law 59
commonwealth 179
communication 6, 117–118, 178; changing environments 118–119; effectiveness 119; graphic communication 122, 124–125, 178; in groups 121; human relationships 119; information technology 118; leadership 174, 178; methods 119–120; missteps and errors 118; oral communication 120–122; population diversity 118; public input 119; in venues of public participation 121–122; written communication 122–124; conclusion 125–126

Index

Computer-Aided Design and Drafting (CADD) 281
Conant, R. W. 326
Consortium for Scenario Planning 85
constitutional law 59
continued professional development (CPD) 23–24, **24**
core curricula design 6, 69–70; different approaches 74–75, **75**; history of the core 70–72, **71**; ingredients 73–74, **74**; and national planning cultures 72–73; why a core? 70; conclusion: the future 75–76
Cornell University 80, 82
Cornwall, A. 156
Cosgriff, B. 223
Creswell, J. W. 127
Cullingworth, B. *et al.* 234
cultural awareness 174, 176–178, 181
cultural competence 156–157
culture, defined 156, 177
culture of leadership 177
Cumming, S. 39–40

Dalton, L. C. 74, 75, 210
Davoudi, S. 32, 209
Dawkins, C. J. 40, 74
"deglobalization" 3
Denmark: Aalborg University Land Management program 221–222; urban planning education 211–212
descriptive validity 158
design leadership 180
digital equity 327
discretionary interpretation 62
diversity 299
Doan, P. L. 107–108, 325
Dominican Republic 97
Dorfman, P. W. *et al.* 176
du Toit, J. 127
Duany, Andres 280
Duara, P. 3
Dunne, T. 316
Durkheim, E. 218

Eaton, M. 301
ecological modernization 243
economic development *see* local economic development planning; local economic development planning: teaching; regional economic development (RED) planning
Edin, K. 157
Edwards, M. M. 73
employment and economic development 327
enabling laws 59–60
environmental impact assessments 242
environmental planning 8, 238–239, 327; under construction 247–248; education 239–240; externalities 238; generic and specific 246–247;
local environmental planning 243–245, 246–247; market-based policy instruments 243; non-governmental stakeholders 243; proactive approaches 242–243; reactive approaches 241–242; social dilemmas 246–247; standards and regulations 240–241, 243, 244–245; tapering effects 244, *244*; voluntary agreements 243
environmental policy integration 242–243, 327
Environmental Systems Research Institute (ESRI) 289
environmental zones 244, 245
Envision Tomorrow 80
epistemology 127
equity 163–165, 299
Ertur, O. S. 270–271
ethics 12, 154–155, 233–234; *see also* the just city
European Council of Spatial Planners 14
European Master in Territorial Development (EuMiTD) 212–213, 222–223
European Spatial Development Perspective 211
European Union 210
exactions 62
experiential learning 220, 222–223
expertise 12
externalities 228, 238

Faga, B. 288
Failer, J. 326
Fainstein, N. 323, 324, 325, 327
Fainstein, S. S. 36, 325
Faludi, A. 72, 208
Farthing, S. M. 127, 128
Federal Emergency Management Agency (FEMA) 81
federal law 59, 60
Feiss, C. 32, 39
Fergusson, E. 106
Fischler, R. 13, 32, 36, 37, 40
flipped classrooms 81, 135
Florida Atlantic University 81
Flyvbjerg, B. 130
food systems planning 9, 332–333; current food systems course assessment 334–335; defined 333; discussion 339–340; identifying current course offerings 333–334, **334**; pedagogical assessment 336–338, **337**; conclusion 340–341
Forester, J. 93
France: APERAU **17**, 18, 20, 22, **22**; L'Institute d'urbanisme de Paris 33; national planning 72; planning history courses 36
Frank, A. *et al.* 15, 72, 97
Frank, A. I. *et al.* 206, 209, 214
Freeman, C. 106
Friedmann, J. 36, 70, 71, **71**, 72, 196, 209
Frisch, M. 325
Fu, Shulan 37
future orientation 174, 175–176

344

Index

Gaber, J. 154
Gaber, S. L. 154
gaining entry 155
Gamble, D. 276
Gans, H. J. **146**
Garber, J. 325
Geddes, P. 33, 176, 288
gender 6, 100; Australia 105; current guidelines 102–106; global context 102; networks 106–107; New Zealand 106; pedagogy, core, and specialisms 101; sources of information 102; structure 100–101; timeline of events **110–112**; United Kingdom **104**, 104–105; United States 102–104, **103**; conclusion 107–108
generalizability 158–159
Genzmer, Felix 276
GeoDesign 289
Georgia Institute of Technology 286, 287
Germany 14; accreditation 16, 18, 24, 25n8; ASAP 20, 22, **22**; European Master in Territorial Development (Leibniz Universität) 212–213, 222–223; national planning 72, 212–213; Technical University of Berlin 276
Getis, A. 167
Gilderbloom, J. I. 268
GIS (Geographic Information Systems) 164, 169, 170, 171, 281, 288; methods 75, 79–80
giving back 156
Gladwell, M. 289
Glasmeier, A. 271n1
Global Planning Education Association Network (GPEAN) 106–107
globalization 3, 254, 327
Goldstein, H. A. *et al.* 217
Gordon, David 39–40
Gouldson, A. 241–242
governmental authority and constraints 59–60
grant proposals 123–124
graph theory 169
graphic communication 122, 124, 178; of concepts and ideas 125; for data analysis 124–125; for illustration and documentation 124; for marketing and identity building 125; for persuasion 125; for visualization 125
the greater good 174, 178–179
Greece 71
Greed, C. 104, 234
Green, K. C. 136
Greenlee, A. J. *et al.* 73
Gropius, Walter 33
group communication 121
Gunn, Zan 38
Gurran, N. 234

Habitat III: New Urban Agenda 100; Sustainable Development Goals (SDGs) 100
Hack, G. 276, 287

Hall, P. 32, 39
Hamin, E. 296, 297
Hammer, J. 332
Handy, S. *et al.* 258, **259**, **260**, 261, 262
Hardin, G. 240
Harrison, B. 190
Harvard University: city planning course 91; Housing Studies 267; planning education 33, 36; studio courses **93**, 94, 95, 285–286; urban design 277, 279
Harvey, D. 323
Haughton, G. 212
Haussman, G.-E. 275
Hayden, D. 105
Healey, P. 4, 130
health care and wellness 327
Hebbert, M. 33–34
Heriot Watt University (UK) 104, 105
Heumann, L. F. 95
Heyda, P. 276
Hise, G. 39
history *see* planning history
Hoard, S. 101
Hoey, L. *et al.* 217, 218, 219, 220
Hong Kong 72
Hopkins, L. D. 176
hornbooks 63
housing and real estate planning 8, 265–266, 326; affordable housing 267–268; creating incentives and removing constraints 269–270; disadvantaged groups 266; expanding homeownership 268–269; working with public/nonprofit organizations 270; conclusion 270–271
Hovden, E. 242
Howard, Ebenezer 276
Howe, D. 325
Huairou Commission 100, 104
Huang, T.-Q. 44, 47
Hudnut, Joseph 33
Hughes, H. J. 301
human capital 201
human relationships 119
human rights 105, 312, 313
Hurlimann, A. C. 240
Hutson, Malo André 36–37
Huxtable, A. L. 278

identification 12
IEDC (International Economic Development Council) 194
immigration 327
Inam, A. 281, 285
India 72, 96
information technology 118, 236, 254
infrastructure 179–180
Institute of Economic Development (IED; UK) 194

Index

Intergovernmental Panel on Climate Change (IPCC) 298
international comparative planning 8, 217–218; active learning in lectures and seminars 220–222, 299–300; case-based learning as integral strategy 219–220; encompassing comparisons 220; individualizing comparisons 219–220; pedagogical approaches 219–223; problem-based learning in student projects 222–223; reasons for teaching 218–219; variation-finding approach 220; conclusion 223–224
International Economic Development Council (IEDC) 194
International Labour Organization 12
International Planning History Society (IPHS) 34
International Society of City and Regional Planners (ISOCARP) 227
International Standard Classification of Education (ISCED) 15, 25n6
interpretative validity 158
Irazábal, Clara 39
Islam, S. 316
ISOCARP (International Society of City and Regional Planners): *International Manual of Planning Practice* 234
Italy 71

Jacobs, J. **146**, 281
Jakabovics, A. *et al.* 270
Jänicke, M. 248
Japan 34, 72
Jepson, E. J. 135, 234
Jin, C.-N. 48
Johnson, D. 234
Jordan, A. *et al.* 243, 248
Jörgens, H. 248
Journal of Planning Education and Research 327
Journal of Planning History 34
the just city 9, 323–324; defining justice and the just city 324–325; desert 325; dialogue as pedagogical approach 324; digital equity 327; employment and economic development 327; globalization and immigration 327; healthcare and wellness 327; housing 326; inequity in domains of planning 326–327; parks, service delivery, environment 327; patterns of diversity: social and economic inequity 326; preparing students to address inequities 325–326; social justice 323; transportation 326–327; what can a planner do? 327–328
justice 154

Kahn, T. 271n1
Karlin, D. 131
Kaufman, J.. L. 332
Kennedy, R. F. 270
Kerr, S. *et al.* 12

Keynes, J. M. 207
Kim, S. 311
Klosterman, R. E. 135, 136
Korea, Republic of 72
Kostof, S. 275
Kotter, J. P. 175
Krieger, A. 277
Krizek, K. **259**, **260**, 261–262
Krueckeberg, D. A. 134
Krumholz, N. 327
Kunzman, K. R. 72

Lafferty, W. M. 242
Land Evaluation/Site Assessment (LESA) 170
land use planning 8, 227; case studies and problem-based learning 236; development control 230, 231, 236; ethics in plan making 233–234; externalities 228; key elements and processes 235; key literature contributions 234; legislation and land use 230–232, 235; making land use plans 235; managing impact of development 232–233; strategic planning 230–231; teaching land use planning and course design: 234–236; theory and methods 228–229; towards sustainable land use planning 229–230; welfare economics 228; zoning 228, 231, 232, 233
land use, "private" control of 61–62
Lande, P. S. 200
Landis, John 40
language 122, 156
Lao Tzu 176
Lavedan, Pierre 33
law *see* planning law
law of contracts 61
Le Corbusier 278
leadership 7, 174; communications 174, 178; cultural awareness 174, 176–178, 181; design leadership 180; future orientation 174, 175–176; the greater good 174, 178–179; infrastructure 179–180; *vs.* management 175; place-based quality of life 180; planners are natural leaders 174–175; public health 180; situational awareness 174, 176; situational leadership 176; specific forums and arenas of planning 179–180; sustainability 180; teacher leadership in planning 180–181; conclusion 181–182
Leavitt, J. 103
legal reasoning 58
Legates, R. T. 275
legislative and quasi-legislative processes 58
Leigh, N. G. 103, 135, 187, 188
Leopold, L. B. 316
LESA (Land Evaluation/Site Assessment) 170
letters 122
Levinson, D. **259**, **260**, 261–262

Li, Hou 39
Lincoln University (New Zealand) 106
Lindblom, C. E. 288
LISA (Local Indicators of Spatial Association) 167, *168*, 169
local economic development planning 7, 187; defining 187–188; developing the local economy profile 189; evolution 190; local economic development theory 189; conclusion 194
local economic development planning: teaching: accreditation 194; analytical methods 193; developing a curriculum 190–193, **191**; further training and professional development 193–194; methods covered 192, **192**; most common topics 192, *192*
local environmental planning 243–245, 246–247
local law 59
Loh, C. G. 313
Long, J. G. 95
Long, T. 327
Lynch, K. **146**, 280, 287

McCann, J. 279
Macdonald, E. 285
McHarg, I. L. 169, 278, 281
McLean, M. 135
management 175
Mandelbaum, S. J. 31
Marcucci, D. 296, 297
Marinescu, L. G. *et al.* 327
Martin, M. 326
Massachusetts Institute of Technology Center for Transportation Studies 263
Masser, I. 217
Massey University 106
Maxwell, J. A. 158
Mayo, J. M. 240
Meadows, D. H. *et al.* 240
memos 122
Meyers, D. J. 326
Miller, C. 40–41
Million, A. 220
Mills, C. W. 129
Mills, M. *et al.* 217
Mingione, E. 326
Minner, J. *et al.* 80
minutes 123
Moglen, G. E. 311
"Moran's I" index 167
Morley, A. 37
Morphet, C. 107
municipal law 59

Nakajima, N. 38–39
Nasr, Joe 35
national law 59
national planning 8; accreditation 9; Denmark 211–212; genesis of planning at national level 206–207; Germany 72, 212–213; influence on fabric of planning education 210–213; initial link between national planning and planning education 208–209; perception of space 209; political ideology and steering role 207–208; reorientations: shifting political ideology 209–210; spatial imagery 211; strategic turn 209; conclusion 213–214
nationalism 3
Needham, B. 234
negotiation 62
Nelessen, A. 279
Nelson, S. 104
Netherlands: land use planning 234; national planning 72; planning history courses 37
Neuman, M. 176, 177–178
New York City 278
New Zealand 14; accreditation 22; environmental planning 239; gender: current guidelines 106; studio courses 96; Women in Urbanism 107
New Zealand Planning Institute (NZPI) **24**, 102, 106
Niebanck, P. L. 3
Nolen, J. 276
nomenclature 9
nuisance 61

Ohio State University 82, 84
Olmsted, F. L., Jr. 33
online courses 281, 286
Opportunity Agenda 326
oral communication 120; body language 121; delivery 120–121; in groups 121; organization 120; preparation 120; in venues of public participation 121–122; visual aids 121
Oranje, Mark 35
Ord, J. K. 167
ordinances 59, 123
organizational culture 177
Osland, A. C. 313
Osypuk, T. L. 327
Otago University 106
Ozawa, C. P. 73, 74–75

Palazzo, D. 278, 287
Palmer, R. N. *et al.* 314
parks 327
Parnell, R. 220
Patton, C. V. *et al.* 135
Peattie, L. **146**
pedagogy 4, 6; *see also* core curricula design; gender; studios and workshops; technology
Pendlebury, J. 32
Pereira, F. C. *et al.* 84
Perloff, H. S. 15, 40, 74, 93, 208–209

Index

Peterson, S. J. 39
Philip II, King of Spain 276
Pigou, A. C. 228
place-based quality of life 180
place culture 178
Planetizen 281, 286
planning culture 177–178
planning education 4, 9–10
planning history 5, 31; accreditation standards 37–38, **38**; assessments 40; city history courses **35**, 37; critical approaches 39; discussion 37–40; distributed courses **35**, 37; in evolving planning curricula 32–34; foci 38–39; history and theory courses **35**, 36; primary sources 39–40; reasons for teaching 31–32; standalone courses 34–35, **35**; texts 39; thematic history courses **35**, 36–37; typology of courses 34–37, **35**; urbanisme courses **35**, 35–36; conclusions 40–41
planning law 5–6, 55–56; case method 59, 63; initial challenges 57; literatures 63–64; pedagogy 63; reading cases 63; statutory interpretation 63; technical skills 62–63; theory and methods 56–57; *see also* planning law: applicable knowledge; planning law: foundational knowledge
planning law: applicable knowledge 61; discretionary interpretation 62; exactions 62; law of contracts 61; negotiation 62; nuisance 61; "private" control of land use 61–62; procedural 62; property law 61; substantive 61–62; trespass 61
planning law: foundational knowledge 57–58; administrative procedures 58; bodies/types of law 59; governmental authority and constraints 59–60; legal reasoning 58; legislative processes 58; origins of legal rules 59; private property 60; procedural 58; quasi-judicial processes 58; social attributes 60–61; structural systems and authorities 60; substantive 58–61
Planning Schools Movement 5
planning skills *see* communication; leadership; qualitative methods; quantitative methods; research design and practice; spatial analysis
Planning Support Technologies (PST) 82
planning theory in Chinese universities 5, 44–45; approaches to theory 51–52; course content 47; course title and type *46*, 46–47; methods 45; overview of current planning theory education 45–47; planning history courses 37; teaching methods 47–48; textbooks and bibliography 47; conclusion 52–53
planning theory in Chinese universities: case studies 48, **48**; course requirements and assignments 50–51; instructors and contents 49–50; purpose 48, 49
Plater-Zyberk, E. 280
Poëte, M. 33

Poland 16
Polanyi, M. 129
police power 59
Politecnico di Milano 287–288
political context 119
population diversity 118
Portugal 35–36
Postel, S. 316
Pothukuchi, K. 332
Potts, R. 105
power of eminent domain 59
Pratt Institute, New York 103–104
Pray, J. S. 33
"private" control of land use 61–62
private property 60
problem-based learning 211–212, 213, 222–223, 236
professional competence *see* accreditation and professional competence
professional titles 14
property law 61
Prud'homme, R. 246
PST (Planning Support Technologies) 82
public health 180
public input as source of information 119
public participation 121–122
"public trust" 179

QA (quality assurance) 16
qualitative methods 7; access 155–156; analysis 152, **152–153**; challenges 154–159; confirmability 157; course design and curriculum placement **159**, 159–160; data availability 147; data collection 148–150, **149–150**; ethics 154–155; feedback 159; formal research 145; generalizability 158–159; giving back 156; inconsistencies 158; interpretation 156–157; justification for teaching 145–147; member checking 159; mixed methods designs 147; outputs 147, *147*, 148; practical investigations 145; question type 146; rapport 155–156; reliability/repeatability 157; sampling and selection 150–152, **151**; selected influential works 145, **146**; standards of rigor 157–159; survey fatigue 156; theory and approaches 147–153; transferability to other contexts 158–159; triangulation 158, 159; trust 155–156; truthfulness 158; utility/usefulness 159; validity 158, 159
quality assurance (QA) 16
quantitative methods 7, 134; analytical methods **142**, 142–143; basic methods 137–138, **138**; computing hardware 135–136; course options 136–137, **137**; database methods **140**, 140–141; discounting **138**, 139; forecasting **138**, 138–139; foundational methods 137–140, **138**; pedagogical approaches 135; reasons for

use 134–135; software 136; statistical methods 141, *141*; textbooks 135; virtualization 136; conclusion 143
quasi-judicial processes 58

Rahder, B. L. 36
Rand, P. 288
Randolph, J. 312, 316
rapport 155–156
Reeves, D. 102
regional economic development (RED) planning 7; acquiring/retaining direct investment in regional industries 198–199; anchoring the regional economy 200–201; clustering the regional economy 199–200; defined 196; educating regional economic development planners 202–203; human capital 201; origins and history 196–197; product space 197; regional innovation systems (RIS) 201; related diversification 197; restructuring the regional industrial base 200; strategy rubrics 198; sustaining the regional economy 201; trade 197
Rennie, H. 106
reports 122–123
research context 157
research design and practice 6–7, 127–128; craft 128, 129–130; epistemology 127; in planning vs social sciences 128; soft skills in unfamiliar places 128, 130–132; tacit knowledge 129–130; trust 127–128, 129–131, 155–156, 179; *see also* qualitative methods; quantitative methods
research merit and integrity 155
resolutions 123
respect 155
Restroom Gender Parity in Federal Buildings Act, Washington, D.C. 101
Rey, S. J. 166
Reynolds, J. 33
Richter, B. 316
Riggs, W. *et al.* 79, 81
Rittel, H. W. J. 288
RMIT (Royal Melbourne Institution of Technology) 51–52
Roberts, M. 104
Roberts, P. 241–242
Robinson, C. M. 33
Robinson, P. 79
Rockefeller Foundation 281
Rodríguez-Bachiller, A. 15, 35, 40
Rodrik, D. 202
Rosenbloom, S. 103
Rosier, J. 218–219, 220, 223
Ross, C. 103
Roy, A. 4, **146**
Royal Institution of Chartered Surveyors (RICS) 22
Royal Melbourne Institution of Technology (RMIT) 51–52

Royal Town Planning Institute (RTPI; UK) 22, **22**; Code of Professional Conduct 23–24, **24**, 266; core principles 323; gender 102; programme accreditation 16, 18–20, **19–20**, 73; transportation planning 257; women 104, **104**
Rutgers University 286, 288
Ryle, G. 129

Sabatier, P. *et al.* 314
Sandercock, L. 34, 39, 239
Sanyal, B. 4–5
Saunders, W. S. 277
Schelling, T. C. 162
Schön, D. 39
Schuster Committee 33
Schweitzer, L. **259**, **260**, 261
SDGs (Sustainable Development Goals) 100
Sedlak, D. 306
self-directed learning 20, 213, 222–223
Seltzer, E. 73, 74–75
Sen, A. 324, 326
Senbel, M. 80, 84
Sennett, R. 129
separation of powers 60
Sert, J. L. 277, 280
Shearer, A. W. 289
Shepherd, A. 223
Silva, E. A. *et al.* 128
Silver, C. 34, 97
Silvers, A. L. 134
Simonis, U. E. 241, 242
Singapore Model 4
Sitte, C. 278
situational awareness 174, 176
situational leadership 176
Sloane Report (2013) 103
Slovakia 16
Smith, S. K. *et al.* 135
social justice *see* the just city
social media 81, 82
social planning 265
Society for American City and Regional Planning History 34
South Africa: National Water Act (NWA; 1998) 312–313, 314–315; planning history courses 35
Southern Cross University (Australia) 105
Spain 25n7
spatial analysis 7, 162–163; equity 163–165; methods 166–171; network analysis *163*, 167, 169; objectives 163–166; site suitability analysis *163*, 169–171, **170**; spatial clusters *163*, 166–167, *168*; spatial dependencies 166; spatial heterogeneity 163, *163*, 164–165; structuring a spatial analysis course 171–172; vulnerability 165–166; final thoughts 172; *see also* GIS (Geographic Information Systems)
spatial imagery 211

standards 12
state law 59
state-led planning 196–197
statutory law 59
Stavins, R. N. 243
Stein, C. 276–277
Steiner, F. 278, 289
Steinitz, C. 289
Stephenson, G. 33
Stern, R. A. M. 280
Stiftel, B. 219
Stimson, R. J. et al. 196
Stübben, J. 32
student projects 211–212, 213, 222–223
studios and workshops 6, 90–91; changing role in American planning schools 92–94, **93**; origins and objectives of studio courses 91–92; practica 92; studio courses today **94**, 94–97, 285–286; teamwork 285; urban design 285; workshops 92; conclusion 97
Susskind, L. 316
sustainable development 229; environmental planning 240, 242; land use planning 229–230; leadership 180; regional economy 201; in transportation planning 256, **256**; urban design 278, 288; *see also* climate change; food systems planning; the just city; water resources planning
Sustainable Development Goals (SDGs) 100
Sutcliffe, A. 31, 32
Sweet, E. 81
Switzerland 14

Taiwan 72
Talen, E. 280
Tang, C.-C. 44, 45
Tang, Y. 287
Tarlock, A. D. 309
Taylor, P. J. 206
Team Based Learning (TBL) 300
technology 6, 78; access and delivery of planning education 81; citizen science 84; courses and use of technology for communication 81–82; creativity 85; critical thinking 84; crowdsensing 84; data mining 84; planning support systems (PSS) 79, 82; Planning Support Technologies (PST) 82–84; quantitative methods 135–136; research methods 80; research on planning education and technology 79–80; conclusion 85–86
Teitz, M. B. 32, 326
Temple University (US) 81
Tendler, J. **146**, 158, 202
Thomas, J. M. 325
Thompson, G. F. 278
Thompson vs. HUD (Baltimore, Maryland) 326
Thompson, W. 199
Throgmorton, J. A. 130

Tian, L. 72
Tobler, W. R. 166
trade 197, 199, 201
traditional subjects of specialization *see* environmental planning; housing and real estate planning; international comparative planning; land use planning; local economic development planning; national planning; regional economic development planning; transportation planning; urban design
translators 157
transparency 179
Transport Planning Society (TPS; UK) 254
transportation planning 8, 253–254, 326–327; challenges for educators 263; civil engineering 254; course topics, theory and skills 258–263, **259**, **260**, **261**; demand forecasting 253–254; local to regional-scale 254–255; "mobility" to "accessibility" 255; private-sector mobility services 255; role in planning education 256–257; sustainable transportation 256, **256**; trends 254–256; urban transportation 253, 254, 255
trespass 61
triangulation 158
trust 127–128, 129–131, 155–156, 179
Turkey 25n2

UN-Habitat 81, 324
United Kingdom 14; gender: current guidelines **104**, 104–105; homeownership 269; land use planning 228, 229, 233, 234; *National Planning Policy Framework* 229; planning history 32, 33–34; planning schools 71, 73; Right to Buy 267–268; *Sustainable Development Strategy Securing the Future* 229; Urbanistas 107; water resources 316n1; Women in Planning 107
United Nations 100, 313
United States 14, 84; (nonprofit) community development corporations (CDCs) 269; affordable housing 266, 267, 268; Alliance for Water Efficiency (AWE) 310; Community Development Block Grant (CDBG) 270; Department of Agriculture 170; environmental impact assessments 242; environmental planning 239; Federal Home Loan Mortgage Corporation (HLMC) 268–269; Federal Housing Administration (FHA) 268–269; Federal National Mortgage Association (FNMA) 268, 269; gender: current guidelines 102–104, **103**; graduate planning schools with urban design **282–284**; housing 268; Housing Opportunity through Modernization Act (2016) 269; land use planning 228, 234; Metropolitan Planning Organizations 255; National Academy of Science 299–300; National Climate Assessment 298; National Congress of Neighbourhood Women 104;

National Housing Trust Fund 270; National Oceanic and Atmospheric Administration (NOAA) 81; National Science Foundation 157; Natural Resources Defense Council 313; Planning Accreditation Board (PAB) 16, 18, 20, **21**, 22, **22**, 56, 73, **74**, 257; planning history 32–33; planning history courses 35, 36–37; Planning Student Organization (PSO) 85; undergraduate planning schools with urban design 281, **285**; water allocation institutions 307–309, **308**; *see also* Association of Collegiate Schools of Planning (ACSP, US); core curricula design; planning law; studios and workshops; water resources planning

University of California, Berkeley 286
University of Chicago 279
University of Cincinnati 287
University of Illinois Urbana-Champaign (UIUC) 73
University of Karlsruh, Germany 208
University of Liverpool 208
University of North Carolina 279
University of Pennsylvania (UPenn) 51–52, 286
University of Texas at Austin 80, 288
University of Westminster (UK) 104
urban design 8, 275–276; City Beautiful movement 276; civic design 276; direct or indirect urban design 279; educating urban designers 278–280; foundations of urban design 276–277; lecture vs studio vs online learning 285–288; localism 278; lofty goals, quotidian challenges 277–278; planning education follows practice 280–281, **282–284**, **285**; sustainability 278, 288; what is the future? 288–289
Urey, G. 80

validity 158, 159
virtualization 136
visual aids 121
vom Hofe R. 135
Vos, J. 75, 240
vulnerability 165–166

Waikato University 106
Walters, D. 278
Wang, X. 135
Wang, Z.-C. 47

Warburton, K. 221
water resources planning 9, 305; equality of access to water 312–314; flooding mitigation 311–312; fracking 313; green stormwater management 312; history of water resource management 306–307; integrated management 306, 317n2; theory, principles and methods 307–309; towards more resilient and sustainable planning 314–315; water allocation institutions in U.S. 307–309, **308**; water conservation and built form requirements 309–310; water efficiency 310; water supply and demand forecasting 310–311; new era in planning education 315–316
Watson, V. 219
Webber, M. M. 288
Weitz, J. 135, 234
welfare economics 228
Wen, M. *et al.* 327
Wetmore, L. B. 95
White, R. 37
White, S. S. 240
Whyte, W. F. **146**
Williams, A. 324
Wittgenstein, L. 340
Wolyjer, J. 104
World Bank 81
World Commission on Environment and Development (WCED) 229, 242
World Health Organisation 238
Wright Wendel, H. E. *et al.* 327
written communication 122; announcements 123; grant proposals 123–124; intent, purpose, and audience 122; letters 122; memos 122; minutes 123; ordinances 123; reports 122–123; resolutions 123

Xing, X.-N. 48

Yonder, A. 103–104
Young, I. M. 324

Zhang, L. 47, 52
Zhang Weng 12 45
Zhao, Z.-F. 48
Zhou, J. **259**, **260**, 261